Encyclopedia of
Modern Asia

Editorial Board

Encyclopedia of
Modern Asia

Volume 6
Turkic Languages to Zuo Zongtang

A Berkshire Reference Work
David Levinson · Karen Christensen, Editors

CHARLES SCRIBNER'S SONS®

New York • Detroit • San Diego • San Francisco • Cleveland • New Haven, Conn. • Waterville, Maine • London • Munich

THOMSON
★
GALE

Encyclopedia of Modern Asia

David Levinson and Karen Christensen, Editors

Copyright © 2002 Berkshire Publishing Group

Charles Scribner's Sons
An imprint of The Gale Group
300 Park Avenue South
New York, NY 10010

Gale and Design™ and Thomson
Learning™ are trademark s used herein
under license.

For more information, contact
The Gale Group, Inc.
27500 Drake Rd.
Farmington Hills, MI 48331–3535
Or you can visit our Internet site at
http://www.gale.com

Since this page cannot legibly accommodate all copyright notices, the acknowledg-
ments constitute an extension of the
copyright notice.

LIBRARY OF CONGRESS CATALOGING-IN-PUBLICATION DATA

Levinson, David, 1947-
   Encyclopedia of modern Asia : / David Levinson, Karen Christensen,
   p. cm.
Includes bibliographical references and index.
   ISBN 0-684-80617-7 (set hardcover : alk. paper)
   1. Asia—Encyclopedias.   I. Christensen, Karen, 1957-   II. Title.
DS4 .L48 2002
950'.03—dc21

                                                                    2002008712

Printed in United States of America
1 3 5 7 9 11 13 15 17 19 20 18 16 14 12 10 8 6 4 2

Contents

List of Maps

Survey of Asia's Regions and Nations

The *Encyclopedia of Modern Asia* covers thirty-three nations in depth and also the Caucasus and Siberia. We have divided Asia into five major subregions and assigned the thirty-three nations to each.

West and Southwest Asia

The West Asian nations covered in detail here are Turkey, Iran, and Iraq. Afghanistan and Pakistan form Southwest Asia, although in some classifications they are placed in Central and South Asia, respectively. Afghanistan, on the crossroads of civilizations for thousands of years, is especially difficult to classify and displays features typical of Central, West, and South Asia.

Despite diversity in language (Persian in Iran, Arabic in Iraq, Turkish in Turkey) form of government (theocracy in Iran, dictatorship in Iraq, and unstable democracy in Turkey) and international ties (Iran to the Islamic world, Iraq to the Arab Middle East, Turkey to the West), there are several sources of unity across West Asia. Perhaps the oldest is geographical location as the site of transportation routes between Europe and Central, East, and South Asia. Since ancient times, people, goods, wealth, and ideas have flowed across the region. In 2002 the flow of oil was most important, from the wells of Iran and Iraq through the pipelines of Turkey. Another source of unity is Sunni Islam, a major feature of life since the seventh century, although Iran is mainly the minority Shi'a tradition and there have long been Zoroastrian, Jewish, Christian, and Baha'i minorities in the region. Diversity is also evident in the fact that Turkey is a "secular" state while Iran is a theocracy, and in the conflict between fundamentalist and mainstream Islam in all the nations.

Another important common thread is the shared historical experience of being part of the Ottoman Empire and having to cope with British and Russian designs on their territory and, more recently, American influence. And, in the twentieth century, all three nations have sought to deal with the Kurdish minority and its demands for a Kurdish state to be established on land taken from all three nations.

Unity across Afghanistan and Pakistan is created by adherence to Sunni Islam (although there is a Shi'ite minority in Afghanistan) and the prominence of the Pashtun ethnic group in each nation. Both nations also experienced British colonialism, although the long-term British influence is more notable in Pakistan, which had been tied to India under British rule. West Asia is the only region in the world never colonized by Britain, although some experts argue that it did experience significant British cultural influence. In all nations resistance to external control—British, Russian, or United States—is another common historical experience.

Across the region (although less so in Afghanistan) is the stark contrast between the traditional culture and the modernity of liberation from imperial rule, still not complete across the region. This contrast is apparent in clothing styles, manners, architecture, recreation, marriage practices, and many elements of daily life.

In 2002 all the nations faced a water crisis of both too little water and water pollution. They all also faced issues of economic and social development, including reducing external debt, controlling inflation, reducing unemployment, improving education and health care, and continually reacting to the ongoing Arab-Israeli conflict, which exacerbates many of these problems. The governments also faced the difficult task of solving these problems while resisting Americanization and also while controlling internal political unrest. Political unrest is often tied to efforts at creating democratic governments and the persistence of elite collaboration with tyrannical governments.

Central Asia

Central Asia is known by many names, including Eurasia, Middle Asia, and Inner Asia. At its core, the region is composed of five states that became independent nations following the collapse of the Soviet Union in 1991: Kazakhstan, Kyrgyzstan, Tajikistan, Turkmenistan, and Uzbekistan. Scholars sometimes include Afghanistan, Mongolia and the Xinjiang province of China within the label Central Asia. For this project, Central Asia is restricted to the five former Soviet countries, while Afghanistan is classified in Southwest Asia, and Mongolia and Xinjiang as part of East Asia. These states have a shared landmass of 1.5 million square miles, about one-half the size of the United States.

The region's unity comes from a shared history and religion. Central Asia saw two cultural and economic traditions blossom and intermix along the famed Silk Road: nomadic and sedentary. Nomadic herdsmen, organized into kinship groupings of clans, lived beside sedentary farmers and oasis city dwellers. Four of the countries share Turkic roots, while the Tajiks are of Indo-European descent, linguistically related to the Iranians. While still recognizable today, this shared heritage has developed into distinct ethnic communities.

The peoples of Central Asia have seen centuries of invasion, notably the legendary Mongol leader Genghis Khan in the thirteenth century, the Russians in the nineteenth and the Soviets in the twentieth century. For better or worse, each invader left behind markers of their presence: the Arabs introduced Islam in the seventh century. Today Islam is the predominant religion in the region, and most Central Asians are Sunni Muslims. The Russians brought the mixed legacy of modernism, including an educated populace, alarming infant mortality rates, strong economic and political participation by women, high agricultural development, and environmental disasters such as the shrinking of the Aral Sea. It was under Russian colonialism that distinct ethno-national boundaries were created to divide the people of the region. These divisions largely shape the contemporary Central Asian landscape.

Today the five Central Asian nations face similar challenges: building robust economies, developing stable, democratic governments, and integrating themselves into the regional and international communities as independent states. They come to these challenges with varied resources: Kazakhstan and Turkmenistan have rich oil reserves; several countries have extensive mineral deposits; and the Fergana Valley is but one example of the region's rich agricultural regions.

Finally, the tragic events of September 11, 2001, cast world attention on Afghanistan's neighbors in Central Asia. The "war on terrorism" forged new alliances and offered a mix of political pressure and economic support for the nations' leaders to suppress their countries' internal fundamentalist Muslim movements.

Southeast Asia

Southeast Asia is conventionally defined as that subregion of Asia consisting of the eleven nation-states of Brunei, Cambodia, East Timor, Indonesia, Laos, Malaysia, Myanmar, Philippines, Singapore, Thailand, and Vietnam. Myanmar is sometimes alternatively classified as part of South Asia and Vietnam as in East Asia. The region may be subdivided into Mainland Southeast Asia (Cambodia, Laos, Myanmar, Thailand, and Vietnam) and Insular Southeast Asia (Brunei, East Timor, Indonesia, Philippines, and Singapore). Malaysia is the one nation in the region that is located both on the mainland and islands, though ethnically it is more linked to the island nations of Indonesia, Brunei, and the Philippines.

Perhaps the key defining features for the region and those that are most widespread are the tropical monsoon climate, rich natural resources, and a way of life in rural areas based on cooperative wet-rice agriculture that goes back several thousand years. In the past unity was also created in various places by major civilizations, including those of Funan, Angkor, Pagan, Sukhothai, Majapahit, Srivijaya, Champa, Ayutthaya, and Melaka. Monarchies continue to be significant in several nation—Brunei, Cambodia, Malaysia, and Thailand—today. Subregional unity has also been created since ancient times by the continued use of written languages, including Vietnamese, Thai, Lao, Khmer and the rich literary traditions associated with those languages.

The region can also be defined as being located between China and India and has been influenced by both, with Indian influence generally broader, deeper, and longer lasting, especially on the mainland, except for Vietnam and Singapore, where influences from China have been more important. Islamic influence is also present in all eleven of the Southeast Asian nations. Culturally, Southeast Asia is notable for the central importance of the family, religion (mainly Buddhism and Islam), and aesthetics in daily life and national consciousness.

In the post–World War II Cold War era, there was a lack of regional unity. Some nations, such as Indonesia under Sukarno, were leaders of the nonaligned nations. Countries such as Thailand and the Philippines joined the U.S. side in the Cold War by being part of the Southeast Asia Treaty Organization (SEATO). A move toward greater unity was achieved with the establishment of the Association of Southeast Asian Nations (ASEAN) in 1967, with the founding members being Indonesia, Malaysia, the Philippines, Singapore, and Thailand. Subsequently other Southeast Asian nations joined ASEAN (Brunei, 1984; Laos, Myanmar, and Vietnam 1997; Cambodia 1999). As of 2002, communism was still the system in Laos and Vietnam and capitalism in Brunei, Cambodia, East Timor, the Philippines Thailand, Indonesia, Malaysia and Singapore. Political, economic, and cultural cooperation is fostered by the Association of Southeast Asian Nations (ASEAN), with headquarters in Jakarta, Indonesia. Economically, all the nations have attempted to move, although at different speeds and with different results, from a reliance on agriculture to an industrial or service-based economy. All nations also suffered in the Asian economic crisis beginning in July 1997.

Alongside these sources of similarity or unity that allow us to speak of Southeast Asia as a region is also considerable diversity. In the past religion, ethnicity, and diverse colonial experience (British, Dutch, French, American) were major sources of diversity. Today, the three major sources of diversity are religion, form of government, and level of economic development. Three nations (Indonesia, Malaysia,

Brunei) are predominately Islamic, five are mainly Buddhist (Vietnam, Laos, Cambodia, Thailand, Myanmar), two are mainly Christian (Philippines and East Timor), and Singapore is religiously heterogeneous. In addition, there is religious diversity within nations, as all these nations have sizeable and visible religious minorities and indigenous religions, in both traditional and syncretic forms, also remain important.

In terms of government, there is considerable variation: communism in Vietnam and Laos; state socialism in Myanmar; absolute monarchy in Brunei; evolving democracy in the Philippines, Thailand, Cambodia, and Indonesia; and authoritarian democracy in Malaysia and Singapore. The economic variation that exists among the nations and also across regions within nations is reflected in different levels of urbanization and economic development, with Singapore and Malaysia at one end of the spectrum and Laos and Cambodia at the other. Myanmar is economically underdeveloped, although it is urbanized, while Brunei is one of the wealthiest nations in the world but not very urbanized.

In 2002, Southeast Asia faced major environmental, political, economic, and health issues. All Southeast Asian nations suffer from serious environmental degradation, including water pollution, soil erosion, air pollution in and around cities, traffic congestion, and species extinctions. To a significant extent all these problems are the result of rapid industrial expansion and overexploitation of natural resources for international trade. The economic crisis has hampered efforts to address these issues and has threatened the economies of some nations, making them more dependent on international loans and assistance from nations such as Japan, Australia, and China. The persisting economic disparities between the rich and the poor are actually exacerbated by rapid economic growth. Related to poverty is the AIDS epidemic, which is especially serious in Cambodia, Myanmar, and Thailand and becoming more serious in Vietnam; in all these nations it associated with the commercial sex industry.

Politically, many Southeast Asian nations faced one or more threats to their stability. Political corruption, lack of transparency, and weak civic institutions are a problem to varying degrees in all the nations but are most severe in Indonesia, which faces threats to its sovereignty. Cambodia and Thailand face problems involving monarch succession, and several nations have had difficulty finding effective leaders. Myanmar's authoritarian rulers face a continual threat from the political opposition and from ethnic and religious separatists.

In addition, several nations faced continuing religious or ethnic-based conflicts that disrupt political stability and economic growth in some provinces. The major conflicts involve Muslim separatists in the southern Philippines, Muslims and Christians in some Indonesian islands and Aceh separatists in northern Sumatra, and Muslims and the Karen and other ethnic groups against the Burman government in Myanmar. Since the economic crisis of 1997, ethnic and religion-based conflict has intensified, as wealthier ethnic or religious minorities have increasingly been attacked by members of the dominant ethnic group. A related issue is the cultural and political future of indigenous peoples, including the so-called hill tribes of the mainland and horticulturalists and former hunter-gatherers of the islands.

In looking to the future, among the region's positive features are the following. First, there is Southeast Asia's strategic location between India and China, between Japan and Europe, and between Europe and Oceania. It stands in close proximity to the world's two most populous countries, China and India. Singapore, the centrally located port in Southeast Asia, is one of two major gateways to the dynamic Pacific Basin (the other is the Panama Canal). Second, there is the region's huge population and related economic market, with a total population approaching that of one half of China's. Indonesia is the world's fourth most populous nation. Third, there is enormous tourist potential in sites and recreational locales such as Angkor Wat, Bali, Borobudur, Phuket, and Ha Long Bay. Fourth, there is the region's notable eclecticism in borrowing from the outside and resiliency in transcending tragedies such as experienced by Cambodia and Vietnam. Fifth, there is the region's significant economic potential: Southeast Asia may well have the world's highest-quality labor force relative to cost. And, sixth, there is the region's openness to new technologies and ideas, an important feature in the modern global community.

South Asia

South Asia is the easiest region to demarcate, as it is bounded by the Hindu Kush and Himalayan ranges to the north and the Bay of Bengal and Arabian Sea to the south. It contains the nation-states of Bangladesh, Bhutan, India, Nepal, and Sri Lanka and the more distant island nations of the Maldives and Mauritius. Myanmar and Pakistan, which are considered part of South Asia in some schemes, are here classified in Southeast Asia and Southwest Asia, respectively.

While the region is diverse economically, culturally, linguistically, and religiously, there is unity that, in some form, has existed for several thousand years. One source of unity is the historical influence of two major civilizations (Indus and Dravidian) and three major religions (Hinduism, Buddhism, and Islam). Regionally, Sikhism and Jainism have been of great importance. There is also considerable economic unity, as the majority of people continue to live by farming, with rice and especially wet-rice the primary crop. In addition, three-quarters of the people continue to live in rural, agricultural villages, although this has now become an important source of diversity, with clear distinctions between urban and rural life. A third source of unity is the caste system, which continues to define life for most people in the three mainland nations. Another source of unity is the nature and structure of society, which was heavily influenced by the several centuries of British rule. A final source of political unity in the twentieth century—although sometimes weakened by ethnic and religious differences—has been nationalism in each nation.

South Asia is diverse linguistically, ethnically, religiously, and economically. This diversity is most obvious in India, but exists in various forms in other nations, except for the isolated Maldives, which is the home of one ethnic group, the Divehi, who are Muslims and who have an economy based largely on tourism and fishing.

The dozens of languages of South Asia fall into four major families: Indo-European, Austroasiatic, Dravidian, and Tibeto-Burman and several cannot be classified at all. Because of its linguistic diversity, India is divided into "linguistic" states with Hindi and English serving as the national languages.

Hinduism is the dominant religion in South Asia, but India is the home also to Buddhism, Jainism, and Sikhism. India also has over 120 million Muslims and the world's largest Zoroastrian population (known in India as Parsis) and Bangladesh is a predominately Muslim nation. India also has about twenty-five million Christians and until recently India had several small but thriving Jewish communities. Nepal is mainly Hindu with a Buddhist minority, and Bhutan the reverse. Sri Lanka is mainly Theravada Buddhist with Hindu, Muslim, and Christian minorities. Mauritius, which has no indigenous population, is about 50 percent Hindu, with a large Christian and smaller Muslim and Buddhist minorities.

Linguistic and religious diversity is more than matched by social diversity. One classification suggests that the sociocultural groups of South Asia can be divided into four general and several subcategories: (1) castes (Hindu and Muslim); (2) modern urban classes (including laborers, non-Hindus, and the Westernized elite); (3) hill tribes of at least six types; and (4) peripatetics.

Economically, there are major distinctions between the rural poor and the urban middle class and elite, and also between the urban poor and urban middle class and elite. There are also significant wealth distinctions based on caste and gender, and a sizeable and wealthy Indian diaspora. There is political diversity as well, with India and Sri Lanka being democracies, Bangladesh shifting back and forth between Islamic democracy and military rule, the Maldives being an Islamic state, and Nepal and Bhutan being constitutional monarchies.

In 2002, South Asia faced several categories of issues. Among the most serious are the ongoing ethnic and religious conflicts between Muslims and Hindus in India, the conflict between the nations of Pakistan and India; the ethnic conflict between the Sinhalese and Sri Lankan Tamils in Sri Lanka; and the conflict between the Nepalese and Bhutanese in both nations. There are also various ethnic separatists movements in the region, as involving some Sikhs in India. The most threatening to order in the region and beyond is the conflict between India and Pakistan over the Kashmir region, as both have nuclear weapons and armies gathered at their respective borders.

A second serious issue is the host of related environmental problems, including pollution; limited water resources; overexploitation of natural resources; destruction and death caused by typhoons, flooding, and earthquakes; famine (less of a problem today), and epidemics of tropical and other diseases. The Maldives faces the unique problem of disappearing into the sea as global warming melts glaciers and raises the sea level. Coastal regions of Bangladesh could also suffer from this.

There are pressing social, economic, and political issues as well. Socially, there are wide and growing gaps between the rich and middle classes and the poor, who are disproportionately women and children and rural. Tribal peoples and untouchables still do not enjoy full civil rights, and women are often discriminated against, although India, Sri Lanka, and Bangladesh have all had women prime ministers. Economically, all the nations continue to wrestle with the issues involved in transforming themselves from mainly rural, agricultural nations to ones with strong industrial and service sectors. Politically, all still also struggle with the task of establishing strong, central governments that can control ethnic, religious, and region variation and provide services to the entire population. Despite these difficulties, there are also positive developments. India continues to benefit from the inflow of wealth earned by Indians outside India and is emerging as a major technological center. And, in Sri Lanka, an early 2002 cease-fire has led to the prospect of a series of peace negotiations in the near future..

East Asia

East Asia is defined here as the nations of Japan, South Korea, North Korea, China, Taiwan, and Mongolia. It should be noted that Taiwan is part of China although the People's Republic of China and the Republic of China (Taiwan) differ over whether it is a province or not. The inclusion of China in East Asia is not entirely geographically and culturally valid, as parts of southern China could be classified as Southeast Asian from a geographical and cultural standpoint, while western China could be classified as Central Asian. However, there is a long tradition of classifying China as part of East Asia, and that is the approach taken here. Likewise, Mongolia is sometimes classified in Central Asia. As noted above, Siberia can be considered as forming North and Northeast Asia.

Economic, political, ideological, and social similarity across China, Korea (North and South), and Japan is the result of several thousand years of Chinese influence (at times strong, at other times weak), which has created considerable similarity on a base of pre-existing Japanese and Korean cultures and civilizations. China's influence was greatest before the modern period and Chinese culture thus in some ways forms the core of East Asian culture and society. At the same time, it must be stressed that Chinese cultural elements merged with existing and new Korean and Japanese ones in ways that produced the unique Japanese and Korean cultures and civilizations, which deserve consideration in their own right.

Among the major cultural elements brought from China were Buddhism and Confucianism, the written language, government bureaucracy, various techniques of rice agriculture, and a patrilineal kinship system based on male dominance and male control of family resources. All of these were shaped over the centuries to fit with existing or developing forms in Korea and Japan. For example, Buddhism coexists with Shinto in Japan. In Korea, it coexists with the indigenous shamanistic religion. In China and Korea traditional folk religion remains strong, while Japan has been the home to dozens of new indigenous religions over the past 150 years.

Diversity in the region has been largely a product of continuing efforts by the Japanese and Koreans to resist Chinese influence and develop and stress Japanese and Korean culture and civilization. In the twentieth century diversity was mainly political and economic. Japanese invasions and conquests of parts of China and all of Korea beginning in the late nineteenth century led to hostile relations that had not been completely overcome in 2002.

In the post–World War II era and after, Taiwan, Japan, and South Korea have been closely allied with the United States and the West; they have all developed powerful industrial and postindustrial economies. During the same period, China became a Communist state; significant ties to the West and economic development did not begin until the late 1980s. North Korea is also a Communist state; it lags behind the other nations in economic development and in recent years has not been able to produce enough food to feed its population. In 2002 China was the emerging economic power in the region, while Taiwan and South Korea hold on and Japan shows signs of serious and long-term economic decline, although it remains the second-largest (after the United States) economy in the world. Mongolia, freed from Soviet rule, is attempting to build its economy following a capitalist model.

Politically, China remains a Communist state despite significant moves toward market capitalism, North Korea is a Communist dictatorship, Japan a democracy, and South Korea and Taiwan in 1990s seem to have become relatively stable democracies following periods of authoritarian rule. Significant contact among the nations is mainly economic, as efforts at forging closer political ties remain stalled over past grievances. For example, in 2001, people in China and South Korea protested publicly about a new Japanese high school history textbook that they believed did not fully describe Japanese atrocities committed toward Chinese and Koreans before and during World War II. Japan has refused to revise the textbook. Similarly, tension remains between Mongolia and China over Mongolian fears about Chinese designs on Mongolian territory. Inner Mongolia is a province of China.

Major issues with regional and broader implications are the reunification of Taiwan and China and North and South Korea, and threat of war should reunification efforts go awry. Other major regional issues include environmental pollution, including air pollution from China that spreads east, and pollution of the Yellow Sea, Taiwan Strait, and South China Sea. A third issue is economic development and stability, and the role of each nation, and the region as a unit, in the growing global economy. A final major issue is the emergence of China as a major world political, economic, and military power at the expense of Taiwan, South Korea, and Japan, and the consequences for regional political relations and stability.

Overview

As the above survey indicates, Asia is a varied and dynamic construct. To some extent the notion of Asia, as well as regions within Asia, are artificial constructs imposed by outside observers to provide some structure to a place and subject matter that might otherwise be incomprehensible. The nations of Asia have rich and deep pasts that continue to inform and shape the present—and that play a significant role in relations with other nations and regions. The nations of Asia also face considerable issues—some unique to the region, others shared by nations around the world—as well as enormous potential for future growth and development. We expect that the next edition of this encyclopedia will portray a very different Asia than does this one, but still an Asia that is in many ways in harmony with its pasts.

David Levinson (with contributions from Virginia Aksan, Edward Beauchamp, Anthony and Rebecca Bichel, Linsun Cheng, Gerald Fry, Bruce Fulton, and Paul Hockings)

Regional Maps

CENTRAL ASIA

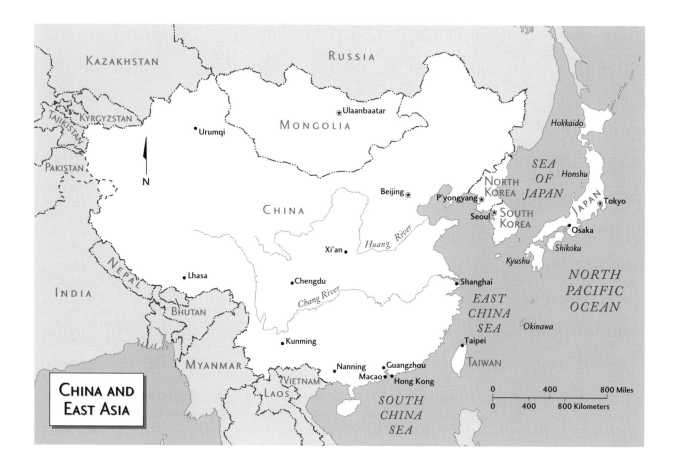

CHINA AND
EAST ASIA

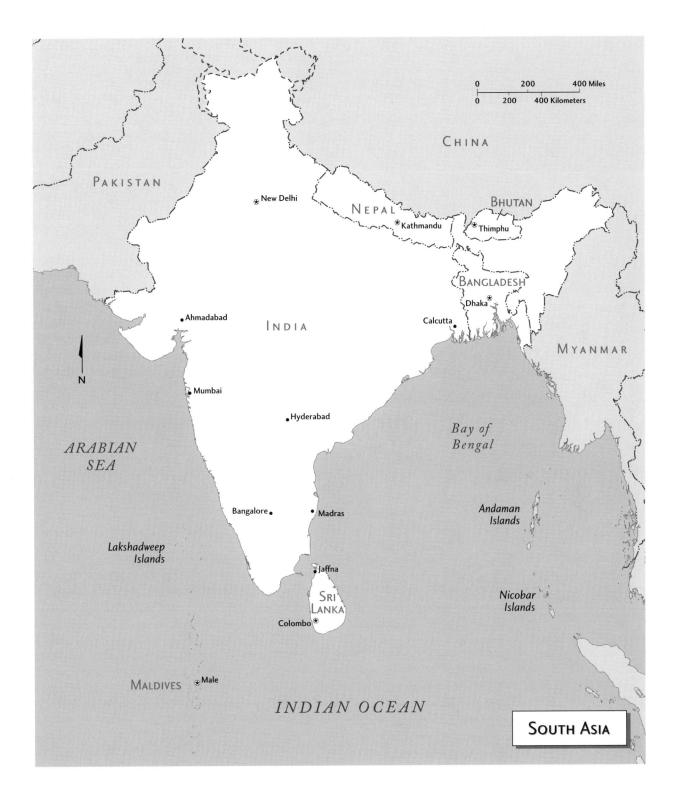

CHINA

PAKISTAN

⊛ New Delhi

NEPAL

⊛ Kathmandu

BHUTAN

⊛ Thimphu

BANGLADESH

Dhaka ⊛

Calcutta

MYANMAR

Ahmadabad

INDIA

ARABIAN
SEA

N

Mumbai

Hyderabad

Bay of
Bengal

Andaman
Islands

Bangalore   Madras

Lakshadweep
Islands

Jaffna

Nicobar
Islands

SRI
LANKA

Colombo ⊛

MALDIVES   ⊛ Male

INDIAN OCEAN

SOUTH ASIA

0   200   400 Miles
0   200   400 Kilometers

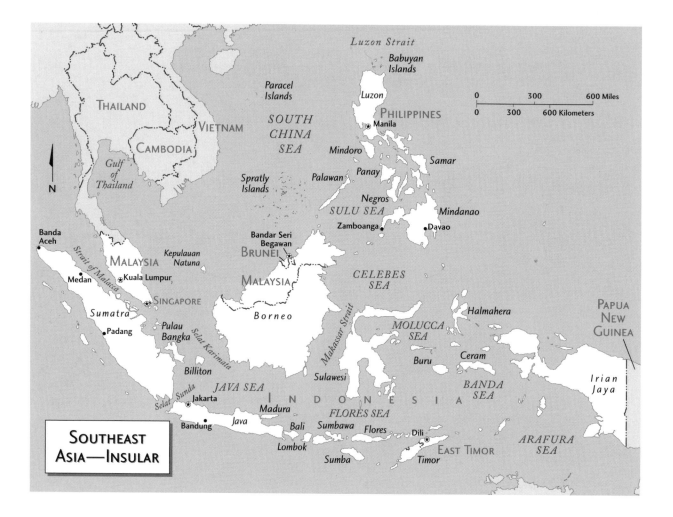

SOUTHEAST ASIA—INSULAR

THAILAND

VIETNAM

CAMBODIA

Gulf
of
Thailand

N

Banda
Aceh

Strait of Malacca

Medan

MALAYSIA

Kuala Lumpur

SINGAPORE

Sumatra

Padang

Pulau
Bangka

Selat Karimata

Kepulauan
Natuna

Billiton

Selat Sunda

Jakarta

Bandung

Java

Madura

Bali

Lombok

Sumbawa

Sumba

JAVA SEA

INDONESIA

FLORES SEA

Flores

Timor

Dili

EAST TIMOR

SOUTH
CHINA
SEA

Paracel
Islands

Spratly
Islands

Bandar Seri
Begawan

BRUNEI

MALAYSIA

Borneo

Sulawesi

Makasar Strait

CELEBES
SEA

Luzon Strait

Babuyan
Islands

Luzon

PHILIPPINES

Manila

Mindoro

Palawan

Panay

Negros

SULU SEA

Zamboanga

Samar

Mindanao

Davao

MOLUCCA
SEA

Buru

Halmahera

Ceram

BANDA
SEA

ARAFURA
SEA

PAPUA
NEW
GUINEA

Irian
Jaya

0	300	600 Miles
0	300	600 Kilometers

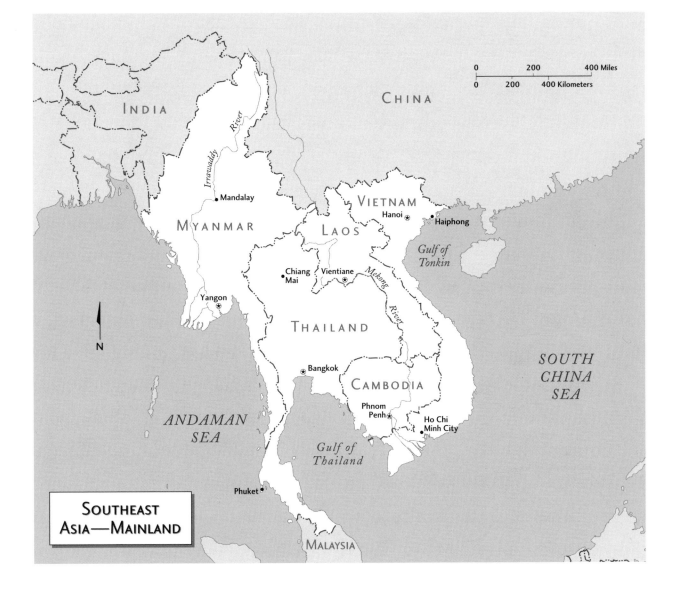

SOUTHEAST ASIA—MAINLAND

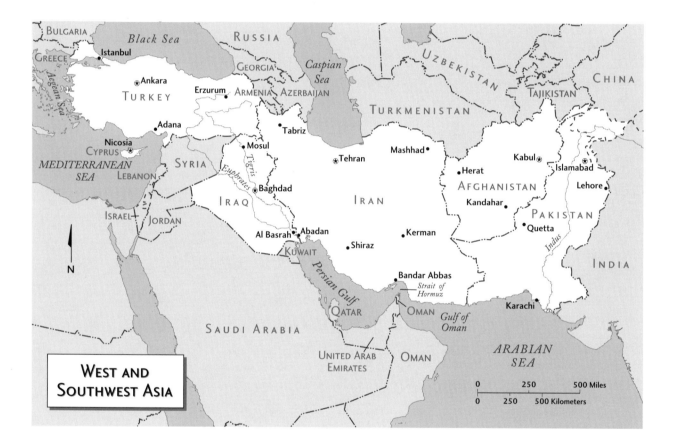

BULGARIA
GREECE
Aegean Sea
Black Sea
Istanbul
⊛Ankara
T U R K E Y
Adana
Nicosia
CYPRUS ⊛
MEDITERRANEAN SEA
LEBANON
ISRAEL
JORDAN
SYRIA
RUSSIA
GEORGIA
Erzurum
ARMENIA AZERBAIJAN
Caspian Sea
UZBEKISTAN
CHINA
TURKMENISTAN
TAJIKISTAN
Tabriz
Mosul
⊛Tehran
Mashhad
Kabul⊛
Islamabad⊛
Tigris
Euphrates
⊛Baghdad
Herat
AFGHANISTAN
Lehore
I R A Q
I R A N
Kandahar
PAKISTAN
Al Basrah
Abadan
Kerman
Quetta
Indus
KUWAIT
Shiraz
Bandar Abbas
Strait of Hormuz
INDIA
N
Persian Gulf
QATAR
OMAN
Gulf of Oman
Karachi
SAUDI ARABIA
UNITED ARAB EMIRATES
OMAN
ARABIAN SEA

WEST AND SOUTHWEST ASIA

0   250   500 Miles
0   250   500 Kilometers

Reader's Guide

ASIA

Arts, Literature, and Recreation

Asian Games
Board Games
Chinese New Year
Jade
Kabaddi
Kites and Kite Flying
Mountaineering
Olympics
Storytelling

Economics, Commerce, and Transportation

Asian Development Bank
Asian Economic Crisis of 1997
Asia-Pacific Economic Cooperation Forum
Automobile Industry
Bogor Declaration
Drug Trade
Export-Led Development
Golden Crescent
High-Technology Industry
Information Technology Industry
Intellectual Property
Islamic Banking
Manila Action Plan
Measurement Systems
Osaka Action Plan
Shanghai Cooperation Organization
Silk Road
Spice Trade
Sustainability
Tin Industry
Tourism
World Bank in Asia

Geography and the Natural World

Air Pollution
Bamboo
Buffalo, Water
Camel, Bactrian
Caspian Sea
Chicken
Cormorant
Deforestation
Duck and Goose, Domesticated
Earthquakes
Endangered Species
Goat
Mangroves
Monsoons
Opium
Pacific Ocean
Pacific Rim
Pig
Rhinocerous, Asiatic
Rice and Rice Agriculture
Soil Loss
South China Sea
Surkhob River
Tiger
Toxic-Waste Disposal
Typhoons
Volcanoes
Water Issues

Government, Politics, and Law

Corruption

International Relations

Africa-Asia Relations
Australia-Asia Relations

EAST ASIA *(continued)*
> **Government, Politics, and Law** *(continued)*
> > *Japan (continued)*

Sendai
Shiga
Shimane
Shipbuilding Scandal
Shizuoka
Showa Denko Scandal
Siemens Incident
Tanaka Giichi
Textbook Scandal
Tochigi
Tojo Hideki
Tokushima
Tokyo
Tottori
Toyama
Wakayama
Yamagata
Yamagata Aritomo
Yamaguchi
Yamamoto Isoroku
Yamanashi
Yoshida Shigeru
Yoshida Shoin
> > *Koreas*

April 19 Revolution—Korea
Chagang Province
Cheju Province
Ch'ongjin
Chun Doo Hwan
Communism—North Korea
Corruption—Korea
Democratization—South Korea
Haeju
Hamhung
Han Yong-un
Inchon
Juche
Kaesong
Kangwon Province
Kim Dae Jung
Kim Il Sung
Kim Jong Il
Kim Pu-shik
Kim Young-sam
Kim Yu-sin
Kwangju
Kwangju Uprising
Kyonggi Province
March First Independence Movement
Namp'o
North Cholla Province

North Ch'ungch'ong Province
North Hamgyong Province
North Hwanghae Province
North Korea—Political System
North Kyongsang Province
North P'yongan Province
Park Chung Hee
Pusan
Pyongyang
Rhee, Syngman
Roh Tae Woo
Sadaejuui
Sejong, King
Seoul
Sinuiju
South Cholla Province
South Ch'ungch'ong Province
South Hamgyong Province
South Hwanghae Province
South Korea—Political System
South Kyongsang Province
South P'yongan Province
Taegu
Taejon
Three Revolutions Movement
Ulchi Mundok
Wang Kon
Yanggang Province
Yi Ha-ung
Yi Song-gye
Yi T'ae-yong
Yu Kwan Sun
Yushin
> > *Mongolia*

Aimag
Batmonkh, Jambyn
Choybalsan, Horloogiyn
Chormaqan, Noyan
Darhan
Erdenet
Genghis Khan
Golden Horde
Gurragchaa, Jugderdemidiyn
Karakorum
Khubilai Khan
Mongolia—Political System
Mongolian Social Democratic Party
Narantsatsralt, Janlavyn
Ochirbat, Punsalmaagiyn
Sukhbaatar, Damdiny
Tsedenbel, Yumjaagiyn
Ulaanbaatar
United Party of Mongolia

Indian Ocean
Indian Subcontinent
Indo-Gangetic Plain
Jhelum River
Jute
K2, Mount
Kangchenjunga, Mount
Kaveri River
Kistna River
Mongoose
Punjab
Reunion Island
Sundarbhans
Tarai
  India
Abu, Mount
Andaman and Nicobar Islands
Bhopal
Chenab River
Dekkan
Eastern Ghats
Ganges River
Godavari River
Hindu Kush
Jumna River
Lion, Asiatic
Mahanadi River
Narmada Dam Controversy
Narmada River
Rann of Kachchh
Satpura Range
Sutlej River
Thar Desert
Tungabhadra River
Vindhya Mountains
Western Ghats
Zebu
  Nepal
Everest, Mount
Kathmandu Valley
  Government, Politics, and Law
Bahadur Shah
Birla Family
Colombo Plan
Hastings, Warren
Humayun
Ibn al-Qasim, Muhammad
Jahangir
Marxism—South Asia
Poros
Raziya
Roy, Rammohan
Shah Jahan
Singh, Jai

Tata Family
Tipu Sultan
  Bangladesh
Awami League
Bangladesh—Political System
Bangladesh Nationalist Party
Chittagong
Dhaka
Ershad, H.M.
Hasina Wajid, Sheikh
Jatiya Party
Rahman, Mujibur
Rahman, Ziaur
Zia, Khaleda
  Bhutan
Thimphu
Wangchuck, King Jigme Singye
  India
Afzal Khan
Agartala
Agra
Ahmadabad
Ajanta
Ajodhya
Akbar
Ali Janhar, Mohamed
Allahabad
Ambedkar, B.R.
Amritsar
Andhra Pradesh
Arunachal Pradesh
Asoka
Assam
Aurangabad
Aurangzeb
Awadh
Azad, Abu'l-Kalam
Babur
Bangalore
Bengal, West
Bentinck, William Cavendish
Bhosle, Shivaji
Bhubaneshwar
Bihar
Bodh Gaya
Bose, Subhas Chandra
Calcutta
Calicut
Canning, Charles John
Chandigarh
Chhattisgarh
Coimbatore
Constitution—India

Ayub Khan
Bhutto, Benazir
Bhutto, Zulfiqar Ali
David, Collin
Hadood
Islamabad
Jama'at-e-Islami
Jinnah, Mohammed Ali
Karachi
Khan, Abdul Ghaffar
Lahore
Mohenjo Daro
Muhajir Qawmi Movement
Multan
Musharraf, Pervez
North-West Frontier Province Sarhad
Pakistan—Political System
Pakistan People's Party
Peshawar
Rahmat Ali, Chauduri
Rohtas Fort
Sehwan
Sind
Zia-ul-Haq, Mohammad
History and Profile
Afghanistan
Afghanistan—History
Afghanistan—Profile
Durrani
Pakistan
Federally Administered Tribal Areas—Pakistan
Pakistan—History
Pakistan—Profile
International Relations
Afghanistan
Afghanistan—Human Rights
Treaty of Gandomak
Pakistan
Bangladesh-Pakistan Relations
India-Pakistan Relations
Pakistan—Human Rights
Language and Communication
Pashto
Afghanistan
Dari
Peoples, Cultures, and Society
Afridi
Baluchi
Brahui
Pashtun
Pashtunwali
Waziri
Clothing, Traditional—Afghanistan
Ethnic Conflict—Afghanistan

Hazara
Pakistan
Sindhi
Siraiki
Women in Pakistan
Religion and Philosophy
Bakhsh, Data Ganj
Islam—Southwest Asia
Shah, Mihr Ali
Shahbaz Qalandar Lal
Sufism—Southwest Asia
Afghanistan
Ansari, Abdullah
Bitab, Sufi
Pakistan
Mawdudi, Abu'l-A'la
Muhajir

WEST ASIA
Arts, Literature, and Recreation
Architecture—West Asia
Architecture, Islamic—West Asia
Cinema—West Asia
Music—West Asia
Rudaki
Shahnameh Epic
Sports—Islamic Asia
Twelver Shi'ism
Iran
Cuisine—Iran
No-ruz
Literature, Persian
Iraq
Cuisine—Iraq
Poetry—Iraq
Turkey
Children's Day—Turkey
Cuisine—Turkey
Guney, Yilmaz
Literature—Turkey
Music—Turkey
Nesin, Aziz
Pamuk, Orhan
Economics, Commerce, and Transportation
Agriculture—West Asia
Industry—West Asia
Oil Industry—West Asia
Organization of Petroleum Exporting Countries
Iran
Iran—Economic System
Iraq
Iraq—Economic System
Turkey
Etatism—Turkey

Encyclopedia of
Modern Asia

TURKIC LANGUAGES The Turkic languages are spoken across Eurasia from eastern Siberia to Iran and from China to Ukraine, but they are concentrated in Central Asia, where groups of two to twenty million are represented; the total number of speakers of Turkic languages exceeds 130 million. Turkish (approximately 57 million speakers) is the largest group. Despite their broad geographic reach, speakers of Turkic languages can usually understand each other. Turkic peoples lived in the paths of countless invasions of Eurasia, and they comprised a large part of the nominally Mongol army. This contact and mobility has rendered classification difficult.

Sound System

Most Turkic languages have eight basic vowels, which may be grouped according to backness (how far back in the mouth the tongue is when they are said), rounding (shape of the mouth), and height (how open the mouth is), such as in Kyrgyz. (See Table 1.)

Some languages have more distinctions (for example, Uighur and Azerbaijani also distinguish an open e [ɛ] and a closed e [e]), and some have fewer (for example, Uzbek and Salar. Yakut, Turkmen, and Khalaj have basic long vowels; many other languages have

TABLE 1

Vowel Phonemes				
	Unrounded		Rounded	
	front	back	front	back
High	i	ï	ü	u
Not high	e	a	ö	o

long vowels in loanwords or from consonant contractions. Reduced vowels are found in Chuvash, Tatar, and Bashkir).

The combination of certain vowels with voiceless consonants have resulted in a "checked" sound (glottalization) in South Siberia (Tuva, Tofa *a"t*, meaning "horse"), and a related sound (preaspiration, or spirantization) in Inner Asia (Uighur *i^{s}kki*, meaning "two").

Syllables tend to have a consonant-vowel (plus optional consonant) shape, maximally CV(V)(C)(C), such as Yakut *küüs*, "force" (CVVC), or *türk*, "Turk" (CVCC, where the first consonant of CC must be a sonorant or fricative). Consonants such as f, v, ž, and ts are atypical, though they occur in many Turkic languages due to contact with other languages. Native initial nasals and liquids are not found, except for the interrogative *ne*, "what?"

The Turkic languages are also known for sound harmony: Native syllables have either all front vowels (*ä, e,i, ö, u*) and consonants (*k, g, γ*), or all back ones (*ï, a, o, u, q*, etc.), as in *kel-*, "to come," or *qal-*, "to remain." There are many exceptions to this principle, however, and the Turkic languages vary widely in the extent of suffix harmony. Most suffixes match the stems in at least voicing and backness (palatal harmony). Some have roundness assimilation (labial harmony) as well, under more restricted conditions. Some languages have a weakened harmonic system, such as Uzbek, due to contact with Iranian.

Morphology and Syntax

Turkic has regular agglutinative suffixation, in which categories for person, number, tense and so on are strung together in a strict order. For example: *Sarïg Yoghur bar-al-γe-mes-dro* is the root verb *go*, with potential-future-negative-third-person-definite endings added on to make "s/he cannot go."

Nouns and verbs each take their own regular suffixes. Turkic nouns have neither gender nor dual number. Noun suffixes are almost uniformly ordered as follows: Uzbek *kitob-lar-im-da*, *book* plus plural-first-person-possessive-locative endings, to yield "in my books." The plural is not marked in collective or numeral expressions. (So *horse* in the Kazakh phrase *at jaqšï* meaning "horse-good" or "Horses are good" is the same in *eki at*, meaning "two horses."). Within the noun phrase, there is no case or number agreement between adjectives and their head nouns. Many particles have case-like functions: *üčün*, meaning "for" and *birle*, meaning "together with," for example.

Nouns can generally function as substantives or adjectives (for example, Chuvash *śută*, meaning both "brightness" and "bright") and many suffixes can be added to both. Only adjectives have comparative forms: Tatar *yaxši-raq*, "better."

Personal pronouns lack a distinction between inclusive and exclusive; honorifics are often formed with plural pronouns, or with the reflexive pronoun in the third person. Demonstrative pronouns usually distinguish three kinds of distance, as with Kazakh *bul* "this (visible)," *sol* "that (invisible)," *osï* "that (further away)." Personal and demonstrative pronouns with genitive suffixes form possessives. Some demonstratives and interrogatives are formed from pronouns with suffixes.

Cardinal numerals are generally based on a decimal system; eleven to nineteen are additive: *on bir* "ten-one" yields "eleven." Exceptions are Sarïg Yoghur and Old Turkic, in which *bïr yigïrmï* ("one-twenty") yields "eleven" and *bïr ohdïs* ("one-thirty") yields "twenty-one." Normally sixty to ninety are multiplicative. Ordinals take a suffix.

Verbal expressions in Turkic comprise partly suffixing "be" verbs and regularly suffixing verbal phrases. In the third person, nonpast copulas are not usually marked (see, for example the Tuvan *ol suruqčï*, meaning "s/he is a student," or the Kazakh *bul adam jaqsï*, meaning "this person is good," to which can be compared *bul jaqsï adam*, meaning "This is a good person." Negative and past copulas are always marked with particles, as in the Turkish *ben değil*, meaning "it isn't me."

Verbal morphology is extensive, with suffixes to express voice, mood, aspect, tense, and possibility or potentiality. Potentiality is often marked with a gram-maticized *al-*, meaning "take" or *bil-*, meaning "know," as in the Turkish *ver-e-bil-ir* "s/he can give."

Verbs fall into two classes, finite and nonfinite. Finite verbs are conjugated, with markers for aspect, mood, and tense, and constitute independent utterances; nonfinite verbs do not carry such markers, and are dependant parts of a sentence (for example, they can be relative clauses). The manner in which an action is carried out is typically expressed by semantically-fused verbal phrases consisting of a nonfinite lexical verb and conjunctor followed by an auxiliary verb. Languages generally have one to two dozen of such grammaticalized combinations of tense, aspect, and modal suffixes.

One important feature of Turkic is inferentiality, which lets the speaker distinguish direct from indirect experience, as in the Uzbek *xatå qïldïm*, meaning "I made a mistake," as opposed to *xatå qïlibman*, meaning "It seems I have made a mistake." The indirective copulas *imiš* and *iken~eken* also exist.

Syntactic typology in Turkic is very consistent and economical. Modifiers always precede what they modify: Noun phrases precede the verb, and verbs come at sentence ends.

Diachronic Development

Before it diverged into distinct languages, a Common Turkic language unity is assumed; some scholars also posit an earlier Proto-Turkic language.

Old Turkic (the first attested) languages include East Old Turkic, Old Uighur, and Karakhanid. East Old Turkic is the oldest known Turkic, attested in runelike inscriptions on stone monuments in the Orkhon and Yenisey valleys in modern-day Mongolia from the second Turkic empire (eighth century); the language of the early Oghuz, Kipchak, and Uighur Turkic peoples was little differentiated at the time. Old Uighur flowered in the Tarim Basin Uighur dynasty under Manichaeanism and Buddhism (ninth through thirteenth centuries); Karakhanid Turkic (eleventh through twelfth centuries), an Islamic literary language centered in Kashgar, was influenced lexically by Persian and Arabic and written in the Arabic script.

Middle Turkic reflects the increasing differentiation of the Turkic branches and the development of literary standards. In the east, Chagatay developed as the premier pan-Central Asian Turkic literary language, written in an Arabic script. In the west, Oghuz Turkic included Old Anatolian Turkish (from the thirteenth century onwards), its successor Ottoman Turkish, and literary Turkmen and Azerbayjani (from the fourteenth and fifteenth centuries onwards, respectively); Kipchak Turkic is exemplified by the fourteenth-century *Codex Cumanicus*.

Modern Turkic comprises six branches, classified on the basis of both genetic and areal-typological features. Early on, Turkic languages in the west with *r* and *l* in some words (the so-called Oghur or Bulghar branch) split off from Turkic languages with *z* and *š* (so-called Common Turkic). Khalaj, spoken today in Iran, represents a further early split. Common Turkic itself has four branches: Southwestern Turkic (Turkmen, Azerbayjani, Turkish, and Gagauz); Northwestern Turkic (Kazakh, Kyrgyz, Karakalpak, Noghay, Tatar, Bashkir); Northeastern (Tuvan, Khakas, Yakut), and Southeastern (Uighur, Uzbek).

Is Turkic Related to Mongolian?

A comparison of Turkic and Mongolian reveals an abundance of lexical cognates, as well as similar suffixation and phonology. Scholars disagree whether the relationship is one of genetic inheritance or borrowing. The former theory posits a common Altaic protolanguage, with three main families: Turkic, Mongolic, and Manchu-Tungusic. Altaicists pointed to regular sound correspondences, common suffixes and personal pronouns, and syntactic similarities. On the other hand, proponents of the now-dominant Turko-Mongolian hypothesis asserted that such similarities were due to borrowing, citing the lack of common numerals, and similarities between Chuvash and Mongolian. Mongolian's *r* corresponding to Old Turkic *z* may indicate that the Mongolian words were borrowed, likely very early on, from an *r*-type Turkic language like Chuvash. Altaicists call into question the claim of unidirectional borrowing from Turkic into Mongolic. Most all scholars agree that Mongolian and Turkic show evidence of heavy bidirectional copying at least since the intensive contact of the thirteenth-century Mongol empire.

The Mongolian influence was particularly strong in Yakut, Tuvan, and other Siberian Turkic languages. Other early loans include Indo-European, Uralic, and Sinitic. In addition, Yakut shows Tungusic and Samoyedic influence, and Salar, Chinese, and Tibetan elements. Uzbek, though a Southeastern Turkic language, shows the effects of contact with Tajik (Iranian) and Kipchak (Northwestern Turkic).

Arienne M. Dwyer

Further Reading

Csató, Éva Ágnes, and Lars Johanson, eds. (1998) *The Turkic Languages*. London: Routledge.

Erdal, Marcel (1991) *Old Turkic Word Formation*. Wiesbaden, Germany: Harrassowitz.

Golden, Peter B. (1992) *An Introduction to the History of the Turkic Peoples*. Wiesbaden, Germany: Harrassowitz.

TURKMEN
The Turkmen are a Sunni Muslim people whose language, Turkmen, belongs to the southwestern, or Oghuz, branch of the Turkic linguistic group. In 1997, about 3.6 million Turkmen lived in the Central Asian country of Turkmenistan, with smaller numbers residing in neighboring countries. About two-thirds of the Turkmen population reside in rural settlements. With the development of Turkmenistan's economy during the post–World War II Soviet period, many non-Turkmen skilled workers and managers immigrated to the republic. The population is distributed unevenly, with few people in the Kara-Kum desert and mountain regions, but large numbers in the oases.

Origins and Early History

The origins of the Turkmen may be traced back to the Oghuz confederation of nomadic pastoral tribes that lived in present-day Mongolia and around Lake Baikal in southern Siberia. The Turkmen probably entered Central Asia in the eleventh century CE and subsequently came under the rule of the Seljuk Turks and the Mongols. Turkmen tribesmen were an integral part of the Seljuk military forces. Turkmen migrated with their families and possessions on Seljuk campaigns into Azerbaijan and Anatolia, a process that began the Turkification of these areas. During this time, Turkmen also began to settle the area of present-day Turkmenistan.

Pre-Russian Social Structure and Livelihood

For centuries the Turkmen were divided into numerous tribes, the largest being the Tekke, Ersari, and Yomut. The Turkmen traditionally lacked paramount leaders and intertribal political unity. Each tribe's elder males formed a committee that discussed matters before embarking on any significant endeavor. They chose their leaders by consensus rather than genealogy.

Prior to the Russian conquest in the late nineteenth century, most Turkmen were pastoral nomads, though during the eighteenth and nineteenth centuries many had settled in the oases and become agriculturalists. The men had reputations as warriors, and many served as mounted mercenaries in various Central Asian and Persian armies. The Akhal-teke breed of horse, world renowned for its beauty and swiftness, is particular to the Turkmen.

Muslim Turkmen in traditional dress and hats praying in a mosque in 1991. (DAVID & PETER TURNLEY/CORBIS)

Prior to Soviet rule, the extended family was the basic and most important social and economic unit among the Turkmen. Small groups of Turkmen families camped together as pastoral nomads in their customary regions. Different camping groups consolidated only in times of war or special celebrations. Camping groups subsisted on their livestock and on agricultural products acquired in trade. In hard economic times, they had to raid sedentary people to survive.

Islam and Life-Cycle Rituals

Although the great majority of Turkmen readily identify themselves as Muslims and acknowledge Islam as an integral part of their cultural heritage, many are not devout practitioners. Most participate in religious traditions associated with life-cycle rituals, such as weddings, burials, and pilgrimages. Islam was spread to the Turkmen in the tenth and eleventh centuries, primarily by Sufi sheikhs rather than by strictly orthodox preachers. These sheikhs reconciled Islam with popular pre-Islamic customs. The people often adopted these Sufis as their "patron saints"—a practice contrary to strict Islam. Among the Turkmen, there developed special holy tribes, known as *ovlat*, which traced their ancestry to the Prophet Muhammad. In the eighteenth and nineteenth centuries, the *ovlat* tribes became dispersed. Their members attended and conferred blessings at important communal and life-cycle events and also acted as mediators between disputing tribes. The *ovlat* institution retains some authority today. Many of the Turkmen who are respected for their spiritual powers trace their descent from an *ovlat*, and it is not uncommon, especially in rural areas, for such individuals to grant blessings at life-cycle and other communal celebrations.

Unlike some Muslim women in the Middle East, Turkmen women never wore the veil or practiced strict seclusion. During the Soviet period, wives often assumed what had been male responsibilities for certain Islamic rites so as to protect their husbands' careers. Many women entered the workforce out of economic necessity, a factor that disrupted some traditional family patterns. Educated urban women entered professional services and careers.

Turkmen place great value on marriage celebrations and life-cycle rituals. In rural areas especially, marriages are often arranged by special matchmakers (*sawcholar*), who seek potential spouses according to their social status, education, and other qualities. The bride's parents traditionally demanded a bride-wealth payment from the groom's family as part of the marriage contract. Turkmen rarely divorce.

Russian and Soviet Periods

In 1881, after conquering the Turkmen, the Russians created the Trans-Caspian oblast (province), which became part of the governorate-general of Turkistan in 1899. The Bolsheviks established control over the area in 1920. In October 1924, when Central Asia was divided into distinct political entities, the Transcaspian Territory and Turkmen Oblast of the Turkistan Autonomous Soviet Socialist Republic became the Turkmen Soviet Socialist Republic. Owing to forced collectivization during the first decades of Soviet rule, the Turkmen were transformed from pastoral nomads into sedentary farmers. They cultivated cotton and bred horses, camels, and karakul sheep. In the oasis strip along the middle Amu Dar'ya, they raised silkworms and grew cotton.

The Communist authorities suppressed religious expression and education. They closed most religious schools and mosques and banned religious observances. Some religious customs, such as Muslim burial and male circumcision, continued to be practiced throughout the Soviet period. Religious customs were preserved especially in rural areas.

Families continued to be close knit and often raised more than five children. It was common for married sons to remain with their parents, living together in an extended one-story clay structure with a courtyard and garden plot. In both rural and urban areas, respect for elders was great; Turkmen still consider grandparents sources of wisdom and spirituality.

The Soviet period dampened but did not suppress the expression of all Turkmen cultural traditions. Turkmen continued to produce their famous carpets; men continued to wear the high sheepskin hats, while women adorned themselves with distinctive Turkmen fabrics and jewelry. Turkmen also maintained their rich musical heritage and oral literature.

Independence

Turkmen leaders declared Turkmenistan's independence from the Soviet Union in 1991. The new government has made efforts to regain some of the cultural heritage lost under Soviet rule. It has ordered that basic Islamic principles be taught in public schools. Saudi Arabia and Kuwait have financed the opening of religious schools and mosques as well as instruction in Arabic, the Qur'an, and Islamic history. Courses on *edep*, or proper moral conduct according to traditional Turkmen and Islamic values, have been introduced in the public schools, and efforts are being made to contact Turkmen living outside Turkmenistan.

Paul J. Magnarella

Further Reading
Capisani, Giampaolo R. (2000) *The Handbook of Central Asia: A Comprehensive Survey of the New Republics.* London: I. B. Tauris.
Esenov, Rakhim. (1982) *Turkmenia.* Trans. by Tamara Mats. Moscow: Novosti Press Agency Publishing House.
Müller, Helga, et al. (1994) *Turkmenistan.* Washington, DC: World Bank.
Smith, Dianne L. (1998) *Opening Pandora's Box: Ethnicity and Central Asian Militaries.* Carlisle, PA: Strategic Studies Institute, U.S. Army War College.

TURKMENABAT

TURKMENABAT (1999 est. pop. 203,000). Turkmenabat (Chardzhou, Charjou, or Charjew before 1999) is a major river port in Central Asia, on the right bank of the lower Amu Dar'ya River, in the eastern part of the republic of Turkmenistan, a Central Asian state. It is the country's second largest city (after the capital Ashgabat) and the administrative center of Lebap Welayat (province). The city was founded in 1886 as a Russian military settlement named Novi Chardzhui (New Chardzhui), when Russia's Transcaspian Railroad, linking the Caspian Sea with the middle of Central Asia, reached the Amu Dar'ya. In 1940, the city was renamed Chardzhou and became the administrative center of the Chardzhou oblast (province) of the Turkmen Soviet Socialist Republic, part of the Soviet Union.

After the dissolution of the USSR in 1991, the city became the center of the Lebap province of the republic of Turkmenistan. In July 1999, it was renamed Turkmenabat (Turkmen City). At present, Turkmenabat is a major rail junction and the largest port on the Amu Dar'ya in Central Asia. The city has cotton-processing, silk-weaving, and chemical industries. It is also famous for its Astrakhan fur manufacturers.

Natalya YU. Khan

Further Reading
Allworth, Edward, ed. (1994) *Central Asia, 130 Years of Russian Dominance: A Historical Overview.* 3d ed. Durham, NC: Duke University Press.

TURKMENISTAN—PROFILE

TURKMENISTAN—PROFILE (2001 est. pop. 4.6 million). The Republic of Turkmenistan is located in southwest Central Asia. The nation shares an eastern border with Afghanistan, a northern border with Uzbekistan, a northwestern border with Kazakhstan, a southern border with Iran, and a western border with the Caspian Sea.

Turkmenistan was annexed by Russia in the last part of the nineteenth century. On 27 October 1924, the Turkmenistan Soviet Socialist Republic was established. It became an autonomous republic of the Soviet Union in May 1925. Turkmenistan became an independent state on 27 October 1991, following the collapse of the Soviet Union.

Geography

Ninety percent of Turkmenistan's area of 488,100 square kilometers is consumed by the Kara-Kum and Kyzyl-Kum deserts, and is largely uninhabited. The Kara-Kum Canal carries water from the Amu Dar'ya westward across the desert to Mary and ultimately to Ashgabat, a distance of about 800 kilometers. The canal water permits irrigated agriculture and industry along the southern margin of the Kara-Kum desert. Temperatures tend toward extremes, with very cold winters and extremely hot, dry summers. Precipitation is low.

People

Turkmenistan had a 2001 estimated population of 4.6 million people. More than one-third of the population is under the age of fifteen. Ethnically, about 73 percent of the population is Turkmen, 9.8 percent is Russian, 9 percent are Uzbek, and 2 percent are Tatar. The population growth rate is high, about 2.1 percent in 2000. Life expectancy is about 61 years. Literacy rates are high, around 98 percent. About 89 percent of Turkmenistan's population practices Islam. Turkmen are traditionally Sunni Muslims. Another 9 percent of the population professes Eastern Orthodox Christianity. Sufi mysticism and shamanism are also visible.

In 1990 Turkmen was declared the official language. The Soviets replaced the traditional Arabic script with a Latin script in 1929, and later Cyrillic in 1940. Independent Turkmenistan has returned to a Latin script.

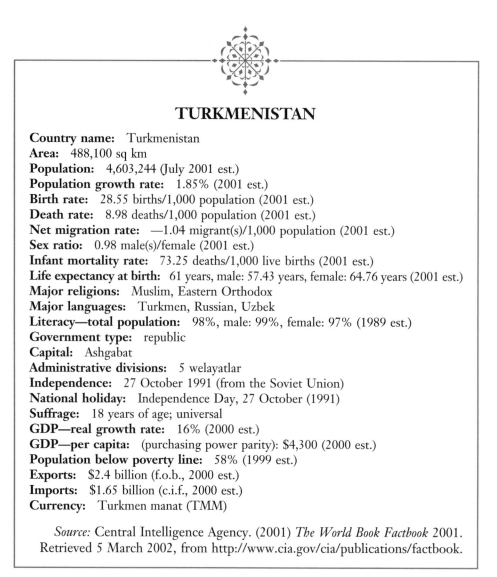

TURKMENISTAN

Country name: Turkmenistan
Area: 488,100 sq km
Population: 4,603,244 (July 2001 est.)
Population growth rate: 1.85% (2001 est.)
Birth rate: 28.55 births/1,000 population (2001 est.)
Death rate: 8.98 deaths/1,000 population (2001 est.)
Net migration rate: —1.04 migrant(s)/1,000 population (2001 est.)
Sex ratio: 0.98 male(s)/female (2001 est.)
Infant mortality rate: 73.25 deaths/1,000 live births (2001 est.)
Life expectancy at birth: 61 years, male: 57.43 years, female: 64.76 years (2001 est.)
Major religions: Muslim, Eastern Orthodox
Major languages: Turkmen, Russian, Uzbek
Literacy—total population: 98%, male: 99%, female: 97% (1989 est.)
Government type: republic
Capital: Ashgabat
Administrative divisions: 5 welayatlar
Independence: 27 October 1991 (from the Soviet Union)
National holiday: Independence Day, 27 October (1991)
Suffrage: 18 years of age; universal
GDP—real growth rate: 16% (2000 est.)
GDP—per capita: (purchasing power parity): $4,300 (2000 est.)
Population below poverty line: 58% (1999 est.)
Exports: $2.4 billion (f.o.b., 2000 est.)
Imports: $1.65 billion (c.i.f., 2000 est.)
Currency: Turkmen manat (TMM)

Source: Central Intelligence Agency. (2001) *The World Book Factbook* 2001. Retrieved 5 March 2002, from http://www.cia.gov/cia/publications/factbook.

Government

Turkmenistan is a republic with executive, legislative, and judicial branches of government, and a new constitution that was adopted on 18 May 1992.

Saparmurat Niyazov, who had been chairman of the Supreme Soviet, has served as Turkmenistan's president since 1991. In 2001, he announced he would retire by 2010, and open presidential elections are not planned until his retirement. Niyazov is often called Turkmenbashi, meaning "head of the Turkmen." Niyazov is the real source of power in the Turkmenistan government. There are two parliamentary bodies, a unicameral People's Council, or Halk Maslahaty. and a unicameral Assembly or Majlis. The constitution guarantees an independent judiciary.

Turkmenistan has five administrative regions (*velayat*s or *welayatlar*): Ahal, Balkan Welayaty, Dash-howuz, Lebap, and Mary. These five are subdivided into fifty *etrap*s, or districts. Ashgabat is the country's capital.

Economy

Turkmenistan is largely desert country with intensive agriculture in irrigated oases. One-half of its irrigated land is planted in cotton, making it the world's tenth-largest producer. Desertification and water pollution pose future concerns. The country has huge gas reserves (the fifth-largest reserves in the world) as well as oil resources. Other natural resources include coal, sulfur, and salt.

Until the end of 1993, Turkmenistan had experienced less economic disruption than other former Soviet states because its economy received a boost from higher prices for oil and gas and a sharp increase in

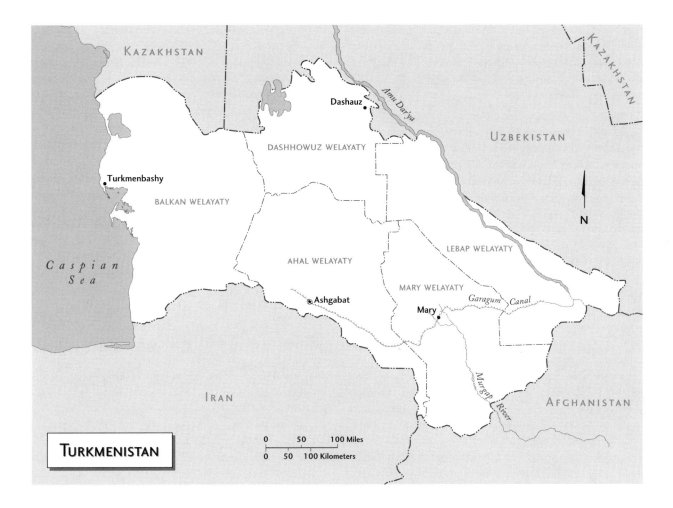

KAZAKHSTAN

KAZAKHSTAN

Dashauz

Amu Dar'ya

UZBEKISTAN

DASHHOWUZ WELAYATY

N

Turkmenbashy

BALKAN WELAYATY

LEBAP WELAYATY

Caspian Sea

AHAL WELAYATY

MARY WELAYATY

Garagum Canal

⊛Ashgabat

Mary

IRAN

Murgap River

AFGHANISTAN

TURKMENISTAN

0   50   100 Miles

0   50   100 Kilometers

hard-currency earnings. This changed in 1994 as the fortunes of its customers in the former Soviet Union continued to decline. The government has been cautious in initiating economic reform measures, including privatization. A regional financial crisis prompted President Niyazov to issue a decree in late 1998 restructuring the banking sector and increasing government ownership.

Turkmenistan's telephone system is poorly developed, with only 363,000 telephone lines in use in 1997. Estimates for radios and televisions in 1997 were 1.225 million and 820,000 respectively. A 2000 estimate showed 2,000 Internet users in the country. There were seventy airports in the country in that same year; thirteen of those had paved runways. In 1989, official statistics showed sixty-six newspaper titles published in Turkmenistan.

About 58 percent of the population of Turkmenistan lived below the poverty line in 1999. Future prospects are uncertain.

Rebecca M. Bichel

Further Reading

UNESCO (2002) *Statistical Yearbook 1999.* Retrieved 1 May 2002, from: http://www.uis.unesco.org/en/stats/stats0.htm.

United Nations (2001) *Statistical Yearbook.* New York: United Nations Statistics Division.

United States Census Bureau. (2002) "IDB Summary Demographic Data for Turkmenistan." Retrieved 1 May 20002, from: http://www.census.gov/cgi-bin/ipc/idbsum ?cty=TX.

TURKMENISTAN—ECONOMIC SYSTEM

The economy of Turkmenistan is dominated by agriculture and by public investment in export-oriented oil and gas. Turkmenistan's economic system is a highly administered, command-style economy, dominated by the government and the ruling political party. Structural market reforms, under way since Turkmenistan became independent upon disintegration of the USSR in October 1991, have proceeded slowly.

Background

Sandy deserts dominate Turkmenistan's terrain. Oases and river valleys have supported civilization since ancient times, but Turkmenistan's inhospitable desert climate created barriers to the development of a modern state until the past century. The contemporary national frontiers of Turkmenistan are a product of the modern period.

Turkmenistan is a predominately Muslim nation in faith and culture. Roughly 90 percent of Turkmenistan's native population speak Turkic, and most speak an Oghuz Turkic variant that is easily understood by a modern Turkish speaker from Turkey. A small percentage of the population in the nation's four major urban areas (Ashgabat, Dashauz, Turkmenbashy, and Mary) are Soviet-era European migrants and post-Soviet-era foreign technical specialists, speaking mainly Russian and English.

Economic Activity during the Transition Period

Turkmenistan's economic activity in ancient times was restricted to oasis agriculture and animal husbandry. During the Soviet period, investment was concentrated in agricultural development and the gas and oil industries. Turkmenistan's agriculture emphasized cotton production. Given the nation's arid environment, expansion of the cotton-based agricultural economy required development of an extensive irrigation system. Diversion of the waters of the Amu Dar'ya River through Turkmenistan's Garagum (Kara-Kum) Canal contributed to the desiccation of the Aral Sea and fueled disagreements among the Central Asian states regarding water use. The Soviet-era economy was organized on the principle of cooperative production, meaning that primary commodities such as raw cotton fiber, oil, and natural gas were transported to manufacturing centers, located primarily in the Russian areas of the USSR, for high-value secondary processing. As a consequence, Turkmenistan served as a supplier of primary commodities, while the associated processing and manufacturing took place in northern industrial centers.

Turkmenistan's Soviet-era economy depended on massive hidden subsidies. When Soviet subsidies ended, many industrial and agricultural enterprises immediately became insolvent. The government of Turkmenistan quickly sought to liberalize prices for external trade while maintaining price supports domestically. The government adopted a development strategy that stressed increasing foreign trade earnings while assuring domestic political stability under the policy of "positive neutrality." First, according to this policy, Turkmenistan sought to maintain as much distance as possible from Russia without giving up access to northern and European gas markets that, during at least the first few years of independence, would con-

tinue to be controlled by Russia by virtue of geography. Second, the policy of positive neutrality implied the expansion of trade with Turkmenistan's southern neighbors on the basis of self-interest. Third, it meant the nation would seek foreign investment to the extent possible to revitalize the gas-related industry and build a Kuwait-style emirate in Turkmenistan.

Economic Activity Today

The cornerstone of Turkmenistan's future economy is its energy wealth. With an estimated 2.7 trillion cubic meters in natural gas reserves and additional potential reserves estimated at 14 trillion cubic meters, Turkmenistan is the second-largest natural gas producer in the former Soviet Union and the fourth-largest producer in the world. Turkmenistan also has an estimated 1 billion metric tons of oil reserves and is the fourth-largest oil producer in the region.

Turkmenistan's hydrocarbon resources offer great potential for economic development but also imply certain developmental vulnerabilities. Turkmenistan was an early beneficiary of price liberalization after the disintegration of the USSR. This enabled Turkmenistan to charge world market prices for the gas it supplied to its former Soviet-era customers in Ukraine, Georgia, Russia, and other nations. On the other hand, Turkmenistan's landlocked position and limited transportation infrastructure made dependent upon customers in nations that were not in a position to pay. Accordingly, gas was supplied sporadically on credit, and a large proportion of Turkmenistan's gas sales was conducted on an inefficient barter basis. This led to serious problems of external arrears and a declining gas output. The total of arrears—mainly to Armenia, Azerbaijan, Georgia, and Ukraine—rose to $1.2 billion, and the government of Turkmenistan interrupted some gas exports in 1997, greatly exacerbating political tensions in the region. Following complex negotiations involving trading partners, governments, commercial banks, and international organizations, many of the debts were rescheduled, and the government resumed gas exports.

In 1998, Turkmenistan produced 13.3 billion cubic meters of gas, down from 17.3 billion cubic meters in 1997. Turkmenistan produced 6,217 tons of oil in 1998, down from 4.4 million metric tons in 1997. Turkmenistan's gas industry is not limited by capacity. Turkmenistan can expand the output of natural gas with the turn of a valve. The constraints on production arise from the physical transport capacity. In late 1997, Turkmenistan began exporting gas to Iran through a newly completed pipeline. The government of Turkmenistan has also sought to develop new pipelines for access to external gas markets. The government has lobbied hard for international cooperation in the construction of a gas pipeline across the Caspian, through Azerbaijan, Georgia, and through the Turkish port of Ceyhan to western consumers.

Although the oil and gas sectors account for a large proportion of foreign-currency earnings, they produce incomes that are restricted to a relatively small circle and form only a small portion of overall employment. Agriculture and animal husbandry, in contrast, account for about 20 percent of gross domestic product (GDP) and more than 60 percent of overall employment. Turkmenistan is among the top ten cotton producers worldwide. The production of cotton increased in 1999 was 1.2 metric tons, up from 700,000 metric tons in 1998 and from 624,000 metric tons in 1997. In an effort to establish food self-sufficiency, Turkmenistan subsidized wheat production, leading to an increase to 1.2 million metric tons, up from 648,000 metric tons in 1997.

Despite some economic gains in recent years, much of Turkmenistan's population (48 percent by World Bank estimates) lives below the poverty level. The government has adopted populist policies to support the social safety net. Since 1992 the government has subsidized housing and related utilities (for example, electricity, water, gas, sanitation, heating, and hot water), making them virtually free, and subsidized key consumer goods (for example, bread, flour, and baby food). According to social indicators, however, the safety net is far from sound. Local gas and water supplies, although without cost to consumers, are frequently interrupted. The nation's infant mortality rate (73.25 per 1,000 live births) is among the highest in the region, and life expectancy (61 years) is among the lowest among former Soviet republics. The 2000 GDP per capita was estimated at $4,300.

The Government and the Economy

The government of Turkmenistan has been unwilling to enact serious post-Communist structural reform by reducing the dominance of the government, liberalizing the price structure, and monetarizing the economy to allow a true private sector to emerge. A weak financial and banking infrastructure continues to hobble economic growth. The government has sought to increase direct foreign investment but has pursued this goal primarily by wooing strategic investors with concessions rather than by establishing a level playing field for economic activity. The government's credit policy has been expansionary, based on "directed credit programs" and sweetheart deals. This has led to lax budget constraints and a predictably high number

of unperforming loans as credit is extended frequently not on the basis of financial merit but on the basis of access to influence and power.

The transfer of the state's most valuable assets to the private sector—privatization—has been slow and unsuccessful. Although small-scale trading and service operations have largely been privatized, the government of Turkmenistan has delayed transfer to the private sector of medium-sized and large-scale enterprises, preferring to hold these as state-managed trusts.

The government of Turkmenistan continues to play a highly interventionist role in the economy. All decisions affecting business involve some political considerations. The fusion of political and economic decision making requires that businesspeople "facilitate" necessary decisions to avoid capricious regulatory delays by offering inducements in the forms of bribes. Rather than create greater oversight, this form of control creates opportunities for corruption.

Faced with declining tax revenues from gas exports, the government has reduced budgetary sending by curtailing some expenditures (wages, pensions, stipends, and medicines are protected) in order to achieve fiscal balance. According to official figures, state budget deficits have not been large. The reported deficit was roughly 1.5 percent of GDP from 1994 to 1996, and a slight surplus was recorded in 1997 and 1998. But these figures are misleading. Turkmenistan's true budgetary picture is hard to assess because of a large number of extrabudgetary funds. A realistic estimate would put the real overall public sector deficit at 10 percent of GDP in 1999.

Future of the Turkmenistan Economy

Turkmenistan has sought to be an attractive partner, particularly for foreign enterprises interested in participating in the development of Turkmenistan's gas, oil, and agricultural sectors. However, the foundation of economic partnership in a market economy is the establishment of fair conditions for trade and commerce, not a system of favors and special treatment for preferred parties. International financial institutions such as the International Monetary Fund (IMF), the World Bank, and the European Bank for Reconstruction and Development (EBRD) have sought to assist Turkmenistan in the development of its economic institutions. Although the IMF has no formal lending program in Turkmenistan, it has provided technical assistance and policy advice. The World Bank has made major institution-building investments in privatization, modernization of the financial and banking sectors, joint-venture administration, training in the energy sector, and improvement in water quality and urban transportation. The EBRD has provided significant investment in key institutional programs.

But by and large the international development community has not been satisfied with Turkmenistan's progress toward the adoption of international standards of policy and practice. In April 2000 the EBRD took the unprecedented step of suspending its public-sector lending programs to Turkmenistan on the basis of the government's unwillingness to implement agreed-upon structural reforms. Turkmenistan's future economic development rests upon the nation's ability to break away from excessive government controls and crony capitalism toward a modern economy based upon international standards.

Gregory Gleason

Further Reading
Akiner, Shirin, and Anne Aldis. (1997) *The Caspian: Politics, Energy, Security.* London: St. Martin's Press.
Bremmer, Ian, and Raymond Taras, eds. (1993) *Nations and Politics in the Soviet Successor States.* Cambridge, U.K.: Cambridge University Press.
Craumer, Peter R. (1943) "Agricultural Change, Labor Supply, and Rural Out-Migration in Soviet Central Asia." In *Geographic Perspectives on Soviet Central Asia,* edited by Robert A. Lewis. London: Routledge, 132–180.
European Bank for Reconstruction and Development. (1999) *Turkmenistan 1999 Country Profile.* London: European Bank for Reconstruction and Development.
Gleason, Gregory. (1997) *Central Asian States: Discovering Independence.* Boulder, CO: Westview Press.
Haghayeghi, Mehrdad. (1995) *Islam & Politics in Central Asia.* New York: St. Martin's Press.
Hopkirk, Peter. (1994) *The Great Game: The Struggle for Empire in Central Asia.* London: Kodansha International.
International Monetary Fund. (1999) "Turkmenistan: Recent Economic Developments." *IMF Staff Country Report* 99, 140 (December).
McChesney, R. D. (1996) *Central Asia: Foundations of Change.* Princeton, NJ: Darwin Press.
Ollcott, Martha Brill. (1993) "Democracy and Statebuilding in Central Asia: Challenges for U.S. Policy Makers." *Demokratizatsiya* 2, 1: 39–50.
Rumer, Boris. (1989) *Soviet Central Asia: "A Tragic Experiment."* Boston: Unwin Hyman.

TURKMENISTAN—EDUCATION SYSTEM Turkmenistan marked ten years of independence from the Union of Soviet Socialist Republics (USSR) on 27 October 2001. From 1924 to 1991, the Ministry of Education of the USSR provided centrally planned curricula and textbooks, determined enrollments, and required teaching in Russian. Since 1991, many reforms have taken place in the educational system of Turkmenistan.

Structure of the Education System
The educational system of Turkmenistan consists of preschools, primary and secondary schools, vocational schools, and institutions of higher education. Preschools are available to children three years of age and older. Formal compulsory education in Turkmenistan begins at the age of seven. Students attend secondary schools for nine years. All secondary schools include elementary schools (grades one through three), where all classes are taught by the same teacher, and general schools (grades four through nine), where different subjects are taught by different teachers. Secondary schools enroll about 95 percent of the seven- to sixteen-year-old age group, evenly divided between girls and boys.

After graduating from secondary school, students may enter either a vocational school or an institution of higher education. The length of study in vocational schools varies according to the type of school, but on average ranges from one to eighteen months.

There are sixteen institutions of higher education in Turkmenistan: fifteen public and one private. The only private institution is the International Turkmen-Turkish University. Most classes at this university are taught in English, and students have to pay tuition to attend. However, attendance is free for those students who receive high scores on admission tests. The public institutions of higher education include one university, eleven institutes, one academy, one college, and one conservatory. The Ministry of Education of Turkmenistan coordinates the operation of all fifteen public institutions of higher education in the country, while the Ministry of Economy and Finances governs their budgets. All the public institutions provide education free of charge. The length of study is four to six years, depending on the specialization. In recent years, Turkmen has replaced Russian as the primary language of instruction.

Policy Making
The educational system of Turkmenistan remains highly centralized. Direction is provided mainly through decrees signed by the president of the country. The Ministry of Education, which plays a leading role in policy making, includes a minister and two assistant ministers.

Challenge for the Twenty-First Century
The major issue facing students and teachers in Turkmenistan is acquiring proficiency in the Turk-

men language. Instruction in 77 percent of secondary schools is provided in Turkmen, and in the very near future, Turkmen will be the exclusive language of instruction at all levels (it is already the only language of instruction at all institutions of higher education in the country). The government is preparing for this change by training teachers to teach in Turkmen.

The available statistics on what percentage of the population speaks Turkmen as a first language is highly misleading (all numbers are too high). The new language policy divides people into two camps: the first group feels that instruction in Turkmen is the right policy because Russian was forced on them many years ago; the other group (mostly those who do not speak Turkmen as a first language) feel that this change is unnecessary and unfair.

Jeren Balaeva-Sawyer

Further Reading

Ataev, M. A., ed. (1999) *Turkmenistan: Eight Years of Independent Development.* Ashgabat, Turkmenistan: Ministry of Economy and Finance of Turkmenistan, National Institute of Statistics and Forecast of Turkmenistan.

Atagarriyev, G. B., ed. (1999) *Turkmenistanin Presidenti Saparmirat Turkmenbashinin "Turkmenistanda durmush-ikdisadi ozgertmelerin 2010–nji yila chenli bash ugri* (The National Program of the President of Turkmenistan Saparmurat Turkmenbashi on "The Strategies of Socioeconomic Reforms in Turkmenistan for the Period until 2010"). Istanbul: Kutlu Publishing & Impex.

National Institute of Statistics and Forecasting of Turkmenistan. (1996) *Turkmenistan—Human Development Report.* Ashgabat, Turkmenistan: UNDP.

———. (1998) *Turkmenistan—Human Development Report.* Ashgabat, Turkmenistan: UNDP.

———. (1999) *Turkmenistan—Human Development Report.* Ashgabat, Turkmenistan: UNDP.

Turkmenistan—Education Sector Review. (1997) Ashgabat, Turkmenistan: UNDP.

TURKMENISTAN—HISTORY
(2000 est. pop. 4.5 million). Turkmenistan in Central Asia is home to most of the worlds Turkmen, a Turkic people: hence the name, which means "land of the Turkmen," or Turkmenia in Russian. In 1924 the newly created Turkmen Soviet Socialist Republic was named Turkmenistan, and this name was retained when the republic first became a sovereign country in 1991 with the breakup of the Soviet Union.

Premodern Turkmen and Oghuz
Turkmen descend from the Oghuz Turks, a political union of Turkic peoples, who in the eighth century migrated westward from the Gok-Turk empire, located in what is today Mongolia. They organized themselves under a *yabghu* (leader), and khans and *begs* oversaw the tribes and clans. By the tenth century the Oghuz were living in the vicinity of the Aral Sea and were one of the most numerous of the Turkic peoples, possessing extensive herds of sheep, camel, and horse.

By the eleventh century, the Turkic (Seljuk) state in Khorasan, in modern Iran, was Islamic. The name "Turkmen," previously used only as a political term, may have come to distinguish those Oghuz who adopted Islam and moved southward with the Seljuks in the eleventh century. Although they were Muslims, the Turkmen retained many aspects of their pre-Muslim beliefs and practices: shamanism, Zoroastrianism, the *Gok* or sky god (Tengri) belief system. Syncretism continues today but does not limit the Turkmen sense of Islamic heritage.

The Seljuk empire (1038–1157) had developed from the Oghuz federation of tribes. Seljuk and several Oghuz tribes moved southward to seek land and pasturage; recognizing the importance of Islam in the region, they converted. The Seljuk empire expanded into the Persian, Arab, and Byzantine lands. Its dominance over the Middle East carried Turkic traditions and customs throughout the region, advancing Persian and Turkish as administrative and cultural languages and diminishing the predominance of the Arabic language in the Muslim world.

The decline of the Seljuk empire led to the rise of principalities, most of which were overwhelmed by the Mongol invasion in the thirteenth century. The Mongol incursions into Turkmen regions pushed the Oghuz peoples farther westward into what is today Azerbaijan and Asia Minor (Turkey), whence the Ottoman empire partly grew.

During the next several centuries most Turkmen continued their traditional nomadic lifestyle, with some moving into Uzbek (another Turkic-speaking people)-dominated urban centers. While culturally and linguistically related to other Turks, the Turkmen saw themselves as distinct, even though they were not a united group. Although they recognized their Turkmen identity, tribal affiliation was even more pronounced and continues to be important. Khan leadership, regard for family genealogies, clan *tagma* (symbol), and oral traditions symbolized the primacy of clan and tribal membership

Imperial Russia
Russia began military incursions into the Turkmen regions in the mid-nineteenth century. In 1879,

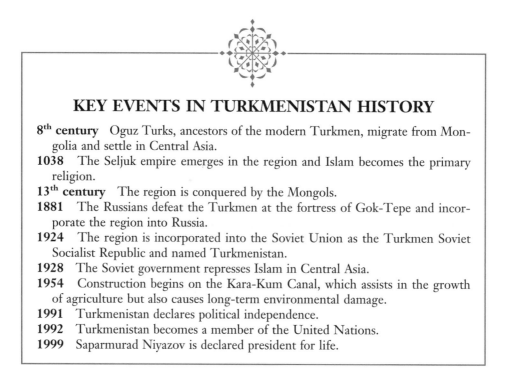

KEY EVENTS IN TURKMENISTAN HISTORY

8th century Oguz Turks, ancestors of the modern Turkmen, migrate from Mongolia and settle in Central Asia.

1038 The Seljuk empire emerges in the region and Islam becomes the primary religion.

13th century The region is conquered by the Mongols.

1881 The Russians defeat the Turkmen at the fortress of Gok-Tepe and incorporate the region into Russia.

1924 The region is incorporated into the Soviet Union as the Turkmen Soviet Socialist Republic and named Turkmenistan.

1928 The Soviet government represses Islam in Central Asia.

1954 Construction begins on the Kara-Kum Canal, which assists in the growth of agriculture but also causes long-term environmental damage.

1991 Turkmenistan declares political independence.

1992 Turkmenistan becomes a member of the United Nations.

1999 Saparmurad Niyazov is declared president for life.

several Turkmen tribes united to repulse the Russians, but the Russians returned in 1881 and on 12 January massacred eight thousand Turkmen at the fortress of Gok-Tepe, a battle that continues to haunt the Turkmen memory and that has been commemorated yearly since 1991. On 6 May 1881, the Turkmen region known in Russian as Transcaspia was named an "oblast" (region). By 1886 the Russian Imperial Transcaspian railroad stretched the length of the Turkmen lands, reinforcing Russian military and economic domination. In 1899 Transcaspia was incorporated into the governor-generalship of Russian Turkistan. In the Russian empire, the Turkmen were categorized as *inorodsty* (alien) or *tuzemtsy* (native), which meant that they were exempt from military service to the czar and were allowed to preserve local custom, but these terms also belittled them for their non-Russianness.

The Soviet Era

In 1917 Turkmen regions were divided among the Khiva khanate, Bukharan emirate, and Transcaspia. Before the Bolsheviks could take control, they had to deal with the Social Revolutionary Transcaspian Provincial Government, the British in Iran to whom the Turkmen turned for assistance, and the Basmachi or Turkmen National Liberation Movement.

On 27 October 1924, the Turkmen Soviet Socialist Republic was created from the regions inhabited primarily by Turkmen, and Turkmen tribal identities were subsumed under a new Soviet national identity. In the 1920s and early 1930s, efforts to bring Turkmen culture and infrastructure in line with the new Soviet society brought many reforms. Agriculture, industry, and the economy were radically reoriented toward Soviet goals, chief among which was continuing the czarist policy of using Turkmenistan as a mass producer of cotton. Turkmen resisted the Soviet program of collectivization, but the traditionally nomadic tribes were eventually forced to settle and work on collectives *(kholkhoz)* and state farms *(sovkhoz)*. Women's lives began to change as educational and professional opportunities grew. In 1928 the Soviet government launched an antireligious campaign against Islam in which most mosques were destroyed and Islamic life was severely hampered. The policy of *korenizatsiia* (fostering indigenous culture) led to the creation of a standardized language and a broadly based educational and literacy campaign—all of which were designed to create a loyal Turkmen proletariat.

By the 1930s, however, Moscow's policies shifted, and *korenizatsiia* was denounced as "national chauvinism." In the 1940s, Soviet policy shifted again, this time away from ideas of internationalism and toward Russification; for example, in 1940 the Turkmen were required to adopt a Cyrillic alphabet. During the 1950s Russification increased, and supranational culture such as *dastan*s (oral traditions) came under attack as a threat to Soviet culture. In 1954 construction began on the Kara-Kum Canal to bring water from the Amu Dar'ya

River to Ashgabat in Turkmenistan. The canal helped increase agricultural and cotton production, but the damage to the ecology was severe. The canal contributed to the draining of the Aral Sea and to the salinization of Turkmen lands.

Although the Soviet system deeply penetrated life in Turkmenistan, the Turkmen managed to retain many aspects of their distinct culture and values. Turkmen carpets continue to be of the highest quality and beauty. Stockbreeding remains an important sector of the economy and allows families to provide their own meat and milk products. Despite pressures, literature and poetry, especially the works of the poet Magtumguly and *dastan*s, remain vital to Turkmen identity.

Post-Soviet Era

On 27 October 1991, Turkmenistan declared political independence. Saparmurad Niyazov, the former chairman of the Supreme Soviet, popularly known as *Turkmenbasy* (head of the Turkmen), became president in 1991, was re-elected in June 1992, and was declared president for life in December 1999. In March 1992 Turkmenistan became a member of the United Nations.

Today Turkmenistan is working to establish a national identity in the international sphere, to rebuild its culture, and to restore its history. After years of suppression, Islam is emerging both in private life and in the public sector. Turkmen culture continues to cultivate many aspects of its past. Mosques are being built and restored, national holidays include the old Zoroastrian springtime celebration of Navruz, and Turkmen women still wear camel-hair bracelets to ward off evil spirits.

Victoria Clement

See also: **Central Asia–Russian Relations; Central Asia—Early Medieval Period; Central Asia—Late Medieval and Early Modern; Central Asia—Modern; Central Asia—Prehistoric; Ethnic Conflict—Central Asia; Great Game; Perestroika; Post–Communism; Russification and Sovietization—Central Asia**

Further Reading
Bartold, W. (1977) *Turkestan down to the Mongol Invasion.* London: Luzac & Company.

Becker, Seymour. (1968) *Russia's Protectorates in Central Asia: Bukhara and Khiva, 1865–1924.* Cambridge, MA: Harvard University Press.

Bennigsen, Alexandre, and S. Enders Wimbush. (1986) *Muslims of the Soviet Empire: A Guide.* Bloomington, IN: Indiana University Press.

Gleason, Gregory. (1997) *The Central Asian States: Discovering Independence.* Boulder, CO: Westview Press.

Golden, Peter. (1973) "The Migrations of the Oghuz." In *Archivum Ottomanicum* (Ottoman Archive). The Hague, Netherlands: Mouton, 45–84.

———. (1992) *An Introduction to the History of the Turkic Peoples: Ethnogenesis and State-Formation in Medieval and Early Modern Eurasia and the Middle East.* Wiesbaden, Germany: Otto Harrassowitz.

Kononov, A. N. (1958) *Rodoslovnaia Turkmen: Sochenenie Abu-l-Gazi Khana Khivinskogo* (Genealogy of the Turkmen: The Work of Abu'l Gazi Khan of Khiva). Moscow-Leningrad: Academy of Sciences.

Leiser, Gary, ed. and trans. (1988) *A History of the Seljuks: Ibrahim Kafesoglu's Interpretation and the Resulting Controversy.* Carbondale, IL: Southern Illinois University Press.

Pritsak, Omeljan. (1981) Two Migratory Movements in the Eurasian Steppe in the 9th–11th Centuries," and "The Decline of the Empire of the Oghuz Yabghu." In *Studies in Medieval Eurasian History.* London: Variorum Reprints, 157–163.

Saray, Mehmet. (1989) *The Turkmens in the Age of Imperialism: A Study of the Turkmen People and Their Incorporation into the Russian Empire.* Ankara, Turkey: Turkish Historical Society Printing House.

Soucek, Svat. (2000) *A History of Inner Asia.* Cambridge, U.K.: Cambridge University Press.

Wheeler, Geoffrey. (1964) *The Modern History of Soviet Central Asia.* Westport, CT: Greenwood Press.

TURKMENISTAN—POLITICAL SYSTEM
Although nominally a republic, Turkmenistan has a highly authoritarian political structure and culture. Turkmenistan's president, Sapamurat Niyazov (b. 1940), popularly known simply as Turkmenbashy, or "head of the Turkmen," leads Turkmenistan's only political party, the Turkmenistan National Democratic Party. During the latter Soviet period (December 1985–December 1991), Niyazov served as first secretary of the Communist Party of Turkmenistan, the highest political office in the country. Niyazov was elected chairman of the Turkmenistan Supreme Soviet in January 1990 and was elected president of the Soviet Socialist Republic of Turkmenistan on 27 October 1991, during the last stages of Gorbachev-era political reform.

After Turkmenistan gained independence in October 1991, Niyazov sought to improve his political legitimacy through popular elections. He was elected president of Turkmenistan for a five-year term in elections held on 21 June 1992, running without opposition. Niyazov's term was extended for an additional five years by a national referendum held on 15 January 1994. On 28 December 1999, Turkmenistan's parliament approved an amendment to the Turkmenistan Constitution allowing the president to remain in office for an unlimited period, effectively making Niyazov president for life.

Turkmenistan has recognized its president by naming numerous institutions, including cities, irrigation canals, schools, streets, and buildings, in his honor. Even the famed Lenin Kara-Kum Canal of Turkmenistan was renamed the Niyazov Kara-Kum Canal. A new medal of Turkmenistan National Distinction was introduced to honor extraordinary service to the Turkmenistan state, and President Niyazov became the first bearer of this new distinction.

Constitutional and Legal Framework

The postindependence Turkmenistan constitution was adopted in May 1992. According to the Turkmen political system, the president is the head of state and the government's chief executive officer. The government is managed on the top-down principle that accountability and responsiveness in Turkmenistan should be maintained not through the electoral process but through the paternalism of the head of state. The cabinet is composed of deputy chairpersons of the cabinet of ministers, usually eight in number, each with responsibilities in a broadly defined area. Beneath the level of the cabinet are the ministers leading ministries defined by functional areas. While the number of ministries varies from time to time, the list includes areas familiar from Soviet-era government administration, such as foreign affairs, defense, internal affairs, justice, finance, education, energy and industry, and oil and gas.

Other high officers of government include the chairpersons of the national parliament, or Mejlis, the members of the Supreme Court, the members of the Supreme Economic Court, and the prosecutor-general. The cabinet members and the other officers of government serve at the president's pleasure. The president appoints judges at all levels and has the power to disband local governing bodies and the Mejlis in the event that a no-confidence vote occurs twice within the Mejlis in eighteen months.

The legislative branch consists of the Khalk Maslkhaty, or People's Council. The Khalk Maslkhaty is meant to be a public information institution rather than a true deliberative assembly. In addition to its fifty elected members, the Khalk Maslkhaty includes the president, the high officers of government (including high court justices), fifty elected members of the Mejlis, from territorially defined single-voter districts, and certain other appointed local officials. In the Mejlis elections held in December 1994, the Central Electoral Commission reported a 99 percent voter turnout. In this election, fifty new Mejlis deputies were elected in noncompetitive, single-candidate districts.

All the candidates were registered members of the Turkmenistan National Democratic Party. In parliamentary elections held on 12 December 1999, the parliamentarians were elected in the same way, and all seats went to candidates of the Turkmenistan National Democratic Party.

The Turkmenistan constitution was the first legal document in any of the Central Asian states to explicitly endorse private property, by guaranteeing citizens the right to capital, land, and other material or intellectual property. However, the constitution had no provisions about the sources from which this private land was to come, nor was a land-holding fund created. A market for land emerged during the early years of independence, but the market has been dominated by local officials who set prices and determine availability, often on the basis of nonmarket factors.

Executive-Branch Functions

The Turkmenistan president is head of state and chief executive officer of the government. There is no vice president or prime minister. While the Turkmenistan constitution pays lip service to the principle of separation of powers, in fact no system of checks and balances functions in the country. Since declaring national independence, Turkmenistan has made only minimal progress in moving toward establishing an independent judiciary, promoting a truly deliberative legislature, conducting competitive elections, promoting institutions of democratic accountability, defending civil rights, and allowing freedom of association. The public and private sectors remain as closely interdependent today as they were during the period of state Communism. This fusion of political and economic decision making in Turkmenistan creates constraints on the normal operation of business and provides a fertile ground for petty economic corruption.

Competitive Politics, Elections, Parties, and Civil Rights

Turkmenistan has not succeeded in recognizing the importance of institutional pluralism in the modern period. Opposition political parties are outlawed, and the government security services deal harshly with small, unofficial parties and opposition movements. Fundamental freedoms of speech, press, assembly, movement, and confession are routinely subordinated by the state to the prevailing definition of the national interests as determined by the president. Only Islam and Russian Orthodox Christianity are registered religions. Authorities have intimidated, arrested, and otherwise persecuted individuals and groups outside these government-supervised structures.

14

The Turkmenistan government maintains that the country is "not ready" for openly functioning political parties openly debating values, ideals, and policies, as in most developed democratic countries. The government prefers to avoid social tensions, conflicts, and bloodshed by outlawing democratic institutions. The elections that have been held in Turkmenistan have been instruments designed to legitimize the existing power structures rather than expressions of the popular will. Turkmenistan does not pass the "election test"; that is, the situation in the country is not one in which, as Bernard Lewis says, "the government can be changed by elections as opposed to one where elections are changed by the government" (Lewis 1996: 53).

Transition to International Standards of Governance

International human rights organizations have been highly critical of Turkmenistan's political system, accusing it of failing to make sufficient progress toward international standards of acceptable governance. The U.S. government and other major world powers have been criticized for turning a blind eye to Turkmenistan's record and instead promoting the development of Turkmenistan's fabulous gas potential.

However, Turkmenistan's negative record is not without consequences. The European Bank for Reconstruction and Development (EBRD) suspended some of its lending programs to the Turkmenistan government in April 2000, claiming that the Turkmenistan government had failed to implement agreed-on structural reforms. The vice president of the EBRD, Charles R. Frank, noted that "the Bank has adopted a graduated approach, in which the scope of its involvement is tied to the progress these countries make in the application of universal democratic values" (Reuters 2000).

Turkmenistan's position in the international community may be determined not by its ability to make the transition to a higher standard of living but rather by its ability to offer its citizens a higher quality of life.

Gregory Gleason

Further Reading

Akiner, Shirin, and Anne Aldis. (1997) *The Caspian: Politics, Energy, Security*. London: St. Martin's Press.

Bremmer, Ian, and Raymond Taras, eds. (1993) *Nations and Politics in the Soviet Successor States*. Cambridge, UK: Cambridge University Press.

Commission on Security and Cooperation in Europe. (2000) *Human Rights and Democratization in Uzbekistan and Turkmenistan*. Washington, DC: U.S. Government Printing Office.

European Bank for Reconstruction and Development. (1999) *Turkmenistan 1999 Country Profile*. London: European Bank for Reconstruction and Development.

Gleason, Gregory. (1997) *Central Asian States: Discovering Independence*. Boulder, CO: Westview Press.

Haghayeghi, Mehrdad. (1995) *Islam & Politics in Central Asia*. New York: St. Martin's Press.

Hopkirk, Peter. (1994) *The Great Game: The Struggle for Empire in Central Asia*. London: Kodansha International.

International Monetary Fund. (1999) *Turkmenistan: Recent Economic Developments*. IMF Staff Country Report no. 99/140 (December). Washington, DC: International Monetary Fund.

Lewis, Bernard. (1996) "A Historical Overview." *Journal of Democracy* 7, 2: 52–63.

McChesney, R. D. (1996) *Central Asia: Foundations of Change*. Princeton, NJ: Darwin Press.

Ollcott, Martha Brill. (1993) "Democracy and Statebuilding in Central Asia: Challenges for U.S. Policy Makers." *Demokratizatsiia* (Democratization) 2, 1: 39–50.

Reuters. (2000) "EBRD Cuts Turkmen Loans, Slams Political System" (18 April).

U.S. Department of State. (2000) *1999 Country Reports on Human Rights Practices*. Washington, DC: U.S. Department of State.

TURKS—WESTERN ASIA

The word "Turk" refers to the members of the great linguistic and cultural family of Turkic peoples extending from China to Europe. Today there are two main groups of Turkic peoples: the western and the eastern. The eastern group is made up of the Turkic peoples inhabiting the areas of present-day Central Asia and the Uygur Autonomous Region of Xinjiang in China. The Turks of Turkey belong to the western group, which also includes the Turks of the Balkans, Anatolia, Cyprus, northern Iraq, and northwestern Iran and Azerbaijan. Almost nine-tenths of the population of Turkey claims Turkish as their first language. In present-day Turkey, however, the word implies not only ethnic, cultural, and linguistic aspects but also designates the politico-cultural group that includes everyone living in the territory of the Turkish state. According to the Turkish Constitution, Turkey is made up of all its citizens without distinction of race or religion.

Origins of Turkic Peoples

The primary ancestors of the Turks of Turkey are the Oguz Turks, who founded an empire in Central Asia in the sixth century CE. By the eighth century, nearly all the Oguz had adopted Islam, which is still the religion of most eastern and western Turks today. Around the tenth century, the Oguz migrated westward and settled southwest of the Caspian Sea, in Iran and Iraq. There the family of Oguz tribes known as Seljuks created an empire, which by the eleventh century extended from the Indus River west to the Mediterranean Sea. In 1071, the Seljuk sultan Alp Arslan defeated the Byzantines at the Battle of Manzikert, and thereafter several million Oguz settled in Anatolia. These Turks came to constitute the majority of the population there and made it part of the Islamic world.

Ottoman Dynasty

An Oguz tribe led by Osman Beg founded the Ottoman dynasty in 1299. The empire reached its zenith during the reign of Suleyman the Magnificent (reigned 1520–1566) and controlled vast areas from northern Africa to southern Russia and from the borders of Austria to the Bay of Basra. Turks spread westward into the Balkans, and their descendants continued to inhabit that region for five hundred years. After the collapse of the empire, most of these Turks returned to Turkey.

European expansion into the Ottoman empire and the rise of nationalism among the ethnic and racial groups of the empire resulted in the Ottoman empire's dissolution in the early twentieth century. Nationalist feelings began to spread among the Turks, and Turkish elite began to call themselves Turks rather than Ottomans and began searching for Turkic origins.

Modern Turkey

Following the partition of the six hundred-year-old Ottoman empire after World War I, Turkish nationalists under the leadership of Ataturk (1881–1938) renounced the Ottoman heritage and founded the Republic of Turkey in 1923 within the borders of the empire's Turkish core–Anatolia and eastern Thrace. To Westernize Turkey, Ataturk launched a series of reforms affecting all aspects of life, from introducing a civil code to changing the alphabet from Arabic to Latin in 1928

A Turkish man with his two daughters in Kayseri, Turkey, c. 1997. (DAVE BARTRUFF/CORBIS)

and, in the 1930s, purifying the Turkish language by removing the foreign words. Ataturk's aim was to forge the identity of the modern Turks and to make them more like Europeans. Ataturk's reforms, based on secularism, nationalism, and modernization, constitute the ideological base of modern Turkey, called Kemalism.

In the process of modernization, the Ottoman structure of social relationships was greatly transformed. Women began to take their place in the public sphere along with men; the nuclear family replaced the extended family, although in most rural areas patrilineal ties and values are still dominant in determining social and kinship relations. Nearly two-thirds of the population live in urban areas and work in industrial and service sectors. The rate of population growth declined after the 1960s due to family-planning policies. Today approximately 3.5 million Turks live in various Western European countries.

Nearly all Turks are Muslim. Thus, while the Turkish state is secular, Islam has had a deep impact on family and social life, although this influence varies according to people's social and economic status. Two dominant sects of Islam, the Sunni majority and the Alevi, divide society vertically. The Alevi originated from Shi'ite Islam, but unlike their Iranian counterparts, are heterodox and have no formal clergy.

The culture of modern Turks has both modern and traditional elements, the latter of which are based on the rich Ottoman legacy apparent in carpet weaving, ceramics, music, architectural forms, and folk arts. Thanks to Ataturk's reforms, modern literature, fine arts, and classical and contemporary music flourish in Turkey. Today, theater, a growing film industry, and book and magazine publications play an important role in Turkish culture.

Most Turkish citizens are ethnically Turk, but very few if any are "pure" ethnic Turks. After the Turkic nomads came to Anatolia in the eleventh century, some settled peoples like the Greeks and the Armenians became Muslim and Turkish. Other Turkish citizens are descendants of those who came from the Balkans and the Caucasus as refugees in the late nineteenth and early twentieth centuries. This long history of intermixing explains the difference in physical appearance between the Turks of Turkey, who are akin to European peoples, and the eastern Turks, who have an East Asian appearance.

The Turkish language spoken by Turkey's Turks belongs to the Ural-Altaic linguistic family and, with Gagauz, Azerbaijani, Turkmen, and Khorasan Turkic, forms the Oguz branch of the Turkic languages. Modern Turkish is also the language of Turkish minorities living in north Cyprus, northern Iraq, Bulgaria, Greece, Macedonia, and Kosovo. Kurdish-speaking people, an estimated one-seventh of the population of Turkey, constitute another major linguistic group in that nation.

Yilmaz Colak

Further Reading

Hotham, David. (1972) *The Turks*. London: John Murray.
Lewis, Bernard. (1966) *The Emergence of Modern Turkey*. London: Oxford University Press.
McCarthy, Justine. (1997) *The Ottoman Turks*. London: Longman.

TURUGART PASS Turugart (Torugart) Pass is a mountain pass in the Tian Shan mountain range of Central Asia, connecting the Republic of Kyrgyzstan with Xinjiang Province in the far northwestern region of the People's Republic of China. A major highway runs through the pass, following one of the main routes of the ancient Silk Road between Europe and China. The road winds south through the smaller At-Bashi mountain range in the central part of the Tian Shan, which is oriented northeast and southwest, forming much of the Kyrgyz and Chinese border. Reaching a height of 3,752 meters at the pass, the road descends to the Chinese city of Kashgar on the edge of the vast Taklimakan Desert. A pristine mountain landscape and high mountain lakes such as Lake Chatyr Kul, virtually untouched by human hands, make the pass an area of environmental concern for the Kyrgyz government and people.

Near the pass, within Kyrgyzstan, sits the tenth-century Tash-Rabat caravanserai, or caravan rest stop, that gave shelter to caravans traveling along the Silk Route between Europe and China. The high mountain pass is growing in importance as a major economic and trading link between Kyrgyzstan and western China. The Kyrgyz form the majority of the population on both sides of the Turugart Pass.

David R. Smith

Further Reading

Gvozdetskij, N. A., and N. I. Mikhailov. (1978) *Fizicheskaia Geografiya SSSR: Aziatskaia Chast'* (Physical Geography of the USSR: Asian part). Third edition. Moscow: Mysl'.
Whittell, Giles. (1995) *Central Asia: The Practical Handbook*. London: Cadogan Books.

TWELVE MUQAM The Twelve *Muqam* are considered the most prestigious music of the Uighur people of Xinjiang in northwest China. In terminol-

ogy, they are allied to the Arabo-Persian *maqam* system; *muqam* is the Turkic-language variant of this Arab term, and many names of individual suites are also drawn from Arabic. Musically, however, the *Muqam* are more closely related to Central Asian art-music traditions, like the Bukharan *Shashmaqam*. Unlike the Arabo-Persian traditions, which involve a degree of improvisation in performance, each of the Uighur Twelve *Muqam* is basically a tripartite suite made up of (1) *chong naghma* (great music)—a series of vocal and instrumental pieces beginning with a meditative unmetered *bash muqam* (introduction); (2) *dastan* (stories)—slower metered pieces; (3) *mashrap* (festival)—fast dance pieces.

The pieces are characterized by rhythmic formulas marked out by the hand-held *dap* (drum). Each of the Uighur Twelve *Muqam* is basically a fixed tripartite musical suite; each has a defining mood and pitch range, but modulation is so frequent that is hardly possible to link a *Muqam* to one mode, in contrast to the Arabo-Persian tradition.

The lyrics of the Twelve *Muqam* are attributed to the great Turkic and Persian poets or drawn from folk poetry; they are imbued with Sufi imagery and ideals. Said to originate in the fifteenth-century Kashgar court, their present form is more realistically traced back to the nineteenth century. *Muqam* may be performed by one singer with bowed or plucked lute (*satar* or *tanbur*) plus drum or with a small group of supporting voices and instruments. Men, women, beggars, and respected religious men may practice this tradition, for enjoyment or religious purposes. The Twelve *Muqam* hold an important place in Uighurs' affections and are often referred to in terms of spiritual necessity and moral authority.

Rachel Harris

Further Reading

During, Jean, and Sabine Trebinjac. (1991) *Introduction au Muqam Ouigour*. Bloomington, IN: Indiana University Press.
Mackerras, Colin. (1985) "Traditional Uyghur Performing Arts." *Asian Music* 16: 29–58.
Trebinjac, Sabine. 2000. *Le Pouvoir en chantent: L'Art de fabriquer une musique chinoise*. Nanterre, France: Societé d'ethnologie.

Recordings

La Route de Soie, Chine, Xinjiang. (1992) Recordings by Anderson Bakewell. France: Playasound PS 65087.
Turkestan Chinois/Xinjiang: Musique Ouigoures. (1990) Recordings by Sabine Trebinjac and Jean During. France: Ocora C559092-93.

Uyghur Musicians from Xinjiang: Music from the Oasis Towns of Central Asia. (2000) Sleeve notes by Rachel Harris. U.K.: Globestyle CDO0BD 098.

TWELVER SHI'ISM

There are two major branches of Islam. After the death of the prophet Muhammad (c. 632 CE), Muslims who followed Abu Bakr, 'Umar, and 'Uthman as the temporal and spiritual heads of Islam came to be known as Sunni Muslims. Those following 'Ali and his descendants came to be known as Shi'ite Muslims. Among the Shi'a, those believing in the twelve imams (spiritual heads of the Muslim faith), beginning with 'Ali and ending with the twelfth imam, are known as *Ithna 'ashariyiah* or Twelver Shi'ite Muslims. This also contrasts with those who only believe in seven imams—the Ismailis. In both Sunni and Shi'ite Islam, there are traditions attributed to the prophet Muhammad about the day of judgment and the coming of the Mahdi (Rightly Guided One). In the Twelver Shi'a theology, the Mahdi and the twelfth imam are one and the same. It is thought that when recognized, the Mahdi will be named after the prophet Muhammad and will be a member of the house of the prophet, one who is a direct offspring of Muhammad.

The twelfth imam is the last imam of the Twelver Shi'ite tradition. Like many of the Shi'a imams, the eleventh imam, Hasan al-Askari (d. 874), was persecuted by the Sunni rulers of his time. The Abbasid caliph Mu'tamid had deported Imam al-Askari from Medina to Samarra (in present-day Iraq) and kept him as a prisoner for much of his short imamate. After Imam al-Askari's death, general confusion erupted among the Shi'ite community because no apparent successor had been appointed by him, nor was he known to have had any sons. As many as twenty factions were formed among the Shi'a, with each adhering to idiosyncratic beliefs. One faction continued to believe that Imam al-Askari was not dead but in a state of occultation (waiting to reappear to humanity). Similar ideas had risen after the death of the seventh imam, Musa al-Kazim (d. 799 CE). Others claimed that Imam al-Askari was childless. Yet others claimed that he had a son, who was the anticipated Mahdi and who has gone into occultation. They claimed that the five-year-old Mahdi was seen searching for his father near his dwelling place when he entered a cavern and was not seen again.

Although the myth or reality of the twelfth imam cannot be fully determined, the Twelver Shi'ism tradition considers him to have existed, to have been named Muhammad, and to have been a son of the eleventh imam, Hasan al-Askari. It is said that even his mother was not aware of her own pregnancy. The twelfth imam is said to have been in danger of being killed by the Abbasids, who were the rulers of his time, because the Abbasids feared that the emergence of the Mahdi would end their tyrannical rule. In order to create dissent within the Shi'a ranks, the Abbasids had even supported one of Imam al-Askari's brothers by the name of Ja'far as the claimant to the office of the imamate.

It is also held that Imam al-Askari smuggled his son, Muhammad, from Samarra to Medina in 873. During his seven-year imamate, Hasan al-Askari lived in occasional imprisonment, hiding, and dissimulation (*taqiyya*), a practice of denying of one's faith used by the Shi'ites to protect themselves from the majority Sunni.

The twelfth imam lived in hiding for sixty-nine years, communicating with and guiding the Shi'a believers through four renowned followers. This period is known as the lesser occultation (874–941 CE). The concept of the *safir* (ambassador or agent) through whom imams communicated with their followers, had been established by earlier Shi'ite imams. After the death of the fourth ambassador, no other significant leader immediately claimed to be an ambassador or direct communicator with the twelfth imam. Another tradition has it that the fourth ambassador also gave the news of the bodily death of the imam to the believers.

The period from the supposed death of the twelfth imam until the day of his resurrection is known as the greater occultation. Many of the Shi'a believe that the twelfth imam is living among humanity but is invisible and that he will choose to reveal himself and rid the world of injustice when he deems it an appropriate time.

During the nineteenth century, several prominent figures are considered to have been the twelfth imam. The most prominent were Shaykh Ahmad al-Ahsa'i (1753–1826), Sayyid Kazem Rashti (d. 1844), and Mirza 'Ali Muhammad (1819–1850) of Shiraz, also known as the Bab ("the Gate"). The Bab announced his status in 1844, exactly one thousand lunar years from the lesser occultation of the twelfth imam (260 CE). Later, Mirza 'Ali Muhammad claimed to be the Mahdi and was eventually imprisoned and executed.

Unlike in the Sunni branch of Islam, in Shi'a clerics are considered more than religiously well-versed people who hold the same status as judges in secular courts. Many Shi'ite Muslims consider their religious figures to speak and deliver judgments in the name of the twelfth imam. This has given substantial powers to Shi'ite clerics. The twelfth imam is also known as the *Muntazar* (the Expected One), the *Hujja* (the Proof), the *Qaim* (the Living), and the *Imam al-Zaman* (the Imam of Time). Today, the birth of the twelfth imam is celebrated throughout the Shi'a Muslim world.

Cyrus Koenberg

Further Reading
Sachedina, Abdulziz A. (1981) *Islamic Messianism: The Idea of the Mahdi in Twelver Shi'ism.* Albany, NY: State University of New York Press.

TWENTY-SIX MARTYRS   The twenty-six martyrs were Japanese and Western Christians crucified at Nishizaka Hill in Nagasaki on 5 February 1597. The twenty-six were ordered executed by Toyotomi Hideyoshi (1536/7–1598), Japan's paramount leader at the time, in response to developments surrounding the stranding of the Spanish galleon *San Felipe* the previous autumn off the island of Shikoku. Hideyoshi, who had long exhibited an erratic policy toward Christianity in Japan, had first banned the religion in 1587 but had not strictly enforced this proscription directed against the Jesuits. Originally, he also welcomed the Franciscans when they began their missionary work in the country in the 1590s, but when a pilot aboard the *San Felipe* boasted that Franciscan friars had in the past served as a vanguard of Spanish invasion forces in foreign territories, Hideyoshi moved quickly against the Franciscans in Japan.

In December 1596, six Western Franciscans from the Kyoto/Osaka area, fifteen Japanese followers of the Franciscan mission, and three Japanese Jesuits were arrested, tried, and condemned to death. The twenty-four were marched overland from Kyoto to Nagasaki for crucifixion. Two Japanese who followed the prisoners to look after their needs were also included among those executed. The deaths of the six foreign missionaries marked the first time that Westerners were executed in Japan for their faith.

The twenty-six were beatified by Pope Urban VIII in 1627 and canonized by Pope Pius IX in 1862. Three years later, to commemorate the martyrdom, French Catholic missionaries built Oura Church facing Nishizaka Hill in Nagasaki. A memorial to the martyrs was built at Nishizaka on the centennial of their canonization. In 1981 Pope John Paul II visited the memorial and paid tribute to the martyrs.

Lane R. Earns

Further Reading
Fujita, Neil S. (1991) *Japan's Encounter with Christianity: The Catholic Mission in Pre-Modern Japan.* New York: Paulist Press.
Yuki, Diego R. (1979) *The Martyrs' Hill Nagasaki.* Nagasaki, Japan: Twenty-six Martyrs Museum.

TYPHOONS   Typhoons or cyclones are large, often destructive tropical storms similar to the western hemisphere's hurricanes. From Japan to India, millions of lives are at risk from typhoons, because of their high wind speeds, intense rainfall, and sea surges.

Since typhoons depend on heat and moisture to sustain them, these storms always form over warm oceans near the equator where sea-surface temperatures are at least 26°C. They originate in the western Pacific above the equator and follow several general tracks—westward across the central Philippines and into central and northern Vietnam, or curving northward to Hong Kong, Taiwan, Japan, and coastal areas of China. The most deadly and damaging of these storms originate in the warm water of the Bay of Bengal, where their northward track drives them into the low-lying and densely settled areas of Bangladesh. These storm occur before (April and May) or after (October–November) the southwest monsoon season and have been accompanied by winds in excess of 145 miles per hour. Although these winds can do great damage and release large amounts of rainfall, it is the storm surge or wall of water pushed ahead of the low pressure eye of the storm as it approaches the shoreline that is most devastating and accounts for most loss of life. The average annual frequency of typhoons in East and Southeast Asia is three or more per year. In the Indian Ocean and Bay of Bengal, where these storms are called cyclones, there may be one or more per year.

Residents with their personal belongings wade through the flooded streets of Nagoya, Japan, in September 2000 following a typhoon. (AFP/CORBIS)

The greatest damages from typhoons or cyclones have occurred in Bangladesh, the Philippines, and Japan. About 10 percent of all tropical cyclones form in the Bay of Bengal. Poverty and overpopulation worsen the devastating effects of cyclones on Bangladesh. Twenty million people live in vulnerable rural communities in the delta at the head of the Bay of Bengal, where much of the more productive rice land is located. In May 1985, a cyclone with a storm surge nine meters high caused more than eleven thousand deaths, although much higher death tolls have been recorded. For example, the storm of 29 April 1991 had an estimated death toll of 150,000–200,000 people and directly affected 15 million residents.

In isolated island groups such as the Philippines and Japan, typhoons can inflict large amounts of property damage, flooding, and loss of life. The concentration of built-up methods and agricultural activities in flood-prone lowlands and along coastlines means that high winds and heavy rainfall can cause damage to crops and buildings and threaten human life. The low-lying and narrow landmass of these island groups tends to intensify the impact of these forces. In 1970, four major typhoons swept central and north Luzon Island in the Philippines with over fifteen hundred lives lost. Typhoon Goring caused millions of pesos in crop damage in 1989.

Japan is hit by an average of four typhoons a year, which cause millions of dollars in property damage, primarily in the southern islands of Kyushu and Fukuoka. Typhoon Vera, which struck central Honshu in 1959, left five thousand dead and over forty thousand injured.

Efforts to mitigate the adverse impact of typhoons vary. Japan has enforced typhoon-resistant building practices in many of the most vulnerable urban areas in Kyushu and southern Honshu Islands and Fukuoka Prefecture for many years. Elsewhere in Asia, evacuation programs and early warning systems are less developed, although governments and international disaster-management agencies are working on developing them.

James Hafner

Further Reading
Alexander, David. (1991) *Natural Disasters.* New York: Chapman & Hall.

Kovach, Robert L. (1995) *Earth's Fury: An Introduction to Natural Hazards and Disasters.* Englewood Cliffs, NJ: Prentice-Hall.

Smith, Keith. (1996) *Environmental Hazards: Assessing Risk and Reducing Disaster.* 2d ed. New York: Routledge.

UCHIMURA KANZO (1861–1930), Japanese writer and religious figure. Uchimura Kanzo was born in Edo (present-day Tokyo) to the samurai class and educated in the English language at Sapporo Agricultural College (now Hokkaido University), where he converted to Christianity. In 1884, he traveled to the United States, studied at Amherst College and Hartford Theological Seminary, and worked at a mental hospital in Philadelphia. His spiritual autobiography, *How I Became a Christian* (1895), describes the racial prejudice, economic injustice, crime, and strident religious sectarianism he found in the United States, all of which he considered contrary to true Christianity. After returning to Japan in 1888, he became a schoolteacher, but was accused by his colleagues of showing disrespect toward the emperor. Unable to continue in education, he became a writer, editor, and religious leader, as well as a prominent pacifist. His *mukyokai* (nonchurch) doctrine sought to avoid reliance upon church buildings, professional ministers, and organizations in favor of more informal and democratic gatherings at individuals' homes. Although motivated in part by a resistance to the hegemony of Western religious institutionalism, his doctrine also emphasized Bible study in small groups, organized along the culturally familiar pattern of *sensei* (teacher or mentor) and *deshi* (student or disciple). While technically a fundamentalist, his beliefs are also seen as nationalistic in their advocacy of a Japanese-led reformation of Christianity.

Matthew Mizenko

Further Reading
Miura Hiroshi. (1996) *The Life and Thought of Kanzo Uchimura, 1861–1930.* Grand Rapids, MI: Eerdmans.

Uchimura Kanzo. (1895) *The Diary of a Japanese Convert.* New York: Revell.
———. (1895) *How I Became a Christian.* Tokyo: Keiseisha.

UIGHURS Uighurs (or Uygurs) are the largest of the Turkic groups in Xinjiang Uygur Autonomous Region of China, with an estimated population in the region of 8 million in 1997. Uighurs account for 46.7 percent of the population of Xinjiang Uygur Autonomous Region, with Han Chinese accounting for 38.4 percent and members of other minority ethnicities accounting for the remaining 14.9 percent. For most of the past ten centuries, these people have lived under the control of the Mongolian peoples. The Uighurs make their living in the Tian Shan mountain range as nomads (though the nomadic population is decreasing), herding sheep, goats, cows, horses, and camels. In oases near the Taklimakan Desert, they engage in farming with the aid of irrigation canals or underground waterways to run meltwater. Wheat, corn, cotton, and fruit (grapes, watermelons, and muskmelons) are popular crops. Trading is actively carried out across borders in the southwestern cities, where people weave traditional carpets.

At present they are Sunni Muslims, but earlier in their history they inclined to Manichaeanism (since the eighth century) and Buddhism (since the tenth century), and originally they adhered to shamanism and believed that Heaven *(tengri)* gave order, power, and wisdom to mankind. Fragments of many kinds of texts on Buddhism, Manichaeanism, and Nestorian Christianity have been uncovered at archaeological sites in Uighur areas. Islam came to Uighur lands along the Silk Road, and almost all Uighurs had become Muslims by the end of the fifteenth century. Since 1978, the Chinese government has maintained an appeasement policy with regard to religious expression, supporting the revival of religious activities, including reconstruction of mosques and religious school, as well as supporting publication of books in Uighur, in an effort to promote reform and an open-door policy. This is in an attempt to mend the damage done by the Cultural Revolution (1966–1976), in which much of the culture of the pre-Communist period was destroyed. Muslims are hopeful that these policies will lead to a resurgence of ethnic and religious autonomy, but their optimism is guarded. They are quite afraid that their ethnic and cultural sovereignty will be overwhelmed by the area's growing Han Chinese population. China, for its part, is very sensitive about matters affecting its sovereignty over the Xinjiang Uygur Autonomous Region.

Early History of the Uighur people

The term Uighur originated as the name of one of the Nine Tribes (Tokuz Oghuz), a confederation of Turkic nomads that first appears in the annals of Chinese historiography in the early seventh century. A clan of the Uighur tribe, the Yaghlakar, established a state (744–840 CE) in what is now Mongolia. This state's most notable contribution was the military rescue of the Chinese Tang dynasty (618–907 CE) from the crises caused by the rebellion of the general An Lushan (703–757). In return, the Chinese emperor bequeathed the Uighur state a large monetary award annually. The Uighurs strengthened their relationship with the Sogdian merchants (Sogdians were a people who lived in Transoxiana, now Uzbekistan) who had a profitable trade of horses from the Uighur state for silk from China. In 763, the Uighurs permitted the Sogdians' Manichaean missionary work. The city Ordubalik ("Town of the Palace"), located on the Orkhon riverside and later named Karabalghasun, enjoyed its greatest flourishing during this time. The Sogdians engaged in commerce with their colonies along the Silk Road leading to China and the Uighur state.

The Uighur ruling classes attempted to strengthen social and economic relations with the Sogdians, which caused unrest among nomadic Uighurs, who were suffering from famine and pestilence, and, in 839, from heavy snowfalls. Probably seeing the opportunity to take advantage of the situation, a large number of Kyrgyz, a Turkic tribe in the upper Yenisey valley, allied with a discontented Uighur general and invaded and burned Ordubalik, bringing down the Uighur government in 840. Both Uighur nomads and nobles of the ruling classes emigrated, eventually settling in the area

from the Tian Shan to Gansu Province in northwestern China. Immigrant Uighurs founded at least two new states, the Uighur kingdom of Ganzhou (890–1028), and the West Uighur kingdom (early tenth century–1284). Descendants of the former Ganzhou Uighurs may be the Yugu in Gansu, traditionally known as the Yellow Uighurs (with a population of approximately 39,000 people in the Autonomous Sunan Yugu Prefecture in 1997).

Rule by the Kara Khitan and the Mongols

The Uighur kingdom of Ganzhou was absorbed by the Tangut people (herdsmen from the Ordos desert area of northern China) into their Xi Xia kingdom in 1028. The West Uighur kingdom fell under the control of the Kara Khitan in the 1130s. In 1209, unable to bear the tyranny of the local Kara Khitan magistrate, the king of the Uighurs had him killed. He was no doubt emboldened by the promise of protection from a new and more powerful overlord: Genghis Khan. The king surrendered the West Uighur kingdom to Genghis Khan in the same year; it survived as a Mongol vassal state until 1284. The Uighurs were originally supposed to provide military service for the Mongol empire but ended up occupying higher positions in various areas of the government.

A succession dispute among the Mongol khans turned the Uighur lands into a battlefield at the end of the thirteenth century, and by the early fourteenth century the castle towns in the Turfan basin were devastated by war. The Uighur royal family and their subordinates took refuge in Gansu in 1284, and the Uighur lands came to be ruled by the descendants of Chagatai Khan, son of Genghis Khan. When the Kashgar Khojas, Islamic nobles, gained power in the seventeenth and eighteenth century, Islam and Islamic culture, for example, the Naqshbandiya order of Sufi Islamic mystics, spread among the Uighur people. Galdan Khan (1645–1697), leader of the Oirats of western Mongolia, occupied the land of the Uighurs for seventy years following an invasion in 1679. In the first half of the eighteenth century, under Galdan's successors, many Uighur farmers (later called Taranchis) of southern Xinjiang were forcibly relocated to the Ili Valley on the northern border.

Rule by China

In 1760, the Uighur lands were conquered by military expeditions of the Chinese Qing dynasty (1644–1912). Approximately forty-five thousand Uighurs moved to Semirechie in Kazakhstan in 1881. The Uighur people in the oases around the Taklimakan desert came under Chinese rule when Xinjiang Province was established there in 1884. After the Uighur rebellion of 1931–1934, the Chinese government at last granted the Uighurs the status of a minority people.

The Uighurs, together with China's Kazakh minority, founded a state (the East Turkistan Republic) in northern Xinjiang in 1944–1949, but the newly established People's Republic of China absorbed it in October of 1949. In 1955 the Chinese set up an administrative office in the Xinjiang Uygur Autonomous Region of China at Urumchi. About sixty thousand people, including Uighurs and Kazakhs, emigrated to Kazakhstan (1962). Today, there are more than 200,000 Uighurs who are citizens of Kazakhstan.

Juten Oda

Further Reading

Allsen, Thomas T. (1983) "The Yuan Dynasty and the Uighurs of Turfan in the 13th Century." In *China Among Equals. The Middle Kingdom and Its Neighbors, 10th–14th Centuries,* edited by Morris Rossabi. Berkeley and Los Angeles: University of California Press, 243–280.

Gansu Province Statistical Bureau, ed. (1998) *Gansu Yearbook: 1997.* Beijing: Zhongguo tongji chubanshe.

Mackerras, Colin. (1990) "The Uighurs." In *The Cambridge History of Early Inner Asia,* edited by Denis Sinor. Cambridge: Cambridge University Press, 320–342.

Warikoo, Kulbhushan. (1998) "Ethnic Religious Resurgence in Xinjiang." In *Post-Soviet Central Asia*, edited by Touraj Atabaki and John O'Kane. Leiden, the Netherlands: Tauris Academic Studies, London, New York in association with the International Institute for Asian Studies, 269–282.

Xinjiang Uygur Autonomous Region Statistical Bureau, ed. (1998) *Xinjiang Statistical Yearbook: 1997.* Beijing: Zhongguo tongji chubanshe.

ULAANBAATAR   (2000 est. pop. 774,000). Ulaanbaatar (also Ulan Bator, Urga, Niislel Huree), situated at an altitude of 1,350 meters in central Mongolia, is the capital of the Mongolian People's Republic and is the country's largest city. Mountains, including the prominent Bogd Uul Ridge (2,200 meters), surround the city, which lies in a long valley of the Tuul River.

The city began in 1639 as the itinerant court of an influential Mongolian prince. Over decades it gradually became a religious and political center for the region, and in the eighteenth century the court settled permanently on the current site of Ulaanbaatar. From this place, the *bogdo-gegen,* Mongolian Buddhism's highest lama, exercised religious and political authority across large areas of modern-day Mongolia. By 1900, as many as twenty thousand lamas were conducting services at more than one hundred temples in

Ulaanbaatar in 1983, while still under Soviet rule. The high-rises on the outskirts of the city were occupied by Russians and Eastern Europeans and contrast with the more traditional architecture of buildings in the foreground of the photo. (DEAN CONGER/CORBIS)

the city. In addition the city was home to six hundred foreign firms and several thousand merchants and craftsmen and prospered from trade between Russia and China.

The first half of the twentieth century was a turbulent time for the city. In 1911, when Outer Mongolia declared independence from China, the city was renamed Niislel Huree ("national capital"). During the following decade, it was variously occupied by Chinese and White Russian troops, and in 1921 a Mongolian militia commanded by Damdiny Suhbaatar captured the city with the aid of the Soviet Red Army. In 1924 leaders of the country's Communist revolution renamed the town Ulaanbaatar, which means "red hero." With Soviet aid, the city built museums, theaters, and several institutions of higher learning, including the National University of Mongolia. To accommodate the fast-growing population, block apartments replaced the traditional Mongolian *ger* (felt tent) and public transportation replaced horses. In 2000 the city produced more than 50 percent of the country's industrial output. Its architecture is an eclectic combination of Soviet-style block apartments, neoclassical public buildings, Tibetan Buddhist temples, and traditional *ger*s. The Trans-Mongolian Railway and an international airport connect the capital to both Beijing and Moscow, and it is the political, cultural, and social center of the Mongolian People's Republic.

Daniel Hruschka

Further Reading
Bawden, Charles R. (1968) *The Modern History of Mongolia.* London: Weidenfeld & Nicolson.

ULCHI MUNDOK (flourished 589–618), general of the Korean kingdom of Koguryo (37 BCE–668 CE). Ulchi Mundok was the hero of the Koguryo repulsion of the Sui Chinese invasion of 612. He is known, however, largely from one short passage in Kim Pu-shik's (1075–1151) *Samguk sagi* (History of the Three Kingdoms), which discusses his cunning defeat of the larger Chinese force. He lured the battle-weary Sui invaders deep into Koguryo territory by feigning defeat in several small skirmishes and sending a poem taunting the Chinese commander. He then trapped and slaughtered the Chinese troops at the Sal River (now Ch'ongch'on) and harassed them all the way back to Liaodong. Winning this great victory saved Koguryo from Chinese conquest. The poem and the Chinese version of story, from which Kim Pu-shik's account derives, are preserved in Wei Zheng's (580–643) *Sui shu* (History of the Sui).

Ulchi Mundok did not become a Korean national hero until the modern era. Traditionally, that honor was accorded to the Shilla kingdom's General Kim Yu-shin (595–673), an important figure in the unification of the Three Korean kingdoms (Koguryo, Shilla, and Paekche) in the 660s. However, nationalist historians have more recently argued that Ulchi Mundok was the real military hero of the period, because he protected Koguryo's ancient possessions in Manchuria and preserved Korea's political and cultural independence by not forming an alliance with Tang China as the Shilla leaders did. Because many present-day Koreans see Korea's historical and cultural roots in Koguryo, Ulchi Mundok has become a symbol of the Korean national spirit.

Richard D. McBride II

Further Reading
Lee, Peter H., trans. (1993) "Ŭlchi Mundŏk" (from Kim Pu-shik's *Samguk sagi* [History of the Three Kingdoms]). In *Sourcebook of Korean Civilization, 1: From Early Times to the Sixteenth Century,* edited by Peter H. Lee. New York: Columbia University Press, 37–38.

UMAR, TEUKU (1854–1898), Acehnese war leader. Born in Meulaboh, Aceh, on the island of Sumatra, Indonesia, Teuku Umar (Teuku Oema) first rose to prominence as a military leader on the western coast of Aceh during the long military struggle against the Netherlands's annexation of the sultanate in 1874. In 1883 he was lured away from the resistance by Dutch promises of money and weapons as part of a policy to create a coalition of pro-Dutch Acehnese forces but deserted them in 1884. He rejoined the Dutch in 1893 and deserted them again in 1896, taking many of their weapons and resuming the armed struggle against them. His action strengthened those among the Dutch arguing for more forceful action in Aceh. In 1898 Colonel J. B. van Heutsz was appointed head of the Dutch civil and military forces with the task of subjugating the region. Van Heutsz's wide-ranging military operations included an ambush at Meulaboh in which Umar was killed.

Although Umar is officially regarded as a hero of the anticolonial resistance, his willingness to collaborate with the Dutch presaged their successful strategy of co-opting *uleebalang* (war leaders) as allies against more radically anticolonial Muslim leaders.

Robert Cribb

Further Reading
Reid, Anthony. (1969) *The Contest for North Sumatra: Atjeh, the Netherlands, and Britain 1858–1898.* London: Oxford University Press.

UNGPHAKORN PUEY (1916–1999), Thai government official, economist, educator. Ungphakorn Puey was known as an honest government official, an economist and educator, a strong promoter of rural development, and an advocate for democracy in Thailand through nonviolent means. Born into a Sino-Thai family, he finished high school at Assumption College in 1933 and received his B.A. from the University of Moral and Political Sciences (Thammasat University) in 1937.

The Japanese occupation of Thailand in 1944 prompted Ungphakorn Puey to volunteer to work with the British Army Pioneer Corps. His main task was to contact leaders of the underground "Free-Thai" movement, and he risked his life by parachuting into Thailand, where he was nearly executed by the Thai police.

Puey received his Ph.D. from the London School of Economics in 1989, graduating with First Class honors, and began his career as an economist and senior government official. He held the post of governor of the Bank of Thailand from 1959 to 1971. While governor, he succeeded in keeping the bank largely free of political influence and thus enabled it to have a sound monetary policy. This allowed Thailand to avoid serious inflation and kept the Thai currency remarkably stable.

In 1964, he offered his resignation as bank governor to become dean of the Faculty of Economics at Thammasat University. A compromise was reached among bank and university officials, and he was allowed to keep both positions. His deanship at Thammasat University was from 1964 to 1972.

In 1972, continuing actions against democracy on the part of the military regime prompted Dr. Puey to write an open letter from Cambridge University, where he was a visiting fellow, to protest against the prime minister, General Kittikhachorn Thanom. The letter, together with a growing protest movement, led to the student uprising of 14 October 1973, and a brief period of freedom and democracy was instituted in Thailand from 14 October 1973 to 6 October 1976. Ungphakorn Puey returned to Thailand and was elected rector of Thammasat University in 1975.

The military regime returned to power on 6 October 1976, and Dr. Puey, because of his personal convictions, was forced into self-exile in England with his English wife, Margaret Smith. He continued with various nonviolent activities against the military regimes in Thailand until his death in London at the age of eighty-three, two years after Thailand's democratic constitution of 1997 was proclaimed.

Apichai Puntasen

Further Reading
Kunatiranont, Thiti, ed. (2000) *A Siamese for All Seasons: Collected Articles by and about Puey Ungphakorn.* 5th ed. Bangkok: Kamol Keemthong Foundation.

UNIFICATION CHURCH Tongil-kyo (*tongil* is the Korean word for "unification"; *kyo* is Korean for "church": thus literally "Unification Church") is the most prominent of Korea's new religions that have Christian origins. Once formally known as the Holy Spirit Association for the Unification of World Christianity, in 1997 the full name of what is still popularly known as the Unification Church was changed to the Family Federation for World Peace and Unification in order to embrace all religions rather than focusing solely on Christianity. The Unification Church was founded in 1954 by Sun Myong Moon (b. 1920), an itinerant Christian preacher who had been imprisoned by Communist authorities in North Korea. Moon moved to South Korea when his prison was liberated during the Korean War. Soon afterwards, in 1954, he established the Unification Church in Seoul and began preaching a revision of traditional Christian theology based on revelations Moon proclaimed he had received.

According to *Divine Principle*, the record of those revelations, Adam and Eve were to be the true parents of mankind. However, Satan seduced Eve, ensuring that she and Adam would not be the sinless progenitors needed to ensure that human beings live in harmony with God's will. God later sent his only son Jesus to earth in another attempt to establish a sinless lineage and erect a heavenly kingdom on earth. However, humanity rejected Jesus, crucifying him before he could marry and father children. In the twentieth century, God allowed a man to be born without sin in order to complete the mission the savior Jesus had begun. That messiah would save the rest of humanity from Satan by marrying a woman equally sinless in order that human beings may finally have true parents who can restore them to the family of God.

In 1992, Moon and his wife Hak Ja Han, whom he had married in 1960, announced publicly that they are those true parents, and that under their stewardship humanity had left behind the New Testament age and embarked upon a new age in human history, the Completed Testament Era. Every year Unificationists celebrate the Moon's wedding anniversary as Parents Day, the date on which humanity began the return to the state of grace that prevailed before Eve's transgression with Satan.

Though the Unification Church is Korean in origin, it is no longer primarily a Korean church. Moon moved to the United States in 1971. Even though a U.S. federal court convicted him of tax evasion in 1982, and he served thirteen months in prison on that charge, he continues to lead the Unification Church from its American headquarters in New York State. In 1999, church officials said that only 220,000 of a claimed 4.5 million members worldwide resided in Korea.

Don Baker

Further Reading
Chryssides, George D. (1991) *The Advent of Sun Myong Moon: The Origins, Beliefs and Practices of the Unification Church.* London: Macmillan.
Holy Spirit Association for the Unification of World Christianity. (1973) *Divine Principle.* New York: HSA-UWC.
Sherwood, Carlton. (1991) *Inquisition: The Persecution and Prosecution of the Reverend Sun Myung Moon.* Washington, DC: Regnery Gateway.

UNIFIED SHILLA KINGDOM   On the Korean Peninsula, the Shilla kingdom (57 BCE–935 CE), with the Tang dynasty (618–907 CE) of China as its ally, was able to overpower the Paekche kingdom (18 BCE–663 CE) and then the Koguryo kingdom (37 BCE–668 CE) in the 660s. It soon became apparent, though, that Tang China had it eyes on this conquered territory for itself and did not recognize the Shilla kingdom's claim to the territory south of the Taedong River, south of Pyongyang (in present-day North Korea), until 676. This excluded much of the former Koguryo territory, and it was to this territory that many Koguryo people migrated and set up the Parhae kingdom (698–926 CE). The Shilla kingdom was thus able to unify most of the Korean Peninsula under its rule but less than half of the land ruled during the Three Kingdoms period of China (220–265 CE).

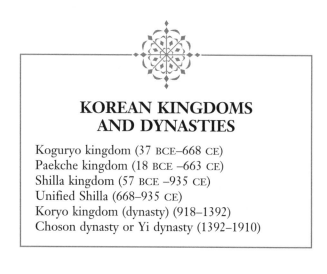

**KOREAN KINGDOMS
AND DYNASTIES**

Koguryo kingdom (37 BCE–668 CE)
Paekche kingdom (18 BCE –663 CE)
Shilla kingdom (57 BCE –935 CE)
Unified Shilla (668–935 CE)
Koryo kingdom (dynasty) (918–1392)
Choson dynasty or Yi dynasty (1392–1910)

The Unified Shilla kingdom (668—935 CE) reached its peak in the middle of the eighth century. With Buddhism already the state religion, the Unified Shilla kingdom attempted to establish the ideal Buddhist nation. To this end, splendid Buddhist temples and shrines were constructed. The most noted of these are the Pulguk Temple and Sokkuram Grotto, both located near the Shilla capital, present-day Kyongju. Extensive woodblock printing of Buddhist scriptures was also undertaken. These included the recently discovered imprint of the *Dharani Sutra*, probably printed in the first half of the eighth century. Overall, the arts and sciences flourished.

After unifying the peninsula, the Unified Shilla kingdom reorganized its administration after that of neighboring China and developed a complex bureaucracy. Most important, there was a growing authoritarianism in the power exercised by the king, which increased to the extent that opposition to the throne was virtually eliminated. The power of the throne was evidenced by changes in military organization. Members of the nation's ten garrisons and national army took oaths of loyalty to the throne and were under the king's direct authority. The Unified Shilla kingdom enjoyed an era of peace with Tang China. In return for being allowed to remain independent of the Tang in internal affairs, the Unified Shilla kingdom sent periodic tribute to the Tang emperor and recognized China's authority in Asian affairs.

As the nobility indulged in easy, luxurious lives, Buddhism as the state religion began to decline in the latter part of the eighth century. A new sect, Son (Zen), began to establish itself in remote mountainous areas. Corruption in the bureaucracy and factional strife in the government became rampant. Rulers became increasingly weak and immoral, and aristocrats abused their power. The situation deteriorated to one of near anarchy, leading to peasant revolts. Leaders of these revolts created rival states—the Later Paekche kingdom (892–936) and the Later Koguryo kingdom (901–918)—backed by strong armies. The Unified Shilla kingdom shrank to its preunification size. The Later Koguryo kingdom, renamed Koryo, gained control of the central part of the peninsula, and the Unified Shilla kingdom, being too weak to resist, handed over power to the Koryo kingdom. In 936, after fierce military resistance, the Koryo kingdom (918–1392) defeated the Later Paekche kingdom to reunify the Korean Peninsula.

David E. Shaffer

Further Reading
Eckert, Carter J., Ki-baik Lee, Young Ick Lew, Michael Robinson, and Edward W. Wagner. (1990) *Korea Old and*

New: A History. Cambridge, MA: Korean Institute, Harvard University.

Han, Woo-keun. (1970) *The History of Korea.* Trans. by Lee Kyung-shik. Seoul: Eul-yoo Publishing.

Henthorn, William E. (1971) *A History of Korea.* New York: Free Press.

Koo, John H., and Andrew C. Nahm, eds. (1997) *An Introduction to Korean Culture.* Elizabeth, NJ: Hollym.

Lee, Ki-baik. (1984) *A New History of Korea.* Trans. by Edward W. Wagner. Seoul: Ilchokak Publishers.

Nahm, Andrew C. (1983). *A Panorama of 5000 Years: Korean History.* Elizabeth, NJ: Hollym.

UNION SOLIDARITY AND DEVELOPMENT ASSOCIATION—MYANMAR

In the absence of a political party popular among the masses, Myanmar's State Law and Order Restoration Council (SLORC) founded the Union Solidarity and Development Association (USDA) on 15 September 1993 as a mass movement to help unite Myanmar (Burma) under its sovereignty. Organized at all levels, from State and Division to village tract level, the SLORC declared the following five formal objectives: (a) non-disintegration of the union, (b) non-disintegration of the unity of the national races, (c) perpetuation of national sovereignty, (d) uplift of national prestige and patriotism, and (e) the emergence of a developed, peaceful, and modern state. Membership in the USDA affords promotion and special privileges, but also compels participation in denunciation of perceived threats, including against the National League for Democracy (NLD) and democratically elected political parties and their leaders. Though a membership in the millions is proclaimed by the authorities, the fact that it is conceived entirely as an instrument of state, and pressures people to join with intimidation, means that this organization is unlikely to play an enduring role if, and when, political reforms are initiated.

Gustaaf Houtman

Further Reading

Steinberg, David I. (2001) *Burma: The State of Myanmar.* Washington, DC: Georgetown University Press.

———. (1997) "The Union Solidarity and Development Association: Mobilization and Orthodoxy in Myanmar." *Burma Debate* 4, 1: 4–11.

UNITED FRONT STRATEGY

The United Front strategy grew from the belief of the Soviet Comintern, or international organization of Communist parties, that Communist groups in nations subject to foreign subjugation should form a united front with nationalists to gain their liberation before beginning their socialist revolutions. "Hostile classes," Lenin believed, "are united by a common interest in opposing foreign exploitation" (Schram 1969: 134). The strategy was first used in China and, after a successful start there, was also attempted in Korea. In the end, both attempts were unsuccessful, and the societal divisions that emerged remain in the divided Korean Peninsula and in the politically divided governments of China and Taiwan.

In China, until the Communist purge in 1927, the union of the Communists and Guomindang (Chinese Nationalist Party) led to the formation of a government with Communist participation; one Russian adviser even observed that members of the right-wing Guomindang were moving toward the left. This observation was premature with the brutal purge of the Communists by Chiang Kai-shek's (1887–1975) nationalist group, ending any hope of a strong united front to challenge Japanese imperialism in China.

In Korea, the United Front strategy was meant to create "a broad national revolutionary front that included handicraftsmen, the intelligentsia, and the petty and middle bourgeoisie along with the workers and peasants" (Scalapino and Lee 1972: 95). The structure for this front was the Korean National Party (KCP), formed in early 1926. This party was organized by Korean Communists in an attempt to form an alliance with Korean nationalists and thus placed Korean Communist Party members at its core. This attempt was weakened by the roundup of many KCP leaders by the Japanese after the funeral of former Emperor Sunjong in June 1926.

The formation of the Singanhoe (New Korean Society) in 1927 marked Korea's best opportunity to unify rival factions. The society, which accommodated a variety of groups ranging from the moderate to the radical, soon established a national network of 386 branches with more than seventy-five thousand members. The beginning of the end of the society came in 1929 when its leaders were rounded up by Japanese police and charged with lending support to the student riots in Kwangju in 1929. The society's subsequent move to the right caused many leftist members to quit, leading to its demise in 1931 and ending hope for a Korean united front against the Japanese.

These efforts by the Soviets to create united fronts in both China and Korea failed due to the political differences facing the leaders of the respective nationalist and conservative parties. These differences eventually erupted into civil wars in both nations, deepening divisions that persist in the twenty-first century.

Mark E. Caprio

Further Reading

Eckert, Carter J., Ki-baik Lee, Young Ick Lew, Michael Robinson, and Edward W. Wagner. (1990) *Korea Old and New: A History*. Cambridge, MA: Korean Institute, Harvard University.

Scalapino, Robert A., and Chong-sik Lee. (1972) *Communism in Korea*. Vol 1. Berkeley and Los Angeles: University of California Press.

Schram, Stuart R. (1969) *The Political Thought of Mao Tse Tung*. Rev. ed. New York: Praeger Press.

UNITED NATIONS   Created in 1945 from the ashes of the failed League of Nations (1920–1946), the United Nations (U.N.) is an international organization dedicated to promoting world peace and cooperation. Although some Asian countries, including Afghanistan, China, India, Thailand, and Japan (until 1935), were members of the League of Nations, the league focused on European problems rather than on Asia; by contrast much work of the United Nations has centered on Asia, where most of the world's population lives.

Political Foundations

When the United Nations Charter took effect on 24 October 1945, China was a permanent member of the Security Council; the only other Asian members of the organization were India, the Philippines, and Thailand; Afghanistan joined in 1946. Japan was not allowed to join until 1956, after the peace treaty of 1951 ended the Allied Occupation.

As decolonization proceeded in Asia, most countries in the region were admitted to membership, but with some anomalies. When members of the government of the Republic of China (ROC) fled to the island of Taiwan in 1949 in the wake of the Communist revolution that established the People's Republic of China (PRC), the ROC continued to occupy the U.N.'s China seat. Upset over the establishment of Malaysia from territories contiguous with Indonesia, President Achmed Sukarno (1901–1970) withdrew his country from the U.N. in 1965, but Indonesia rejoined in 1966 when Sukarno was overthrown. In 1971, the General Assembly voted to have the PRC replace the ROC. North Korea and South Korea were not admitted until 1991. In 1992 former Soviet republics in Central Asia (Kazakhstan, Kyrgyzstan, Tajikistan, Turkmenistan, and Uzbekistan) became the latest Asian countries to join. East Timor is expected to be the next Asian member.

After the United Nations was instituted in 1945, the world was engulfed in two major struggles: decolonization and the Cold War. While the struggle for decolonization united Asian countries, the Cold War, a conflict between Western nations and Communist states allied with the Soviet Union, shattered Asian solidarity. Revolutions brought Communist regimes to power in China, North Korea, and North Vietnam, while anti-Communist Asian states forged alliances with the United States.

When the Cold War conflict became heated in 1961, U. Thant (1909–1974) of neutral Burma (now Myanmar) became the first secretary-general named to the United Nations from outside Europe; he served until 1971.

U.N. Interventions in Asia

After 1946 many countries in transition from colonialism experienced conflicts, and the U.N. often intervened to help restore stability. India and Pakistan became independent in 1947, and cross-border violence erupted. The U.N. Commission for India and Pakistan was dispatched in 1948 to investigate and mediate; when the countries agreed to a cease-fire line in Kashmir in 1949, the U.N. Military Observer Group in India and Pakistan (Unmogip) was established to monitor the peace. Unmogip continues to function today.

The U.N. Temporary Commission on Korea was set up in 1947. Assigned to monitor the 1948 election in South Korea, the body continued in 1949 as the U.N. Commission on Korea. In 1950, while the Soviet Union was boycotting the U.N., war broke out between North Korea and South Korea. The Security Council authorized a U.N. Command (UNC) to help South Korea stop the aggression. The United States coordinated the UNC, with General Douglas MacArthur (1880–1964) commanding until 1951, when General Matthew B. Ridgway (1895–1993) took over. Troops from sixteen countries, including the Philippines and Thailand, fought until a cease-fire was declared in 1953; six countries, including India, sent medical units. To monitor the cease-fire, the UNC Military Armistice Commission was established. Because North Korea withdrew in 1994, only informal Commission meetings have been held.

Subsequently the U.N.'s operations in Asia have included actions involving Irian Jaya (former West New Guinea) (1962–1963), the India-Pakistan War (1965–1966), plebiscites in Sabah and Sarawak in Malaysia (1965), the war in Afghanistan (1988–1990), Cambodian refugees in Thailand (1982–1992), Cambodian elections (1991–1992), the Tajikistan civil war (1994–2000), and East Timor (1999–).

INDIA'S EARLY HOPES FOR THE UNITED NATIONS

The following resolution regarding the United Nations was passed at a session of the All-India Congress, held in Delhi, 18–19 October 1951. It outlines the hopes of India for an international organization that could serve as an effective forum for peace.

The United Nations Organization was formed to provide a common platform for all countries, even though they differed from each other in many ways, and was based on each country having freedom to develop in its own way and not interfering with another. If that basic policy of the U.N.O. is followed, the fear that grips the world today will gradually lessen and a peaceful consideration of problems will become easier. This Congress approves of the policy pursued by the Government of India in seeking friendly relations with all countries and in avoiding any entanglement in military or other alliances which tend to divide the world into rival groups and thus endanger world peace.

In particular, the Congress approved of the decision of the Government of India not to participate in the San Francisco Conference, which was held for the purpose of signing the Japanese Peace Treaty and instead to have a separate treaty with Japan. Peace in the Far East, which has been gravely disturbed by hostilities in Korea and subsequent developments, has to be based on the cooperation of the countries of the Far East and the other countries chiefly concerned. Any partial arrangement which does not include all these countries is likely to increase the tension and lessen the chances of a peaceful settlement.

This Congress hopes that the negotiations for a cease fire in Korea will meet with success and that this will be followed by a larger settlement in the Far East.

The colossal programmes of rearmament, which present-day conditions have led many countries to adopt, give rise international tension and cast a heavy burden on the people of those countries, which results in a lowering of their standards. The progress of the underdeveloped countries of the world is also impeded by these programmes of rearmament. If this vast expenditure on rearmament was diverted towards constructive purpose and to the advance of under-developed countries, that would be a surer guarantee of peace than preparations for war.

The Congress trusts that the United Nations Organization will devote itself to the furtherance of the aims so nobly set forth in its Charter and reorganise itself for this purpose, where this is considered necessary.

Source: Jagdish Saran Sharma. (1965) *India's Struggle for Freedom: Select Documents and Sources.* Vol. 2. Delhi: S. Chand & Co., 190.

Economic Foundations

The polarization of the Cold War diverted attention from the poorest countries of the world. Accordingly India launched a third path, which came to be known as the Nonaligned Movement, among countries that believed that a primary agenda of the U.N. was to alleviate world poverty.

India and the nonaligned countries of Asia and Africa succeeded in directing the U.N.'s attention to economic issues, and several new technical organizations took their place alongside existing specialized U.N. agencies, such as the U.N. Development Program and the U.N. Industrial Development Organization. Nevertheless U.N. headquarters and the specialized agencies were in New York and Western Europe, far from the realities of Asia.

Regionalization

In 1947 China pressed for establishment of a regional economic commission for Asia. Western countries at first opposed the idea, but changed their minds when they realized the advantages of an economic commission for Europe. Accordingly, the Economic Commission for Asia and the Far East (ECAFE) was established in 1947 at Shanghai, but moved in 1949 to Bangkok. Initially the ECAFE region reached from Iran on the west to the Soviet Union on the north and Australia and New Zealand in the southeast. Since 1990, the region has included the nations of Central Asia. ECAFE nations included those U.N. members in the region as well as the colonial powers of France, Britain, the Netherlands (until 1950), and the United States. In 1974 ECAFE was renamed the Economic Commission for Asia and the Pacific (ESCAP), as newly decolonized countries of the South Pacific joined the U.N. and the scope of activities grew to include social concerns.

In 1959 U. Nyun (b. 1910) of Myanmar was appointed ESCAP executive secretary. Realizing that countries outside Asia were dominating discussions in the organization and dealing with Cold War issues, he formulated the principle of the Asian way, which asked countries of the region to do most of the talking, with decisions made by consensus rather than voting. Thus the nonregional powers began to listen to the needs of developing countries and funded worthwhile projects.

ESCAP focuses on development needs in communications, energy, environment, human and natural resources, population policies, rural and urban development, social development, statistics, trade, transportation, and tourism. The mission is carried out primarily by holding conferences that bring together bureaucrats and experts from member countries to formulate regional priorities. ESCAP then promotes projects approved by member countries. In some cases the organization has established the framework for non-U.N. bodies that have subsequently operated on their own. Notable among these spin-offs are the Asian Development Bank, the Mekong River Commission, and commodity organizations focusing on coconuts, jute, natural rubber, pepper, silk, and tin.

In addition to ESCAP, other specialized agencies established regional offices in Asia: the Food and Agriculture Organization (Bangkok) and the World Health Organization (Manila and New Delhi). Other U.N. agencies, particularly the U.N. Development Program, which coordinates technical assistance projects for specialized agencies and other aid sources have field offices in many other Asian countries.

The Future

Asia has been a major focus of attention throughout the history of the U.N. Politically the U.N. has helped to keep peace, though it has not been active in mediating between the PRC and the ROC, perhaps Asia's most serious conflict situation today. The U.N.

technical agencies are expected to continue to support economic development by helping poorer nations of the region to upgrade the quality of goods produced so that these nations will be more competitive in the global marketplace.

Michael Haas

Further Reading

Haas, Michael. (1989) *The Asian Way to Peace: A Story of Regional Cooperation.* New York: Praeger.

Wightman, David. (1953) *Toward Economic Cooperation in Asia.* New Haven, CT: Yale University Press.

UNITED NATIONS IN EAST TIMOR

The involvement of the United Nations (U.N.) in the conflict between East Timor and Indonesia, which invaded and annexed East Timor after East Timor became independent from Portugal in 1975, has taken different forms and been of varying degrees. The adoption of two U.N. resolutions in 1975 was decisive in guaranteeing the East Timorese the right to self-determination because it gave them international legitimacy. After two decades of stalemate between Indonesia and Portugal, when the U.N. was not of much use, the fall of Indonesia's president Suharto in 1998 opened a window of opportunity in which to solve the East Timor question.

Background

During the Portuguese transition to democracy in 1974–1976, the Portuguese government decided to allow the East Timorese to exercise their right to self-determination. Indonesia, whose territory includes contiguous West Timor, opposed that decision and invaded East Timor in December 1975. Portugal immediately appealed to the U.N. for a ruling on the Indonesian invasion. On 12 December 1975, the U.N. General Assembly passed Resolution 3485, and on 22 December 1975, the U.N. Security Council adopted Resolution 384, both demanding Indonesia's military withdrawal from East Timor.

From 1976 until 1982, the U.N. General Assembly passed a new resolution each year reaffirming its initial demand. Confronted with the gradual loss of support in the U.N. voting sessions, Portugal ceased to submit the issue of Indonesia's invasion of East Timor to the General Assembly after 1982.

Starting in 1983, the East Timor question was instead submitted to international dispute mediation by the secretary-general. Between 1983 and 1991, the secretary-general was not able to find a solution to the question. In part, this reflected the refusal of Indonesia and Portugal to bow to each other's demands: Portugal wanted Indonesia to allow the East Timorese to exercise their right to self-determination, while Indonesia wanted Portugal to recognize its sovereignty over East Timor. Only with the Dili Massacre in 1991, when the Indonesian military killed dozens of East Timorese during a funeral while foreign journalists filmed the event, was Jakarta compelled to accept bilateral negotiations with Portugal under the auspices of the secretary-general. Between 1992 and 1996, eight rounds of ministerial negotiations took place under the auspices of the secretary-general.

The U.N. role became more significant under the U.N.'s seventh secretary-general, Kofi Annan, who took office 1 January 1997. During the first post-Suharto ministerial meeting between Indonesia and Portugal under the secretary-general's auspices, on 4–5 August 1998, it became obvious that Indonesia was prepared to discuss granting East Timor wide-ranging autonomy that would fall short of actual independence. On 6–8 October, delegations of both nations met again and discussed U.N. proposals for autonomy. On 8–9 February 1999, Portugal and Indonesia agreed on the overall terms for the wide-ranging autonomy proposal, but they were unable to agree on how to hold a popular consultation (referendum). At last on 11 March Indonesia accepted a direct, secret, and universal ballot. The tripartite agreements were finalized on 23 April and signed on 5 May 1999. According to the agreements, the East Timorese were to accept or reject continued Indonesian rule with wide-ranging autonomy. Before and after the popular consultation, Indonesia would be responsible for maintaining peace and security in East Timor.

United Nations Mission in East Timor

On 11 June 1999, the Security Council adopted Resolution 1246 establishing the United Nations Mission in East Timor (UNAMET). This mission would be responsible for organizing and conducting the popular consultation on East Timor's future status. Despite two delays in conducting the ballot and repeated episodes of violence by East Timorese militias that favored the continued tie with Indonesia, the U.N. gave the green light for the popular consultation to be held on 30 August 1999. On 3 September, Kofi Annan reported to the Security Council that 344,580 voters (78.5 percent of the votes cast) had rejected the special autonomy proposal. This overwhelming defeat triggered a scorched-earth policy by Indonesia-backed East Timorese militia groups that had supported the proposal. At least fifteen hundred East Timorese lost their lives, and the territory's infrastructure was almost totally destroyed.

InterFET

In the days after announcement of the ballot results, it became clear that Indonesia's police and military lacked the ability and will to provide peace and security in East Timor. After several days of intense political pressure, on 12 September 1999 Indonesia accepted a proposal establishing in East Timor a multinational force under U.N. authority. On 15 September, the Security Council adopted Resolution 1264 authorizing the establishment of the multinational force under a unified command structure. Its mission was to restore peace and security in East Timor, to protect and support UNAMET, and to facilitate humanitarian operations in the territory. There was considerable concern that International Force East Timor (InterFET) would face military opposition from East Timorese militia groups. This opposition did not materialize, and InterFET easily fulfilled its goals.

United Nations Transitional Administration in East Timor

The next step in U.N. involvement in the East Timor question came on 25 October 1999, when the Security Council adopted Resolution 1272, which established the United Nations Transitional Administration in East Timor (UNTAET). UNTAET was endowed with overall responsibility for the administration of East Timor and empowered to exercise all legislative and executive authority, including the administration of justice. In other words, UNTAET took responsibility for preparing East Timor for independence. This has not been a small task. Since its establishment, it has had to provide security and maintain law and order; establish an effective administration; assist in the development of civil and social services; ensure the coordination and delivery of humanitarian assistance, rehabilitation, and development assistance; support capacity-building for self-government; and assist in the establishment of conditions for sustainable development. Bearing this in mind, since October 1999, the territory's transitional administration has introduced dozens of regulations.

On 20 May 2002, East Timor becomes an independent state. The U.N. involvement has been important not only to guarantee that the East Timorese could exercise their right of self-determination, but also to create a new sovereign state. In reaching both goals, the U.N. has not always been as effective as it might have been.

Paulo Gorjão

See also: **Dili Massacre; East Timor—Profile**

Further Reading
Cotton, James. (2000) "The Emergence of an Independent East Timor: National and Regional Challenges." *Contemporary Southeast Asia* 22, 1: 1–22.
Gorjão, Paulo. (2001) "The End of a Cycle: Australian and Portuguese Foreign Policies and the Fate of East Timor." *Contemporary Southeast Asia* 23, 1: 101–121.
Gunn, Geoffrey C. (1997) *East Timor and the United Nations: The Case for Intervention.* Lawrenceville, NJ: Red Sea Press.
Maley, William. (2000) "The UN and East Timor." *Pacifica Review* 12, 1: 63–76.
Martin, Ian. (2000) "The Popular Consultation and the United Nations Mission in East Timor." In *Out of the Ashes: The Destruction and Reconstruction of East Timor,* edited by James J. Fox and Dionisio Babo Soares. Adelaide, Australia: Crawford House, 136–148.
Sebastian, Leonard C., and Anthony L. Smith. (2000) "The East Timor Crisis: A Test Case for Humanitarian Intervention." In *Southeast Asian Affairs 2000.* Singapore: Institute of Southeast Asian Studies, 64–83.

UNITED NATIONS TRANSITIONAL AUTHORITY IN CAMBODIA

The United Nations Transitional Authority in Cambodia (UNTAC) was formed following the signing of peace agreements by Cambodia's four warring factions at Paris in October 1991. UNTAC's primary function was to facilitate the creation of a neutral political environment through which "free and fair" elections could be conducted, a constituent assembly elected, a government formed, and a new constitution promulgated. At the time of its creation, UNTAC was the most ambitious peacekeeping operation ever embarked upon by the United Nations. It was composed of seven components (civil administration, civilian police, electoral, human rights, military, rehabilitation, and repatriation), the largest being the multinational military force of sixteen thousand soldiers under the command of the Australian lieutenant general John Sanderson. The UNTAC operation cost the international community more than $2 billion.

The degree to which UNTAC succeeded continues to be debated by scholars and analysts of Cambodian and international affairs. On one side are those who claim that while it was imperfect, UNTAC delivered to the Cambodian people a democratically elected coalition government and provided the cata-lyst to end the civil conflict that had undermined Cambodia's development for more than two decades. Critics point out that by failing to disarm the warring factions, as its mandate dictated, UNTAC failed to provide the environment for the conduct of free and fair elections. These critics point to UNTAC's slow deployment, its acquiescence to the Khmer Rouge, and its failure to deal adequately with intimidation of electoral candidates and their supporters as evidence that the United Nations mission was far from successful.

David M. Ayres

Further Reading
Doyle, Michael. (1995) *UN Peacekeeping in Cambodia: UNTAC's Civil Mandate.* Boulder, CO: Lynne Rienner.
Heininger, Janet. (1994) *Peacekeeping in Transition: The UN in Cambodia.* New York: Twentieth Century Fund Press.

UNITED PARTY OF MONGOLIA

The United Party of Mongolia was officially founded in February 1992 by Sanjaasurengiyn Zorig, the leader of the democratic movement in Mongolia who brought down seventy years of Communist rule in 1990. The United Party (UP) developed from a merger of the Republican and Free Labor Parties and a wing of the Mongolian Democratic Party (MDP) in time to compete in the 1992 first democratic parliamentary elections. The UP was officially registered with the government on 2 April 1992. It allied itself for the June 1992 parliamentary elections with the MDP and Mongolian National Progress Party. Zorig was the only candidate who won a UP seat in that vote. In October 1992 the UP merged with three other small democratic parties to form the present Mongolian National Democratic Party (MNDP).

Alicia J. Campi

Further Reading
Sanders, Alan J. K. (1996) *Historical Dictionary of Mongolia.* Lanham, MD: Scarecrow Press.

UNITED STATES MILITARY BASES—JAPAN

As part of the 1951 U.S.-Japan Security Treaty and related Administrative Agreement signed on 28 February 1952, the United States was granted the right to establish military bases in post-peace treaty Japan. This right continued following the revision of the security treaty in 1960 (Article 6) and the signing of the Status of Forces Agreement regarding the use of bases in Japan. In the early 2000s, there are ninety U.S. exclusive-use facilities in Japan, including thirty-seven in Okinawa. The main bases include Misawa, Yokota, Yokusuka, Zama, Iwakuni, Sasebo, Kadena, and Futenma.

In the 1950s, the United States began scaling down its military presence in mainland Japan due to budgetary considerations and friction, crimes, and accidents involving the bases. Several of these units were moved to Okinawa, which was under U.S. administrative control at the time and thus were not subjected to the same restrictions that existed in mainland Japan under the Security Treaty. Following Okinawa's reversion to Japan in 1972, bases (land area) were reduced some 60 percent in mainland Japan, with a 15 percent reduction in Okinawa. At present, approximately 75 percent (land area) of U.S. bases in Japan are located in Okinawa, which has led citizens in Okinawa to protest the disproportionate share of bases in their prefecture.

Robert D. Eldridge

Further Reading

Aketagawa Toru. (1999) *Nichibei Gyosei Kyotei no Seijishi* (A Political History of the Japan-U.S. Administrative Agreement). Tokyo: Hosei Daigaku Shuppankyoku.
Green, Michael J., and Patrick M. Cronin. (1999) *The U.S.-Japan Alliance: Past, Present, and Future*. New York: Council on Foreign Relations.

UNITED STATES–JAPAN SECURITY TREATY
The United States–Japan Security Treaty, officially known as the Treaty of Mutual Cooperation and Security Between Japan and United States of America, was signed on 19 January 1960 and went into effect on 23 June of that year. It replaced the earlier Security Treaty Between Japan and the United States, signed on 8 September 1951 in San Francisco, two hours after the signing of the Treaty of Peace with Japan. Due to the perception that the 1951 Security Treaty was no more than a continuing of the Occupation by the U.S. military and gave America rights thought to infringe on Japanese sovereignty, criticism within Japan grew and demands for its revision became increasingly strong. In 1957 the Japanese government officially requested revisions to be made, and a joint committee was established, leading to the revised treaty of 1960, which has continued without amendments or revisions since then. Made up of ten articles, the new treaty obliges the United States to defend Japan (Article 5) and Japan to provide bases to

the United States for "contributing to the security of Japan and the maintenance of international peace and security in the Far East" (Article 6). A separate Status of Forces Agreement was also signed regarding the use of facilities in Japan to replace the earlier Administrative Agreement.

Robert D. Eldridge

Further Reading

Green, Michael J., and Patrick M. Cronin, eds. (1999) *The U.S.-Japan Alliance: Past, Present, and Future*. New York: Council on Foreign Relations.
Packard, George R. III. (1996) *Protest in Tokyo: The Security Treaty Crisis of 1960*. Westport, CT: Greenwood Press.

UNITED WA STATE PARTY
The United Wa State Party (UWSP) is the largest of the armed ethnic forces formed in 1989 during mass mutinies that led to the fall of the Communist Party of Burma (CPB). A Mon-Khmer people once feared for their headhunting, the Wa inhabit the mountains along the Shan State frontier with China. Few of these areas have ever been brought under the control of any central government.

The Wa substates became a major war zone after 1968, when the CPB launched an invasion from China. In the next two decades, tens of thousands of Wa were killed. Some villagers joined the CPB's People's Army, others were forced to flee their homes, while still others enlisted in rival insurgent forces. In April 1989, resentment broke out into the open. Wa mutineers, led by Kyauk Ni Lai (b. 1938), seized control of the CPB's headquarters at Panghsang and its well-stocked arsenals. Shortly afterward, the UWSP was formed and a cease-fire agreed with the ruling State Law and Order Restoration Council.

Promised a Wa autonomous region, during the 1990s the UWSP embarked on various development programs in an area designated as Shan State Special Region 2. Its twenty-thousand-strong army also fought battles with the Mong Tai Army of Khun Sa before the MTA's demise and began settling more than fifty thousand villagers along the Thai border, where it was accused of financing its activities through narcotics trafficking. Particular controversy followed the activities of the UWSP's southern leader in the Mong Yawn area, Wei Hsueh-kang (an ethnic Chinese), who was named by international antinarcotic organizations as a principal figure in the illicit opium and methamphetamine trades. In response, despite widespread international skepticism, in 2001 the UWSP pledged to make its territories narcotics-free within five years.

Martin Smith

Further Reading

Lintner, Bertil. (1998) "Drugs and Economic Growth: Ethnicity and Exports." In *Burma: Prospects for a Democratic Future*, edited by Robert Rotberg. Washington, DC: Brookings Institution Press, 165–183.

Scott, James George. (1932) *Burma and Beyond*. London: Grayson & Grayson.

Smith, Martin. (1999) *Burma: Insurgency and the Politics of Ethnicity*. 2d ed. London: Zed Books.

Yan Nyein Aye. (2000) *Endeavours of the Myanmar Armed Forces Government for National Reconsolidation*. Yangon, Myanmar: U Aung Zaw.

UNIVERSITI BRUNEI DARUSSALAM

Universiti Brunei Darussalam was established in October 1985 with an inaugural class of 176 students. It is the only university in Brunei Darussalam. Its emergence can be traced to a review of the sultanate's higher education program in 1976. Nevertheless, it was not until 1984–1985 that active planning began when Sultan Hassanal Bolkiah called for the establishment of a local university in the interest of national development and nation building.

While awaiting the completion of its permanent campus at Gadong, the university utilized a renovated building complex on the outskirts of Bandar Seri Begawan. The Ministry of Education Committee on the Establishment of the University worked in partnership with universities in Malaysia and the United Kingdom to develop the curriculum and programs for a bachelor of arts in both English- and Malay-language courses. Academic and administrative personnel were recruited from Malaysia, Singapore, and the United Kingdom. In 1989 the Sultan Hassanal Bolkiah Institute of Education was added as a division, in addition to Arts and Social Sciences, Science, Management and Administrative Studies, Islamic Studies, and Academy of Brunei Studies.

Universiti Brunei Darussalam has 1,500 students and 300 faculty members and seeks to produce quality graduates who can contribute to nation building. Applied research that is consistent with the nation's interests is promoted. The university also expects that the knowledge and skills of faculty members will be utilized to serve the wider society.

Ooi Keat Gin

Further Reading

Universiti Brunei Darussalam. (1992) *Majlis Perletakan Batu Asas Kampus Kekal Universiti Brunei Darussalam* (Ceremony of the Laying of the Foundation Stone for the Permanent Campus of Universiti Brunei Darussalam). Bandar Seri Begawan, Brunei: Universiti Brunei Darussalam.

———. (1997).*Towards the Next Millennium*. Gadong, Brunei: Universiti Brunei Darussalam.

———. (2002/2003). *Universiti Brunei Darussalam Prospectus*. Gadong, Brunei: Universiti Brunei Darussalam.

UNIVERSITI SAINS MALAYSIA

Universiti Sains Malaysia (University of Science, Malaysia), the second-oldest university in Malaysia, received its first students (fifty-seven in number) on 9 June 1969. Since then, the student population has increased to more than 20,000, and an expanding pool of academic staff numbered more than 1,500 for the 1999–2000 academic session. The idea for another tertiary institution in Malaysia was discussed as early as the 1950s, but it was another two decades before Penang University officially came into existence. The pioneer group of students commenced studies at the Malayan Teachers' College, Gelugor, where only the Schools of Biological Sciences, Chemical Science, and Physics and Mathematics were functioning then. In May 1971, the university moved into its present premises at Minden. In line with Malaysia's emphasis on science education, Penang University became the University of Science, Malaysia (Universiti Sains Malaysia) in April 1972.

From its inception, it was organized to promote an interdisciplinary approach. Currently the university has more than twenty schools, including several in non-science–based fields like humanities, management, the arts, and education. There are also more than twenty institutes, centers, and research units covering diverse fields, from drug research to computer-aided translation. A branch campus at Kubang Kerian, Kelantan state, houses the School of Medical Sciences, while the School of Engineering is at Tronoh, Perak state. By the mid-1990s, Universiti Sains Malaysia emerged as the country's largest university in terms of academic programs, student enrollment, and infrastructure facilities.

Ooi Keat Gin

UNIVERSITY OF INDONESIA

The University of Indonesia (Universitas Indonesia—UI) was established in Jakarta on 2 February 1950, shortly after Indonesia gained its independence from the

Netherlands. Notwithstanding its legacy as a colonial education institution of higher learning, the UI also fulfills the need for a national institute of higher education in a newly independent state.

Four of the university's five original campuses at Bogor, Bandung, Surabaya, and Makassar have become independent universities. The UI teachers' training and education center in Jakarta, established in 1962, became the Institute for Teachers' Training and Education (Institut Keguruan dan Ilmu Pendidikan), and more recently Universitas Jakarta. UI now has two campuses and prides itself on a progressive curriculum that is responsive to the needs of a developing country.

As a national university, UI is under the jurisdiction of the Ministry of National Education. The university employs over three thousand faculty members and enrolls around 40,000 students. Its faculties include medicine, dentistry, mathematics and natural sciences, law, social sciences, political science, economics, letters, psychology, public health, computer science, and nursing. It has a graduate program and a polytechnic. Recognized as a leading Indonesian university, UI celebrated its golden anniversary in the year 2000.

Andi Faisal Bakti

UNIVERSITY OF MALAYA
Situated on the southwest outskirts of Kuala Lumpur, Malaysia, the 750-acre University of Malaya (UM) campus is the premier university in the country. The university came into being in 1949 as a result of the merger of two older educational institutions based in Singapore: King Edward VII (founded in 1905 for medicine) and Raffles College (founded in 1928 for education).

The merger had been proposed ten years earlier by the MacLean commission. With political independence from Britain imminent, and as a result of the Aitken commission, a branch of the university was set up in Kuala Lumpur. In 1962, legislative changes to the constitution saw the installation of the first Malaysian chancellor, Tunku Abdul Rahman Putra al-Haj (1903–1990), also the first prime minister of the country. The Singapore branch became the National University of Singapore in 1965.

The early 1970s were tumultuous years for the university. The charged political climate saw the enactment of the Universities and University Colleges Act (Amended) in 1975, which sought to stifle student activism. The university also assumed an important role in the government's restructuring programs of the new

economic policy. A differential ethnic quota system for entry was implemented in an attempt to remedy the economic and ethnic imbalance between Malays and Chinese in the country, and the medium of instruction changed from English to Malay.

In early 1997, UM was corporatized. Currently, it has eleven faculties, two academies, an Institute of Postgraduate Studies and Research, and a University Hospital. The university motto is Ilmu Punca Kemajuan ("Knowledge is the key to success").

Yeoh, Seng-Guan

UNTOUCHABILITY
Untouchability is an Indian phenomenon based on degrees of pollution and purity probably unrelated to race. Sometime around the fifth century CE castes evolved that were ranked below the fourfold *varna* (caste) system of Brahman (priest), Kshatriya (warrior and king), Vaishya (merchant), and Sudra (laborer or craftsman). In earlier texts the term *chandala* referred to the attendants of the burning ghats, who were despised as unclean because they handled the dead. The range of castes who work with leather or rope, clean night soil, play drums, or attend death sites developed later. Specific names indicate specific, large untouchable castes. *Bhangis* or *valmikis* are scavengers; *camars* or *chamarkars* work with leather; pariahs were traditional drummers; and

An elderly "untouchable" man and children in Mysore, India, in 1929. (E. O. HOPPE/CORBIS)

RITUAL IMPURITY AND UNTOUCHABILITY

The segregation and low status experienced by untouchable castes in India is based on the notion of ritual impurity. Because they work with polluting materials and perform polluting work, they must keep apart from the higher castes, as is the case with the Nadars and other untouchable castes in South India described below.

The Nadars were defiled by their ritually impure calling as toddy-tappers. They were forbidden entry into Hindu temples, and their use of public wells was strictly prohibited. Although the Nadars, unlike the Pallan and Paraiyan untouchables, had access to the streets of the Brahmin quarter, the agraharam, they did share with them the prohibitions of spatial distance. As a "half-polluting" caste, in villages where they numbered only a small minority the Nadars lived in separate habitations just outside the main village, though not in so remote a site as the untouchables' cheri. As their middling position was spatially represented in the location of their house sites, so the Nadars were, by traditions, forbidden to approach nearer than a specified number of paces to a man of higher caste, though they might come closer than the Paraiyan or Pallan.

Source: Robert L. Hardgrave, Jr. (1969) *The Nadars of Tamilnadu: The Political Culture of a Community in Change.* Berkeley and Los Angeles: University of California Press, 22

---

*mahar*s were all-around servants of the village. Approximately 12 percent of the population of India belong to one of the Scheduled Castes (former untouchables), and over four hundred such castes exist, each usually limited to one language area.

Names Denoting Untouchability

The titles of untouchables as a group indicate the history of the phenomenon. *Avarna* (without caste) was a traditional name. In a speech in 1908 the maharaja Sayajirao (1875–1939) of Broda, India, was the first to use the term "untouchable" in this context. The phrase "depressed classes" came into use when reform began in the early part of the twentieth century. Mohandas K. Gandhi (1869–1948) coined the word "harijan"(people of god) in the early 1930s to indicate his concern, but Bhimrao Ramji Ambedkar (1891–1956) a *mahar* and the chief organizer of untouchables, rejected that term as patronizing and unrealistic. "Scheduled Castes" came into use in 1935, when the government of India created a schedule or list to indicate which castes were eligible for benefits and for reserved places in parlia-

mentary bodies. "Dalit"(downtrodden, ground down), a proud term indicating that external oppression rather than any polluting quality is responsible for the inferior status of untouchables, has gained currency since 1970. Some cultural developments have incorporated the term, such as the Dalit Panthers, a militant group in Maharashtra and Tamil Nadu, and Dalit literature, a burgeoning field of poetry, prose, and drama. The use of the term "Dalit" usually suggests a politically awakened group of untouchables or writing by others that recognizes that awakening. "Harijan" remains in use, especially among Gandhians and some groups of rural untouchables in the south of India. The nineteenth-century word "outcaste" is inaccurate, since untouchables are within castes even though they are outside the classical Hindu *varna* system.

Discrimination and Political Activism

Restrictions on untouchables have included exclusion from Hindu temples, homes, and Brahman rituals; prohibitions against using the village well or studying in the village school; and a prohibition against touching any Hindu or any material or food that could convey the untouchables' supposed pollution. In some areas untouchables could not own land, although in other areas some castes held some land as part of their village contract. They were generally confined to traditional occupations and agricultural labor.

The first voices of untouchables came from the bhakti (devotional religion) movement, which brought Nandanar of the Tamil Vaishnava movement into a circle of saints in the seventh century CE and Tirupan Alvar into the Shaivite legends of piety a little later. Cokhamela, of the Marathi-speaking area, and his entire family are featured in hundreds of songs performed by the devotees of the god Vithoba in Maharashtra. Their fourteenth-century voices contain notes of distress and protest as well as joyous devotion. In the fifteenth century Ravidas, who lived in the Hindi-speaking area of the north, told of his low-status leather work as well as his faith. The British brought some change in terms of servant positions in British homes, recruitment into the army, and later new kinds of work on the railways, in the mills, and on the docks. Social reform, however, did not begin until the end of the nineteenth century. When army recruitment stopped and pensioned soldiers pleaded for readmission, efforts at education and social betterment were made within the untouchable *mahar* caste itself and among such high-caste Hindu religious reform groups as the Brahmo Samaj in Bengal, the Arya Samaj in the Punjab and the United Provinces (now Uttar Pradesh), and the Depressed Classes Mission in the former province of Bombay. A Buddhist movement among untouchables in Tamil Nadu in south India became an awakening force, and beginning with Ambedkar in 1956, conversion was widespread.

A number of untouchable leaders appeared in the second quarter of the twentieth century, and Ambedkar was chief among them. His voice for political representation in all government institutions, educational opportunities, and a general awakening initiated massive changes. India reserves places for Scheduled Castes in all elected bodies, in government institutions, in educational institutions, and on the teaching staffs of colleges and universities run by the government. Among the important untouchable political parties is the Bahujan Samaj Party (BSP or the party of the majority) founded by Kanshi Ram(b. 1934), an untouchable Sikh from the Punjab. With Mayavati (b. 1956), a *camar* woman, as its chief voice, that party is very powerful in Uttar Pradesh. The Republican Party founded by Ambedkar just before his death in 1956 holds some power on the local level in Maharashtra

and a few state and national seats when it combines with other political parties. Tamil Nadu also has a strong political movement. As untouchables become politically and socially active, however, they frequently face violence. A report by Human Rights Watch in 1999 entitled *Broken People* indicates that acts of rape, arson, and murder committed against untouchables have increased since independence. If one Dalit oversteps what is expected, runs off with a caste Hindu girl, or challenges higher castes economically, the entire Dalit section of the village may suffer revenge. Another persistent show of anger at Dalit actions is attacking the ubiquitous statues of Ambedkar found everywhere in untouchable quarters and, in recognition of his importance, in city centers. Nevertheless, the progress among Dalits in some areas is remarkable, and because of the reservation system, a sizable literate middle class has emerged.

Eleanor Zelliot

See also: **Caste**

Further Reading
Deliège, Robert. (1999) *The Untouchables of India*. Translated from the French by Nora Scott. Oxford: Berg Publishers.

Keer, Dananjay. (1962) *Dr. Ambedkar: Life and Mission*. Bombay, India: Popular Prakashan.

Mendelsohn, Oliver, and Marika Vicziany. (1998) *The Untouchables: Subordination, Poverty, and the State in Modern India*. Cambridge, U.K., and New York: Cambridge University Press.

Narula, Smita. (1999) *Broken People*. New York: Human Rights Watch.

Singh, K. S. (1993) *The Scheduled Castes*. Delhi: Anthropological Survey of India with Oxford University Press.

Zelliot, Eleanor. (1996) *From Untouchable to Dalit: Essays on the Ambedkar Movement*. New Delhi, India: Manohar Publications.

UPANISHADS   The Upanishads constitute the fourth and final stratum of the corpus of Vedic literature (early Hindu sacred writings), traditionally held to be *shruti*, or the revealed and eternal divine word. The Upanishads are chiefly concerned with metaphysical speculations about the nature of reality and the destiny of the human soul. The term is normally understood to mean a dozen or so esoteric and speculative texts, in prose and in verse, that are associated with the four great Vedic textual traditions or schools and are thought to date, in the main, from the sixth century BCE to perhaps the first centuries CE. These texts come chronologically at the end of the Vedic corpus and they represent, broadly speaking, the culmination of the development of Vedic thought from a relatively straightforward ritualism to an interiorization of the ritual and speculation on the underlying principle of the cosmos. For these reasons they are sometimes referred to collectively as the Vedanta or end (*anta*) of the Veda. The term *Upanishad* is, like many words in the later Vedic texts, subject to a variety of etymological interpretations. However, scholars generally understand it to derive from a verbal root meaning "to sit down near" and to convey the sense of disciples seating themselves at the feet of a master to imbibe the esoteric doctrines that characterize these texts.

Such is the power and influence of these and other Vedic texts that (like the name Veda itself) the term *Upanishad* has been extended to a variety of post-Vedic texts such as the Sannyasa Upanishads, which lay down the rules of conduct for religious renunciants, while other important religious texts such as the *Bhagavad Gita* are sometimes also considered to be Upanishads.

The original Upanishads vary in length and are diverse in character, consisting of a variety of materials including dialogues of a spiritual or metaphysical character, genealogies of spiritual teachers and disciples, narratives involving gods, demons, men, and, in some cases talking animals, and rituals and spells for the acquisition of power, long life, wealth, sex, and progeny.

Atmavada Doctrine in the Upanishads

Deriving as they do from the various Vedic schools, each with their particular interests and preserving a broad diachronic spectrum of legendary, ritual, philosophical, theological, physiological, and psychological materials, the Upanishads do not put forward a single, consistent set of principles or doctrines.

Nonetheless, the single most dominant and most frequently articulated philosophical focus of the Upanishads is the so-called Atmavada or Brahmavada, the doctrine of the universal world Self or Soul. Simply stated, this doctrine holds that there exists only one, single, limitless, irreducible, and unchanging real entity. This is called the Atman, or Self, the Paramatman, or Supreme Self, or Brahman. This entity which is pure existence (*sat*), pure consciousness (*cit*) and pure bliss (*ananda*) is the innermost essence of all things. Indeed the apparent diversity of the universe and indeed the real existence of any of its apparent constituents is illusory and arises as a result of a kind of cosmic illusion (*maya*) and is perpetuated by our ignorance (*avidya, ajnana*) of the true nature of things. True knowledge (*vidya, jnana*) consists in the profound inner realization that all apparent individuation, in-

cluding the all but universal perception that we are separate autonomous entities, is false. This realization is in effect a profound inner understanding of the esoteric correspondences that link the Vedic ritual, the human body, and the phenomenal universe. It is to be accomplished through the cultivation of detachment from the world of the senses. In this the Atmavada is similar, although far from identical, to many of the early brahmanical and nonbrahmanical religious systems of early India.

This rigorously nondualist philosophy forms the underlying principle around which was developed the major philosophical school of Advaita (nondual) Vedanta most closely associated with its greatest exponent Sankaracarya (c. 788–820 CE), among whose most seminal works is his magisterial *Upanishadbhashya*, or collection of commentaries on the principal Upanishads. This school, although it is just one of many different religious and philosophical schools to have been developed in ancient India, has often come to be seen and represented in more modern times as the dominant and most characteristic, if not the only strand of Indian philosophy. This attitude has enhanced the prestige of the Upanishads as the foundational scripture of Hinduism.

Although the Upanishads constitute a diverse body of often obscure and highly esoteric late Vedic belief and speculation, they have come, by virtue of their promulgation of the important doctrine of the Atman and its realization as the unique path of spiritual liberation, to be canonized as one of the principal fonts of Hindu thought and practice.

Robert P. Goldman

Further Reading
Deussen, Paul. ([1906] 1966). *The Philosophy of the Upanishads*. Reprint ed. New York: Dover.

Hume, Robert Ernest. (1968) *The Thirteen Principal Upanishads: Translated from the Sanskrit*. 2d ed. Madras, India: Oxford University Press.

Keith, A. B. (1925) *The Religion and Philosophy of the Veda and Upanishads*. Harvard Oriental Series, vol. 32. Cambridge, MA: Harvard University Press.

Olivelle, Patrick. (1996) *Upanishads*. Oxford: Oxford University Press.

URALIC LANGUAGES The Uralic languages, including both the Finno-Ugrian and the Samoyedic groups, constitute a large family of languages of Europe and Northern Eurasia. Finno-Ugrian languages are spoken mostly in Europe; three of them, Finnish, Estonian, and Hungarian, are major literary and national languages of independent states. All other Finno-Ugrian languages are spoken by people in Russia. Mari (or Cheremis), Mordvin, Udmurt (or Votiak), and Komi (or Zyryene) are spoken by numerous peoples who live between the river Volga and the Ural Mountains.

The closest relatives of Hungarian, however, the Ob'-Ugrian languages, are spoken in the Asiatic part of Russia, east of the Ural Mountains, in the basin of the river Ob'. The two languages of this group are Khanty (or Ostiak) and Mansi (or Vogul). Nowadays Khanty is spoken by about 13,000 people; Mansi has approximately 3,000 speakers. Khanty and Mansi are the titular nationalities of the semiautonomous National Territory of the Khanty and Mansi, which forms part of the Tiumen'skaia Oblast' (province) of Western Siberia.

All Samoyedic languages are spoken by people living in Siberia. This group is commonly subdivided into a Northern and a Southern subgroup. Northern Samoyedic languages are Nganasan (Tawgy-Samoyed), spoken by around 1,000 members of the northernmost nationality of Russia, in fact of all of Asia, on the Taymyr Peninsula; Nenets (Yurak-Samoyed) has around 30,000 speakers north of the Arctic Circle to the west and east of the Ural Mountains, and the obsolescent Enets (Yenisey-Samoyed) is spoken by less than 100 people in a few villages on the bank of the river Yenisey. Southern Samoyed is today represented only by Sel'kup (Ostiak-Samoyed; 1,500 speakers); other Southern Samoyed languages, now extinct, were recorded in the eighteenth and nineteenth centuries as far south as the Sayan Mountains (Mator, Koibal, Kamass).

The genetic relationship of the Finno-Ugrian languages was established as early as the eighteenth century; the Samoyedic languages were added to the Uralic family by the mid-nineteenth century.

Uralic languages, especially the eastern members of the family, show a marked typological similarity to Altaic languages (e.g., verb-final word order, vowel harmony, lack of word-initial consonant clusters) in the nineteenth century this similarity gave rise to the so-called Ural-Altaic hypothesis, which tried to describe Uralic, together with Turkic, Mongolian, and Tungus, as members of one great family of languages. Because more accurate descriptions of these languages became available, and the methods of comparative linguistics were improved, specialists had largely abandoned this view during the twentieth century.

Stefan Georg

Further Reading

Abondolo, Daniel, ed. (1998) *The Uralic Languages*. London and New York: Routledge.

Collinder, Björn. (1957) *Survey of the Uralic Languages*. Stockholm, Sweden: Almqvist & Wiksell.

Hajdú, Péter. (1992) *Introduzione alle lingue Uraliche* (Introduction to Uralic languages). Turin, Italy: Rosenberg & Sellier.

Sinor, Denis, ed. (1988) *The Uralic Languages: Description, History, and Foreign Influences*. Leiden, Netherlands: E. J. Brill.

URDANETA, ANDRES DE

URDANETA, ANDRES DE (1498–1568), Spanish Augustinian friar and navigator. Andres de Urdaneta was born in 1498 in the Basque region of Spain. At seventeen he became a sailor and served as a page to Garcia Jofre de Loaysa's expedition to the Moluccas. He spent eight years in Malaka (Moluccas), where he figured in several encounters with the Portuguese, Spain's rivals in colonizing Malaka, until the members of the expedition surrendered and were later repatriated to Spain via Lisbon in 1536.

In 1553 Urdaneta joined the Augustinian order in Mexico after a long, distinguished military career following his return to Spain. In 1559, King Philip II, interested in the Philippine Islands, which were named after him by the Villalobos expedition, sought out Urdaneta's services. Since his priestly status forbade him to command an expedition, Urdaneta recommended that the king appoint Miguel Lopez de Legazpi, a distinguished official in Mexico, to command the expedition. The expedition left Navidad, Mexico, in 1564 and, through Urdaneta's guidance, it reached Philippine shores in February 1565. After establishing a settlement, Legazpi sent Urdaneta back to Mexico to deliver samples of Philippine spices discovered and to find a more expedient route. Urdaneta sailed far north near Japan before turning east, where the winds were favorable. He reached Acapulco after sailing for four months. The passage he discovered was later called the Urdaneta Passage. Years later the galleons of the Manila-Acapulco trade followed this route.

When his mission was over, Urdaneta returned to his Augustinian order in Mexico. Although he expressed a desire to return to the Philippines to undertake missionary work, his superior did not grant him permission to do so due to his old age. He died on 3 June 1568 in Mexico at the age of sixty.

Aaron Ronquillo

Further Reading

Agconillo, Teodoro. (1990) *History of the Filipino People*. 8th ed. Quezon City, Philippines: Garotech Publishing.

Arcila, Jose, S. J. (1984) *Introduction to Philippine History*. 3d ed. Manila, Philippines: Ateneo de Manila University Press.

Mitchell, Mairin. (1964) *Friar Andres de Urdaneta, OSA*. London: MacDonald & Evans Ltd.

URDU. See **Hindu-Urdu.**

URFA (2002 est pop. of province 1.5 million). Urfa, a province and a city (1995 pop. approximately 365,000) in southeastern Turkey, was known as Edessa in antiquity; its Arabic name was al-Ruha. Under the republic of Turkey it became known as Sanliurfa ("glorious Urfa"), the capital of the province of the same name.

The city was occupied as early as 3500 BCE by the Hurrians and then successively by the Hittites, Assyrians, Seleucids, Romans, and Byzantines. In the third century the city adopted Christianity, and by the early fourth century it was a center of Syriac Christianity. The city surrendered to the Arabs in c. 639 and subsequently lost its political and religious importance. The town was attacked by the Byzantines in 959–960; by the Turks in 1065–1966 and 1066–1967, and by the Seljuk sultan Alp Arslan for 50 days in 1070. After the battle of Manzikert (1971), the city was supposed to be handed over to the Seljuks, but instead it remained under Constantinople's control until 1086–1087, when it was given to the Seljuk sultan Melikshah.

Urfa was ruled by various dynasties in the following centuries until it was conquered by Sultan Selim I, probably in 1517. In the sixteenth century it became part of the province of Diyarbakır. During this time it was located on a caravan route to Aleppo and was a transit point for goods traveling from Anatolia to Persia and Iraq. Urfa was occupied by the French in 1919–1920 and officially became part of the Turkish Republic under the Treaty of Lausanne (1923). Today Urfa is largely an agricultural city producing wheat, barley, and beans. A college of the Dicle University in Diyarbakır is located here.

Tipi Isikozlu-E. F. Isikozlu

Further Reading

Faroqhi, Suraiya. (1960) "al-Ruha." In *Encyclopaedia of Islam*. 2d ed. Leiden, Netherlands: E. J. Brill, 589–593.

Statistical Yearbook of Turkey, 1998. (1999) Ankara, Turkey: Devlet Istatistik Enstitusu.

URGENCH Urgench was an ancient city that was an important trade center and the capital of Khwarizm until its destruction by the Mongols in the thirteenth century. It was rebuilt only to be again destroyed by Timur in the fourteenth century; for most of the sixteenth century it was the capital of the khanate of Khiva (1511–1920). It was abandoned later in the century after the Uzbeks conquered the area. Today the town of Kunya-Urgench (or Konye-Urgench) in modern-day Turkmenistan rests on the site. Visitors can see the Kutlug Temir minaret, which is the largest minaret in Central Asia, mausoleums, and other ancient ruins.

Today, there is another Urgench, the capital city of the Khorezm oblast of Uzbekistan. It had an estimated population of 169,000 in 2002, is situated on the Amu Dar'ya River and the Shavat Canal, and houses cotton and food processing industries. Kunya-Urgench in Turkmenistan is about 140 kilometers northwest of Urgench, Uzbekistan.

Rebecca M. Bichel

USTYURT PLATEAU The Ustyurt Plateau is a 160,600-square-kilometer (62,000-square-mile) desert plateau in Central Asia between the Caspian Sea to the west and the Aral Sea to the east. It lies mostly in the southern part of Kazakhstan and the northern part of the Karakalpak Republic and Turkmenistan. The plateau's elevation ranges from 150 to 365 meters (490 to 1,200 feet), with an average elevation of 200 meters (656 feet), and it drops steeply to the Aral Sea and surrounding plains. A largely uniform desert landscape, the plateau provides little pasture for the sheep, goats, and camels raised by its small seminomadic human population. Transport networks are poor due to both natural conditions and long-term neglect.

Oil and natural gas deposits are located in the western portion of the plateau. It is estimated that there are more than 4 billion tons of hydrocarbons in the region. Exploration and production is set to continue as the region increases its contribution to the world supply of hydrocarbons. Mining activities are likely to improve air links across the Caspian Sea and stimulate further regional economic development.

Warwick Gullett and Daniel Oakman

Further Reading

Garnett, Sherman, Alexander Rahr, and Koji Watanabe. (2000) *The New Central Asia: In Search of Stability*. New York: The Trilateral Commission.

Olcott, Martha Brill. (1996) *Central Asia's New States: Independence, Foreign Policy, and Regional Security*. Washington, DC: United States Institute of Peace Press.

USUBALIEV, TURDAKUN USUBALIE-VICH

USUBALIEV, TURDAKUN USUBALIE-VICH (b. 1919), Kyrgyz politician. Turdakun Usubalievich Usubaliev led the Kyrgyzstan Soviet Socialist Republic from 1961 to 1985 as the first secretary of the Communist Party. Born in Naryn (a remote eastern province of the republic) in 1919, he spent his entire career in the Communist Party apparatus, becoming one of the republic's most influential politicians for almost three decades in the late Soviet era. From 1955 to 1956 he worked as editor of the leading national newspaper, *Sovettyk Kyrgyzstan*, and later held various party posts before assuming leadership in the republic. He viewed Soviet policy (reflected in his writing) as an important mode of modernization of a traditional "backward" country and measured it purely in the terms of economic development and state-led industrialization. These views largely shaped Kyrgyzstan's political and economic setting in the 1960s and 1970s.

Usubaliev belonged to the cohort of Central Asian leaders who were most loyal to the Soviet political system and to Moscow's leadership. As Kyrgyzstan's leader he contributed to the vigorous implementation of the policies of Russification and "internationalism." However, it was his success in attracting huge investment in the industrialization of the republic that won him nationwide recognition and respect.

In 1985, with the introduction of Gorbachev's policy of glasnost, Usubaliev was forced to leave his post and was charged with patronage, corruption, and mismanagement; however, these accusations have never been brought to court. Turdakun Usubaliev remains one of the most popular politicians in post-Soviet Kyrgyzstan and a prolific writer (mainly memoirs). In 1992 he returned to the political arena as a member of the Jogorku Kenesh (Parliament), supporting moderate nationalism and remaining highly critical of the Westernization of Kyrgyz society.

Rafis Abazov

Further Reading
Huskey, Eugene. (1995) "The Rise of Contested Politics in Central Asia: Elections in Kyrgyzstan, 1989–90." *Europe-Asia Studies* 47, 5 (July): 813–834.

Usubaliev, T. U. (1995) *Epokha, sozidanie, sud'by* (Epoch, Creation, Destinies). 2 vols. Bishkek, Kyrgyzstan: Izdatelstvo Sham.

UTAI *Utai* (also called *yokyoku*) is the vocal music of the Japanese classical theater form called Noh. It is monophonic music influenced by Buddhist chant, especially of the *shomyo* tradition of the Tendai and Shingon esoteric sects that came to Japan from China in the Heian period (794–1185). Notation called *gomafu* or *gomaten* (literally, "sesame seed marking," from the way the notation marks look) developed from this same tradition and was consolidated in the Edo period (1600/1603–1868), with each mark having a slightly different form and a definite meaning for each of the Noh schools. Although the language and sometimes pronunciation, too, are classical and not always easily understood, the performance of *utai* is studied by amateurs of all ages as well as by professionals.

A Noh text develops through the progression of combinations of units of prose and of poetry in a 7/5-syllable meter. An actor speaks prose lines in *kotoba* (inflected speech) or chants lines solo or in exchanges with other characters. The chorus (*ji-utai*) expresses a character's speech or thoughts as well as describes a scene or narrates action during mimed sections.

Utai as chant is characterized by rhythm, pitch, and mode. The rhythm (*nori*) of Noh can be divided into *hyoshi-awazu* (incongruent) and *hyoshi-au* (congruent) chant to the drum patterns in an eight-beat system. *Hyoshi-awazu* chant may be found in short poetic sections. There are three kinds of *hyoshi-au* (congruent) chant. *Hira-nori*, the most common form, distributes the twelve syllables of the 7/5 meter over eight beats, with the syllables on the upbeat of the first, third, and fifth beats held. *Chu-nori*, also called *shura-nori* as it is often used in descriptive passages in *shura-mono* (warrior plays), distributes sixteen syllables of text over eight beats and is characterized by stress on every second beat. *O-nori* places one syllable per beat and is often used when the *taiko* (stick drum) is played for a strong or dynamic effect. Variations of syllables in lines in each of these styles create interesting syncopation. The pitch of *utai* goes through three centers: *jo* (high), *chu* (center), and *ge* (low), each a perfect fourth apart, following conventions of movement and embellishment for each section of the text. The chorus follows the pitch set by its leader, the *ji-gashira*. The two modes of *utai* express a wide range of emotions: *yowa-gin*, a weak or melodic mode for lyric passages, and *tsuyo-gin*, a strong, dynamic mode that uses microtonal pitch changes.

Ogamo Rebecca Teele

See also: **Noh-Kyogen**

Further Reading
Komparu, Kunio. (1983) *The Noh Theater, Principles and Perspectives.* New York: Weatherhill/Tankosha.

Malm, William P. (1959) *Japanese Music and Musical Instruments*. Rutland, VT: Charles E. Tuttle.

Tamba, Akira. (1981) *The Musical Structure of Noh*. Trans. by Patricia Matoreas. Tokyo: Tokyo University Press.

UTTAR PRADESH (2001 est. pop. 166.1 million).

Uttar Pradesh is located centrally in the Indo-Gangetic Plain southeast of New Delhi. The area measures 243,286 square kilometers. It has been under one administration, at first as part of Bengal Presidency, since 1877, and in 1902 became known as the United Provinces of Agra and Oudh. This became, simply, United Provinces in 1935, a name translated into Hindi as Uttar Pradesh after Independence in 1947. This state was made up of the former United Provinces and the princely states of Benares, Tehri-Garhwal, and Rampur. The capital is Lucknow (or Laknau). Not only was this area the center of the army uprising known as the Indian Mutiny (1857); Lucknow also was the focal point of the movement for an independent Pakistan. In 2000 the new state of Uttaranchal was carved out of Uttar Pradesh.

Uttar Pradesh is governed by a legislative council and a legislative assembly. The state has a mixed, mostly rural, population of Hindus and Muslims, who speak Hindi, Urdu, and English; the official language is Hindi. Traversed by several rivers and canals, especially the Ganges and Jumna, the fertile state is the largest producer of food grains in India. In addition, sugar and edible oils are important farm produce. There is considerable industrialization—among goods produced in Uttar Pradesh are paper, chemicals, glass, distilled spirits, farm implements, leather and footwear, textiles, copper, coal, limestone, bauxite, silica, phosphorite, and pyrophillite.

Paul Hockings

Further Reading

Spate, O. H. K. (1972) *India and Pakistan: A General and Regional Geography*. 3rd ed. New York: E. P. Dutton & Co.

Wadley, Susan S. (1994) Struggling with Destiny in Karimpur, 1925–1984. Berkeley and Los Angeles: University of California Press.

UTTARANCHAL (2001 est. pop. 8.5 million).

Uttaranchal is an Indian state that was created in 2000 from the northern quarter of Uttar Pradesh. It consists of thirteen hill districts bordering on Nepal to the east, with the lower Himalayas in the north, and the states of Haryana and Himachal Pradesh to the west and northwest respectively. It has an area of 51,125 square kilometers.

Dehra Dun is the state capital, and the population of the individual districts is primarily tribal. The state is home to four of the most revered Hindu sites in India: Badrinath, Kedarnath, Gangotri, and Yamunotri. All attract thousands of pilgrims every month. In the pre-Independence period, the numerous districts of present Uttaranchal were ruled over by several petty hill princes, who owed their formal allegiance to the British. Among the prominent nationalist figures who came from this region is the Congress leader Dr. Govind Ballabh Pant (1887–1961). (The town of Pantnagar in Nainital district has been named after him.) Since the 1980s, the region has been at the forefront of the Indian environmental movement, spearheaded by the Chipko Movement of Sunderlal Bahuguna and Chandi Prasad Bhatt. There also has been vocal opposition to the proposed Tehri Dam in the district of Tehri Garhwal, a construction that threatens to wipe away entire villages.

Paul Hockings

Further Reading

Berreman, Gerald D. (1972) *Hindus of the Himalayas: Ethnography and Change*. Berkeley and Los Angeles: University of California Press.

UZBEKISTAN—PROFILE (2001 est. pop. 25.1 million).

Uzbekistan is the most populous former Soviet state in Central Asia and the third most populous of all former Soviet states, after Russia and the Ukraine. It declared its independence on 1 September 1991 and is officially called the Republic of Uzbekistan.

Geography

With an area of 449,601 square kilometers, Uzbekistan is almost 42 percent desert. In North Central Uzbekistan lies the vast Kyzyl Kum desert, 297,850 square kilometers in size. Spurs of the Tian Shan and Pamir Mountains rise to the east and northeast; the highest elevation in Uzbekistan is 4,643 meters, and earthquakes are common.

Because rainfall is scarce except on the mountain sides, agriculture elsewhere in the country is possible only with irrigation. In mountainous areas live snow leopards; desert monitors, lizards that can grow longer than 1.5 meters, inhabit the desert. The two main rivers—the Amu Dar'ya (Oxus) and Syr Dar'ya (Jakartes), which flow into the Aral Sea—as well as the Zarafshon River and the Fergana Valley form the core of the relatively limited populated areas.

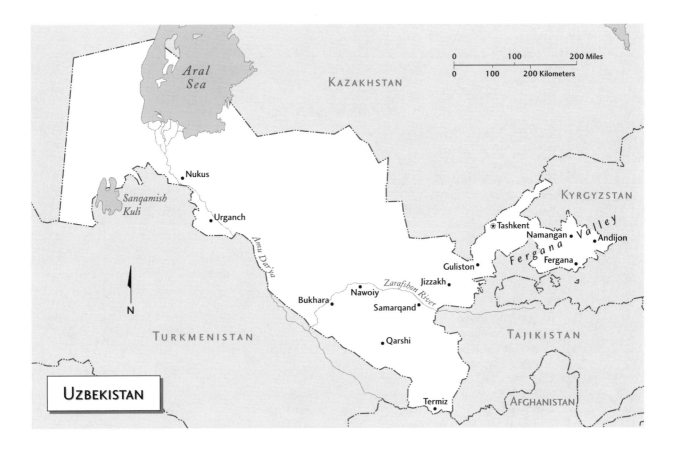

The country is divided into twelve *wiloyatlar* (regions), one city (Tashkent, the capital), and the Karakal Autonomous Republic, located in northwestern Uzbekistan. These entities are further divided into smaller units; at each level elected and appointed officials have constitutional responsibility, but most power rests in the central state apparatus.

Population

Almost 3 million people live in the capital city of Tashkent, which is the largest city in Central Asia and the fourth largest among former Soviet cities. The country has over one hundred nationalities, although almost 80 percent are ethnic Uzbeks, a Turkic-speaking Muslim people. Other significant ethnic groups include Russians, Tajiks, Kazakhs, Karakalpaks, Turkmen, and Tatars. The Russians are the largest minority, but their numbers decreased after independence, when many moved to Russia and other countries.

History

Uzbekistan has a rich and long history, and Uzbeks lived in the Central Asian region for many hundreds of years, but until 1925 there was no political entity named "Uzbekistan." Known as the ancient Persian province of Sogdiana, the region was conquered by Alexander of Macedon in the fourth century BCE. Arabs conquered it in the eighth century as did the Mongol empire in the thirteenth century; Timur (Tamerlane) developed his "local" Mongol empire in the fourteenth and fifteenth centuries; Shaibani Khan introduced Uzbek authority to the region in the sixteenth century.

The final conquerors—the Russians—appeared only in the nineteenth century and consolidated their power by the 1860s and 1870s. In the face of stiff guerrilla resistance, the Soviets took over in the 1920s and eventually formed new political entities, parceling out the territory according to ethnic groups. The delimitation of 1925 saw Uzbekistan appear as a Soviet Socialist Republic. In 1929 the Tajik Socialist Soviet Republic was formed from a portion of Uzbekistan; the Karakalpak Autonomous Republic became part of Uzbekistan in 1936.

The Soviet period was particularly difficult; despite advances in education, health care, and treatment of women, the Uzbeks suffered during the purges and collectivization campaigns of the 1930s, and cultural

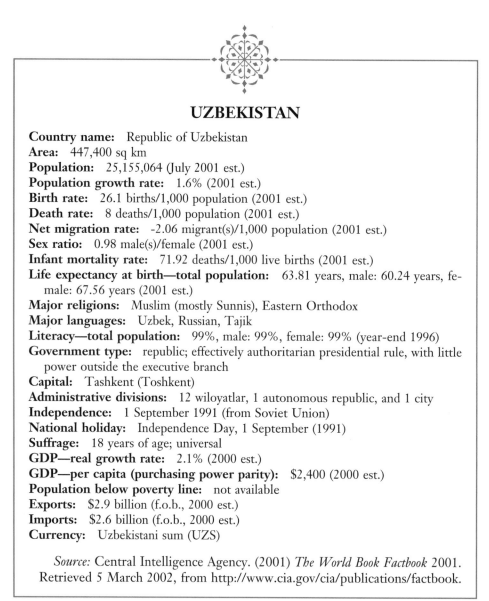

UZBEKISTAN

Country name: Republic of Uzbekistan

Area: 447,400 sq km

Population: 25,155,064 (July 2001 est.)

Population growth rate: 1.6% (2001 est.)

Birth rate: 26.1 births/1,000 population (2001 est.)

Death rate: 8 deaths/1,000 population (2001 est.)

Net migration rate: -2.06 migrant(s)/1,000 population (2001 est.)

Sex ratio: 0.98 male(s)/female (2001 est.)

Infant mortality rate: 71.92 deaths/1,000 live births (2001 est.)

Life expectancy at birth—total population: 63.81 years, male: 60.24 years, female: 67.56 years (2001 est.)

Major religions: Muslim (mostly Sunnis), Eastern Orthodox

Major languages: Uzbek, Russian, Tajik

Literacy—total population: 99%, male: 99%, female: 99% (year-end 1996)

Government type: republic; effectively authoritarian presidential rule, with little power outside the executive branch

Capital: Tashkent (Toshkent)

Administrative divisions: 12 wiloyatlar, 1 autonomous republic, and 1 city

Independence: 1 September 1991 (from Soviet Union)

National holiday: Independence Day, 1 September (1991)

Suffrage: 18 years of age; universal

GDP—real growth rate: 2.1% (2000 est.)

GDP—per capita (purchasing power parity): $2,400 (2000 est.)

Population below poverty line: not available

Exports: $2.9 billion (f.o.b., 2000 est.)

Imports: $2.6 billion (f.o.b., 2000 est.)

Currency: Uzbekistani sum (UZS)

Source: Central Intelligence Agency. (2001) *The World Book Factbook* 2001. Retrieved 5 March 2002, from http://www.cia.gov/cia/publications/factbook.

identity was often suppressed. Not until the 1980s could Uzbeks openly discuss their own non-Soviet history and Muslim identity. Ironically these issues are still problematic in post-Soviet Uzbekistan.

Politics

Islam Karimov was president even before independence, having been elected on 24 March 1990. Constitutionally he is afforded a wide range of powers and can legislate by decree. He has successfully curtailed potential rivals' efforts by constantly shuffling regional leadership and removing key individuals from office, including his former vice president, Shukhrulla Mirsaidov. Karimov was reelected in January 2000 with an overwhelming majority (even the token opposition candidate voted for Karimov).

Uzbekistan's 250-member legislature, the Oliy Majlis, is a relatively weak entity that has never challenged the presidential authority. The court system and regional governments are also fairly compliant. The country is technically multiparty, and four parties are registered. Each, especially the dominant People's Democratic Party, swears allegiance to President Karimov and acts simply as an advocate for a specific constituency in Uzbek society.

Opposition—secular and religious—is severely curtailed. Most opposition leaders have fled the country, as was the case with the leaders of the opposition movements Birlik (Unity) and Erk (Will) in the 1980s and 1990s. The religious-based opposition parties, Adolat (Justice) and the Islamic Renaissance Party, were never even allowed to register. These and other movements have been prohibited from becoming legal entities since 1992. As a result they either remain underground or maintain a base in exile. In the summer of 1999, a relatively new movement—the Islamic Movement of Uzbekistan (IMU), under the leadership of Jumaboi Namangani—emerged as a threat to the Karimov regime. In that summer and in the summer of 2000, IMU units attacked positions in Kyrgyzstan and southern Uzbekistan. It is feared that in subsequent years this movement will increase its activities in Uzbekistan and could become a long-term problem for President Karimov.

Economy

Uzbekistan's economy is based largely on cotton (which was introduced in imperial Russian times despite Uzbek protests about resulting food shortages and loss of land) and on agriculture in general. Although only 31 percent of the country's gross domestic product (GDP) comes from agriculture, over 40 percent of all working-age Uzbekistan citizens are employed in this sector. Uzbekistan is the largest cotton exporter in the world, but because agriculture is concentrated in cotton, the country must import much of its food. The industrial and service sectors are slowly developing, with the latter now responsible for 42 percent of the country's GDP.

The major obstacles to economic growth are geography, infrastructure, and program execution. Because Uzbekistan is landlocked, it must often transit goods across international borders—a serious problem because customs duties and procedures are not consistently enforced in Central Asia. The infrastructure is in the process of moving from the Soviet-era system that was in place, although the pace of development has not kept up with the deterioration of the old infrastructure. Last, the opaque maze of regulations and the lack of openness have made it difficult for local, joint-venture, and foreign-owned businesses to establish themselves and to develop effectively. The weak currency is also a detriment to economic growth. Finally, corruption has become a deterrent to the successful creation of new companies.

Foreign Policy

Because of its geography, Uzbekistan is a key actor in the geopolitics of Central Asia. Sitting among the other Central Asian states of Kyrgyzstan, Kazakhstan, Turkmenistan, and Tajikistan, as well as Afghanistan to the south, Uzbekistan is a key transportation and communications hub. As a strategic country, it has been involved in peace processes in Tajikistan and Afghanistan. In an effort to strengthen its position as an independent state, Uzbekistan has joined a range of associations and organizations. Ties with Russia are still important and have slowed the emergence of a free market in the country. Uzbekistan's abysmal human-rights record is often noted as a cause for U.S. concern and has been a point of contention between the two countries.

The national prospects for Uzbekistan are tied to President Islam Karimov. In his early sixties, Karimov is fit and appears poised to continue as president for the foreseeable future. The lack of a successor, of strong political actors and parties, and of a politically active population suggests that Uzbekistan's political system will not develop into a democracy any time soon. In addition to suffering from continuing economic problems, the IMU insurgency of the past two years persists unabated. While Uzbekistan has the benefits of resource wealth and an educated population, problems loom over the horizon. How Uzbekistan addresses these problems will shape the future success or failure of the country.

Roger D. Kangas

Further Reading

Allworth, Edward. (1990) *The Modern Uzbeks: From the Fourteenth Century to the Present, a Cultural History*. Stanford, CA: Hoover Institution.

Bohr, Annette. (1998) *Uzbekistan: Politics and Foreign Policy*. London: RIIA.

Gleason, Gregory. (2001) "Uzbekistan." In *Nations in Transit 2001*, edited by Adrian Karatnycky, Alexander Motyl, and Amanda Schnetzer. New York: Freedom House, 406–416.

Kangas, Roger. (2000) *Uzbekistan in the Twentieth Century: Political Development and the Evolution of Power*. New York: St. Martin's Press.

Karimov, Islam A. (1997) *Uzbekistan on the Threshold of the Twenty-First Century*. Tashkent, Uzbekistan: Uzbekistan Publishers.

Khalid, Adeeb. (1999) *The Politics of Muslim Cultural Reform: Jadidism in Central Asia*. Berkeley and Los Angeles: University of California Press.

MacLeod, Calum, and Bradley Mayhew. (1999) *Uzbekistan: The Golden Road to Samarkand*. Hong Kong: Odyssey.

Melvin, Neil. (2000) *Uzbekistan: Transition to Authoritarianism on the Silk Road*. Amsterdam: Harwood.

UZBEKISTAN—ECONOMIC SYSTEM

Uzbekistan, the most populous and best developed of the newly independent states in Central Asia, occupies the dominant geographical, political, and cultural position in the region. It is home to Central Asia's most productive agricultural oases, river valleys, and irrigated lowlands.

Uzbekistan is a landlocked country, and each bordering country is itself a landlocked state. The southern border with Turkmenistan is partly defined by the watercourse of the Amu Dar'ya River, one of Central Asia's most important natural resources. To the north the country's border with Kazakhstan is defined by the watercourse of the Syr Dar'ya River. In the northwest the Aral Sea, dying from overuse of the region's water resources, defines the country's border. The Fergana Valley, lying in the protected eastern part of the country between Kyrgyzstan and Tajikistan, is one of the most productive agricultural regions in the world. The oases and river valleys of Bukhara and Samarqand have supported civilization and agriculture since ancient times.

Postindependence Economic Functioning

Uzbekistan's population is well educated and technically trained. The country is rich in a variety of natural resources, including coal, copper, gold, natural gas, oil, silver, and uranium. Primary commodities, together with cotton fiber, account for about 75 percent of merchandise exports, with cotton alone accounting for about 40 percent. Uzbekistan's 1998 gross national product was estimated at $870 per person, placing it among lower-middle-income economies.

At the time of independence the Uzbek economy was more diversified than the economies of the other four Central Asian states and included agriculture, light and heavy industry, and important branches in primary commodities. Following the disintegration of the Soviet Union, Uzbekistan's economy was insulated from much of the economic decline that afflicted other former Soviet states, due to its labor-intensive economy based on agriculture and mineral extraction. Rapid growth in 1992–1995 in oil and gas production allowed Uzbekistan to eliminate oil imports and increase gas exports. Additionally, Uzbekistan shifted some of its crop acreage from cotton to grains to boost food self-sufficiency. While these were positive outcomes, they resulted in delaying the structural reforms that Uzbekistan's neighbors, particularly Kazakhstan and Kyrgyzstan, implemented.

Economic Policy of Stabilization

The Uzbekistan government, under the leadership of President Islam Karimov, quickly embraced the idea of market-based commercial relations. Uzbekistan announced that it was "pro-business," and the Soviet system was immediately rejected. Replacing it, however,

was an indigenous, state-controlled economy with many structural parallels to the Soviet system, except on a smaller, regional scale.

The Uzbekistan government has stressed a gradual, step-by-step approach to macroeconomic and market-oriented structural reforms. This conservative transition strategy has emphasized establishing self-sufficiency in energy and food grains, exporting primary commodities, particularly cotton and gold, and creating an internally oriented services market. In the early years of independence the government approached questions of structural reform cautiously and relied on administrative measures and controls to soften the shock of the interruption of Soviet-era commerce.

More recently the Uzbekistan government has made limited progress in implementing structural reforms in some areas, including privatization and the financial sector. In late 1998 the government announced an accelerated program for the case-by-case privatization of large strategic enterprises. At the same time it announced that restructuring and subsequent privatization of banks were to be undertaken. Yet fundamental agricultural reforms such as farm restructuring, land registration, changes in state procurement policies, and export-marketing arrangements continued to be delayed.

Reform Process and Currency Convertibility

In September 1996 in connection with a shortfall in foreign reserves, the Uzbekistan Ministry of Finance imposed a system of import contract registration. The goal of the system was to ensure that scarce foreign currency was used primarily to import capital rather than to buy consumer goods, particularly luxury goods. In practice, however, the system severely limited the availability of foreign exchange for all sectors of the economy and retarded economic activity. In subsequent years the Ministry of Finance periodically acted to make the system yet more rigorous as foreign currency reserves continued to dwindle. In 1998 the number of importers given convertibility quotas was cut by one-third of the number two years before. The remaining importers saw their quotas slashed in half.

Foreign companies in Uzbekistan reported that the currency restrictions constituted the most serious obstacle to doing business in the country. Foreign companies or foreign joint ventures importing capital goods with their own funds held outside Uzbekistan have also in effect been subject to the import registration system, although a 1998 presidential decree exempted joint ventures from the registration requirement. Nevertheless foreign businesses have continued to experience bureaucratic hurdles with payments and settlements. In addition customs clearance remains a tedious and capricious bureaucratic process. Capital equipment imports for U.S.-Uzbek joint ventures have been subject to substantial processing delays and often remain in customs for months at a time. Delays can be substantial and expensive, and no procedure has been established for releasing goods under bond.

In May 2000 the government devalued the official exchange rate for government transactions by about 50 percent to bring it into line with the commercial exchange rate. But the economy remains hampered by adherence to these bureaucratic constraints.

The Future of the Uzbekistan Economy

An overvalued currency tends to channel trade into narrow and easily managed sectors and thus may appear to offer a solution to capital flight, but it is also associated with great efficiency losses. Financial transactions must be strictly regulated, which imposes a heavy burden of monitoring and sanctions. Well-connected parties with access to cheap, government-financed foreign exchange and import licenses benefit greatly from this situation. These parties can be expected to lobby to maintain the situation, despite the efficiency losses and corresponding damage to the public interest.

The bureaucratic burden of maintaining strict currency controls can be expensive and unavoidably creates an unfavorable climate for trade. A policy of overvaluation provides a rationale for extending police sanctions even to the extent of replacing the goal of public safety with that of regulating private behavior. Such a policy can produce an incentive structure in which private parties have an interest in avoiding or evading the legal framework through various forms of side payments and inducements. An overvalued currency can also lead to the depletion of foreign reserves, which, in turn, can bring about pressures for severe import restrictions and, eventually, the collapse of the free-trade policy.

Stressing economic self-sufficiency and state-sponsored welfare programs, the Uzbekistan government has resisted counsel from international organizations and economic specialists to liberalize prices, abandon government subsidies, adopt a tradable currency, and open its borders to trade. Instead Uzbekistan has maintained restrictions on trade and currency movement, closed its borders with war-torn Tajikistan, established government-controlled trading companies, and developed an elaborate system of subsidies and price supports for industry and agriculture.

There are indications that Uzbekistan's foreign economic policies are changing. In June 2001, President Islam Karimov signed a decree designed to liberalize the currency market, modernize the republic's monetary system, and strengthen the banking system. The Afghanistan war drew a considerable amount of attention from foreign governments and international organizations. Faced with the potential for dramatic economic modernization spurred by international assistance, the Uzbekistan government redoubled its efforts after the beginning of the antiterror campaign in Afghanistan to bring its currency and macroeconomic policies into line with international standards.

Gregory Gleason

Further Reading

Akiner, S. (1999) "Emerging Political Order in the New Caspian States. " In *Crossroads and Conflict: Security and Foreign Policy in the Caucasus and Central Asia*, edited by Gary K. Bertsch, Cassady B. Craft , Scott A. Jones, and Michael D. Beck. New York: Routledge, 90–128.

Gleason, Gregory. (1997) *The Central Asian States: Discovering Independence*. Boulder, CO: Westview Press.

International Monetary Fund. (1999) *Uzbekistan: Recent Economic Developments*. IMF Staff Country Report no. 99/140 (December). Washington, DC: International Monetary Fund.

Karimov, Islam. (1998) *Uzbekistan on the Threshold of the Twenty-First Century*. New York: St. Martin's Press.

Kaser, M. (1997) *The Economies of Kazakhstan and Uzbekistan*. London: Royal Institute of International Affairs.

McCagg, W. O., and B. Silver, eds. (1979) *Soviet Asian Ethnic Frontiers*. New York: Pergamon Policy Studies.

Pomfret, R. (1995) *The Economies of Central Asia*. Princeton, NJ: Princeton University Press.

Rumer, B. Z. (1989) *Soviet Central Asia: "A Tragic Experiment."* Boston: Unwin Hyman.

UZBEKISTAN—EDUCATION SYSTEM

Uzbekistan has a comprehensive system of education that embraces the entire population. Although the lands that now constitute Uzbekistan have been centers of higher learning for centuries, the system of education as it exists today has its roots in the Soviet era and thus follows the modern European model of state-based, free, compulsory, universal, and secular instruction.

Traditional Uzbek Education

Before the Soviet era, every residential neighborhood in Central Asia had a *maktab* (primary school), where a teacher, usually the imam of the mosque, taught basic texts to neighborhood boys. The purpose of the *maktab* was to inculcate culturally accepted norms of behavior and to have students memorize certain basic texts of the area's Islamic tradition. The teacher received gifts from the parents of the boys he taught. Girls were usually taught at home. Beyond the *maktab*, education took place in practical contexts of apprenticeships or in *madrasahs* (religious schools). Those who aspired to work in the nexus of administration, justice, and religion entered the *madrasah*, where they could learn the art of textual interpretation from a recognized master in a system that had marked similarities to apprenticeship. *Madrasahs* were funded by income from endowments *(waqf)* established by various individuals. Bukhara's *madrasahs* were renowned and drew students from as far away as Tatarstan (a region on both sides of the Volga River) and India. This pattern of traditional education survived the Russian conquest of the 1860s and 1870s. A network of Russian schools emerged, but it attracted few local students.

After the turn of the twentieth century the *maktab* and the *madrasah* came under intense attack from a new group of modernist intellectuals, the Jadids, who accused them of not meeting the needs of the age. The Jadids advocated a new method of education, in which the *maktab* would focus on imparting functional literacy and a basic knowledge of arithmetic, history, geography, and hygiene. For higher education, the Jadids advocated a curriculum of technical and vocational education to equip future generations with the skills necessary for survival in the vastly new circumstances introduced by the Russian conquest. Lack of material resources and hostility from both the state and conservative elements in local society meant, however, that "new-method" schools remained few in number before the Russian Revolution of 1917.

Uzbek Education under the Soviets, 1917–1991

Real change came during the Soviet period. The Bolsheviks who took power after the Russian Revolution shared the Jadids' critique of traditional Central Asian education, although their agenda was far more radical. For the Bolsheviks, economic backwardness—in Russia as much as in Central Asia—could be overcome only through combating cultural backwardness. They therefore expended substantial energies on campaigns against illiteracy and for the establishment of a ramified system of educational institutions. Crash courses to train primary teachers and to abolish illiteracy among adults began with the advent of Soviet power. A network of Soviet primary schools offering

a basic modern education faced substantial difficulties, however, and did not become a reality until late in the 1920s. Only in 1930 did education become universal and compulsory. The Soviet commitment to universal education meant that girls were brought into the educational system. By the 1930s, coeducation was the norm in Uzbek schools.

Education was the key to the remaking of society and culture, in the Bolshevik view. One of the first Soviet decrees concerned the separation of church and school. The Soviets saw religion as an ideological cloak that prevented the full realization of human reason; religious elites were also potential political opponents. This notion was applied in Central Asia as well, although *maktabs* were tolerated for much of the 1920s until enough Soviet schools could be built. The triumph of the Soviet school spelled the end of traditional Islamic education in Uzbekistan. Soviet primary schools replaced the *maktab*, while *madrasahs* were destroyed by the early 1930s through the nationalization of their *waqf* property, which was given over to the use of new state-run schools. Traditional Islamic education was pushed underground by the mid-1930s. In 1941, a *madrasah* with a radically transformed curriculum and modern pedagogical methods was opened to train small numbers of officially sanctioned clergy; a second one followed in 1970.

Soviet policy called for provision of education in the vernacular for all nationalities. The new schools operated in the Uzbek language, with Russian taught as a second language. In the cities with substantial Russian populations, Russian-language schools were also built. These were open to non-Russians, and since a knowledge of Russian was a vital skill, many ambitious Uzbek parents sent their children to Russian schools. Higher education, especially in technical fields, operated only in Russian, and after World War II the Uzbek regime emphasized the importance of Russian as the lingua franca of the USSR. Moreover Uzbekistan's higher education was closely linked with Soviet networks, with the most prestigious institutions being those in Moscow.

Higher education evolved along parallel tracks of teaching and research. The Central Asian Communist University (called Tashkent State University since 1960), established in Tashkent in 1920, was the first institution of modern higher learning in Uzbekistan. Over time, universities were established in Samarqand, Bukhara, and Nukus. A number of specialized institutes, teacher-training colleges, and vocational schools existed alongside the universities. Research-oriented education was based in the Uzbekistan Academy of

TABLE 1

Uzbekistan's Educational Statistics, 1999

	Institutions	Teachers	Students
Pre-Primary	n/a	96,100	1,071,400
Primary	8,500	92,400	1,905,693
Secondary		332,300	3,104,400
Teacher training	n/a	2,464	35,411
Vocational	440	7,900	214,500
Higher	53	24,787	321,682

SOURCE: UNESCO (1999).

Sciences (established 1943), with numerous affiliated institutes. Access to higher education was through university entrance examinations.

Soviet education achieved nearly universal literacy by the 1970s. In other indicators, Uzbekistan lagged behind all-Soviet levels, at least partly because of relatively low levels of urbanization. According to the last Soviet census (1989), Uzbekistan had 817 "specialists" per 10,000 population, as compared with the USSR average of 1,271. These figures are nevertheless impressive.

Uzbek Education after Independence, 1991

The basic structure of Uzbekistan's education system survived the breakup of the USSR. After nine years of compulsory education, students continue in vocational or academic streams, on the basis of their examination results. The infrastructure of primary and secondary education remains in place. Five million children study at school, and more than a million are enrolled at kindergarten level. (See Table 1.) In other ways, however, there have been drastic changes.

The end of central planning has necessitated new ways of funding education, and such resources have not always been forthcoming. Material difficulties, such as poor physical plants, shortages of textbooks and supplies, and low salaries for teachers, pose the largest threat to the system. Other problems arise from the disruption of contacts with academic institutions in the former USSR, which have not always been replaced by new ones. The government has also sought to downplay the public visibility of Russian, while emphasizing Uzbek-language education. Nevertheless Russian remains the only foreign language most people know. Russian schools continue to exist, and Russian remains a compulsory subject in non-Russian schools. Although the government would like to replace Russian with English as the means of communication with the outside world, such a switch remains

highly unlikely given the shortages of teachers. Higher education has suffered from brain drain as well as from shortages.

Another significant feature of the period since independence has been the reemergence of Islamic education. The government acknowledges Islam as part of the spiritual heritage of the nation, but it is also wary of political challenges from a religious opposition. It therefore keeps tight control over religious education. Only schools under the supervision of the Muslim Religious Board of Uzbekistan, a government department, are allowed to operate, and their curricula meet basic requirements set by the Ministry of Education. State schools remain resolutely secular, with no religious instruction whatsoever.

Adeeb Khalid

Further Reading

Bendrikov, K. E. (1960). *Ocherki po istorii narodnogo obrazovaniia v Turkestane* (Sketches from the History of Public Education in Turkestan). Moscow: Akademiia pedagogicheskii nauk.

Medlin, William K., William M. Cave, and Finley Carpenter. (1971) *Education and Development in Central Asia: A Case Study on Social Change in Uzbekistan.* Leiden, Netherlands: E. J. Brill.

UNESCO. (1999*) Statistical Yearbook, 1999.* Paris: UNESCO.

UZBEKISTAN—HISTORY
Uzbekistan is a former Soviet republic and now a member of the Commonwealth of Independent States (CIS). Its official name is the Republic of Uzbekistan. The history of Uzbekistan covers more than 2.5 millennia. During this period, various ancient states rose and fell in Central Asia, such as Bactria, Khorezm, Sogdiana, and Parthia.

The Ancient Period

From the sixth century to the fourth century BCE the territory belonged to the Iranian Achaemenid empire founded by Cyrus the Great (c. 585–c. 529 BCE). Alexander of Macedon (356–323 BCE) invaded Central Asia in 334 BCE and destroyed the Achaemenid empire. Inhabitants of the territory tried in vain to defeat him; a revolt under the leadership of Spitamen was one of the great battles.

After the death of Alexander in 323 BCE his empire was divided. Between the third and the second centuries BCE, the Graeco-Bactrian state, becoming independent from Alexander's empire, incorporated the

KEY EVENTS IN UZBEKISTAN'S HISTORY

6th–4th centuries BCE The region is under the control of Persia.

3rd–2nd centuries BCE The region is under the control of Graeco-Bactrian state.

1st–4th centuries CE The region is ruled by the Kushan empire.

552–745 The Turks rule Central Asia.

7th century Muslim Arabs conquer the region.

819–1001 The region is ruled by the Samanid dynasty.

1000 The Ghaznavid and Karakhanid dynasties begin to displace the Samanid dynasty in the region.

1097 The Anushtegin dynasty emerges in western Uzbekistan.

13th century The Mongols conquer the region.

14th century Timur displaces the Mongol rulers and establishes a capital at Samarqand.

16th–18th centuries Various Uzbek dynasties compete for power in the region.

1860 The Russians invade and then conquer Central Asia.

1924 The Soviet Socialist Republic of Uzbekistan is founded.

1991 Uzbekistan becomes an independent nation.

greater part of present-day Uzbekistan. From the first to the fourth century CE, the territory of Uzbekistan was under the control of the Kushan empire, which also controlled present-day Afghanistan, northern India, and part of Pakistan.

The Turks ruled Central Asia between 552 and 745 CE and played a great role in consolidating nomadic tribes in the Central Asian steppes and oases. By the end of the sixth century, due to local wars their empire was divided into two parts: the Eastern and Western Kaganates.

Before Arab conquests of Central Asia, there were several small states in the territory. Then, in the seventh century CE, Arabs conquered Central Asia under the leadership of Qutaybah ibn Muslim (d. 715) and brought Islam with them. The territory between the Amu Dar'ya (Oxus) and Syr Dar'ya (Jaxartes) Rivers was named Mawaraannahr (Transoxiana) by the Arabs and included in the Arab caliphate. Under the Abbasid caliphs of Baghdad, Islamic influence became domi-

nant in the cities of Central Asia. Arab conquest played a positive role in the development of Mawaraannahr.

The Samanid and Karakhanid Dynasties

At the beginning of the ninth century, the caliphate's power began to wane, and local dynasties ruled in provinces. The Samanid dynasty ruled Mawaraannahr from 819 to 1001. This period in Central Asian history was marked by a great upsurge in economy and culture. Cities and some rural areas turned into great commercial and cultural centers. For instance, Samarqand was renowned even outside of Central Asia for the production of high-quality glass and paper. Famous scholars such as the astronomer al-Biruni (973–1048), the mathematician Khorezmi (c. 780–850), the physician Ibn Sina (Avicenna; 980–1037), and many others lived at this time.

In 999, the Karakhanid dynasty began to supplant the Samanids in Samarqand and Bukhara. The new rulers even pushed south of the Amu Dar'ya, but Mahmud of Ghazna (971–1030) stopped them, and the river became the dividing line between Khorasan and Mawaraannahr. Thus, by the end of the tenth century the territory of the Samanids was occupied by the Karakhanid and Ghaznavid dynasties.

In Khwarizm, in the western part of present-day Uzbekistan, a new Muslim dynasty was founded in 1097 CE by Qutb al-Din Muhammad bin Anushtegin. This Turkic dynasty, which was called the Anushtegins (Khorezmshahs) in historical sources, gradually attained great power and became independent from another Turkic tribe, the Seljuks, in 1127. The Anushtegins were able to control the huge territory of Central Asia. During their rule, culture, economy, and science flourished.

The Mongol Era and the Reign of Timur

Mongols conquered Central Asia between 1219 and 1221 under the leadership of Genghis Khan (c. 1162–1227), and his second son, Chagatai (d. 1241), ruled the region. Mongols destroyed many cities and killed and enslaved thousands of peasants and craftsmen. In 1238, a great revolt against the Mongols started in Bukhara under the leadership of Mahmud Tarabi. However, it was suppressed.

In the middle of the fourteenth century, a battle against the Mongol empire began in Mawaraannahr under the leadership of Timur (1336–1405), who had once fought with Chagatai. Timur created a great kingdom from India to the Volga River and from the Tian Shan Mountains to Bosporus. Timur chose

Samarqand, one of the oldest cities in Central Asia, as the capital and built many great mosques and gardens. His rule and the rule of his descendants were marked by the development of irrigation, arts and crafts, trade, literature, science, and art in Samarqand and Mawaraannahr. Timur was a cruel conqueror. He slaughtered thousands of inhabitants of the cities that rebelled against him, especially at Delhi.

The Sixteenth to Eighteenth Centuries

At the beginning of the sixteenth century, nomadic Uzbeks, the Shaybanids, conquered most of Central Asia and ruled until the Ashtarkhanids, the group from the ruling house of Astrakhan (the town near of the mouth of the Volga), came to power in 1601. In 1753, the dynasty of the Mangits, an Uzbek tribe that was dominant in the central regions of Mawaraannahr, came to power in Bukhara and ruled until 1920.

At the beginning of the eighteenth century, Fergana became independent from Bukhara, and there the khanate of Quqon was founded. In the first quarter of the nineteenth century, it possessed Tashkent and the region of Syr Dar'ya. In 1511, the khanate of Khorezm was founded at the northwestern part of present-day Uzbekistan, and by the end of the century Khiva was chosen as its capital. Thus, there were three states in Central Asia before the Russian conquest: the Bukhara, Quqon, and Khiva khanates.

Nineteenth-Century British-Russian Rivalry

In the nineteenth century, Central Asia became an object of rivalry between Russia and Britain. Czarist Russia strove to capture Central Asia's raw materials and to prevent British penetration into the territory. In 1860, Russia invaded Central Asia and conquered it by the end of the nineteenth century. In 1876, the Russians dissolved the khanate of Quqon but allowed the khanates of Khiva and Bukhara to remain as protectorates. The Russians created the province of Turkestan, with its center at Tashkent. It was ruled by a governor-general.

On 30 April 1918, the Turkestan Autonomous Republic under the Russian federation was founded. In February 1920, Soviet power came to Khorezm, and the Khorezm People's Soviet Republic was established. In September of that year, the Bukhara People's Soviet Republic was also proclaimed.

In October 1924, following the establishment of the Union of Soviet Socialist Republics, the Soviet Socialist Republic of Uzbekistan (SSRU) was founded. It included Samarqand, Syr Dar'ya, the Fergana regions, and the territories of Bukhara and the Khorezm People's Soviet Republic. Tajikistan was a part of the SSRU until 1929, when it became an autonomous republic. In 1936, the Karakalpak Autonomous SSR was joined with Uzbekistan. In 1956 and 1963, the Mirzachul Steppes were transferred in portions from Kazakhstan to Uzbekistan. Some of the area was returned in 1971.

During the Soviet period, Russia exploited Uzbekistan for its tremendous productivity in cotton and for its other natural resources. Moscow controlled Uzbekistan's economic and political contacts with the rest of the world. The Republic of Uzbekistan became independent on 1 September 1991, following the collapse of the Soviet Union. On 2 March 1992, Uzbekistan joined the United Nations.

Akram Khabibullaev

Further Reading

Akhmedov, Erkin, and Zuhra Saidaminova. (1998) *Republic of Uzbekistan*. Tashkent, Uzbekistan: Uzbekistan Publishing House.

Allworth, Edward. (1990) *The Modern Uzbeks: From the Fourteenth Century to the Present: A Cultural History*. Stanford, CA: Hoover Institution Press.

Bakhtiyar, Nazarov, and DeWeese Devin, eds. (1993) *Essays on Uzbek History, Culture, and Language*. Bloomington, IN: Indiana University Press.

Calum, Macleod, and Mayhew Bradley. (1999) *Uzbekistan: The Golden Road to Samarkand*. Hong Kong: Odyssey Publications.

Tomas, Paul. (1992) *The Central Asian States—Tajikistan, Uzbekistan, Kyrgyzstan, Turkmenistan*. Brookfield, CT: Millbrook Press.

UZBEKISTAN—POLITICAL SYSTEM

Uzbekistan is home to the Uzbek nation, a Turkic-speaking people with a proud history and rich culture. While Uzbekistan's multinational population includes Kyrgyz, Tajiks, Turkmen, Kazakhs, Karakalpaks, Slavs, and many other groups, Uzbek national identity has undergone a significant revival since national independence in 1991. In December, 1998 Uzbekistan symbolically celebrated the re-creation of its past by awarding the country's highest honor, the Order of Emir Timur, to Uzbekistan's president, Islam Karimov (b. 1938). The award was intended to mark the country's achievements in creating a sovereign state, increasing respect for Uzbekistan around the world, strengthening civil peace and national accord, and promoting Uzbek cultural values.

Islam Karimov, while rhetorically championing democratic values and market reform, has steered a course toward concentration of executive powers. A financial specialist and former head of the Uzbek republic's Communist Party during the Soviet period, Karimov established himself as the strongman of Central Asia in the first period of Uzbekistan's independence. In 1983, Karimov was named minister of finance. In 1986, he was named vice chairman of the Council of Ministers and chairman of the State Planning Committee. In June 1989, he was appointed first secretary of the Uzbekistan Communist Party Central Committee. In March 1990, he was elected president of the republic by the Supreme Soviet (a legislative appointment—not a popular election). In December 1991, he was elected by popular vote. Karimov's supporters see his rule as reinforcing "Central Asian values"; critics view his leadership as reinforcing authoritarianism and despotism. Karimov justifies the severe paternalism of his government in his book *Uzbekistan on the Threshold of the Twenty-First Century*.

Constitutional and Legal Framework

The preamble of Uzbekistan's constitution (adopted 8 December 1992) states that one of the principal goals of the people of Uzbekistan is to "create a humane and democratic rule of law." The constitution guarantees the rights of freedom of speech, assembly, and religion, as well as the right to express one's national heritage.

The constitution specifies a branch system of government with a division of powers. The president directs the executive branch. The legislature is the Oliy Majlis (Supreme Council). Uzbekistan's three-tiered judiciary system is composed of the Constitutional Court, the Supreme Court, and the Arbitrazh Court (Commercial Court). There are local courts as well at the municipal level.

In theory the judiciary is independent, but in practice its capacity to function as an independent branch of government is limited. While the constitution describes the legislature as the highest organ of power, in fact the country has a unitary presidential form of government. Furthermore the branches are not coequal or balanced; the executive branch is dominant in virtually all matters. The president acts as the head of state and executive authority in the republic, and there are no meaningful lower tiers of independent authority (for instance, no federal divisions).

Executive-Branch Functions

The president's executive powers are extensive: he has the right to form a government; direct the government; appoint and dismiss the prime minister and cabinet ministers; appoint and recall diplomats; establish and dissolve ministries; appoint and dismiss the procurator-general and his or her deputies; nominate appointees to the Constitutional Court, Supreme Court, and board of the Central Bank; appoint and dismiss judges of regional, district, city, and arbitration courts; appoint and dismiss *hakim*s (governors or mayors) for violations of the law; suspend or repeal acts of *hakim*s; sign all laws of the Oliy Majlis or return them for reconsideration; declare a state of emergency; serve as commander-in-chief of the armed forces; declare war; award orders and medals; rule on matters of citizenship; issue amnesties and pardons; and appoint and dismiss heads of the national security service.

The president is elected by direct, secret, but not necessarily competitive, election for a term of five years. According to the constitution, a president can hold office for no more than two terms. After state service, the president becomes a lifetime member of the Constitutional Court. Islam Karimov was elected president in March 1990 by Uzbekistan's Soviet-era parliament. He was reelected in December 1991 in a popular election, running opposed and winning 86 percent of the votes. A March 1995 referendum extended the president's term of office to January 2000, matching the terms of the Oliy Majlis deputies (parliamentarians) and allowing Karimov to stand again for election. In December 2001, the Oliy Majlis adopted a resolution calling for a presidential election. If the resolution is implemented in 2002, a referendum may be held allowing Karimov to remain in office until 2007.

The three-tiered judicial system is subordinated to the Ministry of Justice. The court system is funded from the state budget. To avoid partisanship, no judge may be a member of any political party. The procurator's office represents the prosecutorial arm of the justice system and is responsible for public observance of the laws. Procurators are appointed by the president and are restricted from belonging to any political party or participating in party activity during their period of service. Local and neighborhood conflict-resolution committees—the Mahalla—are reported to function effectively on a local level in many areas, particularly rural areas.

In Uzbekistan, the parliament, the Oliy Majlis, serves as an advisory and legitimating instrument, not as a deliberative body. The core of Uzbekistan's government is not the parliament or the courts, but the system of administration that relies on the twelve *veli-atlar* (former oblasts or regions) headed by *hakim*s. Of the *hakim* appointments announced in March 1994, all were ethnic Uzbeks; all had previously been oblast-level Communist Party committee secretaries, and all were members of the People's Democratic Party of Uzbekistan, the party headed by Karimov. The system is prefectoral. Each *hakim* administers his or her territory as representative, or prefect, of the president.

Competitive Politics, Elections, Parties, and Civil Rights

Politics is not pluralistic in Uzbekistan: the political process is carefully monitored and controlled. The Central Electoral Commission (CEC) is a fourteen-member board established by the Oliy Majlis on the advice of the president. The CEC is responsible for oversight of the nomination process and of campaigning and for the organization of the election. Campaign financing and campaign publicity are also managed by the CEC. According to an election law passed in December 1993, the right to nominate candidates is reserved to registered political parties, the *veliat* legislative councils, and the Karakalpakastan parliament in the Karakalpak Autonomous Republic in Uzbekistan. Political parties must also satisfy the additional condition of having been registered with the ministry of justice no less than six months before the election, and they must have collected fifty thousand voters' signatures supporting the party's participation in the election. These and other restrictions on the nomination process make it possible for the government to exercise a determinative influence on the preselection of candidates.

The People's Democratic Party (PDP), the successor to the Communist Party, is the dominant party and explicitly supports the president and the government. Other political parties include the Fatherland Progress Party, the Adolat Social Democratic Party, the Democratic National Rebirth Party, and the Self-Sacrificers Party (Fidoskorlar). In 1996 Karimov withdrew from the PDP, claiming that the president should be above partisan politics.

In Uzbekistan, as in many authoritarian contexts, personalities play a more significant role than do principles. When independence occurred—not as part of an organic internal development but as the outcome of a deal brokered by the disintegrating Communist Party of the Soviet Union—the existing power structures reconstituted themselves as an independent government.

A political opposition did emerge on independence, but the leading faction of the beneficiaries of the old Soviet system used their established influence to brush the opposition aside. Uzbekistan embarked on a course of national consolidation that emphasized the state as the leading and guiding force of society. The constitution adopted in December 1992 merely institutionalized the existing political system. The government publicly emphasized the Central Asian tradition of strong but benign leadership. In private the government relied on and even refined Soviet-style techniques of manipulation and intimidation.

The Uzbekistan government's record on human rights is considered poor by most international human-rights organizations. Rights of speech, assembly, and religion routinely are circumscribed by government agencies that identify social stability and security as the principal goal. In numerous documented cases the security forces have arbitrarily arrested or detained human-rights activists, religious activists, and ethnic-group activists on false charges, by allegedly planting narcotics, weapons, or forbidden literature on them. Prison conditions are poor, and detention can be prolonged. Police routinely infringe on citizens' rights, and officials responsible for documented abuses are rarely punished. After five terrorist bombs exploded near government targets in Tashkent on 16 February 1999, Uzbekistan security forces launched a campaign of arrests and intimidation against many seen as opposing the government. Also arrested were members of the secular opposition, human rights activists, and Muslim believers.

President Karimov has argued that economic development, not European-style civil rights, is the true fruit of national independence. Uzbekistan, stressing welfare authoritarianism, has resisted counsel from international organizations to embrace democratic principles and processes.

Gregory Gleason

Further Reading

Akiner, S. (1999) "Emerging Political Order in the New Caspian States." In *Crossroads and Conflict: Security and Foreign Policy in the Caucasus and Central Asia*, edited by Gary K. Bertsch, Cassady B. Craft, Scott A. Jones, and Michael D. Beck. New York: Routledge, 90–128.

Allworth E., ed. (1994) *Central Asia: 130 Years of Russian Dominance*. Durham, NC: Duke University Press.

Anderson, John. (1997) Elections and Political Development in Central Asia." *Journal of Communist Studies and Transition Politics* 13: 28–53.

Bennigsen, A., and C. Lemercier Quelquejay. (1967) *Islam in the Soviet Union*. London: Praeger.

Cavanaugh, Cassandra. (1994) "Historiography in Independent Uzbekistan: The Search for National Identity." *Central Asian Monitor* 1: 30–32.

Fierman, William. (1997) "Political Development in Uzbekistan: Democratization?" In *Conflict, Cleavage, and Change in Central Asia and the Caucasus*, edited by Karen Dawisha and Bruce Parrott. New York: Cambridge University Press.

Gleason, Gregory. (1991) "Fealty and Loyalty: Informal Authority Structures in Soviet Asia." *Soviet Studies* 43: 613–628.

———. (1997) *The Central Asian States: Discovering Independence*. Boulder, CO: Westview Press.

———. (1997) "Uzbekistan: The Politics of National Independence." In *New States, New Politics: Building the Post-Soviet Nations*, edited by Ian Bremmer and Ray Taras. New York: Cambridge University Press.

Haghayeghi, Merhdad. (1996) *Islam and Politics in Central Asia*. New York: St. Martin's Press.

Human Rights Watch. (1999) *World Report 1999: Kyrgyzstan, Uzbekistan*. New York: Human Rights Watch.

Karimov, Islam. (1998) *Uzbekistan on the Threshold of the Twenty-First Century*. New York: St. Martin's Press.

Manz, B. F., ed. (1994) *Central Asia in Historical Perspective*. Boulder, CO: Westview Press.

Massell, G. (1975) *The Surrogate Proletariat*. Princeton, NJ: Princeton University Press.

McCagg, W. O., and B. Silver, eds. (1979) *Soviet Asian Ethnic Frontiers*. New York: Pergamon Policy Studies.

UZBEKS

The Uzbeks are a Central Asiatic people who speak a language belonging to the Chagatay branch of the Turkic language subfamily. In 1998, an estimated 18 million Uzbeks lived in the independent republic of Uzbekistan, located mainly between the Syr Dar'ya and Amu Dar'ya Rivers in Central Asia. Uzbekistan has an area of 447,400 square kilometers. Its estimated 1998 population was 24.1 million, of whom approximately 76 percent were Uzbek, 6 percent other Turkic, 6 percent Russian and Ukrainian, 5 percent Tajik, and 7 percent other. Smaller numbers of Uzbeks also inhabit Afghanistan, other Central Asiatic Turkic republics, and Russia.

Most Uzbeks are devout Sunni Muslims. They are the least Russified of the Turkic peoples formerly under Soviet rule, and virtually all of them still claim Uzbek as their primary language. Parents typically give their children Uzbek rather than Russian names. The majority of Uzbeks live in rural areas, where extended family households are common. Only two-fifths of the population of Uzbekistan live in urban areas, and a disproportionately high number of these urbanites are Slavic peoples. In the late 1980s and early 1990s, many Russians and Jews emigrated from Uzbekistan, thereby changing the country's ethnic composition and opening up more technical and management jobs for Uzbeks.

Uzbekistan's population is youthful. Uzbeks have a high birth rate and large families. Of all the former Soviet republics, Uzbekistan has the greatest number of mothers with ten or more living children under the age of twenty years. In 2001, life expectancy at birth was estimated to be sixty-four years.

The Early Uzbeks

The Turkic-Mongol tribes known as Uzbeks originated in Siberia and entered the land of present-day Uzbekistan in the fourteenth century. They may have adopted the name "Uzbek" from the Muslim ruler of the Golden Horde, Oz Beg (Uzbek) Khan (reigned 1312–1341). The Uzbeks entered Central Asia under the leadership of Abu al-Khayr Khan, a descendant of the great Mongol leader Genghis Khan. Abu al-Khayr Khan led the Uzbek tribes southeastward to the north bank of the Syr Dar'ya.

In the late fifteenth century, the Uzbeks conquered key portions of Transoxania (the region between the Amu Dar'ya and Syr Dar'ya Rivers) and occupied the major cities of Bukhara, Khiva, Samarqand, and Khujand. Uzbek khans gained wide recognition for their Sunni religious orthodoxy and cultured patronage of the arts. They sponsored the construction of architectural monuments, such as mosques, Islamic seminaries, palaces, and bridges.

Over the centuries, the territory of what is now Uzbekistan produced great scholars, poets, and writers. In the fifteenth century, the astronomer and mathematician Ulugh Beg founded a famous observatory in Samarqand, and the scholar, poet, and writer 'Ali Shir Nava'i greatly advanced Turkic-language literature.

During the reign of 'Abd Allah Khan II (1557–1598), Uzbek rule was expanded in Balkh, Samarqand,

A Uzbek grandmother holds her grandchild outside their dwelling in the desert. (BUDDY MAYS/COPRBIS)

Tashkent, and Fergana. Uzbek hegemony extended eastward as far as Badakhshan in present-day Afghanistan and East Turkistan (roughly today's Xinjiang Uygur in northwestern China) and westward to Khorasan and Khwarizm in present-day northern Iran. Thereafter Uzbek power and influence declined, reaching a low point by the mid-1700s, with military defeats by the Iranian ruler Nadir Shah. Three Uzbek-dominated polities, known as khanates, emerged in the eighteenth century at Ququn in eastern Uzbekistan, Bukhara in southern Uzbekistan, and Khiva on the lower Amu Dar'ya.

Russian and Soviet Rule

Czarist Russian forces advanced southward, conquering Bukhara in 1868, Khiva in 1873, and Ququn in 1875. The Russians incorporated the Uzbek lands into the province of Turkistan and linked it to the rest of the empire via telegraph, telephone, and the press. Railroads reached Samarqand and Tashkent by 1905. Despite being ruled by czarist colonial administrators, the Uzbek intelligentsia and clergy of Bukhara and Khiva resisted the influence of Russian educational, religious, economic, and governmental institutions. At the same time, however, a group of reformers known as Jadids worked with the support of Russian governors to prepare a number of young urban intellectuals for change in their economy and society. The Jadid era (1900–1920) produced a number of modern poets and writers, who produced many of the first indigenous plays, stories, and novels of Central Asia.

The Russian Revolution of 1917 caused instability and conflict in Turkistan, as Muslim resistance and attempts to establish an autonomous government were defeated by the Red Army. By 1921, Communist-dominated politicians held power. In 1924–1925, they designated the region of Central Asia with an Uzbek population majority as Uzbekistan and incorporated it into the Union of Soviet Socialist Republics. The authorities soon granted Uzbekistan the formal status of constituent republic of the USSR. Uzbeks constituted a minority in the capital city of Tashkent and were underrepresented in the Soviet bureaucracy and administration; Slavic peoples—Russians, Ukrainians, and Belorussians—constituted the majority.

The Communist political purges of the 1930s exacted heavy casualties, especially among Uzbekistan's relatively small class of intelligentsia and leaders. World War II brought major demographic changes, as the Soviet authorities moved thousands of Russian, Polish, and Jewish technicians, managers, and teachers to the towns and villages of Uzbekistan.

During the 1980s, Islamic religious practice surged, transforming many aspects of Uzbek life, especially in the towns of the Fergana Valley and other concentrations of Muslim believers. This resurgence affected the republic's cultural life through the increased activities of religious schools, neighborhood mosques, religious orders, and religious publishing ventures and through the Islamic Renaissance Party.

Throughout most of the Russian and Soviet eras, the Uzbeks maintained significant portions of their cultural traditions. In athletics, wrestling, horse riding, and team competitions continued to be popular. In rural areas, both men and women continued to wear distinctive Uzbek dress. For their homes, Uzbeks continued to prefer simple, one-story structures, like those of the past, built around courtyards planted with fruit trees and gardens open to the skies but closed off from the streets.

At the same time, many Uzbeks acquired Russian as a second language, and compulsory school attendance raised the literacy rate for both males and females to above 90 percent. Until the 1980s, most Soviet Uzbek authors produced tendentious novels, plays, and verse in line with official Communist Party themes. Since the 1990s, however, younger Uzbek poets and authors have broken away from the sloganeering characteristic of Soviet Socialist Realism. Attempts are also being made to revive classical Uzbek musical forms.

Postindependence

Uzbek political leaders declared Uzbekistan's independence from the Soviet Union in 1991. However, the Uzbek Communists retained political power and prohibited opposition parties from participating in the 1991 and 1994 elections. The government's human rights record has drawn international criticism, although the government has promoted the reclamation, renovation, and reconsecration of many smaller old mosques. Communist authorities had relegated these to serve as garages, storehouses, shops, slaughterhouses, or museums. Muslim artisans have accurately reconstructed these damaged buildings as part of a comprehensive drive to recreate the Islamic life suppressed by the Communists between 1920 and 1990.

Paul J. Magnarella

Further Reading

Allworth, Edward. (1990) *The Modern Uzbeks: From the Fourteenth Century to the Present: A Cultural History*. Stanford, CA: Hoover Institution Press.

———. (1964) *Uzbek Literary Politics*. The Hague, Netherlands: E. J. Brill.

Critchlow, James. (1991) *Nationalism in Uzbekistan: A Soviet Republic's Road to Sovereignty*. Boulder, CO: Westview Press.

Kalter, Johannes, and Margareta Pavaloi, eds. (1997) *Uzbekistan: Heirs to the Silk Road*. London: Thames and Hudson.

Karimov, Islam A. (1998) *Uzbekistan on the Threshold of the Twenty-First Century: Challenges to Stability and Progress*. New York: St. Martin's Press.

VALIKHANOV, CHOKAN (1835–1865), nineteenth-century Kazakh explorer and scholar. Regarded by many scholars as the first Kazakh intellectual, Chokan Valikhanov was born in 1865. A grandson of Ablai Khan (1711–1781), the last great khan of the Kazakh Middle Horde, Valikhanov (also known as Mukhammed Khanafiia) was initially educated at home, and in 1847 he entered the newly opened Omsk Kadet Korpus as the first Kazakh admitted to the institution. While there he studied history, geography, mathematics, and classics of Russian and Western literature. Graduating in 1853, he worked for the office of the governor-general of Western Siberia, where he became a close friend of the Russian novelist Fyodor Dostoyevsky (1821–1881), recently released from internal exile in Siberia and assigned to serve five years in a disciplinary battalion, and Petr Semonov-Tian-Shanskii (1827–1914). In 1856 he participated in an expedition to Semirechye province, where he became the first person to write down parts of the great Kirgiz oral epic *Manas*. Two years later he undertook a clandestine journey to Kashgar in Xinjiang, where he gathered economic and political information for the Russian government. His reports were published in the journal of the Russian Geographic Society and translated into German and English. Honored for his accomplishments, in 1860 he was assigned to the Asiatic department of the ministry of foreign affairs in the capital, St. Petersburg. His health weakened by the arduous journey to Kashgar, he returned to the Kazakh steppe to recuperate from complications due to tuberculosis. He died near present-day Almaty in April 1865. In 1904 an edited volume of his collected works was published by the Ethnographic Section of the Russian Geographic Society.

Steven Sabol

Further Reading

McKenzie, Kermit. (1989) "Chokan Valikhanov: Kazakh Princeling and Scholar" *Central Asian Survey* 8: 1–30.
Strelkova, Irina. (1983) *Valikhanov*. Moscow: Young Guards.
Valiakanov, Chokan. (1958) *Izbrannye proizvedeniia*. Almaty, Kazakhstan: Kazakh State Publisher.

VAN (2002 est. province pop. 851,000). The city of Van (estimated 2002 pop. 253,000), the capital of the province of Van, is located in eastern Turkey on the eastern shore of Lake Van; the population is now largely Kurdish. The city, with an altitude of 1750 meters, is in the valley of the Nemrut and Suphan mountains. During the thirteenth through seventh centuries BCE the Urartean empire flourished in this area, and Van was its capital in the eighth century BCE.

After Nineveh, capital of the Assyrian empire, fell in 612 BCE, the city was successively occupied by the Medes, Persians, and kings of Pontus in northeastern Asia Minor. During the first century BCE it was part of the kingdom of the Armenian king Tigranes I (c. 140–c. 55 BCE). The Romans, Sasanids, and Arabs all sought to conquer Van in the seventh century CE; it fell to the Arabs.

During the eighth century the region came under the rule of the Armenian Bagratid dynasty, and the city later became the capital of Vaspurkan, an independent Armenian state. The city of Van was occupied by the Byzantines in 1021 and then fell to the Seljuks after the battle of Manzikert (1071). The Ottoman sultan Süleyman I conquered Van in 1543, and the city remained under Ottoman control until the Russians occupied it from 1915 to 1917, during World War I. The years 1896 and 1913 were times of terrible massacres and deportations of Armenians in this area.

Remnants of Armenian churches, Seljuk and Ottoman mosques, and the citadel still exist. North of the city lies the site of Toprakkale, an ancient Urartean city that has been excavated.

Lake Van is the largest body of water in Turkey and the second largest in the Middle East. Its natural beauty has recently begun to attract tourism. The economy of the province of Van is based on the production of fruits, vegetables, skins, and grains.

T. Isikozlu-E. F. Isikozlu

VARANASI (2001 est. pop. 1.1 million). Varanasi (also Banaras, Benares, or Kasi) is for Hindus the most sacred city in India. Located at a bend of the River Ganges, it lies on the left bank, near the eastern border of Uttar Pradesh State, and nearly 700 kilometers east-southeast of Delhi. Although the devout commonly equate its extreme sanctity with extreme antiquity, dubbing it "the oldest city on earth," archaeology shows that it had its origins during the Iron Age, in the eighth century BCE.

The biggest attraction in the city, for pilgrims and tourists alike, is the celebrated ghats, broad steps that lead down to the river and that feature a constant commerce in ritual bathing, religious teaching, cremation of the dead, or—for very poor families—launching of corpses into the river current. Of all the ghats, the Manikarnika Ghat is considered the most sacred and is consequently the one most pictured. It is one of five celebrated places of pilgrimage within the city. Buildings of note within Varanasi include hundreds of temples and shrines, preeminently the Durga Temple

Hindus bathe in the Ganges River in the holy city of Varanasi. (ALISON WRIGHT/CORBIS)

(miscalled by Europeans the Monkey Temple) and Benares Hindu University. The city has a wide range of handicrafts and is especially noted for its brasswork, silks, shawls, and embroidery. Because of the thousands of pilgrims and so many old people who come here in the expectation of dying, the city does a brisk business in cheap hotels and hospices.

Just outside the city (7 kilometers) is the site of Sarnath, where Buddha preached his first sermon in about 530 BCE. Its Deer Park is still maintained as an important archaeological site.

Paul Hockings

Further Reading
Eck, Diana. (1982) *Banaras: City of Light.* Princeton, NJ: Princeton University Press.
Michell, George, and Philip Davies. (1989) "Varanasi." In *The Penguin Guide to the Monuments of India.* New York: Viking Press, vol. 1, 195–98; vol. 2, 260–64.

VEDDA The Vedda (also Vadda, Veddah, Veddha, Vaddo) are an indigenous people of Sri Lanka. They are divided into three groups: The Bintenne Veddas, the Anuradhapura Veddas, and the Coast Veddas. The Bintenne Veddas live in an area in the southeastern region of the island, the Anuradhapura Veddas live in North Central Province, and the Coast Veddas live on the central coast. The Vedda population is small, though an accurate number has yet to be recorded. A 1970 census counted more than 6,600 Anuradhapura Veddas. Bintenne and Coast Vedda populations are probably significantly smaller.

Until recently, many Vedda maintained a way of life based on hunting and gathering and shifting agriculture. The increase in the population of Sri Lanka and the modern importance of cash cropping rather than trade and reciprocity has changed Vedda subsistence activities a great deal. The Anuradhapura Vedda, traditionally shifting agriculturists, now obtain most of their income as agricultural wage laborers outside their own villages. The Coast Veddas fish, practice some shifting agriculture, and also work as casual wage laborers. The Bintenne Veddas still maintain hunting and gathering as a way of life. In recent years, they have asked for land to be set aside on Sri Lanka as a Vedda reservation. The government has provided assistance by way of agricultural cooperatives and development societies.

Traditional villages consisted of huts of wattle and daub or plaited palm with packed earth floors. Recently, the government has begun subsidizing the construction of tin-roofed brick houses with concrete floors. Within the villages, kinship provides the major social structure. Vedda caste specialization, hunting, and spirit mediumship are important in interaction with the Tamil and Sinhalese.

Vedda religious beliefs, like their language, have been strongly influenced by their Tamil and Sinhalese neighbors. Vedda groups located near the Tamil tend toward Hinduism, while those located near the Sinhalese tend toward Buddhism. All three groups use some form of religious or ritual medicine, although the state also provides free access to Western medicine.

Stephanie L. Ware

Further Reading
Brow, James. (1978) *Vedda Villages of Anuradhapura District: The Historical Anthropology of a Community in Sri Lanka.* Seattle, WA: University of Washington Press.

Dart, Jon. (1985) "Ethnic Identity and Marginality among the Coast Veddas of Sri Lanka." Ph.D. diss. University of California, San Diego.

VEENA In classical texts on Indian music, the term veena refers to almost any string instrument, and at least forty different types of veena are listed. Today, the term refers to a particular type of stringed instrument, of which about two or three closely related variants are in existence. Like other stringed instruments in Indian classical music, the veena consists of a large round wooden base and a narrower and longer body also made of wood. On this body are attached brass or silver frets, usually enough in number to cover two octaves. There are about seven strings, of which at least three exist to create a drone. Usually, only two of the main strings are played on, by plucking. The veena is held either horizontally across the player's knees or slanting against the shoulders. While these broad features characterize a number of string instruments in India, the veena group stands out in details of construction, position of the main string, richness of sound, antiquity, and association with vocal music. Of all stringed instruments, the veena has been the closest to vocal music traditions; its repertoire has had much in common with that of vocal music, and the veena has often been played and taught by great singers themselves.

Tirthankar Roy

Further Reading
Krishnaswamy, S. (1965) *Musical Instruments of India.* Delhi: Publications Division, Government of India.

VELEYET-E FAQIH *Veleyet-e faqih* literally means "the authority or governance of the jurist" in Arabic and "rule of the religious jurisprudent" ("jurisprudent" referring to one who is learned in law) in Persian. In essence, it is the belief that an ideal government is one that is run by Islamic clergy who are well versed in Islamic law, history, and theology. It is a doctrine whose origins date back to 939 CE at the beginning of the Twelfth Imam's major occultation or absence from earth. It was determined that scholars of Shi'a Islam were the most qualified to conduct government services during the Twelfth Imam's occultation, which continues to the present.

Theoretically, *veleyet-e faqih* was contemplated in the nineteenth century as a definite legal consideration, but it became a political reality in Iran only under Ayatollah Khomeini after the Iranian Revolution in 1979. The ayatollah originally began developing this concept in his first work titled *Kashf al-Asrar* in 1944 when he asserted the right and duty of Shi'a scholars to lead. During his exile in Iraq, he worked out the details more fully in lectures, which were eventually published as *Hokumat-e Eslami* (*Islamic Government*). When Ayatollah Khomeini rose to power in 1979, an Assembly of Experts was assigned to take on the task of making his ideas into a viable political structure. The result was a government structure headed by the *faqih*, who would be an Islamic theologian overseeing the executive, legislative, and judiciary branches of government. Ayatollah Khomeini was Iran's first *faqih*, followed by the 2000 *faqih*, Ayatollah Khameni.

Houman A. Sadri

Further Reading
Algar, Hamid. (1991) "Religious Forces in Twentieth-Century Iran." In *The Cambridge History of Iran*, volume 7, edited by Peter Avery, Gavin Hambly, and Charles Melville. Cambridge, U.K.: Cambridge University Press, 732–64.

Khomeini, Ruhollah. (1981) *Islam and Revolution: Writings and Declarations of Imam Khomeini.* Trans. by Hamid Algar. Berkeley, CA: Mizan Press.

———. (1978) *Veleyet-e Faqih.* In Persian. Tehran, Iran: Amirkabir Book.

Rahnema, Ali, ed. (1994) *Pioneers of Islamic Revival.* London: Zed Books.

Sachedina, Abdalaziz A. (1988) *The Just Ruler in Shiite Islam.* New York: Oxford University Press.

VIENTIANE (2000 pop. 233,000). The city of Vientiane (or Viangchan, in Lao) is the capital of Laos and central to the cultural, commercial, and political life of Laos. It is situated in central Laos, along the

Mekong River, and covers about 180 square kilometers. Archaeological findings in the area have included Mon artifacts related to the practice of Theravada Buddhism. The earliest known settlement near present-day Vientiane was Chandapuri (City of Sandalwood). The Mon lived in the area until about 1006. The Vientiane region became a part of Cambodia during Khmer rule (802–1431). King Xetthathirat (flourished 1540s) made the city of Vientiane the capital of Lan Xang, transferring the capital there from its previous capital, Luang Prabang, and constructed the famous shrines of Vat Phra Kaeo (1565) and That Luang (1566), the latter being the national symbol of Laos.

The city remained the capital of Lan Xang through the Lao-Siamese wars (1779 and 1826–1828). Following Siam's victory and the destruction of the city, Laotian residents were forcibly relocated to Siam, and the city became a ghost town. In March 1867, French explorers found only a few residents, including monks who were living in ruined monasteries.

The French made the city the capital of French Laos. The city is comparable to Saigon in its colonial French architecture. The French, in addition to providing their rulers and armies with accommodation, erected monasteries and restored the ancient temples. Under French rule, the population was largely Vietnamese. The Japanese briefly assumed control of the city during World War II; the French reassumed control in April 1946, and the nation was taken into the French Union.

Laos gained independence in October 1953. It soon had its own troubles, including war and civil unrest. Vientiane was, like much of Laos, bombed throughout both the war with France (French, or First, Indochina War, 1946–1954) and the Vietnam War (Second Indochina War, 1954–1975). The Pathet Lao, a Communist revolutionary group, seized power in 1975 and retained Vientiane as the capital of the Lao People's Democratic Republic.

Tourism has flourished at traditional architectural sites, such as Buddhist monasteries and monuments. These include That Luang; Patousai (1958), a monument patterned on the Arc de Triomphe; and Vat Sisaket, the only temple to survive the Siamese sacking of the city in 1828 and Laos's oldest surviving temple.

Linda Dailey Paulson

Further Reading

Davies, Ben. (2001) *Laos: A Journey beyond the Mekong.* Bangkok, Thailand: Asia Horizon Books.

Dubus, Arnaud. (1995). *Eternal Vientiane: Contemporary Portrait of a Timeless City.* Hong Kong: Fortune Images Ltd. for Les Editions d'Indochine.

Kremmer, Christopher. (1998) *Stalking the Elephant Kings: In Search of Laos.* Honolulu, HI: University of Hawaii Press.

Mansfield, Stephen. (1995) *Laos: A Portrait.* Hong Kong: Elsworth Books.

VIETNAM—PROFILE (2001 est. pop. 79.9 million). Vietnam occupies the eastern portion of the Indochinese peninsula, bordered on the north by China, on the west by Laos and Cambodia, and on the east by the South China Sea. The area of the country is slightly smaller (329,560 square kilometers) than the state of California, although, in terms of people, for every one Californian there are about two and a half Vietnamese.

Geography

All Vietnamese children are taught in school that their country takes the form of an elongated letter S,

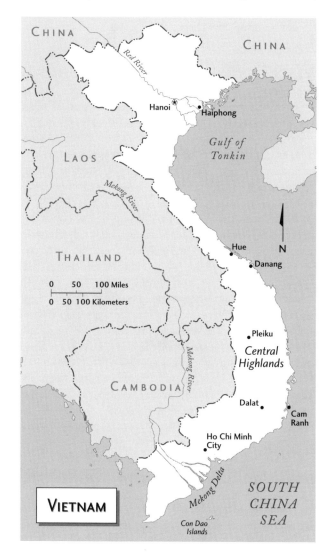

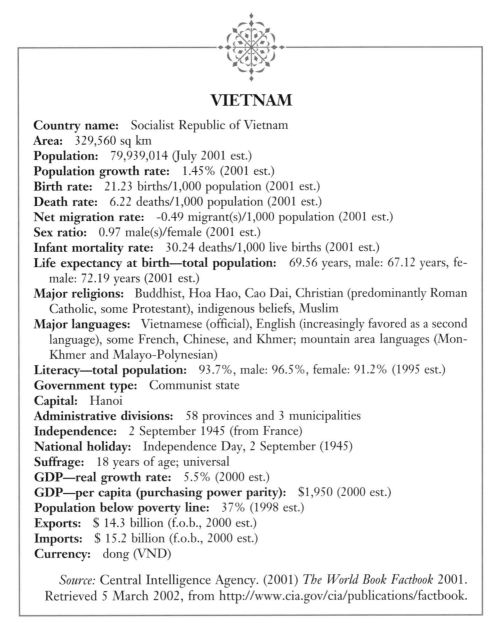

VIETNAM

Country name: Socialist Republic of Vietnam

Area: 329,560 sq km

Population: 79,939,014 (July 2001 est.)

Population growth rate: 1.45% (2001 est.)

Birth rate: 21.23 births/1,000 population (2001 est.)

Death rate: 6.22 deaths/1,000 population (2001 est.)

Net migration rate: -0.49 migrant(s)/1,000 population (2001 est.)

Sex ratio: 0.97 male(s)/female (2001 est.)

Infant mortality rate: 30.24 deaths/1,000 live births (2001 est.)

Life expectancy at birth—total population: 69.56 years, male: 67.12 years, female: 72.19 years (2001 est.)

Major religions: Buddhist, Hoa Hao, Cao Dai, Christian (predominantly Roman Catholic, some Protestant), indigenous beliefs, Muslim

Major languages: Vietnamese (official), English (increasingly favored as a second language), some French, Chinese, and Khmer; mountain area languages (Mon-Khmer and Malayo-Polynesian)

Literacy—total population: 93.7%, male: 96.5%, female: 91.2% (1995 est.)

Government type: Communist state

Capital: Hanoi

Administrative divisions: 58 provinces and 3 municipalities

Independence: 2 September 1945 (from France)

National holiday: Independence Day, 2 September (1945)

Suffrage: 18 years of age; universal

GDP—real growth rate: 5.5% (2000 est.)

GDP—per capita (purchasing power parity): $1,950 (2000 est.)

Population below poverty line: 37% (1998 est.)

Exports: $ 14.3 billion (f.o.b., 2000 est.)

Imports: $ 15.2 billion (f.o.b., 2000 est.)

Currency: dong (VND)

Source: Central Intelligence Agency. (2001) *The World Book Factbook* 2001. Retrieved 5 March 2002, from http://www.cia.gov/cia/publications/factbook.

its two enlarged extremities filled by the fertile deltas of the Red River in the north and the Mekong River in the south. Central Vietnam is constituted by very narrow stretches of coastal plains that are hemmed in on one side by the elongated chain of mountains called the Long Mountains (Truong Son) and on the other side by the Pacific Ocean. The stylized profile of the country as it is drawn on maps evokes the image of the long bamboo pole with two baskets suspended at both ends that is carried by peasants on their way to and from the market.

The two main rivers of Vietnam are the Red and the Mekong, which is called the Nine Dragons River. The Red River owes its name to the red dirt that it carries over its course all the way from the southern Chinese province of Yunnan to the Gulf of Tonkin. The Mekong is a long river, linking together all five countries of mainland Southeast Asia: Myanmar (Burma), Laos, Thailand, Cambodia, and Vietnam. The soil of the two deltas is fertile from the presence of rich alluvium; in the rest of the country, principally in the highlands, the soil is rather poor, because nutrients are leached out by a combination of rushing rain water and scorching sun. Only about one-third of the Vietnamese land is good for farming.

The mountains of Vietnam are not high. In general their elevation ranges from 600 to 1,500 meters, with the exception of the Fan Si Pan, situated in the northwest, which rises up to approximately 3,060 meters. Rain forests, shielding a great variety of species of trees, some of which are hardwood such as teak and mahogany, cover virtually the entire mountainous region. These forests fit well the definition of the word "jungle," if they are complemented with their exotic fauna: monkeys, tigers, and elephants.

Rain, more than extremes of temperature, defines the seasons, although the north sees a temperature range from the high thirties (Celsius) in the summer to about 10° or 5°C in the winter months of January and February. Elsewhere, a moist and hot 30°C plus endures pretty much the whole year round, except on the slopes of mountains and possibly during the months of December and January, when the atmosphere seems somewhat less oppressive. That discrepancy is due to the influence of seasonal winds called monsoons, which regulate the dry-cold and rainy-hot portions of the year. The northeast monsoon that brings cold and dry air from the Asian continent weakens as it reaches the Hai Van Pass in central Vietnam. Consequently, the southern half of Vietnam has a more equally distributed, fresher weather through roughly six months of the year. The other six months, from about April or May to September or October, a hot and humid wind blows from the ocean around the equator toward the peninsula, bringing with it both heat and rain.

People

Many different ethnic groups share the land of Vietnam. The official census divides them into two general categories: the "plains" people and the ethnic minorities who generally occupy the highlands (with the exception of the Cham, Chinese, and Khmer minorities). There are up to sixty different groups, speaking as many different languages. The plains people consist of the Vietnamese who, from north to south, the speak one common tongue. Vietnamese is an Austroasiatic language that does not belong to the same linguistic family as Chinese, although 70 to 80 percent of its vocabulary is derived from Chinese words.

Traditionally, the Vietnamese were essentially a small-agriculture, rural people. Villages constituted their primary social units. Usually three elements figure in every village: a communal house, a pagoda, and a pond. The communal house, called *dinh*, serves as a meeting place for all activities common to all the villagers: administration, justice, police, jail. It is also a place of worship in honor of the protecting genie, who generally was an inhabitant of that village who accomplished some illustrious feat benefiting the coun-

try: a general, a writer, an artist, a person of virtue. The presence of the pagoda testifies less to the number of Buddhist followers than to the patrons of past dynasties, who manifested their devotion by erecting shrines in almost every village of the realm. Although the majority of the villagers may claim to be Buddhists or may go to the pagoda on the first and the fifteenth of the lunar month, they all practice the cult of ancestors mixed with a tinge of Taoism and Confucianism. In the past fifty years, a fourth component surfaced in almost every village: a cemetery-memorial to bury and honor the villagers who have sacrificed their lives for the country.

Since the majority of villagers are peasants, life in the countryside centers around the agricultural cycle, which starts about a month before the first monsoonal rains and ends with the drying of the unhusked rice. In certain areas, the weather and the fertility of the land permitting, that cycle repeats itself once or even twice. Rural people can afford few days of rest. All celebrate the three days of Tet, the lunar New Year. Another two or three days' rest occurs on the birth or death day of the deity who is worshipped in the *dinh*; in celebration, games, competitions, races, and theatrical performances are organized.

Cities, such as Hanoi, the present capital, and Hue, that of the Nguyen dynasty in the nineteenth century, were rare phenomena in the past. Many of the more modern cities, like Ho Chi Minh City (Saigon), Da Nang, and Can Tho are products of the modernization process that took place during the French colonial period.

Economy

Vietnam is classified as a developing country, and the average annual income of its citizens remains among the lowest in the world ($333 in 1998). The economic development of Vietnam suffers from three serious impediments. During the time they controlled Vietnam, the French developed only those economic sectors that brought profit to the French themselves; long wars have marred recent history; and a decade of unfortunate postwar socialist experimentation with a centralized economy has left deep scars. Since 1986 the government has adopted a new policy called *doi moi* (renovation), which replaced a planned economy with a market economy, allowed private ownership of the means of production, and encouraged private investments from all sources. Since then, Vietnam has become an exporter of rice, and the economic growth stood for many years at around 10 percent until it was drastically reduced by the Asian economic crisis of the mid-1990s.

The Future

Due to the tight control the government exercises over foreign investments, Vietnam suffered only mildly from that crisis. By 1998, the situation had remarkably improved, with an increase in the production of crude oil and some agricultural products such as rice, pepper, and coffee. A bilateral trade agreement with the United States that took effect in 2001 will facilitate the importation of Vietnamese goods into the huge American market and thereby ease the pains of a growing economy in the time of globalization.

Truong Buu Lam

Further Reading

Dao Duy Anh. (1992) *Viet Nam Van Hoa Su Cuong* (Outlines of Vietnamese Culture). Ho Chi Minh City, Vietnam: School of Teachers Training.

Hodgkin, Thomas L. (1981) *Vietnam: The Revolutionary Path*. New York: St. Martin's Press.

Jamieson, Neil. (1995). *Understanding Vietnam*. Berkeley and Los Angeles: University of California Press.

Phan Ke Binh. (1990) *Viet Nam phong tuc* (Vietnamese Customs). Ho Chi Minh City, Vietnam: Ho Chi Minh City Presses.

Toan Anh. (1991) *Phong Tuc Viet Nam: Tho Cung To Tien* (Vietnamese Customs: Ancestor Worship). Hanoi, Vietnam: Social Sciences Presses.

———. (1969) *Phong-tuc Viet-Nam: tu ban-than den gia-dinh* (Vietnamese Customs: From Self to Family). Saigon, South Vietnam: Khai-Tri Bookstore.

VIETNAM—ECONOMIC SYSTEM Vietnam is a poor, densely populated country, whose economy is based on agriculture—primarily wet rice cultivation. More than 80 percent of the country's 80 million people are engaged in farming. There have been numerous attempts to industrialize, but the country's infrastructure was devastated after decades of war, while aid was wasted due to poor economic planning.

Post–World War II

In 1945, Vietnam inherited an economy from the French that was poor, underdeveloped with a weak infrastructure, woefully exploited, and geared to serving the colonial regime. The French, who had colonized Vietnam from the 1860s, had changed landholding patterns, creating millions of landless peasants and day laborers who worked on French-owned plantations, and had imposed taxes and corvée duty that kept the peasantry in a cycle of indebtedness. State monopolies and limited attempts to industrialize also distorted the economy, which was then shattered by nine years of anticolonial war between 1946 and 1954.

Following the 1954 Geneva Peace Accords that saw Vietnam divided into two halves at the seventeenth parallel, the two competing regimes implemented substantially different economic policies. In North Vietnam, the Communist regime under the Lao Dong Party (LDP) began to socialize the economy rapidly. In the countryside, the LDP implemented a two-phase land reform program to radically redistribute land and abolish landlordism. The implementation of this policy was marked by mass violence as class labels were applied. After two years, massive peasant unrest caused the party to slow down the implementation of land reform. Despite an increase in the amount of collectivized land, per-capita agricultural output actually fell. The state monopolized the harvest and marketing of the rice, paying the peasantry below-market prices for their crops, so that the urban proletariat could receive subsidized food.

The urban economy of the north was also socialized through a strategy of Stalinist industrialization. Private enterprise was abolished, trade was monopolized by the state, and the north began a process of heavy industrialization with massive amounts of Chinese and Soviet aid. Between 1955 and 1965, North Vietnam received $457 million and $364 million in Chinese and Soviet aid, respectively. Central economic planning was adopted and the country was put on Soviet-style five-year plans. The fact that all economic resources were directed to the war against U.S.-backed South Vietnam, especially after 1963, caused terrible economic dislocations and massive shortages.

In South Vietnam, the economy was a quasi-capitalist system. Unlike North Vietnam, land in South Vietnam was inequitably distributed, which infuriated the peasants who supported the communist-backed Viet Cong National Liberation Front (NLF), which promised land reform. The South Vietnamese regime's base of support came from the landlord class, which resisted land reform, and the peasants suffered under absentee landlordism, high rates of landlessness, and high taxation.

The South Vietnamese regime was increasingly dependent on U.S. economic aid, which by 1963 amounted to more than $1 billion. But unlike North Vietnam, South Vietnam invested little of that aid in industrialization; the economy remained overwhelmingly agrarian. As in the North, the war caused massive dislocations. The government became increasingly dependent on U.S. aid, having lost much of its own revenue. The economy was also racked by inflation and smuggling, and was dominated by an enormous black market.

Much of Vietnam's farming still relies on human labor and manual tools. In 2000, two women irrigate their rice field with water transferred from a canal with a wooden paddle irrigator. (AFP/CORBIS)

Reunification of the Two Vietnams

Following reunification under North Vietnam in 1976, Hanoi decided to socialize the southern economy rapidly: private enterprise was abolished; land was collectivized; and wholesale, retail, and foreign trade were nationalized. The ethnic Chinese, who dominated the South Vietnamese commercial sector, were persecuted and fled en masse. Additionally, radical currency reform wiped out capital holdings. There was a postwar economic malaise following the loss of Chinese aid in 1978, the imposition of an international trade embargo after Vietnam's December 1978 invasion of Cambodia, and the huge domestic expenditures (amounting to one-third of Vietnam's budget) for the Cambodian occupation.

Although Vietnam joined the Soviet-led trade block, the Council for Mutual Economic Assistance (CMEA), in 1978 and received approximately $1 billion in Soviet economic aid annually during the 1980s, much of the aid was wasted, and the country suffered huge trade deficits. The leadership believed that the collectivization of agriculture in the South would lead to net gains in output, but there were food shortages, as output could not keep pace with the postwar baby boom. In 1982 agriculture in the South was decollectivized, and Hanoi began to experiment with Chinese-style agricultural production contracts. In 1986 the country was wracked by triple-digit inflation and food shortages.

The sixth party congress of December 1986 adopted an economic reform program known as *doi moi*, or renovation. Agriculture was completely decollectivized, and fifteen-year contracts for individual production units were granted. As a result, Vietnam went from a net importer of rice to the world's third largest exporter within two years, between 1986–1988. Vietnam also became the world's second largest producer of coffee robusta. Market forces were introduced and central planning was eliminated for all but essential commodities. Vietnam rejected a model of heavy industrialization in favor of sectors in which its economy had a comparative advantage: agricultural commodities (rice, coffee, rubber), natural resource (oil and natural gas) exploitation, and labor-intensive manufacturing. The labor market was freed up. Foreign investment was courted, and the government began to market the country as an offshore center for manufacturing. Currency reform eliminated the inflationary forces caused by an overvalued currency and the black market. Having withdrawn from Cambodia in 1989, Hanoi began to renew ties with the international community. Embargoes were eased, and bilateral and multilateral lending and development assistance resumed. This was essential, because Hanoi lost all Soviet aid and subsidies by 1991.

The Vietnamese economy slowed down by the mid-1990s, hampered by its half-capitalist, half-socialist system. Vietnamese authorities slowed implementation of the structural reforms needed to revitalize the economy and produce more competitive, export-driven industries. Although the government had embarked on reforming woefully inefficient state-owned enterprises (SOEs) and had pledged to shut some down, eliminate subsidies, and equitize other SOEs, it failed to implement a comprehensive solution. Although there are now only 5,300 SOEs, down from 12,000, they remain a terrible burden on the economy. Privatization of state enterprises remains bogged down in political controversy, while the country's dynamic private sector is denied both financing and access to markets. There is concern over high rates of unemployment. Complicating SOE reforms is a banking crisis, brought on by triangular debts and nonperforming loans. In addition, the revenue base remains small and tax collection sporadic.

The Asian Economic Crisis that began in August 1997 was a serious blow to the Vietnamese economy. Some 60 percent of Vietnam's exports went to Asian states, but with the sharp decline in the currencies of neighboring countries, Vietnam faced greater competition from its neighbors. Its gross domestic product (GDP), which grew by 8.5 percent in 1997, fell to 4 percent in 1998 and rose slightly to an estimated 4.8 percent in 1999.

Refusal to liberalize trade has led to smuggling and huge trade deficits. In October 2000 Vietnam signed a bilateral trade agreement with the United States that greatly liberalizes the Vietnamese trade regime, ends state subsidies, and paves the way for Hanoi's entry into the World Trade Organization.

The initial reforms that decollectivized agriculture greatly improved the standard of living in the countryside; beginning in the late 1990s, however, there was widespread unrest as a result of corruption, inequitable distribution of land, and the many new taxes and fees. Despite the early gains of the reform program that saw a rise in agricultural production and incomes, these gains have leveled off, and the country is now confronted with a rapidly rising urban-rural income gap. As a result, there is both increased tension as well as a rapid rise in urban migration. Although the economy grew at an average 6.7 percent annually in the 1990s, Vietnam remains one of the least developed countries in the world.

Zachary Abuza

See also: **Doi Moi; Mekong Project; New Economic Zones**

Further Reading
Fforde, Adam, and Stefan de Vylder. (1996) *From Plan to Market: The Economic Transition in Vietnam*, Boulder, CO: Westview Press.
Norlund, Irene, Cu Cao Dam and Carolyn Gates, eds. (1995) *Vietnam in a Changing World*. Surrey, U.K.: Curzon Press.

VIETNAM—EDUCATION SYSTEM

Since Vietnam was occupied by China between 111 BCE and 939 CE, the Vietnamese education system was initially developed resembling the Chinese hierarchic Confucian examination system. This system mainly served for the recruitment of loyal civil servants, who were trained according to Confucian morals and ethics. The main educational content of the system was taken from the Chinese Five Classics (*Yi jing*, or Classic of Changes; *Shu jing*, or Classic of History; *Li ji*, or Book of Rites; *Shi jing*, or Classic of Poetry; and *Chunqiu*, or Spring and Autumn Annals), and the Confucian Four Books (*Da xue*, or Great Teaching; *Zhong yong*, or Doctrine of the Mean; the Analects, and *Mengzi*, or Mencius.) However, Mahayana Buddhism also had some important influence on the system.

Because the Vietnamese language originally lacked its own script, the civil-service examination system used Chinese characters as a teaching and learning medium. During the thirteenth century, Vietnamese scholars developed the first national script system *(nom)*, which, while based on Chinese characters, was built around the Vietnamese pronunciation of words. However, this script did not spread among the common population, because it demanded extensive knowledge of written Chinese. In the sixteenth century, Christian Portuguese and French missionaries arrived in Vietnam and later developed the currently used *quoc ngu* script, which uses Latin alphabet with diacritical signs. During colonial occupation, the French proclaimed Vietnamese, written in *quoc ngu*, and French the two official languages.

Education in the Colonial Period
After several changes, the colonial education system eventually comprised three years of elementary school (*certificat d'études élémentaire indigène*), three years of primary school (*certificat d'études primaires franco-indigène*), four years of complementary primary school (*diplôme d'études primaires supérieurs franco indigène*), and three years of secondary school (*baccalauréat local*). Serving the extensive needs of the colonial government for low-paid civil servants, the colonial education system focused on practical training and on the acquisition of the French language. In addition, although the final official Confucian examinations were held in 1918, during most of the colonial period traditional Confucian instruction continued to exist, as did Buddhist education, provided for future monks.

Education in the Two Vietnams
During the separation of the country between 1954 and 1975, two different education systems developed. In the North, President Ho Chi Minh (1890–1969) launched large literacy campaigns that were highly successful. Educational reforms were aimed at establishing a socialist education system, modeled on the Soviet model. The school system was composed of nine (later ten) years of schooling in total (4-3-2, later 4-3-3). Various vocational secondary schools and training centers developed that provided personnel for lower-level careers in the state sector. Higher education was provided by highly specialized, small-enrollment universities, polytechnical universities, and colleges. Postgraduate education was mainly conducted in the Soviet Union, East Germany, Poland, and Czechoslovakia. Education was organized by five- and one-year state plans and served the national demand for qualified labor. After graduation, students were directly transferred to diverse positions in the state sector.

In the South, a twelve-year system was promoted by the government. Vocational secondary schools, vocational training centers, and on-the-job training opportunities were established to serve the labor market. Universities such as the universities of Saigon and Can Tho, as well as colleges, developed on the American model.

Education after Reunification

Vietnam was reunified in 1975, and the third education reform was initiated in 1979. Efforts were undertaken to unify the two different school systems and to establish a national education system according to the principles of free education for all, polytechnic education following the socialist model, and priority for socialist ideology and practical work in all teaching curricula. This brought about the closing of approximately 2,500 private educational establishments in the South. Higher-education students were selected according to their personal curriculum vitae and social origin, and student exchange programs were almost exclusively organized with countries from Eastern Europe and the Soviet Union. Foreign-language teaching focused on Russian and German.

Since the official promulgation of the *doi moi* ("renovation") reform policy program in 1986 the national education system has adapted to new circumstances. Today it is composed of the following components: public kindergarten establishments, which serve children from three months to four years, public preschools for children of at least five years of age, public primary schools for children between six and ten (five years' duration), public lower secondary schools for children between eleven and fourteen (four years' duration), vocational training centers at lower secondary level (under one year's duration), upper secondary schools for students between fifteen and seventeen, secondary vocational schools at the upper secondary level (three to four years' duration), secondary technical schools at upper secondary level (three to four years' duration), and vocational training centers at upper secondary level (one to two years' duration). In addition, different opportunities for on-the-job training courses are offered by the labor market. Higher education is composed of universities (three to six years' duration) and colleges (two to four years' duration). Written and oral examinations are held to transfer pupils from one level to the next, and final examinations after grade 12 are followed by entrance examinations to universities and colleges. Postgraduate education consists of master and doctoral programs.

When the Sixth Party Congress of the Vietnamese Communist Party liberalized the economy and proclaimed more market-oriented reform measures, one of the immediate consequences was a decline in education at all levels. Income-raising opportunities forced people to decide between children's contribution to the family income or education. In addition, there were educational reform measures, which reflected the overall transition to a multisector economy. The reform measures can be grouped into five categories: the diversification of financial resources, efforts to internationalize the education system through reform of the structural organization of higher education, the withdrawal of the state-promoted plans for the decentralization of decision making in Vietnamese education, an overall increase in legal documents accompanying the transformation and culminating in the promulgation of the first national education law in 1999, and methods of encouraging the development of educational elites, which resulted in the reestablishment of schools and classes for especially gifted students.

These transformation processes were paralleled by trends among the general public. The trends include making extensive efforts and investment to gain additional instruction and preparation for their offspring to improve their chances for a future career (including sacrifices to allow their children to study overseas in other Southeast Asian nations, Australia, the United States, and Europe); educational stratification resulting from the overall differentiation of income structures, especially between urban and rural areas; reorientation of students in their choices of disciplines (preferences for English, Chinese, communication technology, computer sciences, law, economics, public administration, and so forth); a change in values and increased popularity of diplomas and certificates; and brain drain from higher education toward higher-paying jobs in the developing market economy.

Ursula Nguyen

Further Reading

Berlie, Jean. (1995) "Higher Education in Vietnam: Historical Background, Policy, and Prospect." In *East Asian Higher Education: Traditions and Transformations.* Issues in Higher Education Series, edited by Albert H. Yee. Oxford: Pergamon Press, 155–165.

Kelly, Gail P. (1978) "Colonial Schools in Vietnam: Policy and Practice." In *Education and Colonialism*, edited by Philip G. Altbach and Gail P. Kelly. New York: Longman, 96–121.

Nguyen The Long. (1995) *Nho hoc o Viet Nam: Giao duc va thi cu* (Confucianism in Vietnam: Education and Examination). Hanoi, Vietnam: NXB Giao Duc.

Pham Minh Hac, ed. (1994) *Education in Vietnam 1945–1991.* Hanoi, Vietnam: NXB Giao Duc.

Sloper, David, and Le Thac Can, eds. (1995) *Higher Education in Vietnam: Change and Response.* Singapore: Institute of Southeast Asian Studies.

VIETNAM—HISTORY The creation myth of the Vietnamese people places their founding in the northern sector of the Indochinese peninsula. Lac Long Quan (the Dragon) and Au Co (the Immortal) were said to have engendered the founders of the Vietnamese nation in the form of the eighteen Hung kings of the Hong Bang dynasty, which reigned over Van Lang (Vietnam) from 2879 to 258 BCE. The rule of this dynasty stretched from the end of the Neolithic period through the civilization of Dong Son, with its famously decorated bronze drums, down to the Iron Age.

In 258 BCE, the legendary King An Duong was able to overthrow the last Hung king because he used weapons—mainly arrowheads—made of bronze and iron. The effectiveness of these weapons was said to have been increased a thousand times by a magic claw given to King An Duong by a local deity, the Golden Turtle, and his country, now renamed Au Lac, became impregnable.

Chinese Influence

According to legend, Qin Shi Huang Di (c.259–210 BCE), the emperor who unified China, sent one of his generals, Zhao Tuo, to invade Au Lac toward the end of the third century BCE. Zhao Tuo, however, remained powerless against the magic claw held by

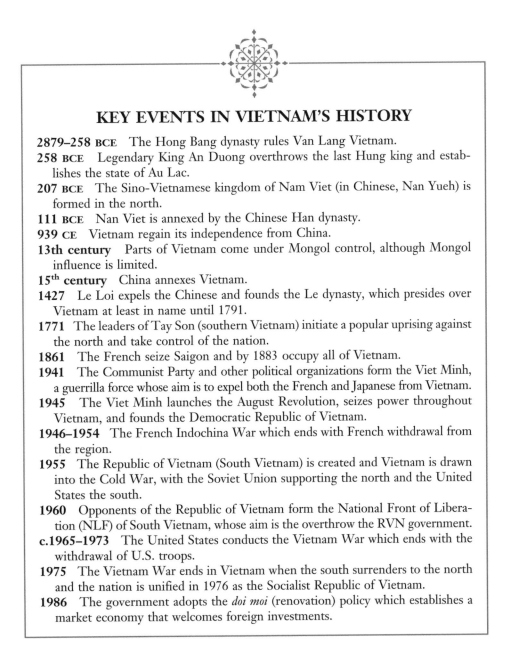

KEY EVENTS IN VIETNAM'S HISTORY

2879–258 BCE The Hong Bang dynasty rules Van Lang Vietnam.

258 BCE Legendary King An Duong overthrows the last Hung king and establishes the state of Au Lac.

207 BCE The Sino-Vietnamese kingdom of Nam Viet (in Chinese, Nan Yueh) is formed in the north.

111 BCE Nan Viet is annexed by the Chinese Han dynasty.

939 CE Vietnam regain its independence from China.

13th century Parts of Vietnam come under Mongol control, although Mongol influence is limited.

15th century China annexes Vietnam.

1427 Le Loi expels the Chinese and founds the Le dynasty, which presides over Vietnam at least in name until 1791.

1771 The leaders of Tay Son (southern Vietnam) initiate a popular uprising against the north and take control of the nation.

1861 The French seize Saigon and by 1883 occupy all of Vietnam.

1941 The Communist Party and other political organizations form the Viet Minh, a guerrilla force whose aim is to expel both the French and Japanese from Vietnam.

1945 The Viet Minh launches the August Revolution, seizes power throughout Vietnam, and founds the Democratic Republic of Vietnam.

1946–1954 The French Indochina War which ends with French withdrawal from the region.

1955 The Republic of Vietnam (South Vietnam) is created and Vietnam is drawn into the Cold War, with the Soviet Union supporting the north and the United States the south.

1960 Opponents of the Republic of Vietnam form the National Front of Liberation (NLF) of South Vietnam, whose aim is the overthrow the RVN government.

c.1965–1973 The United States conducts the Vietnam War which ends with the withdrawal of U.S. troops.

1975 The Vietnam War ends in Vietnam when the south surrenders to the north and the nation is unified in 1976 as the Socialist Republic of Vietnam.

1986 The government adopts the *doi moi* (renovation) policy which establishes a market economy that welcomes foreign investments.

FRANCE TAKES CONTROL IN VIETNAM

The Treaty of Alliance and Peace of 15 March 1874 extracted below formalized French control of much of mainland Southeast Asia including Vietnam.

Article 2. His Excellency, the President of the French Republic, recognizing the sovereignty of the King of Annam and his complete independence in regard to any foreign power whatsoever, promises him aid and assistance and engages to give him, on request and freely, the support necessary to maintain order and tranquility in his States, to defend himself against all attacks, and to destroy the piracy which desolates a part of the coasts of the Kingdom.

Article 3. In acknowledgement of this protection, His Majesty the King of Annam engages to make his foreign policy conform to that of France and to change nothing in his present diplomatic relations.

This political engagement does not extend to commercial treaties. But in any case, His Majesty the King of Annam cannot make with any nation whatsoever a commercial treaty in disagreement with that concluded between France and the Kingdom of Annam, and without having informed the French government beforehand.

Article 5. His Majesty the King of Annam recognizes the full and complete sovereignty of France over all the territory currently occupied by France and including the following frontiers:

To the east, the China Sea and the Kingdom of Annam (Binh-Thuan Province);

To the west, the Gulf of Siam;

To the south, the China Sea;

To the north, the Kingdom of Cambodia and the Kingdom of Annam (Binh-Thuan Province) . . .

Source: John M. Maki, ed. (1957*) Selected Documents Far Eastern International Relations (1689–1951).* Seattle: University of Washington Press, 50.

King An Dong until he married his son to one of King An Duong's daughters. The son-in-law quickly stole the device, and Zhao Tuo easily defeated King An Duong. Zhao Tuo then combined Au Lac with his own territory to form the kingdom of Nam Viet (in Chinese, Nan Yue) in 207 BCE. Subsequently, the rulers of the Han dynasty (206 BCE–220 CE) annexed Zhao's kingdom into the Chinese empire in 111 BCE. Vietnam was not to regain its independence until 939 CE.

Throughout the thousand years of Chinese rule, there were frequent independence struggles; some were successful for short periods, others resulted in utter failure. The decisive battles against China's colonial control began in the beginning of the tenth century; they were fought by Vietnamese local officials. The struggle culminated in 938 with the naval victory on the Bach Dang River scored by Ngo Quyen over the fleet of the Nan Han Kingdom of southern China, which was the then suzerain of Vietnam. In the following year, Ngo Quyen proclaimed himself king and thereby inaugurated the monarchical tradition for a newly established kingdom that was independent from China. From then on, Vietnamese leaders endeavored to differentiate themselves from the Chinese and to nurture a culture that, although deeply influenced by

China, was Vietnamese. They wanted the Chinese authorities to renounce their conviction that Vietnam was an integral part of China's national territory.

In the eleventh century, while fighting the invading armies of the Chinese Song dynasty (960–1267), which sought to reincorporate Vietnam into the Chinese empire, a Vietnamese general of the Ly dynasty (1010–1225) fired up the emotions of his troops by reciting to them a song that, while establishing a separate destiny for Vietnam, asked also the fateful question: "How dare those foreigners come to invade our country?" In the thirteenth century, Mongol armies came to occupy parts of Vietnam. A harmonious relationship between the Tran monarchy (1225–1400), the army, and the people allowed Vietnam to successfully repel repeated attacks by the invader. In the beginning of the fifteenth century, the Chinese, now under the Ming dynasty (1368–1644), once again annexed Vietnam. In 1427, after ten years of resistance, Le Loi (d.1443) expelled all Chinese occupiers to inaugurate the Le dynasty, which presided over the destinies of Vietnam, at least in name, until 1791.

Internal Factionalism

The decline of the Le began with the sixteenth century. The Trinh and Nguyen families gained increasing ascendance over the Le emperor, who finally became a mere puppet. The two factions soon confronted each other; weaker, the Nguyen petitioned the emperor in 1558 to be sent to govern the southern part of Vietnam. In 1627, the Trinh-Nguyen rivalry broke out into open warfare, and after fifty years of indecisive battles, they resigned themselves to coexistence on opposite sides of the Gianh River, approximately at the seventeenth parallel.

From the village of Tay Son, southern Vietnam, three brothers, Nguyen Nhac, Nguyen Hue and Nguyen Lu, set in motion one of the mightiest popular uprising, starting around 1771. After overpowering the ruling Nguyen family faction, they turned their weapons against the Trinh. The Le emperor fled to China, and, on the pretext of reinstating him on his throne, the emperor of the Qing dynasty (1644–1912) ordered the invasion of Vietnam. In 1789, the Tay Son army took Hanoi by surprise and routed the Chinese expeditionary corps, which it found still blithely indulging in the New Year festivities. The Tay Son reign was not to be a long dynasty, however. The sole survivor of the former Nguyen lords of the south regained rapid control of Vietnam, and in 1802 he founded the last dynasty and transferred his capital to Hue.

European Colonialism

The Nguyen came to power at a time when European colonialism was experiencing a revival of interest in Asia. In 1861, the French seized Saigon. In 1882, they took Hanoi, and from there they spread out to occupy all of Vietnam a year later.

As with the Chinese period, the French colonial times were fraught with uprisings and rebellions. The pre-1930 anti-French struggles all ended in failures. Finally, the Vietnam Nationalist Party (Viet Nam Quoc Dan Dang, commonly referred to as the VNQDD), organized along the same principles as Sun Yat Sen's Nationalist Party in China and composed mainly of the new western-educated middle class, and the Dong Duong Cong San Dang, or Indochinese Communist Party (ICP), which counted among its members a great number of peasants and workers, discovered that they had to organize far more thoroughly before they could hope to threaten the colonial master.

During World War II, the colonial administration in Indochina managed to keep its authority while accommodating a small contingent of Japanese occupation troops in Indochina for five years. In the meantime, in 1941 the ICP led various national organizations in the formation in southern China of the Viet Minh, a guerrilla force whose aim was to expel both the French and Japanese from Vietnam. Two days after the Japanese surrender on 15 August 1945, the Viet Minh launched the August Revolution, which allowed it, less than a fortnight later, to seize power throughout Vietnam. On 2 September 1945 in Hanoi, Ho Chi Minh (1890–1969), the leader of the ICP and of the Viet Minh, proclaimed the independence of his country and the founding of the Democratic Republic of Vietnam (DRV)

The government set up by the Viet Minh was not to enjoy independence for long. The French were determined to reconquer their Indochinese colonial empire, and war broke out in December 1946, to end only in 1954 with the signing of the Geneva Accords that divided Vietnam into two temporary zones.

In violation of the Geneva Accords, elections were not held in 1956 for the reunification of the two zones, which had meanwhile become embroiled in the global Cold War between the Soviet Union, which supported the DRV, and the anti-Communist bloc led by the United States, which buttressed the Republic of Vietnam (RVN) it helped to create in 1955. The RVN quickly spawned a totalitarian, corrupt government. In December 1960, opponents of the RVN gathered together to form, with the active cooperation of the

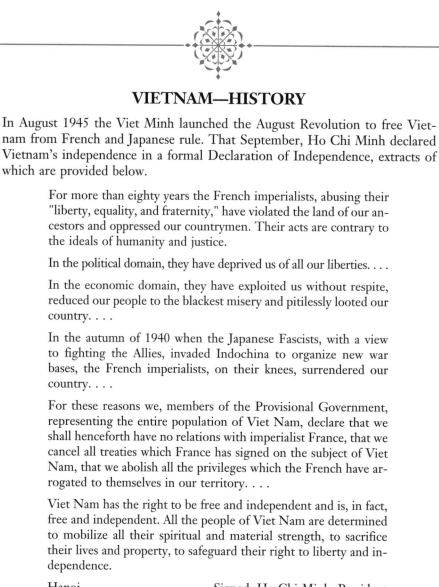

VIETNAM—HISTORY

In August 1945 the Viet Minh launched the August Revolution to free Vietnam from French and Japanese rule. That September, Ho Chi Minh declared Vietnam's independence in a formal Declaration of Independence, extracts of which are provided below.

For more than eighty years the French imperialists, abusing their "liberty, equality, and fraternity," have violated the land of our ancestors and oppressed our countrymen. Their acts are contrary to the ideals of humanity and justice.

In the political domain, they have deprived us of all our liberties. . . .

In the economic domain, they have exploited us without respite, reduced our people to the blackest misery and pitilessly looted our country. . . .

In the autumn of 1940 when the Japanese Fascists, with a view to fighting the Allies, invaded Indochina to organize new war bases, the French imperialists, on their knees, surrendered our country. . . .

For these reasons we, members of the Provisional Government, representing the entire population of Viet Nam, declare that we shall henceforth have no relations with imperialist France, that we cancel all treaties which France has signed on the subject of Viet Nam, that we abolish all the privileges which the French have arrogated to themselves in our territory. . . .

Viet Nam has the right to be free and independent and is, in fact, free and independent. All the people of Viet Nam are determined to mobilize all their spiritual and material strength, to sacrifice their lives and property, to safeguard their right to liberty and independence.

Hanoi

September 2, 1945

Signed: Ho Chi Minh, President

[Fourteen additional signatures]

Source: Harold M. Isaacs (1945) *New Cycle in Asia*, as translated from *La Republique*, No. 1 (1 October): 163–165.

DRV, the National Front of Liberation (NLF) of South Vietnam, whose aim was to overthrow the RVN government. The NLF soon launched armed attacks against the government, and the movement grew rapidly to present a formidable challenge. After the failure of massive economic, technical, and military aid, the United States came to the aid of the RVN with more than half a million of its own troops. The United States thereby made itself a party in what, in the view of many, had been essentially a civil war and, by the same token, gave the people who fought against the RVN an age-old incentive, that of a struggle against foreign intervention.

Unification

The war ended in 1973 for the United States when it signed a treaty with the DRV committing itself to withdraw its troops from Vietnam. For Vietnam, the war ended only in 1975 when troops of the NLF and the DRV entered Saigon to receive the RVN's surrender from the hands of its last president. In 1976, the National Assembly, composed of newly elected representatives, voted to unify the country, now called the Socialist Republic of Vietnam and placed under the firm control of the Communist Party of Vietnam.

The building of socialism did not succeed because the economic situation went from bad to worse, until the government decided, in 1986, to apply the policy of *doi moi* (renovation). *Doi moi* did away with the planned and supposedly self-sufficient economy in which all enterprises had been under the control of the state and established in its place a market economy that welcomed foreign investments and allowed the formation of private enterprises, with the aim of eradicating poverty and backwardness. Many problems still beset the development of the country, and today, after more than sixteen years under the renovation regime, Vietnam remains one of the poorest countries in the world.

Truong Buu Lam

Further Reading

Hodgkin, Thomas L. (1981) *Vietnam: The Revolutionary Path*. New York: St. Martin's Press.
Karnow, Stanley. (1991) *Vietnam: A History*. 2d ed. New York: Viking Press.
Lich Su Viet Nam. (1971 and 1989) 2 vols. Hanoi, Vietnam: Social Sciences Publishing House.
Taylor, Keith W. (1983) *The Birth of Vietnam*. Berkeley and Los Angeles: University of California Press.

VIETNAM—INTERNAL MIGRATION

The emperors of Vietnam's Nguyen dynasty (1802–1955) used resettlement policies to secure both population and territory. The French colonial authorities, whose presence in Vietnam lasted from 1859 to 1954, tried and failed to do so. After independence (1954), the government of the Democratic Republic of Vietnam (DRV) established a migration program, extending it to the south after the country's reunification (1975). Over four decades, 5 million inhabitants of the plains were relocated into highland and border areas. One million people moved from the cities of the south after 1975. The program has transformed the highlands and influenced the pace of urban development.

Internal Migration under the Nguyen Dynasty

The emperors of the Nguyen dynasty realized ambitious resettlement policies. Prisoners and vagabonds were exiled to the south and to Cambodia, where they joined soldiers and migrant farmers on military farms, clearing land, founding villages, and guarding the frontier. These policies predated the Nguyen rulers by many centuries: the Ly (1010–1225), Tran (1225–

1400/1414) and Le (1428–1788) emperors consolidated their conquests of Champa and Cambodia by promoting migration. The present shape of Vietnam, formed from one thousand years of southward expansion, owes much to these policies.

Internal Migration under the French

The expansion of settlement continued under the French colonial administration after 1859. Construction of canals attracted spontaneous settlers to the western Mekong Delta. Programs of organized migration provided labor for economic development. Laborers moved to build railways in the north and work plantations in the south and Cambodia. Land grants were made to settlers in the northern hills. Yet owing to competing objectives in the colonial administration, few of these initiatives enjoyed sustained success, and the independence war (1946–1954) ended them. The Geneva Agreement (1954) divided the country in two, confronting Vietnamese with the choice between residence in the north, under Communist rule, or the south, which became the Republic of Vietnam (RVN). This agreement created the largest internal migration in Vietnam's history. One million people opted to go south, and about 140,000 moved north.

There was little policy continuity between colonial and postcolonial administrations. After independence, the RVN's resettlement policy was led by the imperatives of nationalism and war, while the DRV's program was modeled on Soviet experiences of collective farming and drew from the lessons of the precolonial past.

Under the DRV, resettlement was organized in two directions. Lowlanders headed to the hills, to develop sparsely populated regions. Urban folk headed to the countryside, in implementation of the socialist model of limited urban development. Planned economic development was one purpose of the program. With the country divided, national security also became an important objective of resettlement policy. The highlands were filled with "loyal" lowlanders, while potentially turbulent cities were restricted in their growth. Both policies were extended after U.S. bombing started (1965), as the population's security depended on dispersal. The policies persisted after reunification, as the borders were attacked from Cambodia and China, and internal security was threatened by ethnic insurgency in the Central Highlands and dissatisfaction in southern cities.

Development of the Settlement Model

The settlement model evolved gradually. From 1954, plantations became state farms. These large-scale collective enterprises were used widely in agriculture and forestry, sometimes run by the army in a model reminiscent of precolonial military farms. From 1960, lowland villagers established cooperatives in the hills. From 1968, ethnic-minority highlanders were persuaded to abandon slash-and-burn farming, which required large areas of land for extensive cultivation. The policy, known as sedentarization *(dinh canh dinh cu)*, aimed to bring the minorities under closer state control while making space for the newcomers. In the 1970s, district towns became a focus for local government and economic activity. Areas in which this four-prong model were used came to be known as New Economic Zones (NEZs). An NEZ consisted of migrant cooperatives, settled minority villages, and a district town, under the leadership of a state farm or forestry enterprise. The NEZ model transformed the Central Highlands after reunification, replacing the land development and strategic hamlet policies initiated in the 1950s by the RVN and disrupted by the war.

The migrants formed two communities, by their origin and the method of their recruitment. On the one hand, mobilization teams motivated village migrants with talk of patriotism and economic progress. On the other, inhabitants of the southern cities were required, under post-reunification policy, to return to their villages or move to NEZs, with very little choice in the matter. Recruitment in both contexts was enforced by a system of household registration, whereby essential goods and services were available only in a registered place of residence. Cutting registration created an incentive for departure, but could not ensure settlement on arrival. More than 50 percent of migrants abandoned their NEZ, moving back to the village or city from which they had come, drifting elsewhere, or joining the boat people exodus of the 1980s.

Internal Migration in the Reform Era

Economic reform in the 1980s changed the dynamics of migration. The resettlement program remained, but people's economic survival no longer depended on their household registration. Free migrants headed to the cities (in search of work) and the highlands (in search of land). While registration requirements in the cities limited urban growth, there were no restrictions in the hills. Settlers planted coffee and other commercial crops, which now found markets within Vietnam and abroad. By creating networks between previous migrants and inhabitants of the plains, the resettlement program facilitated a new, uncontrolled movement of spontaneous migration, especially to the Central Highlands, where people could

take advantage of market reforms to grow and sell coffee and other cash crops.

Results of Internal Migration

Population resettlement has changed both the cities and the highlands. Vietnam's urban population remains low, and neither Hanoi nor Ho Chi Minh City may be compared with the metropolis cities of Bangkok, Manila, or Jakarta. Meanwhile, the highland population has grown rapidly. Networks of roads and towns now service a population of migrants from the plains. Forests have given way to farms. In the northern highlands, environmental stress caused by population pressure (itself caused by previous decades' resettlement programs) has provoked migration to the Central Highlands, which will experience environmental difficulties in the years to come. And the highlanders, now minorities in their own provinces, have responded by joining the national economy, retreating to remote regions, converting to Protestantism, or organizing peaceful protests against the loss of their land. All four reactions are the signs of the migration program's achievement of its long-term objectives. Intended to transform these forested havens of insurgency and underdevelopment, resettlement has brought about widespread economic, social, and landscape change in the highlands. As a result, and in spite of the strains, these outlying regions are now integrating into the Vietnamese nation.

Andrew Hardy

Further Reading

De Koninck, Rodolphe. (1996) "The Peasantry as the Territorial Spearhead of the State in Southeast Asia: The Case of Vietnam." *Sojourn* 11, 2: 231–258.

Evans, Grant. (1992) "Internal Colonialism in the Central Highlands of Vietnam." *Sojourn* 7, 2: 274–304.

Hardy, Andrew. (2002) *Red Hills: Migrants and the State in the Highlands of Vietnam*. Richmond, U.K.: Nordic Institute of Asian Studies.

Jamieson, Neil J., Le Trong Cuc, and A. Terry Rambo. (1998). *The Development Crisis in Vietnam's Mountains.* Honolulu, HI: East-West Center.

Li Tana. (1996) *Peasants on the Move, Rural-Urban Migration in the Hanoi Region.* Singapore: Institute of Southeast Asian Studies.

Thrift, Nigel, and Dean Forbes. (1986) *The Price of War: Urbanisation in Vietnam, 1954–1985.* London: Allen and Unwin.

Turner, Sarah, Andrew Hardy, and Jean Michaud, eds. (2000). "Migration, Markets, and Social Change in the Highlands of Vietnam." Special Issue of *Asia Pacific Viewpoint* 41, 1.

United Nations Development Programme. (1998) *The Dynamics of Internal Migration in Viet Nam.* Hanoi, Vietnam: UNDP Discussion Paper.

VIETNAM—POLITICAL SYSTEM In order to put Vietnam's current political system in perspective, it is helpful to consider briefly the political systems that were in use prior to Vietnam's reunification in 1975. The political system of the Republic of Vietnam (South Vietnam, 1955–1975) was quite different from that of the Democratic Republic of Vietnam (North Vietnam, 1945–1975).

Republic of Vietnam (1955–1975)

After French colonial forces were defeated in the First Indochina War (1946–1954), Vietnam was partitioned along the seventeenth parallel, the north under the control of Ho Chi Minh (1890–1969) and the Communists, the south under the U.S.-supported Ngo Dinh Diem, an intellectual Christian who was appointed president of South Vietnam in October 1955. He was considered a nationalist intent on eradicating the Communists in the North. Diem won initial respect from the public and the United States by subduing the South's various military factions and religious sects that were threatening to overthrow the government. His 1959 land reform policy was seen as inequitable, however, and he soon lost his popularity.

Furthermore, Diem's government was characterized by nepotism. His eldest brother, Ngo Dinh Thuc, was a Roman Catholic bishop, and as such wielded considerable power. Another brother, Ngo Dinh Nhu, became Diem's special adviser. The youngest brother, Ngo Dinh Can, exercised political control in central Vietnam. Moreover, Nhu's wife, Le Xuan, was also involved in political and social activities. As Diem and his family used military power to suppress political and religious protests, the United States began losing interest in supporting him.

On 1 November 1963, Diem and Nhu were killed in a conspiracy led by General Duong Van Minh.

Minh was not capable of maintaining his paramount position for long, however, and was succeeded by Nguyen Khanh in January 1964. The military regime that General Minh set up was more compliant with U.S. interests, but faced protest from religious groups, interest groups, and political activists, and Minh lost control over South Vietnam in less than a year. General Nguyen Cao Ky and his comrade General Nguyen Van Thieu seized power in February 1965, and maintained military rule over the South until 1975.

Democratic Republic of Vietnam (1945)

The political situation in the North was equally chaotic. On 25 August 1945, Bao Dai (1913–1997), the last Emperor of Vietnam, reluctantly handed over the

The mausoleum of Vietnamese leader Ho Chi Minh in Hanoi. His body is preserved in a glass sarcophagus inside. (STEVE RAYMER/CORBIS)

imperial seal and symbolic golden sword to the National Liberation Committee headed by the Communists. On 2 September 1945, Ho Chi Minh declared Vietnam's independence and announced the birth of the Democratic Republic of Vietnam. Not many countries recognized it, however, and Ho failed to gain support from the United States and other Western countries. He was forced to fight the French, who wanted to reassert their colonial authority. Although he defeated them at the battle of Dien Bien Phu (1954), he failed to gain control of the South.

Socialist Republic of Vietnam (from 1975)

On 30 April 1975, North Vietnamese forces took control of Saigon. With reunification, the South came under the rule of the central government. Since then, Vietnam's politics have been dominated by the Vietnamese Communist Party (VCP), whose ideology closely follows Marxist-Leninist doctrines and Ho Chi Minh's thoughts.

PREAMBLE TO THE CONSTITUTION OF VIETNAM

Adopted 2 July 1976 (revised 1992)

In the course of their millennia-old history, the Vietnamese people, working diligently, creatively, and fighting courageously to build their country and defend it, have forged a tradition of unity, humanity, uprightness, perseverance and indomitableness for their nation and have created Vietnamese civilisation and culture.

Starting in 1930, under the leadership of the Communist Party of Vietnam formed and trained by President Ho Chi Minh, they waged a protracted revolutionary struggle full of hardships and sacrifices, resulting in the triumph of the August Revolution. On 2 September 1945, President Ho Chi Minh read the Declaration of Independence and the Democratic Republic of Vietnam came into existence. In the following decades, the people of all nationalities in our country conducted an uninterrupted struggle with the precious assistance of friends throughout the world, especially the socialist countries and the neighbouring countries, achieved resounding exploits, the most outstanding ones being the historic Dien Bien Phu and Ho Chi Minh campaigns, defeated the two wars of aggression by the colonialists and the imperialists, liberated the country, reunified the motherland, and brought to completion the people's national democratic revolution. On 2 July 1976, the National Assembly of reunified Vietnam decided to change the country's name to the Socialist Republic of Vietnam; the country entered a period of transition to socialism, strove for national construction, and unyieldingly defended its frontiers while fulfilling its internationalist duty.

In successive periods of resistance war and national construction, our country adopted the 1946, 1959, and 1980 Constitutions.

Starting in 1986, a comprehensive national renewal advocated by the 6th Congress of the Communist Party of Vietnam has achieved very important initial results. The National Assembly has decided to revise the 1980 Constitution in response to the requirements of the new situation and tasks.

This Constitution establishes our political regime economic system, social and cultural institutions; it deals with our national defence and security, the fundamental rights and duties of the citizen, the structure and principles regarding the organisation and activity of State organs; it institutionalises the relationship between the Party as leader, the people as master, and the State as administrator.

In the light of Marxism-Leninism and Ho Chi Minh's thought, carrying into effect the Programme of national construction in the period of transition to socialism, the Vietnamese people vow to unite millions as one, uphold the spirit of self-reliance in building the country, carry out a foreign policy of independence, sovereignty, peace, friendship and cooperation with all nations, strictly abide by the Constitution, and win ever greater successes in their effort to renovate, build and defend their motherland.

Source: Government of Vietnam. Retrieved 8 March 2002, from: http://home.vnn.vn/english/government/constitution/preamble.html

---

The new Constitution of Vietnam was issued on 15 April 1992. All people eighteen years of age or older have the right to vote, with the exception of criminals. Elections are held every five years at national, provincial, and local levels. Vietnam's government has three branches: legislative, executive, and judiciary. The Communist Party is effectively a "fourth branch," involved in all activities of the government.

Legislative Branch The unicameral National Assembly consists of 450 delegates elected in the general

election. It is the highest organ of the state and possesses both constitutional and legislative powers. It makes all decisions on domestic and foreign policies, sets socioeconomic goals, and deals with national defense and security issues.

Previously, only members of the Communist Party were qualified to stand for the election. However, since 1997 independent candidates have been eligible. In the latest election, in 1997, about 92 percent of the seats in the parliament were occupied by Communist

TABLE 1

The Cabinet in 1997

Position	Name
Prime Minister	Phan Van Khai
First Deputy Prime Minister	Nguyen Tan Dung
Deputy Prime Minister	Nguyen Cong Tan
Deputy Prime Minister	Ngo Xuan Loc
Deputy Prime Minister	Nguyen Manh Cam
Deputy Prime Minister	Pham Gia Khiem
Other Ministers	(24 others)

Party members, with independent candidates holding the rest.

The National Assembly's Standing Committee is permanent and consists of the chairman (in 1999, Nong Duc Manh), the vice chairman, and members who are determined by the National Assembly. A member of the Standing Committee cannot occupy another position in the government.

The president of the National Assembly is elected by its members and serves a five-year term. As head of state, the president represents Vietnam both at home and in foreign countries. Tran Duc Luong was elected president on 25 September 1997. From 1992, the vice president has been Nguyen Thi Binh.

Executive Branch Vietnam has a parliamentary system in which a prime minister heads the cabinet. In actual fact, however, the general secretary of the Communist Party holds greater power, due to the nature of one-party government.

The president appoints the prime minister from among the members of the National Assembly. The prime minister then appoints the deputy prime ministers and other ministers.

Judicial Branch The legal system is based on the French civil law and consists of the Supreme People's Court, the Provincial Courts and the District People's Courts. The chief justice is nominated by the president and voted on by the National Assembly. Trinh Hong Duong has been the presiding judge since 1997. His term is for five years.

In addition, there is the Supreme People's Procuracy, which supervises and controls law enforcement at all levels of society, from the central government down to the individual citizen.

The one-party political system has been stable for a long time, though some fragmentation exists. With economic reform and Vietnam's integration into re-gional and international organizations such as the Association of Southeast Asian Nations (ASEAN) and the Asia-Pacific Economic Cooperation Forum (APEC), the political system is expected to become more open, transparent, and accountable.

Ha Huong

Further Reading

Cable News Network. (1998) "Vietnam." In *Cold War*. Retrieved 12 March 2000, from: http://cnn.com/SPECIALS/cold.war/episodes/11/recap.

Dang Phong and Melanie Beresford. (1998) *Authority Relations and Economic Decision-Making in Vietnam*. Copenhagen, Denmark: NIAS.

Ellis, Claire. (1996) *Culture Shock! Vietnam*. Singapore: Times Books International.

Engelbert, Thomas, and E. Christopher Goscha. (1995) *Falling out of Touch*. Warrnambool, Australia: Amazon Press.

Hunt, H. Michael. (1996) *Lyndon Johnson's War: America's Cold War Crusade in Vietnam, 1945–1968*. New York: Hill and Wang.

Kamm, Henry. (1996) *Dragon Ascending—Vietnam and the Vietnamese*. New York: Arcade Publishing.

Karnow, Stanley. (1997) *Vietnam: A History*. New York: Penguin Books.

National Geographic Atlas of the World Revised Sixth Edition (1995). Retrieved 12 March 2000, from: http://amsworldwide.com/facts/vie-fax.html.

Nugent, Nicholas (1996) *Vietnam: The Second Revolution*. Brighton, U.K.: In Print Publishing Ltd.

Vietnamese Embassy (United States). (1999) Retrieved 15 March 2000, from: http://www.vietnamembassy-usa.org.

Vietnam Insight. (1999) "Vietnam Communists Say to Keep Single-Party System." Retrieved 12 March 2000 from: http://www.vinsight.org/1999news/0802d.htm

Wright, David. (1995) *Causes and Consequences of the Vietnam War*. London: Evans Brothers.

Young, B. Marilyn. (1991) *The Vietnam Wars 1945–1990*. New York: HarperPerennial.

VIETNAM COMMUNIST PARTY The origins of the Vietnam Communist Party (VCP) date back to 1925 when Comintern official and Vietnamese nationalist leader Ho Chi Minh (1890–1969) founded the Revolutionary Youth League in southern China. Hobbled by factionalism, the group was defunct by May 1929. After uniting feuding Communist groups operating in southern China, Ho founded the Indochina Communist Party (ICP) in 1930. The group operated clandestinely, because French colonial authorities imprisoned many of its leaders. The ICP grew, however, into the preeminent anticolonial force in Indochina.

To widen the party's appeal, Ho created a broad nationalist united front, known as the Viet Minh, under the ICP's leadership in 1941. Viet Minh troops waged a guerrilla war against the Japanese and Vichy French troops. Following Japan's surrender, Ho's Viet Minh marched into Hanoi and declared the founding of the Democratic Republic of Vietnam (DRV) on 2 September 1945. To assuage fears that Communist forces would not dominate the new coalition government, Ho dissolved the ICP. With the return of French colonial forces and the breakdown of a series of negotiations in 1946, the Viet Minh began a guerrilla war, culminating in the 1954 defeat of French forces at Dien Bien Phu. Materially aided by the People's Republic of China after April 1950, the Viet Minh leadership was encouraged to restore the Communist Party. In February 1951, the Lao Dong Party (LDP) was founded.

Under Chinese, Soviet, and French pressure, the DRV accepted the temporary division of Vietnam at the 17th parallel as part of the Geneva Accords and anticipated winning nationwide elections in 1956–1957. The LDP was the sole political force in the north and began to implement a Communist political and economic system. The LDP's land reform program, implemented in two phases between 1954 and 1960, was particularly brutal and had a negative effect on production. At the advice of Chinese advisers, "people's courts" were established and "class labels" were applied to all members of society to aid identification and liquidation of the landlord class. Wide-scale violence and peasant unrest led the LDP to sack its general secretary and revise its policies. The LDP also imposed a strict system of control over its writers and artists, beginning in 1954.

In May 1959 the LDP Politburo authorized support for southern revolutionaries to defeat the regime of Ngo Dinh Diem (1901–1963). In 1963, the LDP ordered the infiltration of North Vietnamese troops into the south of the country. The LDP continued its policy to take over the south following Ho's death in 1969 and eventually negotiated peace with the United States in 1973. In 1974, the Politburo again ordered the use of force to take over the south. Formal reunification occurred in October 1976, at which point the LDP changed its name to the Vietnam Communist Party.

From 1976 to 1986, the VCP consolidated its rule but led the country into an economic malaise and diplomatic isolation, following the December 1978 intervention into Cambodia. In 1986 the party embarked on a radical course of economic reform, known as *doi moi*, or renovation, that had a positive impact on the economy. The decollectivization of agriculture caused Vietnam to go from being a net importer of rice to the world's third largest exporter of rice by 1988. Likewise, per capita GDP doubled in the first fifteen years

of the reform program. The VCP remains the sole legal party in Vietnam today. It is ruled by an 18-person Politburo and a 170-member central committee.

Zachary Abuza

See also: **Communism—Vietnam; Ho Chi Minh; Vietnam—Economic System; Vietnam—History; Vietnam—Political System**

Further Reading

Duiker, William J. (1981) *The Communist Road to Power in Vietnam.* Boulder, CO: Westview Press.

———. (2000) *Ho Chi Minh.* New York: Hyperion.

Khanh Huynh Kim. (1982) *Vietnamese Communism, 1925–1945.* Ithaca, NY: Cornell University Press.

Jamieson, Neil L. (1993) *Understanding Vietnam.* Berkeley and Los Angeles: University of California Press.

Marr, David G. (1981) *Vietnamese Tradition on Trial, 1920–1945.* Berkeley and Los Angeles: University of California Press.

Porter, Gareth. (1993) *Vietnam: The Politics of Bureaucratic Socialism.* Ithaca, NY: Cornell University Press.

Tin, Bui. (1995) *Following Ho Chi Minh: Memoirs of a North Vietnamese Colonel.* Honolulu, HI: University of Hawaii Press.

VIETNAM WAR

VIETNAM WAR   From 1954 to 1975, America fought its longest and costliest war. The Vietnam War created massive disruption to Southeast Asia and massive turmoil in American society.

The Human Cost of War

The major product of war is the number of casualties: the killed, wounded, or missing in action (MIA). Although the numbers are tainted by exaggeration or error, the estimated total of military casualties from 1954 to 1975 was 1.75 million killed and at least 3 million wounded. By the end of the war, there were 10,173 captured and missing in action. Total civilian casualties for Vietnam, Laos, and Cambodia numbered well over 500,000. In addition, after the war thousands of Vietnamese died trying to flee Communist rule, and nearly 2 million Cambodians were killed by the Communist Khmer Rouge led by Pol Pot (c. 1925–1998).

American forces suffered 47,382 killed in action, 10,811 noncombatant deaths, 153,303 wounded in action (some 74,000 survived as amputees), and about 3,000 MIAs. (In April 1995 the U.S. Department of Defense listed 1,621 Americans missing in Vietnam and 2,207 for all of Southeast Asia.)

The greatest causes of deaths in the U.S. Army were small-arms fire (51 percent) and artillery shells, mortar, and grenade fragments (35 percent). Twelve generals and eight women were killed in action. Seventy percent of all American enlisted casualties were twenty-one years of age or younger. African Americans and Hispanics suffered more casualties per enlistee than whites did.

Casualties for the Viet Minh (Communist irregulars) are undocumented. Allegedly, during the period of French control, 300,000 lost their lives in combat. The U.S. Central Intelligence Agency's (CIA) Phoenix program (1967–1972), which identified and eliminated the Viet Cong infrastructure in South Vietnam, claimed official responsibility for "neutralizing" 81,740 Communist cadres, of whom 26,369 were executed. General Vo Nguyen Giap (b. 1911), general and commander of the People's Army of Vietnam (PAVN) from 1946 to 1972, estimated that 500,000 soldiers died in battles with Americans during the years from 1964 to 1969. The combined forces of the army of North Vietnam (the NVA) and the Viet Minh of South Vietnam in the Easter Offensive of March 1972 lost over 100,000 lives. The Americans estimated that 50,000 of these soldiers were killed by saturation bombing. Moreover, tens of thousands of Laos's Pathet Lao Communists and Cambodia's Khmer Rouge were killed in the secret bombings that began in 1969 and intensified in the joint South Vietnamese-American incursions into their territories in the early 1970s.

Background to the War

French colonization of Indochina—consisting of Vietnam, Cambodia, and Laos—began in 1859 with the capture of the city of Saigon, although the first French campaign (at Tourance/Danang) began in 1858. The termination of World War II introduced a worldwide period of anticolonial movements and wars. During the final months of the Pacific war, Japan occupied Indochina and turned it into a protectorate, ousting the French, who had still ruled it throughout most of the war. Upon Japan's surrender in August 1945, Indochina's independence became a geopolitical problem. On 25 September, Ho Chi Minh (1890–1969), a leader of the Indochinese independence movement, proclaimed the creation of the Democratic Republic of Vietnam (DRV). The United States and its allies agreed to send British troops to disarm the Japanese and obtain control of southern Vietnam and to send Chinese and French troops to administer postwar programs in the city of Hanoi. Soon the French were allowed to negotiate full control of Vietnam. In March 1946, the French declared Vietnam an independent state within the French union. In November 1946, with the French naval bombardment of the seaport of Haiphong, the French challenged the authority of the DRV under the vague framework of the March agreement. This engagement launched the First Indochina War (1946–1954).

Ho Chi Minh and his Viet Minh troops retreated from Hanoi and launched a guerrilla war. Finally, in 1950, the anticolonial movement became integrated into the Cold War: The Soviet Union and the People's Republic of China recognized Ho Chi Minh, and the United States and Britain recognized the French-sustained state of Vietnam. The United States reluctantly provided military and economic aid for the French pacification effort. President Eisenhower endorsed the Domino Theory, which predicted that the fall of one nation to Communism would result in the fall of other nations. The French made it clear that their support and participation in the North Atlantic Treaty Organization depended on Washington's support of France in Indochina. Consequently, France received 85 percent of its Indochinese budget from the United States.

In May 1954, the Vietnamese Communist forces decisively defeated the French at the Battle of Dien Bien Phu. To resolve the issue of control over Indochina, an international conference met in Geneva in the summer of 1954. After much disagreement about the issues of French withdrawal and who was the rightful representative of the government of South Vietnam, Russia, China, France, and Hanoi signed the Geneva Agreements, which partitioned Vietnam at the seventeenth parallel pending a national referendum within two years. The agreements' legitimacy was challenged when the South Vietnamese and American representatives refused to sign.

The Communist Revolution and the Pursuit of National Independence

The leaders of the Communist revolution in Vietnam were Ho Chi Minh, Vo Nguyen Giap, and Truong Chinh (1907–1988). They developed Hanoi's unique method of fighting the wars against the French and the Americans. "Uncle" Ho combined a fervid loyalty to Vietnam's independence and nationalism with a Marxist-Leninist commitment to class struggle, land reform, social revolution, and socialist economics. Depending on the political context, he could charismatically organize policies of allegiance to seemingly contradictory goals. Some scholars argue that his power and ideology were solidified with his 1941 announcement of the formation of a united front called the League for the Independence of Vietnam (Viet Minh). This front tried to unite the moderate elements of all social classes to promote land reform and anti-imperialism—against both the French and the Japanese.

The Viet Minh organization was the predecessor of the National Liberation Front for the Liberation of South Vietnam (NLF). This term designates groups in South Vietnam who were disaffected by the rule of President Ngo Dinh Diem (1901–1963). Diem became prime minister of southern Vietnam in 1954 and, with the help of the U.S. government, established the independent state of South Vietnam and declared himself president. Diem's power base relied on Catholic refugees from northern Vietnam, wealthy and powerful landlords and merchants, and foreigners. His aloofness and familial authoritarianism estranged him from the nationalists, peasants, and Buddhists. The National Liberation Front had organized professionals such as lawyers and physicians, as well as peasants, urban workers, and Buddhists to resist Diem's rule. Mass demonstrations in the summer of 1963 fueled a coup against him. He fled from the Presidential Palace but was caught and murdered by his South Vietnamese bodyguard on 2 November 1963.

The NLF also organized a military arm, the People's Liberation Armed Forces (technically the PLAF but commonly called the Viet Cong). During the late 1950s and early 1960s, Ho Chi Minh became identified with the classical military approach to the war—conventional forces, armed confrontations, and great patriotic sacrifices. His conventional approach resulted in horrendous carnage and loss of life. After the war, many survivors suffered psychologically from this approach.

Vo Nguyen Giap, general and commander of the war, promoted the ideology of "people's war" advocated by China's Mao Zedong (1893–1976). Tactically, this ideology viewed the revolutionary war in terms of mobilization and coordination of the nation's military, psychological, diplomatic, and economic resources. The war was not to be limited to the battlefield. Giap's greatest success was the 1968 Tet Offensive. Although the offensive was a military disaster for the Communists, its psychological impact convinced the United States that the war could not be won.

Truong Chinh ranked second only to Ho Chi Minh in the political structure. An adherent of Mao's harsh revolutionary programs, he advocated vigorous policies of class struggle that ultimately led to a disastrous land reform campaign. He remained a true believer in the guerrilla strategy of people's war, even when a more conventional approach was more suitable.

The conflicting approaches of the leadership led to many bitter arguments, but by focusing primarily on the war itself and making use of multiple strategies,

they strengthened their chances of victory despite their contradictory policies. The emphasis on people's war was a costly but effective way to mobilize the Vietnamese military and civilians against the Saigon government. Neither conventional nor guerrilla warfare alone could force the United States to succumb militarily, however. After the United States withdrew its military support in 1973, Hanoi's tactics changed from a guerrilla war that stressed mobilization to a conventional war of massive troop movements that stressed destroying South Vietnam's military and seizing the government in Saigon.

U.S. "Soft" Intervention: 1954–1964

President Eisenhower manifested his support for Saigon's anti-Communist Ngo Dinh Diem by publicly praising him and providing military and economic assistance. In September 1954, Eisenhower's secretary of state, John Foster Dulles, completed the establishment of the Southeast Asia Treaty Organization (SEATO), whose major function was to support Saigon. In October, the French military left Vietnam, and the United States took over the job of creating a strong southern government. In 1955, Diem rejected the Geneva Agreements, refused to call nationwide elections, and declared the establishment of the sovereign Republic of Vietnam.

Washington established economic support and sent military advisers to help Diem's forces train and modernize. Economic aid was so immense that Diem, no longer dependent solely on tax collection for his finances, did not need to appeal to the populace and therefore did not engage in meaningful land reforms or industrial development. His *agroville* (a strategic hamlet) campaign of 1959 forcibly relocated entire rural villages into fortified settlements, depleted the rural economy and destroyed the cohesiveness of peasant families and villages. The result was the beginning of vast migration to cities, where peasants increased the rolls of the unemployed.

From 1960 to 1963, Diem's rule became more dictatorial and repressive. His National Assembly Law allowed police to arrest and execute (by a portable guillotine) suspected Communists or anti-French nationalists. Intellectuals and professional groups petitioned Diem to step down or democratize his rule. An unsuccessful coup in 1960 made Diem even more repressive. At the beginning of 1963, the poor performance of the South Vietnamese army against the local Communist guerrillas at the Battle of Ap Bac revealed the incompetence and low morale of the South Vietnamese fighting forces and the need to change course. Soon after this battle, Buddhist demonstrations grew in number and vehemence, forcing Diem to use military force to squelch them. In June, the first of seven Buddhist monks committed self-immolation to protest Diem's policies. The most vivid expression of the public's hostility to Diem's rule occurred after the protest suicide of Nguyen Tuong Tam on 7 July. Tam, born in 1906, was one of the greatest modern writers in Vietnam and an anti-Communist, nationalistic advocate of a greater Vietnam. His funeral was accompanied by the largest demonstration ever held in Saigon. Within weeks, Vietnamese military leaders plotted to end Diem's rule with the tacit approval of the U.S. government. On 2 November 1963, just weeks before John F. Kennedy's assassination, Diem and his brother Ngo Dinh Nhu were shot to death while trying to escape from Saigon.

The year 1964 was the turning point for America's commitment in Vietnam. In June, General William C. Westmoreland replaced General Paul D. Harkins (1904–1984) as commander of American armed forces in Indochina. In August, President Lyndon Johnson informed Congress that North Vietnamese patrol boats had attacked American ships in the international waters of the Gulf of Tonkin. Decades later, the reports of these incidents were revealed as having been questionable at best and shams at worst. Nevertheless, Congress was convinced that the president should be given full authority to challenge North Vietnam and to support South Vietnam by any means. The Gulf of Tonkin Resolution (August 1964) legitimized America's decision to engage in military activities in Indochina. The resolution served as an unofficial declaration of war. The U.S. Air Force began raids on North Vietnam's facilities, and U.S. ground troops pursued Viet Cong attacking U.S. bases.

Search and Destroy: 1965–1968

President Johnson's war quickly ratcheted the level of violence but without sufficient Vietnamese support and interaction. Relying on the managerial expertise of Secretary of Defense Robert McNamara, the narrow military mind of General William Westmoreland, and the diplomatic arrogance of Ambassadors Henry Cabot Lodge and Ellsworth Bunker, Johnson disallowed any serious criticism of his policies. Westmoreland's strategy was to destroy the enemy, its logistical support in production and transportation areas, and its reliance on agricultural supplies and protection in local villages. After the costly battle in the Ia Drang Valley in the summer of 1965, Westmoreland announced his policies of attrition: (1) to destroy the enemy in such numbers that it could not replace or resupply sufficient men or materiel to fight the war

and (2) to establish a favorable ratio of killing—more enemy and fewer U.S. soldiers. Quantitative measures of success were provided by body counts, destroyed supply depots, destruction of protective ground cover, and removal of populations who supported enemy activity. Westmoreland knew that the South Vietnamese army could not win the war by itself or with its own equipment. His strategy called for the first use of B-52s for tactical support of U.S. troops and massive search-and-destroy missions against enemy targets. During this period, helicopters equipped with rapid-fire machine guns and rockets became key to fighting the war as well as transporting troops and picking up the wounded and stranded.

Johnson sent the first combat troops into Vietnam in March 1965. By 1968, there were over five hundred thousand troops in Vietnam, and Westmoreland was calling for more. Johnson's military strategy was hobbled by his domestic initiatives. Increased budget requests for the Great Society were dented by requests for huge amounts of money to fight the war. Johnson also was aware that tax increases to support the war would be denied or would be unpopular because his opponents would accuse him of feathering the Great Society programs at the expense of the war. To avoid a clear run into the war, Johnson implemented a strategy of "graduated response." He and his advisers believed that at some point when the price was too great, the north would relinquish its attempt to reunify the south. His refusal to use taxation to fund the war led to borrowing strategies that resulted in an increase in the Consumer Price Index, a growing international trade deficit, and eventually a high rate of inflation and unemployment.

Westmoreland, McNamara, and Secretary of State Dean Rusk predicted that the war would soon come to an end. It was thus a psychological shock to the American public when, in January 1968, the Communists initiated a nationwide uprising in South Vietnam. After months of hard fighting and tremendous destruction, General Westmoreland claimed a military victory yet asked for two hundred thousand more soldiers. The destruction of the imperial city of Hue, the burning of villages, and the slaughter of Vietnamese civilians had been seen on American television (the My Lai massacre had occurred right after the first Tet Offensive but was not publicized until November 1970). The Tet uprising had clearly been a great psychological victory for the Communists. President Johnson declared he would not run for a second term, announced the cessation of bombing of North Vietnam, appointed McNamara to direct the World Bank, and replaced Westmoreland with General Creighton Abrams.

Pacification and Vietnamization: 1969–1971

Richard Nixon was elected president in November 1968 on the promise that he had a secret plan to end the war. Nixon won election during a year of great domestic and international turmoil: in April, Martin Luther King, Jr., was assassinated; in May, while American diplomats were negotiating in Paris with Hanoi, the Communists launched a second Tet Offensive; in June, Robert F. Kennedy was assassinated, and the military outpost of Khe Sanh, the centerpiece of Westmoreland's strategy of massive destruction and attrition of enemy soldiers, was abandoned; in August, the riotous Democratic National Convention was held in Chicago while the Communists staged their third Tet Offensive. Clearly, policies in Vietnam and the United States were exacerbating military and civil unrest.

Nixon's Vietnamization of the war strategy (that is, his turning over of control of the war to the Vietnamese) installed a new core of leaders: Ambassador Ellsworth Bunker, General Creighton Abrams, and William Colby guided political, military, and pacification programs. Nixon's "plan" gave full military control over to the Vietnamese army. The Americans began to withdraw troops—150,000 in 1970 and an additional 100,000 in 1971. The United States provided economic, technical, and material assistance to the government of South Vietnam but would not direct the war or engage in undue combat. Colby's pacification programs (including the notorious Phoenix program) concentrated on quietly destroying the infrastructure of the Communists and their influence in South Vietnam by rooting out Communist cadres and spies and imprisoning or executing them. American and Vietnamese civic action teams, particularly in the Mekong Delta, improved the quality of agricultural yields, health programs, and local defense.

American support missions were focused on destroying the caches of supplies that the Communists stored up for future battles and support. Nixon's illegal bombings of and incursions into Cambodia (April 1970) and Laos (January 1971) were an attempt to destroy Hanoi's ability to wage war and to give time to Saigon to build its military strength and morale.

True, the intensive training and support increased the South Vietnamese army's expertise, but the emphasis on self-reliance hindered its logistical and communication ability to engage in complex maneuvers and to coordinate its battle plans with American forces. These problems were evident during the poorly coordinated South Vietnamese attack in Laos in January 1971. This was the last time that a significant number of American ground personnel helped the South Vietnamese army. Aware of the South's inadequacies, in March 1972, the North Vietnamese army launched a threefold attack on targets in South Vietnam. Although General Abrams credited the Vietnamese with fighting a good battle, in truth, the North Vietnamese were repelled by the massive B-52 bombing of the battlefield.

Nixon's plan to Vietnamize the war actually increased the number of American casualties. The American public was traumatized by media coverage of the death and destruction. Domestically, the antiwar movement grew to immense proportions, destabilizing American society. Moratorium antiwar protests began in early 1970 with mass demonstrations in Washington, D.C., in April. On 4 May, opposition to the Cambodian incursion caused nationwide demonstrations and resulted in four deaths and nine wounded by the Ohio National Guard at Kent State University in Ohio. The November trial of Lieutenant William Calley for the 1968 massacre at My Lai lasted five months and provided even more reason for demonstrations and antiwar activity. Congress felt the pressure and in December 1970 repealed the Gulf of Tonkin Resolution.

The year 1971 brought even greater protests. In June of that year, the *New York Times* began publishing the "Pentagon Papers," which provided an insider's account of how decisions were made to fight the war. The evidence of deception coupled with the administration's attempt to censor the account resulted in widespread antiwar sentiment. Nixon finally withdrew all U.S. ground troops in August 1972 and won reelection in November. In January 1973, the draft ended.

The year 1972 witnessed the dismal results of Nixon's strategy of Vietnamization. As the responsibility of fighting the war was turned over to the Saigon regime, the Communist troops became more confident of winning the war. As the United States continued to withdraw troops and limit direct military cooperation with the South Vietnamese army, its room to maneuver or affect the talks became more limited. A snag in the talks in the autumn of 1972 raised the level of frustration. On 18 December, unable to redeploy troops to Vietnam, Nixon ordered the most concentrated B-52 bombing campaign of the war on North Vietnam. This two-week so-called Christmas bombing forced the North Vietnamese to resume peace talks. By 23 January, a peace agreement was initialed by Henry Kissinger and Le Duc Tho (1910–1990), founder of the Indo-Chinese Communist Party and chief negotiator at the Paris talks, along with representatives from the Republic of Vietnam

(Saigon) and the Provisional Revolutionary (Communist) government in South Vietnam. In 1973, the Nobel Prize Committee in Sweden declared that Le Duc Tho and Kissinger should receive the Nobel Peace Prize. However, Le Duc Tho refused to accept the award because the war had not yet ended in Vietnam.

In the last years of the war, Nixon changed the war goals from rescuing South Vietnam from the Communists to ending the war honorably. This meant that the new focus was on getting American POWs back and discovering the whereabouts of MIAs. In February 1973, the Communists released 588 POWs; a month later the last U.S. military personnel left Vietnam; and in April, the last POWs were released. After the war ended, the U.S. government claimed that not all U.S. servicemen were accounted for. Hanoi was instructed to provide detailed information on MIAs and possible POWs. Without full disclosure, diplomatic recognition and normalization of relations would not be possible.

"The Decent Interval": 1971–1973

By 1971, President Nixon had realized that a victory in South Vietnam was not possible. He and Henry Kissinger devised the plan to provide Saigon with enough strength in 1973 to stand on its own against the North Vietnamese. Between the time that American troops would leave South Vietnam and the time that Saigon would fall to the North or would establish a form of accommodation, there would be a "decent interval." Saigon would bear the responsibility for its political future, and the United States would not be blamed for "losing" Vietnam, like it had been blamed for losing China.

The specific scenario for this plan was to pressure Hanoi militarily and politically to give Saigon freedom of maneuver. South Vietnam could strengthen its military forces, organize its economy, and create popular policies in rural areas—especially in the Mekong River delta south of Saigon. The "decent interval" was never achieved. Soon after America's withdrawal, North Vietnam ordered its divisions to march south in conventional military offensives, complete with tanks and artillery attacks on towns and civilians. Once American air power was halted, Saigon's army could not repel Hanoi's offensive. Furthermore, Saigon was unable to reform itself—rampant corruption, military defection, and uncontrollable dissent shattered any hopes for its continued existence against enemy threats.

Congress and public opinion choked off Nixon's strategic policies and options. Congress reduced Vietnam's economic aid package from $2.3 billion to $1 billion. In 1973, Congress cut off all funding for further U.S. air operations and for any further military operations in Southeast Asia. By 1974, the Pentagon could no longer authorize or budget replacement of Vietnam's military equipment. Congress belligerently overrode the president's veto of the War Powers Act, which limited the president's prerogative to declare war or to send troops abroad for more than sixty days without congressional approval.

Following Cambodia's surrender to the Khmer Rouge on 16 April 1975, Saigon surrendered to Hanoi's troops on 30 April. In the last few days of April, U.S. Ambassador Graham Martin remained publicly optimistic in order to prevent panic. Thus, there was no preparation for the evacuation of the many Vietnamese personnel who had sided with the American forces. The television news coverage showed the chaotic retreat by helicopter of American personnel from the roof of the U.S. embassy. The war was over.

Controversies Surrounding the War

The most common reason given for American commitment to South Vietnam is that the United States was obsessed with anti-Communist ideology. The aggression of the Soviet Union in Eastern Europe and the Korean War, the successful Communist revolution in China, and the nuclear arsenal of Moscow forced the United States to conclude that the whole globe was in danger of Communist domination. The battle for Vietnam was a proxy for the war between the West and Communism—between the United States and the Soviet Union and China.

Domestically, the American public engaged in energetic efforts to cleanse the nation of Communism. On 19 June 1953, just thirteen months before the fall of Dien Bien Phu, Julius and Ethel Rosenberg were executed for high treason against the United States. Their crime was providing the Soviet Union with secrets to produce an atomic bomb. Senators Joseph McCarthy and Pat McCarran held years of public hearings that denounced Communists in government, the foreign service, universities, labor unions, and Hollywood. Many of the accused lost their jobs or went into exile abroad; a few committed suicide. The disruption to American society was felt for decades.

An apologetic view of why the United States maintained the war is that the United States had entered a quagmire and could not get out. Author David Halberstam advanced this view after reporting on the Battle of Ap Bac (January 1963). Essentially, American pride, faith in technology, ignorance of Vietnamese culture, and refusal to develop a noncorrupt and com-

People travel on the Ho Ci Minh Trail in November 2000. During the Vietnam War, the trail was an important supply route for the North Vietnamese. (REUTERS NEWMEDIA INC./CORBIS)

petent ruling force shoved U.S. forces more deeply into the morass of Vietnam.

In the 1970s, Vietnam veterans and critics of the war felt that the government had lied to them about the war. The radical left and the leaders of the antiwar movement criticized American capitalism and imperialism for profiting from the war and crushing the Third World's aspirations to, and sacrifices for, liberation and revolution. These groups aligned themselves with foreign anti-imperialist leadership. They also criticized the U.S. government for creating a national security bureaucracy and an international investment program that attacked dissent at home and impoverished farmers and workers abroad. The most authoritative criticism was voiced by the Committee of Concerned Asian Scholars. Organized by graduate students and professors who specialized in Asian history, the committee's *Bulletin of Concerned Asian Scholars* provided the most thorough criticism of the war in Indochina.

Why Did Hanoi Win?

The United States lost the war mostly because politicians controlled the strategy of the war. The war could have been won if the Pentagon had been given freedom to bomb where, when, and as much as it wanted. Rather than slowly escalating the war, as Johnson did, maximum firepower should have been used immediately against North Vietnam and the Communist-held areas of South Vietnam. The devastating Christmas bombing of 1972 proved that overwhelming force could bring Hanoi to its knees. But it was too late. The final rout of South Vietnam's forces in the spring of 1975 could have been reversed if Congress had released funds for the war effort and had not

declared that all U.S. bombing and military support must end.

The rebuttal to this argument is that such tactics in the mid-1960s would have brought retaliation from China or the Soviet Union. The memory of China's entrance into the Korean War was still a vital force in the strategic decision-making process. The South Vietnamese government was too corrupt, the military too incompetent, and the populace too disloyal to expect that a military victory alone would solve the problems of Vietnam. The thorough destruction of North Vietnam would have sparked uncontrollable anger in the population and would have brought demands that the United States colonize the area with troops and administrators for an unlimited time.

In 1995, twenty years after the war, Robert S. McNamara, secretary of defense under Kennedy and Johnson, pinpointed eleven failures that led to defeat. Among them were that the United States (1) misunderstood the enemy and exaggerated the dangers of the Cold War, (2) misjudged the strengths and weaknesses of its allies, (3) relied too much on the promises of high technology, and (4) failed to organize the executive branch to deal with the political and military issues in an open and critical manner. Even in the twenty-first century, the Vietnam War is still affecting lives in the United States and in Southeast Asia.

Richard C. Kagan

Further Reading
Addington, Larry H. (2000) *America's War in Vietnam: A Short Narrative History*. Bloomington, IN: Indiana University Press.
Duiker, William J. (1994) *Sacred War: Nationalism and Revolution in a Divided Nation*. New York: McGraw-Hill.
———. (2000) *Ho Chi Minh*. New York: Hyperion.
Hynes, Samuel. (1997) *The Soldiers' Tale: Bearing Witness to Modern War*. New York: Penguin Books.
Jamieson, Neil. (1998) *Understanding Vietnam*. Berkeley and Los Angeles: University of California Press.
Kutler, Stanley, ed. (1996) *Encyclopedia of the Vietnam War*. New York: Charles Scribner's Sons.
McNamara, Robert S. (1995) *In Retrospect: The Tragedy and Lessons of Vietnam*. New York: Random House.
Tucker, Spencer, ed. (1998) *The Encyclopedia of the Vietnam War: A Political, Social, and Military History*. Oxford: Oxford University Press.

VIETNAM–UNITED STATES RELATIONS Communism, Containment, the Vietnam War, the end of the Cold War, and globalization have shaped the relations between Vietnam and the United States since 1945. Opinion within the United States and throughout the world was sharply divided as the Vietnam War escalated in the 1960s, and the consequences of this war still linger on.

1945–1956

The Viet Minh, the organization lead by Ho Chi Minh (1890–1969) that was devoted to securing Vietnam's independence from France, controlled Hanoi and six provinces of Vietnam during the Japanese occupation and cooperated with the United States in the common fight against the Japanese. Ho Chi Minh proclaimed the Democratic Republic of Vietnam in September 1945, but the cause of Vietnamese independence was foiled by the Allies at Potsdam in July 1945. The French regained control of their former colony, and the First Indochina War began from 1946. The United States was alarmed by the expansion of Communism in the Cold War period, and in response, Containment became the hallmark of American policy. The United States supported the French, and by 1954 it was bearing 80 percent of the colonial war burden. In 1949 the French had set up the rival Republic of Vietnam (South Vietnam) under Emperor Bao Dai (1913–1997), and the United States recognized it.

With the humiliating defeat of the French at Dien Bien Phu on 7 May 1954, colonial rule was over. The already-convened Geneva Conference partitioned the country at the seventeenth parallel. The question of reunification was to be decided by election two years later. South Vietnam, Laos, and Cambodia were designated as associate states under the protective umbrella of SEATO (Southeast Asia Treaty Organization), which was formed in September 1954. Within a year, U.S. advisers arrived to help President Ngo Dinh Diem (1901–1963) of South Vietnam. The administration of President Dwight D. Eisenhower (served 1952–1960) blocked elections in 1956.

1956–1963

The United States mistakenly believed that Diem was a nationalist alternative to Ho Chi Minh. Eisenhower wrote in his memoirs that 80 percent of the people would have voted for Ho in 1956. Diem was becoming unpopular by alienating all major sections of the population. The Viet Cong, a Communist guerrilla force seeking to reunify the two halves of Vietnam, set up the National Liberation Front (NLF) in December 1960 from the Communist cadres of South Vietnam. From the American viewpoint, the situation was becoming alarming, and the new president, John F. Kennedy (served 1961–1963), picked up where his predecessor had left off. The U.S. administration

made an all-out effort to check Communist expansion in South Vietnam. The two countries signed a treaty resulting in arrival of American support troops, and the U.S. Military Assistance Command was set up.

American aid to South Vietnam from 1955 to 1961 had amounted to $1.8 billion; for the 1962–1963 year alone, it was $700 million. The United States was underwriting half of South Vietnam's government budget, including the full salary of its armed forces. U.S. military advisers numbered 17,000. The NLF increased its strength, and the situation deteriorated in South Vietnam. The Viet Cong controlled about two-thirds of the rural areas. After Diem's assassination, a succession of military generals ruled in South Vietnam. The political instability worsened. The new U.S. president, Lyndon Baines Johnson (served 1963–1968), also believed in what was known as the Domino Theory. If South Vietnam fell to Communism, the reasoning went, so would the rest of Southeast Asia.

1964–1968

The covert operation against North Vietnam, code-named Operational Plan 34A, began in February 1964 with U-2 spy plane missions and commando raids. The U.S. Congress gave sweeping powers to the president in August 1964 after a U.S. naval vessel reportedly was fired upon in the Gulf of Tonkin. North Vietnam saw the United States as the main obstacle to reunification of Vietnam. The United States began bombing North Vietnam in February 1965 in what later was to become a regular feature under Operation Rolling Thunder. U.S. fighter-bombers dropped a total of about 8 million tons of bombs, flown in about 3 million sorties, during the Vietnam War. The Ho Chi Minh Trail, the main supply route to the Viet Cong, came under severe bombing, as did Hanoi and Haiphong Harbor. By 1967 the number of U.S. troops in South Vietnam rose to half a million. The Tet Offensive of January 1968 produced a military stalemate. In March President Johnson announced that he would not be seeking reelection and ordered a partial halt to bombing over North Vietnam. The My Lai massacre of 300 Vietnamese on 16 March 1968 outraged world opinion, and the pictures of carnage from the massacre haunted generations of Americans. Domestic dissent increased in the United States, and the antiwar movement spread among students, liberal clergy, journalists, U.S. senators, and intellectuals. In October a complete bombing halt was declared. About 30,000 American soldiers had lost their lives by 1968. In spite of heavy bombing over the Ho Chi Minh Trail area, 150,000 North Vietnamese soldiers had infiltrated South Vietnam, and supply convoys went on.

HO CHI MINH'S NATIONAL DAY SPEECH

On 2 September 1957 Ho Chi Minh delivered a speech marking the twelfth anniversary of the founding of the Democratic Republic of Vietnam. In the speech he outlined national progress and noted the threat posed by the United States.

Dear compatriots . . .

During the past three years, our people in the north have made great efforts to overcome difficulties and to carry out production through labor. They have recorded great successes in healing the wounds of war, restoring economy, and starting the development of culture, thereby lessening difficulties in the life of the popular masses and gradually improving their living standards, in the delta regions as well as in the mountainous areas. Land reform has fundamentally been completed, the correction of errors committed and the work of developing the success obtained during that reform have been fruitfully carried out in many localities. Agriculture has visibly surpassed the prewar level. In industry, old factories have been restored and new ones built. Order and security have been ensured and national defence strengthened. On behalf of the Party and Government, I congratulate the personnel of branches at all levels for their ardour in serving the people and in building up the fatherland.

Our task for this year is to further increase production and the practice of economy, to strive to fulfill the State Plan, to restore basically North Vietnam's economy, thereby progressively improve the living conditions of our people, and prepare conditions for us to advance in 1958 toward building the north under a long-term plan.

While the north of our country is becoming stronger and stronger, in the south, the American imperialists are intensifying their intervention, increasing their military personnel, catching hold of the South Vietnam economy. Together with the southern authorities, they have been sabotaging the Geneva agreements and the peace and unity of our country. They have resorted to all means of terror and repression with the aim of quenching the patriotism and the will for reunification of our southern compatriots. However the latter, always heroic, have unceasingly broadened their solidarity and struggle for the improvement of their standard of living, for democratic liberties, and for the peaceful reunification of their fatherland. Our government has recently proposed once again to the southern authorities contacts between the two zones and the re-establishment of normal north-south relations with a view to reaching a consultative conference on general elections to reunify the country. However, the southern authorities have obdurately persisted in their refusal, thus going counter to the deep aspirations of the entire people.

Source: Vietnam Information Bulletin. (1957) Rangoon: News Service of the Vietnam Democratic Republic (25 September), no. 38.

1968–1975

Although the Paris peace talks began on 25 January 1969, the Vietnamization program of President Richard Milhous Nixon (served 1969–1974) continued to wage war, using South Vietnamese ground forces and U.S. air power without U.S. ground troops. The Vietnam War became a truly pan-Indochina war when Laos and Cambodia became involved. The publication of the Pentagon Papers in 1971 revealed the covert operation of the secret war in Vietnam, Laos, and Cambodia. The Paris talks made very slow progress, and North Vietnam began the March 1972 Easter Offensive to conquer South Vietnam. The mining of North Vietnam's harbors and the bombing of roads and bridges in May 1972 brought vehement international criticism and renewed antiwar protests in the United States.

In January 1973 the U.S. negotiator Henry Kissinger and North Vietnam's Le Duc Tho resumed stalled negotiations, and the major differences between the opposing sides were solved. On 27 January the United States, North and South Vietnam, and the Provisional Revolutionary Government (PRG), representing the Viet Cong, signed the Paris Peace Accords. Major provisions of the agreement included withdrawal of American troops, a cease-fire, return of prisoners of war, and unification of the North and South. This provided a temporary respite for the corrupt and repressive regime of South Vietnam. On 30 April 1975 Saigon fell, and Vietnamese unification took place in July 1976. The casualty figures in the Vietnam War included 50,000 Americans, 400,000 South Vietnamese, and 900,000 Communists.

1975–Present

Postwar relations between Vietnam and the United States have revolved around the prisoners of war/missing in action (POW/MIA) issue, the establishment of diplomatic relations, American aid for reconstruction of Vietnam, and the refugee problem. Vietnamese premier Pham Van Dong (1906–2000) called for normalization of relations with the United States and requested payment of $3.3 billion for reconstruction as secretly promised by President Nixon after signing the Paris agreement. The United States declined and put forth its own condition of full accounting of the MIAs. Two years later, the United States relaxed its stand to a good-faith attempt at accounting and sent a mission to Hanoi. The prospects of bilateral relations improved in 1978, when Hanoi did not put forth a precondition of economic assistance. The Vietnamese invasion of Cambodia and the Chinese invasion of Vietnam complicated the matter. In 1985 Vietnam

permitted the excavation of a B-52 crash site and began to return the remains of dead American soldiers. A presidential envoy, General John W. Vessey, visited Hanoi in August 1987; Vietnam agreed to cooperate on the MIA issue, and the United States officially agreed to provide humanitarian assistance.

Vietnam's domestic and foreign policies saw a marked change in late 1980s and early 1990s, which paved the way for a better relationship with the United States. The process of economic liberalization, Vietnam's withdrawal from Cambodia, and Vietnam's gain of access to regional and international organizations facilitated normalization of Vietnamese-U.S. relations. POW/MIA accounting, resettlement for Vietnamese boat people, human rights, and religious freedom were key issues. In 1993 the United States supported international bodies helping Vietnam and lifted its economic embargo of the nation. A liaison office was opened in Hanoi in 1994. The United States announced establishment of diplomatic relations on 11 July 1995. Pete Peterson, a former U.S. congressman and POW, became the U.S. ambassador to Vietnam. In January 1997 Vietnam and the United States reached agreement on the resettlement of Vietnamese refugees from countries of first asylum like Thailand and Hong Kong. Bilateral trade agreement negotiations commenced in 1996. Vietnam joined the Asia Pacific Economic Cooperation forum (APEC) in 1998.

Vietnam also sought integration into the world economy and initiated sweeping economic reforms. Trade between Vietnam and the United States amounted to $750 and $900 million respectively in 1998 and 1999. Limited military contact was established along with a program of colonel-level exchange visits. In September 1999 the secretary of state visited Vietnam. A new phase of Vietnamese-U.S. relations was marked with a bilateral trade agreement signed on 13 July 2000. This agreement provided greater mutual market access for Vietnamese and U.S. companies, recognition of and respect for intellectual property rights, and protection of U.S. investment. The transparency clause of the agreement made Vietnamese laws in areas concerning the agreement public, and it included the right of appeal by U.S. citizens. Vietnam insisted on retaining control over telecommunications, not allowing foreign investors more than a 50 percent stake in any investment project.

The first visit by a U.S. president to Hanoi took place in November 2000 and was marked by cordiality. President William Jefferson Clinton (served 1993–2001) had discussions with Vietnamese president Tran Duc Luong (b. 1937) and prime minister Phan Van Khai (b. 1933) regarding mutual concerns. The president paid warm tribute to the Vietnamese people and urged opening of a new era in U.S.-Vietnamese relations. The United States promised $2 million each year over the next three years to help Vietnam implement the trade agreement of July 2000. The United States opened a consulate in Ho Chi Minh City (Saigon).

The election of the conservative Republican U.S. president George W. Bush in 2001 came without Congress having ratified the July 2000 trade pact, however. The U.S. Commission on International Religious Freedom suggested that the trade pact be linked to human rights. Pending ratification of the July 2000 trade pact, Hanoi had waived the 50 percent surcharge on U.S. products, but it has threatened to reimpose it.

Vietnam is slowly moving away from authoritarian control, which would help it in establishing close bilateral relations with the United States. The government has made progress toward allowing religious freedom, recognizing the Vietnam Buddhist Church, the Vietnam Catholic Church, the General Council of Protestant Churches of the South, and other religious organizations. The International Labor Organization has opened an office in Hanoi, and Vietnam has ratified three labor conventions. The authorities are tolerating critical public expression, which was unheard earlier. Nong Duc Manh of the Tay ethnic minority was appointed to the top post of secretary-general of the Communist Party in April. National Assembly members are openly criticizing some of the policies of the government. Not all in the National Assembly are members of the Communist Party, and a former South Vietnamese military officer has been elected to that body.

In spite of lingering Vietnamese and American grievances, the Vietnamese Foundation Act of 2000 had attracted more Vietnamese students to study in American universities. Both countries have moved forward in the process of normalizing relations. The hard-liners in Vietnam and the United States may be skeptical of close relations, but the mutual perception is changing.

Patit Paban Mishra

Further Reading

Addington, Larry H. (2000) *America's War in Vietnam: A Short Narrative History.* Bloomington, IN: Indiana University Press.

Halberstam, David. (1964) *The Making of a Quagmire.* New York: Random House.

Kaiser, David. (2000) *American Tragedy: Kennedy, Johnson, and the Origins of the Vietnam War.* Cambridge, MA: Harvard University Press.

Karnow, Stanley. (1983) *Vietnam: A History.* New York: Viking Press.

McNamara, Robert. (1999) *Argument without End: In Search of Answers to the Vietnam Tragedy.* New York: Public Affairs.

VIETNAMESE With a population of more than 79.9 million (2001 est.), Vietnam ranks as the fourteenth most populous country in the world. In Vietnam's 1999 census, the population was found to be 23.5 percent urban and 76.5 percent rural. Many people still earn their living from agriculture. Over 10 percent of the people (and almost one-third of the urban population) live in either Ho Chi Minh City, formerly Saigon (with a population of over 5 million), or in Hanoi (with a population of almost 3 million). Over 86 percent of the population is ethnic Vietnamese, now known as Kinh.

The non-Kinh population of Vietnam was more than 10.5 million in 1999. There are officially fifty-four ethnic groups in Vietnam, including the Kinh majority. Four of these groups have over a million people: the Tay (once called the Tho), the Thai, the Muong, and the Khmer. Four other groups have well over half a million people: the Chinese (officially known as the Hoa), the Nung, the Hmong (formerly known as the Meo), and the Dao (or Dzao or Yao). Other groups are small in size. Twelve groups have populations under five thousand. Some (such as the Ro-Man, the O Du, and the Brau) number only a few hundred.

Vietnam's population is very diverse. The fifty-four ethnic groups belong to five language families: Austroasiatic, Austronesian (Malayo-Polynesian), Thai-Kadai, Sino-Tibetan, and Hmong-Dao. The Kinh majority and many other groups speak languages within the Austroasiatic family. A cluster of groups speaking Austronesian (Malayo-Polynesian) languages and having matrilineal kinship, the Ede (Rhade), Gia Lai (Jarai), Cham, Raglai, and Chu-ru (Chru), live mainly in and around the central highlands. Some small groups speaking Sino-Tibetan languages are found along the Chinese border in the northern uplands. Only four of these fifty-four groups have historically lived in the lowlands: The Khmer (mainly in the lower Mekong Delta), the Cham (mostly in the central coastal plain), the Chinese (mainly in urban areas), and the majority Kinh population.

Traditionally, ethnic Vietnamese lived in lowland areas and lived mainly by growing rice in paddy fields. Very few Vietnamese lived in the uplands. Lack of paddy fields, fear of malaria and other dangerous diseases, the presence of sometimes-unfriendly tribal groups, and the periodic appearance of bandit gangs made Vietnamese very reluctant to live in upland areas.

But with population pressure rising, modern medicine available, and the security provided by the modern nation-state, in the past fifty years over 4 (perhaps 5) million Kinh have, often under state-organized programs, moved into upland areas previously inhabited only by non-Kinh groups; many of the immigrant Kinh live in urban areas, along main highways, or in and around state farms and forest enterprises. Population movement continues, especially from rural to urban areas, from north to south, and from lowlands to uplands. There is also some spontaneous migration of non-Kinh ethnic households (that is, Nung and Tay) from portions of the northern mountain region (that is, Cao Bang) to the central highlands (especially Dak Lak and Lam Dong Provinces). The rest have traditionally lived in upland areas.

Characteristics of the Vietnamese (Kinh) Majority

The Vietnamese family has long been the most important and most stable part of Vietnamese society. Descent through the male line (patrilineal descent) is very important. Even today, some families still gather to celebrate the death anniversaries *(ngay gio)* of shared male ancestors, especially fathers and grandfathers. These are not usually sad occasions, but happy times in which people remember their shared roots and build solidarity among living family members.

Children are raised to appreciate the tremendous importance of the family as the primary and most reliable source of identity, emotional support, and help in time of need. As children learn to speak, they are taught about family relationships and the proper terms of address and self-reference that accompany them. Vietnamese have no general term equivalent to the English "you," and they rarely use the word for "I" or "me." Instead Vietnamese children address other people in the family as "mother" or "father" or "father's older brother" or "father's younger brother" or "mother's brother" or "father's sister" and so on. They refer to themselves not as "I," but as "child" or "niece" or "nephew." They call older siblings "older brother" or "older sister" and refer to themselves as "younger sibling."

As children grow up, go to school, and meet a wider range of people, they call most other people by kin terms much of the time, as if all of society were one big family. Choice of which kin term to use with which person is guided by gender, relative age and status, degree of intimacy or friendship, and the nature of the occasion. What a Vietnamese calls someone and the way he or she refers to himself or herself influences the way the two people will behave toward each other and what they can expect from each other.

A Vietnamese girl on her moped in Hanoi in 1995. (CATHERINE KARNOW/CORBIS)

This way of talking with each other is an important part of being Vietnamese. Vietnamese often seem to be less concerned about their own individual feelings and desires than many other people. But they may also be somewhat less concerned with universal principles and with people in general. What they are greatly concerned with is a very particular set of interpersonal relationships with specific people. Their identity and sense of self-worth are intimately connected to their relationships with parents, family, neighbors, teachers, classmates, colleagues, and coworkers.

Within this complex web of relationships people must perform many roles, always adjusting their behavior to fit the particular position they are in within a specific social context. Vietnamese society is hierarchical. One is expected to defer to those who are older or who have higher status, and to nurture and to instruct those younger or of lower status. These significant other people in one's life are always evaluating the way one performs one's various social roles. The acceptance, approval, and admiration of these people are very important to most Vietnamese and many people often gladly modify their behavior to achieve this kind of social recognition.

Over the past fifty years or so a number of mass organizations have been created and many (but far from all) people belong to one or more of them. There are organizations for women, for farmers, for youth, for the elderly, for veterans. These organizations extend from the national level down to the village. They are guided and coordinated by the Fatherland Front, an umbrella organization that in turn receives guidance from the Communist Party and includes senior party officials in its leadership as well as representatives of a variety of religious and ethnic groups. To a large extent these organizations, in addition to government structures and Communist Party organization, incorporate all of Vietnam's ethnic groups and regions into one national society.

Characteristics of Non-Kinh Ethnic Groups

More than 10.5 million citizens of Vietnam, nearly 14 percent of the population, are categorized as non-Kinh persons. The official set of fifty-three ethnic categories other than Kinh seems to lump together some groups that may well be considered to be separate ethnic groups. In any case, however these groups are categorized and labeled, the reality is that there are hundreds of relatively small local groups with somewhat distinctive dialects and ways of life. Although some of these groups may have similar cultures and share a common ethnic identity, the extent to which they form a meaningful social unit is problematic.

The three non-Kinh ethnic groups who live mainly in the lowlands are distinctive. The Khmer, who lived in the Mekong Delta long before the arrival of the Kinh, number over a million and are Vietnam's fifth-largest ethnic group. Most still live in the lower half of the Mekong Delta. Most Khmer follow a form of Buddhism similar to that found in Cambodia, Laos, Thailand, and Myanmar called Theravada or Hinayana Buddhism. This is in contrast to the Mahayana Buddhism that is predominant among Kinh Buddhists. The Buddhist pagoda is usually the center of Khmer community life, and monks often are highly influential and respected community leaders.

The Chinese (Hoa), who number about 870,000, making them Vietnam's sixth-largest ethnic population, are among Vietnam's most highly urbanized groups. They have levels of income, life expectancy, and education that are comparable to those of the Kinh majority. There is a large ethnic Chinese population in Ho Chi Minh City.

The Cham, of whom there are only a little over 130,000, live mostly in villages along the central coast, especially in Ninh Thuan and Binh Thuan, although there is a Cham community in the Mekong Delta near the Cambodian border. The Cham have a matrilineal kinship system, tracing descent through the female line, and a young married couple usually lives with or near the bride's parents rather than those of the groom. Cham religion contains combinations of Hindu (Brahman) and Islamic influences that survive from earlier periods and veneration of indigenous spirits.

The remaining forty-nine ethnic non-Kinh groups in Vietnam have traditionally lived in upland areas, and the vast majority of them still do. It is difficult to generalize about them because both within and between groups there are many differences in economic levels, social organization, health status, ecological conditions, religion, and ways of life. And almost everywhere change is occurring at a rapid pace. In fact, one might say that the two most important characteristics of ethnic non-Kinh upland areas now are diversity and change.

The great majority of upland ethnic nationalities live in one of two big areas. The first is the northern mountain region, extending along the border with Laos from about Vinh and along the border with Laos and then China all the way back to the sea. The second area is usually called the central highlands in English and Tay Nguyen (Western Plateau) by the Vietnamese. It is composed of upland areas along the border with Cambodia. Between Hue and Vinh the ethnic minority population is very small because the terrain is highly broken and mountain slopes are very steep, while the flat plain is densely populated by Kinh. Fifty or sixty years ago most of the uplands were densely forested and most people lived there much as they had for centuries.

Family, kin, and community still make up the meaningful social worlds of most ethnic minorities. Most of these people traditionally lived in relatively small villages, made up of sometimes only four or five houses and rarely as many as a hundred. Most houses were built on stilts with wooden beams, bamboo walls, and thatch roofs.

The majority of upland people lived by cutting down and burning small patches of forest and then planting in the ashes, a practice often called swidden, or "slash and burn," agriculture. A cleared field would typically be used for two to four years and then abandoned for five to twenty years. Although sometimes erroneously called nomads, most people moved only from spot to spot within a fixed area. These upland fields were usually planted with rice or corn, interplanted with a variety of beans as well as gourds and other crops. Pigs and chickens were commonly raised, but in small numbers. Other domesticated animals commonly found in upland areas were oxen, water buffalo, ducks, goats, and dogs. The particular mix in the way each group earned a living was determined by local conditions. Some groups who lived in valleys cultivated wet rice in paddy fields. In some places, people created terraced fields on hillsides. Farming was supplemented by hunting, fishing, and gathering wild vegetables and tubers from the forest.

The forest not only provided much of people's food, but also was a source of medicine, building materials, fuel, and water. Few if any villages were completely isolated. There was always some trade, but more were relatively self-sufficient. Life was difficult in some ways, but very satisfying in others.

Over recent decades, however, change has been taking place at an accelerating rate. These changes have disrupted familiar ways of life, causing problems and providing benefits. Access to modern medicine and other innovations (such as mosquito nets and iodized salt) has reduced infant mortality rates and increased life expectancy. Access to education has increased significantly. Many people now have electricity in their homes. Many own radios, flashlights, raincoats, kitchen utensils, and other consumer goods that make life more convenient. Quite a few have bicycles, and some have television sets, and even VCRs and motorcycles. Upland ethnic minorities are still poorer than the average Vietnamese, but they are better off in many ways than they once were.

At the same time, population density is much higher than before, because of both in-migration and natural increase in population. The forests have been reduced both in size and in quality. Biodiversity has plummeted. It is much more difficult for people to hunt and fish and gather wild food. Water and decent agricultural land are in short supply in many places. There is little room to increase wet rice paddies, and in swidden fields the yields are declining because the fragile upland soils are overworked.

The uplands contain many opportunities and many challenges. People do not always agree on how much change they want, at what rate, or how to achieve it. But it is difficult for members of an ethnic group, or even for uplanders as a whole, including Kinh, to work together to devise common solutions to shared problems. Throughout much of the uplands, but especially in the northern mountain region, ethnic groups are scattered across different districts and provinces.

Villages are grouped to form a commune, the lowest administrative unit in Vietnam, and communes are combined to form a district, which is like a county. Out of 109 districts, 59 contain 10 or more different ethnic groups, and 8 contain 15 or more ethnic groups. And in the northern mountain region 97 percent of all communes contain more than one ethnic group. Since people are scattered in villages that are within different communes and districts, even provinces, with dozens of other ethnic groups, also scattered, living around them, their meaningful social world is usually still limited to family, kin, and village. The basic model of social structure in the uplands is one of hundreds of rather tightly knit local groups, unevenly overlaid with national institutions that reach out from Hanoi.

Religion in Vietnam

It is difficult to say how many Vietnamese follow any particular religion. The religious beliefs and practices of most Vietnamese do not fit neatly into any single category. And this does not bother them. Estimates of how many people in Vietnam "follow" a particular religion vary widely, depending on how terms are defined.

The 1999 census reported that over 80 percent of the population of Vietnam had "no religion." This estimate counted only those who are formal, practicing members of an officially recognized religious organization and can be misleading. Other estimates, however, are often rather high, usually based upon a very loose definition of "religion" and without any sound empirical basis.

Buddhism is by far the largest organized religion in Vietnam. Although the 1999 census counted only a little over 7 million Buddhists, other estimates go above 20 million. Mahayana Buddhism is predominant among the Kinh, whereas over a million people (mostly in the Mekong Delta and mostly Khmer) follow Theravada Buddhism. Most Vietnamese have been influenced by Buddhist thought, however, and it is difficult to draw a line between Buddhists and non-Buddhists.

The second-largest organized religion in Vietnam is Christianity, which gained a foothold in the seventeenth century. There may be as many as 8 to 10 million Catholics in Vietnam, although the 1999 census counted only a little over 5 million. Protestantism came to Vietnam much later, but it has experienced rapid growth since the late 1980s, especially among upland ethnic minority groups. The 1999 census counted only 261,000 Protestants, but by some estimates there are as many as 2 million.

The 1999 census counted only 63,000 Muslims. Other estimates, which range up to 1 million, seem high. There seem to be few, if any, Kinh who follow Islam. Most Muslims in Vietnam are Cham, Khmer, or expatriates from Islamic countries.

Hoa Hao, a reformed Buddhist sect stressing simplicity of worship, is sometimes estimated to have as many as 2 million followers. The 1999 census counted about 1.2 million Hoa Hao. Most Hoa Hao are concentrated in the western portion of the Mekong Delta, mainly in and around the city of Long Xuyen in An Giang Province.

Cao Dai is an eclectic religion, drawing on Buddhism, Christianity, and Vietnamese tradition. It probably has 1 to 2 million followers, mainly in Tay Ninh Province and in the Mekong Delta.

Vietnamese in the Twenty-First Century

Vietnam is still a poor country. Its growing population is already stressing its environment and will continue to do so in coming decades. Under these conditions, the Vietnamese are aspiring to achieve rapid economic growth that is both equitable and sustainable and simultaneously to attain more democracy and greater rule by law. Such aspirations not only require changes in laws and policies, which are already taking place, but also ultimately will require changes in institutions, in behavior, and in ways of looking at the world.

At the same time, there is a strong desire to preserve a distinctive Vietnamese identity that retains the best elements of Vietnamese culture and tradition. This ambitious agenda will pose an immense challenge to the Vietnamese people in the twenty-first century. But they have made progress in recent years and are determined to continue to move forward.

Neil L. Jamieson

Further Reading

Borton, Lady. (1995) *After Sorrow: An American among the Vietnamese.* New York: Viking.

Dang Nghiem Van, Chu Thai Son, and Luu Hung. (2000) *Ethnic Minorities in Vietnam.* Hanoi, Vietnam: World Publishers.

Do Phuong. (1998) *Vietnam: Image of the Community of 54 Ethnic Groups.* Hanoi, Vietnam: Ethnic Cultures Publishing House.

Duong Thu Huong. (1993) *Paradise of the Blind.* Trans. by Phan Huy Duong and Nina McPherson. New York: Penguin Books.

Gourou, Pierre. (1955) *Peasants of the Tonkin Delta.* New Haven, CT: Human Relations Area Files.

Hickey, Gerald C. (1964) *Village in Vietnam.* New Haven, CT: Yale University Press.

———. (1993) *Shattered World: Adaptation and Survival among Vietnam's Highland Peoples during the Vietnam War.* Philadelphia: University of Pennsylvania Press.

Hiebert, Murray. (1996) *Chasing the Tiger: A Portrait of the New Vietnam.* New York: Kodansha America.

Ho Anh Thai. (2001) *Women on the Island.* Seattle, WA: University of Washington Press.

Jamieson, Neil L. (1993) *Understanding Vietnam.* Berkeley and Los Angeles: University of California Press.

Kamm, Henry. (1997) *Dragon Ascending.* New York: Arcade Publishing.

Luong, Hy Van. (1992) *Revolution in the Village.* Honolulu, HI: University of Hawaii Press.

VIETNAMESE LANGUAGE The origins and affinities of the Vietnamese language are complex and have long been debated by scholars. The language now appears to have developed from the Mon Khmer family within the larger Austroasiatic language group. There are indications of influence from Tai languages, especially the use of tones. It also seems to exhibit some Austronesian influence, perhaps from ancient relatives of the Cham and Ede (Rhade) in prehistoric times.

In historical times there has been a very strong Chinese influence, especially in vocabulary. The word *Viet* comes from the Chinese word *yue*, which was used broadly to refer to non-Chinese ethnic groups south of the Chang (Yangtze) River. *Nam*, or *nan* in Chinese, means "south" or "southern." Some terms have been thoroughly Vietnamized and now are no longer perceived as foreign terms. Examples would include the word for "citizen," which is *cong dan*, and the word for "virtue" or "morality," which is *dao duc*. But other terms and phrases are still considered to be Sino-Vietnamese. These expressions are still heard, but not as much as they used to be.

More recently some French words have come into common use, with some of them becoming what now seem to be purely Vietnamese words. For example, the Vietnamese word for "station," *ga*, comes from the French *gare*. Similarly, the word for "doll," *bup be* comes from the French *poupée*. The word for "pump" (*bom*) comes from *pompe*; the word for "chocolate" (*so co la*) from *chocolat*. English vocabulary has even more recently been entering the language, but to a much lesser extent than Chinese or even French words. Many English-language words have appeared quite recently and have not yet been Vietnamized. One occasionally sees in Vietnam today words like *club*, or *computer*, or *video*, even though Vietnamese already have words that mean exactly or much the same thing.

Because each syllable is written separately and usually has a meaning (as in Viet Nam), Vietnamese seems to be, and is often called, a monosyllabic language. But compound and psuedocompound words are quite common. The words for "citizen," "virtue," and "Viet Nam" are compound words in Vietnamese. The Vietnamese word for "airplane," for example, is *may bay*. *May* means "machine" and *bay* means "to fly."

Vietnamese is also uninflected. There are no endings to distinguish tense or number or gender, subject from object, and so on. But future tense can be indicated by adding *se* in front of the verb. Thus "will fly" would be *se bay*. The past tense of "fly," "flew," would be *da bay*. Vietnamese speakers, however, use *se* and *da* sparingly, usually adding them only when necessary to avoid misunderstanding. Whether some action has already happened or will happen in the future is usually quite clear from context.

Vietnamese is also a tonal language. There are six distinct tones in the north and five in the south. In the example given above, the syllable *may*, which with a high rising tone means "to fly," would mean "eyebrow" with a low falling tone, or "lucky" with a level tone. The tone is thus an integral part of the word.

For many centuries, Vietnamese used the Chinese writing system. Classical Chinese was the official language of government and a common vehicle for literary expression. A system of writing called *Nom*, which recombined elements of Chinese characters to represent Vietnamese words, gradually evolved. By the thirteenth century it had begun to take shape as a useful system of writing and by the fifteenth century it had become a respectable and thoroughly adequate means of writing prose and poetry of the highest order. In the seventeenth century, Christian missionaries developed a phonetic, Romanized alphabet for writing Vietnamese. Early in the twentieth century this alphabet came into popular use. It soon replaced both *Nom* and Chinese characters. This writing system is now known as the "national language" (*quoc ngu*). Very few Vietnamese can now read Chinese characters and *Nom* can now be read only by a few dozen professional scholars.

In Vietnamese a person's family name (*ho*) comes first, and one's given name (what is often called the "first name" in English) comes last. Vietnamese are known mainly by their given names rather than by their family name. Let us take, for example, a Mr. Nguyen Van Ba. Nguyen would be his family name, Van his middle name, and Ba his given name. He would typically introduce himself and be addressed and referred to by others as "Mr. Ba" (*Ong* Ba). One reason for this may be that some family names (like Nguyen) are so common that most people would know many men with the family name of Nguyen but far fewer with the given name of Ba.

A final aspect of the language worth noting is the way Vietnamese address and refer to others and refer to themselves. The first person singular pronoun, "I" or "me" in English, *toi* in Vietnamese, is not often used in daily speech by native speakers of Vietnamese. There is not even a single word like the all-purpose pronoun "you" to use to address the person to whom one is speaking in Vietnamese. Instead of using somewhat neutral and impersonal pronouns like "I" or "me" or "you," Vietnamese usually use terms of kinship that express a relationship they have to the person to whom they are speaking.

In English, a child will address his or her mother as "mother." A Vietnamese child will not only do this, but will also refer to himself or herself (replacing both "I" and "me") as "child" (*con*). Even when speaking with people who are not relatives, kin terms are normally used, both for address and for self-reference. For example, older men are often addressed by one of several terms Vietnamese have for what we call "uncle." Depending on relative age, status, and degree of intimacy, a young Vietnamese may address an older man as "father's older brother" (*bac*) or "father's younger brother" (*chu*). He or she would then refer to himself or herself as *chau*, which can mean "niece" or "nephew" or "grandchild." Other common forms of address that take the place of "you" are "older brother" (*anh*), "older sister" (*chi*), and "father's sister" (*co*). The speaker would refer to himself or herself as *em* (meaning "younger sibling") or *chau*. Children are taught to make fine distinctions when using such terms with a wide variety of people as they are learning to talk.

As these examples clearly show, there are different terms for mother's relatives and father's relatives, and for older and younger siblings in the speaker's generation and his parents' generation. People also always take account of the relative age and status of the people to whom they are speaking. The Vietnamese language is thus hierarchical in nature. The English terms "I" and "you" imply a relationship of relative independence and equality, while Vietnamese speak in ways that express inequality and relationship. For some time, the Communist Party in Vietnam tried to introduce the use of the word "comrade" (*dong chi*) to reduce the sense of hierarchy in Vietnamese interpersonal relationships, but today the word is hardly ever spoken outside of party circles.

Neil Jamieson

Further Reading
Herbert, Patricia, and Anthony Milner. (1989) *South-East Asia Languages and Literatures: A Select Guide*. Honolulu, HI: University of Hawaii Press.

VIETNAMESE, OVERSEAS

VIETNAMESE, OVERSEAS In the early part of the twentieth century, the *Viet Kieu* (Vietnamese sojourners abroad) living in small settlements around the Indochina peninsula could be counted in thousands of families. By the century's end, they numbered 3 million in approximately seventy countries around the world.

Precolonial and Colonial *Viet Kieu*

Before French colonization (1859–1954), most *Viet Kieu* lived in Laos, Cambodia, Thailand, and southern China. While short-distance moves were usually made for economic reasons, long journeys often had a political or religious dimension. Diplomats and artisans traveled to China, while many Vietnamese in Siam (now Thailand) were refugees from nineteenth-century religious persecutions. With the exception of Vietnamese Catholic villages along the Mekong River in Thailand, few traces remain of these precolonial movements. Today's Vietnamese diaspora is made up of twentieth-century migrants.

Their first community was formed as a result of French colonialism. Ocean travel opened emigration to destinations beyond the Indochina peninsula. The French transported prisoners to New Caledonia and the New Hebrides, followed in later years by plantation and mine workers. During the two World Wars, workers were sent to French factories in Europe. Between the wars, students were sent to universities in France. And a small number of Vietnamese simply traveled to France. Among these was the man later known as Ho Chi Minh (1892–1969), who learned his Communism in Paris (1910s), returned home with it (1940s), and led an independence war that ended with the French withdrawal (1954). On independence, some Vietnamese associated with the colonial power went to France. Traditions of study in Paris persisted during the war against the United States, as some families sought to spare their children from military conscription. By the end of the war (1975), France was home to over fifty thousand *Viet Kieu*.

Prior to independence, other political dissenters also chose the route of emigration. Intellectuals joined Phan Boi Chau (1867–1940) in Japan (1905–1909). Independence activists worked in southern China and Thailand. Existing communities of Vietnamese in Thailand were later joined by fifty thousand *Viet Kieu* from Laos, who fled the French army's violent reoccupation of Laos (1946), crossing the Mekong into Thailand. However, the refugees' support for Ho Chi Minh and Thailand's alliance with the United States made their presence there increasingly awkward. Some returned to North Vietnam (1960–1964). Others were subject to restrictions on their civil rights, becoming eligible for Thai nationality only after Vietnam's 1995 entry into the Association of Southeast Asian Nations.

Postcolonial *Viet Kieu*

A second community was formed in the wake of the Vietnam War. At the end of the war, 140,000 Vietnamese fled with the U.S. forces. They formed the nucleus of today's population of more than 1 million Vietnamese in the United States. Later refugees also went to Australia, Canada, China, France, Great Britain, and West Germany. They traveled by boat, via refugee camps in Southeast Asia, by land into China and Cambodia, and by airplane in a program designed to stem the flow of boat people. Yet the flow continued for twenty years. At first, most refugees were people associated with the old regime in South Vietnam. In the late 1970s, they were ethnic Chinese, expelled as a result of Vietnam's conflict with China (1979). By the 1980s, many boat people were northerners, tired of the failures of Communism and attracted by dreams of "paradise" in the West.

Resettlement policies varied. In China, the 300,000 refugees were sent to state farms near the border. Western countries, however, attempted to disperse them. Inhabitants of towns throughout North America, Australia, and Europe remember the arrival of a few Vietnamese families during the boat-people crisis. They also remember their departure, as they moved on to California (Orange county's Little Saigon), Sydney (the suburb of Cabramatta), and Paris (the thirteenth arrondissement). But many *Viet Kieu* are now reluctant to stay in Vietnamese suburbs. Socioeconomic success, acquired through commerce and education, is expressed in a move away and integration into a local middle class. For many, the Little Saigons have now become places to shop rather than live. They

HOI AN—WORLD HERITAGE SITE

A UNESCO World Heritage Site since 1999, the Vietnamese port city of Hoi An is a colorful demonstration of the divergent cultural influences on Vietnam between the fifteenth and nineteenth centuries.

A Vietnamese grocery store in Garden Grove, California, in 1986. (JOSEPH SOHM; CHROMOSOHM INC./CORBIS)

are places, too, from where the *Viet Kieu* send remittances to their relatives in Vietnam, which since the early 1980s have had an important impact on the country's economy.

Gradual integration also characterized the political outlook of the *Viet Kieu*. On arrival, many sought to hasten their return home, forming organizations dedicated to the overthrow of the Communist government. In Vietnam, the term *Viet Kieu* became associated with anti-Communism. In the 1990s, however, many *Viet Kieu* returned to Vietnam, holding Western passports stamped with tourist or business visas issued by the Vietnamese government. Sentiments of anti-Communism are now expressions of community membership more often than strong political beliefs.

A third *Viet Kieu* community was formed beginning in 1980, through Vietnam's repayment of its national debt to the Soviet Union with the labor of 300,000 workers in the factories of the Soviet Union, Czechoslovakia, and East Germany. After the collapse of European Communism, many stayed behind. Leaving the factories, they established trading businesses and played an influential role in Central Europe's underground economies. Many retain Vietnamese passports and—untainted by anti-Communism—they are not known as *Viet Kieu*. The current term *nguoi Viet Nam o nuoc ngoai* ("Vietnamese living abroad") includes this "loyal" population in a broader category, distinguishing them from politicized communities.

Overseas Vietnamese in the Twenty-First Century

The overseas Vietnamese make up three communities, formed as a result of Vietnam's relations with its former colonial ruler (France) and the Cold War

superpowers (the United States, the Soviet Union, and China). These relations, of collaboration or opposition, molded the attitudes of the expatriate community toward Vietnam. But in the twenty-first century, as their socioeconomic integration proceeds and memories of the Cold War fade, the depoliticization of these communities is underway. Meanwhile, new overseas migrations are taking place, with journeys of marital union and family reunion. Contract workers travel to Taiwan, Korea, Laos, and Samoa, and prostitutes seek lucrative markets in Cambodia, Malaysia, Singapore, and Hong Kong. The overseas Vietnamese used to resemble the Cubans in Florida, defined by their opposition to Communism. Vietnam's twenty-first-century emigrants may better be compared to those of other Southeast Asian countries. Most are contract workers, illegal immigrants, and businesspeople.

Andrew Hardy

Further Reading
Alley, Rewi. (1980) *Refugees from Vietnam in China.* Beijing: New World Press.
Bousquet, Gisèle L. (1991). *Behind the Bamboo Hedge: The Impact of Homeland Politics in the Parisian Vietnamese Community.* Ann Arbor, MI: University of Michigan Press.
Dang, Phong. (2000) "The Vietnamese Diaspora: Returning and Integrating into Vietnam." *Revue Européenne des Migrations Internationales* 16, 1: 183–205.
Goscha, Christopher E. (1999) *Thailand and the Southeast Asian Networks of the Vietnamese Revolution, 1885–1954.* Richmond, U.K.: Curzon Press.
Hardy, Andrew. (2000) "Des Valeurs de l'amitié: Esquisse ethnographique des travailleurs vietnamiens dans les pays socialistes de l'Europe." *Revue Européenne des Migrations Internationales* 16, 1: 235–246.
Kelly, Gail Paradise. (1977) *From Vietnam to America: A Chronicle of the Vietnamese Immigration to the United States.* Boulder, CO: Westview Press.
Poole, Peter A. (1970) *The Vietnamese in Thailand: A Historical Perspective.* Ithaca, NY, and London: Cornell University Press.
Robinson, W. Courtland. (1998). *Terms of Refuge: The Indochinese Exodus and the International Response.* London and New York: Zed Books.
Thomas, Mandy. (1999) *Dreams in the Shadows: Vietnamese-Australian Lives in Transition.* Saint Leonards, Australia: Allen and Unwin.
Wain, Barry. 1981) *The Refused: The Agony of the Indochinese Refugees.* New York: Simon & Schuster.

VIJAYANAGARA EMPIRE Vijayanagara, the "City of Victory," the greatest of all medieval Hindu capitals, was founded in 1336 CE by Hukka and Bukka, two princes of a local family, the Sangama. This dynasty rapidly extended its control over the whole of southern India. The power vacuum left in this region after the disruption caused by the Muslim invaders in the early years of the fourteenth century created the ideal political situation for the emergence of a new ruling house.

The Vijayanagara empire, until 1565, the year of its fall, was ruled by three dynasties, the Sangama (1336–1485), the Saluva (1485–1505), and the Tuluva (1505–1570). The most distinguished king, not only in Vijayanagara history but also in the history of medieval India, was Krishnadevaraya (1509–1529). His campaigns against both the sultans of the Deccan in the north and the Gajapati dynasty of Orissa in the east were successful. At the same time, he maintained good relations with the Portuguese on the west coast. Krishnadevaraya was an accomplished scholar and poet in Sanskrit and Telugu, and his reign saw arts, architecture, engineering, and learning flourish. He renovated and built temples throughout the empire to which he gave generous gifts; he also endowed religious institutions.

Krishnadevaraya's half-brother Achyutaraya (1529–1542) succeeded him and continued the same enlightened policy. However, in the power struggle following his death, the faction led by Ramaraya, Krishnadevaraya's son-in-law, triumphed, and Sadashiva, Krishnadevaraya's nephew, was placed on the throne with Ramaraya as regent. The regent became involved in rivalries among the Deccan sultans with fatal consequences. At the end of a long series of alliances and wars, resulting in territorial gains and increased political power for Vijayanagara, the Deccan sultans buried their differences and in a joint action defeated Ramaraya in a decisive battle at Talikota (now in northern Karnataka) in January 1565. The invading armies of the sultans occupied, sacked, and torched the capital for six months. The Vijayanagara state never fully recovered, and Vijayanagara ceased to be the capital. Two years later, tigers were reportedly roaming through the ruins.

It has often been stated that Vijayanagara was founded in an attempt to establish a new political and moral order based on traditional Hindu cultural values. Although the wars against the sultans of the Deccan were frequent, their cause was more political and economical than religious. On the one hand, the victims of Vijayanagara expansion were not always Muslim, but often were minor Hindu dynasties. On the other hand, a strong contingent of Muslim troops was crucial for the successes of the Vijayanagara army. The Vijayanagara power, however, limited the expansion of the Muslim power in the Deccan for over two centuries and created the conditions for the flourishing of Hindu culture and institutions.

A. L. Dallapiccola

Further Reading

Dallapiccola, Anna Libera, ed. (1985) *Vijayanagara: City and Empire*. Stuttgart, Germany: Franz Steiner Verlag.

Michell, George. (1995) *Art and Architecture of Southern India, Vijayanagara and the Successor States*. London: Cambridge University Press.

Stein, Burton. (1989) *Vijayanagara*. Cambridge, U.K.: Cambridge University Press.

Verghese, Anila. (1995) *Religious Traditions at Vijayanagara, as Revealed through its Monuments*. New Delhi: Manohar and American Institute of Indian Studies.

VINDHYA MOUNTAINS

The Vindhya Mountains, an east-west range in central India, divide the subcontinent into two major geographical zones, the Indo-Gangetic Plain to the north and the Deccan Plateau to the south. The range reaches heights of 500–1,500 meters, and forms the northern edge of the Narmada Valley. Uniting the Eastern and Western Ghats at its two extremities, the range forms one side of the triangle known as the Deccan Plateau. The Vindhyas contain some of the oldest rocks in India—granites, schists, and marbles—and are geologically the northern front of Gondwanaland where it abuts the Himalayas. The Indo-Gangetic Plain is the infilling of a trough between the two.

The Vindhyas have been of crucial importance in the historical geography of India because they were sufficiently high to dissuade most invading groups from pushing further south into the Deccan Plateau, instead deflecting invaders eastward along the Gangetic Plain. The Vindhyas are largely inhabited by such important Scheduled Tribes as the Bhils.

Paul Hockings

VISAYAN ISLANDS

(2000 est. pop. 15.5 million). Surrounded by the Visayan Sea and the Philippine Sea, the Visayan Islands lie in the central part of the Philippine archipelago, between Luzon and Mindanao Islands. The group includes several major islands: Bohol (land area 3,865 square kilometers), Cebu (land area 4,422 square kilometers), Leyte (land area 7,214 square kilometers), Negros (land area 12,705 square kilometers), Panay (land area 11,515 square kilometers), Samar (land area 13,080 square kilometers), and Masbate (land area 3,269 square kilometers). There are also hundreds of small islands in the group.

The Visayas are traditionally divided into three geographic areas: the Eastern Visayas (Samar and Leyte) with a population of 3,610,355 (2000 census); the Western Visayas (Negros and Panay) with a population of 6,208,733 (2000 census); and the Central Visayas (Bohol and Cebu) with a population of 5,701,064 (2000 census).

The Eastern Visayas are the least-developed and least-populated islands in this group, due to frequent typhoons during the wet season; because they act as a buffer, the other Visayas enjoy a mild climate suitable to intensive agriculture. The population in the Eastern Visayas relies largely on fishing and agriculture (abaca or Manila hemp, a fiber from the banana leafstalk; coconuts; rice; and corn). Copper mining, deforestation, and industrial development have caused serious ecological problems on Samar Island.

Better developed due to the mild climate, the Western Visayas are important commercial and agricultural centers for the Philippine economy and produce sugar (both for internal consumption and for export), abaca, coconuts, corn, tobacco, minerals, and timber.

The Central Visayas are among most developed and most densely populated regions in the Philippines. Cebu, the first capital of the Philippines, is situated here. The Central Visayas host many industries, including textiles, footwear, mining (coal, copper, limestone, silver), food processing, and furniture. This area is also a major tourist attraction.

For centuries before European colonization, Malays from the Malay Peninsula and Borneo Island successfully traded with the Philippine Archipelago and often settled there. The modern history of the Visayas began on 7 April 1521, when Ferdinand Magellan (c. 1480–1521), the Portuguese explorer, landed on Cebu Island. Almost half a century later, the Spanish, led by Miguel Lopez de Legazpi (c. 1510–1572), established a settlement and a Catholic mission on Cebu Island on 27 April 1565, making Cebu City a major center for the further colonization of the archipelago.

Rafis Abazov

Further Reading
Guillermo, Artemio R., and May Kyi Win. (1997) *Historical Dictionary of the Philippines.* Lanham, MD: Scarecrow Press.
Schirmer, Daniel, and Stephen Rosskamm Shalom, eds. (1986) *The Philippines Reader: A History of Colonialism, Neocolonialism, Dictatorship, and Resistance.* Boston: South End Press.
Steinberg, David J. (1994) *The Philippines.* 3d ed. Boulder, CO: Westview Press.

VISHAKHAPATNAM (2001 est. pop. 1.1 million). Vishakhapatnam (Vizagapatam, or Vizag) is an important industrial city and seaport on the east coast of India, and the headquarters of Vishakhapatnam District in the northeast corner of Andhra Pradesh state. The city lies on a small bay 600 kilometers northeast of Madras and includes the old resort of Waltair, reputed to have the finest beach in India. The population was 752,000 in 1991, having grown eighteenfold since the beginning of the century. Vishakhapatnam has a large oil refinery and a shipbuilding industry. Manganese ore, rice, and sugar are also produced in the area.

A British factory, established in Vishakhapatnam, early in the seventeenth century, was captured by the French in 1757, but was recovered within a few months. There was a minor sepoy revolt in 1780; otherwise, the town has been remarkably peaceful and prosperous in modern times. Sixteen kilometers north of the city is the thirteenth-century sanctuary of Simhachalam, with a stupa and monastery secluded in the wooded Kailasa Hills. The monastery remains a popular site of Hindu worship.

Paul Hockings

VIVEKANANDA, SWAMI (1863–1902), Indian philosopher and religious leader. Swami Vivekananda (meaning "the bliss of spiritual discrimination") is the monastic name of Narendranath Datta. He was a major philosopher, author, social reformer, and religious and intellectual leader of India and the world. He brought back its original universalism to Hinduism, made it available to India and the world, and included service to humanity as an integral element of personal salvation.

Narendranath Datta was born in an affluent Westernized Bengali family in 1863. He received his bachelor's degree from Calcutta University in l884. He was an accomplished classical musician and singer and knew Bengali, English, Sanskrit, Hindi, and French well. A member of the Brahmo sect, a vigorous monistic reformed version of Hinduism, Datta came in contact with Ramakrishna Paramhansa (1836–1886) in 1881. Ramakrishna was not formally learned but had an immense knowledge of all religions and accepted their validity as paths for personal salvation, though he was mainly a worshiper of the Omnipresent in the form of the goddess Kali. After much conflict, personal and with Ramakrishna, Datta finally accepted Ramakrishna as his spiritual adviser (guru) in 1885. He renounced the world, became a Sannyasi (Hindu monk), and commenced an intense study of philosophy and religion.

From 1890 to 1893, Vivekananda traversed all of India on foot and met people of all classes of society. He was moved by the poverty, ignorance, and ill health he saw. With the encouragement and support of the raja of Khettry, Vivekananda traveled to the United States to attend in September 1893 the World Parliament of Religions held in Chicago. His initial speech overwhelmed the audience. Through his many speaking engagements and his dynamic personality, he attracted many followers in the United States and later in Britain when he visited that country. Vedanta centers, or societies, were established in the West, and on his return to India, he established both a monastic order (the Ramakrishna Math) and a missionary society (Ramakrishna Mission), which manages hospitals, schools, colleges, and so forth, and which sends monks and devotees to disaster-stricken areas. Currently there are seventy such organizations in India, nineteen in the United States, and fourteen in other countries. Vivekananda's unique blend of Hindu universalism, personal salvation, and service to humanity form the philosophic backbone of these organizations.

Ranès C. Chakravorty

Further Reading
Isherwood, Christopher. (1994) *Ramakrishna and His Disciples.* Calcutta, India: Advaita Ashrama.
Rolland, Romain. (1965) *The Life of Vivekananda and the Universal Gospel.* 6th ed. Calcutta, India: Advaita Ashrama.

VO NGUYEN GIAP (b. 1911), general and commander of the People's Army of Vietnam. Vo Nguyen Giap is best known as the general and commander of the People's Army of Vietnam (PAVN) during the Vietnamese resistance against France and the United States between 1946 and 1973. Giap is widely recognized as an expert in military science and particularly in logistics, tactics, and strategy. His personal style of conducting war, crafted from a wide array of sources and field experiences, enabled the Vietnamese armies under his command to oust both the French and U.S. military forces from his country.

Giap was born in Quan Binh Province in 1911 to a poor family that was fervently anti-French. After reading the writings of Ho Chi Minh (1890–1969), he joined the underground Communist Party in his teens and, because of his anti-French activities, was imprisoned by the French at the age of sixteen. After he was released, he entered the National University in Hanoi and earned a Bachelor of Law degree. After graduation, Giap became a public member of the Communist Party in 1937, coauthored the influential study

Retired General Vo Nguyen Giap in 1991. (VITTORIANO RASTELLI/CORBIS)

The Peasant Problem with Truong Chinh (1907–1988) in 1938, and in 1939 published *The Question of National Liberation in Indochina,* which stressed the importance of protracted warfare for defeating a foreign military adversary. He professed that revolutionary warfare passed through three stages: guerrilla warfare, strategic defensive, and counteroffensive, and worked later to follow this process against the French and the United States.

In 1940 he fled to China after the French banned the Communist Party. There he began a long relationship with Ho Chi Minh. Ho appointed Giap head of the anti-French guerrilla forces, later to be known as the Viet Minh, and ordered Giap to the mountainous region in northern Vietnam, where he successfully recruited and trained hill tribes and lowland Vietnamese for the anti-French cause. Giap's forces made their first attacks against French installations in December 1944 and later, after learning of the Japanese surrender in August 1945, marched his troops into Hanoi. The Viet Minh was able to claim control from the Red River to the Mekong Delta between 19 and 30 August, which enabled Ho to proclaim the new Democratic Republic of Vietnam (DRV) in September 1945. Giap became the minister of the interior in the new government and later was promoted to the rank of full general and commander of all Viet Minh military forces.

During the ensuing Vietnamese-French war beginning in 1946, Giap shaped the new People's Army of Vietnam (PAVN) into a strong and motivated fighting force with rigorous military training and a program of political indoctrination and education. He depicted Vietnam's war for independence as a political war first and a military one second, a people's war that involved total commitment from the population. His victory at Dien Bien Phu against the French in 1954 ensured his international recognition. After the French ouster from Indochina, Giap led the DRV forces against the Republic of Vietnam and the United States during the 1960s and 1970s. After Ho's death in 1969, Giap shared power in Hanoi with Le Duan (1908–1986) and Pham Van Dong (b. 1906). In 1972, after the failed Easter Offensive, Giap was replaced as commander of DRV forces but retained his position of minister of defense, which he held until 1980. In 1982 he lost his seat on the Politburo but remained very popular with the Vietnamese public. He spent the next years making trips to other Communist countries and in 1992 was awarded the Gold Star Order, Vietnam's highest decoration.

Richard B. Verrone

Further Reading

Currey, Cecil B. (1997) *Victory at Any Cost: The Genius of Viet Nam's Gen. Vo Nguyen Giap.* Washington, DC: Brassey's.

Davidson, Phillip B. (1988) *Vietnam at War: The History, 1946–1975.* Novato, CA: Presidio Press.

Giap, Vo Nguyen. (1962) *Dien Bien Phu.* Hanoi, Vietnam: Foreign Languages Press.

———. (1967) *People's War People's Army: The Viet Cong's Insurrection Manual for Underdeveloped Countries.* New York: Praeger.

———. (1975) *Unforgettable Months and Years.* Translated by Mai Elliot. Ithaca, NY: Cornell University Press.

———. (1978) *Unforgettable Days.* Hanoi, Vietnam: Foreign Languages Publishing House.

VO VAN KIET (b. 1922), Vietnamese prime minister.

Vo Van Kiet, considered a leading reformer, was born in 1922 in the city of Can Tho in southern Vietnam. He became involved in anticolonial and revolutionary activities in the 1940s. Following the August Revolution of 1945, Vo Van Kiet became an important member of the Vietnam Communist Party in southern Vietnam. In the early 1970s, he served as secretary of the Saigon Municipal Party Committee. After reunification in 1975, he was named chairman of

Ho Chi Minh City's People's Committee and in 1976 replaced Nguyen Van Linh as chairman of the Ho Chi Minh City Party Committee, a position he held until 1982. During this time, Vo Van Kiet established more liberal trade and commercial policies, which later became part of Vietnam's *doi moi* period. He became a member of the Politburo in 1982. He was named acting prime minister following the death of Pham Hung (1912–1988) but was defeated in an election for that post later that year. He was vice premier and chairman of the State Planning Commission in 1986 and then served as prime minister from 1992 to 1997. In 1997 he chose not to run for office and was replaced by Phan Van Khai (b. 1933).

Micheline R. Lessard

Further Reading

Duiker, William J. (1995) *Vietnam: Revolution in Transition.* Boulder, CO: Westview Press.

Kolko, Gabriel. (1997) *Vietnam: Anatomy of a Peace.* London: Routledge.

VOLCANOES

Of the more than 1,500 potentially active volcanoes in the world, eight to ten are erupting at any given moment. On the bottom of the seabed circling the Pacific basin lies a series of volcanic arcs and oceanic trenches coinciding with the edges of one of Earth's main tectonic plates. This zone is called the Ring of Fire, because of its frequent earthquakes and volcanic eruptions. About 80 percent of these volcanoes are located in countries in Pacific Asia. The most volcanically active country in Asia is Indonesia, which has seventy-six historically active volcanoes, four-fifths of which erupted in the last century. Ten have erupted since 1990.

Volcanoes form when a break in Earth's crust allows magma (molten rock) and hot gas to reach the surface under pressure, resulting in dangerous eruptions. The main threats in the immediate area of these eruptions are high-speed, superheated toxic gases and debris (pyroclastic flows), blast effects, lava flows, volcanic earthquakes, landslides, and lahars (mudflows). Ash clouds or deposits and tsunamis (tidal waves) can be hazardous over a greater distance. Volcanoes can cause immense destruction to crops, forests, roads, and entire towns, resulting in many evacuees who must be sheltered, fed, and resettled.

While Japan's cone-shaped Mount Fuji presents an image of a volcano's majestic beauty, the volcanoes of the Philippines have earned the reputation of being the most deadly and costly in the world. On average

UJUANG KULON NATIONAL PARK—WORLD HERITAGE SITE

A UNESCO World Heritage Site since 1991, Ujuang Kulon National Park is located on the southwest tip of the Indonesian island of Java. Ujuang Kulon is home to a treasure trove of rare species and spectacular inland volcanoes.

over 13 percent of volcanic eruptions cause fatalities and 22 percent cause damage. The 1991 eruptions of Mount Pinatubo, for example, caused an estimated US$260 million in damage. The series of eruptions lasted for months, producing the largest cloud of climate-modifying gases since mighty Krakatau erupted in Indonesia in 1883. Scientists estimated that Pinatubo's eruption added more aerosols (light gases and particles) than all human activity since the industrial revolution. The cooling effect of these particles on the atmosphere lasted for two years and temporarily more than offset any global-warming effect.

Many Asian countries have increased their volcano research and monitoring, to provide greater warning time of likely eruptions and to broaden natural-hazard management programs. Although these efforts help to mitigate the impacts of volcanic eruptions on humans and property, volcanic eruptions will persist as a significant natural hazard throughout countries located in Asia's Ring of Fire.

James Hafner

Further Reading

Kovach, Robert L. (1995) *Earth's Fury: An Introduction to Natural Hazards and Disasters*.Upper Saddle River, NJ: Prentice-Hall.

Merrits, Dorothy, Andrew De Wet, and Kirsten Menking. (1998) *Environmental Geology: An Earth System Science Approach*. New York: W. H. Freeman.

Simkin, Tom, and Lee Siebert. (1994) *Volcanoes of the World*. 2d ed. Washington, DC: Smithsonian Institution.

Smith, Keith. (1996) *Environmental Hazards: Assessing Risk and Reducing Disaster*. 2d ed. London and New York: Routledge.

VOLKSRAAD From the 1870s until the first half of the twentieth century, concern was expressed in the Netherlands over people's welfare in the Dutch East Indies (now Indonesia). There were also calls within the Indies itself for greater self-government. This gave rise to the Ethical Policy, whereby the Netherlands tried, among others, to bring indigenous elements into the colonial service, provide education, develop agriculture, establish health programs, and decentralize authority. This last objective saw the establishment of a Volksraad (People's Council), a single-chamber debating forum that lasted from 1918 to 1942.

Established on 18 May 1918, the Volksraad comprised both elected and appointed officials. Apart from being a place to voice ideas and criticisms, the council had no official powers, merely functioning in an advisory capacity. Dutch authorities were able to dominate the council through appointment of sympathetic elements and Dutch settlers. However, indigenous members (under 50 percent of the representatives) were able to communicate their desire for self-determination at this body, notably through insisting that Bahasa Melayu (Malay) be used alongside Dutch as a working language. In the year of the Volksraad's establishment, Dutch colonial authorities vaguely promised self-government in the "November Promise," which gave moderates hope of an evolutionary path to independence.

After its first decades, the council was strongly influenced by the political wing of Budi Utomo, an organization prepared to work within Dutch rule to achieve independence. However the failure of emergent political parties, such as Budi Utomo, to effect real change working within the Dutch administration leant greater credence to those, like Sukarno (Indonesia's founding president in 1945), who chose noncooperation. In 1936, council member Sutardjo proposed self rule within ten years, but the proposal was obfuscated and dropped, disappointing those who favored working within the colonial administration. From then on the Volksraad was a dead letter.

The Volksraad had little impact on Dutch rule, as the Netherlands continued to solidify its grip on the archipelago, increasingly interfering in the everyday lives of the people. However the Volksraad was a factor in the emergence of a "pan-Indonesian" consciousness among the diverse peoples of the archipelago.

Anthony L. Smith

Further Reading

Penders, Chris L. M., ed. and trans. (1977) *Indonesia: Selected Documents on Colonialism and Nationalism, 1830–1942*. Queensland, Australia: Queensland University Press.

Von Albertini, Rudolf. (1982) *European Colonial Rule, 1880–1940: The Impact of the West on India, Southeast Asia, and Africa*. Westport, CT: Greenwood.

WAHID, ABDURRAHMAN (b. 1940), president of Indonesia. Born in East Java in 1940, educated (although without formal degrees) in the Middle East and Europe, and heir to Muslim elite, Abdurrahman Wahid became the head of Nahdatul Ulama, Indonesia's largest Islamic organization, gained broad national respect for leadership and candor in criticizing the dictator Suharto in the 1990s, and finally established the National Awakening Party (PKB) to compete in 1999 in Indonesia's first relatively open parliamentary election in forty-four years.

Urbane, multilingual, courageous, and ecumenical, Abdurrahman Wahid (commonly called Gus Dur) was elected president of Indonesia in October 1999 by the National Assembly (MPR), which also forced him from office less than two years later. Initially he was widely heralded as the perfect reformer and balm to deep national wounds from decades of autocracy, oppression, and corruption. In reality he faced crippling obstacles.

Voting irregularities and confusion in the constitutional process raised serious questions of legitimacy in Wahid's election. Military supremacy in actual governmental authority (the legacy of decades of dictatorship), pervasive institutional corruption, general economic implosion, and the marginality of his own electoral and political party base fatally constrained his presidential authority and influenced selection of his cabinet. Physical (and, reportedly, psychological) problems from recent strokes left him with sharply diminished motor coordination and energy, as well as near blindness. Soon, despite whirlwinds of international travel, jocularly effective cultivation of media and domestic publics, cheerleading about Indonesia's future, and a few reformist flourishes, Wahid proved incapable of governing. Erratic behavior, scapegoatism, and allegations of corruption accumulated quickly and led to his ouster by the MPR and replacement by his vice president, Megawati Sukarnoputri.

Roger Paget

President Wahid at a press conference in Jakarta in November 1999. (AFP/CORBIS)

WAKAYAMA (2002 est. pop. 1.2 million). Japan's Wakayama Prefecture is situated in the central part of the island of Honshu. Its 4,723 square kilometers encompass the almost completely mountainous terrain of the western Kii Peninsula. Wakayama is bordered by the Pacific Ocean, Kumano Sea, and Kii Channel, and by Osaka, Nara, and Mie prefectures. Once known as Kii Province, it assumed its present name and borders in 1871.

The prefecture's capital is Wakayama, which grew up around a castle erected in 1585 by Toyotomi Hideyoshi (1536–1598), one of Japan's three national unifiers. The prefecture has long been the home of the Koyasan Buddhist monastic complex and the Shinto Kumano Sanzan shrines. It was ruled through the Edo period (1600/1603–1868) by a branch of the Tokugawa family. The prefecture's other important cities are Tanabe, Kainan, and Singu.

The prefecture produces rice and mandarin oranges, and supports fishing and forestry. When the Hanshin Industrial Zone was extended southward from Osaka, it brought chemical, steel, and electrical equipment plants to supplement Wakayama's traditional spinning, and furniture-making and papermaking industries. Visitors are drawn to the area's coastal scenic attractions and to sacred Nachi Falls, one of the nation's highest.

E. L. S. Weber

Further Reading
"Wakayama Prefecture." (1993) *Japan: An Illustrated Encyclopedia*. Tokyo: Kodansha.

WAKHAN Wakhan is a high, narrow valley in the Pamir Mountains of northeastern Afghanistan, between Tajikistan and Pakistan. It is located in northeastern Badakhshan Province around the Wakhan River and extends from Ishkashim in the west to China in the east. The Great Silk Road passed through Wakhan, and Marco Polo is said to have stopped there on his way to China.

In 1896, the Anglo-Russian Boundary Commission awarded this area to Afghanistan in order to create a buffer zone between British India and Russia; thereafter, the area became known as the Wakhan Corridor. Previously, it had been an autonomous region ruled by an independent emir (prince) until 1882, when it came under the administrative control of the governor of Badakhshan.

The region is known for its biodiversity. It has an alpine fauna, which provides a good habitat for the famous Marco Polo sheep, ibex, snow leopard, and brown bear. The area is also rich in lapis lazuli, the rare, bright blue semiprecious stone much prized in antiquity.

Its inhabitants are the Wakhis and Tajik, who live along the upper reaches of the Panj River and who speak an Indo-Aryan language. The main occupations are farming (wheat, barley, and legumes), and herding (cattle, sheep, and goats). As well, there are Kyrgyz herders, who have domesticated the yak. Both the yak and the two-humped Bactrian camel are important beasts of burden in the region.

Before the Marxist coup in 1978 (known as the Saur Revolt), the Corridor attracted hunters who came for the Marco Polo sheep, as well mountain climbers. Few outsiders currently venture into the area, but this may change as the region stabilizes.

Nirmal Dass

Further Reading
Faizi, Inayatullah. (1996) *Wakhan: A Window into Central Asia*. Islamabad, Pakistan: Al-Qalam.
Gopalakrishnan, Ramamoorthy. (1980) *The Geography and Politics of Afghanistan*. New Delhi: Concept.

WALI ALLAH, SHAH (1703–1762), Indian theologian. Shah Wali Allah Dihlawi, a leading Muslim theologian and intellectual of India, was born in Delhi to an important family at the court of the Mughal emperors. An exceptional student, in 1719 Wali Allah succeeded his father as head of the religious college, Madrasah Rahimiyya, in Delhi. In 1731 he made the pilgrimage to Mecca, where he remained for fourteen months before returning to Delhi. During his stay in Arabia he studied Islamic law, hadith (narratives of Muhammad's life), and mysticism with eminent scholars who influenced his religious beliefs.

During the next thirty years he dedicated himself to teaching and writing on hadith traditions and Islamic law, in Arabic and Persian. Wali Allah is considered the father of Indian Islamic modernism and a major figure in the Islamic intellectual revival. He used a systematic historical approach to try to renovate traditional religious thought organized around the doctrine of *tatbiq* (conciliation)—a method for mitigating the conflict between Sufi mystical doctrines and theological dogmatism.

In his analyses Wali Allah underlined the importance of social and economic welfare, linking the degeneration of Islamic thought and practices to the economic and social decadence of Indian Muslims. His ideas influenced several religious and political revolutionary movements in the Indian subcontinent in the eighteenth and early nineteenth centuries.

Riccardo Redaelli

Further Reading

Baljon, J. M. S. (1986) *Religion and Thought of Shah Wali Al-lah Dihlawi 1703–1762*. Leiden, Netherlands: E. J. Brill.

WAN AHMAD (d. 1914), ruler of the Malay state of Pahang. Wan Ahmad was the all-powerful *benda-hara* (1863–1887) and first sultan (1887–1914) of the peninsular Malay state of Pahang, who for two decades resisted British influence. Born into the hereditary line of *bendahara* (prime ministers), Wan Ahmad was the son of Bendahara Tun Ali (1806–1857). He had to struggle in a bitter, devastating six-year civil war (1858–1863) against his half-brother, Tun Mutahir. He prevailed in May 1863 and having assumed the title of *bendahara*, ruled Pahang with an iron fist.

The rumored potential economic resources of Pa-hang and the fear that other European powers (notably France and Germany) might gain a foothold there made it imperative for the British to pressure Wan Ahmad to accept the Residential system. Through the efforts of Hugh Clifford, Wan Ahmad signed a treaty in October 1887 to accept a British Agent; the British in turn recognized him as sultan of Pahang. Although some quarters perceived Wan Ah-mad to be kind and generous, others, including Clif-ford, saw him as ruthless.

In 1888, Wan Ahmad bowed to British pressure and agreed to receive a British Resident. Theoretically the British Resident served as an adviser to the sultan on all matters excluding those relating to Malay customs and the Islamic faith. In practice, however, the Resi-dent exercised executive power. After 1889, Wan Ah-mad, who detested the new regime, withdrew to the background, but lent his tacit support to disaffected Pahang Malay chiefs, whose dissatisfaction with the British system of governance erupted in an anti-British resistance in the 1890s.

Ooi Keat Gin

Further Reading

Aruna, Gopinath. (1991) *Pahang 1880–1933: A Political History*. Kuala Lumpur, Malaysia: Malaysian Branch of the Royal Asiatic Society.
Gullick, John Michael. (1992) *Rulers and Residents: Influence and Power in the Malay States, 1870–1920*. Kuala Lumpur, Malaysia: Oxford University Press.
Linehan, William. (1973) *A History of Pahang*. Kuala Lumpur, Malaysia: Malaysian Branch of the Royal Asiatic Society.

WANDERING SOULS   In Vietnam obsequies customarily have been performed to ward against the possibility of the deceased's becoming an errant, male-volent being, or "wandering soul." The Vietnamese have traditionally believed that the souls of those who have died have influence over, and can be influenced by, ac-tions and events in the world of the living. It is thought that when they die, the departed want and need ritual support from the living. For almost everyone, this sup-port is provided by their family. Vietnamese under-stand "family" to extend across many generations, including both the living and the dead.

A series of rituals are held for the decreased. The full set, now often simplified by many people, would include rituals held immediately after death, at the fu-neral, at burial (sometimes reburial), at weekly inter-vals for seven weeks, and finally after one hundred days. Additionally, ritual celebrations are still held for departed family members on the anniversary of their death, and rituals are organized on New Year's Eve to welcome the ancestors who, it is believed, come to share in this big family celebration. Important events are reported to the ancestors.

Under ideal circumstances, the deceased remain participating members of the family—contented, happy, quiet, invisible. They are often thought to pro-vide their descendants with advice, warning of danger, or good luck. But those unfortunate people who die without descendants, or violently, or far from home, or for any reason lack the necessary assistance of in-cense and offerings may become errant spirits, or wan-dering souls. These spirits are believed to be miserable, discontented, and sometimes dangerous to the living. Vietnamese have always had some means of guarding against these spirits and of helping them to find peace.

Well into the twentieth century, on the outskirts of many Vietnamese villages, a plot of land was set aside as a burial ground. Beside the burial ground there was often a modest building known as the "temple of wan-dering souls" *(am chung sinh)*. Such temples were sim-ply a place to make sacrifices to wandering souls. Often, an older woman, sometimes a shaman, lived at or near the temple and made periodic offerings to wandering souls. Village groups or individual households put out rice gruel and made other ritual offerings to the souls, especially on the fifteenth day of the seventh lunar month. On this day, in various ways, individually and in groups, villages commemorated wandering souls and tried to placate them and even help them find peace. Some of these practices have become rare in recent decades, or have been greatly simplified.

Even now, on this day, exactly the middle of the lu-nar year, a special ceremony, usually the most impor-tant of the year, is organized in Buddhist pagodas throughout Vietnam. Many Vietnamese associate this day and this Buddhist tradition with the tale of Mu Lien, a Buddhist monk who went into hell to plead successfully for the release of his mother. But in this case, offerings are made to plead for the salvation of all discontented spirits, including those in hell, in the Buddhist spirit of charity.

Neil Jamieson

See also: **Ancestor Worship—East Asia**

Further Reading
Hickey, Gerald C. (1964) *Village in Vietnam*. New Haven, CT: Yale University Press.
Van Huyen, Nguyen. (1995) *The Ancient Civilization of Vietnam*. Hanoi, Vietnam: The Gioi Publishers.

WANG JINGWEI (1883–1944), leader of China's Nationalist Party. Wang Jingwei was an early leader of China's Nationalist Party (Guomindang), whose fierce rivalry with Chiang Kai-shek (1887– 1975) led him to collaborate with the Japanese during World War II. Born in Guangzhou (Canton), Wang won a government scholarship to study in Japan, where he received a degree from Tokyo Law College in 1906. While in Tokyo, he joined Sun Yat-sen's (1866–1925) National Revolutionary Alliance (Tongmenghui) in 1905. Wang, who demonstrated considerable writing and speaking skills, quickly rose to a prominent position in the movement. Imprisoned for participation in a plot to assassinate the Qing regent Prince Chun in 1910, Wang was released after the fall of the Manchus, or Qing dynasty (1644–1912).

Although Wang was hailed as a hero for his revolutionary activities, he left China in 1912 after the assumption of power by the militarist Yuan Shikai (1859–1916). Returning in 1917, Wang rejoined Sun in Guangzhou, where they worked to reorganize the Nationalist Party (Guomindang, as the Tongmenghui had been renamed) and build an army with the ultimate goal of reunifying China. Sun's death in 1925 left Wang seemingly positioned to take control of the Party, but his path was blocked by a new rival, Chiang Kai-shek. Although Chiang was a relative newcomer to the Nationalists and lacked Wang's revolutionary credentials, he did control the army. This would prove decisive in the coming power struggle.

As the Nationalists and their allies (including the nascent Chinese Communist Party) embarked on the Northern Expedition to reunify China, Wang emerged as the leader of the left wing of the Party (favoring the alliance with the Communists), while Chiang headed the right wing, which opposed the alliance. This dispute led briefly to the formation of separate Nationalist governments headed by Wang in Wuhan and Chiang in Nanjing. Wang later broke with the Communists and mended fences with Chiang in a show of unity following the Japanese invasion of 1931.

As titular head of the Nationalist government in Nanjing from 1932 to 1935, Wang was forced to appease the Japanese, while Chiang led the army in a campaign to exterminate the Communists. To recover from an assassination attempt, the disillusioned Wang resigned and left China in 1935. He returned after the outbreak of the Sino-Japanese War in 1937 and pessimistic about China's military prospects, attempted to persuade Chiang to make peace with Japan. After escaping another assassination attempt by Nationalist agents, Wang fled to occupied China, where the Japanese Army installed him as head of the puppet "Reorganized Nationalist Government" in Nanjing in March 1940. Wang's hopes of presenting himself as a credible alternative to Chiang, however, were dashed by the harsh reality of Japanese military domination. Wang died on 10 November 1944, while undergoing medical treatment in Nagoya, Japan.

John M. Jennings

Further Reading
Boyle, John Hunter. (1972) *China and Japan at War, 1937–1945: The Politics of Collaboration*. Stanford, CA: Stanford University Press.
Bunker, Gerald E. (1972) *The Peace Conspiracy: Wang Ching-wei and the China War, 1937–1941*. Cambridge, MA: Harvard University Press.

WANG KON (877–943), founder of the Koryo dynasty, Korea. Wang Kon, posthumously known as T'aejo, was born in Songak (modern Kaesong, North Korea). He came from a prominent merchant family that had built up its wealth in the China trade. At the start of the tenth century, Wang Kon became a major lieutenant to a regional lord, Kungye (d. 918). Under him, Wang Kon proved to be both an able soldier on land and a skilled commander at sea. In 918, wearied by Kungye's tyrannical acts, Wang Kon overthrew Kungye and founded a new dynasty called Koryo (918–1392).

From his capital at Songak, Wang Kon struggled to unify the Korean peninsula. In 935, the former

Shilla kingdom (57 BCE–935 CE) peacefully surrendered to Koryo, and then in 936 Wang Kon forced the other rival state, Later Paekche (18 BCE–663 CE), to submit. With the kingdom unified, Wang Kon spent the remainder of his reign stabilizing the dynasty. He married twenty-nine women from various parts of the peninsula, used both indigenous techniques and political institutions modeled on Chinese practices, and turned to Buddhism as ways to unify the country. Before he died, he issued Ten Injunctions instructing his descendants how to govern so as to ensure the success of the dynasty. These Ten Injunctions serve as an excellent political and intellectual statement of the era. Three of Wang Kon's sons succeeded him as monarchs.

Edward J. Shultz

Further Reading
Lee, Ki-baik. (1984) *A New History of Korea*. Boston, MA: Harvard University Press.

Lee, Peter H., ed. (1993) *Sourcebook of Korean Civilization*. New York: Columbia University Press.

WANG YITING (1867–1938), painter and businessperson. Wang Yiting was born in Shanghai and began life as an apprentice in a picture-mounting shop, later becoming a comprador for a Japanese company. He was extremely successful in his business career and served as chairperson of the Shanghai Chamber of Commerce.

Wang Yiting was also a generous supporter of artists and helped to found many important art societies in Shanghai. He was proficient in painting historical figures, folk legends, birds with flowers, animals, and landscapes and was particularly renowned for his Buddhist figures and dragons. In later life, Wang became a devout Buddhist and once served as the president of the Chinese Buddhist Association.

Kuiyi Shen

Further Reading
Andrews, Julia, Claudia Brown, David Fraser, and Kuiyi Shen. (2000) *Between the Thunder and the Rain: Chinese Paintings from the Opium War through the Cultural Revolution, 1840–1979*. San Francisco, CA: Echo Rock Ventures and Asian Art Museum of San Francisco.

Tsao, Hsing-yuan. (1998). "A Forgotten Celebrity: Wang Zhen (1867–1938), Businessman, Philanthropist, and Artist." In *Art at the Close of China's Empire*, edited by Ju-hsi Chou. Phoenix, AZ: Phoebus Occasional Papers in Art History 8, 94–109.

WANGCHUCK, JIGME SINGYE (b. 1955), King of Bhutan. Fourth of the Wangchuck dynasty founded by Ugyen Wangchuck in 1907, King Jigme Singye Wangchuck was born in Dechenchholing Palace, Thimphu (the capital of Bhutan), on 11 November 1955 and was educated in Bhutan and in England. He ascended the throne in 1972, following the premature death of his father, Jigme Dorje Wangchuck. He was crowned in 1974, the coronation allowing the outside world a rare glimpse of the remote Himalayan kingdom. The Wangchuck family claims descent from the most famous Bhutanese saint, Pema Lingpa (1450–1521). In 1988 the king married four sisters related, according to tradition, to an incarnation of the founder of the Bhutanese state, Shabdrung Ngawang Namgyal (1594–c. 1651). The crown prince is the king's eldest son, Jigme Khesar Namgyal (b. 1980).

The king maintains a policy of balancing modernization with tradition, called Gross National Happiness. He believes that as a small, landlocked, and undeveloped country, Bhutan must promote national unity based on the Bhutanese cultural heritage, including environmental awareness, while expanding its international role in the U.N., South Asian Association for Regional Cooperation, or SAARC (which includes

King Jigme Singye Wangchuck. (ALAIN LE GARSMEUR/CORBIS)

India, Pakistan, Sri Lanka, Maldives, Bhutan, Bangladesh, and Nepal), and other bodies.

Although a proactive ruler, the king has gradually yielded more power to his ministers. Since 1998 a rotating chairman of the Council of Ministers functions as head of government. The king has also reduced the powers of the civil service, privatized many state enterprises, and devolved decision making to the local level. He has also pledged to make himself personally responsible for the solution of the so-called southern problem of Bhutanese refugees in Nepal and has toured the country repeatedly requesting southern Bhutanese not to leave.

Michael Kowalewski

Further Reading
Aris, Michael. (1994) *The Raven Crown*. London: Serindia.
Rose, Leo. (1977) *The Politics of Bhutan*. Ithaca, NY: Cornell University Press.

WARRING STATES PERIOD—CHINA
The name "Warring States" *(Zhanguo)* refers to a period of Chinese history ending with the unification of China under the first emperor of the Qin dynasty in 221 BCE. While there is universal agreement that the Warring States period ended in 221, the date of its beginning is a matter of convention: some place it in 481, when the chronicle known as *Chunqiu* (Springs and Autumns) draws to a close; others in 453, when the state of Jin was divided into three territories; still others in 403, when each of these three new states was formally recognized by the Zhou king. For the purposes of this book, the Warring States period begins in 475 BCE, the first year of the reign of Viscount Xiang of Zhao, one of the three states that supplanted Jin. The Warring States period constitutes the second half of the Eastern Zhou dynasty (770–221 BCE), while the first half of the Eastern Zhou dynasty is known as the Spring and Autumn period (770–476) BCE, after the chronicle of the same name.

The Eastern Zhou kings were recognized as the Heaven-ordained rulers of the terrestrial world, but they were forced over the centuries to cede more and more power to the feudal lords occupying the lands around them. During this time, the most powerful of the semi-independent statelets gradually conquered and annexed their neighbors, so that by the Warring States period, only eight contenders remained: Zhou, Qin, Qi, Chu, Zhao, Wei, Han, and Yan. In 256 BCE, the last Zhou king, who was by this time nothing more than a figurehead, was finally deposed,

and the Chinese world awaited the final victory of the state of Qin.

Political Changes in Warring States Times
The political landscape of the Warring States period was determined by the intensification of several interrelated geopolitical processes that began in the Spring and Autumn period: the ongoing decline of centralized power, the rise of warlike and expansionist states with their own domestic and foreign policies, and the continual diminution in the number of autonomous states as the weakest were annihilated by the strongest. By Warring States times, these underlying historical forces had brought about pervasive political, economic, social, and intellectual changes that radically transformed the character of Chinese life.

"Agriculture and war" became a popular slogan, as states recognized the substantial benefits of a healthy economy and a mighty army. As the stakes of battle rose, the conception of war necessarily changed from a ritualized competition between educated aristocrats (as in the Spring and Autumn period) to a lawless and bloody struggle between infantry armies as large as could be mustered.

The logistical problems associated with raising, training, and supplying a massive army induced rulers to rethink their approach to governing their territories. Those rulers who could most fully exploit their resources gained a sizable advantage in the theater of war. Thus the demands of battle led to the restructuring of the state as a vast production ground of people and munitions, maintained by an efficient and organized administration and serving a single king, to whom the entire population owed unquestioning allegiance. Kinship ties, ritual obligations, and traditional practice, which had been significant considerations guiding human action in earlier times, were now subordinated to the material requirements of the "warring state." In this manner, the imperial model of Chinese statecraft was being forged even before the establishment of the empire itself. The governments of the Qin and Han dynasties were largely based on the precedents of the Warring States.

Birth of Chinese Philosophy
The Warring States period is celebrated as the foundational era of Chinese philosophy. Historians sometimes ask why such a tumultuous and perilous time provided the context for some of the most sophisticated philosophers in Chinese history, but the reasons for this intellectual burgeoning are not obscure. The competing lords valued any resource that

CHINA—HISTORICAL PERIODS

Xia dynasty (2100–1766 BCE)
Shang dynasty (1766–1045 BCE)
Zhou dynasty (1045–256 BCE)
    Western Zhou (1045–771 BCE)
    Eastern Zhou (770–221 BCE)
Spring and Autumn period (770–476 BCE)
Warring States period (475–221 BCE)
Qin dynasty (221–206 BCE)
Han dynasty (206 BCE–220 CE)
Three Kingdoms period (220–265 CE)
North and South dynasties (220–589 CE)
Sui dyansty (581–618 CE)
Tang dynasty (618–907 CE)
Five Dynasties period (907–960 CE)
Song dynasty (960–1279)
    Northern Song (960–1126)
    Southern Song (1127–1279)
Jurchen Jin dynasty (1125–1234)
Yuan dynasty (1279–1368)
Ming dynasty (1368–1644)
Qing dynasty (1644–1912)
Republican China (1912–1927)
People's Republic of China (1949–present)
Republic of China (1949–present)
Cultural Revolution (1966–1976)

might aid them in their quest for world dominion, and so they were willing to listen to new ideas. The old ways, after all, were leading the Zhou dynasty to assured extinction. The demand for original thinkers resulted in the growth of a new profession: "wandering persuaders" *(youshui)*, who traveled freely from state to state in search of landed patrons, earning their bread alongside diplomats, generals, diviners, and other educated specialists.

The two foremost philosophical schools in Warring States times were those of the Confucians and the Mohists. The former were followers of the ethical worldview laid down by Confucius (Kong Qiu, 551–479 BCE); the latter group was founded by Mozi, or Master Mo (Mo Di, c. 480–c. 390 BCE), who preached a philosophy of "universal love" *(jian'ai)*. The Confucians and Mohists were irreconcilable enemies—Confucians could never accept the Mohist tenet that one should love the father of one's neighbor as one loves one's own father—but they were alike in that their doctrines did not always coincide with the desires of the lords whom they served. Confucians, for example, believed that loyal advisers should remon-

strate *(jian)* with their lord when he was in error, and their outspoken criticism often alienated their superiors. Mohists, for their part, believed that human acquisitiveness was at the root of all suffering in the world, and they actively disrupted campaigns of conquest in the hope of deterring warlords from preying on their neighbors.

Other philosophical orientations were more amenable to the aspirations of rulers. Political philosophers such as Shan Buhai (flourished 354–340 BCE), Shen Dao (b. c. 360 BCE), and Han Fei (d. 233 BCE) formulated an ideal of statecraft (often misleadingly called "legalism") that relied on standardized laws, protobureaucratic administrative systems, and unfailing adherence to the protocols of reward and punishment. The political aspect of philosophy was so important that even the *Laozi* (or *Daode jing*), a text whose primary purpose is to elucidate the benign cosmological notion of "the Way" *(dao)*, takes pains to point out the political applications of its teachings.

Paul R. Goldin

Further Reading
Cho-yun Hsu. (1965) *Ancient China in Transition: An Analysis of Social Mobility, 722–222 B.C.* Stanford, CA: Stanford University Press.
Graham, A. C. (1989) *Disputers of the Tao: Philosophical Argument in Ancient China.* La Salle, IL: Open Court.
Lewis, Mark Edward. (1990) *Sanctioned Violence in Early China.* Albany, NY: State University of New York Press.
Li Xueqin. (1985) *Eastern Zhou and Qin Civilizations.* Trans. by K. C. Chang. New Haven, CT: Yale University Press.
Loewe, Michael, and Edward L. Shaughnessy, eds. (1999) *The Cambridge History of Ancient China: From the Origins of Civilization to 221 B.C.* Cambridge, U.K.: Cambridge University Press.

WAT XIENG KHOUAN Wat Xieng Khouan or the Buddha Park is a cement sculpture garden of religious, mythological, and secular beings located approximately 20 kilometers south of Viengchan by the Mekong River in Laos. The creator of the sculpture garden, Luang Pou Bounluea Salithat (1920?– 1996), studied both Buddhism and Hinduism but never completed his ordination into Buddhist monkhood. Based on his prophetic dreams and meditation practice, he developed a religious community of Lao, Thai, and foreign laypeople.

In the late 1950s, he oversaw the creation of the images for the park—phantasmic imagery that includes the Buddha in different postures, other gods in the Hindu and Buddhist pantheons, mythological animals such as the *naga* or serpent god, and humans who were prominent religious figures. One unique sculpture is a life-size pumpkin containing three levels. The lower level is hell; the middle level is the earth; and the upper level is heaven.

Wat Xieng Khouan was never a Buddhist temple, but received its name from all the religious images it contains. The socialist government presently runs Wat Xieng Khouan as a public park and a tourist attraction.

After the Communist takeover in 1975, Luang Pou Bounluea left Laos and went to live across the border in Nongkhai, Thailand. He then commenced to create a second sculpture park on the Mekong River bank in Thailand, opposite the original park.

Linda McIntosh

Further Reading
Gilliand, Donald. (1998) "A Pleasant Hell in Laos." Retrieved 10 December 2001, from: http://www.thingsasian.com/goto_article/article1198.html.

WATER ISSUES For the people who live in Asia, daily life depends on the freshwater that reaches their fields, serves their households, and provides means of transportation. Agriculture consumes 70 percent of freshwater available around the world. Water scarcity and quality have emerged to threaten public health, economic productivity, and even food security in parts of the continent.

Water has become an increasingly critical natural resource for many Asian states' residents, technicians, and leaders. The continent's greatest challenge is to ensure sustainable access to freshwater resources. The specific water issues discussed here bear witness to the vulnerability of ecosystems to change in the domestic and international political environments.

Governance entails management of water resources at the regional, national, and local levels. Water governance refers to a range of economic, political, and administrative systems put in place to develop and manage water resources, as well as to provide water services. Water governance draws on issues in the public sphere, invoking the interventions of state and, increasingly, multilateral parastatal institutions.

Throughout the second half of the twentieth century in particular, public and multinational officials sought to promote economic and social development through intervention in water distribution for use in agriculture and industry. Interventions dedicated to the storage and seasonal management of Asia's fresh-water—ranging from hydroelectric dams to forestry and intensive agriculture programs—are the topic of public discussions among Asian political communities. Modernist visions for quality of life include access to potable water and services as well as intensive agricultural cultivation. Considered in the light of water governance, these interventions generated water-management issues specific to Central Asia.

Urban Drinking Water, Sanitation, and Material Quality-of-Life Indicators
Water issues are central to the expansion of modern infrastructure serving Asia's residents. Officials argue the value of such interventions in raising the quality of life for Asia's residents, citing that of the 3.5 billion people living in Asia in 1995, 830 million lacked access to treated drinking water, and 2 billion had no access to sanitary waste disposal.

Demographers note that Asia's population growth is increasingly concentrated in large cities, as a result of population growth and rural-urban migration. It is projected that following the year 2020, the developing world's population growth will occur mainly in urban areas. By the middle of the twenty-first century, villages will cease to exist in many countries—including in Asia—and poverty will have been transferred to urban areas.

In Asia's modern states, water systems are centralized, depending on public investment and transfers of resources from central governments. Yet the large cities of Asia are characterized by permanent, informal settlements with restricted access to modern facilities. Consequently, residents are less likely to have access to potable water and private toilets than are people in smaller towns and even villages.

Data from many developing-states' cities suggest that the substantial progress in improving water and sanitation in recent decades is now being reversed. For this reason, analysts suggest that future water and sanitation policies and strategies be directed to urban areas, particularly to periurban areas and satellite towns where the most disadvantaged people live.

Decreasing Volume of Available Water Resources
There is a drastic decrease in the amount of water available in the Aral Sea basin, located between Uzbekistan and Kazakhstan. Kazakhstan's western area, along the Syr Dar'ya River to the Aral Sea, is relatively unpopulated, with large stretches of uncultivated desert landscape; the concentration on few commodi-

ties has resulted in common water issues shared among Central Asian communities.

In 1960, the Aral Sea was the world's fourth-largest sea. Since that time, its volume has decreased by 75 percent and its surface area by 50 percent, so that it is currently ranked eighth largest. A closed hydrological system, it receives water from two tributaries (the Amu Dar'ya entering from the south and the Syr Dar'ya from the east). Until the 1960s, the Syr Dar'ya and Amu Dar'ya Rivers' combined outflow into the Aral Sea totaled about 6 cubic kilometers per year. During the next twenty years, the sea came to release more water than it received, via perennial irrigation networks, seepage, and evaporation.

In opening up new lands for cultivation, Turkmenistan's navigable Kara-Kum Canal contributed to the drying up of the Aral Sea. The canal, under construction between 1954 and 1988, diverted a significant amount of the Amu Dar'ya's waters along its 1,100-kilometer length through and into the Kara-Kum Desert in Turkmenistan and through and beyond the republic's capital of Ashkhabad. The canal's primitive design allows almost 50 percent of its water to escape via seepage and evaporation.

The amount of water available to the Aral Sea's hydrological system has decreased as a direct result of the expansion of irrigation drawing on the Aral Sea basin's freshwater resources between the 1960s and the 1980s. Increased water usage for agriculture in the Aral Sea basin caused the amount of water reaching the sea to drop by as much as 90 percent over this period. Consequently, by 1989, 28,000 square kilometers of the Aral Sea floor had dried up, exposing salt beds. At present, the sea contains less than half the amount of water that it did in 1960.

As the inland sea shrinks, salt-laden dust from the exposed seabed blows to locations more than 300 kilometers distant, ruining the soil and killing plants wherever it lands. The sea's salinity has increased to the destruction of a once-thriving local fishing industry. The drying of the Aral Sea has negatively affected well water used by residents along its shores. Also, the loss of the sea's water mass, which once moderated temperatures by absorbing heat in the summer and releasing it in the winter, has affected the local climate.

Decrease in the Quality of Water Resources

While industrial demands for single-crop cultivation increased during the second half of the twentieth century, the contamination of the Aral Sea serves Central Asian states as a negative patrimony from the Soviet Union. Agricultural-industrial monocultures took

A traditional irrigation well in a field in central Turkey in the 1990s. (CHRIS HELLIER/CORBIS)

on a qualitative transformation during the last quarter of the century, marked by the mechanical and chemical invasive forms of cultivation required by the Green Revolution, which in turn affected water quality.

Kazakhstan harvested 23.1 thousand metric tons of rice in 1967, increasing to 654 thousand metric tons by 1987. Cotton was sown on 1,450 thousand hectares of Uzbek land in 1960, which increased to 2,108 thousand hectares by 1987—making Uzbekistan the world's fifth-largest cotton producer.

In keeping with the technical requirements of modern agriculture, petroleum-based fertilizers, chemical pesticides, and artificial defoliants were poured onto cotton fields. In Uzbekistan, an average of 146.8 kilograms of chemical fertilizers was distributed over each hectare of agricultural land in 1965, increasing to 238.3 kilograms by 1975, and doubling to 305.6 kilograms in 1987.

These rates can be compared with only 122.1 kilograms per hectare for the whole Soviet Union (1987).

Central Asian cultivators applied fertilizers at much lower rates following the end of Soviet agricultural chemical subsidies in 1991 and the consequent upward spiral in the price of fertilizers and other additives. However, the earlier period of widespread use of fertilizers in cotton and rice cultivation led to an increase in traces of contaminants of fertilizer origin in irrigation water and field runoff, eventually compromising the quality of the Aral Sea's contents.

Fertilizer contaminants were not the only threat to the quality of the Central Asian water supply. Industrial pesticides and herbicides were also dumped onto Uzbekistan's cotton fields. During the late 1970s, the average hectare of Uzbekistan's cultivated land received between 30 and 35 kilograms of insecticides and defoliants. This high rate of application was unique to Central Asia and can be contrasted with the rest of the Soviet Union. While Soviet centralized planning required industrial-agricultural methods, Uzbekistan's insecticide- and defoliant-application rates were just short of thirty times higher than the average used in the rest of the Soviet Union during the same period.

Leading them was the chlorinated organic insecticide DDT, as well as the lindane insecticide benzene hexachloride. These were supplemented by the insecticides octamethyl and gamma benzene hexachloride. Pesticides included methyl mercaptans, phosphide pesticides, mitocide (known under the trade name Milbex), Lenacil, Aldrin (also referred to as Aldrex, Aldrite, and Octalene), and molinate (also known as Hydram, Ordram, and Yalan). Herbicides and defoliants included butifos and the cycloate herbicide ronit (also known by the registered trade name Ro-Neet). Phosalone was used as an insecticide and acaricide, and sodium trichloroacetate was used as both pesticide and herbicide.

Contaminants originating in fertilizers, pesticides, defoliants, and insecticides entered the Aral Sea by leaching off fields into drainage canals, then emptying into the sea's tributary rivers. Thus, the closed hydrological system of the Aral Sea basin was under a double stress: at the same time as the sea's outlet was increased for monocrop irrigation, its two tributaries entered heavily laden with pollutants. The end result was to concentrate contaminants in the sea's decreasing volume.

Declining Quantity and Quality of Water Resources Threaten Residents' Health

The adverse effects of intensive monocrop cultivation were identified in the declining health of Central Asia's residents. Central Asian infant mortality became the highest among the former Soviet republics. High rates of disease prevalence were attributed to the en-

vironmental degradation caused by cotton cultivation. Those living in Kazakhstan's Qyzylorda subdivision, closest to the sea, experienced a rapid deterioration in living standards as the Aral Sea shrank. Salts and pesticides contaminated the region's water and soil and affected the health of the population.

Health professionals attest that local populations are characterized by remarkably high rates of throat and lung cancers, kidney disease, hepatitis, asthma, bronchitis, gastrointestinal ailments, infant mortality, birth defects, anemia, and tuberculosis. During the 1970s and 1980s, Kazakhstan showed a 3.29-fold rise in total morbidity due to various infectious and somatic diseases associated with the drastic worsening of the ecological situation in the Aral Sea region. At the same time, child and maternal mortality rates increased significantly.

The Aral Sea crisis has come to threaten local residents' food security, as well as their long-term health. Investigations at the Institute for Regional Nutritional Problems of the Soviet Academy of Medical Sciences showed that pesticides, mineral fertilizers, and various microorganisms and their toxic metabolites were major pollutants of food products in all regions of Kazakhstan. It is alleged that discharge of agricultural chemicals into the water environment accumulates toxins in local fish.

In addition, since early 2000, regions surrounding the Aral Sea basin, including the Karakalpak Autonomous Republic in Uzbekistan and Khorezm, a subdivision in the same country, have undergone the worst droughts in recent memory. Local authorities report substantial losses to rice, cotton, and other crops, as well as a severe impact on animal husbandry, affecting 1 million residents' access to food. Drastically decreased rains during 2000 meant that Uzbekistan farmers produced just 3 million tons of grain, against an expected harvest of 4.89 million tons.

Neighboring States Share Water Issues

A second water issue encountered in the post-Soviet Central Asian states, in addition to the degradation and diminution of freshwater resources, is a shared dependence on common sources of water. Between 1967 and 1987, Uzbekistan, Kazakhstan, and Tajikistan used water resources located in Kyrgyzstan. Their mutual membership in the Union of Soviet Socialist Republics exempted them from any requirement for formal remuneration. The emergence of new states after the collapse of the Soviet Union in 1991 requires the renegotiating of preexisting water-management mechanisms.

Soviet authorities built seven large hydroelectric and irrigation facilities to serve the four republics of Uzbekistan, Kazakhstan, Tajikistan, and Kyrgyzstan. These provided access to primary water resources, such as irrigation, as well as secondary water resources, like electrical power and transport. These installations enabled the direct, perennial irrigation of 400 thousand hectares. In addition, these facilities augmented rainfall on an additional 918,000 hectares across the four then-Union republics.

While providing regional benefits, agricultural productivity through perennial and seasonal irrigation was incurred at the expense of Kyrgyzstan. Among the seven installations, the Toktogulsk hydro knot alone removed 12,000 hectares of Kyrgyz agricultural land from use, drowned under its reservoir. Likewise, industrial productivity in the surrounding republics was incurred at Kyrgyz expense. While the hydro knot's dams served local needs for electrical power, 2.4 million kilowatt-hours of energy were used outside the republic.

Political developments upset the region's means of distributing water resources. As a result of the dissolution of the Soviet Union in 1991, remuneration for water use emerged as an international political issue. Central Asian states had to develop new means to recompense water transactions. Kyrgyzstan demanded compensation for maintaining reservoirs on the Syr Dar'ya River complex during 2001, for the first time pressuring neighboring Kazakhstan to conclude a barter deal exchanging fuel for water.

Asia's Water Issues and Parastatal Organizations

The United Nations Development Programme (UNDP) and similar parastatal organizations have emerged as advocates for implementation of integrated water-resources management (IWRM) in Asia. Rather than depending on technological advances or identifying new sources of freshwater supply, the IWRM approach advocates innovation in water-resources governance. According to parastatal organizations, the participation of users in water-resource management and use will result in the creation of appropriate policy frameworks to allocate and manage water among competing users.

Parastatals' policies emphasize public accountability, focusing on the political process of achieving effective water governance. In particular, parastatals call for adequate institutional capacity and accountability within regulatory and management institutions as necessary for sustainable development and management of water resources. Appropriate tariff structures for water use, in particular, will both raise the revenues necessary to provide services and will extend participation to economically unempowered countries and regions.

The UNDP, the International Council for the Environment (ICLEI), and the Global Water Partnership (GWP) particularly seek to address the politics of water management through governance dialogue. The institutionalized discussion is intended to facilitate communication between political decision makers, water technicians, and users in different nations, to highlight real processes and actual cases, and to identify the next steps culminating in the governors' meeting of the Inter-American Development Bank in South America in March 2002, the World Summit on Sustainable Development in September 2002, and the Third World Water Forum in Japan during March 2003.

Elizabeth Bishop

Further Reading

Anonymous. (1997) "In Asia, Water Is Worth Blood." *Focus Central Asia* 52, 21–22 (November).

Asian Development Bank. (1999) *Water in the 21st Century*. Annual Report. Retrieved 30 April 2002, from: http://www.adb.org/Documents/Reports/Water/default.asp.

Catley-Carlson, Margaret. (2000) "Why We Must Invest in Urban Water and Sanitation." *Habitat Debate UNCHS (Habitat)* 6, 3.

Deichmann, Uwe. (3 May 1996) *Asia Population Database Documentation*. Santa Barbara, CA: National Center for Geographic Information and Analysis. Retrieved 30 April 2002, from: grid2.cr.usgs.gov/globalpop/asia/intro.html.

Gallagher, Susan. (1998) "The Syr Darya River Basin of Central Asia: Economic Development, Environmental Crisis, Regional Conflict, and Reform." Talk presented at the Sixth Annual Central Eurasian Studies Conference, Indiana University, Bloomington, IN, March.

Glazovsky, Nikita F. (1995) "The Aral Sea Basin." In *Regions at Risk: Comparisons of Threatened Environments*, edited by Jeanne Kasperson, Roger Kasperson, and B. L. Turner. New York: United Nations University Press, 52.

Kobori Iwao, and Michael H. Glantz, eds. (1998) *Central Eurasian Water Crisis: Caspian, Aral, and Dead Seas*. Tokyo: United Nations University.

Micklin, Philip P. (1991) "The Water Management Crisis in Soviet Central Asia." Carl Beck Papers in Russian and East European Studies, no. 905. Pittsburgh, PA: University of Pittsburgh.

Pannier, Bruce. (2000) "Central Asia: Water Becomes a Political Issue." Radio Free Europe/Radio Liberty (3 August).

United Nations Development Programme. (2002) *Dialogue on Effective Water Governance*. Retrieved 30 April 2002, from: http://www.gwpforum.org/gwp/library/Governance.pdf.

WAYANG BEBER

Wayang beber is one variety of Javanese puppet shadow play *(wayang)*. Painted pictures on a long strip of leather, bark, paper, or cloth are rolled from one supporting pole to another. The size of the strip varies, but it is usually around 20 centimeters wide and 12 meters long. Each spool contains sixteen scenes.

As the storyteller unrolls the spool scene by scene, he narrates the story accompanied by Javanese traditional music orchestra or gamelan. Traditional *wayang beber* tales include *Panji* stories or a story based on the mythical Javanese Jenggala Kingdom, or the *Mahabharata* and *Ramayana* epics. Gamelan orchestration is allowed only if the performance is held at the court compound. Outside the court a rebab (a kind of violin) was the traditional accompaniment. *Wayang beber* is performed very rarely because of the sacred nature of the performance. It was only performed at specific occasions following some rituals to ward off evil and epidemics. Some scholars argue that *wayang beber* is the oldest variety of *wayang* and has been performed since the early twelfth century. However, this kind of performance is rare, and the art form is near extinction. Some original scrolls are preserved at Wonosari, Yogyakarta; Mangkunagaran museum; and Pacitan. In 1986, it was reported that only two painters of *wayang beber* were still active.

Andi Achdian

Further Reading
Koentjaraningrat. (1985) *Javanese Culture.* Singapore: Oxford University Press.

WAYANG GOLEK

Wayang golek refers to two main genres of puppet theater in West Java, Indonesia, both of which use wooden rod puppets. One genre, *wayang golek cepak*, was created in the north coast region of Cirebon, West Java, in the late sixteenth century and is thought to have been used to convert people to Islam. *Wayang golek cepak* (also called *wayang golek menak* or *wayang bendo*) is still performed in the Cirebon Javanese language, and its repertoire includes stories about Amir Hamza (Muhammad's uncle, who brought Islam to the Arab world), the Islamic conversion of Java, and the history of legendary Javanese kingdoms.

The other genre, *wayang golek purwa*, is performed in the Sundanese language and is thought to be based on a type of *wayang kulit* (shadow-puppet play) practiced in the area of Tegal on the north coast of central Java. This *wayang golek* was brought to the Sundanese city of Bandung to entertain Sundanese aristocrats in the early to mid-nineteenth century. The main repertoire of tales is based on the *Mahabharata* and the *Ramayana*. Puppets range from 15 to 30 inches in height. The head, body, and arms are carved from soft wood and painted in a wide variety of colors. The costumes are made of velvet and other colored fabrics, batik cloth, and sequins. About sixty puppets are used in a single performance. Puppets are organized into four groups, including refined aristocrats, warriors and demon-kings, clowns, and ogres.

In both types of puppetry, the main performer is the *dalang* or puppeteer, who manipulates the puppets, nar-

Wayang golek puppets in Solo, Indonesia, in the 1990s. (LINDSAY HEBBERD/CORBIS)

rates the tale, sings many of the songs, and directs a troupe of musicians who play the instruments of the gamelan (Indonesian percussion instruments). *Wayang golek* blends puppetry, narrative, dialogue, song, instrumental music, movement, and dance. Performances are all-night affairs that play a central role in Sundanese cultural and civic life. A *wayang golek* performance coincides with a *hajat*, a ritual feast in which food is served, prayers are recited, and spirits are asked to bless the feast's host. The most common *hajat* are weddings and circumcisions. Performances are also held for ritual purification ceremonies *(ruatan)*. *Wayang golek* performances are opportunities for people to gather and reflect on issues that affect their everyday lives.

Andrew Weintraub

Further Reading
Foley, Kathy. (1979) "The Sundanese Wayang Golek: The Rod Puppet Theatre of West Java." Ph.D. diss., University of Hawaii.
Weintraub, Andrew. (2001) *Wayang Golek: The Sound and Celebration of Sundanese Puppet Theater.* Six-compact-disc set and accompanying forty-four-page booklet. Vermont: Multicultural Media.

WAYANG KULIT A *wayang kulit* performance features puppets made from parchment-like buffalo skin and horn. Such performances belong to the cultural tradition of various ethnic groups in the Indonesian archipelago. The puppeteer sits behind the cotton cloth screen, which is fixed in a wooden frame with a banana-trunk base; he or she manipulates the skillfully painted puppets that cast their shadows onto the screen in the light of an oil lamp. Most famous and sophisticated are those of the Central-Javanese courts and those on Bali, dating back to the period of the ancient Hindu-Javanese kingdoms (tenth–sixteenth centuries). They dramatize stories from the Old Javanese adaptations of the ancient Indian epics *Ramayana* and *Mahabharata* and are staged mostly in a ceremonial context (especially during life-cycle rituals). In Bali, the audience sits in front of the screen; in Java, only the women watch from the front, while the men enjoy the colorful puppets and the large gamelan (Indonesian percussion instruments) orchestra directed by the puppeteer from behind. The vast aesthetic and spiritual knowledge, obtained in years of study, makes the puppeteer a highly revered member of traditional society. His advice and comments on local affairs, which are put into the mouths of the clown-servant puppets, are enjoyed as well as feared.

Martin Ramstedt

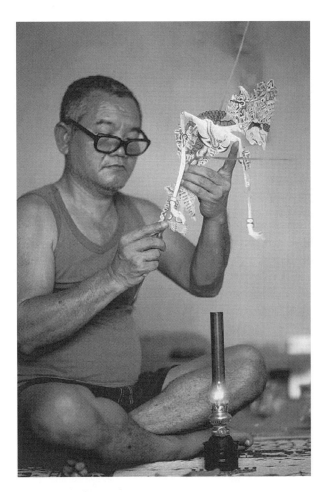

A man in Yogyakarta, Java, making a shadow puppet. (OWEN FRANKEN/CORBIS)

Further Reading
Brandon, James R. (1970) *On Thrones of Gold: Three Javanese Shadow Plays.* Cambridge, MA: Harvard University Press.
Hobart, Angela. (1987) *Dancing Shadows of Bali.* London and New York: KPI.
Keeler, W. (1987) *Javanese Shadow Plays, Javanese Selves.* Princeton, NJ: Princeton University Press.
Mellema, R. L. (1988) *Wayang Puppets: Carving, Colouring, Symbolism.* Amsterdam: Royal Tropical Institute.
Zurbuchen, Mary S. (1987) *The Language of Balinese Shadow Theater.* Princeton, NJ: Princeton University Press.

WAYANG TOPENG *Wayang topeng* is a classical Javanese dance-drama genre, in which dancers use elaborately carved and painted masks to perform stories from the romantic Panji cycle. These stories, which relate the adventures of the handsome mythical prince Panji and his fiancée, Princess Candra, are thought to have occurred during the last Hindu-Javanese kingdom, the Majapahit (thirteenth to fifteenth centuries).

Tradition has it that *wayang topeng* was created in the sixteenth century by Sunan Kalijaga, one of the nine legendary Muslim saints who converted Java to Islam by using the highly popular performing arts of the destroyed Hindu-Javanese courts to attract people to their sermons. Following the model of a *wayang kulit* (shadow-puppet play) enacting the Panji romance, Sunan Kalijaga is said to have created masks for nine dancers who were directed, as was also the case for the shadow-puppet play, by a *dalang*, or puppeteer.

Nowadays, the performers include a large number of dancers who are accompanied by a huge gamelan (Indonesian percussion instrument) orchestra. Their appearance onstage is introduced and commented on by the *dalang* in speech and song. Clowns entertain the audience with their jokes and mockeries in interludes between the acts. *Wayang topeng* has incorporated elements from other classical dance genres like the Serimpi or the Kiprah mask-dance, revered classical Javanese dances, whose origins might date to the time of the Majapahit kingdom. The Serimpi is danced by four girls, usually princesses; the Kiprah is a lively courting dance in which a male dancer impersonates a king. *Wayang topeng* has been preserved in the court tradition of Surakarta in central Java until today.

Martin Ramstedt

Further Reading

Rebling, Eberhard. (1989) *Die Tanzkunst Indonesiens.* Wilhelmshaven, Germany: Florian Noetzel Verlag, Heinrichshofen-Bücher.

Soedarsono. (1984) *Wayang Wong: The State Ritual Dance Drama in the Court of Yogyakarta.* Yogyakarta, Java, Indonesia: Gadjah Mada University Press.

WAYANG WONG *Wayang wong* is a classical dance-drama genre in Java and Bali, in which stories from the Old Javanese versions of the ancient Indian epics *Ramayana* and *Mahabharata* are performed, for entertainment as well as in ritual contexts. The earliest record of *wayang wong* occurs in a central Javanese inscription dating to 930. This ancient form either developed from or evolved at the same time as the *wayang kulit*, the shadow-puppet play, replacing the puppets with human dancers.

The contemporary Javanese *wayang wong*, however, was created in 1755 at the courts of Yogyakarta and Surakarta in Java, with the intention of continuing an ancient Javanese tradition. Stories from both the *Mahabharata* and the *Ramayana* are dramatized. The elaborate dance movements of the actors, who wear elaborate makeup, are accompanied by a large gamelan (Indonesian percussion instrument) orchestra.

The Balinese version of *wayang wong* was created at the end of the eighteenth century at the royal court of Klungkung on the east coast of south Bali, using ancient masks from the sacred heirlooms of the family of the Dewa Agung and drawing on the dance movements of the classical Gambuh dance drama. According to indigenous sources, the Gambuh is the oldest court dance-drama of Bali; it features stories from the Panji cycle, the adventures of the handsome mythical prince Panji and his fiancée Princess Candra, which supposedly occurred during the last Hindu-Javanese kingdom, the Majapahit (thirteenth to fifteenth centuries). Dramatizing only stories from the *Ramayana*, the Balinese *wayang wong* is accompanied by a special music ensemble, the gamelan *Batel* (probably "of warriors"), consisting of metallophones, gongs, cymbals, and drums.

Martin Ramstedt

Further Reading

Arps, Bernard, ed. (1993) *Performance in Java and Bali: Studies of Narrative, Theatre, Music, and Dance.* London: School of Oriental and African Studies, University of London.

Bandem, I. Made. (1986) *Wayang Wong in Contemporary Bali.* Ann Arbor, MI: University of Michigan Press.

———, and Frederik Eugene deBoer. (1995) *Balinese Dance in Transition: Kaja and Kelod.* Kuala Lumpur, Malaysia: Oxford University Press.

De Zoete, Beryl, and Walter Spies. (1973) *Dance and Drama in Bali.* Kuala Lumpur, Malaysia: Oxford University Press.

Soedarsono. (1984) *Wayang Wong: The State Ritual Dance Drama in the Court of Yogyakarta.* Yogyakarta, Indonesia: Gadjah Mada University Press.

WAZIRI The Waziris are a tribe living on the border of Afghanistan and Pakistan. Although they have their own tribal affiliation, the Waziris of Afghanistan are a subgroup of the larger Ghilzai (or Ghiljai in Farsi) branch of the Pashtun tribe. Their language is Pashtu, and they practice Pashtunwali or the Code of Conduct for Pashtun tribal members. The terrain in which they live is so remote that it is difficult to meet a Waziri outside of his or her home. Some Waziris live in tents along the Khyber Pass, and others live as pastoral nomads herding sheep throughout the mountains. Historically, the Waziris' homeland was referred to as Wana. However, after the British mandate to separate Pakistan, India, and Afghanistan, this area has been referred to as South Waziristan.

Because their tribe is spread out across the border of Afghanistan and Pakistan, the Waziris also have much in common with their Pakistani neighbors.

Their tribe is much larger on the Pakistani side. Waziris are divided into two subgroups: the Darwesh Khel (Darwish Khal) and the Mahsuds (Mahsoods). In the early 1900s, it was these two groups who led the largest and most difficult resistance against British rule in Afghanistan, which was called the Third Afghan War. Many joined with the Taliban after the post-Soviet civil war in Afghanistan.

Jennifer Nichols

Further Reading
"Afghanistan." (1993) *Encyclopedia Iranica*. Costa Mesa, CA: Mazda Publishers.
Elphinstone, Mountstuart. ([1815] 1998) *An Account of the Kingdom of Caubul*. Reprint ed. Columbia, MO: South Asia Books.
Rashid, Ahmed. (2000) *Taliban: Militant Islam, Oil and Fundamentalism in Central Asia*. New Haven, CT: Yale University Press

WELD, FREDERICK (1823–1891), British colonial administrator. Sir Frederick Aloysius Weld was born in 1823 in England and immigrated to New Zealand in 1843, joining his cousins as a sheep farmer. Entering politics in 1848 when he joined the Wellington Settlers' Constitutional Association, he was elected in 1853 from Wairau to the House of Representatives. In 1860–1861, he served as minister for native affairs and in 1864–1865 as premier. In 1867, he returned to England, but in December 1868, he was appointed governor of Western Australia (1869–1874), after which he became governor of Tasmania (1875–1879). In 1880, he went to Singapore, where he was governor of the Straits Settlements from 1880 until his retirement in 1887. During his term of office his stated ambition was to extend British control as far as possible over the peninsula south of Siam (Thailand). His successful expansionist policy was carried out by a group of ambitious young men, the most notable of whom was Sir Frank Swettenham (1851–1946). Weld's dispatch on education in 1882 initiated the growth of a Malay vernacular educational system in the Protected Malay States. In 1883, he coined the term "British Malaya" as a geographical and political expression for the peninsular states. Weld died in England on 20 July 1891.

Edwin Wieringa

Further Reading
Stevenson, Rex. (1975) *Cultivators and Administrators: British Educational Policy towards the Malays 1875–1906*. Kuala Lumpur, Malaysia: Oxford University Press.

Turnbull, C. Mary. (1989) *A History of Malaysia, Singapore and Brunei*. Sydney: Allen & Unwin.
Watson Andaya, Barbara, and Leonard Y. Andaya. (1982) *A History of Malaysia*. Basingstoke, U.K., and London: Macmillan Education.

WEST PAPUA. See **Irian Jaya.**

WESTERN GHATS The Western Ghats, (or Sahyadri in Sanskrit), are a chain of mountains forming the rim of western India, and running parallel to the coast of the Arabian Sea. Their length is about 1,600 kilometers. Their northern end is in Rajasthan, and the southern limit Cape Comorin (Kanyakumari), and in most places the Ghats are within sight of the coast. They thus form the western perimeter of the Dekkan Plateau, and average 800 to1,000 meters in elevation. The geological formation is trap in the northern parts and gneiss in the more southern. This range is the source of nearly all the rivers in the Indian peninsula. Unlike the Eastern Ghats, the Western are a continuous chain, with only one significant break, the 40-kilometer-wide Palghat Gap, through which trains and roads connect Cochin with Coimbatore and Madras. Just to the north of this gap the Eastern Ghats fuse with the Western in the Precambrian formation of the Nilgiri Hills. Anai Mudi Peak (2,695 meters), the highest point along the Western Ghats, lies nearby, in the Cardamom Hills of Kerala. The entire range is subject to intense rainstorms during the southwesterly monsoon, June through August each year. Consequently, much of the range is still covered with dense tropical forests, which, however, are being rapidly depleted by loggers.

Paul Hockings

Further Reading
Nair, K. S. S., R. Gnanaharan, and S. Kedharnath, eds. (1986) *Ecodevelopment of Western Ghats*. Peechi, India: Kerala Forest Research Institute.

WESTERNIZATION—CENTRAL ASIA
There was little evidence of Western—that is, European—cultural concepts and values penetrating into either Central Asian nomadic or sedentary societies in the aftermath of the Russian conquest in the mid- to late nineteenth century. The exception was the small handful of Central Asian intellectuals who became Russified. In some cases—Kazakh thinkers such as the writers Shokan Valikhanov and Abai Qonanbaev were a case in point—they sought closer acquaintance with Russian culture so as take from it those things that

would benefit Central Asians while preventing the destruction of their own traditional cultures.

The other means by which a degree of Westernization penetrated Central Asia was through the activities of the Jadidists, the primarily Tatar educators and journalists who sought to spread their Western-oriented educational philosophy through the Muslim regions of the Russian empire.

Westernization under the Soviet Union

The effects of pre-Soviet efforts at Westernization in the Central Asian parts of the Russian empire were largely lost through the destruction of the Central Asian intelligentsia during Stalin's purges of the 1930s. But at the same time, the Soviet regime undertook active efforts to create a "New Soviet Man" in Central Asia, through massive forced culture change. This had the effect of bringing a degree of Europeanization to the region, albeit filtered through Soviet ideology and Russian culture. Central Asians living in urban areas, particularly members of the intellectual and political elites, were under continual pressure to adopt Russian cultural values and to replace their own languages with Russian. By state policy, the non-Russian nationalities of the Soviet Union were expected to receive world culture through the Russian language. This was in fact the case due to lack of direct contact with the outside world as well as lack of knowledge of foreign languages other than Russian.

The degree of pressure on Central Asians to become Russified varied and was particularly intense in the later years of the Brezhnev era (1964–1982). The result was an intellectual class that had assimilated a Western orientation, while developing some degree of sentiment for their own history and traditional cultural heritage. The growth of national consciousness in Central Asia was at least partly in reaction to most Russians' view of Central Asian cultures as primitive and backward.

Residents of rural settlements were much less affected by the Russification campaigns, not least of all due to a lack of resources, including an adequate supply of teachers of Russian. Some acquaintance with Western-style culture seems to have penetrated the rural parts of Central Asia more extensively with the spread of radio and television. According to Soviet sources, however, some of the remoter areas of Central Asia were unable to receive broadcasts until the late 1980s.

Postindependence Western Influences

When the Soviet Union disintegrated in 1991 and the Soviet Central Asian republics became independent, the new countries' first instinct was to turn toward Europe for recognition and assistance—somewhat to the surprise of the international community. Later the Central Asian states also sought to establish ties with the Muslim world, following the model of Turkey, which is both Muslim and Western. In the immediate postindependence period, the United States and some European countries actively urged the Turkish model on the Central Asians. Their response was to accept politely Turkish economic assistance and then to inform the Turks that the new countries had no desire to exchange one "Big Brother"—Russia—for another. But the Turkish connection was to prove fruitful for the new Central Asian states, not only as a source of economic aid and investment, but also of assistance in the development of education, military training, transport, and communications. At the same time, the Turkish connection provided—as the West had hoped—an indirect channel for Western ideas and values to reach Central Asia.

The Central Asian postindependence orientation toward Europe and North America was based partly on economic realism—these countries were seen as the most reliable sources of aid and investment. But it was also based on instincts developed during the Soviet era. Though the Soviet Union was marginal to Europe, it still belonged in the general European cultural sphere. A European commissioner was astonished to be asked in 1992 by Kazakhstan's President Nursultan Nazarbaev how his country should go about getting itself on the list for membership in the European Economic Community. It was pointed out to the commissioner that Turkey was being given serious consideration as a potential member of the European Community, and more of Kazakhstan is geographically part of Europe than is the case with Turkey.

Security was another attraction the Western world held for the new states of Central Asia. Europe and the United States were viewed as potential guarantors of the countries' independence. Initially dependent on the Russian Federation for help in creating their own military establishments and border-guard forces, most Central Asian countries eventually looked to the West as a counterbalance to the Russian desire to restore hegemony over the region. Starting with Turkmenistan, all the Central Asian states except Tajikistan joined the NATO-sponsored Partnership for Peace (PfP). Consideration of Tajikistan's membership was delayed until the civil war had been resolved, and the country was admitted to the PfP program in May 2001. Some Central Asian states, in particular Uzbekistan and Kyrgyzstan, considered even closer security ties with the West, not only as a counterweight to Russia and China but as a source of assistance in countering terrorist groups based in Afghanistan. In the wake of the events of 11 September 2001 in New York, Uzbekistan, Kyrgyzstan, and Tajikistan agreed to a U.S. and European military presence in their territories, to the distress of some Russian political figures and commentators who believed that these countries were being drawn into the Western world.

Western cultural influence, which had become well established with urban young people in the last years of the Soviet era, developed even more rapidly after independence as domestic radio and television stations broadcast Western music and films, and increasing numbers of Central Asian youths had opportunities to travel and study abroad.

Central Asian membership in the primarily European Organization for Security and Cooperation in Europe (OSCE) exposed the ruling elites and intellectuals in the region to Western political values and human-rights standards, especially after the establishment of a permanent OSCE presence in each Central Asian state. The European Bank for Reconstruction and Development, the European Union's Technical Assistance to the CIS (TACIS) program, and the U.S. Agency for International Development through its network of contractors, as well as other Western assistance groups both large and small, were instrumental in promoting familiarity with and acceptance of Western political and social standards. The agencies of the United Nations sought to promote acceptance of universal human-rights standards, which were identical with Western standards. Most Central Asian leaders asserted that they aspired to achieve Western standards though they sometimes protested that they were really Asians and so needed time to assimilate European values.

The Westernization of Central Asia—in the sense of the adoption of a Western cultural orientation—may be expected to continue as the countries of the Central Asian region intensify their contacts with Europe and North America. Western tastes and attitudes adopted by the urban population are likely to spread as rural young people make their way to the cities in search of work. Western political values are likely to take longer to become rooted in the region, as is the case in most former Soviet possessions.

Bess Brown

Further Reading

Brown, Bess. (1995) "Die Angst Zentralasiens vor dem russichen Baeren." *Internationale Politik* 11 (November): 51–56.
European Bank for Reconstruction and Development. (1992) "Political Aspects of the Mandate of the European Bank for Reconstruction and Development." London: European Bank for Reconstruction and Development.
Snyder, Jed C., ed. (1995) *After Empire: The Emerging Geopolitics of Central Asia*. Washington, DC: National Defense University Press.

WESTERNIZATION—EAST ASIA

Westernization in Asia has been defined as the broad interaction between Asian values and behaviors and the external influences of Western colonial or national powers, such Great Britain, France, Germany, Portugal, the Netherlands, and the United States, that have exercised control, partial or otherwise, over Asian societies. Western influences have permanently altered practically all the societies in Asia. This process of Westernization in Asia began in the final years of the fifteenth century and continued to grow in terms of vigor and strength well into the twentieth century. The historical process of Westernization ended just after World War II with the assertion of independent nationhood by many Asian societies. Because modernization in many ways overlaps with the processes of Westernization, much of the historical influence of the West has continued with markedly expanding effects.

Western impact varied with the geographical proximity of the different Asian societies to the major areas of Western power. The nations of East Asia—China, Japan, and Korea—supposedly have had less exposure to the impact of Western influences and power than India because they are farther from Europe than is India. Two major processes have been identified through which Western power was asserted in Asia: colonization and the imposition of unequal treaties.

Colonization of Hong Kong and Macau

Early colonization by Western powers such as Portugal and Spain, who first colonized parts of India, the Philippines, Burma, and Malaya, had little impact on Asian culture because the colonizers had little contact with the indigenous people. The second wave of colonization was spurred on by rapid industrialization in the West during the early nineteenth century. British and Dutch colonial influences started, for example, in the coastal areas of India, Malaya, and Indonesia before spreading inland. A growing market for new food products, such as tea, coffee, and sugar, as well as the expanding demand for raw materials, such as rubber, tin, and oil, encouraged the Netherlands and Great Britain to extend their colonial control in Malaya, Indonesia, and Burma. The drive for raw materials and markets for Western manufactured goods stimulated Dutch and British interest in China and Japan.

An important dimension of Westernization in Asia was the education of the Asian indigenous elite in Western liberal and scientific thought. While the main colonial purpose was to train enough indigenous personnel to staff administrative and commercial positions, this elite also spread Western values and modes of behavior to broader segments of the local population. Some colonial governments, such as France in relation to Vietnam, reserved places in the universities for local people who were fluent in the Western languages of instruction and who were sympathetic to colonial rule.

Unequal Treaties

Some Asian countries, such as Japan and China, staved off actual colonialization by accepting unequal treaties that granted special concessions to Western powers. This made possible, for example, the spheres of influence different Western powers maintained in portions of Chinese territory. Western enclaves on Chinese soil were established by treaties, and their occupants remained outside the jurisdiction of the Chinese government. Each Western concession imposed its own laws on the residents living within its authorized territory.

Western norms in China were communicated by the large numbers of Western nationals in advisory positions in the Chinese government and engaged in trade and missionary activity. At the same time, Western political and legal institutions served as models for political and legal modernization. Although the Western powers did not have a unified program of Westernization, their actions were often synergistic. For example, the United States led the negotiations to open Japan to Western influence and interactions, and then Great Britain provided naval vessels for the modernization of Japan's fleet and British technicians to act as advisers in newly created Japanese industries. Similarly, France cooperated with Great Britain and the United States in reorganizing the Chinese customs services in the 1850s, and the French led the expansion of Western cultural influences in China by obtaining extraterritorial rights for foreign missionaries to work in the interior of the country.

Educational Systems

Educational systems were often vehicles of Westernization. Prior to the West's intrusion into China, indigenous Chinese higher education consisted of Confucian academies and specialized schools to train Confucian scholars. Following the arrival of the West, until the Nationalist regime established a few universities in China in the late 1920s, many Chinese youth attended the secondary schools and universities run by

The façade of a McDonald's fast food outlet in Beijing in the 1990s. (EYE UBIQUITOUS/CORBIS)

As Western colonialism spread, competition among the Western powers sometimes prevented one or another from achieving its goals, as was the case for the Germans in China. The Germans obtained a sphere of influence in the Shandong Peninsula, but their attempts to expand it were blocked by Russia, Great Britain, and the United States.

Colonial administrations in Asia favored the introduction of Western languages for instruction in educational establishments. Colonial economic policies also left permanent fixtures in the Asian landscape, including ports, highways, railroads, water-control projects, research facilities, and bridges. While often built with revenues generated in the colonies themselves and for the benefit of the colonial economy, the ports and other facilities became the infrastructure upon which the independent Asian nation-states depended in their early years of independence. Colonial social policies attempted to impose Western values on Asian societies.

Christian missionaries in China or pursued education in Europe or the United States. East Asian scholars returned from their sojourns in the West having mastered a Western language and having internalized Western values, and many of these overseas-trained elite spearheaded the nationalist movements in East Asia and led the drives to modernize their respective countries. Education in the West has continued to bring Western influences into East Asia.

Backlash

In many instances modern East Asian societies have reacted against Western behavioral norms and values. People have decried the fact that continuing exposure to stimuli from the West, with its technological superiority and its wealth, has eroded traditional ways of life and traditional virtues, such as respect for authority, a sense of familial duty, and individual sacrifice for the larger common good, whether that be the good of the family or even the nation. Nevertheless, the lure of wealth and technological advancement have continued to entice the East Asian populace, assuring the continued health of Westernization.

Kog Yue Choong

Further Reading

Apter, David E. (1965) *The Politics of Modernization.* Chicago: University of Chicago Press.

Beasley, W. G. (1963) *The Modern History of Japan.* London: Weidenfeld and Nicolson.

Darling, Frank C. (1979) *The Westernization of Asia: A Comparative Political Analysis.* Boston: G. K. Hall.

Fairbank, John K. (1971) *The United States and China.* Cambridge, MA: Harvard University Press.

Franke, Wolfgang. (1967) *China and the West.* New York: Harper and Row.

Han, Sung-Joo. (1998) "Asian Values: Asset or Liability?" In *Globalisation, Governance, and Civil Society.* Tokyo: Japan Centre for International Exchange, 63–71.

Lamb, Beatrice Pitney. (1968) *India: A World in Transition.* New York: Frederick A. Praeger.

Latouche, Serge. (1996) *The Westernisation of the World.* Oxford: Polity Press.

Pannikar, K. M. (1953) *Asia and Western Dominance.* London: George Allen and Unwin.

Sansom, G. B. (1965) *The Western World and Japan.* New York: Alfred A. Knopf.

Ware, Edith E. (1932) *Business and Politics in the Far East.* New Haven, CT: Yale University Press.

WESTERNIZATION—SOUTH ASIA

The term "Westernization" alludes to more than just the social effects that Western civilization has produced in non-Western societies. In the South Asian context it also tacitly admits the hegemony of Western paradigms of thought and practice. Hence, some sensitive scholars and social thinkers in South Asia vigorously oppose Westernization. Yet opposing Westernization is an uphill task, if not an altogether futile exercise. Nirad Chaudhuri, an Indian writer in English and a self-proclaimed admirer of the British empire, dramatically highlights the tacit Indian acceptance of Western hegemony by recounting Robert Clive's victory procession in Murshidabad after he won the Battle of Plassey in 1757. He notes that if each of the gathered native onlookers had hurled a stone at the procession, Clive and his entire army would have been submerged under a mountain of stones! Anthropologists prefer to view such acquiescence as a reflection of the Indian genius for adaptation. This view glosses over the altered social and cultural framework within which such adaptation occurs. It also hides the fundamental change in the mental outlook of the people; in fact, the urge to oppose Westernizing trends is itself a Westernized response to Westernization.

In this article, the focus will be mainly on the Indian experience because the colonial penetration was deeper and more widespread in India than in the other countries of the region. The experience of other South Asian countries will be used to point to divergences from the central tendencies.

Values and Ideologies

The values and ideologies of the Western civilization have made a deep and long-lasting impression on the people of South Asia, particularly on those exposed to Western knowledge and education. These values and ideologies of liberty, individual freedom, equality, citizenship, and democracy stood in stark contrast to the holistic and hierarchical values of the South Asian cultures and triggered indigenous impulses toward social reforms. Of course, the lofty ideals that Western civilization cherished could not justify colonial rule. As Nirad Chaudhuri noted in his dedication to his book *Autobiography of an Unknown Indian*, the British denied Indians the status of British citizenship and considered them as mere British subjects. To justify such differential treatment and their rule of India they evolved the credo of the civilizing mission and of the White Man's Burden. Guided by such dual value schemes, British rule generated mixed and ambiguous responses from its subjects. The constant reminder of subjugation in everyday life tempered their admiration for Western culture.

According to French anthropologist Louis Dumont, the ideology that distinguishes Western civilization is individualism. The interests of the individual gain priority over the interests of the group or community to which he or she belongs. The individual is free to pursue his own interests and inclinations so long as he does not abridge the interests of others in doing so. The other important ideas associated with the West, such as liberty, equality, citizenship, democracy, separation of the secular realm from that of the sacred, and rationality are all derived from the importance accorded to the individual. Individualism is the bedrock of capitalism, which has institutionalized private property and free labor.

Several Indians who acquired Western education were profoundly influenced by the works of Enlightenment thinkers. Such men as Raja Ram Mohan Roy, Jotiba Phule, Mahatma Gandhi, E. V. Ramaswamy Naicker, and Dr. B. R. Ambedkar were the more prominent Indians who launched vigorous campaigns to rid society of its superstitious practices and institutions. As is well known, the seeds of nationalist struggles and movements for the establishment of democratic regimes owe much to the lessons that the people in South Asia learned from the West.

Some scholars point out that many of the Western ideals that created social stirrings in India were not new to the country; indeed, historical evidence suggests that many profoundly liberating and universal ideals originated in India. Yet these ideals remained secondary to the ethos of hierarchy and authoritarianism. The failure of several bhakti (devotional) sects in fighting the evil of caste discrimination and hierarchy and their own subsequent conversion into castes testifies to the dominance of hierarchy in India.

It is necessary to point out that the South Asian societies have not been as favorably disposed to the ideology of individualism as they have been to the ideology of equality. Even Ambedkar, who as chairman of the drafting committee of the 1949 Indian Constitution incorporated individual liberty in the constitution's section on fundamental rights, realized the need to qualify the rights of individuals to serve the collective interests of certain oppressed castes and tribes. He believed that liberty would be meaningless to members of the oppressed castes unless their interests were protected through special constitutional provisions. Hence, the Scheduled Castes and Scheduled Tribes were given special privileges in India's constitution. Individualism is looked upon with suspicion in Islam, which is after all a communitarian religion. There is the general apprehension in South Asia that the Western concept of individual freedom encourages individuals to question the authority of traditional institutions and customs and promotes a culture of decadence and hedonism. By adopting an Islamic con-stitution, Pakistan chose to oppose individualism at the ideological level. Yet a major dilemma confronting Pakistan as well as other South Asian societies is the inability to reverse trends toward individualization that are inherent in market-oriented models of development adopted by all the countries in the region.

The ideology of equality has had profound effects on India despite the fact that British rule in actual practice strengthened authoritarian and hierarchical values and institutions in India. The credo of the civilizing mission not only helped the British to justify their rule in India but also it allowed them to slip easily into the patron-client or *mai-baap* relationship with the local population. In effect, the Westerners simply replaced the nawabs they had earlier overthrown. The new form of authoritarianism tended to take on racial overtones, as was blatantly visible in the whites-only clubs that sprouted in urban centers and hill stations in India. In the tea plantations of Bengal, and in the indigo plantations of Champaran in Bihar, the patronage system gave rise to repressive labor practices. While the British rule did promote modern industrialization to a limited extent, the colonial government favored and protected European investors in India, resulting in discrimination against local Indian entrepreneurs. Such glaring inequities fueled the nationalist movement.

British rule reinforced the consciousness of caste by generating the politics of caste. The decision to enumerate castes in the Indian censuses heightened the awareness of customs and markers of social status that differentiate castes. It also promoted a new sense of solidarity among castes sharing similar social or occupational traits, even when there was no social interaction among them. More important is the caste politics generated by caste enumeration. Castes competed with each other to be ranked as superior castes. Later, educated and politically conscious members of underprivileged castes launched movements demanding reservations in educational institutions and the government so that their members could overcome their social disabilities.

For administrative convenience, the British used certain stereotypes about castes and communities. For instance, because certain tribal communities that were displaced from their habitats due to government policies resorted to petty theft and robbery for their survival, they were categorized as criminal tribes and an officially sponsored folklore about their ruthlessness and innate criminal tendencies was constructed. The stereotype colored the attitude of the police as well as of the mainstream society, thereby further alienating and isolating the members of these unfortunate communities. Similarly, the decision to declare certain communities as martial and favor recruitment of their members in the army resulted in the dominance of particular communities in the army. The Muslim weavers of the United Provinces belonging to the Julaha caste who lost their livelihoods because of cheap British imports of machine-made cotton cloth were administratively classified as "bigoted" because their economic vulnerability was exploited by vested interests to incite them to violence against the Hindus. A by-product of such state-sponsored stereotyping was the reinforcement of caste and community sentiments and corresponding constriction of the scope for individualism.

The work of various European scholars, missionaries, and administrators considerably shaped the self-image of South Asians, just as it kindled the Western romance with exotic India. The Orientalists learned Sanskrit and other ancient Indian languages, which tended to highlight the greatness of ancient India and its long history. Several European scholars and travelers wrote about the unique features of the Indian village and the caste system. European missionaries learned Indian languages and wrote authoritative dictionaries that gave birth to new literary trends in these languages. Orientalist scholarship nurtured by the Europeans aroused the consciousness of educated Indians about their rich cultural heritage. The translation of several rare manuscripts written in Sanskrit and Pali, archaeological discoveries at Harappa and Mohenjo Daro, and the unearthing of numerous Buddhist relics scattered all over the country deeply affected educated Indians. These discoveries provided the Indians with the raw materials to construct a new national identity. Nationalists used the Europeans' scholarly contributions to redefine Hinduism as a great and tolerant religion so that they could forge a semblance of unity across the divisions of caste, religion, ethnicity, and language. The works of European philologists who traced links between Sanskrit and European languages and speculated about the Aryan-Dravidian division in India also fueled the powerful Dravidian movement in the south, with its separatist overtones. Several revivalist and anti-Western movements were also kindled by Oriental studies initiated by Western scholars, along with the notion that reconstructing the glorious past necessitated a rejection of the Western influence that only bred inferiority complexes and sapped creative energies.

Institutions and Interactions

The British evolved a mammoth and stable administration in India that made possible the large-scale mobilization of human and material resources to collect revenue and maintain law and order. Administrative decisions became more predictable and provided greater social stability. The introduction of modern

A young woman reads a Western fashion magazine on a street in New Delhi, India, in 1990. (ARVIND GARG/CORBIS)

systems of transport and communications, the systems of modern medical care, Western education, law and justice, and the establishment of a modern bureaucracy provided benefits to the people. The system of Western medicine and health care provided cures for several diseases and stemmed epidemics that used to take a huge toll of life. The Western system of education in English unlocked the doors to knowledge of modern science, technology, Western literature, and philosophy and opened up employment opportunities for the educated. These visible benefits camouflaged the effects of colonial exploitation so well that the British rule even acquired considerable legitimacy in the eyes of numerous Indians. The "backward classes" and the depressed castes viewed British rule as delivering them from the age-old oppression of the caste system and hence were reluctant to join the freedom struggle.

After Independence

After India gained independence, the influence of Britain gradually waned while the influence of the United States and the Soviet Union increased dramatically. The influence of the Soviet Union was pronounced at the ideological and policy levels. The Soviet Union's experiment with socialism and with economic planning provided the template for India's development. The government of India set up the National Planning Commission to prepare five-year plans to steer the Indian economy firmly toward the socialist pattern. The socialist strategy, with its accent on equity, enlarged the bureaucracy and invested it with considerable discretionary power. One consequence of these policies was that socialist ideals and ideas of equality became firmly entrenched in the Indian political firmament. Socialism became the rhetoric of party politics, with different political parties espousing their own versions. As it evolved through the politics of India, socialism took on the idiom of caste; the theme of social justice for the socially and educationally deprived castes and communities gained prominence on the political agenda. Politics of caste reinforced caste identities, instead of diluting them as was fondly hoped by several socialist ideologues.

It could be inferred that Westernization in both the colonial and postcolonial contexts strengthened caste and community solidarities. This seeming continuity, however, hides the qualitative change that has occurred in the nature of caste society. In the colonial era, competition between castes was mainly over relative ranking in the status hierarchy. The census officials of the colonial era confronted representatives of castes who brought with them documentary evidence substantiating their claims to superior ranking vis-à-vis other proximate castes. After independence, castes competed with each other for the special privileges provided by the government to the deprived castes, ostensibly to abolish caste hierarchy itself. In contemporary India, the talk of one caste being superior to another is not part of politically appropriate speech. Notions of caste hierarchy surface mainly in private spheres and in informal conversations.

Although the Soviet Union was the officially sponsored model for independent India, the United States proved to be the popular model of Westernization. While the leading politicians and government officials in India were espousing the merits of socialist, indigenous models of self-reliant development and were even sharply critical of the policies of the United States, their children were forming long lines at the U.S. embassy and its consulates in India for visas to study or work in the United States. The preference for green-card holders (persons who are officially granted the status of resident aliens by the federal government of the United States) and NRIs (nonresident Indians) settled in the United States expressed in matrimonial advertisements in prominent Indian newspapers reflect the fascination of the Indian middle class with the American way of life.

Fashion, like all other elements of culture, is also a site of controversy. In this context, it is important to note that some of the American fashion trends that have shaped the culture of the Indian youth in urban elite families are in fact derived from the African-American trends that mock and debunk the culture of the white elite in America. By adopting some of the Western dress codes, young women from urban middle classes have been able to break free of the repressive dress codes that kept their mothers secluded from pubic life. Western styles also made it possible for members of marginalized castes to erase humiliating markers of their low social status. Defiance is more sharply articulated in American pop songs that have influenced the tastes of urban Indian youth. In India, television channels such as MTV and VTV, which play pop music, have even developed Indian versions of pop culture that pungently and wittily expose the hypocrisy of the mainstream traditional culture.

The influence of television on the youth and the consequent weakening of indigenous traditions have triggered strong reactions from conservative sections of society. Such strong reactions have given birth to militant movements attacking the Western way of life as decadent, hedonistic, and morally repugnant. Some of these movements resort to the use of force to wipe out corrupting Western influences and conserve traditional values and practices. In recent years, beauty contests, films allegedly portraying Indian women in a negative light, and the celebration of Valentine's Day have been targeted by organizations ostensibly seeking to defend traditional Indian culture and values.

The British rule also had a liberating impact on women in India. It was during the British rule that the practice of suttee or immolation of the widow in the funeral pyre of her dead husband was abolished. Western values inspired several educated Indians to launch movements against child marriage and to actively promote widow remarriage and women's education. The constitution of independent India by adopting adult franchise and by making special provisions for the welfare of women sought to promote the idea of gender equality. Yet, during the early years of independence a woman's sphere of influence continued to be mainly within the household. Women were encouraged to go to schools and colleges and even take up jobs outside the family, but these extramural roles only complemented their main role, which was the care of their families.

The impact of postcolonial Westernization on women has been complex and uneven. While the Western ideas of feminism and gender equality have encouraged some urban middle-class women to become educated and compete with men in various professions, Indian women face new obstacles in their quest for gender equality. In urban middle-class families, young men were encouraged to pursue prestigious careers in the government bureaucracy or as high-salaried professionals in various public-sector and private-sector concerns or, better still, migrate abroad, preferably to the United States, for lucrative jobs. They were sent to prestigious English schools and professional colleges and institutes to prepare them for successful careers. Although their sisters were encouraged to study and go to English schools and convents, the main objective was to make them attractive and eligible brides for successful grooms. For women, career was only a secondary option. Further, as a family consisting of unmarried young women loses its social status, parents of young women became anxious to find grooms for their daughters as soon as they came of age. Under the circumstances, the institution of dowry—previously confined to certain upper castes—became almost universal in India. Dowry even spread to those castes that had traditionally required grooms to pay a bride-price. As the institution of dowry gained in popularity, dowry demands also started mounting. Parents of eligible young men perched in a successful career could demand huge amounts of money and other gifts from parents desperate to marry off their daughters. Reports of dowry deaths, invariably involving the avaricious groom and his parents forcibly setting the woman on fire, appeared so frequently in newspapers and magazines that the government passed an act banning the practice of dowry and changed the rules regarding the registration of evidence to ensure that the accused parties will not escape prosecution owing to procedural technicalities. Linked with the issue of dowry is the practice of female feticide and infanticide that is taking new forms. For instance, sex determination tests using ultrasound techniques are extensively used, despite a legal ban on conducting such tests, so that female fetuses can be aborted. Demographers point out that the persistence of an adverse female-male sex ratio in the Indian population even after more than five decades of attaining independence does not augur well for gender equality.

The trend of rising dowry demands compelled parents to encourage their daughters to study and become eligible for jobs so that they could help in accumulating the dowry fund. Also as "working girls" are now preferred to "homely brides," a trend that began in the 1970s, marriage prospects for women holding jobs improve considerably. As women go out of their homes to study and work, they get opportunities to mix freely with other men and become autonomous enough to contract love marriages that violate the rules of caste endogamy. Such marriages may not be acceptable to the parents of the couple, but in urban India the popularity of commercial Hindi films that celebrate love marriage has ensured the social acceptability of such unions. Recent newspaper reports mention incidents of love marriages violating rules of caste endogamy and hierarchy from rural areas. These reports also describe the hostile reaction of caste *panchayat*s (traditional institutions governing caste affairs) to such marriages. The offending couple are punished with banishment from the village, a ban on social interaction, or even a death sentence carried out without legal sanction.

The feminist movement in India that arose in the 1970s had indigenous roots, but the rise of feminist ideology in the West provided inspiration for Indian intellectuals to investigate the condition of women in India. They launched campaigns to bring to light the plight of women in India and sensitize the public about gender issues. Indian feminists viewed women's oppression as a societal problem and focused their attention on ways of overcoming the constraints imposed by patriarchal traditions by creating a general social awareness of women's problems (in marked contrast to the strategy of confrontation with men that several Western feminists advocated). Despite this strategy, the feminists have been unable to reverse the adverse trends in gender relations. For instance, despite vigorous campaigns to reserve seats for women in the Indian Parliament, and despite the express commitment of the ruling government and the leading opposition party to have the constitution amended suitably for the purpose, the Parliament has been unable to take up the relevant bill for discussion. A prominent male Member of Parliament who had vigorously supported the policy of reservations for the "backward classes" opposed the introduction of the bill on the ground that it only promoted the cause of women who had bobbed their hair—a pejorative reference to Westernized women. The statement of this Member of Parliament only reflected his antagonism to the Westernization that has encouraged Indian women to reject traditional restraints on their sexuality by adopting the liberal views of Western women. It is true that several revivalist groups and movements strongly oppose Westernization because they are convinced that it corrodes traditional morality, values, and institutions. What is more significant is that this view is tacitly endorsed by even some of the progressive political parties and intellectuals.

Westernization Outgrown?

It is clear that it is not possible to trace linear trends of Westernization in South Asia. Considering that the Western encounter has been deeply felt for over two centuries, contradictory trends and processes generated by Westernization are bound to be encountered. Westernization has not succeeded if we assess the phenomenon in terms of English writer Thomas Macaulay's dream of converting Indians into Englishmen in tastes and habits. Western culture has been consciously resisted, and there have been several instances of sharp backlash against Westernization. Individualism has not been able to cut through the dense tangle of bonds of family and kinship, caste, religion, and language. A dissonance has emerged between the ideology of equality and its practice. In practice, measures taken to reduce social inequality have often proved to be counterproductive. This change in discourse is nevertheless radical; hierarchy that was only a few decades ago accepted as an inevitable feature of society in India has now been displaced by the principle of equality.

Some recent trends in globalization are now challenging the ideology of individualism. Western societies are increasingly attracting migrants from non-Western societies to bolster their economies. The presence of these immigrants and their growing political importance have compelled the major political parties in Western countries to pay special attention to the problem of immigrant minorities. The migrants' rights as citizens and their rights to preserve their cultural identity have now become vital political issues. Consequently, the discourse of individual rights and rights of citizenship around which law and order is structured is increasingly proving to be inadequate to guide political governance. Further, as the cultural interaction between the native Westerners and the immigrants intensify and as the ethos of multiculturalism spreads, Western culture is itself caught in the vortex of radical transformation. The usefulness of the concept of Westernization cannot any longer be taken for granted.

M. N. Panini

See also: **Marriage and Family—South Asia; Orientalism**

Further Reading

Chaudhuri, Nirad C. (1951) *Autobiography of an Unknown Indian.* London: Macmillan.

———. (1975) *Clive of India: A Political and Psychological Essay.* London: Barrie & Jenkins.
Gupta, Dipankar. (2000) *Mistaken Modernity: India between Worlds.* New York: HarperCollins.
Madan, T. N. (1996) *Pathways: Approaches to the Study of Society in India.* Delhi: Oxford University Press.
Srinivas, M. N. (1966) *Social Change in Modern India.* Berkeley and Los Angeles: University of California Press.

WESTERNIZATION—SOUTHEAST ASIA

In reflecting on the Westernization of Southeast Asia, it is first important to define carefully the term itself. By "Westernization" is meant specific economic, sociocultural, and political influences on the region emanating from the West (that is, Europe, the United States, and Australia and New Zealand). The earliest external influences on the region (pre-sixteenth century) were not from the West, but from India, China, and the Islamic world. These influences were primarily in religion, culture, art, and political systems.

The first Western contact with Southeast Asia was through European exploration such as that by the Dutch and Portuguese. In 1511, the Portuguese captured Melaka and had arrived in the Moluccas. The explorers were followed by missionaries who were active throughout the region. These early contacts paved the way for colonization of the entire region, except for Siam (Thailand). Dutch trader Gerritt van Wuysthoff traveled up the Mekong River in 1641–1642 to the Lao capital, Vientiane. The French mistakenly anticipated that the Mekong River would be a navigational gateway to the riches of China, and this partially explained their interest in colonizing Vietnam, Laos, and Cambodia. Among famous explorers of the region who often left detailed records of their travels and observations were Ferdinand Magellan (who died in the Philippines), Stamford Raffles (founder of Singapore), Francis Garnier (who explored the Mekong River), Joseph-Fernand Grenard, Henri Mouhot, August Pavie, and David Livingston. Among important missionaries who were active in the region were Father da Cruz, Henri Langenois, Dan Beach Bradley, Alexander de Rhodes (who developed a system, *quoc ngu*, for romanizing the Vietnamese language, 1624–1630), and Samuel McFarland. A number of Western novelists such as Joseph Conrad, Somerset Maugham, Pierre Loti, and in more recent decades Graham Greene, Eugene Burdick, Marguerite Duras, Anthony Burgess, C. J. Koch, Blanche d'Alpuget, and Robert Drewe were inspired by their experiences in the region. They left powerful Westernized and often distorted images of the region. Their literary works, however, provide rich insights into the complex nature of the Westerners' encounters with Southeast Asia.

TABLE 1

Colonization

Nation (current name)	Former colonial name	Date colonized	Colonizing country	Date of independence
Brunei	Brunei	1888	Protectorate of the United Kingdom	1984
Cambodia	Cambodge; formerly part of French Indochina	1863 (French protectorate established)	France	1953
East Timor		1860, 1893, 1914	Portugal	1975 (from Portugal); 1999 (from Indonesia)
Indonesia	Dutch East Indies	End of seventeenth century	The Netherlands	1949*
Laos	Formerly part of French Indochina	1893	France	1949
Malaysia	Straits Settlements; Malaya	1867	United Kingdom	1957
Myanmar	Burma; also formerly part of Greater India	1885	United Kingdom	1948
The Philippines (name derives from the name of a Spanish king)	The Philippines	Late sixteenth century; 1898 (United States)	Spain and then United States	1946
Singapore	Formerly part of Straits Settlements; Malaysia	1819	United Kingdom	1963 (joined independent Malaysia); 1965 (from Malaysia)
Vietnam	Part of French Indochina	1884; French Indochina established in 1887	France	1945, 1954,* 1975*

*Independence involved violent struggle.

Western Colonization of Southeast Asia

Competition was intense among the Western colonialists for Southeast Asian territories. (See Table 1.) In mainland Southeast Asia, the primary competitors were the British coming from the west (Burma and India) and the French coming from the east (coastal Vietnam). In insular Southeast Asia, the competition was primarily among the Dutch, British, and Portuguese. The United States replaced Spain as the colonial power in the Philippines as a result of the Spanish-American War. In so doing, the United States thwarted an indigenous Filipino revolution fighting for independence.

Siam

Siam represents a fascinating case of selective Westernization without colonization. Siam was the only nation in the region not to be colonized. The Siamese kings of the nineteenth century evolved astute diplomatic strategies for avoiding colonization and playing the British and French off against each other by becoming a buffer state between the two colonial powers. In a major act of compromise, the Siamese ceded important territories in what are now Laos and Cambodia to the French. The Siamese historically were also open to outsiders, and prominent Dutch, Greeks, and Portuguese were allowed to play important roles in the Siamese court. Later in the nineteenth and twentieth centuries, various Westerners contributed to the modernization of Siam. Missionaries such as Dan Beach Bradley contributed to the development of the Siamese printing industry and modern health practices. Missionaries also contributed to the establishment of excellent schools, which are still prominent to this day. Germans were invited in to help develop a modern rail system; British advisers helped with the development of modern financial institutions. The basic strategy was to make Siam sufficiently open to Westerners that there would be no need to colonize it.

Westernization after Independence

The Asia-Pacific theater of World War II, in which the Japanese invaded and took control of much of Southeast Asia, helped awaken powerful forces of local nationalism. The Japanese demonstrated to the Southeast Asians the possibility of opposing the West successfully. Thus, within the first two decades after World War II, all the nations of Southeast Asia had received their independence, except for East Timor, a colony of Portugal that was later absorbed by Indonesia, and Brunei, which remained a protectorate of the United Kingdom until 1984.

Political Westernization Despite achieving political independence, the Southeast Asian nations continued to feel the force of Westernization in various domains. In the political arena, Southeast Asia became a battleground of the Cold War, with the USSR, China, and the United States fighting for influence among Southeast Asian nations. Communist insurgencies supported by the Marxist-Leninist USSR emerged in the Philippines, Malaya, Thailand, Vietnam, Cambodia, and Laos. Indonesia at one point also had a very large communist party, the PKI. The West intervened politically in these areas to try to stop the spread of communism, ironically itself a Western influence. Communism failed in the Philippines, Malaya, Singapore, Indonesia, and Thailand, but it succeeded in Cambodia, Laos, and Vietnam. Politically, the United States continues to support actively the development of democracy and civil society in the major nations of the region.

Cultural Westernization Southeast Asian culture also continues to feel the effect of Westernization. Popular Western dress, music, film, and fast food permeate the urban areas of most parts of Southeast Asia. The powerful forces of transnational corporations and advertising have also contributed to a growing materialism. Reflective of this new value placed on material goods is the common pattern of evaluating people's status based on their possession of those goods. In the early 1960s, U.S. advisers called for Bangkok, Thailand, to become an automobile city. Many canals were replaced by highways, and the "Venice of the East" became a highly urbanized, congested, and polluted city. Possession of automobiles, and importance attached to the prestige of the type of vehicle owned, has become an integral part of the growing materialistic culture.

Throughout much of the region there is the pervasive influence of modern transnational corporations such as IBM, Coca-Cola, KFC (Kentucky Fried Chicken), McDonald's, Nike, and Philip Morris (Marlboro cigarettes, especially prominent in Cambodia, which has a large potential youth market). Nike has outsourced significant production to subcontractors in Indonesia, Thailand, and Vietnam, with a presence also in Cambodia and Laos. Sometimes Brunei is referred to as the Shell-fare state, given the prominence of the Royal Dutch/Shell Group in that nation.

A prominent building in old Bangkok is the headquarters of the East Asiatic Company, a major Scandinavian trading company, which has been active in the region for many decades. Thailand is becoming the "Detroit of Southeast Asia" with the major presence of Western automobile manufacturers such as General Motors.

Technological influences from the West are also pervasive, especially in modern urban areas. Personal cell phones (many Nokia or Motorola) are ubiquitous in the cities of Southeast Asia. Cable television and Internet services have dramatically expanded, especially in urban areas. Southeast Asians appear extremely open to the adoption of new Western technologies in all arenas of life.

The physical infrastructure of Southeast Asian nations shows Western influence in the buildings that survive from colonial days. Laos, Cambodia, and Vietnam are all noteworthy for their colonial French architecture. In fact, the policy of Laos is the total preservation of such distinctive cream-colored architecture as an important and unique historical legacy.

The British colonies of Singapore and Malaysia also benefited from important physical and human infrastructure (modern bureaucratic structures) as a legacy of British rule. Even in Yangon (formerly Rangoon), the capital of Myanmar, there is evidence of an important physical infrastructure left behind by the British colonial masters.

The growth of the tourism industry is another by-product of Westernization. Among major attractions are Bali in Indonesia; Thailand, with its many famous beaches and excellent tourist infrastructure; and Angkor Wat temple in Cambodia, the world's largest religious monument. Vietnam also has excellent tourism potential. Tourism represents in the region a major earner of foreign exchange from the West.

Educational and Economic Westernization Two important interrelated areas of Western influence are economic aid and international education. Many Southeast Asian young people educated in the West returned to play leading roles in overturning traditional political systems. Examples of such individuals are Ho Chi Minh, Pol Pot, Pridi Banomyong, and Pibul Songkram. During the post–World War II period, many educated youth from the region have aspired to study in the West. Apart from skills learned, study in the West brings great prestige and status. Many leading intellectuals, technocrats, and some politicians in the region were educated in the West. Among prominent political leaders educated in the West are Thaksin Shinawatra, prime minister of Thailand; Corazon Aquino, former president of the Philippines; President Gloria Macapagal Arroyo of the Philippines; and Lee Kuan Yew, former leader of Singapore. Universities in the West are active in recruiting students from the region, and some are offering education in the region itself with offshore programs.

Because Southeast Asia is a region primarily of developing nations, nearly all nations (except wealthy Brunei and Singapore) have been major recipients of international development assistance from the West. Currently, transitional economies such as those of Cambodia, Laos, and Vietnam are also receiving significant economic assistance from the West.

These postcolonial Western influences, especially materialism, have given rise to the growth of anti-Western movements. Several key intellectuals in the region, including Sulak Sivaraksa in Thailand, Renato Constantino in the Philippines, and Syed Hussein Alatas in Malaysia, have been highly critical of the pervasive influence of Western materialism. Sulak, for example, calls for a return to core traditional Buddhist values. Despite the prolific writings and the social activism of those opposing Westernization and globalization, they have had little impact in stemming the tide of rising Western materialism and modern popular culture and their growing influence throughout the region.

Gerald W. Fry

Further Reading

Coedes, George. (1968) *The Indianized States of Southeast Asia.* Edited by Walter F. Vella and translated by Susan Brown Cowing. Honolulu, HI: East-West Center.

Darling, Frank C. (1979) *The Westernization of Asia: A Comparative Political Analysis.* Boston: G. K. Hall.

King, Victor T. (1995) *Explorers of South-East Asia: Six Lives.* New York: Oxford University Press.

May, Glenn A. (1991) *Battle for Batangas: A Philippine Province at War.* New Haven, CT: Yale University Press.

Multatuli. (1982) *Max Havelaar, or, The Coffee Auctions of the Dutch Trading Company.* Trans. by Roy Edwards. Amherst, MA: University of Massachusetts Press.

Orwell, George. (1967) *Burmese Days: A Novel.* London: Heinemann.

Reid, Anthony. (1999) "Heaven's Will and Man's Fault: The Rise of the West as a Southeast Asian Dilemma." In *Charting the Shape of Early Modern Southeast Asia,* edited by Anthony Reid. Chiang Mai, Thailand: Silkworm Books, 246–271.

———, ed. (1993) *Southeast Asia in the Early Modern Era: Trade, Power, and Beliefs.* Ithaca, NY: Cornell University Press.

Sioris, George A. (1998) *Phaulkon: The Greek First Counsellor at the Court of Siam: An Appraisal.* Bangkok, Thailand: The Siam Society.

Sulak Sivaraksa. (1985) *Siamese Resurgence: A Thai Buddhist Voice on Asia and a World in Change.* Bangkok, Thailand: Asian Cultural Forum on Development.

WESTERNIZATION—WEST ASIA The nations of West Asia (Turkey, Iran, and Iraq) are considered part of the Middle East, the home of Islam, and they have a distinct history, culture, and civilization. There is a close nexus between religious authority and society. Of the three West Asian nations of the Middle East, Turkey is among the most secular and Westernized, whereas Iran and Iraq are less so, though they are almost as different from each other as they are from Turkey. Contradictions in the regime structures, political ideologies, and institutional goals of these nations have provided a fertile ground for the growth of radicalism. The state has turned out to be a most powerful institution, the final arbiter in matters of politics and societal structure.

Over the centuries, conservative and radical Arab nationalism has been a mainstream influence on state, social, and political institutions in the Middle East. By pushing people toward Islamic fundamentalism, Arab nationalism has restricted the development of a progressive outlook.

The process of Westernization in the Middle East, insofar as it has occurred, has been gradual, complex, and painful, carried out over decades to bring about transformation in patriarchal, feudal, and conservative societies. In Iran, the regime (1921–1941) of Reza Shah Pahlavi (1878–1944) in Iran began the modernization process under which he diverted major resources to expanding and strengthening the military apparatus to ensure the continuation of the absolute monarchy. To this end, he modernized military apparatus, built roads, improved the transportation system, and invested oil-based revenues in defense. The process opened up Iran's oil-based economy to Great Britain and the United States.

The inroads Reza Shah made in modernizing Iran did not extend to Westernizing it, however. In fact, his regime imposed strict censorship on the press and limited freedom of speech and expression. He deployed secret police to eliminate progressive-minded political leaders. His autocratic policies failed to create a cohesive socioeconomic base to bring about attitudinal changes among masses, and his style of autocratic regime was incompatible with liberal and democratic values.

It is paradoxical that Westernization and radical Arab nationalism have coexisted. For Middle Eastern nations, the admirable aspects of Western society are modern political concepts such as legitimacy, adult franchise, and gender equality. The Middle East's intellectuals and educated citizenry have not been so accepting what they perceive as an excessive focus on

An Iranian family drinks Coca-Cola outside a cold drink shop in Bam, Iran, in 1997. (EARL & NAZIMA KOWALL/ CORBIS)

individualism and materialism. The ruling elites in the oil-rich Middle East are also affected by the impact of science and information technology, globalization, and the opportunities presented by trade and investment. Some recognize that economic reforms, political moderation, and social change can bring economic growth, employment, and an improved standard of living for their populace.

Turkey

Turkey, with a population of 61.8 million (1997 census), is a democratic and secular country. The Turks constitute approximately 80 percent of the population; of them, 66 percent are Sunni Muslims and 33 percent are Alevi (Shi'ite) Muslims. Agriculture provides 50 percent of the nation's jobs. Early on, Mustafa Kemal Ataturk (1881–1938) championed Westernization. He ordered the adoption of Western clothing, replaced the Arabic alphabet with the Roman alphabet, and emphasized a secular state. By and

large, the nation has followed that path ever since, although in the 1990s Islamists came to have a stronger voice of opposition.

As a result of modernization programs launched by the government, Turkey's economy is being steadily liberalized. Transportation and communication facilities are fast expanding. Industrial growth contributes more than 30 percent of GDP, and 33 percent of employment in the labor sector. More significantly, the Turkish government has abolished Sufi orders and closed down *madrasah*s (Islamic religious schools), which are associated with radical Islam. The fast expansion of basic education has brought the country's literacy rate to more than 81 percent. Cumulatively speaking, Turkey has become an ideal model of a progressive and modern state in the Middle East, although its human-rights record still leaves much to be desired. The people of Turkey do not consider themselves Westernized in the strict liberal sense of the term, however.

Iran

The Constitutional Revolution (1906), the nationalist movement of 1951–1953, and the Islamic Revolution of 1978–1979 were Iran's three major political movements during the twentieth century. They opposed the unjust and illiberal monarchy, and granted Western-style individual freedom and rights within the framework of Islamic ideology. In March 1979, the Islamic Republic proposed by Ayatollah Khomeini (1900–1989) was overwhelmingly endorsed by the people (98.2 percent) in a referendum. But the Islamization measures undertaken under the Khomeini's regime were anti-Western, aimed at reversing liberal reforms, social progress, and women's rights. Socioculturally and psychologically, Westernization was seen as antithetical to Islamic ideology.

In the 1990s, after the death of Khomeini, a process of political reform started. Iranian people favored individual freedom and rights. Reformists launched a political campaign to promote democratic values. Hashemi Rafsanjani (b. 1934), a champion of modernization and political reform, was elected as president in July 1989. He made efforts to revamp the economy and emphasized the necessity for liberal education in schools and colleges. The 1997 election of his successor, Muhammad Khatami (b. 1943), proved beyond doubt that the people were not in favor of conservatives and radicals. The government has demonstrated that it is not opposed to the new sources of legitimacy. In 1999, three hundred women out of a total of five thousand women candidates won local elections. Like men, women are entitled to vote at the age of fifteen. Women continue to face discrimination in employment and the social sector, however.

The new regime in Iran today is keen to introduce secular values. Nevertheless, radical forces are still very active in Iran; these forces question the legitimacy of Western values, which they think are antithetical to Islamic ideology. In addition, there is the difficult task of blending modernity with social justice.

Iraq

Iraq has been under a long spell of the presidential dictatorship. It has suffered a lot almost on all fronts under the regime of Saddam Hussein (b. 1937), who came to power in 1968. He is opposed to Western values tooth and nail, and considers the West, especially the United States, to be the enemy of Islam. The people in Iraq have virtually no individual freedom or rights. Nor is there gender equality. The press is fully under the control of the government. All these have contributed to the reversal of the Westernization program of the 1950s and the 1960s. Economically, Iraq has suffered as a result of the Persian Gulf War (1990–1991). Unemployment is estimated at 50 percent.

When applying the yardstick of Westernization in terms of broad social and cultural outlook, expansion of education, economic development, growth of technology and mass media, and improved living and health standards, West Asia can hardly be described as Westernized. It is still hamstrung by conservatism, feudalism, and religious radicalism, which prevent people from imbibing the liberal democratic values of human freedom and dignity. Traditionally, the impact of Islamic beliefs and practices is so strong as to make it extremely difficult for people to change. There is still a long road to liberal democracy and secularism in the Middle East. Many regimes are not prepared to grant political freedom and rights. However, the acceleration of the process of economic reform and privatization, along with increased foreign investment, may make possible gradual political openness, economic development, and inter- and intrareligious tolerance.

B. M. Jain

Further Reading
Beinin, Joel, and Joe Stork, eds. (1996) *Political Islam: Essays from Middle East Report.* Berkeley and Los Angeles: University of California Press.
Bogle, Emory C. (1996) *The Modern Middle East: From Imperialism to Freedom, 1800–1958.* Upper Saddle River, NJ: Prentice Hall.
Choueiri, Youssef M. (2000) *Arab Nationalism: A History.* Oxford: Blackwell Publishers.
Esposito, John L. (1998). *Islam and Politics.* 4th ed. Syracuse, NY: Syracuse University Press.
Halliday, Fred. (1996). *Islam and the Myth of Confrontation: Religion and Politics in the Middle East.* New York: I. B. Tauris
Lee, Robert D. (1991). *Overcoming Tradition and Modernity: The Secret for Islamic Authenticity.* Boulder, CO: Westview.
Lewis, Bernard. (1984) *The Shaping of the Modern Middle East.* New York: Oxford University Press.
Owen, Roger. (2000) *State, Power and Politics in the Making of the Modern Middle East.* New York: Routledge
Hoiris, Ole, and Sefa Martin Yurukel, eds. (1997) *Contrasts and Solutions in the Middle East.* Aarhus, Denmark: Aarhus University Press.

WHALING—JAPAN Japan has a long history (dating back to 10,000 BCE) of whaling. Whalebones have been found in ruins from the Jomon period (10,000—300 BCE). A description of whales appeared first in the *Kojiki,* the oldest Japanese written record (712 CE). Whale meat was in supply from the Muromachi period (1333–1573).

Whaling became a prosperous endeavor in the middle of the Edo period (1600/1603–1868), and whale meat continued to be eaten. During this period, the main whaling stations were in Taiji, Koza (Wakayama Prefecture), Tsuro, Fubotsu (Kochi), Ikitsuki, Waniura, Tsushima (Nagasaki), and Awa (Chiba). Harpooning by hand was the method used. Toward the end of the seventeenth century, techniques of net whaling were developed in Taiji and continued to dominate until the end of the nineteenth century. In 1662, whaling ships were painted, and fifteen-member crews used eight sets of oars. The whales caught were grays, rights, humpbacks, fins, and probably some minkes. Temples and shrines were built to commemorate the souls of whales drowned in nets.

By 1900, through Russian whaling, the Norwegian method of using a motorized fleet was introduced to Japan. This led to the development of modern coastal whaling. Whaling traditions spread from southern Japan to the northern coast of Hokkaido, and whaling took place not only along the coast but also in the open seas of the North Pacific and Antarctic. After World War II, the people of Japan became more and more dependent on whale meat because of a food crisis and the lack of other sources of protein. In 1951, Japan signed the International Convention for the Regulation of Whaling of 1946. Japan gave up commercial whaling following the international moratorium in 1986 but has engaged in research, such as a whaling program to study southern ocean minke whales and the Antarctic ecosystem since 1987. The Institute of

Cetacean Research, created in 1987, is implementing this program with the Japan Whaling Association. Conservationists view this institute's activities, through its whaling research program, as a cover for commercial whalers. In 1993, Japan hosted the Forty-Fifth Annual Meeting of the International Whaling Commission (established in 1948) in Kyoto. The meeting resolved to work to alleviate distress to Japanese coastal whaling communities resulting from the moratorium. Today, there are four Japanese whaling communities, Taiji (population 3,900), Wada (population 6,000), Ayukawa (population 4,000), and Abashiri (population 44,000).

Nathalie Cavasin

Further Reading

Kalland, Arne, and Brian Moeran. (1992) *Japanese Whaling: End of an Era?* London: Curzon Press.

Morita, Katsuhaki. (1994) *Kujira to hogei no bunkarei* (Cultural History of Whales and Whaling). Nagoya, Japan: University of Nagoya Press.

WHITE RAJAS The White Rajas of Sarawak were British adventurers who ruled as enlightened paternal despots for more than a century, from 1841 to 1946. Three generations of the Brooke family maintained Sarawak as a multiethnic, agrarian state until they turned it over to Great Britain following World War II. The Brookes worked with the leaders from the native and immigrant populations to protect the region's traditional way of life.

The History of the White Rajas

The rule of the White Rajas began in 1841, when James Brooke (1803–1868) was granted the territory of Sarawak, then covering the Lundu, Sarawak, and Sadong River basins, by Sultan Omar Ali Saifuddin II of Brunei, as a reward for putting down a revolt staged by the Malays and Bidayuhs (Land Dayaks) of the area.

By the time that Brooke died in London, he had extended the boundaries of Sarawak eastward to the Bintulu River (1861). His nephew, Charles (1829–1917), succeeded him, and during his long reign from 1868 until his demise in 1917, Sarawak assumed its present-day configuration through acquisitions from Brunei of the Baram (1881), the Trusan (1885), the Limbang (1890), and the Lawas (1905) Rivers. Charles, together with his son and successor, Vyner (1874–1963), molded Sarawak into a semblance of a modern state, despite its isolation.

Following World War II, it was deemed financially burdensome and beyond the means for the modestly endowed Brooke government to undertake rehabilitation and reconstruction. Vyner decided that the practical option was the cession of Sarawak to the British government. In June 1946, Sarawak became a British Crown colony.

Characteristics of the Brookes

While James Brooke was courageous, charming, and charismatic, at ease with royalty as well as common people, his successor Charles was remote, reserved, uneasy, and lacking social graces in the company of high society. Unlike Charles, who was a consummate hands-on administrator, extremely thrifty and almost parsimonious, James Brooke had been a poor administrator and an even poorer financier. Vyner Brooke was shy and introverted; he disliked public appearances and pomp and ceremony. He was indecisive and had an aversion for day-to-day administration, but at the same time he was unable to delegate authority effectively. Vyner's younger brother, Bertram (1876–1965), who shared the rajaship in accordance with the will of Charles Brooke, was deferential and cautious about not upstaging Vyner. Bertram displayed no personal ambition and undertook his role as a matter of duty.

The Brookes' Principles of Governance

All the Brookes were steadfast to the principles of governance laid down by James Brooke, which became enshrined as the traditions of the White Rajas of Sarawak. These traditions emphasized the principles of trusteeship whereby Sarawak belonged to the indigenous peoples and the Brookes administered the territory on their behalf. The maintenance of the status quo in all spheres—political, economic, sociocultural—was emphasized. Change was discouraged, particularly radical transformation; if necessary or inevitable, the process of change was to be gradual and was not to affect adversely the way of life of the indigenous inhabitants.

Although the White Raja was an absolute monarch, he ruled through consultation with native chiefs, namely the Malay *datu* (nonroyal chieftains). This practice was institutionalized in 1855 with the establishment of the Supreme Council. If the raja consulted the *datu*, his European officers in the outstations relied on their respective native officers, drawn from the *perabangan* (sons of *datu*), for advice and discussion. Moreover officers at the district level were expected to seek advice and guidance from, and consult with, local native leaders. The advice and views given were not binding; nonetheless the act of consultation served the purpose of gaining the native perspective on issues. Despite being basically a public relations exercise, the General Council (instituted in 1867), a triennial gathering of native chiefs and Brookes officers with the raja, represented the formal aspect of personal rule.

The raja also consulted with Chinese communal leaders from the various dialect groups (Hokkien, Teochew, Cantonese) on matters pertaining to the Chinese community. In the Chinese court, established in 1912, Chinese communal leaders presided as magistrates to deal with civil cases involving Chinese customs, traditions, and practices.

In the economic sphere, the development of trade and commercial activities and exploitation of natural resources were to be carried out without unduly disrupting the traditional pattern of native subsistence and way of life. The indigenous peoples were to be shielded from exploitation by outsiders—European and Chinese—particularly on the issue of land. Raja Charles Brooke equated land with *darah daging* (flesh and blood) of the natives. Under no circumstances were the natives to part with this heritage. Moreover the backbone of the economy, the Brookes insisted, was to be the tilling of the land. Agriculture was the means of improving native welfare. Ideally, as Raja Charles envisioned, family-owned and family-managed smallholdings of food crops (rice) and some commercial crops (rubber, pepper, tropical fruits) were to be established. The sago-producing coastal Melanau districts were to maintain their traditional way of life.

European capital investment and Chinese labor and entrepreneurial skills, if cautiously applied, would gradually develop the resources of Sarawak. The Chinese were allowed to engage in gold mining and in trade and commerce; subsequently they dominated the country's retail trade. The Chinese also developed commercial agriculture (pepper, gambier, rubber) on a smallholding scale. The limited number of European enterprises was confined to the extractive industries (gold, oil) and plantation agriculture (rubber).

The Brookes eliminated traditional abusive practices such as *serah dagang* (forced trade), bondage, all forms of slavery, and headhunting. Although they had mixed feelings about the effects of Western-style education on the native peoples, the Brookes provided government-sponsored Malay schools and allowed Christian missionaries to establish urban English-medium and rural vernacular schools. The Brookes were dubious about the influence of Christian missions on the indigenous peoples and forbade proselytizing among the Muslims (Malays, some Melanaus, Kedayans).

After a century of White Raja rule, Sarawak was a thinly populated, tranquil, virgin country, barely touched by influences from without. The multiethnic native population remained largely in rural-based subsistence farming communities. There were also Chinese-managed commercial smallholdings of pepper, gambier, and rubber. The Chinese dominated trade and commerce. Aside from the extractive industry (oil and gold), there was a conspicuous absence of European large-scale capitalist enterprise. Equally nonexistent were native landlessness and indebtedness.

The White Rajas fostered a form of enlightened paternal despotism that jealously protected the interests of the native inhabitants and the preservation of their traditional ways of life. Consequently, economic development was sluggish, and there was no apparent significant improvement in the livelihood of the indigenous population. The provision of education and public health care barely touched the vast majority of native inhabitants. Infrastructure development was minimal.

Nonetheless, the indigenous peoples and the Chinese inhabitants revered the Brooke regime that maintained a stable administration and a peaceful country. However, heightened nationalistic feelings consequent of the brief but significant Japanese military occupation (1941–1945) of Sarawak and the changing postwar geopolitical situation made Brooke paternal rule an anachronism. When Sarawak was ceded to the British government and became a crown colony (1946–1963), a small sector of the Malay community opposed it; the majority of the population, however, viewed cession favorably. British rule brought some improvement particularly in the development of infrastructure and in the social services, such as education and public health.

Ooi Keat Gin

Further Reading

Crisswell, Colin. N. (1978) *Rajah Charles Brooke: Monarch of All He Surveyed.* Kuala Lumpur, Malaysia: Oxford University Press.

Ooi Keat Gin. (1997) *Of Free Trade and Native Interests: The Brookes and the Economic Development of Sarawak, 1841–1941.* Kuala Lumpur, Malaysia: Oxford University Press.

Pringle, Robert. (1970) *Rajahs and Rebels: The Ibans of Sarawak under Brooke Rule.* London: Macmillan.

Reece, R. H. W. (1982) *The Name of Brooke: The End of White Rajah Rule in Sarawak.* Kuala Lumpur, Malaysia: Oxford University Press.

WHITE TERROR

"White terror" was the name given to the terror regime established by the Chinese Nationalist Party (CNP, or Guomindang) after its capture of Shanghai in 1927. The violence, which drove a permanent wedge between the Nationalists (the white party) and the Communists (the red party), was directed at the labor unions and their leaders but later turned into extortion of Shanghai's privileged classes.

Background

From the time of the collapse of China's last imperial dynasty in 1911 and the establishment of the Republic of China in 1912, China's political landscape had been fragmented; by the early 1920s Sun Yat-sen (1866–1925) led the CNP from its principal base in Guangzhou (Canton), while the Chinese Communist Party (CCP) was founded in Shanghai in 1921 by Chen Duxiu (1879–1942). In 1923 Sun Yat-sen's favorable impression of the Bolshevik revolution in Russia and the communist belief that a socialist revolution would follow a nationalist revolution led to the Communists and the Nationalists forming an uneasy alliance against the local warlords who held large parts of China. Michael Borodin (originally named Mikhail Gruzenberg, 1884–1951), who was a Comintern agent in China from 1923 to 1927 and who was one of the architects of the alliance between the CCP and CNP, became one of Sun Yat-sen's special advisers. At a CNP conference in January 1924, Communist delegates accounted for fewer than 20 percent of those present, but already in January 1926, Communists and their supporters in the CNP constituted the majority of the delegates at a conference held in Guangzhou. Following the death of Sun Yat-sen in 1925, Chiang Kai-shek (1887–1975), commander of the Whampoa Military Academy south of Guangzhou, soon emerged as the new leader of the CNP.

Although Guangzhou had become a Communist stronghold, powerful anti-Communist factions of the CNP existed all over China, and under the new CNP leadership, the pro-Soviet line was abandoned. The tensions between the CCP and the CNP surfaced in March 1926 when Chiang Kai-shek felt provoked by the presence of a gunboat commanded by a Communist and imposed martial law in Guangzhou. Soviet advisers were arrested, and workers and Communists were disarmed. After some days, martial law was lifted, and after negotiations involving Borodin, the CNP-CCP alliance continued, but with a weakened Communist position. By the end of 1926, the armies controlled by the CNP and Chiang Kai-shek had conquered most of southern China and established headquarters in Nanchang, while the CCP and its supporters were based in Wuhan.

Shanghai 1927

In the 1920s the central part of Shanghai was divided into a number of foreign settlements surrounded by Chinese neighborhoods. The foreign concessions were legislatively and administratively independent of China, and they could even overrule the legal system of the Chinese government. The city was a booming center of industry and trade, and Communist leaders had been very successful in organizing workers on the docks and in the factories in labor unions. In May 1925 strikes involving several hundreds of thousands of workers in Shanghai spread to the rest of China, and the riots were stopped only when Japanese and British troops opened fire and killed numerous Chinese workers.

In February 1927, at the same time Chiang Kai-shek was contemplating a move on Shanghai, the Communist leaders in the city, Zhou Enlai (1899–1976) and Li Lisan (1899–1967), organized a general strike that paralyzed the busy port and the industry. Again, numerous workers were arrested and executed, but in March the strike turned into an armed rebellion against the CNP and the authorities in the Chinese part of Shanghai, and police stations and other key buildings in the city were occupied. Chiang Kai-shek delayed his advance on Shanghai in the hope that foreign troops or Shanghai's local Chinese commander would crush the Communists, but when that failed to happen, the CNP armies arrived on 26 March.

White Terror

One of Chiang Kai-shek's main motives for taking over the rich city of Shanghai was to secure financial support for his campaign to conquer the northern provinces, which at that time were controlled by independent warlords. At the same time, he wanted to curb the influence of the CCP headquarters in Wuhan and the strong Communist organization in Shanghai. The city's industrial leaders, powerful businessman, foreign concessions, and underworld entrepreneurs occupied with gambling, prostitution, kidnapping, and opium trade shared Chiang's opposition to the CCP. The illegal activities in Shanghai were controlled by a secret society known as the Green Gang (Qingbang), led by Huang Jinrong, a senior officer in the French police. The nature of Chiang Kai-shek's connection with the Green Gang remains undisclosed, but it is generally agreed that an alliance was formed between the Nationalist occupying forces and the secret society to strike against labor unions and Communists.

At 4:00 A.M. on 12 April, while Chiang was away to set up his capital in Nanjing, a well-orchestrated attack on union headquarters around Shanghai was carried out by a militia led by associates of Huang. The militia, which consisted of approximately one thousand men, was heavily armed and wore plain blue clothes and white armbands with the Chinese character for labor *(gong)*. In several instances, they were assisted by Nationalist troops, and they were allowed to pass freely through the foreign settlements. Hundreds of leading labor unionists and Communists were shot or arrested and turned over to the Nationalist troops, who executed them. A few leaders, among them Zhou Enlai, narrowly escaped. The next day, the labor unions responded with huge strikes and demonstrations that were dispersed with machine guns, bayonets, and swords.

The white terror spread to other cities held by the CNP, and several Communist attempts to establish city communes were suppressed. Having put an end to Communist activities in Shanghai, Chiang Kai-shek began to collect payment from the privileged classes for his services. Assisted by criminals of the Green Gang, the CNP forced the rich to donate money or extend "loans" to finance its armies. Those who refused were imprisoned and only released in return for huge sums of money or had their property confiscated or their children kidnapped.

The white terror in Shanghai and other urban Communist strongholds had a crucial influence on the further development of Communist strategy in China. Having lost its influence in the cities, the CCP concentrated its focus on the large and richly populated rural areas and based its revolution on the peasants rather than the industrial workers.

Bent Nielsen

See also: **Guomindang**

Further Reading
Coble, Parks M., Jr. (1980) *The Shanghai Capitalists and the Nationalist Government, 1927–1937.* Cambridge, MA: Harvard University Press.
Martin, Brian G. (1996) *The Shanghai Green Gang: Politics and Organized Crime, 1919–1937.* Berkeley and Los Angeles: University of California Press.

WIJAYA, PUTU (b. 1943), Indonesian playwright, film director, writer. Born in Bali in 1943, Putu Wijaya has developed a style that blends traditional Balinese influences with elements drawn from Antonin Artaud (1869–1948) and avant-garde Western theatre. His stage works often use a very Balinese blend of music, choreography, and dramatic action to present plots that leave a very Western impression of disturbing uncertainty. His theatrical works mostly have one word

titles, such as: *Edan* (Mad), *Aduh* (Ouch), *Awas* (Beware), *Aib* (Dishonor), and *Dor* (Bang). Putu Wijaya works mostly with his own theater company, Teater Mandiri (Independent Theater). His novels and short stories are best-sellers in Indonesia and are written to confront and shock readers and thereby grab their attention. Among his popular works are *Blok* and *Prrotes*. His plays are also performed outside Indonesia as a leading example of modern Indonesian drama.

Tim Byard-Jones

Further Reading
Putu Wijaya. (1992) "Blood." *Menagerie 1.* Jakarta, Indonesia: Lontar Foundation, 179–191.
———. (1988) *Bomb: Indonesian Short Stories by Putu Wijaya.* Edited by Ellen Rafferty and Laurie J. Sears. Madison, WI: Center for Southeast Asian Studies, University of Wisconsin.
——— and Ellen Rafferty. (1989) *Putu Wijaya in Performance: A Script and Study of Indonesian Theatre.* Monograph No 5. Madison, WI: Center for Southeast Asian Studies, University of Wisconsin.

WOMEN IN CENTRAL ASIA Central Asian women represent more than twenty different ethnic groups, speak variations of the Turkic and Tajik languages, and live in five countries: Kazakhstan, Kyrgyzstan, Tajikistan, Turkmenistan, and Uzbekistan. Nevertheless, they share many common characteristics. Most Central Asian women are Muslims of the Sunni sect. They were raised under Soviet ideals of gender equality; they share high literacy rates, maintain close ties to their extended families, and are navigating the immense economic and social upheaval of the post-Soviet era.

Pre-Soviet Society
Little is recorded about Central Asian women prior to the Soviet period. Sparse descriptions in travel journals note that women of the nomadic Kazakh and Kyrgyz groups rarely were veiled. In comparison, their more sedentary agricultural neighbors, the Uzbeks, practiced female seclusion and adhered to the custom of *parandzha*, face and body veiling. Women of nomadic tribes wore male apparel since girls and women were expected to perform tasks as competently as their male counterparts, whether horseback riding, hunting, or herding. Such expectations stemmed from the seasonal cycle of nomadism, which required that men and women live separately for months at a time. While men grazed cattle on the highest pastures, women were the de facto masters of the lower-altitude camps,

performing all the duties that men performed when they were there. Since the nomadic groups of Central Asia were not Islamized until the 1800s, these women had few restrictions on their daily lives. Nevertheless, both nomadic and sedentary women had few opportunities to be educated, little freedom in choosing a mate, and few property rights.

The Soviet Period

Beginning in 1926 the Soviets initiated a campaign of female emancipation in Central Asia called (in Uzbek) *hujum* or assault. This campaign advocated that, for the good of the young Soviet nation, Muslim women become the equals of men, be allowed to work, and be educated outside the home. One of the most radical steps in the campaign was do away with the custom of veiling. The Soviets organized large assemblies so thousands of women could "unveil" at the same time. For the Russians the veil symbolized oppression and ignorance, but for Central Asians the veil was an integral part of their lives. In urban settings it provided protection from the desert heat and dust; it also represented the definitive divide between the spaces accorded to men and women. Men were the public face of the family, and women remained secluded in their homes with their children.

Over the course of a decade Central Asians slowly shed the veil. They were given an education, and, as a first step toward employment outside the home, the Soviets established female cooperatives for textile and agricultural training. It became understood during the Soviet period that education and employment were not only their right but also their duty to their country.

In spite of Soviet norms and restrictions, many traditional customs survived. Central Asian women in many ways lived dualistic lives. They performed their duties as Soviet citizens in public while privately attending to the numerous traditions and rituals that reflected the central role of family in their society. Perhaps only in the realm of childbearing did the Soviet agenda and Central Asian traditionalism overlap. In Central Asian society children are considered a family's wealth; a woman who bears many children is regarded highly. During World War II, the Soviets encouraged reproduction, presenting medals of honor to women bearing more than five children. Central Asian women were by far the most decorated "mother heroines," even as they continued to work outside the home and boosted literacy rates to 98 percent.

Post-Soviet Dilemmas

With the dissolution of the Soviet Union in August 1991, five new states emerged from the former Soviet republics. "Democracy" and "market economy" became code words for the transition away from socialism. Instead of ushering in a new era of freedom and opportunity, as hoped, the last decade of the twentieth century was particularly arduous for women. Many of the state enterprises and collective farms, which had previously employed a large percentage of women, were privatized or eliminated. Official and unofficial unemployment have become rampant. Further, many preschools and medical supports for the aged were curtailed because of limited governmental funds. Without state provisions for child care, elder care, and other benefits, women become primary caregivers for their extended families. At the end of the twentieth century, Central Asian women also played a pivotal role in nongovernmental organizations. In lieu of formal employment, they were active in the informal marketplace, especially in buying and selling goods at local bazaars.

In summary, the ethnic diversity of Central Asian women is mitigated by the fact that they share the customs of Islam. Likewise, the common experience of seventy years under Soviet rule gave women the opportunity to be educated and to work outside the home. Nevertheless, women continue to be expected to maintain family traditions. The economic woes resulting from the independence of the Central Asian countries placed an unusually heavy burden on women, since they were primarily responsible for the physical and social well-being of the family and for supplying an income.

Kathleen Kuehnast

Further Reading

Akiner, Shirin. (1997) "Between Tradition and Modernity: The Dilemma Facing Contemporary Central Asian Women." In *Post-Soviet Women: From the Baltic to Central Asia*, edited by Mary Buckley. New York: Cambridge University Press, 261–304.

Massell, Gregory J. (1974) *The Surrogate Proletariat: Moslem Women and Revolutionary Strategies in Soviet Central Asia, 1919–1929*. Princeton, NJ: Princeton University Press.

Olcott, Martha Brill. (1991) "Women and Society in Central Asia." In *Soviet Central Asia: The Failed Transformation*, edited by William Fierman. Boulder, CO: Westview Press, 235–254.

Tabyshalieva, Anara. (1997) "Women of Central Asia and the Fertility Cult." *Anthropology and Archeology of Eurasia* 36, 2: 45–62.

WOMEN IN CHINA

WOMEN IN CHINA Women figure significantly in Chinese history and had a unique status for two reasons. First, the orthodox system of Confucianism that ordered the Chinese imperium from its earliest dynasties until the twentieth century considered the family to be the basic political unit. Women's roles as wives, household managers, and educators of the young thus served not only the family but also the state. Second, although Confucius (551–479 BCE) emphasized the hierarchical relationships between ruler and subject, father and son, and husband and wife, he also taught the reciprocal responsibilities of each. Thus, while a wife was bound to obey and serve her husband, he was equally bound to treat her with dignity and respect. Through the complex interweaving of official and private lives, Chinese women had opportunities to exercise informal power not known to women in other patriarchal societies.

Women's Roles in Early China

Confucianism ordered the lives of women from their birth to their death through three sets of principles. The earliest was penned by the great woman scholar Ban Zhao in *Lessons for Women* during the Han dynasty (206 BCE–220 CE). Ban Zhao instructed women to be guided by womanly virtue, correct speech, proper deportment, and womanly work. These were known collectively as the "four womanly virtues." Also central was the concept of the "three obediences"—obeying one's father when young, one's husband when married, and one's son when widowed. Finally, there was the principle of *bie* or separateness. Men and women each had their own spheres. For elite men, this was the world of study, civil-service examinations, and official careers. For peasants, it was the field. The home was a woman's sphere whether she was rich or poor. The separate spheres of men and women in China, however, must not be confused with similar concepts in the West. Because the family was the basic political unit in the Confucian system, the state had a vested interest in the lives of women. Thus, although women led private lives, their lives were a public matter.

Although Confucian China was a patriarchal society, its moral code applied equally to men and women. One of the five basic Confucian relationships was that between husband and wife. While husbands were placed over their wives, the principle of reciprocity required that husbands treat their wives with respect if they expected to be served well in return. The principle of filial piety also elevated a woman's position. From boyhood sons were bound to their mothers through both maternal ties and the Confucian principle of filial piety, which required them to honor and serve both parents throughout their lives and after their deaths. Practical aspects of the Confucian bureaucracy also provided elite women with unusual status and power in the family. The arduous task of studying for

the examinations that led to officialdom occupied men, from their youth often through middle age. Because Chinese statesmen could not hold office in their home province, after they won official appointment they could be sent away from home for years at a time. Wives bore the responsibility of managing the household itself and often the entire family estate as well.

Because Confucianism bolstered the patriarchal state and endorsed, at least in theory, women's subservient position to the men in the household, it provided little solace for women. To find spiritual satisfaction and harmony, women turned to Buddhism and Taosim, both considered "heterodox" religions because they ran counter to the orthodox system of beliefs in Confucianism. They studied Buddhist sutras and Taoist writings and made pilgrimages to local shrines. Older women and widows might hand over control of their households to their oldest daughter-in-law and retire into seclusion to pray and meditate. The fact that women traveled on pilgrimages testifies to the hold on the public imagination of heterodox religions as well as the toleration of Confucianism. The fact that a family matriarch could withdraw from daily responsibilities and devote herself to prayer if she wished speaks to the importance of hierarchical relationships within the family and the respect given to family elders.

Certain female practices, however, lay outside the domain of the dominant Confucian culture. The custom of foot binding, the painful practice of binding a young girl's feet so that they did not grow but took on the form of a lotus flower is often offered as evidence of Chinese women's extreme subjugation. Yet while widely accepted, foot binding was not condoned in orthodox Confucian literature. A patriarchal society may have approved of the fact that women with bound feet were more easily controlled, and men may have regarded women's tiny feet as erotic, but in actuality foot binding was part of the female culture.

Foot binding began as a courtesan fashion during the Song dynasty (960–1279) and was soon imitated in court circles. The practice evolved slowly into a status marker in elite society, and a woman's beauty and desirability were judged by how tiny her feet were. Because it was the custom in China for men to marry women of lower social standing, foot binding eventually spread to peasants, where it was a means of upward mobility for daughters. Foot binding was a private female ritual: mothers bound the feet of their daughters. Young girls embroidered intricate slippers as part of their trousseau and wrote poems about their tiny feet. Bathing and rebinding feet became a lifelong part of women's daily toilet. Except for her husband, no man ever saw a woman's feet, and even he never saw his

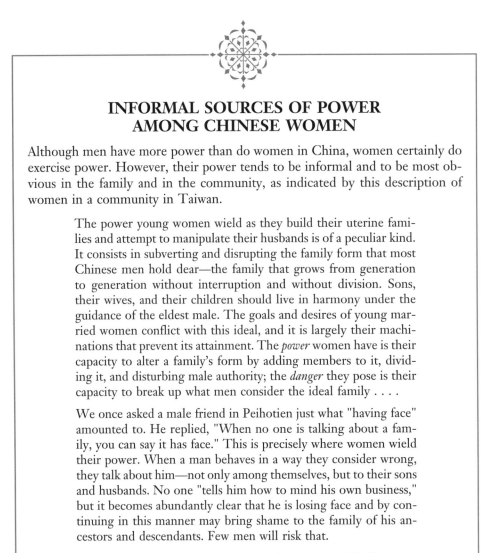

INFORMAL SOURCES OF POWER AMONG CHINESE WOMEN

Although men have more power than do women in China, women certainly do exercise power. However, their power tends to be informal and to be most obvious in the family and in the community, as indicated by this description of women in a community in Taiwan.

The power young women wield as they build their uterine families and attempt to manipulate their husbands is of a peculiar kind. It consists in subverting and disrupting the family form that most Chinese men hold dear—the family that grows from generation to generation without interruption and without division. Sons, their wives, and their children should live in harmony under the guidance of the eldest male. The goals and desires of young married women conflict with this ideal, and it is largely their machinations that prevent its attainment. The *power* women have is their capacity to alter a family's form by adding members to it, dividing it, and disturbing male authority; the *danger* they pose is their capacity to break up what men consider the ideal family . . . .

We once asked a male friend in Peihotien just what "having face" amounted to. He replied, "When no one is talking about a family, you can say it has face." This is precisely where women wield their power. When a man behaves in a way they consider wrong, they talk about him—not only among themselves, but to their sons and husbands. No one "tells him how to mind his own business," but it becomes abundantly clear that he is losing face and by continuing in this manner may bring shame to the family of his ancestors and descendants. Few men will risk that.

Source: Emily M. Ahern. (1978) "The Power and Pollution of Chinese Women." In *Studies in Chinese Society*, edited by Arthur P. Wolf. Stanford, CA: Stanford University Press, 276–277.

wife's feet unbound. As with other cultural rituals no longer practiced, it is difficult to unravel its meaning and importance in the lives of women, but the practice of foot binding belonged to the female sphere.

Women as Producers and Reproducers in Later China

While patriarchal systems legitimized male power over women, they also defined male and female roles in relation to what was necessary for the state and society to prosper. In China the adage "Men till, women weave" was more than a statement of gender roles. In early imperial China, taxes were paid in rice and woven cotton cloth. Because women contributed a portion of the annual tax levy, both elite and peasant women gained status as economic producers. Reforms in the tax system and the commercialization of weaving at the beginning of the late imperial period altered women's status. From the Song to the Qing dynasties, technological advances in loom design, the introduction of silk and silk damasks, and the increasing demand for more intricately patterned cloth resulted in the decline of weaving as a cottage industry and its growth as a commercial enterprise. While domestic weaving was marginalized in the economy, culturally the adage "Men till, women weave" emphasized the importance of work over leisure, even for women in elite households.

Arguably, the downward spiral of women's social status in late imperial China, especially from the Ming dynasty onward—which was also reflected in changes in the legal code and in the increasing cultural importance of foot binding to both men and women—started with women's loss of economic power vis-à-vis the family and the state. This shift led women to find new, informal means of exercising power. One way was through motherhood.

Being indentured as servants, sold into slavery or prostitution, or abandoned at nunneries was a possible fate for peasant girls and even girls from elite households that were gradually descending into poverty, but most women married. Producing children, although valued in all traditional societies, had certain special implications in Chinese society. Sons were desired because they would care for their parents in their old age. In elite households sons were also prized because they could bring honor, prestige, and wealth to their families if they were successful in the civil-service examinations and fortunate in their careers.

From earliest childhood girls were groomed for their future roles as wives, mothers, and daughters-in-law. They were taught to read and write, some becoming proficient enough to write poetry. They were schooled in womanly virtues and taught all the practical aspects of household management. Marriage was a social contract, arranged between families. A bride and groom never saw each other before the wedding, and the hooded bridal gown prevented them from seeing each other even during the ceremony. A bride's primary relationship was with her mother-in-law. Many tales of the cruelty of mothers-in-law to their daughters-in-law have come down in popular Chinese literature, much like stories of evil stepmothers in fairy tales in the West. How true these stories were is impossible to tell. What is certain, however, is that relations among the many women in an extended family compound were complicated. Hierarchy among women was dictated by age and marital status. A woman's position was also determined by her beauty, talent, and virtue, or by her skill in compensating for the lack of such attributes. The great social novel *Dream of the Red Chamber* (*Hunglou meng*, 1792) provides the classic example of how much intrigue as well as genuine friendship there was among women in the extended Chinese family.

One complication in the Chinese household that has no direct counterpart in the West was concubinage. A concubine was a second or third wife who had no legal standing as a wife. The practice was officially condoned as long as a man's first wife produced no male heir. Among the affluent, the practice of taking more than one concubine as a mark of wealth became prevalent. Not only did a concubine have no legal standing as a wife, but also she could not even consider her children to be her own. Even if she was fortunate enough to produce the desired male heir, the first wife was considered the child's mother.

Thus motherhood and the status motherhood brought with it were conferred only on the legitimate, first wife. The child owed filial obedience only to his or her socially recognized mother. The gain for some women and the loss for others in this social arrangement cannot be overstated. As the mothers of successful bureaucrats, elite women were able to reestablish a link between themselves and the state. By the Ming dynasty, no longer important as producers, they gained importance and honor as Confucian mothers.

Women's Modern Transformation

After the Opium Wars of the mid-nineteenth century, Western powers forced themselves on China. From 1840 to 1949 China was a country in transformation, and women were caught up in it. The late nineteenth century saw the beginning of serious attempts to reform society. Every aspect of Chinese life came under challenge, including the limited social, political, and economic roles of women.

Western missionaries led the way in educating Chinese girls, one of their true contributions to Chinese society. Even before universal education was established in 1907, many gentry families had opened Western-style schools for girls or sent their daughters overseas to receive higher educations.

CHAIRMAN MAO ON WOMEN

"In order to build a great socialist society, it is of the utmost importance to arouse the broad masses of women to join in productive activity. Men and women must receive equal pay for equal work in production. Genuine equality between the sexes can only be realized in the process of the socialist transformation of society as a whole."

Source: Mao Zedong. (1976). *Quotations from Chairman Mao Tsetung.* Beijing: Foreign Language Press, 297.

With its large population a major economic resource, China has work teams that are continually building and maintaining public resources throughout the country. Here, three women working on a new water main from Miyun to Beijing take a rest. (DEAN CONGER/CORBIS)

Education was the key to women's transformation. The first generation of Chinese feminists received their higher educations abroad. With the introduction of higher education in China, first through Christian union colleges for women, founded between 1905 and 1915, and then through universities, later female leaders were more likely to have been educated entirely in China. It was not only those with advanced educations who played a pivotal role in women's struggle for a share of China's progress. Many more women with middle-school educations entered the teaching ranks than did college-educated women.

Other professions were slow to open up for women. In the 1920s women worked as doctors and educators. Gradually women entered government service. Political rights were even more elusive. Both the Nationalist and the Communist Parties were essentially patriarchal. The New Life Movement, an ideological campaign launched by General Chiang Kai-shek in the early 1930s, actually emphasized the four womanly virtues and sought to curtail women's public roles by promoting domesticity. However, in the 1930s, a civil law code was finally passed that granted women many civil rights, such as the right to divorce and hold property.

Much of the progress women made in the first half of the twentieth century affected only women in urban centers. In the rural countryside that made up most of China, life changed more slowly. Foreign wars, internal revolts, devastating famines and floods, and a spiraling population plunged the majority of Chinese women into unimaginable poverty. Infanti-

cide and the selling of little girls into various forms of bondage was prevalent. Young girls became part of the trade in labor for mills in industrializing coastal cities. Not until the Communists won the civil war in 1949 did many of these practices end.

At the time of the Communist victory, a core of women from various women's organizations formed the All-China Women's Federation (ACWF). Quasi official in nature, the ACWF provided women with their first collective voice in their own affairs and those of their country. Although ideologically bound to the Communist Party, the ACWF was and still is exclusively a women's forum that monitors women's lives, lobbies the government on their behalf, and helps enforce government policy at regional and local levels. The organization represents a step forward for women still bound in large part by patriarchal principles.

The past twenty years have brought significant changes to the lives of women in urban China, but again less so to women in rural villages. Education and economic security are still key to women's progress and, as more and more women gain both, their status and power in society should improve.

For years, all that was known about the lives of women in China came from the writings of men. Historians now realize that such writings cannot be interpreted literally because they represented only the male view of how society should function, rather that the lived experiences of women. The discovery of thousands of poems written by women finally furnished scholars with a female perspective and furthered the study of women in China.

Primary among the results of the significant new findings that have transformed the previous superficial understanding of women's lives and shattered many long-standing stereotypes is that historians and other social scientists now realize that they cannot assume that all traditional patriarchal societies are the same. Confucianism, while fundamentally patriarchal, provided certain protections for women not found in other parts of the world. The question is no longer "Who had power?" but "How did people, especially women, use the types of power available to them?" Scholars also realize that other universal categories, like motherhood, need to be carefully situated in the context of specific cultures and periods of history. When studying the lives of women, it is just as important to understand the relations between women themselves as it is to understand the relations between women and men.

Elizabeth A. Littell-Lamb

Further Reading

Croll, Elizabeth. (1978) *Feminism and Socialism in China.* London: Routledge & Kegan Paul.

Honig, Emily. (1986) *Sisters and Strangers: Women in the Shanghai Cotton Mills, 1919–1949.* Stanford, CA: Stanford University Press.

Kwok, Pui-lan. (1992) *Chinese Women and Christianity, 1860–1927.* Atlanta, GA: Scholars Press.

Mann, Susan. (1997) *Precious Records: Women in China's Long Eighteenth Century.* Stanford, CA: Stanford University Press.

Pruitt, Ida. (1945) *A Daughter of Han: The Autobiography of a Chinese Working Girl.* New Haven, CT: Yale University Press.

Spence, Jonathan. (1981) *The Gate of Heavenly Peace: The Chinese and Their Revolution, 1895–1980.* New York: Penguin Books.

Stockard, Janice E. (1989) *Daughters of the Canton Delta: Marriage Patterns and Economic Strategies in South China, 1860–1930.* Stanford, CA: Stanford University Press.

Tsao Hsueh-chin. (1958) *Dream of the Red Chamber.* New York: Anchor Books.

Wolf, Margery. (1985) *Revolution Postponed.* Stanford, CA: Stanford University Press.

WOMEN IN JAPAN This entry focuses on the situation of women in the period from 1945. Under the political system of Imperial Japan (from 1890 to 1945) women's and men's situations were determined by their status as gendered subjects of the emperor.

Under the feudal system which was in place until the late nineteenth century, men and women's lives were primarily determined by their place in the feudal hierarchy of the imperial family, samurai, peasants, artisans, merchants and outcasts. Japanese women and men now enjoy the highest life expectancy rates in the world. High life expectancy rates and low birth rates have led to the development of distinctive life-cycle patterns in Japan's highly prosperous postwar society. Women in Japan also enjoy a legal environment that guarantees them basic political and civil rights, although they are still campaigning for social change on several fronts. The low birth rate and the steadily decreasing numbers of people of working age have been linked with problems in the delivery of care and welfare benefits to the aged.

Although women in Japan have relatively high rates of participation in the labor force, they are concentrated in part-time and casual labor rather than full-time permanent positions. Labor force participation rates show a distinctive M-shaped curve, with highest participation rates in the twenties and late forties. The curve dips in the years when women are most likely to be engaged in childbirth and childcare. In recent years, however, the M-shaped curve has been flattening.

The age of marriage for both men and women is steadily increasing. In 1975 the average age of first marriage was 24.7 for females and 27 for males. In 1998 the average age had risen to 26.7 for females and 28.6 for males. Since the postwar baby boom of 1947 (33.8 births per 1,000 population), birth rates have declined. Between 1955 and 1975, the birth rate fluctuated between 17.1 and 18.8, but has steadily declined since, reaching 11.9 in 1985. Falling birth rates and a trend toward nuclear households have resulted in a steady decline in household size, from 4.97 in 1955 to 3.17 in 1985. Later marriage and lower birth rates mean that women are spending fewer years engaged in full-time childcare.

Women have been able to vote and stand for public office since April 1946. The revised constitution of 1947 includes a clause outlawing discrimination on the grounds of sex, status, or religion, and the Civil Code was revised in 1947 in line with the new constitution. The Labor Standards Law of 1947 included the principle of equal pay for equal work. Marriage, divorce, and inheritance laws were also revised on more egalitarian lines, unlike prewar family law, which had been based on patriarchy (the rule of the father) and primogeniture (inheritance by the eldest son).

Equal-opportunity legislation was passed in 1985 and became effective in 1986, with revisions taking place in 1997. In response to Japan's ratification of the Convention on the Elimination of All Forms of Discrimination Against Women (CEDAW) and recognition of the Beijing Platform of Action, recent years

GIRLS' LIVES: REAL AND IDEAL

This poem dating to the 1930s points out the contradictions in girls' lives in Japan. Girls learned English in schools, but the only use they could make of it was to write love letters.

High-school girl, beautiful as a flower bud,
Before her parents writes a love letter in English.
The two parents, not knowing it to be a love letter,
Praise her for studying so much.

Source: John F. Embree. ([1939] 1979) *Suye Mura: A Japanese Village.* Chicago: The University of Chicago Press, 195.

Japan's Naoko Takahashi leads the field in the women's marathon at the 2000 Summer Olympics in Sydney. Takahashi won the race with a time of 2:23:14.

have seen further legislation directed at creating a more equitable society. In 1994 the Headquarters for the Promotion of Gender Equality was organized within the prime minister's office. This developed into the Office for Gender Equality and the Council for Gender Equality. In 1996 the latter submitted a report, Vision of Gender Equality—Creating New Values for the Twenty-first Century to the prime minister. In June 1999 the Basic Law for a Gender-Equal Society was passed by Japan's legislature, the Diet, and became effective on 23 June 1999.

Recent years have also seen important legislation concerning the conditions of working women, the harmonization of family and working life, and the provision of care for the elderly. Nevertheless, women have campaigned for over a century for improvement in their situation, and feminist campaigns have continued into the twenty-first century.

Women's Movements for Change

Feminist thought and activism in Japan dates back to the late nineteenth century. As part of a more general development of notions of human rights, women's rights (joken) were debated beginning in the 1880s. Socialist thinkers also debated the "woman question" (fujin mondai) in the first decades of the twentieth century. The feminist literary journal, Seito (Bluestocking), edited first by Hiratsuka Raicho and then Ito Noe, appeared from 1911 to 1916. Until 1922, Article Five of the Public Peace Police Law prevented women from attending, holding, or speaking at political meetings or belonging to political organizations. After the modification of Article Five in 1922 it became possible for women to form organizations to lobby for suffrage. The League for the Attainment of Women's Suffrage was formed in 1924, led by Ichikawa Fusae. Bills for women's suffrage passed the lower house of the Diet in 1930 and 1931 but failed in the House of Peers. Autonomous women's organizations were gradually co-opted under the total national mobilization system during World War II.

In postwar Japan, women were initially active in such organizations as the Hahaoya Taikai (Mothers' Convention), consumer groups, pacifist organizations, and the Shufuren (Housewives' Association). In the 1970s, women's organizations took on a more explicitly feminist character. Some women participated in the New Left and student left organizations that protested the renewal of the U.S.-Japan Security Treaty in 1960, and which brought universities to a standstill in 1968 and 1969. Women, however, became disillusioned with the sexism of the men in leftist organizations, and formed their own women's liberation groups in the 1970s to explore issues of sexuality, reproductive control, and identity, and to oppose moves to amend Japan's relatively liberal abortion law.

International Women's Year in 1975 and the subsequent United Nations Decade for Women provided a focus for reformist activities. After Japan's ratification of CEDAW, there was reform of the Nationality Law, so that both women and men could pass on Japanese nationality to their children. There was also enactment of legislation to promote equal employment opportunities, and reform of the education system so that there would be no subjects solely for boys or solely for girls.

Current issues involve the consideration of the relationships between men and women in Japan and men and women in other Asian countries, prompted by an interest in the situation of immigrant workers in Japan and workers in the tourism industry and multinational factories in Southeast Asia.

Women's Studies and Women's History

The current wave of women's studies in Japan can be traced to the women's liberation movements that grew out of the activism of the 1970s, and to broader reformist feminist movements. Although there are now several women's studies associations and several academic journals devoted to women's studies, most teachers in the field are on the fringes of the academy, reflecting the already marginal place of women in most colleges and universities. As in many other countries, courses on women's studies survive thanks to the dedication of groups of feminist researchers who find solidarity in networks that cross institutions and bring together academics, activists, journalists, and other professionals. In addition to women's studies based in the academy, there is also a range of community-based, grassroots women's studies activity, which often takes the form of newsletters, journals, or monographs produced on a collaborative basis. Women's history, in particular, has developed such grassroots, community-based ways of writing history, while other community-based research is tied to specific issues such as sexual harassment, domestic violence, the situation of part-time and immigrant workers, or support for claims for compensation by women forced into military prostitution during World War II. Local women's centers, established during the International Women's Decade, host adult education classes on women's studies and women's history, and provide a focus for local study groups.

Vera Mackie

Further Reading

Bernstein, Gail Lee, ed. (1991) *Recreating Japanese Women, 1600–1945.* Berkeley and Los Angeles: University of California Press.

Fujimura-Fanselow, Kumiko, and Atsuko Kameda, eds. (1995) *Japanese Women: New Feminist Perspectives on the Past, Present, and Future.* New York: The Feminist Press.

Hunter, Janet, ed. (1993) *Japanese Women Working.* London: Routledge.

Imamura, Anne E., ed. (1996) *Re-Imaging Japanese Women.* Berkeley and Los Angeles: University of California Press.

Lebra, Joyce, Joy Paulson, and Elizabeth Powers, eds. (1976) *Women in Changing Japan.* Stanford, CA: Stanford University Press.

WOMEN IN KOREA Women have enjoyed considerable freedoms throughout much of premodern Korean history. Confucianism, however, hindered women's status from the sixteenth century onward. Today, Korean women continue to be restricted by traditional mores and social structures, but they are closer to gaining equal opportunities in education, employment, and law.

Premodern Korea

Social rank was of utmost importance in the Shilla kingdom (57 BCE–935 CE). The bone-rank system divided all people into one of the following ranks: royal hallowed bones (*songgol*), aristocratic true bones (*chin'gol*), and headranks six to one. One's hereditary social class was based on both parents' positions, with the offspring taking the lower parent's status. The hallowed-bone class declined in number due to this hereditary rigidity. As the last two members of the hallowed-bone rank, two queens (Sondok, ?–647, and Chindok, ?–654) ruled in their own right before the throne passed to true bones. Chinsong (?–897), a third *yowang* ("queen in her own right"), reigned 887–897. The strictness of the hereditary social status is cited as one of the reasons for the eventual decline of the Shilla kingdom. Married women in Shilla often lived with their natal families for some time before moving to their in-laws' homes.

In the Koryo dynasty (918–1392), as in Shilla, women generally did not have public roles, but daughters shared equally in inheritance or division of property because of siblings' collective responsibilities in

CRIMINALIZING ADULTERY IN KOREA

According to *AsiaWeek*, South Korea, along with Greece, Switzerland, Taiwan, and Austria are the only non-Muslim nations that criminalize adultery, with Criminal Law Article 241 allowing imprisonment for up to two years. In 2001, the Constitutional Court upheld the law by an 8 to 1 vote, although it did allow that the government should consider abolishing the law in view of changing Korean attitudes about sexual behavior. Those who support the law claim that it protects married women and sets a moral standard for Korean society. Opponents, including most women's groups, argue that it has little effect on sexual behavior and is an infringement on personal privacy.

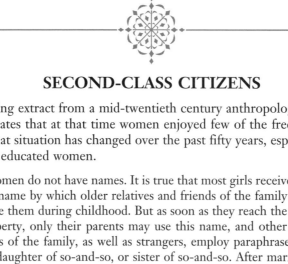

SECOND-CLASS CITIZENS

The following extract from a mid-twentieth century anthropological report on Korea indicates that at that time women enjoyed few of the freedoms enjoyed by men. That situation has changed over the past fifty years, especially in cities and among educated women.

Women do not have names. It is true that most girls receive some surname by which older relatives and friends of the family designate them during childhood. But as soon as they reach the age of puberty, only their parents may use this name, and other members of the family, as well as strangers, employ paraphrases such as daughter of so-and-so, or sister of so-and-so. After marriage a woman no longer has any name. Her own parents usually designate her by the name of the district where she was married, and her husband's parents by the name of the district where she lived before she was married. Sometimes she is called simply the house of so-and-so (the husband's name). When she has sons, convention requires that one use the designation mother of so-and-so. When a woman is forced to appear before the courts, the mandarin officially imposes a name on her for the duration of the case in order to facilitate debate.

Source: Christopher Dallet. (1954) *Traditional Korea*. New Haven, CT: Human Relations Area Files, 115–116.

caring for older family members and performing ancestor rituals. Koryo women had considerable freedom, with rights to marry, divorce, and remarry at will. Married women of Koryo had close ties with their natal families, even when they lived with their in-laws.

Although early Choson society was largely similar to Koryo society, the Choson dynasty (1392–1910) is characterized by the Neo-Confucian transformation of society that began in the sixteenth century. Neo-Confucian social restructuring had a strong impact on women's status. According to Neo-Confucian social rules, a woman's identity came from her place in hierarchical and patriarchal relationships within the family. A woman was also bound by "The Three Followings"—she had to obey her father during childhood, her husband after marriage, and her son in her old age. Married women had limited ties with their natal families.

Choson women lost most of their inheritance rights and were not permitted to participate in ancestor rituals. There was also a stigma against remarried widows and their sons. Other Choson marriage restrictions included bans on endogamy (marriage between people of the same surname and same clan seat) and marriage between matrilateral cousins.

Although the Neo-Confucian transformation seems stifling to women, it improved women's status in certain ways. With the increased stratification of the inner quarters, primary wives and mothers of sons became more powerful. Aristocratic (*yangban*) men were also duty bound to treat their wives with respect. Concubines or secondary wives, however, had a precarious position in society and were denied the rights accorded primary wives. For example, a man could acquire or discard secondary wives at will, whereas he could divorce his primary wife only in certain situations. Children born of *yangban* fathers by secondary wives were considered illegitimate and faced social discrimination for most of the Choson period. A separate social class of *chungin* ("middle people"), just below *yangban*, was formed largely of *soja* (descendants by secondary wives) and limited to specific clerical positions. Women who had public roles were at the bottom of the social status system in Choson. *Kisaeng* (courtesans) and shamans were part of the lowest social order, ranking only above slaves.

Yangban homes had separate inner quarters for women and outer quarters for men. Due to practical considerations, commoners did not have to maintain the same degree of separation between the sexes, since their houses were smaller and women had to work in the fields alongside the men.

The promulgation of the *Hunmin chongum* (hangul) writing system in 1432 enabled more *yangban* women to be literate because the new writing system was easier to learn than literary Chinese, which required years to master. Women were denied formal education, but they were indoctrinated in Confucian morality through informal, family-centered education and books for women such as *Naehun* (Inner Teachings) and *Samgang haengsilto* (The Three Followings).

Modern Korea

Formal education for women began with the arrival of Christian missionaries, who established Christian schools in the late nineteenth century. Enlightenment thinkers of the late nineteenth century, who had been influenced by Western society as well as Japanese and Chinese modernization paradigms, also advocated women's rights. The Japanese-engineered Kabo reforms of 1894–1895 abolished social-class distinctions and allowed sons by secondary wives to succeed their fathers.

Korean women were influenced by women's movements in Japan and the West. Both women and men saw education as an important means to modernization. But gender discrimination continued under Japanese colonialism (1910–1945). Among Koreans, women's issues were generally subjugated to the larger issue of nationalism. Korean women made a noticeable difference in anticolonial efforts, including the March First Independence Movement of 1919. Yu Kwan-sun (1904–1920), a student at Ewha Haktang ("academy"), a women's school, took part in March First demonstrations in Seoul and in her hometown in Ch'ungch'ong Province. She became a symbol of the nationalist movement when she was arrested and killed by police.

The World War II "Comfort Women" issue is one of the most controversial, unresolved aspects of Japanese colonialism. In the final years of the colonial period, some 200,000 women, most of them Korean, were "conscripted" into sexual slavery for the "Comfort Corps" (Chongsindae) to provide sexual services to the Japanese military. Korea and Japan have yet to settle issues of responsibility and reparations.

Industrialization also changed women's roles. From the early twentieth century, women entered the modern workforce by working in factories. Women educated in Korea, Japan, and the West also became

In the 1990s, several South Korean women emerged as leading players on the women's professional golf tour. Here Se Ri Pak tees off at the 1999 women's U.S. Open in West Point, Mississippi, in defense of her 1998 title. (AFP/CORBIS)

pioneers in fields such as education, medicine, and journalism during the early twentieth century.

North Korea

With the end of World War II in 1945, Korea was divided into North and South under Soviet and American occupations, respectively. The Democratic People's Republic of Korea (North Korea) and the Republic of Korea (South Korea) were established in 1948.

Although women are guaranteed full equal rights under the North Korean Communist system, men still dominate society, and gender discrimination is commonplace. Women and men may compete equally for low- and middle-level jobs, but women are generally scarce in high-level jobs and politics. Women are further burdened by the triple duty of full-time work, their roles as wives and mothers, and volunteer work for the Korean Communist Party.

South Korea

In South Korea as well, women have access to higher education, but discrimination continues to

In Pyongang, North Korea, in 1979, a female police officer controls traffic on a main thoroughfare. (BETTMANN/CORBIS)

prevail because of patriarchal practices in the family, workplace, and society.

The post-1970 economic surge opened up many new jobs for women and men, but such jobs usually entailed low wages and difficult conditions. The Equal Employment Act of 1987 and its 1989 revision protect women's equal rights in the workplace and provide penalties for violation of the law, but the law is not strictly enforced. Wage differentials, sexual harassment, and inequalities in the workplace continue to hinder women. Women are generally expected to stay at home to raise children, and women who do pursue careers receive lower pay and are the first to be laid off. In recent years, rural communities have seen an exodus of young men who go to cities in search of work. This has left women to fill the void in farming.

Long-term efforts to revise the Korean Family Law in 1992 brought about legal revisions granting women the right to sue for divorce, gain custody of children, and inherit equally. There is also considerable effort by women's nongovernmental organizations to establish hot lines and shelters for female victims of domestic and sexual violence.

Despite lingering discrimination, women have been making strides toward gender equality through legal changes, greater social awareness, and combined efforts by women's groups. Women's Studies is a growing academic discipline, and there have been recent efforts to increase pan-Asian and other international cooperation among feminists.

Jennifer Jung-Kim

Further Reading

Gelb, Joyce, and Marian Lief Palley, eds. (1994) *Women of Japan and Korea: Continuity and Change.* Philadelphia: Temple University Press.

Hunter, Helen-Louise. (1999) *Kim Il-song's North Korea.* Westport, CT: Praeger.

Kim, Yung-Chung. (1976) *Women of Korea: A History from Ancient Times to 1945.* Seoul: Ewha Womans University Press.

WOMEN IN PAKISTAN   Two perceptions describe the basic understanding of gender relations in Pakistan: Women are subordinate to men, and a man's honor resides in the actions of the women of his family. Social life in Pakistan revolves around family, and social status revolves around the honor of a family's women. As in other orthodox Muslim societies, women are responsible for adhering to respectable norms of conduct and for limiting contact between the sexes and thereby ensuring a family's honor. To ensure women's proper behavior, society limits their mobility and restricts their acceptable behavior and activities.

Space is allocated to and used differently by men and women in Pakistan. Traditionally, a woman was regarded as needing protection from the outside world, where her respectability—and therefore that of her family—was at risk. Women in many parts of the country still live under traditional constraints associated with purdah (seclusion; literally curtain), which necessitate the separation of women's activities from those of men, both physically and symbolically.

Thus male and female spheres are differentiated: most women (except for those of the urban upper classes) spend most their lives physically within their homes; they go outside only when there is a substantive purpose. Life outside the home generally revolves around the actions of men. In most parts of the country—with the exception of Islamabad, Karachi, and wealthier parts of a few other cities—people consider a woman (and by extension, her family) to be shameless when no restrictions are placed on her mobility.

Traditional Context

Purdah is practiced in various ways, depending on family traditions. The most extreme forms are found in remote parts of the North-West Frontier Province (NWFP) and Baluchistan, where a woman essentially never leaves her home except at the time of her marriage and never meets with unrelated men. While gender relations are somewhat more relaxed among most people in Punjab and Sind, nowhere (traditionally) do unrelated men and women mix freely. Poor urban women in close-knit communities, such as the old cities of Lahore and Rawalpindi, generally observe some form of purdah and wear either a *burqa* (fitted body veil) or a chador (loosely draped cotton cloth) when they leave their homes. This practice becomes less compelling in rural areas, though rural women still take care to dress modestly.

Two important factors differentiate the degree to which women's mobility is restricted: class and rural versus urban residence. Poor rural women in Punjab and Sind have traditionally enjoyed a great degree of mobility if for no other reason than sheer necessity. These women characteristically are responsible for transplanting rice seedlings and weeding crops and are often involved in activities such as raising chickens (and selling eggs) and stuffing wool or cotton into local blankets. When a family's level of prosperity rises and it begins to aspire to a higher status, often the first social change is that its women put on veils and are placed into some form of purdah.

The common perception that women are to remain confined within their homes so that neighbors do not gossip about their respectability has important implications for women's productive activities. Rural women are generally engaged in production for exchange at the subsistence level and do not earn a countable wage. In both urban and rural contexts, women's economic contributions are often included as part of the total family's labor, with government data crediting women's contributions to the male earners.

There is less of an urban-rural divide among purdah practices of wealthier classes. Rather, family traditions have more to do with whether women observe purdah and, if they do, the kind of veil they wear. In some cases, women simply observe "eye purdah," in which they tend not to mix with men, and when they do, they avert their eyes when interacting with them. Bazaars in wealthier areas of cities in Punjab differ from those in poorer areas by virtue of the greater proportion of unveiled women shopping in them. Bazaars in cities throughout NWFP, Baluchistan, and the interior of Sind are markedly devoid of women in general; when a woman does venture out into a bazaar in these areas, she always wears some sort of veil.

Political Challenges and Responses by Women

The women's movement in Pakistan has done much to raise public awareness about the conditions confronting women, as well as playing an important advocacy role in lobbying the government to change laws that discriminate against women. In Pakistan's first three decades, the most significant legal success was the 1961 Muslim Family Law, which regulated mar-

riage, divorce, and polygamy. There were marked increases in female literacy, labor-force participation, and political activities prior to the coup by Mohammad Zia-ul-Haq (1924–1988) in July 1977. Following this, however, in 1979, Zia's military regime promulgated a series of controversial laws, which, it claimed, were based on Islamic law. Women protesting against the 1979 Enforcement of *Hudood* (Islamic Laws) Ordinances focused on its lack of distinction between adultery *(zina)* and rape *(zina-bil-jabr)* and claimed that enforcing the law discriminated against women. Four years later, they protested against the promulgation of the proposed 1983 Law of Evidence, which did not give equal weight to men's and women's legal testimony. While this has been applied only to matters pertaining to economic transactions, the resultant effect is that women are not equal economic actors with men in the eyes of the law.

The issue of evidence became central to the concern for women's status, and matters such as mandatory dress codes for women and whether females can participate in international sports competitions underscored the reality that Zia's Islamization program was having a comprehensive effect on women's lives. The traditional concept of the gendered division of space continues to be perpetuated in broadcast media. Women's subservience is consistently shown on television and in films, while popular television dramas raise controversial issues such as women working, seeking divorce, or even having a say in family politics. What is often depicted, however, is the image that when a woman strays from traditional norms, she faces insurmountable problems and becomes alienated from her family. Indeed, families provide a virtually complete package of economic and social support, provided that members abide by its norms. If a man violates a social norm, it may raise some concern, but

Pakistani women carry torches during a ceremony marking Women's Day in Islamabad on 8 March 2001. (AFP/CORBIS)

143

if a woman violates virtually any social norm, it becomes a calamitous event for her family, with disastrous results for the woman's future.

Since the restoration of democracy in 1988, nearly all political parties in Pakistan have embraced the rhetoric of women's empowerment. While women today actively participate in the economy, less progress has occurred in the political arena. Pakistan became a state party to the U.N. Convention on the Elimination of All Forms of Discrimination Against Women (CEDAW) in 1996, yet none of the discriminatory laws promulgated under Zia's Islamization program have yet been reversed.

Anita M. Weiss

Further Reading
Amesty International. (1995) *Women in Pakistan: Disadvantaged and Denied Their Rights.* New York: Amnesty International.

Mumtaz, Khawar, and Fareeda Shaheed. (1987) *Two Steps Forward, One Step Back?* London: Zed Press; Karachi, Pakistan: Vanguard Books.

Weiss, Anita M. (1996) "The Slow Yet Steady Path to Women's Empowerment in Pakistan." In *Islam, Gender, and Social Change,* edited by Yvonne Yazbeck Haddad and John Esposito. New York: Oxford University Press, 124–143.

———. (1992) *Walls within Walls: Life Histories of Working Women in the Old City of Lahore.* Boulder, CO: Westview Press.

WOMEN IN SOUTH ASIA In the late twentieth century, South Asian women launched a struggle for social reform against millennia of strict patriarchal control. Traditionally a woman had few rights. She was always under the control of her father, her husband, or if a widow, her sons. Even women who took Buddhist or Jain vows were subordinate to the males of the order. A growing body of evidence, however, demonstrates that the lives of women were not always severely restricted and that early civilizations on the subcontinent accorded some women social freedom and spiritual status that were curtailed at a later time.

The Early Pre-Vedic Period
Archaeological remains of the earliest urban culture of the region, the Indus Valley, or Harappan civilization (3000–1800 BCE), include numerous terra-cotta images of females, perhaps mother goddesses. Female figures wearing the horns of a water buffalo on various steatite seals have been identified as a goddess who may have been the precursor of one of the forms of the great goddess of later Hinduism. Because the

Harappan civilization was an agrarian-based culture, it seems logical that the Harappans accorded an earth goddess paramount importance. It was typical in early farming cultures that the fertility of the earth was linked with feminine fecundity. The goddess gave birth to the world, and the mystery of creation was mirrored in the creative capacity of women. Such fertility cults were concerned with sexuality, birth, and the larger realm of increase. Some historians hypothesize that the Harappan culture was matrilineal and endogamous and that women may have served a goddess as priestesses. Archaeological finds suggest that women enjoyed high status and that the culture experienced neither an imbalance between the sexes nor social stratification into distinct classes. Indus skeletons and teeth show no differences among the diets of any of the inhabitants, suggesting that food distribution did not favor any particular group.

The Vedic Period (c. 1500–600 BCE)
The Harappans were succeeded by the so-called Indo-Aryans, whose religious and social milieu was significantly different. Archaeological evidence suggests that the Aryans, a warrior people who formulated the caste system to consolidate their superior social and religious position, introduced warfare to the subcontinent. The Harappan religion of the goddess was supplanted by the patriarchal religion of the Aryan Vedas. Despite patriarchal notions, the early Vedic culture accorded women a degree of freedom and religious distinction. Some twenty female seers and authors were cited as having composed sections of the Vedas. Viewed as an integral part of a hierogamy in which marriage was a requirement for both sexes, wives and husbands were partners in religious rites. Women also participated in theological discussions. Many women were educated, and some women were teachers (*brahmavadinis*) of philosophy and theology. Gargi (c. ninth century BCE) was a particularly well-known female theologian who engaged in a pivotal debate recorded in the *Brihadaranyaka Upanishad* (c. 600 BCE). The Vedas also record that men and women of any age interacted with relative freedom.

Sometime in the middle of the first millennium BCE, however, the position of women diminished so drastically that in subsequent ages they were regarded as unfit for exposure to the sacred Vedas and equivalent in status to the lowest caste, regardless of their caste at birth. The classical law text known as *Manusmriti* (c. 200 CE) unequivocally declared the inferiority of women and the necessity for controlling their thoughts, choices, and movements. Although a woman had limited rights to property, her husband controlled it. Discouraged from religious life, women's functions were limited to caring for her husband and his family and children. Women had no power outside of marriage. Brahman priests' concerns regarding ritual purity caused them to stigmatize women as polluting and dangerous because of their menses. Ritual taboos began to influence the secular world, and women ultimately were viewed as corrupting and debilitating.

Historians have proposed various reasons for the usurpation of women's freedom and authority in the latter part of the first millennium BCE. Developing notions of reincarnation and karma (fate) in the late Vedic age may have been a key component. Religious leaders faced mounting pressures to find a resolution for the soul enduring an endless cycle of births, deaths, and rebirths. Renunciation was viewed as a way to end the cycle, and as such it was a process of closing out and closing down, of decreasing. The ontological opposite of the indigenous fertility cults, renunciation stressed the avoidance of family ties, emotional bonds, and sexuality, all of which were associated with women. As a result women, as the agents of birth, came to be viewed as mentally, morally, hygienically, and biologically inferior.

Under Hinduism (c. First Century CE–Present)

While strong religious assertions promoted the efficacy of renunciation, by the first century CE non-Vedic indigenous cults, particularly fertility cults, reasserted themselves with vigor and merged with Vedic religion to form the pantheon of Hindu deities. A great goddess, Devi, emerged into prominence. She took various forms, including mother, warrior, and one who grants blessings, children, and enlightenment. Coeval with the emergence of the goddesses was the notion of Shakti, female power that animates all things in the universe. While the mythic model could have affected the status of women and led to increasing authority and improved status, such did not end up to be the case. For Hindu women the goddess has served mainly as a model of virtue. The most important mythical model was Sita (literally furrow), the ideal wife, who was meek, obedient, and saintly. In the *Ramayana*, the great Hindu epic (c. 300 BCE), Sita follows her husband into exile and endures a brutal kidnapping, only to have her fidelity and chastity disputed upon her release. She survives trial by fire again and again as proof of her innocence. While many literary passages extol the virtues of wives and mothers and propose that they should be regarded with honor and esteem, great discrepancies existed between the stated textual ideal and women's lot in daily life.

As is expected in a patriarchal society, female children were not welcomed as were males, who were val-

Women in Madurai, India, carrying food in baskets on their heads to workers. (ENZO & PAOLO RAGAZZINI/CORBIS)

ued as an economic asset. Caste was passed only through the male line of descent. Males also were required to perform for the father the funerary rites that guaranteed his ascent to heaven. The partiality ultimately led to female infanticide in some sectors of Hindu society, particularly from the medieval period (c. 900–1600 CE) until the nineteenth century.

Marriage in Hinduism In early times girls married around the age of fifteen or sixteen, but by the fourth century BCE the standard age for girls to marry was between six and ten. In addition to ensuring their virginity, the young age meant that the girls were too young to have formed strong personalities, opinions, or desires and thus were easily controlled by the husband and his family. The prevalence of child marriages coincided with restrictions on the remarriage of widows. Because young girls married older males, widowhood and child widows were widespread.

During the first century CE the plight of widows became severe. Shunned by society, a widow was regarded as bad luck for her husband's family. Denied the opportunity of remarriage, a widow was expected to lead an ascetic life, to remove all ornaments, to shave her head, to sleep on the floor, and to consume a restricted diet consisting of one meal per day. She spent her time in prayer and observing rituals. The only alternative to such a circumscribed existence was sati (immolation on her husband's funeral pyre). Sati was regarded as an auspicious act benefiting the family and the community, though it was practiced only in sectors of society that considered female labor of no great value.

The dowry custom apparently was not a standardized social convention in early or classical India. The literature recommends that the bride be given suitable ornaments for her wedding, but the precise nature of the gift was left to the discretion of the father. The dowry was connected with ancient notions of gift giving, in which the bride was accompanied by a gift to the groom's family. In the medieval period the dowry system began to assume extraordinary proportions. Changes resulting from industrialization under the British particularly led to competition to obtain well-educated husbands of social standing and steady incomes. Thus the sizes of dowries escalated.

Notable Hindu Women in History Only privileged Hindu women received educations. Nonetheless, some gifted women made contributions in various fields. Among the more renowned female poets were Shila-bhattarika of Kanauj, who in the ninth century was honored as the equal of the famous classical poet Bana (flourished seventh century); Rupamati of Malwa (sixteenth century CE), who was an accomplished poet and musician; and Molla (sixteenth century CE), who wrote a moving version of the epic *Ramayana*. A number of famous female mystics were known for their profound devotional hymns. Karaikkal Ammaiyar (c. sixth century CE), Kodai Andal (c. ninth century CE), Lalla (late fourteenth century CE), and the deeply inspired Mira Bai (c. 1450–1547) were all passionate devotees of the divine. Many women were patrons of religion and art, such as the tenth-century queen Sembiyan Mahadevi, who raised countless temples throughout the southern Chola empire.

Among the accounts of heroic Hindu women, the most famous is the Rajput queen Padmini (d. 1303), who along with ten thousand female subjects endured self-immolation rather than be taken prisoner by enemy forces. Rani Lakshmi Bai (d. 1858), the famous queen of Jhansi, inspired fierce rebel fighting against British control in the Indian Mutiny of 1857. Fighting alongside her men, she finally was killed in battle.

Under Jainism

In Jainism women had more freedom than in Hinduism. Jain texts suggest that women with spiritual commitment and aptitude far outnumbered men with similar inclinations and abilities. Historically in Jainism the number of women taking vows outnumbered men by more than two to one. Jainism emphasized renunciation, and both men and women formed monastic orders. The founder of the religion, Mahavira (c. 599–527

BCE), was considered the twenty-fourth Jina or Tirthankara, an enlightened being. Mythological references point to at least two female Jains who attained enlightenment long before the time of Mahavira: Marudevi, the mother of the Tirthankara Rishabha, and the Jina Malli, the nineteenth Tirthankara.

Chandana (c. sixth century BCE) was Mahavira's first female disciple and the first head of an order of Jain nuns. Yakini Mahattara (eighth century CE) was renowned for defeating in debate the boastful Brahman scholiast Haribhadra Suri, one of the most esteemed minds of his day. Haribhadra was so impressed with Yakini's reasoning and mental skill that he eventually converted to Jainism.

While early Jainism accorded women freedom of choice and movement, nuns eventually became dependent on male authority, and regulations eventually restricted all aspects of their lives. The liberalism toward females that had characterized the early centuries was eventually influenced by the pan-Indian prejudices against women. A schism produced two sects, the Digambaras and the Svetambaras. The Svetambaras allowed the possibility of female enlightenment and endorsed the female Jina Malli. The Digambaras, on the other hand, claimed that women lacked the adamantine body necessary for spiritual liberation and refuted the story of Malli altogether.

Under Buddhism

The Buddha (c. 563–483 BCE) initially did not permit the ordination of women. He accepted monks but not nuns, a surprising fact given that his first spiritual teacher was a woman: His aunt, Mahaprajapati Gotami, insisted on forming a women's order. Submitting to social pressures, the Buddha finally allowed women to renounce their earthly ties and become nuns. Generally nuns, no matter what their level of accomplishment, were expected to defer to monks of all ranks. Women of the order were enjoined to bow to all monks. Under no circumstances were nuns allowed to admonish monks, although monks were free to upbraid nuns. Nuns endured far stricter requirements than their male counterparts. The rules for nuns numbered 311, compared with only 227 for monks. Some inviolable rules applied to both sexes, such as avoidance of killing, stealing, and sexual indulgence.

Buddhist women and men received the same education on the principles of Buddhism. Buddhist women generally were literate. One remarkable literary work, the *Theragatha*, is a collection of verses composed within five hundred years of the life of the

146

IMPROVING THE LIVES OF SOUTH ASIAN WOMEN THROUGH POLITICAL REFORM

Mohandas Gandhi, the leader of the Indian independence movement, was a strong supporter of women's rights, and the Indian National Congress political party advocated for reforms to afford women rights and to protect women's rights. The following resolution from the sixtieth meeting of the Congress at Avadi in 1955 summarizes their position.

1. This Congress is strongly of the opinion that all social and legal disabilities as well as reactionary customs and usages to which women are at present subject and which retard their development and prevent them from taking their rightful place in the various activities of the nation should be removed and ended. The history of India contains numerous examples of women who have shown their greatness in many fields of activity. In the struggle for freedom, women took an active and effective part. It is, therefore, not only desirable but essential in the national interest that they should have full opportunities of growth and service and should also have rights of inheritance so that they might not suffer from any legal or social disability.

2. The welfare of children is of paramount importance and should be given first place in the plans for national development.

3. The Congress appreciates the efforts made by the various governments in India for the welfare of women and children and urges them to pay even greater attention to them. In particular, the Congress welcomes the Hindu Law Reform Bills at present before Parliament, and trusts that they will be enacted at an early date.

Source: The Indian National Congress. *Resolutions Passed at Various Annual Sessions, A.I.C.C. and Working Committee Sessions held at various places up to 1963.* Delhi.

Buddha by several nuns of the earliest order who attained nirvana. The contributions are songs stemming from the hearts of women who discovered ultimate bliss. The more liberal attitudes of the early period were abandoned eventually, and women were pushed into the background. The lack of later literature composed by Buddhist women attests to their great anonymity, and in time Buddhist theologians became equivocal on the subject of female enlightenment. It was written that being born a woman was considered a cause for special suffering; for a woman to be reborn as a man was considered the greatest merit. Occasional records document that later Buddhist women achieved enlightenment, but given their obstacles, the nuns are impressive in their demonstrations of devotion.

Under Islam

Islam, a faith imported from Arabia, brought with it severe laws regarding women set down in the seventh century by the Prophet Muhammad. The Qur'an endorses polygamy and insists on a woman's obedience to her husband. A woman's distinction was based solely on her childbearing abilities. Generally, from puberty until death, Islamic women in most parts of South Asia wore veils (*parda*) and were screened from the sight of all males except close family members. Families arranged marriages, and women spent their lives in strict confinement. Islamic law allowed a woman to have and control her own property, however, and she could inherit from her parents and her husband.

Members of the All India Democratic Women's Association protest in New Delhi for legislation that would reserve one-third of seats in parliament for women. (AFP/CORBIS)

Muslim women received little education if any. Their immobility and anonymity provided scant record of their individual lives. Women in households of the ruling class generally were literate, and a few notable women even held political influence. For example, Raziya Sultan (d. 1240), the daughter of the Slave king Iltutmish, was named by her father to succeed him. In 1236 she cast off her veil and ruled until rebels, discontented with a woman as their ruler, killed her. Gulbadan Begum (early sixteenth century CE), daughter of the first Mughal ruler, Babur (1483–1530), left a history of her father and her brother, the next emperor, Humayun, in the *Humayun-nameh* (sixteenth century CE). Nur Jahan (d. 1645), the wife of the emperor Jahangir (1569–1627), was the de facto ruler of the Mughal empire (1526–1857) for years. A more able administrator than her husband, who was primarily concerned with art and alcohol, she issued *firmans* (official orders) under her own seal. Jahan Ara Begum (seventeenth century), the daughter of Shah Jahan (1592–1666), served as an adviser to her father in his last years. One courageous female, Rokeya Sekhawat Hossain (1880–1932), a severe critic of Muslim patriarchy, spearheaded a movement at the beginning of the twentieth century for education and liberal treatment of Muslim women.

The Modern Period

The progressive leader Mohandas (Mahatma) Gandhi (1869–1948) was extremely critical of the traditional treatment of women and encouraged them to join the independence movement. In his book *Women and Social Injustice* (1942), he declared women superior to men and championed the abolition of child marriages, cruel treatment of widows, and prostitution. Encouraging full equal rights for women, he was in-

strumental, along with the feminist activist Sarojini Naidu (1879–1949), in developing a comprehensive plan for female advancement, and they argued for equal rights guarantees in the constitution. At the time of independence from Britain in 1947, India, West Pakistan (now Pakistan), and East Pakistan (now Bangladesh) granted adult women full suffrage.

While a number of early reformers worked for constitutional equity, beginning in the 1970s women's unions and organizations coordinated at all levels of society to ensure that women were not barred from practicing their rights. Women's activism affected various sectors of the populations of India, Sri Lanka, Nepal, Bangladesh, and Pakistan. Generally, more women began to receive some education, and a greater number of women earned professional degrees in all fields. In India and Sri Lanka large numbers of women entered the workplace, many in white-collar positions. Wider access to social contacts through the workplace encouraged more marriages of choice and fewer arranged marriages. Family planning also allowed women more freedom. Nonetheless, the prevailing attitude remained that a woman's status depends on motherhood. Islamic South Asian women in particular have been less visible in the workforce, with only a slight increase in the late twentieth century.

In addition to gaining constitutional protections, women in the late twentieth century battled the more insidious forms of control exerted by communal social pressures. For example, divorce was an option for few women because of its social stigma. In the late twentieth century, however, more women extricated themselves from abusive situations, though leaving was still difficult for them in many areas, especially Pakistan. Women of South Asia also became active in politics, and both India and Bangladesh reserve a share of the parliamentary seats for women. Six women became the political leaders of their nations in the twentieth century: Sirimavo Bandaranaike (b. 1916) of Sri Lanka was the world's first woman prime minister, and her daughter subsequently became prime minister. In addition Indira Gandhi (1917–1984) of India, Benazir Bhutto (b. 1953) of Pakistan, and Begum Khaleda Zia-ur-Rahman (b. 1945) and Sheikh Hasina Wajed (b. 1947) of Bangladesh served their nations as prime ministers.

Katherine Anne Harper

Further Reading

Altekar, A. S. (1987) *The Position of Women in Hindu Civilization.* Delhi: Motilal Banarsidass.
Bose, Mandakranta, ed. (2000) *Faces of the Feminine in Ancient, Medieval, and Modern India.* New York: Oxford University Press.

Hussain, Irfan, ed. (1997) *Pakistan.* London: Stacey.

Jaini, Padmanabh S. (1991) *Gender and Salvation: Jaina Debates on the Spiritual Liberation of Women.* Berkeley and Los Angeles: University of California Press.

Jeffery, Patricia. (1979) *Frogs in the Well: Indian Women in Purdah.* London: Zed.

King, Karen L., ed. (1997) *Women and Goddess Traditions.* Minneapolis, MN: Fortress.

Leslie, Julia, ed. (1991) *Roles and Rituals for Hindu Women.* Rutherford, NJ: Fairleigh Dickinson University Press.

Murcott, Susan. (1991) *The First Buddhist Women: Translations and Commentary on the Therigatha.* Berkeley, CA: Parallax.

Paul, Diana. (1979) *Women in Buddhism: Images of the Feminine in Mahayana Tradition.* Berkeley, CA: Asian Humanities Press.

Roy, Manisha. (1975) *Bengali Women.* Chicago: University of Chicago Press.

WOMEN IN SOUTHEAST ASIA

The position of women in Southeast Asia is often cited as evidence that women are not universally subjugated to men. Women's high status in the region is said to derive from their important role in agriculture; it is reflected in the bilateral kinship systems which predominate and in which male and female descent lines are equally followed in determining ancestry; the widespread phenomenon of land inheritance by women; control of household finances by women; and so on. Even amongst Chinese groups and the Vietnamese (or *kinh*), whose societies are traditionally patriarchal, women in Southeast Asia are in many ways strikingly more highly valued than women in many other parts of the world. However, in recent times, with the increased pace of urbanization and industrialization, women do not seem to be benefiting from development to the same extent as men.

Traditional Roles

The position of women in Southeast Asia in relation to men has often been described as one of complementarity: in traditional societies the roles of men and women are generally seen as equal in importance and mutually supportive. This idea reflects a symbolic dualism in the conceptualization of the world. Origin myths as well as the division of labor in such societies often demonstrate this principle. Thus creation myths often oppose textile equipment with weapons, magic, or writing, with women being defined by the former and men the latter. Among groups such as the Nagas (located in India and adjacent sections of Myanmar), in which men traditionally proved their maturity through headhunting, women may gain adult status through proving themselves as accomplished weavers.

In Buddhist societies in which maturity is achieved for a man through being a monk, motherhood and accomplishment in weaving were also the traditional ways to express a woman's maturity. This is not to say that the two spheres were always separate, and a degree of cooperation in some activities is also found, in gathering in the rice harvest, for example. Men who are for some reason without a wife may happily perform "female" tasks.

The high status held by women often derives from their symbolic importance as a source of fertility, and women often have a special role to play in relation to rice cultivation. In traditional methods of agriculture, although men may prepare the land to receive the seed, women often do the actual planting. Similarly, in many societies only women may enter the rice granary. In both mainland and maritime Southeast Asia this symbolic association of women with fertility often seems to apply also in the field of human reproduction, so that even in patrilineal societies such as the Bataks of northern Sumatra, the lineage of a bride is regarded as superior to that of the husband, since it is the woman who brings greater life force to the marriage.

In many Southeast Asian societies women have traditionally held positions of some power. Thus among the Minangkabau of West Sumatra, although legal and administrative power may be held by men, land and clan membership pass down the female line. In other societies, in which clan membership relates to male descent groups and ancestral lands are held in common following a patrilineal pattern of kinship, women's positions were in many ways less strong. In most Southeast Asian societies, however, kinship is reckoned along both male and female lines, and there is a degree of inheritance on both sides.

Postmarital residence is another factor that may affect a woman's position. Where a young bride must move in with her husband's parents, the possibility of exploitation of her labor exists; where a man traditionally lives with his parents-in-law it is he who may be subservient to his wife's family. In most but not all Southeast Asian societies, the practice is for the newly married couple to move in with the parents of the wife. When they do set up a home of their own, it is often near the wife's mother's house, and clusters of related women form strong networks in many of the villages of Southeast Asia.

In contemporary Southeast Asia many of these traditional patterns are changing, though the legacy of these perceptions often means that attitudes towards women are respectful, especially within the home, which throughout the region is regarded as the woman's domain. Changes brought about by colonization and later through administrative arrangements under independence have often failed to recognize such traditional roles. Land that was once owned by women was in many cases registered in the names of their husbands; household censuses listed the senior male as head of the household, and in some cases village headmen were appointed in places where villages had in the past been run by councils consisting of household heads, both male and female. The declining importance of women as textile producers in the face of industrialization has also tended to diminish the status of women, though where ritual textiles are still regarded as necessary for rites of passage, this symbolic importance remains.

Religion

The introduction of world religions into the region has also affected the role of women. Where Buddhism is the main religion—in Thailand, Cambodia, Laos, and Myanmar—the chief way for a man to make merit and thus earn respect is through ordination as a monk. In some areas, women do serve as nuns, but they cannot achieve the same status as the monks in the Buddhist priesthood; nor do they receive the same training in the scriptures. However, outside the monastery, women are able to make a considerable contribution to Buddhist society. It is the women who prepare and present gifts of food and textiles to the monks, and they also attend services and observe the precepts. All these activities provide women with the means of making merit both for themselves as individuals and for their families. Women are also responsible for the care of tutelary spirits in the home and for other essential lay duties. The ability to make merit gives women access to a degree of social mobility.

There is a fundamental difference, however, between the spheres in which women and men make merit. Men's involvement in the priesthood removes them from the material world and from relationships with their families, and this removal from the world of desire is associated with a higher plane of religious experience. A woman's route to merit making strengthens her link with the world of material things and with her role as a mother. For her, the major act of merit making is providing a son for ordination as a monk. Women are thus more likely to be involved in trade and financial matters than men, who are more distanced from their families and from the material world.

Islam has affected the position of women in Southeast Asia to a lesser degree than is the case in some Middle Eastern countries, but where Islamic law is called on, for example in settling disputes over inheritance, women receive less equal treatment than they enjoyed under traditional law, or *adat*, as it is known in the Indo-Malay archipelago. However, Islam as practiced in Southeast Asia does not discriminate against women in terms of their religious status or worth. Women, like men, pray five times a day, and both follow the five pillars of Islam. While men attend Friday prayers at the mosque, women may belong to a Qur'an reading group that meets at a member's house. Although men are more frequently prayer leaders than women, a woman may occasionally take on this role if she is the best qualified to do so in terms of her knowledge of the teachings of Islam. Literacy has always been an important element in Islamic societies, and although in the past boys were more likely to receive a formal education than girls, national education policies in Brunei, Malaysia, and Indonesia, the countries with the greatest percentage of Muslims in the region, have gone a long way towards their aim of giving boys and girls equal access to education.

In areas where Christianity achieved dominance, the position of women was also affected. In precolonial times, the status of men and women in the Philippines was probably for the most part equal and complementary. The male-centered Spanish regime, however, placed a great many constraints on women. This had greater consequences for women in lower socioeconomic groups than it did for those belonging to the upper classes. Among the better off, precolonial domestic patterns proved relatively resilient and many women took advantage of the opportunities presented by the economic developments of the postcolonial era. Thus they have been fairly well represented in professional, clerical, and administrative occupations.

Education

Everywhere in Southeast Asia, adult literacy levels are higher for males than for females, though the discrepancy varies from country to country. The greatest discrepancies are in Cambodia and Laos; the least discrepancy is found in the Philippines, which has a very high literacy rate.

Girls' participation in schooling in Southeast Asia is high in comparison with developing countries in other parts of the world. In Malaysia, Brunei, Myanmar, and Indonesia there is very little difference at all between participation rates for boys and girls at primary level, though the picture is less good in Cambodia and Laos. In the latter two countries female participation is lower at secondary level than at primary level, as is the case in Indonesia. In Myanmar, Malaysia, and Brunei the rate of enrollment for males and females is roughly comparable at secondary level.

In Malaysia, equal rights to education for boys and girls are written into the law, but in practice girls' education lags behind that of boys.

Politics

In recent times, a number of notable women have reached the top level of political office in Southeast Asia. However, their achievement has nearly always resulted from a family connection (that is, they have either been the wife or daughter of a prominent male politician). Men dominate the political arena everywhere, although the picture does vary from country to country. In Thailand, women have had the right to vote and to be elected to political office since 1932, but the percentage of women in the cabinet is still very low. In all other countries in Southeast Asia apart from Brunei, women gained the right to vote at or soon after independence. Only in the Philippines, however, are a substantial number of women involved in government. It was also in the Philippines that the first woman was elected to parliament, in 1941.

However, this is not to say that women do not have an important influence on political life in Southeast Asia. In Thailand and the Philippines in recent years, women from the urban elite have become increasingly active in the political arena. Furthermore, although women are much less numerous than men in formal political institutions, they are very active politically in a broader sense. There are many women's organizations in Southeast Asia that provide a vehicle for the expression of opinion, and women have become adept at organizing and finding a voice for themselves, albeit in a restricted sphere. In Indonesia, women's organizations are active in the area of welfare and income generation at the grassroots level. In the Philippines, many professional women's associations have emerged, and in Thailand women's nongovernmental organizations have been invited to participate in decision making and policy making by the government and by U.N. agencies in areas of life that are seen to relate specifically to women.

In Vietnam, women played an important role in the struggle for independence, and this seems to have led to a recognition that women have a contribution to make in the political arena. There was a steady growth in the number of women in the National Assembly between 1946 and 1975. After this date, however, both the number of women representatives and their percentage of the total fell. The fact that the decline coincided with the period of unification has led to the suggestion that the decline resulted from the relatively strong influence of feudal thinking in the South. A similar pattern occurred also at provincial, district, and village levels. Despite this fall, women in Vietnam play an active role in political life, with 118 women deputies in the National Assembly as compared with 332 men.

Economy

Generally in Southeast Asia, motherhood and care of the family are assumed to be the first responsibility of women. However, women are not prevented from engaging in economic activity as well, and their traditional participation in agricultural work alongside men means that the division of labor is not as clear cut as in many other developing countries. Everywhere in Southeast Asia, the proportion of earned income contributed by women is lower than that contributed by men. In Cambodia the proportion earned by men and women is most closely comparable; in Brunei there is the greatest disparity. Despite these earning disparities, women occupy high-status positions throughout Southeast Asia. They compete successfully with men in entrepreneurial roles as well as in the armed forces, the ranks of the police and civil servants, and in the academic world. There are highly educated women who are professionals and who occupy executive and administrative positions in both the public and the private sector, but in all cases they are in the minority.

Women form a large proportion of migrant workers in Southeast Asia, traveling both within the region and outside it. Industrial development in the cities, particularly medium-sized or large-scale domestic or multinational operations, attracts young unmarried women and girls from the countryside, especially in Cambodia and Thailand. Few women who have worked for any length of time in the city return to the countryside, and many find husbands in the city. Out of a sense of duty and obligation towards their parents, most young women who work in the city send money home to their families, who may be unaware of or turn a blind eye to the fact that their daughters may be involved in prostitution. For girls who have found work in Bangkok, it is quite easy to find evening classes to further their education, and this is an added attraction for girls from rural areas. The trappings of modern city life are also an attraction. In Indonesia, it is chiefly Javanese girls who leave home, often to work in the domestic sphere in wealthier households within Indonesia or overseas. Philippine migrant workers also include a high proportion of women, many of them in domestic service overseas.

Although young women's wages are not high, their ability to contribute to household income in a modernizing economy has had an effect on intrahousehold relations in many cases. As they grow older and are able to find employment, unmarried daughters often begin to expect their views to be heard, especially in relation to their own employment. The traditional pattern of deference of younger to older, woman to man in these cases is beginning to be challenged.

Fiona Kerlogue

Further Reading

Dube, Leela. (1997) *Women and Kinship: Comparative Perspectives on Gender in South and Southeast Asia.* Tokyo, New York, and Paris: United Nations University Press.

Eisen, Arlene. (1984) *Women and Revolution in Vietnam.* London: Zed.

Helliwell, Christine. (1993) "Women in Asia: Anthropology and the Study of Women." In *Asia's Cultural Mosaic: An Anthropological Introduction,* edited by Grant Evans. Singapore: Prentice Hall and Simon & Schuster, 260–286.

Keyes, Charles. (1995) *The Golden Peninsula: Culture and Adaptation in Mainland Southeast Asia.* Honolulu: University of Hawaii Press.

Lebra, Joyce, and Joy Paulson. (1980) *Chinese Women in Southeast Asia.* Singapore: Times Books.

Manderson, Lenore, ed. (1983) *Women's Work and Women's Roles: Economics and Everyday Life in Indonesia, Malaysia, and Singapore.* Development Studies Centre Monograph, no. 32. Canberra, Australia: Australian National University.

Ovesen, Jan, Ing-Britt Trankell, and Joakim Öjendal. (1996) *When Every Household Is an Island: Social Organisation and Power Structures in Rural Cambodia.* Uppsala Research Reports in Cultural Anthropology, no. 15. Uppsala, Sweden: Uppsala University.

United Nations Development Programme. (1998) *Human Development Report 1998.* New York: Oxford University Press.

van Esterik, Penny, and John van Esterik, eds. (1992) *Gender and Development in Southeast Asia.* CCSAS Proceedings, no 20. Vol 2. Ottawa, Canada: Canadian Council for Southeast Asian Studies.

WOMEN IN WEST ASIA

Women in West Asia constitute a diverse population. Notwithstanding stereotypes concerning the status and roles of the predominately Muslim and Arab women of West Asia, women's social positions within and across nations vary by social class, ethnicity, age, education, and location (urban or rural). Other important factors are a nation's social structure and stage of development, as well as the nature of the nation and its economic, social, and cultural policies. These sociodemographic and structural factors shape the opportunities available to women, their legal status, and the structure of gender relations in any given society in West Asia.

Despite this diversity, however, there are some common characteristics that are particularly noticeable when comparisons are made with women in other regions. These common characteristics are relatively high (although declining) fertility rates, gender gaps in literacy so that women have lower literacy rates than men, relatively limited access to paid employment (except in Israel), and underrepresentation in the political system. Moreover, women in nearly all the nations of West Asia experience second-class citizenship due to certain provisions in Muslim family law and to patriarchal cultural practices and norms. The persistence of a patriarchal system that favors men is itself partly the result of the influence of Islamist movements in recent decades. To address these problems, women in West Asia have formed a dynamic women's movement that seeks to challenge patriarchal gender arrangements; expand women's civil, political, and social rights; and empower women economically and politically.

Women constitute about half of the population of the nations in West Asia, whether in the small Persian Gulf sheikhdoms such as Bahrain, Kuwait, and the United Arab Emirates or the large nations such as Iran

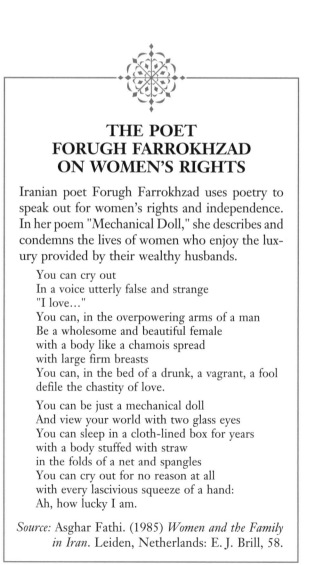

THE POET FOROUGH FARROKHZAD ON WOMEN'S RIGHTS

Iranian poet Forugh Farrokhzad uses poetry to speak out for women's rights and independence. In her poem "Mechanical Doll," she describes and condemns the lives of women who enjoy the luxury provided by their wealthy husbands.

> You can cry out
> In a voice utterly false and strange
> "I love..."
> You can, in the overpowering arms of a man
> Be a wholesome and beautiful female
> with a body like a chamois spread
> with large firm breasts
> You can, in the bed of a drunk, a vagrant, a fool
> defile the chastity of love.
>
> You can be just a mechanical doll
> And view your world with two glass eyes
> You can sleep in a cloth-lined box for years
> with a body stuffed with straw
> in the folds of a net and spangles
> You can cry out for no reason at all
> with every lascivious squeeze of a hand:
> Ah, how lucky I am.

Source: Asghar Fathi. (1985) *Women and the Family in Iran.* Leiden, Netherlands: E. J. Brill, 58.

WOMEN AND MEN—SEPARATE LIVES

This extract of text from an ethnographic study of a farming village in central Turkey describes a pattern typical of husband-wife relations in rural West Asia, in which there is little contact except in family financial and sexual matters.

Women do not look to their husbands for companionship; still less do the men look to their wives. It is taken for granted that there is no common ground for conversation. A man must never show affection for his wife in front of anyone else. When a soldier returned to the village after years of absence, his kin and neighbours gathered round him to welcome and embrace him. The ceremony often lasted for hours, as one person after another heard the news and hastened to the guest room. His greeting for his wife was left over till bedtime—she could not even see him until all the others had finished with him. When men left Elbasi on their way to Mecca, their sisters and mothers embraced them publicly and histrionically at the boarding of the lorry—but not their wives. Within the household, before close kin, the taboo on public affection is even stronger. Nobody talks about 'love' except occasionally in cases of adultery and elopement. The relationship is limited to economic co-operation and to sexual intimacy. Women frequently said to my wife that they did not love their husbands—not only in specific cases, but as a general description of village life. Men spoke very little of their relationship to their wives, and when they did, it was of the common bed, of their prowess therein, and of their large families that they boasted. More than once, men remarked to me in jest: "We love our wives at night."

Source: Paul Stirling. (1965) *The Village Economy*. London: Charles Birchall, 113.

and Turkey, although in some countries the existence of an adverse sex ratio is a cause for concern. A growing number of countries in the region are now predominantly urbanized, but there remain sizable rural populations in countries such as Jordan, Turkey, and Iran. The marriage rate remains high in the region, and the fertility rate of women in West Asia tends to be higher than in other nations at similar stages of development. Fertility rates correlate with a mother's educational attainment and employment status—themselves a function of social class and location—but they also reflect the nation's stage of development and the government's family-planning policy. And in many nations, a woman's age at marriage has been rising, a result of both economic pressures and rising educational attainment. Thus fertility rates range from lows of 2.2–2.7 births per woman in Iran, Turkey, Lebanon, and Israel to highs of about 6 births per woman in

Saudi Arabia, Yemen, and Palestine (the West Bank and Gaza)—where adolescent fertility rates are also very high.

Gains in Education

Educational attainment is growing among women in West Asia, and the gender gaps are narrowing. Although illiteracy is common among women in the older age groups, and universal schooling has yet to be achieved in some of the poorer nations (notably Yemen), enrollment rates for girls in primary and secondary schools are rising and nearly at a par with those for boys. Some nations have made tremendous progress in the past two decades. For example, in 1980 the expected number of years of schooling for girls in Oman and Saudi Arabia was only two and five years, respectively, but by 1997 it had increased to nine years, according to World Bank figures. In Iran and the

United Arab Emirates, girls can expect to complete at least eleven years of schooling. Iran has had a tremendous increase in the population of educated urban and rural females, and about half of university students are now women. In Bahrain, Qatar, and the United Arab Emirates, the majority of university students are female. Less is known about the quality of education that women receive, although some research shows that government cutbacks have resulted in crowded classrooms, fewer qualified teachers, and poor instructional materials in the state-owned schools.

Women in the Workforce

Rising educational attainment, as well as declining household budgets after the oil boom era, has led to growing involvement by women in the formal and informal sectors of the economy, and their share of the labor force increased significantly between 1980 and 1997. This is particularly true in nations such as Jordan, Kuwait, Oman, Saudi Arabia, and the United Arab Emirates, where women's participation in the labor force was previously negligible and the economies relied on foreign contract labor. In the 1990s, women's employment increased in Turkey and Iran, largely in the teaching and health professions, to a lesser extent in sales and services. Improved methods of counting the range of women's economic activities have also yielded higher percentages of women in agriculture as well as in urban informal occupations. In Jordan, Iran, and Turkey, businesses owned by women are a growing trend. As elsewhere in the world, however, much of the work available to working-class women is irregular and ill paid, and even middle-class women in the civil service have seen the real value of their salaries deteriorate considerably. An elite corps of professional women may be found in both public and private sectors, but their numbers in the highest administrative and managerial categories are small.

Women in Politics

Women in West Asia have always been involved in political movements (for example, independence, national liberation, socialist, and feminist movements), but their involvement in formal political structures (in political parties or as elected officials) has been more recent and remains limited. In contrast to Turkey, where women were given the right to vote in 1930, other nations granted women voting rights in the 1950s (Lebanon, Syria), the 1960s (Iran), or the 1980s (Iraq). This has partly to do with the relative novelty of elections, partly with the experience of colonialism, and partly with the patriarchal gender system.

Although women are found in the rank-and-file and leadership of political parties (for example, in Turkey, which also had a woman prime minister), nowhere have they reached a critical mass (30 percent), and their appointment to party or government positions is largely a form of tokenism. Women are certainly elected to parliament, but their share of parliamentary seats in 1999

Filling a traditional women's role, women in Turkey collect water for their households. (ED KASHI/ CORBIS)

Iranian women performing at the opening ceremony of Iran's women's sports championships in Tehran in August 2000. (AFP/CROBIS)

ranged from zero in Jordan to 10 percent in Syria; Israel's share of women was 12 percent. The female share of parliamentary seats in Egypt and Lebanon was 2 percent, in Turkey 4 percent, in Iran 5 percent, and in Iraq 6 percent. (By contrast, women in Vietnam and Argentina had a 27 percent share.) Women's organizations have been keen to increase women's political participation by encouraging women to run in national elections, supporting women's involvement in local elections, and insisting that more women be appointed to ministerial and subministerial positions. They hope that women politicians will be more likely to draft or support legislation that would improve the status of women in family law and labor law. But barriers to women's participation in formal politics remain formidable.

Women's Organizations

Partly because of women's underrepresentation in government and political parties, women have formed their own organizations to lobby and advocate for women; to conduct research on women, gender, and social issues; or to deliver services to poor women and their children. There has been a veritable explosion of women's organizations in West Asia; these include feminist or women's rights organizations, professional associations, nongovernmental organizations focusing on women in development, charities run by women that cater to women, institutes and research centers devoted to women's studies, and associations of women workers. These organizations have their own agendas, constituencies, and modes of operation, and their strength or weakness varies depending on the country, but they may be said to constitute a growing women's movement throughout West Asia. The movement has many voices, but the major goals of organized women in West Asia may be summarized as follows: (1) the modernization of family law to attain gender equality in marriage, divorce, child custody, and inheritance; (2) nationality rights for women so that they may retain their own nationality or pass it on to their children; (3) the crimialization of violence against women, including domestic violence, so-called honor crimes (killing a female relative for a real or imagined sexual or cultural transgression), and the public harassment of women by men; and (4) an increase in women's economic opportunities and their participation in political decision making. In addition to the preceding, Muslim women are reclaiming their religion, questioning traditional (or patriarchal) interpretations of the Qur'an and hadith, and emphasizing the egalitarian or emancipatory messages of the holy texts. This is especially true of "Islamic feminists" in Iran. In Israel, women are heavily involved in the peace movement and are engaged in a feminist rereading of the Torah and of Jewish history. And in Turkey, feminists' organizations have confronted and worked against the growing influence of Islamist movements and political parties.

Women in West Asia are divided politically and ideologically as well as socially and economically. Some are more aligned with their governments and regimes, whereas others are critical; some women prefer the separation of religion from politics and the legal framework, whereas others prefer that religion continue to have a strong presence in society. All of them would probably agree, however, that women's status and roles are in need of advancement.

Valentine Moghadam

Further Reading
Gerner, Deborah, ed. (2000) *Understanding the Contemporary Middle East.* Boulder, Colorado: Lynne Rienner.

Joseph, Suad, and Susan Slyomovics, eds. (2001) *Women and Power in the Middle East.* Philadelphia: University of Pennsylvania Press.

Moghadam, Valentine M. (1993) *Modernizing Women: Gender and Social Change in the Middle East.* Boulder, CO: Lynne Rienner Publishers.

United Nations. (2000) *The World's Women: Trends and Statistics (Annual).* New York: United Nations.

WOODWORKING—CENTRAL ASIA   A
significant sector of the economies of Central Asian countries, woodworking produces a variety of products, the most important of which are round logs, lumber, wood-based panels, paper and paperboard, wood pulp, and furniture.

Forest and other wooded land in Central Asia account for 5 percent of the total land area, and constitutes less than 1 percent of the world's forest cover. Turkmenistan has the highest percentage of forest cover (8.0 percent) while Tajikistan has the lowest percentage (2.8 percent); all of the latter's forests are classified as not available for wood supply. To a great extent the demand for forest products in Central Asia is met by imports, mainly from the Russian Federation.

Kazakhstan has the biggest woodworking establishments and accounts for most of the region's production. The forest and woodworking industry plays a significant role in its industrial complex, especially in East Kazakhstan, which is rich in forests. Most of the country's woodworking plants are concentrated in the north and northeast, in Semey, Astana, Petropavl, and Aktobe; a big furniture factory is located in Ust-Kamenogorsk. In south central Kazakhstan, the most important woodworking centers are Chymkent, Almaty, and Zhambyl. In the other Central Asian countries the most important woodworking centers are Ashkhabad, Mary, and Sarakhs in Turkmenistan; Tashkent, Kokand, Andizan, Bukhara, Samarkand, and Karshi in Uzbekistan; Bishkek, Naryn, and Osh in Kyrgyzstan; and Namangan and Dushanbe in Tajikistan.

Forestry practice in Central Asia has remained relatively small-scale and less technologically advanced than in Western Europe. This has been highly beneficial in preserving species diversity. At the same time, most of the indigenous forests in Central Asia disappeared long ago as a result of human activities. The process began during the early Middle Ages in connection with the mining industry and has continued until the present. The effects of deforestation are apparent in the intensification of erosion, higher incidence of avalanches, more arid conditions, air pollution by dust, and melting of the glaciers. In some parts of the Central Asian region, rural poverty causes wood to be used as a primary source of energy, which leads to local deforestation.

Dimitar L. Dimitrov

Further Reading
Alibekov, L. A. (1990) "Deforestation of the Mountains of Central Asia and the Problem of Agriculture and Forest Amelioration." *Vestnik.* Moskovskogo Universiteta. Seriya Geografiya 4: 53–57.

Kaser, Michael. (1997) *The Economies of Kazakstan and Uzbekistan.* Former Soviet South Project Paper. London: Royal Institute of International Affairs.

WORKERS' PARTY—SINGAPORE   The
Workers' Party is a major opposition party in Singapore, where the People's Action Party (PAP) has won every majority since 1965. The Workers' Party was formed in November 1957 by David Marshall (1908–1995), a lawyer and the first chief minister of Singapore. The party's guiding principles of *Merdeka* (independence) are democracy, socialism, and improving the conditions of workers.

Since its inception, the party has been plagued by intraparty differences, which ultimately led to Marshall's resignation in 1963. The party machinery was small and ineffective until Joshua Benjamin Jeyaretnam (b. 1926), a dynamic lawyer, injected life into it in 1971. Jeyaretnam broke the PAP's parliamentary monopoly by winning the 1971 Anson by-election, gaining 7,012 votes, or 51.93 percent of the total valid votes.

In the 1999 general elections, the Workers' Party's Low Thia Khiang was returned as member of parliament for Hougang for a second time. In the Cheng San Group Representative Constituency, the Workers' Party team won 45.2 percent of the valid votes, but lost to the PAP team. Since the Workers' Party candidates obtained the highest percentage of votes among all the unelected opposition candidates, they became eligible to take up the nonconstituency member-of-parliament seat. The Workers' Party team elected the party's secretary-general, J. B. Jeyaretnam, to take up the seat.

Workers' Party officeholders have been repeatedly threatened with defamation suits by the PAP government. Many observers perceive both the Workers' Party officeholders and Jeyaretnam as political victims of the PAP's vindictive course of action.

Khai Leong Ho

Further Reading

Ho, Khai Leong. (2000) *The Politics of Policy-Making in Singapore.* Singapore: Oxford University Press.

Singh, Bilveer. (1992) *Whither PAP's Dominance? An Analysis of Singapore's 1991 General Elections.* Selangor, Malaysia: Pelanduk.

WORLD BANK IN ASIA
The World Bank is an internationally funded development lender, a specialized agency of the United Nations. The Bank was a product of the 1944 Bretton Woods Conference, at which the imminently victorious allies—notably the United States and Great Britain—sought to lay the basis for postwar reconstruction of the world's monetary system. Since the 1960s, it has been a prime lender to the newly industrializing countries (NICs) of Asia.

Founding and Early Years of the World Bank

When discussions were under way at Bretton Woods for the creation of the World Bank, U.S. distaste for the "beggar-thy-neighbor" protectionism of the 1930s that had contributed to the worldwide economic depression and subsequent rise of totalitarianism had a large influence. The United States, possessing a flourishing and ultracompetitive industrial plant, championed free trade, monetary stability, and elimination of tariff barriers. Great Britain, the other leading western industrial power at war's end, was not as unreservedly in favor of free trade, having adopted an Imperial Preference scheme a few years earlier at the Westminster Conference in order to protect Empire and Commonwealth markets. U.S. economic predominance meant, though, that its vision would prevail.

The Bank eventually evolved into five major components, each of which had its own function in promoting international economic development. These units are the International Bank for Reconstruction and Development; the International Development Association; the International Finance Corporation; the Multilateral Investment Guaranty Agency; and the International Centre for Settlement of Investment Disputes.

The Bank's immediate postwar task was to assist with the reconstruction of Europe. By the mid-1950s, Europe had fully recovered and the Bank turned its developmental interest elsewhere. Its interest was global, but Asia received special attention. Asian countries were just emerging from colonial status and now assumed full responsibility for their own economic development. This, naturally, prompted an urgent need for development capital and financial expertise. In addition, this same era saw the end of American occupation of Japan, and that country, already a major economic power, faced the task of full and peaceful integration into the postwar economic order. Also, the communist takeover of China prompted concern in Western capitals that the newly independent Asian countries have an alternative model for economic progress. The mission of the Bank in Asia was to act as a catalyst for economic development among the Asian NICs, many of which were newly independent. However, it differed from commercial lenders in that its goal was not simply profit but rather to help develop institutions and industries that would, in turn, further the long-term maturation of local economies. In this sense, the Bank provided "seed money" for future growth.

From Project-Oriented Policy to Structural Change

During the 1960s and into the 1970s, the Bank was essentially project-oriented. Typical ventures were a series of dams constructed in Asia. These dams were not conceived of as profit-making entities and, as such, would have held little attraction for investors looking for an immediate return. They did, however, offer the potential to control flooding and enhance agriculture, as well as generating electric power that might fuel industrial development. Such projects were well in line with the Bank's vision of investing in projects that would generate long-term wealth. Examples in Asia include the 1960s Phasom Dam Project in Thailand and the Tarbela Dam Project in Pakistan. The increase in agricultural production derived from these efforts caused a rise in rural living standards, while electrification made possible a considerable expansion of industry. Besides money, the Bank provided technical expertise and experienced personnel.

A change in the Bank's *modus operandi* occurred during the late 1970s and into the following decade as it increasingly concentrated on structural change in Asian economies. Whereas, in an earlier period, the obstacles to economic growth were seen as chiefly material—lack of electrical generation or flood control, for example—attention now focused on government policies that impeded capital formation and its effective utilization. A government that shielded inefficient industries through subsidies or tariffs, and thus impeded the more efficient use of capital, was seen as at least as great an impediment to economic growth as a material lack. This shift occurred at a time when economic theory in Western nations moved away from Keynesian government "pump-priming," in vogue during the immediate postwar era, toward monetarist policy that emphasized profound economic reform, not individual projects underwritten by government.

The new orientation of the Bank put it in conflict with local Asian economies. For instance, from independence India had adopted a socialist economic model that stressed extensive government ownership of key industries and state-directed economic growth. Foreign investment was discouraged and import substitution was selected as a growth mechanism, which meant protective tariffs. For the favored industries, this approach produced pockets of prosperity along with stable employment. Such local stability was, however, more than offset by sluggish overall economic performance at the national level.

Bank economists became convinced that project lending was of relatively little good if financed within a national economy made stagnant by inefficient industries that were kept afloat only by wasteful government subsidies, nationalist import-substitution strategies, protective tariffs, and overvalued currencies. The emphasis of the Bank thus changed to "structural reform," by which was meant an end to statism in economic planning, the elimination of state subsidies to inefficient industries, lowering of protective tariffs, and revaluation of national currencies at realistic levels. Such restructuring might be painful in the short term but, it was believed, would open the Asian nations to broad and sustained future growth and further their integration into the world economy.

Structural Reform and Its Consequences

As part of structural reform, the Bank stressed export-oriented industrial growth, privatization of industry, curtailment of state economic planning, and currency devaluation. It was hoped that these changes would encourage exports, halt wasteful subsidizing of weak import-substitution industries, lessen bureaucratic interference, and increase international demand for local products through depreciated currencies.

This program was so in line with the economic interests of the developed countries, the United States in particular, that some charged that the Bank ignored indigenous Asian needs in favor of the creation of a world economic order that simply slotted Asian economies into western capitalism. Local effects of this restructuring, in some instances, were devastating. Currency

devaluation made essential imports hugely expensive and contributed to inflation. Local industries lost their umbrella of tariff protection, failed, and threw thousands out of jobs. The mild global slowdown of the 1980s left the new export industries without markets. One academic observer dealing with the Philippines, wrote in 1988, "Structural adjustment has also been . . . a disaster for the majority of the Third World, that is, for most workers, peasants, and small entrepreneurs producing for the domestic market" (Broad 1988: xviii).

These charges were amplified when the Asian economies were hammered during the late 1990s by the so-called Asian financial crisis. Some have noted that Malaysia's prime minister, Matahir Mohamad, refused to follow many of the Bank's prescriptions and that his nation's economy was spared some of the worst hardships.

Nevertheless, the general restructuring sought by the Bank has generally occurred. India, formerly a quasi-socialist, protectionist economy, moved toward an open-market economy with overall positive results. In the long run, it may be that the undoubted pain brought about by the Bank's change in philosophy enabled the Asian NICs to become competitive in the new global economy.

Robert Whalen

Further Reading
Broad, Robin. (1988) *Unequal Alliance: The World Bank, the International Monetary Fund, and the Philippines.* Berkeley and Los Angeles: University of California Press.

The East Asian Miracle: Economic Growth and Public Policy. (1993) Published for the World Bank. New York: Oxford University Press.

Guhan, Sanjivi. (1995) *The World Bank's Lending in South Asia.* Washington, DC: Brookings Institution.

Vines, David, and Christopher L. Gilbert, eds. (2000) *The World Bank: Structure and Politics.* New York: Cambridge University Press.

WORLD WAR I
The main theater of World War I was in Europe and no major battles were fought in Asia; nevertheless, Turkey, Japan, China, and the Asian colonies of the imperial powers were involved in the conflict, and its impact was immense in unleashing forces of nationalism and self-determination.

East Asian Region
East Asia was connected not with the immediate causes of World War I, but with such tertiary factors as militarism and nationalism. Japan saw the war as a chance to occupy the German settlements in the Pa-

JAPAN DECLARES WAR ON GERMANY

"We, by the Grace of Heaven, Emperor of Japan, on the throne occupied by the same Dynasty from time immemorial, do hereby make the following proclamation to all Our loyal and brave subjects.

"We, hereby, declare war against Germany and We command Our Army and Navy to carry on hostilities against that Empire with all their strength, and We also command all Our competent authorities to make every effort in pursuance of their respective duties to attain the national aim within the limit of the law of nations.

"Since the outbreak of the present war in Europe, the calamitous effect of which We view with grave concern, We, on our part, have entertained hopes of preserving the peace of the Far East by the maintenance of strict neutrality but the action of Germany has at length compelled Great Britain, Our Ally, to open hostilities against that country, and Germany is at Kiaochau, its leased territory in China, busy with warlike preparations, while her armed vessels, cruising the seas of Eastern Asia, are threatening Our commerce and that of Our Ally. The peace of the Far East is thus in jeopardy.

"Accordingly, Our Government, and that of His Britannic Majesty, after a full and frank communication with each other, agreed to take such measure as may be necessary for the protection of the general interests contemplated in the Agreement of Alliance, and We on Our part, being desirous to attain that object by peaceful means, commanded Our Government to offer, with sincerity, an advice to the Imperial German Government. By the last day appointed for that purpose, however, Our Government failed to receive an answer accepting their advice.

"It is with profound regret that We, in spite of Our ardent devotion to the cause of peace, are thus compelled to declare war, especially at this early period of Our reign and while we are still in mourning for Our lamented Mother.

"It is Our earnest wish, that, by the loyalty and valour of Our faithful subjects, peace may soon be restored and the glory of the Empire be enhanced."

Source: John V. A. MacMurray, ed. (1921) *Treaties and Agreements with and Concerning China, 1894-1919.* Vol. 3. New York: Oxford University Press, 1153.

cific and in China. The Anglo-Japanese alliance of 1904 did not include any obligation that Japan join the Allied powers (Britain, France, Serbia, Russia, Japan, the United States, and China). Japan joined the war to increase its international prestige. On 23 August, Japan declared war on the Central powers (Germany, Austria-Hungary, Bulgaria, and Turkey) and entered the Chinese port of Qingdao (Tsingtao). The German settlements in China were occupied, and Japan established itself on the Shandong peninsula. Japan's navy, along with the British, occupied such German islands as the Marianas, Carolines, and Marshalls in the Pacific.

The city of Constantinople ablaze in 1916. (HULTON-DEUTSCH COLLECTION/CORBIS)

China joined the war in 1917 and sent labor forces to France, West Asia, and Africa. China was disappointed with the results of war and refused to sign the treaty of Versailles that ended it. The Chinese government and people refused to recognize the Shangdong provisions, which granted Japan special rights on the peninsula, and large-scale demonstrations were held.

Japan had already obtained pledges from the Allied powers for its claim to Shandong and the German islands in the Pacific. Japan had hoped for parity with the Western Allies as a reward for joining the war, but its demand for a basic principle of racial equality was not included in the covenant of the League of Nations. Although the Japanese claim of racial equality among nations was not granted by the Western powers, the end of war saw a tremendous increase in Japan's power and prestige. The country benefited economically: cotton exports trebled, and the merchant-fleet tonnage doubled. Japan's trade with Asian countries also increased. Japan was able to establish hegemony in East Asia and to have its claims to special rights in Manchuria and its annexation of Korea recognized by the major powers.

West Asian Region

In West Asia, the Turkish Ottoman empire sided with Germany, and the Arabs, having been given a vague promise of freedom from colonization, were persuaded to join the Allies. Turkey joined the war in November 1914 and posed a threat to the oil fields in the Persian Gulf region. The British landed at Gallipoli but were repulsed by Turkish troops. British Indian troops occupied Basra and marched along the Tigris River to Baghdad. The British forces surrendered in April 1916 to the Turkish troops. However, these initial Turkish victories did not save the Ottoman empire.

The Turks could not take the Suez Canal, and the British exploited the Arab dislike for the Turks to British advantage. Colonel T. H. Lawrence (known as Lawrence of Arabia) led a series of desert campaigns in Western Asia. By the end of 1917, the British had taken Baghdad and Jerusalem; Edmund Allenby, the British general, entered Jerusalem on 8 December. He was helped by reinforcements from India and by Arab revolts. After the British offensive in Palestine, Turkey concluded an armistice on 30 September 1918.

The British, along with the French, played devious diplomacy. Publicly they supported the Arabs in their drive for independence. However, as a result of the Sykes-Picot Agreement of 9 May 1916, which decided the spoils of war, Britain gained control over Palestine, Transjordan (present-day Jordan), and Iraq, while the French were established in Syria and Lebanon. To gain the support of the Jews, the Balfour Declaration of November 1917, which was issued by the British secretary of state, promised creation of a national homeland for them.

The war was over, but its impact was momentous in changing the history of West Asia. The Turkish empire was in tatters after the loss of Palestine, Arabia, Transjordan, Iraq, and Syria. The cotton plantations and oil fields were gone. Nevertheless, a national state for the Turks was emerging under the leadership of Kemal Ataturk (1881–1938). The Jews felt disillusioned, as Palestine was to be a mandated territory rather than an independent Jewish state. As for the Arabs, they found they had achieved liberation from the Turks only to come under the yoke of the British and French. Arab nationalism took a new turn, and the Arabs set out on the path to independence.

South and Southeast Asia

The military action of the war in South and Southeast Asia was confined to Madras, India, and Penang, in what was then Malaya (now Malaysia). However, it brought about a crucial change in the political life and socioeconomic condition of the colonial people of the region.

The president of the Thai foreign ministry, Prince Dewawongse, saw the end of the war as an opportune moment to further Thai interests. The motive was to prevent Anglo-French occupation (French and British colonial possessions surrounded Thailand) and to abolish German extraterritorial rights. When the tiny Thai forces returned from France after the war, they were full of new ideas and experiences.

The same was true of the 150,000 Vietnamese who had participated in the war as laborers and soldiers. Nguyen Ali Quoc (Ho Chi Minh, 1890–1969) pleaded in vain for self-determination for Indochina (Vietnam, Cambodia, and Laos). Vietnamese nationalism took a new turn with active resistance to French rule. The British colony of Malaya felt the impact of war economically. Rice exports had been disrupted because of wartime shipping shortages, and this led to agricultural discontent in present-day Myanmar (Burma), which was being administered as part of India.

The nationalist leaders of India had initially supported the war efforts of the British government in the mistaken belief that the colonial rulers would be grateful for their loyalty. As the war went on, however, attitudes changed. The Congress Party passed a resolution of self-government on December 1916. This was a period of Hindu-Muslim unity, and the Congress Party accepted the principle of a separate electorate for the Muslims. The entry of Turkey into the war had generated anti-British feelings in the Muslim commu-

nity, which was sympathetic to the plight of fellow Muslims. Indian politics received a new zest after Annie Besant, an English theosophist who emigrated to India, set up the Home Rule League demanding home rule. Revolutionary and terrorist activities surged.

Price rises and scarcity of agricultural products brought untold misery upon the Indian people. Meanwhile, about 120,000 men from British India were fighting in West Asia and Eastern Africa, which caused hardship for their families at home. Britain also had to depend on Indian industries to help meet its wartime needs; the jute and textile industries, in particular, flourished during this period. Britain thus felt the necessity to grant some concession to the colony, and in August 1917 the announcement was made that there would be gradual development of self-governing institutions. War brought agitation for constitutional reforms in Sri Lanka, and the Ceylon National Congress was set up.

Postwar Rise of Asian Consciousness

The end of World War I on 11 November 1918 and the defeat of the Central powers formed a watershed in Asian history. The prestige of the Western powers suffered drastically. The mutual bickering and fratricidal struggle among European powers convinced the Asian countries that the Western nations were not at all superior. A new Asian self-consciousness developed. Arabs, Jews, Indians, Vietnamese, and others felt deceived by the double-dealing of the colonial powers. With renewed zeal, they strove hard to oust the imperial powers. The Fourteen Points of the U.S. president Woodrow Wilson, particularly the principle of self-determination, had raised high hopes. However, these ideas were applied in Eastern Europe only. Another important development was the proliferation of new industries in Asia at the expense of Europe, whose economy had been directed to war purposes. A change in economic relations between Asia and Europe occurred. An exhausted Europe was losing self-confidence, and the new ideas and experiences that Asia had gained changed the course of world history in the postwar period.

Patit Paban Mishra

Further Reading
Chavan, R. S. (1973) *Nationalism in Asia*. New Delhi: Sterling.
Lowe, Norman. (1999) *Mastering Modern World History*. Delhi: Macmillan.
Pati, Budheswar. (2000) *India and the First World War*. New Delhi: Atlantic.
Romein, Jan. (1962) *The Asian Century*. London: Allen and Unwin.

WORLD WAR II

WORLD WAR II World War II in Asia was very different from the war in Europe. The Asian experience included Japanese colonial expansion into the Asian mainland, which preceded the involvement of European and North American nations, as well as the civil war in China. For some Asian nations, the world-wide aspect of the war was secondary to their own conflicts with Japan.

The war came at a time when some nations were involved either in the war in Europe or in other demographic upheavals, such as the Soviet Union's relocation of ethnic Koreans (who had fled from Japanese-occupied Korea into eastern Siberia) to Uzbekistan. In this instance, some 190,000 Koreans were moved west. Although many ethnic Russians had also been relocated to the Central Asian republics from the 1880s on as a means to counter growing Islamic influence there, such relocations were not part of Soviet wartime relocation policy.

Japanese Expansionism

The "War in the Pacific," as the conflict is known in many Asian countries, took place from 1939 to 1945. However, the military actions and colonial efforts that set the stage for this period began with the termination of World War I. At the end of that war, Japan had acquired territories in China and the Pacific formerly held by Germany. (Japan's expansionist policy had begun even before World War I, with the acquisition of Taiwan following Japan's victory in the Sino-Japanese War of 1894–1895 and the annexation of Korea in 1910.) Japan's aim was one of strategic security, a "Greater East Asia Coprosperity Sphere" stretching some 1,600 kilometers from the Japanese islands, which would remove the Western powers from Asia. Western imperialism had undermined China, and by the mid-1930s, Japan had begun to remove Western influence there by dividing China through the establishment of a puppet government in Manchuria. However, open armed conflict in China escalated in 1937.

In July of that year, Japanese forces attacked Peiping (modern Beijing); they attacked Shanghai in August. At that time, Japan was fighting the forces of the Nationalist government of China; the Nationalists leaned more toward the West in matters of trade and foreign policy than did the Chinese Communists, the Nationalists' adversaries. Unable to stop the Japanese, the Nationalists retreated westward to the city of Nanking (modern Nanjing), where in December Japanese forces captured the city and massacred some 300,000 civilian residents. The "Rape of Nanking,"

more than any event, brought about international condemnation of Japan's expansion into Asia and shaped the policies of Japan's opponents.

In Southern Asia, the war came to India as a consequence of British rule there. When Great Britain declared war on Germany, the Indian viceroy did the same, but the Indian Congress did not support him. While war raged in East Asia and Europe, India was at first little more than a source of men for the African front and for the British in Singapore as well as a supply base for operations in the Middle East.

India's situation changed with the Japanese attacks in the Pacific and on the Asian mainland. Indian soldiers who had been sent to reinforce British territories in East Asia were killed or captured by the Japanese once fighting began, leading India to return to British allegiance, at least in the short term.

U.S. Entry

At this time, the United States was still formally neutral and was selling Japan steel and oil, materials Japan needed for its military expansion. America had accepted Japan's annexation of the Korean peninsula, and in the United States, ethnic Koreans were considered to be Japanese. The American focus was on the growing conflict in Europe, not Asia. While the United States provided some assistance to the Nationalist Chinese, the Soviet Union actually provided China more operational support with Soviet aircraft and pilots until 1939, when those assets were recalled to fight Germany. The major U.S. support to China after that was the effort to construct the Burma Road from Lashio, Burma (present-day Myanmar), to Kunming, China, begun in 1938 to provide a western route into China for military supplies. U.S. policy at the time was to avoid conflict in the Pacific, because conflict there would divert assets from the Atlantic. Only in 1940, in response to further Japanese expansion in China, did the United States institute an economic embargo of oil and steel against Japan. This was expanded in mid-1941 to a complete end to all trade with Japan; Japan then had to seize the sources of materials necessary for its strategic survival.

In Southeast Asia, Japan had continued its program of replacing Western influence with its own. The French colonial government in Indochina (Vietnam, Laos, and Cambodia) capitulated to Japan in 1940, after France fell to Germany. Thailand accepted Japan's presence in the region as a means of reacquiring territory lost to Cambodia, Laos, and Malaya. The outbreak of armed conflict with Western forces in December 1941 led to the occupation of Malaya

CREATING THE AXIS POWERS

The Mutual Assistance Pact signed by Japan, Germany, and Italy in Berlin on 27 September 1940 created the so-called Axis Powers and ceded control of Asia to Japan.

> The Governments of Japan, Germany, and Italy, considering it as the condition precedent of any lasting peace that all nations of the world be given each its own proper place, have decided to stand by and co-operate with one another in regard to their efforts in Greater East Asia and the regions of Europe respectively wherein it is their prime purpose to establish and maintain a new order of things calculated to promote mutual prosperity and welfare of the people concerned.
>
> Furthermore, it is the desire of the three Governments to extend co-operation to such nations in other spheres of the world as may be inclined to put forth endeavors along lines similar to their own, in order that their ultimate aspirations for world peace may thus be realized. Accordingly, the Governments of Japan, Germany and Italy have agreed as follows:
>
> Article I. Japan recognizes and respects the leadership of Germany and Italy in the establishment of a new order in Europe.
>
> Article II. Germany and Italy recognize and respect the leadership of Japan in the establishment of a new order in Greater East Asia.
>
> Article III. Japan, Germany and Italy agree to co-operate in their efforts on the aforesaid lines. They further undertake to assist one another with all political, economic and military means when one of the three Contracting Parties is attacked by a power at present not involved in the European War or in the Sino-Japanese Conflict.
>
> Article IV. With a view to implementing the present Pact, joint Technical Commissions the members of which are to be appointed by the respective Governments of Japan, Germany and Italy will meet without delay.
>
> Article V. Japan, Germany and Italy affirm that the aforesaid terms do not in any way affect the political status which exists at present as between each of the three Contracting Parties and Soviet Russia.
>
> Article VI. The present Pact shall come into effect immediately upon signature and shall remain in force for ten years from the date of its coming into force.
>
> At proper time before the expiration of the said term the High Contracting Parties shall, at the request of any one of them, enter into negotiations for its renewal.
>
> *Source: Far East Year Book.* (1941) Tokyo: Far East Yearbook, 93–94.

(modern Malaysia), Burma, and the Dutch East Indies (present-day Indonesia) and began the conquest of the Philippines.

While the Japanese attack on Pearl Harbor on 7 December 1941 is viewed by most Americans as the beginning of World War II in Asia, this event came thirty-one years after the annexation of Korea, ten years after the establishment of Japanese rule in northern China, four years after the massacre at Nanking (Nanjing), and a year after much of Southeast Asia had come under Japanese domination. To Japan, however, the initiation of armed conflict against the United States was in response to an undeclared war that the United States had initiated with its embargo of critical materials.

Early Japanese Successes

Japan's attack on Western holdings in Asia and the Pacific resulted in tremendous early successes. American military power in Hawaii was blunted, Hong Kong fell, Burma and the Philippines were taken, and at the far reaches of Japanese power, islands in Alaska's Aleutian chain, the Solomon Islands, and the Gilbert Islands were captured. The Solomon and the Gilbert Islands consolidated Japan's holdings acquired by League of Nations mandate after World War I. By mid-1942, the Western powers were close to defeat in Asia and the Pacific. However, the same technological forces that had permitted Japan's rapid military expansion began to work in favor of the Allied forces, due in part to what must be considered a stroke of luck that took place before the attack on Pearl Harbor.

Change in U.S. Naval Strategy

Before December 1941, U.S. naval strategy had been based on the use of battleships in naval combat, but after Pearl Harbor, the aircraft carrier became the linchpin of U.S. naval strategy. The aircraft carrier was an untested experiment until it was used with tremendous success by the Japanese navy. At the time of the Japanese attack, the U.S. Navy's three aircraft carriers were out of port, but its battleships were at Pearl Harbor, where they were destroyed. This forced the United States to adopt a naval strategy based on the aircraft carrier for the Pacific theater of operations, because the primary focus of the war effort was still Europe and replacements for its battleships would not be available for some time. The new strategy would have to counter the advances Japan had already made in the Pacific and would rely on America's industrial capacity (once mobilized), technological advantage, and innovative tactics.

Japan's strategy, however, had been one of quick successes that would give it the advantage in establishing dominance over East Asia before the United States and the Western powers could retaliate. Japan's prime minister, General Tojo Hideki (1884–1948), had no misperceptions regarding America's capacity; even he recognized that a long conflict would work against Japan's long-term goals. As the Allied forces became able to maintain their holdings and then to advance toward the Japanese home islands, the resources available to the Allies (and denied to the Japanese), technology, and tactics swung in favor of the Allies.

Battle for China

On the Asian mainland, however, Japan was still the dominant force. In China, the Nationalists under Chiang Kai-shek (1887–1975) and the Communists under Mao Zedong (1893–1976) had been at odds since 1926, and this competition at times undermined Chinese efforts to defeat the Japanese. While Chinese forces avoided complete defeat at Shanghai in 1932, Japan was able to establish a puppet government in Manchuria (called Manchuguo). Chiang spent the next five years building up his Nationalist army, while the Communists withdrew to northwest China on the Long March (1934–1935) from Jiangxi province to Shaanxi province, covering approximately 9,600 kilometers. Mao rebuilt his forces over the next year and sought a united effort of both Communists and Nationalists against the Japanese. Chiang, however, sought to defeat the Communists first, then deal with the Japanese. In late 1936, Chiang was kidnapped by one of his own generals while on a visit to Xi'an, and as a condition of his release he had to agree to work with the Communists to fight the Japanese. Subsequently, Japanese forces dramatically increased their efforts, leading to the Nanking Massacre and to victories at Wuhan and Guangzhou (Canton) in 1938.

Even as both Chinese factions worked against the Japanese, their efforts were seen as a means for each to dominate the other. Chiang believed that the Japanese would wear down the Communists so that he would be able to deal with them after the Japanese were defeated, and Mao viewed Nationalist action against the Japanese as an opportunity for his Communist forces to rest. Both sides expanded their forces in preparation for a civil war once the Japanese were defeated.

U.S. support for China began only after years of fighting by Chinese forces, but in March 1941 the Lend-Lease Program (which had been used to support European nations fighting against Hitler since 1939) was extended to China. This and other aid were sig-

JAPAN AND THE SOVIET UNION NEUTRALITY PACT

On 13 April 1941 Japan and the Soviet Union signed the Neutrality Pact between Japan and the Union of Soviet Socialist Republics. For the Japanese the benefit of Soviet neutrality was a reduced threat to their holdings in China and Korea.

The Presidium of the Supreme Soviet of the Union of Soviet Socialist Republics and His Majesty the Emperor of Japan, guided by a desire to strengthen peaceful and friendly relations between the two countries, decided to conclude a pact of neutrality, for the purpose of which they appointed as their representatives:

For the Presidium of the Supreme Soviet of the Union of Soviet Socialist Republics, Vyacheslav Molotov, Chairman of the Council of People's Commissars and People's Commissar for Foreign Affairs.

For His Majesty the Emperor of Japan, Yosuke Matsuoka, Minister of Foreign Affairs, Ju San Min, Cavalier of the Order of the Sacred Treasure, First Class; and Yoshitsugu Tatekawa, Ambassador Extraordinary and Plenipotentiary in the Union of Soviet Socialist Republics, Lieut. Gen., Ju San Min, Cavalier of the Order of the Rising Sun, First Class, and the Order of the Golden Kite, Fourth Class.

Who, after the exchange of their credentials, which were found in due and proper form, agreed on the following:

Article I. Both Contracting Parties undertake to maintain peaceful and friendly relations between them and mutually respect the territorial integrity and inviolability of the other Contracting Party.

Article II. Should one of the Contracting Parties become the object of hostilities on the part of one or several third Powers, the other Contracting Party will observe neutrality throughout the duration of the conflict.

Article III. The present Pact comes into force from the day of its ratification by both Contracting Parties and remains valid for five years. In case neither of the Contracting Parties denounces the Pact one year before the expiration of the term, it will be considered automatically prolonged for the next five years.

Article IV. The present Pact is subject to ratification as soon as possible. Instruments of ratifications shall be exchanged in Tokyo as soon as possible.

In confirmation whereof the above-named representatives signed the present Pact in two copies, drawn up in the Russian and Japanese languages, and affixed thereto their seals.

Done in Moscow, April 13, 1941, which corresponds to the 13th day of the 4th month of the 16th year of Showa.

Signed by:

Molotov

Yosuke Matsuoka

Yoshitsugu Tatekawa

Source: Harold S. Quigley. (1942) *Far Eastern War: 1937–1941.* Boston: World Peace Foundation, 296.

---

nificantly expanded after the Japanese attack on Pearl Harbor eight months later.

Broadening of the War

The attack on the U.S. base in Hawaii dramatically changed the war for Japan. Despite its early successes in late 1941 and 1942, Japan lacked the resources necessary for a long war. An early attack on Tokyo made by American bombers launched from an aircraft carrier in April 1942 unnerved Japan. This raid, led by Lieutenant-Colonel James Doolittle, was launched primarily for psychological reasons. For the United States, it provided some good news after a succession of defeats; for Japan, it showed that not even Tokyo was safe.

The new aircraft carrier–based U.S. strategy, instead of being oriented solely against Japanese naval forces, used "island-hopping" as a means of advancing on the Japanese home islands. After the United States defeated Japanese naval forces at the battle of Midway and at Guadalcanal in 1942, Allied forces moved

THE YALTA AGREEMENT

On 4–11 February 1945 Winston Churchill of Great Britain, Franklin Roosevelt of the United States, and Josef Stalin of the Soviet Union met at Yalta in the Crimea to discuss post–World War II Europe. They also agreed secretly that the Soviet Union would attack Japan and would regain territory taken by Japan as detailed below.

The leaders of the three Great Powers—the Soviet Union, the United States of America and Great Britain—have agreed that in two or three months after Germany has surrendered and the war in Europe has terminated the Soviet Union shall enter into the war against Japan on the side of the Allies on the condition that:

1. The *status quo* in Outer Mongolia (The Mongolian People's Republic) shall be preserved;

2. The former rights of Russia violated by the treacherous attack of Japan in 1904 shall be restored, viz:

(a) the southern part of Sakhalin as well as all the islands adjacent to it shall be returned to the Soviet Union.

(b) the commercial part of Dairen shall be internationalized, the preeminent interests of the Soviet Union in this port being safeguarded and the lease of Port Arthur as a naval base of the USSR be restored.

(c) the Chinese Eastern Railroad and the South Manchurian Railroad which provides an outlet to Dairen shall be jointly operated by the establishment of a joint Soviet-Chinese Company, it being understood that the preeminent interests of the Soviet Union shall be safeguarded and that China shall retain full sovereignty in Mongolia;

3. The Kuril Islands shall be handed over to the Soviet Union.

It is understood that the agreement concerning Outer Mongolia and the ports and railroads referred to above will require concurrence of Generalissimo Chiang Kai-shek. The President will take measures in order to obtain this concurrence on advice from Marshal Stalin.

The heads of the three Great Powers have agreed that these claims of the Soviet Union shall be unquestionably fulfilled after Japan has been defeated.

For its part the Soviet Union expresses its readiness to conclude with the National Government of China a pact of friendship and alliance between the USSR and China in order to render assistance to China with its armed forces for the purpose of liberating China from the Japanese yoke.

Source: Occupation of Japan: Policy and Progress. (1946) Washington, D.C.: U.S. Department of State.

through the Gilbert Islands and New Guinea in 1943, then on to the Marianas Islands and the Philippines in 1944. By attacking Japanese strong points that might threaten Allied operations and seizing those islands necessary for operations while bypassing others, the Allied forces were able to prepare for what would have been the final assault on Japan in 1945.

Farther west, the Japanese imperial army had opened a front to invade Burma to counter American and British activities there. This expanded in mid-1944 to an effort to defeat the British and Indian forces in east India, resulting in the overextension of Japanese supply lines and the eventual destruction of the Japanese Fifteenth Army.

Also in 1944, a volunteer corps of American fliers in China, known as the "Flying Tigers," began to attack Japanese forces there. Although the Flying Tigers diverted Japanese attention away from the fight with Chinese forces, Chiang Kai-shek did not capitalize on the diversion, much to the irritation and anger of the senior American in China, Brigadier General Joseph Stillwell. The friction between Chiang and Stillwell soon caused President Franklin D. Roosevelt (1882–1945) to recall Stillwell to the United States.

By 1945, a campaign of strategic bombing of Japanese cities was being waged from island bases in the Pacific. Massed attacks by the U.S. Air Force targeted both Japanese military forces and cities and resulted in tens of thousands of civilian casualties and massive destruction (as had the Allied attacks against German cities). The firebombing of Tokyo on the evening of 9 March 1945, for example, killed up to 120,000 Japanese. The U.S. doctrine at the time was one of "total war" against the Japanese population, in preparation for a final Allied push against Japan, which was to be a massive amphibious assault against the islands of Kyushu (Operation Olympic) in December 1945 and Honshu (Operation Coronet) in March 1946. These assaults were to use forces made available by the defeat of Germany, forces that, in many cases, already were in transit to the Pacific region. As many as 5 million soldiers, primarily American, would have been involved. The Soviet Union would also take part in the invasion of Japan.

Planning for Operation Olympic had begun in 1944 as Allied forces moved toward Japan. By early 1945 it was estimated that approximately 300,000 Japanese soldiers were on the Japanese islands; by August this estimate had risen to over a half million, including a significant number of combat units. The U.S. experience in attacking islands held by the Japanese was that Japanese soldiers and civilians would fight to the death to avoid capture, resulting in very heavy casualties inflicted on U.S. forces. Estimates for the invasion were as high as 1 million Allied casualties and possibly three times that number of Japanese. The losses for Japan would include both military and civilian personnel and might well have resulted in the end of Japan as a nation.

End of the War

Discussions regarding the Allied focus on Japan were held by the leaders of the United States, the Soviet Union, and Great Britain in February 1945 at Yalta in the Crimea. This conference resulted in an agreement that the Soviet Union would enter the war against Japan once Germany was defeated, and that upon Japan's defeat, those areas in China formerly held by Russia but captured by Japan in 1904 would be turned over to the Soviet Union. President Roosevelt kept the agreement secret from even Vice President Harry Truman (1884–1972) on his return from Yalta, but Roosevelt died within two months. The decision to proceed with the plans made earlier then fell on Truman.

Truman met with the British prime minister Winston Churchill (1875–1975) and the Soviet premier Joseph Stalin (1879–1953) at Potsdam, Germany, in July 1945 to discuss further the treatment and disarmament of Japan once it had been defeated. While at Potsdam, Truman learned of the successful test of a new weapon that might shorten the war. That weapon was the atomic bomb. He informed Churchill of the weapon, but not Stalin.

The atomic bomb used against Japan eliminated the need for the invasion. On 6 August 1945 a single aircraft dropped a single ten-thousand-pound bomb on the Japanese city of Hiroshima, resulting in an explosion equal to twenty thousand tons of conventional explosives. Hiroshima had been chosen because it was an industrial target that had not been damaged by earlier attacks, which would permit estimations of the bomb's effectiveness. The bomb instantly killed some 130,000 people, injured as many, and destroyed four-fifths of the buildings in the city. Three days later, a second atomic bomb was dropped on the Japanese city of Nagasaki. By that time, the Soviet Union had declared war on Japan and invaded Manchuria.

Although the two weapons used on Hiroshima and Nagasaki instantly killed approximately 200,000 people and thousands subsequently died from injuries and radiation poisoning, these attacks had not been as damaging as the combined earlier attacks on other major cities. For President Truman, the atomic bomb was simply a weapon of war, not an element of a greater strategy. Its use worked; on 14 August, the Japanese government accepted the guidelines of the Potsdam Declaration. The Soviets refused to accept the Japanese proposal, because it did not contain an order to the Japanese military to surrender; only the official signing of the documents on 2 September 1945 was accepted by the Soviet Union.

The War in the Pacific cost over 11 million Chinese and 2.5 million Japanese lives, plus countless others in the occupied nations of the region. Casualties among the Allied forces—the United States, Great Britain, Australia, New Zealand, India, and Canada—were comparatively light; approximately 200,000 were killed in Asia, the majority of whom were American.

Thomas P. Dolan

Further Reading

Alperovitz, Gar. (1967) *Atomic Diplomacy: Hiroshima and Potsdam.* New York: Vintage.

Buss, Claude A. (1964) *Asia in the Modern World.* New York: Macmillan.

Chang, Iris. (1997) *The Rape of Nanking.* New York: Basic Books.

Dallek, Robert. (1979) *Franklin D. Roosevelt and American Foreign Policy, 1932–1943.* Oxford: Oxford University Press.

Gallagher, Matthew P. (1963) *The Soviet History of World War II.* New York: Praeger.

Harries, Meirion, and Susie Harries. (1991) *Soldiers of the Sun: The Rise and Fall of the Imperial Japanese Army.* New York: Random House.

Hsu, Immanuel C. Y. (1990) *The Rise of Modern China.* 4th ed. New York: Oxford University Press.

Kim, Young Hum. (1966) *East Asia's Turbulent Century.* New York: Appleton-Century-Crofts.

Lattimore, Owen. (1949) *The Situation in Asia.* Boston: Little, Brown.

Lederer, Ivo J., ed. (1962) *Russian Foreign Policy: Essays in Historical Perspective.* New Haven, CT: Yale University Press.

McNelly, Theodore, ed. (1967) *Sources in East Asian History and Politics.* New York: Appleton-Century-Crofts.

Paterson, Thomas G., J. Garry Clifford, and Kenneth J. Hagan. (2000) *American Foreign Relations.* 2 vols. Boston: Houghton Mifflin.

Ulam, Adam. (1974) *Expansion and Coexistence: Soviet Foreign Policy, 1917–73.* 2d ed. New York: Holt, Rinehart, and Winston.

Van Alstyne, Richard W. (1973) *The United States and East Asia.* New York: Norton.

WRAPPING CLOTHS. See **Pojagi.**

WU An estimated 85 million people, living predominantly in the provincial-level municipality of Shanghai as well as in the Zhejiang and Jiangsu Provinces in China, speak the various dialects of Wu. The Wu speakers in Jiangsu Province live primarily south of the Chang (Yangtze) River. A few enclaves of Wu speakers are located at the north of the mouth of this river.

The Wu region is different in a variety of ways from the other regions in which the major Sinitic sublanguages hold sway. In the Wu region, there are several culture centers, whereas in the other sublanguage groups, there is one major "local" capital. This is a population center that sets the cultural as well as linguistic pattern for the rest of the group. For example, the Yue have Guangzhou, while the Minnan of Fujian Province have Xiamen. The scattered Hakka also look to Meixian as their geographic, cultural, and linguistic center.

In comparison, the Wu people are far more diverse. Shanghai, the sublanguage's largest population center, does not really play the role of the center for the Wu people, because it is a new city, relatively speaking, and is subject to Western influences. Furthermore, the population in Shanghai has come from various Wu-speaking districts as well as from Nanjing and beyond. Centers such as Suzhou, Hangzhou, and Shaoxing have all played major roles in the history of the Wu, but none can truly be said to be its center.

The Wu people are also different from other Chinese in that they would not usually describe their subethnic identities in terms of their province of origin. This is because only the southern third of Jiangsu Province is Wu speaking. There is great diversity in Zhejiang Province itself and the people are not all Wu speakers. So the Wu people of Zhejiang have tended to identify themselves by their native prefectures, which are subprovincial political units. Unlike the Yue, Hakka, and Min people to the south, the Wu people did not join the modern migration of Chinese abroad on any major scale, and Wu speakers have only a minor representation in the overseas Chinese population.

The Wu language had its origin in Suzhou—one of the cultural centers of the imperial period. The sociolinguistic evolution of the Wu region, however, is not well established. From the center of its origins, the language spread to regions south of the lower Chang River. It is a language that has gained importance because of the rise of Shanghai as a metropolitan center and one of the treaty ports that was ceded to the Western powers—Britain, France, and Germany.

Origins of Wu

The Chinese character for *wu* was possibly first applied to people living around the mouth of the Chang River who spoke a non-Sinitic language that was largely incomprehensible to those speaking the various Sinitic sublanguages. The other meaning given to the word *wu*, and rarely so, is "clamorous" or "yelling." This might be a reference to the rather loud and emphatic nature of the Wu people's way of speaking. To many early Han Chinese, the language might have also sounded strident. The mention of the kingdom of Wu first appeared in Chinese annals around the seventh century BCE. Historical linguists have been uncertain how to classify the ancient Wu dialect, which could not yet be considered a Sinitic sublanguage at that time. There is a widespread assumption that the language is related to the Tai languages. But the probability is that it is more of a Sino-Tibetan language. The kingdom of Wu started to adopt aspects of the evolving Chinese culture during the Zhou dynasty (1045–256 BCE). Subsequent warfare led to the complete incorporation of the kingdom into the Sinitic political world.

Sinitic Wu culture is thought to have reached its highest point during the Southern Song period (1126–1279). This would have been the period when the Wu region was at the geographical core of what has been considered to be the most highly cultured state in China, if not in the world. The Wu-speaking people left a major legacy for human civilization. The Southern Song, with its capital at present-day Hangzhou, played an important role in transmitting Buddhism and other cultural and artistic values to neighboring countries such as Japan.

Distinguishing Features of the Wu Sublanguage

Many of the archaic features to be found in the Wu sublanguage help distinguish it sharply from modern Mandarin. Principal among these is the continuing use in the sublanguage of the series of voiced initial consonants that have been lost in other Sinitic sublanguages. Most forms of Wu will have *b, d, dzh, g, p,* and *z* as initials. Another feature is a special voiced *h* (a bit like the guttural German *r*), which is contrasted in Wu with the normal, or unvoiced, *h*, according to Leo Moser.

There are fewer diphthongs in Wu than in most other Sinitic sublanguages, and the phonetics are deemed to be somewhat closer to the Old Xiang, or *Laoxianghua,* of Hunan. Wu is different from other sublanguages like the Yue, Minnan, Gan, and Hakka, particularly in the simplified endings of its syllables. While Mandarin has also simplified its endings, it has done this differently from those of Wu, with varying results. Hence, the ancient final syllables such as, *p, t,* and *k* appear in neither Mandarin nor Wu.

Final consonants of Wu dialects typically include only one or two nasal endings with perhaps the glottal stop. It is a pattern that more closely resembles the dialects of Minbei and some forms of Eastern Mandarin. The Wu vernaculars are characterized by complex patterns of tone sandhi in which the tone of one syllable is modified in speaking by that of the syllable that falls next to it. ("Sandhi" is a linguistic term meaning the modification of the sound of a morpheme in certain phonetic situations or contexts.) While tone sandhi in the Min-speaking areas has been deemed to be complex, it is even more so among the Wu dialects.

Wu also differs from other Sinitic sublanguages in grammatical and structural ways. In particular, the Wu dialects differ from Mandarin by putting the direct object before the indirect object when both appear in a sentence. That characteristic makes Wu similar to Cantonese, but different from the intervening Min vernacular tongues, which tend to have an ordering that resembles more that of Mandarin.

The Wu dialect tends to vary by stages over the larger region mainly as a consequence of the pluralism of standards in the sublanguage. The isoglosses (geographical boundaries that delimit the area within which a linguistic feature is found) overlap in what has been found to be a complex pattern. In spite of such variations within the region of Wu-speaking peoples, however, there is generally intercomprehensibility among the so-called Shanghai dialects, of which Suzhou Wu is one example.

One exception to the intercomprehensibility of the Wu dialects is the dialect spoken in the port city of Wenzhou, located in the south of Zhejiang. This Wenzhou dialect and some of the dialects spoken by people living inland from the port are considered extremely different from other Wu dialects. This has led some linguists to suggest that the Wenzhou dialect should be treated and recognized as a Sinitic language that is separate from the rest of Wu.

The vernacular of Shanghai represents a fusion of various forms of Northern Wu and other dialectical influences, including even Eastern Mandarin. Other Wu speakers have traditionally treated the Shanghai vernacular somewhat contemptuously as a mixture of Suzhou and Ningbo dialects. Shanghainese have been portrayed as strategic, smart thinkers, interested in new ideas, and in new words to add to their language. Yet the Shanghainese people have long resisted the Communist government's efforts to make them speak the universally accepted Mandarin dialect.

Ooi Giok Ling

Further Reading

Chao, Yuen Ren. (1967) "Contrastive Aspects of the Wu Dialects." *Language* 43: 92–101.

———. (1968) *A Grammar of Spoken Chinese.* Berkeley and Los Angeles: University of California Press.

Forrest, R. A. D. (1948) *The Chinese Language.* London: Faber and Faber.

Moser, Leo J. (1985) *The Chinese Mosaic: The Peoples and Provinces of China.* Boulder, CO: Westview.

Parker, Edward H. (1884) "The Wenchow Dialect." *The China Review* 12: 162–175, 377–389.

Whitaker, Donald P., Rinn-Suip Shinn, Helen A. Barth, Judith M. Heimann, John E. MacDonald, Kenneth W. Martindale, and John O. Weaver. (1972) *Area Handbook for the People's Republic of China.* Washington, DC: U.S. Government Printing Office.

WU CHANGSHI (1844–1927), innovative early-twentieth-century Chinese painter and calligrapher. The career of Wu Changshi represents the process of evolution from the artistic patterns of late imperial China to those of the modern era. Born into a declining scholarly family in Anji, Zhejiang, he moved to Shanghai and became a professional painter. Wu was best known for his calligraphy in the *zhuan* (seal) and *shigu* (stone drum) scripts. His calligraphy and painting were famed for their *jinshiqi,* or antiquarian epigrapher's taste.

In his youth, Wu studied briefly with Ren Yi (1840–1895), but was mostly self-taught as a painter. Although his favorite themes were usually flowers and rocks, Wu's pictures are to be seen not as images from nature but as arrangements of plants and rocks in an abstract space. Conventions of calligraphy and painting were brought together in his loosely brushed artwork. Thus, despite his commercial market, the ultimate ideal of literati painting—to combine poetry, calligraphy, and painting—was realized in his work.

Kuiyi Shen

Further Reading

Andrews, Julia, and Kuiyi Shen. (1998) *A Century in Crisis: Modernity and Tradition in the Art of Twentieth Century China.* New York: Guggenheim Museum and Abrams.

Cahill, James. (1988) "The Shanghai School in Later Chinese Painting." In *Twentieth-Century Chinese Painting,* edited by Mayching Kao. New York: Oxford University Press, 54–77.

WU ZETIAN (625–705), Chinese emperor. Wu Zetian was the only woman to rule in China as an emperor in name. She entered the Chinese imperial court at the age of thirteen as a lowly ranked concubine to Emperor Taizong (reigned 626–649) of the Tang dynasty (618–907 CE), but when he died she became concubine and later empress to her stepson, Emperor Gaozong (reigned 650–683). When Gaozong died, she declared herself emperor after deposing her sons and attempting to found her own dynasty. She turned to the Buddhist establishment and invented about a dozen characters with a new script to legitimize her position as emperor.

Her overall rule did not result in a radical break from Tang domestic prosperity and foreign prestige. But she changed the composition of the ruling class by removing the entrenched aristocrats from the court and gradually expanding the civil service examination to recruit men of merit to serve in the government. Although she gave political clout to some women such as her capable secretary, she did not go as far as to challenge the Confucian tradition of excluding women from participating in the civil service examinations. Already in 674, she had drafted twelve policy directives ranging from encouraging agriculture to formulating social rules of conduct. She maintained a stable economy and a moderate taxation for the peasantry. Her reign witnessed a healthy growth in the population; when she died in 705 her centralized bureaucracy regulated the social life and economic well-being of the 60 million people in the empire.

Overall, Wu Zetian was a decisive, capable ruler in the roles of empress, empress dowager, and emperor. She was allegedly cruel in her personal life, murdering two sons, a daughter, and other relatives who opposed her. As a woman ruler, she challenged the traditional patriarchal dominance of power, state, sovereignty, monarchy, and political ideology. Her experience reflected a reversal of the gender roles and restrictions that her society and government had constructed for her as appropriate to women. While surviving in the male-ruled and power-focused domain, she showed strengths usually attributed to men, including political ambition, long-range vision, talented organization, and hard work. Later historians have been hostile to her, describing her as a despotic usurper of the throne. According to these historians, the reign of Wu Zetian ended in corruption, drinking, and the elderly ruler delighting in sexual relations with young men who enjoyed all imaginable favors and honors. In 705, she was forced to abdicate, her son Zhongzong was again enthroned, and the Tang was restored.

Jennifer W. Jay

Further Reading

Jay, Jennifer, W. (1990) "Vignettes of Chinese Women in Tang Xi'an (618–906): Individualism in Wu Zetian, Yang Guifei, Yu Xuanji, and Li Wa." *Chinese Culture* 31, 1: 78–89.

Wills, John E., Jr. (1994) "Empress Wu." In *Mountains of Fame: Portraits in Chinese History.* Princeton, NJ: Princeton University Press, 127–148.

WUDANG SHAN Wudang Shan (Mount Wudang) is located in northwest Hubei province, central eastern China, near the city of Shiyan. It is also known as Taihe Mountain. The highest peak, Tianzhu Feng (Heaven-Supporting Pillar), rises 1,612 meters above sea level, and the mountain includes seventy-two peaks, cliffs, ravines, caves, and water pools. One of

WUDANG SHAN—WORLD HERITAGE SITE

Designated by UNESCO as a World Heritage Site in 1994, Wudang is a complex of ancient palaces and temples in China. First begun in the Ming dynasty, the site demonstrates the highest artistic and architectural craft from the Ming, Yuan, and Qing dynasties.

the most sacred places in Taoism, the mountain is famous for its complex of palaces and temples, which date from the Yuan, Ming, and Qing dynasties. The oldest of the Taoist temples, Wulong (Five Dragon Temple), dates from the early Tang dynasty (618–907). The Ming emperor Cheng Zu, a Taoist, began the construction of thirty-three halls and monasteries in 1412. The temple complex covers more than 1.6 million square meters. Wudang is also known as the birthplace of Wudang shadow boxing, or *wudang taiyi wuxing*. This martial art, known as Tai Chi in the West, was most likely developed by the Wudang Taoist Zhang Sanfeng (1391?–1458?). The palace and temple complex on Wudang was inscribed on the World Heritage List in 1994.

Michael Pretes

Further Reading

Kuan Yu-Chien and Petra Häring Kuan. (1987) *Magnificent China: A Guide to Its Cultural Treasures.* Hong Kong: Joint Publishing.

"Wudangshan Mountain." (1989) In *Information China,* vol 1, edited by Caradog Vaughn James. Oxford: Pergamon, 113.

WULINGYUAN

Wulingyuan, known as "China's Yellowstone," is a spectacular karst landscape near Dayong City in western Hunan Province. Its designated Scenic Area covers 265 square kilometers and incorporates China's first national park, Zhangjiajie, as well as the Tianzishan and Suoxiyu nature reserves. The impressive scenery includes more than 3,000 quartzite sandstone pillars, many over 200 meters high, as well as ravines, gorges, streams, pools, waterfalls, caves, and natural bridges. The Zhoutian Dong cavern is thought to be the largest in Asia, and the Tianqia Shengkong natural bridge, the world's highest. Wulingyuan has both subtropical and temperate vegetation and contains numerous endangered plants and animals, including dove trees *(Davidia),* Chinese giant salamanders, Chinese water deer, Asiatic black bears, Asiatic wild dogs, and clouded leopards. Wulingyuan was inscribed on the World Heritage List in 1992.

Michael Pretes

Further Reading

Hunan sheng di fang zhi bian zuan wei yuan hui bian (Hunan Province Local History Editorial Committee). (1998) *Wulingyuan feng jing zhi* (Wulingyuan Scenery). Changsha, China: Hunan ren min.

Li Wenhua and Xianying Zhao. (1980) *China's Nature Reserves.* Beijing: Foreign Languages Press.

WUSHU

Wushu is the generic label for all indigenous martial arts in China. In the West, kung fu is often used as a synonym, although in China it refers to the time and effort given to an activity and can be applied to any activity, not just martial arts. Martial arts forms emerged in China several thousand years ago and have continued to appear and develop ever since. There are now hundreds of different martial arts in China. They are typically classified by region (Northern/Southern), religion (Buddhist/Daoist), or place of origin. Chinese martial arts have also influenced the development of martial arts in other Asian nations such as Japan, Korea, and Indonesia. In the twentieth century they have also become popular in the West. Martial arts using both body parts and weapons developed initially as forms of defense and offense. In the twentieth century, they have become more specialized and are used as forms of exercise and relaxation, in military training, in drama, and as a form of competitive sport.

Michael A. DeMarco

Further Reading

Donohue, John. (1994) *Warrior Dreams: The Martial Arts and the American Imagination.* Westport, CT: Bergin and Garvey.

Holcombe, Charles. (1992) "Theater of Combat: A Critical Look at the Chinese Martial Arts." *Journal of Asian Martial Arts* 1, 4: 64–79.

WUYI, MOUNT

Mount Wuyi looms at the northern end of China's Fujian Province, bordering Jiangxi Province. The magnificence of the landscape has inspired poets, painters, philosophers, and geologists for centuries. Its tree-covered granite mountains and caves of various shapes, its bustling waterfalls and tranquil mountain streams, and its abundance of plant, flower, animal, bird, and fish species caught the attention of a Chinese emperor in the eighth century CE, who ordered the area to be protected. A visitor to Mount Wuyi today can flow down the 9,500-meter-long Nine-Bend Stream on a bamboo raft, for a spiritual or therapeutic experience. Wuyi Yan Cha (Wuyi Rock Tea) has a distinctive taste of sunburned mountain rocks, which has captivated emperors and common folk alike.

Rich in cultural history, Mount Wuyi saw human activity as early as 2100 BCE. The Min Yue people built a city here 2,300 years ago. Cedar coffins of this ancient people, placed on seemingly inaccessible cliffs, still keep researchers wondering. The Neo-Confucian scholar Zhu Xi (1130–1200) lived and taught in Wuyi for about five decades. More than 100 pieces of writing by Zhu Xi during his residency at Mount Wuyi established him as a master of Neo-Confucianism, which has had a fundamental influence on China to the present day. Mount Wuyi was listed as both a natural and cultural UNESCO World Heritage Site in 1999.

Jian-Zhong Lin

XAYABURY (2000 pop. 333,000). The mountainous province of Xayabury, with an area of 16,389 square kilometers, is situated in the northwestern part of Laos. It shares borders with the Vientiane and Luang Prabang Provinces in the east and six provinces of Thailand in the west. Xayabury was under the empire of Lan Xang before it disintegrated into three kingdoms in 1713. Xayabury then became a part of the Luang Prabaang kingdom and was handed over to the French by Thailand under the Franco-Siamese settlement of 1907. France surrendered it to Thailand in January 1941, which caused resentment in Laos.

The province's capital is Sayabouri, located on the banks of river Nam Hung. Annual rainfall is 100–150 millimeters. Rice, watermelons, cabbages, and sugarcane are produced in the fertile regions of Ban Fainamtan, Ban Nakhem, and Ban Nampoui.

Buddhist monuments such as Wat Ban Thin, Wat Ban Phapoon, and Wat Natomoy are situated in the province. A paradise for nature lovers, the province is dotted with thick forests, beautiful meadows, scenic waterfalls, and magnificent peaks. An important tourist attraction is the 1,150-square-kilometer sanctuary Nam Phoun National Biodiversity Conservation Area, which is inhabited by the Asiatic black bear, elephant, guar, gibbon, Malaya sun bear, and Sumatran rhino.

Patit Paban Mishra

Further Reading
Mishra, Patit Paban. (n.d) *Laos: Land and Its People*. New Delhi: Indian Centre for Studies on Indochina.
Toye, Hugh. (1968) *Laos: Buffer State or Battleground*. London: Oxford University Press.

XI'AN (2002 est. pop. 2.7 million). Xi'an is the provincial capital of Shaanxi Province in central China. The city, which is the largest in the province, is situated in the central part of Shaanxi in the Wei River

The Lesser Wild Goose Pagoda in Xi'an. (KEREN SU/CORBIS)

valley north of the Qinling Range. The area around Xi'an has been inhabited for thousands of years; the remains of a stable village from around 5,000 BCE has been found at Banpo. The Xi'an area was also chosen as the capital of the first empire, the Qin dynasty (221–206 BCE), as well as of the Han (206 BCE–220 CE) and the Tang dynasties (618–907 CE). The city was then known as Chang'an. The site of the famous terra-cotta soldiers of the First Emperor of the Qin (Qin Shi Huangdi) is located about thirty kilometers east of the city, and many other archaeological sites dot the area.

For hundreds of years, Xi'an was the gateway to the Silk Route to Central Asia, and during the Tang dynasty it was the largest and most cosmopolitan city in the world. The Big Goose Pagoda, which was completed in 709, still stands sixty-four meters tall, and the old part of Xi'an, with a drum tower, a bell tower, and a magnificent mosque dating to the eighteenth century, is surrounded by one of the best-preserved city walls in China. The walls date to the fourteenth century and were originally fourteen kilometers long and measured twelve meters in height and eighteen meters in width. The modern city has a major textile industry and some electrical industries, and important food processing factories are located in a rich agricultural region in the river valley. Tourism is a major source of income. Xi'an also has important universities and colleges.

Bent Nielsen

Further Reading

Xiang, Yang. (1992) *Xi'an, ancienne capitale de la Chine*. Beijing: Editions en langue étrangères.

XI'AN INCIDENT

XI'AN INCIDENT   The Xi'an Incident, an important event in modern Chinese history, temporarily ended open hostility between the Communist and Nationalist movements and enabled China to present a unified opposition to Japanese aggression.

The incident emerged in 1935, in the aftermath of the Long March of 1934, when the Communists, now located in Yenan province in the northwest, urged all Chinese factions to unite to resist Japanese aggression. Chiang Kai-shek (Jiang Jieshi, 1887–1975), the Nationalist leader, wanted to continue his anti-Communist campaign and to destroy that threat before dealing with the Japanese.

The Communist call for a united front appealed to many Chinese, including General Zhang Xueliang (1901?–2001) and his army, who longed to return to

their homes in Manchuria, now occupied by the Japanese. Chiang ordered Zhang and General Yang Hucheng and their armies to attack the Yenan redoubt of Mao Zedong (1893–1976), but neither the generals nor their troops showed much cooperation.

On 3 December 1936, Chiang flew to Zhang's and Yang's headquarters in Xi'an to put pressure on them to launch a military offensive. Nine days later, Zhang arrested Chang and presented eight demands that centered on a united front against Japan and a halt to the anti-Communist campaign. The crisis worsened when Nationalist generals in Nanjing threatened to attack the two generals in Xi'an and then perhaps launch an all-out offensive against the Communists. It appeared to many that China might break down into chaos.

At this point, the Communist leader Zhou Enlai (1898–1976) offered to negotiate, for the Communists had decided that the threat of civil breakdown was worse than Chiang's continuing in power. Zhang agreed to restore Chiang to power, and Chiang nominally agreed to pursue a united front. Zhang then accompanied Chiang to Nanjing to explain the situation and perhaps to apologize for his actions, but Zhang was arrested, tried, and eventually sentenced to house arrest that lasted until 1962. Zhang later moved to the United States, where he died.

Charles Dobbs

Further Reading

Kataoka, Tetsuya. (1974) *Resistance and Revolution in China: The Communists and the Second United Front*. Berkeley and Los Angeles: University of California Press.
Wu, Tien-wei. (1976) *The Sian Incident: A Pivotal Point in Modern Chinese History*. Ann Arbor: University of Michigan Press.

XIANG

XIANG   The term "Xiang" refers to the people and the local sublanguage used in Hunan, a province in southeast-central China; Xiang is derived from the older literary name of Hunan. It is estimated that more than 25 million Chinese (most of them living in Hunan Province) speak Xiang today. Several early leaders of the Chinese Communist Party came from Hunan, and the linguistic influence of people thinking in Xiang or in Xiang-accented Mandarin appears to have affected the forms selected to simplify the characters used in the Chinese language.

The Xiang are one of the three subgroups of Han Chinese (the other two are the Gan and the Wannan) who settled south of the Mandarin-speaking people in China but not on the coast. The sublanguage spoken by the Xiang has not been considered as significant as the Mandarin forms spoken in the north, and the Xiang have not contributed in a major way to Chinese migration overseas. The Xiang, like the Gan and Wannan, have generally been considered to be Chinese who speak Mandarin, but pronounce it very badly.

Xiang is a complex language with numerous dialects. While it has similarities with Mandarin, it differs from other sublanguages of Han Chinese mainly because of the way the dialects and subdialects relate to each other. The dialects that have similarities with Mandarin are grouped together as the New Xiang or the Xinxianghua. Local histories suggest that the complexity of the Xiang sublanguage arose in part because most of the population now living in Hunan Province originated in other provinces. Migration has thus contributed greatly to the complex pattern of subgroups in Hunan Province.

Linguists find it easier to divide the sublanguage in terms of time into New Xiang and Old Xiang, rather than describing the geographical distribution of the various forms. Old Xiang, or Laoxianghua, has been described as a conservative form of the Xiang sublanguage and hence much closer to the Middle Chinese of the Tang dynasty (618–907) than is new Xiang. Some linguists have suggested that there are ties between Old Xiang and the Wu dialects of the region around Shanghai. It is not surprising that Old Xiang is spoken only in rural districts and some of the smaller cities of central Hunan Province. New Xiang, on the other hand, is spoken mainly in most of the larger cities and towns.

New Xiang

Linguists consider that New Xiang has evolved much further from the Middle Chinese norm than has Old Xiang. The development of New Xiang has generally paralleled that of southwestern Mandarin. Indeed, this form of Mandarin is supposed to have been the strongest influence on New Xiang, partly because southwestern Mandarin is spoken in Hubei Province, located directly to the north of Hunan Province. New Xiang is therefore phonetically much closer to Standard Mandarin than is Old Xiang. Yet both Old and New Xiang have been in use together and coexist in many towns. Complicating the geographical distribution of the speakers of Old and New Xiang are the divisions seen generationally: elderly speakers usually speak Old Xiang, and their younger family members speak New Xiang.

New Xiang that is spoken in Changsha, the capital of Hunan Province, has generally lost the voicing of the initials *b-*, *d-*, *dz-*, *dzh-*, and *gh-*, like the other sur-

TABLE 1

Corresponding Terms in English, Standard Chinese, and New Xiang (Changsha)

English	Standard Chinese	New Xiang (Changsha)
Tomorrow	*Mingtian*	*min-zi*
This year	*Jinnian*	*chin-nie*
We	*Women*	*ngo-men*
This	*Zhege*	*ko-ko*
What	*Shenme*	*mo-tsi*
Cold	*Leng*	*Len*
Person	*Ren*	*Zen*

SOURCE: Moser (1985)

rounding forms of Han Chinese. These initials have been retained in the Old Xiang spoken in the smaller city of Shuangfeng. Therefore, linguists consider Old Xiang an island of linguistic conservatism. New Xiang is expected to change Old Xiang in time, bringing it more into conformity with Standard Mandarin and Mandarin-like speech forms.

The nature of spoken New Xiang can be seen in the list of words used in the provincial capital of Changsha. In new Xiang subdialects, the personal pronouns used are similar to those used in Mandarin. Hence, him or he, *t'a*, is similarly pronounced in New Xiang and Mandarin. Similarly, you, *ni*, is pronounced in the same way in New Xiang and Mandarin. According to scholar Leo Moser, the Changsha vernacular as described in the *Hanyu Fangyan Cihui* has, compared with Standard Mandarin, first of all, no retroflex series of consonants. Second, there are no words ending in *-ng*, although some people in Changsha do use retroflex consonants as well as some syllables ending in *-ng*. Third, there are words beginning with *ng-* and *z-*. Fourth, there are six tones rather than four. Fifth, there are nasalized vowels and, sixth, there is a pattern of consonant liaison that may modify medial sounds in two-syllable phrases. Finally, there are different grammatical particles somewhat differently employed. Words in the Changsha subdialect can also start with an *h-* and an *f-* . These characteristics make the Changsha dialect different from most forms of Xiang. (See Table 1.)

In northern Hunan Province, the Yiyang subdialect is another form of New Xiang. It shares many characteristics with the Changsha subdialect but has five tones and words ending in *ng-*. The subdialect has also developed a pattern of inserting *l*-like sounds in many words.

Linguists have observed that the Xiang sublanguage differs from most other Sinitic sublanguages. Hunanese do not appear to take pride in their local dialect, since

TABLE 2

Corresponding Pronouns in English, Standard Chinese, Old and New Xiang

English (and Standard Chinese)	Old Xiang (Shuangfeng)	New Xiang (Changsha)
I, me *(wo)*	*Ang*	*Ngo*
we, us *(wo-men)*	*ang-nga*	*ngo-men*
he, him *(ta)*	*To*	*Ta*
is not *(bushi)*	*pu dzih*	*pu-sih*
boy *(nanhaizi)*	*ngo-chi*	*nga-tsih*
skin *(pi)*	*Bi*	*Pi*
time *(shihou)*	*dzih-ghie*	*sih-heu*

SOURCE: Moser (1985)

there does not seem to be uniform pronunciation of, say, Changsha, even within the city itself.

Old Xiang

Linguists consider Shuangfeng dialect a good example of Laoxianghua, or Old Xiang. The vernacular of Shuangfeng lacks the *f-* and the initial *j-*, although there are the initial consonants *n-*, *ng-*, and the voiced *h* or *gh-*. According to Wade-Giles Standard Chinese, the word *"liang"* ("two," or "a couple") is *niang* in Shuangfeng, while *jou* (meat) becomes *ñiu*. The tendency to conserve old forms with voiced consonants and other ancient language habits has led to the comparison of Old Xiang and the Wu dialects.

Pronouns in Shuangfeng differ widely from Standard Chinese in both sound and formation. Several pronouns do not share the pluralizing element, *men*, of Standard Chinese. (See Table 2.)

In the far south of Hunan Province, a zone of eleven counties, the Southern Xiang, or Xiangnan, dialect is spoken. Some have assumed that this dialect was influenced by Cantonese, the sublanguage spoken south of the border, but in fact the pronunciation shows a heavy influence of southwestern Mandarin.

Ooi Giok Ling

Further Reading

Chao, Yuen Ren. (1968) *A Grammar of Spoken Chinese.* Berkeley and Los Angeles: University of California Press.

Ho, Ping-Ti. (1959) *Studies on the Population of China, 1368–1953.* Cambridge, MA: Harvard University Press.

Moser, Leo J. (1985) *The Chinese Mosaic: The Peoples and Provinces of China.* Boulder, CO, and London: Westview Press.

Whitaker, Donald P., Rinn-Suip Shinn, Helen A. Barth, Judith M. Heimann, John E. MacDonald, Kenneth W. Martindale, and John O. Weaver. (1972) *Area Handbook for the People's Republic of China.* Washington, DC: U.S. Government Printing Office.

XINJIANG (2002 pop. 19.0 million). Located in northwestern China, the Uighur Autonomous Region of Xinjiang is bordered by Mongolia to the northeast; the Chinese provinces of Qinghai and Gansu to the east; the Tibetan Autonomous Region to the southeast; India and Afghanistan to the south and southwest; Kazakstan, Kyrgyzstan, and Tajikistan to the west; and Russia to the north. Xinjiang is the largest political unit in the People's Republic of China, covering an area of 1.6 million square kilometers (617,800 square miles). Despite its size, it is one of the least populated regions of China: in 1997 it had a total registered population of only 17.18 million. Xinjiang's climate and geography help explain its low population density. Much of the southern half of the region is covered by the great Taklamakan Desert, while the center is dominated by the uninhabitable Tian Shan mountain range.

Xinjiang has long served as China's gateway to Central Asia. As far back as the Han (206 BCE–220 CE) and Tang (618–907) dynasties, the oasis towns that are scattered throughout this region formed the backbone of the great Silk Road, a highway over which merchants brought luxury goods from the Chinese empire to the kingdoms of Central Asia and the Arab empires of the Middle East. Despite its strategic location, Xinjiang retained a great deal of independence for much of its history. The region's current name, which in Chinese translates as "New Frontier," can be traced to the conquest of the area by the Manchu armies of the Qing dynasty in the mid-eighteenth century. But even after 250 years of Chinese control, Xinjiang retains a lot of its traditional culture. The largest ethnic group in the region continues to be the Muslim Uighurs, while several other minority nationalities, including Kazakhs, Uzbeks, and Tajiks are also present in sizable numbers. In 1997, the "minority" population of Xinjiang was recorded to be 10.58 million, or 61.6 percent of the region's total population. This figure is all the more remarkable because, since 1949 when the Chinese Communist Party arrived to take over the governing of Xinjiang, the central authorities have followed a policy of settling large numbers of Han (ethnic Chinese) in the territory in an effort to solidify their rule.

Since the mid-1980s, this official policy, combined with arrival of hundreds of thousands of Chinese economic migrants from the eastern provinces and the rise of Islamic fundamentalism in Central Asia, has resulted in the development of a separatist movement among Xinjiang's Muslim. During the 1990s movement extremists launched a terrorist campaign against the local authorities in the region's capital city of

Urumqi, and against symbols of the Chinese "occupation" throughout the territory. In an effort to prevent the separatists from obtaining external support, during the late 1990s the Chinese government negotiated a number of treaties and agreements with neighboring states to jointly develop the region's natural resources and to promote trade. The authorities in Beijing hoped to curtail support for the Uighur nationalists by promising economic prosperity to the Islamic nations of Central Asia. The region is to be a central element of China's "Developing the West" program announced by Premier Jiang Zemin in 2000.

Robert John Perrins

Further Reading

Besson, Linda, Justin Rudelson, and Stanley W. Toops. (1994) *Xinjiang in the Twentieth Century*. Washington, D.C.: Woodrow Wilson International Center for Scholars.

Bovingdon, Gardner, and Dru C. Gladney. (2000) *Inner Asia: Special Issue—Xinjiang*. Cambridge, MA: White Horse Press.

Dillon, Michael. (1995) *Xinjiang: Ethnicity, Separation, and Control in Chinese Central Asia*. Durham, U.K.: University of Durham, Department of East Asian Studies.

McMillen, Donald H. (1979) *Chinese Communist Power and Policy in Xinjiang, 1949–1977*. Boulder, CO: Westview Press.

State Statistical Bureau. (1998) *China Statistical Yearbook*. Beijing: China Statistical Publishing House.

Weng, Weiquan. (1986) *Xinjiang, the Silk Road: Islam's Overland Route to China*. New York: Oxford University Press.

XIQU Shamanic and court rituals, song and dance folk forms, and entertainments such as story-telling and the presentation of simple skits have existed in China for many centuries. Various aspects of each of these activities evolved over time into the classical theater forms known as *xiqu* (Chinese opera).

The folk culture of presenting song and dance, telling stories, and enacting skits began in unknown ages in China. Certainly shamanic exorcisms and spirit-courting dances were practiced in the Shang dynasty (1766–1045 BCE), if not earlier. Chinese ministries to oversee song and dance performances in the courts of the Eastern Zhou dynasty (770–221 BCE) rigidly enforced the development of presentational traditions according to philosophical beliefs that performances combining music, dance, props, and costumes had a powerful influence over human behavior.

The royal courts continued to sponsor entertainments and ritual performances during the Qin (221–206 BCE) and Han (206 BCE–220 CE) dynasties, setting up a *yuefu* (performance bureau) to recruit and supervise musicians and dancers for state functions. During the following centuries, music, dance, and variety-show acts from throughout China and allied regions were documented and incorporated into courtly events.

By the Tang dynasty (618–907 CE), the Li Yuan (Pear Garden Academy) was established to train musicians and dancers, and *jiaofang* (instructional institutes) were organized at central and regional courts to supervise presentations of theatrical skits and other song-dance activities, as well as to stage shamanic exorcisms. By this time, many elements that would eventually combine to produce Chinese opera were evident in song-dance forms and in ever more complex theatrical sketches involving song and dance. Also, noncourt performances flourished during this period. Early monks began to preach the Buddhist religion to musical accompaniment, and thereafter the genre evolved into a source of entertainment; variety acts were popular in the marketplace and also featured in the private banquets of the wealthy.

Growth of Traditional Forms

During the Song dynasty (960–1279), urban performances of theatrical entertainments, most featuring music and dance and presented on mat-covered stages, attracted crowds in the metropolitan communities surrounding the courts. *Zaju* (assorted drama), composed primarily of plays narrated through song and accompanied by dance, comic bits, acrobatics, and a musical finale, was popular in the Northern Song (960–1126) capital.

Zaju evolved further after the Jurchen Tartars usurped control in 1126; it flowered fully under the Mongol Yuan emperors (1279–1368), when it became the preferred entertainment of the court and a popular pastime of Han (that is, ethnic Chinese) literati, who wrote increasingly complex dramas. *Nanxi* (southern theater) emerged during the Southern Song dynasty (1127–1279) out of the folk songs and ballads of Zhejiang Province and declined during the Yuan dynasty. Soon after, another southern form, *chuanqi* (marvel tales), moved into the limelight. By the end of the Ming dynasty (1368–1644), a form called *kunqu* (Kun opera) was attaining prominence in the south. Although *zaju* continued to develop during the Ming dynasty, it was overshadowed by southern theater forms in the final century of this dynasty, subsequently dwindled, and finally disappeared around the start of the Qing dynasty (1644–1912). *Kunqu*, however, persisted and had a significant impact on subsequent theatrical development.

Chinese Opera *(Xiqu)*

Kunqu is one of the oldest extant styles of *xiqu*. Arising when *zaju* was melded with traditional songs and music of Jiangsu and Zhejiang provinces, it characteristically displayed elegant movement sequences; involved plots featuring poetic dialogue and lyrics; and had a marked vocal style. Considered an art form of the elite, *kunqu* continued to be recognized as China's most popular operatic genre until Beijing opera usurped its place in the late eighteenth century.

During the Ming and Qing eras, many forms of regional *xiqu* (modeled after the Kun opera since the sixteenth century) evolved to share Yuan and Ming plays and other classical novels as repertoire. Performance features common to *xiqu* include the dividing of actor technique into the four areas of song, speech, dance-acting, and stage combat. Although drawing generally on three important musical systems, the various ways of using these systems and combining them with local tune styles serve as the primary means of differentiating the many regional forms. Common to all is the bringing together of song, musical accompaniment, dance, acting, use of costumes and props, and storytelling. Another common feature is the conventionalized use of costuming, properties, scenic items, and performer movement to impart dramatic information to spectators.

The dramas and actor role-types are usually aesthetically classified as either *wen* (civil) or *wu* (military) genres. These two basic genres were initially used to distinguish dance performance style in the Zhou dynasty (1045–256 BCE), at first indicating the duality of ruling through diplomacy and martial means, but by the Yuan dynasty they were being used to identify both performing skills (*wen* actors specialize in song, speech, and dance-acting, whereas *wu* actors specialize in stage combat and to a lesser degree in speech and dance-acting) and dramatic style (*wen* plays are usually about romantic intrigues, whereas *wu* plays are usually about historic or legendary military heroes). Dramatic characters in *xiqu* are divided into role-types (called either *hangdang* or *jiaose*) and based on *wen* and *wu* classification; the four primary *hangdang* common to many *xiqu* forms are *sheng* (male), *dan* (woman), *jing* (warrior or deity), and *chou* (clown). Furthermore, *hangdang* are subdivided into multiple categories, each of which has even more precise requirements of performance skill; for example, the *dan* role-type, among its many subdivisions in any given regional form, might include the subcategories of *wudan* (a woman warrior specializing in combat skills) and *qingyi* (literally, "blue-green clothing," a virtuous young heroine who specializes in singing and dance-acting). The methodology of dividing training and performance according to *hangdang* allows for the highly specialized display of song, speech, dance-acting, and acrobatics present in *xiqu*.

Today there are close to four hundred types of Chinese opera. After the establishment of the People's Republic of China in 1949, the government attempted to eradicate "feudal" aspects from *xiqu* dramas, resulting in the creation of newly arranged historical operas depicting the proletarian struggles. During the Cultural Revolution (1966–1976), historical dramas were banned in favor of a handful of operatic plays collectively known as *yangbanxi* (model-dramas), which blended modern dress and revolutionary content with classical song and movement techniques. However, *xiqu* was reinstituted in the late 1970s, and recently many of the traditional dramas have been restored, with new plays even being created around ancient Chinese legends.

Contemporary Forms

As in neighboring Asian nations, *huaju* (spoken, realistic drama) was introduced in China during the early years of the twentieth century; in China, *huaju* arrived via Chinese scholars who brought the form from Japan. By the 1920s, realistic drama had established a stronghold in urban areas, and by the 1930s the works of modern Chinese dramatists such as Cao Yu and Lao She were being staged in front of audiences who also frequented foreign plays in translation.

New forms of dance also developed during the last half of the twentieth century. The most important indigenous form has been *wuju* (dance-drama), combining Chinese folk dance, Chinese opera dance-acting, and modern ballet in classical as well as modern revolutionary story lines. Western-style ballet companies have been established in the larger cities since the 1980s, and modern dance companies were organized in the 1990s.

Dallas L. McCurley

Further Reading

Bodde, Derk. (1975) *Festivals in Classical China: New Year and Other Annual Observances during the Han Dynasty, 206 B.C.–A.D. 220*. Princeton, NJ: Princeton University Press.

Crump, James I. (1990) *Chinese Theater in the Days of Kublai Khan*. Ann Arbor: Center for Chinese Studies, University of Michigan Press.

Mackerras, Colin, ed. (1983) *Chinese Theater: From Its Origins to the Present Day*. Honolulu: University of Hawaii Press.

Tung, Constantine, and Colin Mackerras, eds. (1987) *Drama in the People's Republic of China*. Albany: State University of New York Press.

Wang Kefen. (1985) *The History of Chinese Dance*. Beijing: Foreign Language Press.

XU BEIHONG

XU BEIHONG (1895–1953), founding father of modern Chinese painting. Born in Yixing, Jiangsu Province, China, in 1895, Xu Beihong began drawing at an early age and by 1915 was discovered selling cheap fan paintings in Shanghai and sent by a sponsor to Japan to study art. From 1919 to 1927 Xu again studied abroad, this time in Paris and Berlin, immersing himself in European Classical and Renaissance art while disdaining the post-Impressionists. He would later argue against the influence of these art forms in China.

Xu himself excelled at figure drawing and painting, and he attempted with mixed results to meld Chinese and Western styles of art. In particular, Xu adopted the French academic mode to portray well-known Chinese historical scenes, such as in *Tian Heng and His 500 Retainers* (1928). His signature work, however, became realistic paintings of galloping horses done in Chinese brush and ink.

A lifelong educator, Xu acted as the director of the Central Art Academy in Beijing from 1946 until his death in 1953. The Xu Beihong Memorial Museum was established in Beijing in 1954 to house his extensive art collection, which his family donated to the state.

Alexa Olesen

Further Reading

Clunas, Craig. (1997) *Art in China*. New York: Oxford University Press.
Fong, Wen C. (2001) *Between Two Cultures*. New Haven, CT: Yale University Press.

XU GUANGQI

XU GUANGQI (1562–1633), Chinese official and scholar. Born in Shanghai, China, in 1562, Xu Guangqi was baptized by Jesuit missionary Matteo Ricci in 1603 and took the name Paul. He spent the next three years collaborating with Ricci in translating Western texts on mathematics, astronomy, and geography into Chinese. Their most famous translation was Euclid's *Elements*, which exerted a great influence on Chinese mathematics. Xu also wrote original works on trigonometry and agriculture, notably the *Book of Agriculture*, which advocated the adoption of Western agricultural practices, such as surveying, mapping, and irrigation. His interest in practical subjects marked a departure from the dominance of neo-Confucian thought. After he became a high official in the Ming court, Xu sponsored the Jesuit missionaries in China.

Xu believed that Western scholarship, particularly geometry, could complement Confucianism and replace Buddhism by undermining the tendency toward vague speculation. In 1629 Xu demonstrated the use of Western science for predicting solar eclipses and other astrological events. When the Manchus invaded China in 1630, he convinced the emperor to use Western armaments to defend the capital.

Daniel Oakman

Further Reading

Engelfriet, Peter. (1998) *Euclid in China: The Genesis of the First Chinese Translation of Euclid's Elements, Books I–VI (Jihe yuanben, Beijing, 1607) and Its Reception up to 1723.* Boston: E. J. Brill.
Jami, Catherine, Peter Engelfriet, and Gregory Blue. (2001) *Statecraft and Intellectual Renewal in Late Ming China: The Cross-Cultural Synthesis of Xu Guangqi, 1562–1633.* Boston: E. J. Brill.

XU ZHIMO

XU ZHIMO (1897–1931), modern Chinese poet. Born in Zhejiang Province, Xu Zhimo studied law at Beijing University in 1917 before attending Columbia University in the United States and then Cambridge University in England. During his stay in England, he began to write poems under the influence of English Romantic poetry. After he came back to China in 1922, he formed a cultural organization called the Crescent Society with writer and reformist Hu Shi, scholar Zhang Junmai, and others in 1923. Their society was the origin of the Crescent poetry school, which was one of the most important literary schools of China in the twentieth century.

Deeply influenced by English Romantic poetry, Xu developed his own unique writing style. His poems are bright, graceful, and full of musicality, reflecting his love of nature with great enthusiasm. As a Romantic poet, he pursued beauty and love and dreamed of a poetic life. Xu also made a great contribution to modern Chinese poetry by developing a new poetic form. During the early decades of the twentieth century, modern Chinese poets made a persistent effort to break away from the shackles of the traditional poetic mode. In their eagerness to experiment with new forms and to achieve free expression, the new poets often disregarded meaning and formal beauty. Xu Zhimo and his colleagues corrected this. He paid much attention to the arrangement of the lines and to meter and rhyme. He and other poets of the Crescent school pursued regularity of form and harmony of rhyme. And they found the importance of poetic meter in modern Chinese poetry. Because of their effort in developing new forms of Chinese poetry, they had a wide influence in modern Chinese literature. Xu published three collections of poetry during his lifetime: *Zhimo's Poems, One Night in Florence,* and *The Fierce Tiger.* Many of his poems have become classics, such as "Farewell to Cambridge Again" and "Farewell to a Japanese Girl." In 1931, Xu died in an airplane crash when he was flying from Nanjing to Beijing.

She Xiaojie

Further Reading
Bian Zhilin. (1984) *The Person and the Poetry.* Beijing: Sanlian.

Leo Ou-Fan Lee. (1983) "Literary Trends: The Road to Revolution, 1927–1949." In *The Cambridge History of China,* edited by Denis Twitchett and John K. Fairbank. Vol 13. New York: Cambridge University Press, 421–491.

Lin, Julia. (1972) *Modern Chinese Poetry: An Introduction.* Seattle: University of Washington Press.

Lu Yaodong. (1986) *Critical Biography of Xu Zhimo.* Xi'an, China: Shanxi People's Publishing House.

XUNZI (c. 298–c. 230 BCE), Chinese philosopher. Although often overlooked by Western scholars, Xunzi (Hsun-tzu) was an important systematizer of pre-Qin (before 221 BCE) philosophy and considered to rank third after Confucius (Kong Qiu, 551–479 BCE) and Mencius (Mengzi, c. 371–c. 289 BCE). Commonly known as Minister Xun or Xun Qing, Xunzi was born in the state of Zhao. The traditional dates for his life may be incorrect, if evidence showing that he lived well into his nineties is accurate. He may have lived from 310 to 213 BCE.

Xunzi began his career at the Jixia academy in the state of Qi when he was fifteen years old. The syncretic approach employed at the academy left a lasting impression on him, as he mastered rhetoric, argumentation, and teachings of the various masters. In his early works, Xunzi critiqued the Jixia scholars and ideas associated with Zhuangzi, Huizi, Shen Dao, Shen Buhai, and others. After Qi was attacked in 284 BCE, Xunzi fled to Chu. There he came in contact with Mohist logic (developed by Mozi, 470?–391? BCE, who used rationalism to evaluate the truth) and sharpened his own skills.

His growing notoriety gained him invitations to other states. Xunzi was the teacher of Lisi (280?–208 BCE) and Han Feizi (d. 233 BCE). Lisi went to Qin in 247, and Han Feizi may have left Xunzi shortly thereafter. Han Feizi became the systematizer of Legalism *(fajia),* which emphasized the authority of rulers and the state's power, while Lisi assisted the state of Qin in the unification of the empire, becoming a high minister and then chancellor under the first emperor.

Between 246 and 240 BCE, Xunzi was caught up in court intrigue and dismissed, then reappointed. When his sponsor was assassinated in 238 BCE, he was again dismissed. His disillusionment with the world is vividly expressed in his poetry. Although Xunzi continued to adhere to the Confucian approach, his later thought turned to the more practicable art of rulership, emphasizing methods and laws, fixed standards for punishments, and control of expenditures, ideas usually associated with Legalism. When Lisi came to power, he offered his aged teacher a minor post. In his wisdom, Xunzi foresaw coming disaster and refused.

Xunzi proposed that human nature is basically bad or socially deviant. Xunzi's position was a direct attack on the view of Mencius that people are basically good. Xunzi's overall position, however, may not be all that distant from Mencius's. Mencius claimed that human nature is basically good but that a "lost mind" leads people to do wrong. Xunzi, on the other hand, argued that people are basically bad but that a properly trained mind leads people to do good. Mencius emphasized the goodness of human nature, and Xunzi stressed the goodness of the human mind. Both Mencius and Xunzi emphasized the need for education and ritual action to develop moral goodness.

Xunzi is noted for his realistic, down-to-earth philosophy. He advocated naturalism and argued against supernaturalism, superstitions, and belief in spirits and demons. He used Mohist argumentative techniques to refute the Taoists and logicians of his day. His syncretic approach including Legalist ideas influenced Confucianism as it developed in the Han (206 BCE–220 CE) dynasty.

James D. Sellmann

Further Reading
Graham, Angus C. (1989) *Disputers of the Tao.* La Salle, IL: Open Court.

Knoblock, John, trans. (1988) *Xunzi: A Translation and Study of the Complete Works.* Stanford, CA: Stanford University Press.

Loewe, Michael, and Edward L. Shaughnessy, eds. (1999) *The Cambridge History of Ancient China from the Origins of Civilization to 221 B.C.* New York: Cambridge University Press.

Nivison, David, S. (1996) *The Ways of Confucianism: Investigations in Chinese Philosophy,* ed. by Bryan W. Van Norden. Chicago and La Salle, IL: Open Court.

YAK Yak (female, *nik*; *bos grunniens*) is a species of bovid native to the high Tibetan Plateau. Though vanishing in the wild, where it usually does not descend below 4,300 meters, it is much domesticated and so is widely used as a beast of burden in Tibet, Nepal, Kashmir, Ladakh, and Sikkim, in the Himalayan Mountain area, normally between 4,270 and 6,100 meters. It also served as a pack, draft, and saddle animal.

The wild yak is very dark brown all over, with some white around the muzzle; but the domesticated variety is often piebald or dun-colored. The adult bull stands 170 centimeters high at the withers, and weighs up to 545 kilograms. Both sexes grow horns that sweep upwards to a length of 75 centimeters. Because of the cold plateau climate, the body is covered in very long, silky hair, which hangs down almost to the ground. Even the tails are hairy, and are used as fly-whisks in the lamaseries. The yak is also adapted to desert conditions, being able to survive on sparse grass and thorn bushes, and eating snow when there is no water. Wild yaks live in small herds, and are very shy. They rely for protection on a strongly developed sense of smell rather than on their eyesight. The rutting season is in late autumn, with calving in April after a nine-month gestation.

The animal was domesticated in prehistoric times and, aside from some color change, it is chiefly distinguishable from the wild variety by shorter horns. The *nik*'s milk and butter are crucial in the Tibetan diet; domestic yaks are used for both milk and beef. The yak's hide is made into leather, and the dried dung of the yak is the only fuel on the high plateau.

There are also smaller domestic cattle called *zho* or *zomo*, which are a hybrid between female yaks and domestic cattle or zebu. Like the yak, these are generally used as pack animals and so are important economically; the male *zho* is sterile.

Paul Hockings

Further Reading
Prater, S. H. (1971) "Yak." In *The Book of Indian Animals.* 3d ed. Bombay, India: Bombay Natural History Society, 246–247.

YAKUSHIMA ISLAND (1994 est. pop. 14,000). Yakushima Island is sixty kilometers south of Osumi Peninsula in Kagoshima Prefecture in southern Kyushu. The island is 500 square kilometers in size. Yakushima is characterized by a hot and humid climate and has the heaviest precipitation in Japan, with an annual rainfall of 400 centimeters in the coastal regions and 1,000 centimeters in the mountains. This rainfall has promoted the use of waterpower to produce electricity.

Yakushima Island is a mountainous island. Miyanouradake (1,935 meters) in the central part is the highest peak in Kyushu. Forestry makes up a major portion of the economy. However, 80 percent of the forests became assets of the Japanese national government at the beginning of the Meiji period (1868–1912). The Japanese cedar (*Yakusugi*) tree grows here and many of them are over one thousand years old. The variety of plants growing in any given locale on the island changes with the altitude and ranges from species indigenous to subtropical zones to those of cold temperature zones. Agricultural products are sugarcane, sweet potatoes, and Ponkan oranges (*Citrus reticulata*). One-third of the

YAKUSHIMA ISLAND— WORLD HERITAGE SITE

A UNESCO World Heritage Site since 1993, Yakushima counts exceedingly rare lichens, ancient Japanese cedar trees, and the last Japanese remnant of warm-temperate forest among its varied vegetation.

island forms the principal part of the Kirishima-Yaku National Park, which contains twenty-three volcanic peaks. In 1993 Yakushima became the first place in Japan to be designated as a World Heritage Site, and 196,500 tourists visit annually.

Nathalie Cavasin

Further Reading
Kagoshima Prefecture. (1996) "Yakushima." Kagoshima, Japan: Kagoshima Prefecture.
Takahashi Yoshinobu. (1997) "Economy of Yakushima and Natural Environment." *Tropics* 6, 4: 467–477.

YAMAGATA (2002 est. pop. 1.2 million). Yamagata Prefecture is situated in the northeast of Japan's island of Honshu. Covering 9,326 square kilometers, its primary geographical features are the Ou, Dewa, and Asahi mountain ranges, with level areas located along the Mogami River (Mogamigawa). Yamagata is bordered by the Sea of Japan and by Akita, Miyagi, Fukushima, and Niigata prefectures. Once part of Dewa Province, it assumed its present name and borders in 1876.

The prefecture's capital is Yamagata city, which flourished during the Edo period (1600/1603–1868) as a castle town and post station known for producing *beni*, a precious crimson safflower dye used to color handspun silk fabric. Today the city is home to Yamagata University. The prefecture's other important cities are Yonezawa, Tsuruoka, Sakata, and Tendo.

Once the land of the aboriginal Ezo people, the region was ruled by the northern Fujiwara family beginning in the Heian period (794–1185) and then by a series of warlords who controlled smaller domains. Still comparatively rural, Yamagata is one of Japan's greatest rice producers and its many orchards grow cherries and other fruit. The main industries include sake brewing, food processing, textiles, woodworking, cast-iron goods, small machines, and chemicals. Visi-

tors are drawn to the prefecture's Zaozan skiing area, scenic mountain parks, and many hot spring resorts.

E. L. S. Weber

Further Reading
"Yamagata Prefecture." (1993) *Japan: An Illustrated Encyclopedia*. Tokyo: Kodansha.

YAMAGATA ARITOMO (1838–1922), Japanese soldier and politician. Yamagata Aritomo was a military man and politician from the feudal domain of Choshu (modern Yamaguchi Prefecture). He is not only considered the principal architect of Japan's modern military, but was also one of the most influential figures in Japanese politics during the Meiji (1868–1912) and Taisho (1912–1926) eras.

Yamagata was born on 14 June 1838 into a low-ranking samurai family in Hagi, the castle town of Choshu. He became one of the leaders of the radical loyalist movement to overthrow the Tokugawa shogunate and commanded the Kiheitai, a semimodern mili-

General Yamagata c. 1905. (HULTON-DEUTSCH COLLECTION/CORBIS)

tia unit, in the civil wars of 1867–1868. After the Meiji Restoration of 1868 he went abroad to study European military systems. Upon his return in 1873, he assumed leadership of the Army Ministry. He became the driving force behind the introduction of conscription and the reorganization of the army along Prussian-German lines.

In the 1880s, Yamagata started an astonishing political career. He served as home minister from 1883 to 1889, during which time he reorganized the ministry, the police, and local government systems. He also served as prime minister from 1889 to 1890 and again from 1898 to 1900.

In his later years, Yamagata retired from active politics but remained a major force behind the scene as the most influential "elder statesman" (genro), the nominal president of the influential Privy Council, and head of a strong political faction including Katsura Taro (1848–1913), Terauchi Masatake (1852–1919), Tanaka Giichi (1863–1929), and others. Yamagata died on 1 February 1922.

Sven Saaler

Further Reading

Dickinson, Frederick R. (1999) *War and National Reinvention: Japan in the Great War, 1914–1919.* Cambridge, MA: Harvard University Press.

Duus, Peter. (1968) *Party Rivalry and Political Change in Taisho Japan.* Cambridge, MA: Harvard University Press.

Hackett, Roger F. (1971) *Yamagata Aritomo in the Rise of Modern Japan.* Cambridge, MA: Harvard University Press.

Lone, Stewart. (2000) *Army, Empire, and Politics in Meiji Japan: The Three Careers of General Katsura Taro.* New York: St. Martin's.

YAMAGUCHI

(2002 est. pop. 1.5 million). Yamaguchi Prefecture is situated in the west of the Japanese island of Honshu. Occupying an area of 6,108 square kilometers, Yamaguchi is bordered by the Sea of Japan, the Inland Sea, and the Hibiki Sea and by Shimane and Hiroshima prefectures. The terrain is low but mountainous and is intersected by plateaus and by Japan's largest limestone tableland, Akiyoshidai, the site of one of the world's vastest limestone caverns. Yamaguchi's rugged coastline is frequently swept by typhoons. Once divided into Suo and Nagato provinces, then combined into the domain of Choshu, the prefecture assumed its present name and borders in 1871.

The prefecture's capital is Yamaguchi city, which was founded in the fourteenth century as a castle town by the territorial warlord Ouichi Hiroyo (d. 1380),

who was awarded lands in western Honshu as payment for service to the Ashikaga shogunate (military government of Japan from 1333 to 1573). It developed into a splendid provincial capital made wealthy by trade with China. During the Onin War (1467–1477), many Kyoto imperial court aristocrats took refuge there. In 1550, the Jesuit missionary Francis Xavier preached Christian doctrine in the streets of Yamaguchi. Soon after, the Ouchi overlords were overthrown, and the capital was moved to Hagi, but in 1863, Yamaguchi again became the capital. The prefecture's other important cities are Shimonoseki, Ube, Tokuyama, Iwakuni, and Hofu.

The prefecture is the site of numerous Yayoi-period (300 BCE–300 CE) burials and artifacts. In ancient times, it was among the first regions to develop, influenced by close trade ties to the Korean peninsula. The powerful Mori warrior clan ruled Choshu throughout the Edo period (1600/1603–1868). Rebeling against the Tokugawa shogunate, Choshu samurai led the movement to return power to the emperor in the Meiji Restoration (1868).

Economically, Yamaguchi relies on rice and fruit production and on heavy and chemical industries in the southern industrial zone. Visitors are drawn to the area's coastal scenery and to its hot spring resorts.

E. L. S. Weber

Further Reading

"Yamaguchi Prefecture." (1993) *Japan: An Illustrated Encyclopedia.* Tokyo: Kodansha.

YAMAMOTO ISOROKU

(1884–1943), Japan's foremost World War II naval officer. Born in Niigata Prefecture, Yamamoto Isoruku graduated from the Japanese Naval Academy in time to see service in the Russo-Japanese War and was severely wounded at the Battle of Tsushima in 1905. In 1919 Yamamoto was sent to the United States for graduate study, which was followed by a year of service at the Japanese embassy in Washington, D.C. He returned to the United States in 1926 for a two-year tour of duty as naval attaché in Washington.

As international tensions mounted in the 1930s, Yamamoto criticized Japan's alliance with Nazi Germany, fearing that it would lead to hostilities with the United States. Nevertheless, he was appointed commander in chief of the Combined Fleet in 1939, and in that capacity he oversaw preparations for war. With a keen appreciation of American industrial might, Yamamoto proposed launching a surprise attack on the U.S. Pacific Fleet based at Pearl Harbor in an effort to avoid a protracted war. Although the attack in December of 1941 was successful, Yamamoto's hope for a quick peace settlement was in vain, and his bid for a decisive victory at Midway failed disastrously in June 1942. Yamamoto was killed in the Solomon Islands on 18 April 1943 when American fighter pilots shot down his plane.

John M. Jennings

Further Reading
Agawa, Hiroyuki. (1979) *The Reluctant Admiral: Yamamoto and the Imperial Navy.* Tokyo: Kodansha.

Hoyt, Edwin P. (1990) *Yamamoto: The Man Who Planned Pearl Harbor.* New York: McGraw-Hill.

Potter, John Deane. (1965) *Admiral of the Pacific: The Life of Yamamoto.* London: Heineman.

YAMANASHI (2002 est. pop. 898,000). Yamanashi Prefecture is situated in the central region of Japan's island of Honshu. Occupying an area of 4463 square kilometers, the prefecture has several mountain ranges, including Kanto, Misaka, and Akaishi, with Mount Fuji, the nation's highest peak, bordering Shizuoka Prefecture on the southeast. On Fuji's northern slopes are the Fuji Five Lakes: Yamanakako, Kawaguchiko, Saiko, Shojiko, and Motosuko, all created by lava flows. The rivers Fuefukigawa and Kamanashigawa form the central Kofu Basin. Yamanashi is surrounded by Tokyo, Kanagawa, Shizuoka, Nagano, and Saitama prefectures. Once known as Kai Province, it assumed its present name and borders in 1871.

The prefecture's capital city is Kofu, which grew as the castle town of the ruling Takeda family in the sixteenth century and flourished in the Edo period (1600/1603–1868). The prefecture's other important cities are Otsuki, Tsuru, and Fuji Yoshida; a smaller city named Yamanashi lies in the central area.

During feudal times, the province was ruled by a series of military families, including the Kai Minamoto, Takeda, and Asano. In the Edo period, the Tokugawa shogunate (military government) took over its administration.

Today the nation's premier grape-growing and wine-producing prefecture, Yamanashi also raises large crops of rice, vegetables, and other fruit, including peaches. Long the fabricator of crystal ware and textiles, it now also produces precision instruments, electrical goods, and machinery. Many visitors are drawn from nearby Tokyo, especially to Mount Fuji and the Five Lakes. Other attractions are the prefecture's three national parks, its various hot spring resorts, and the Minobusan Buddhist temple, headquarters to the Buddhist Nichiren sect.

E. L. S. Weber

Further Reading
"Yamanashi Prefecture." (1993) *Japan: An Illustrated Encyclopedia.* Tokyo: Kodansha.

YAMATO DAMASHII *Yamato damashii* refers to the essential and inexplicable nature of being Japanese that is at the core of beliefs in Japan's uniqueness. The term appears in several contexts, most of them of nationalistic origin, and had its greatest impact during the years of Japanese imperialism, especially in the decades leading up to and during World War II.

In premodern Japan, *wakon* (Japanese native spiritual essence) was ideally complemented by *kansai* (Chinese learning). This evolved, during the period of Japanese nationalism starting in the late eighteenth century, into an idealization of the "Japanese spirit." Japanese intellectuals have historically extolled the special nature and characteristics of Japan's inner spirit. While rarely clearly defined, the idea is prevalent in the theories of premodern intellectuals (for example, Kitabatake Chikafusa and Motoori Norinaga), as well as in the writings of twentieth-century scholars such as Suzuki Daisetz and Umesao Tadao.

Since Word War II, *Yamato damashii* has often been viewed as related to the principle of *seishin* (self-cultivation), implying that it is a spiritual, internal, and subjective experience. Before and during the war, it was more closely associated with *bushido* (way of the warrior), a martial philosophy first formally expressed in the Edo period (1600/1603–1868), but elaborated upon and publicized outside Japan by Meiji-period (1868–1912) writers and ideologists. During World War II, Japanese ideologists emphasized that, notwithstanding Japan's material inferiority to the West, and particularly the United States, it could triumph by virtue of its superior *Yamato damashii*.

The nature of *Yamato damashii* is difficult to define precisely, since its expression is nonverbal and opaque to non-Japanese people, and the characterizations vary from writer to writer. The key to understanding *Yamato damashii* lies in the linguistic understanding of *Yamato kotoba*, that is, Japanese words as distinct from *gairaigo* (loanwords from Chinese and other languages) that have become part of spoken and written Japanese language. Most Japanese exponents of *Yam-*

ato damashii believe that this key is inherently inaccessible to people who are not Japanese.

Michael Ashkenazi

Further Reading
Dale, Peter N. (1986) *The Myth of Japanese Uniqueness.* London: Routledge.

YANGBAN

Yangban were the elite of Choson Korea (1392–1910), with characteristics of a hereditary aristocracy. The term originated in the Koryo dynasty (918–1392) and indicated the two ranks of officials, civil (*tongban*) and military (*soban*). Later it came to denote officeholders and their families and, thus, to indicate social status.

Only about 10 percent of the population, *yangban* monopolized the political process, economic wealth, and Confucian learning. This learning played a central part in *yangban* culture, as did government position, but since *yangban* status was not legally defined, a clear delineation is difficult. However, basic criteria were: a clear line of descent documented through a genealogy (*chokpo*), a distinguished ancestor, a clear geographic area within which such a status was recognized, close marriage ties with other persons of reputable lineage, and a special way of life.

As *yangban* were exempted from corvée labor and military service, the late Choson period, especially the nineteenth century, saw an increase in people claiming *yangban* status. This period also saw an erosion of local *yangban* authority and a clear distinction between nationally powerful lineages (*polyol*), local lineages without government positions (*byangban*), and ruined *yangban* (*chanban*).

Even though *yangban* today have lost their political and economic monopoly through educational and land reforms, modernization, and urbanization, in South Korea there is still a strong awareness of *yangban* ancestry, and descendants of respected families exert a strong influence, especially locally.

Anders Karlsson

Further Reading
Deuchler, Martina. (1992) *The Confucian Transformation of Korea: A Study of Society and Ideology.* Cambridge, MA: Council on East Asian Studies, Harvard University.
Duncan, John. (2000) *The Origins of the Choson Dynasty.* Seattle: University of Washington Press.
Palais, James. (1996) *Confucian Statecraft and Korean Institutions: Yu Hyongwon and the Late Choson Dynasty.* Seattle: University of Washington Press.

———. (1984) "Confucianism and the Aristocratic/Bureaucratic Balance in Korea." *Harvard Journal of Asiatic Studies* 44: 427–468.

YANGGANG PROVINCE

(2002 est. pop. 805,000). Yanggang (also Ryanggang) Province (Yanggangdo or Ryanggangdo), with an area of 13,888 square kilometers, is located inland along the Yalu (Amnok) and Tumen (Tuman) Rivers in North Korea (Democratic People's Republic of Korea). The province takes its name ("both rivers") from the two rivers that form the border between North Korea and China (People's Republic of China). The province was established in October 1954 with the division of Hamgyong Province into Yanggang and North and South Hamyong Provinces. In addition to Hyesan, the province's capital and only city, there are eleven counties (*kun*).

Yanggang has been called Korea's "rooftop" because of its high mountains, ranges, and plateaus. The highest peak is Mount Paektu (2,750 meters), straddling both Yanggang province and China. Kaema Plateau, with an average elevation of 1,339 meters, is located in central and western Yanggang, northwestern South Hamgyong, and eastern Chagang provinces. Measuring 14,300 square kilometers, it is the largest plateau on the Korean peninsula. There are also numerous other rivers and tributaries.

The region has much indigenous vegetation, such as conifers and grasses, and is also amenable to agriculture, particularly potatoes, cabbage, radishes, apricots, and ginseng. The province is also abundant in minerals such as iron, cooper, tungsten, and gold.

Jennifer Jung-Kim

Further Reading
Cho, Chung-Kyung, Phyllis Haffner, and Fredric M. Kaplan. (1991) *The Korea Guidebook.* 5th ed. Boston: Houghton-Mifflin.
Storey, Robert, and Alex English (2001). *Korea.* 5th ed. Berkeley, CA: Lonely Planet.

YANGON

(2002 est. pop. 4 million). Yangon is the capital of the Union of Myanmar (Burma) and of Yangon Division (2002 est. pop. 5.7 million). Located on the Yangon River, some 30 kilometers (21 miles) from its mouth on the Gulf of Martaban, Yangon is Myanmar's largest city and principal seaport, with Mingaladon airport its main international entry point.

Yangon was originally an ancient Mon settlement known latterly as Dagon (derived from an ancient Pali term meaning "three pots"), a name commemorated in that of Burma's famed Buddhist temple, the Shwedagon, which has stood for centuries on Singuttara Hill. Dagon was renamed Yangon (meaning "end of strife") by King Alaungpaya (reigned 1752–1760), who conquered Lower Burma in 1755. Under British colonial rule, Yangon—its name anglicized to Rangoon—developed rapidly as a major seaport and cosmopolitan commercial center. In the 1850s the British constructed a new city on a grid plan on delta land, bounded to the east by the Pazundaung Creek and to the south and west by the Yangon River. By the 1890s Yangon's increasing population and commerce necessitated land reclamation work at its riverine boundaries, while prosperous residential suburbs developed to the north of the royal lakes (Kan-daw-gyi) and the Shwedagon. Colonial Yangon, with its spacious parks and lakes and mix of modern buildings and traditional wooden architecture, was known as "the garden city of the East." Before World War II, almost half of Yangon's population was Indian.

Yangon suffered heavy damage in World War II and, in the decades since Burma regained independence (1948), the city has expanded and changed in character. Satellite towns were built to create a Maha Yangon (Greater Yangon) and names of streets and parks were changed from old colonial appellations to more patriotic nationalist names. The greatest transformation occurred in the 1990s, following both the military government's adoption of an open-door market economy under strong state control and an influx of investment. Many colonial-period buildings were demolished to make way for multistory hotels, office buildings, and shopping developments, and some inner-city inhabitants relocated to new satellite towns. Major road- and bridge-building programs were undertaken, including construction of a bridge across the river to Syriam (Thanlyin) and its industrial hinterland.

The 99.4-meter-high (326-foot-high) golden Shwedagon is the city's major landmark, and the country's largest and most revered Buddhist shrine. Legend links its foundation to the time of the Buddha, and for centuries it has been the focus of state as well as private patronage and devotion. Other temples are the waterfront Botataung (destroyed in 1943, but rebuilt as an exact replica) and the octagonal Sule in the heart of Yangon. Notable twentieth-century temples include the Kaba Aye (World Peace), completed under U Nu's government in 1952; the six-story Kyauk-htat-gyi, containing a huge reclining Buddha; the Melamu; and the Maha Wizaya (Great Victory), completed in 1986. The Azani Beikman (Martyrs' Mausoleum), containing the tombs of Burma's independence hero Aung

San and six cabinet colleagues (assassinated 19 July 1947), is an important national monument.

Patricia M. Herbert

Further Reading

Pearn, Bertie Reginald. ([1939] 1971) *A History of Rangoon.* Reprint ed. Farnborough, U.K.: Gregg.

Renault, Thomas, and Bénédicte Brac de la Perrière. (1998) *Eternal Rangoon: Contemporary Portrait of a Timeless City.* Paris: ASA.

Singer, Noel F. (1995) *Old Rangoon: City of the Shwedagon.* Gartmore, U.K.: Kiscadale.

YANGON DIVISION (2002 est. pop. 5.7 million). The Yangon Division (formerly Rangoon Division) is dominated by the national capital of Myanmar (Burma), Yangon, which is located at its center. The division measures 10,171 square kilometers in area. The Irrawaddy (Ayeyarwady) Division lies to the west, the Gulf of Martaban to the south, and the Pegu (Bago) Division to the east and north. The Pegu Yoma range slightly protrudes into the north of the Yangon Division, but most of the territory is lowland plain, watered by a number of rivers and tributaries.

The majority of the population are Burmans, but there are also more than 230,000 Karens, 50,000 Rakhines, and 500,000 inhabitants of other nationalities, including Chinese and Indians. More than half the inhabitants live in Yangon, Insein, Syriam (Thanlyin), and surrounding urban areas. Other towns include Hlegu and Twante as well as the satellite new towns of Hlaingthayar and Dagon, which the State Law and Order Restoration Council attempted to develop during the 1990s.

Reflecting its strategic position, the Yangon Division is the most developed region of Myanmar. It is Myanmar's main communications center as well as international gateway for air and sea traffic. Numerous light industries are located around the Yangon city area, which was targeted for major economic expansion in the twenty-first century. The division is also important for agriculture. Consisting of 39 townships and 1,444 wards or village tracts, it remains one of the major paddy-producing areas in Myanmar. Other important crops include jute, pulses, rubber, sugarcane, and groundnut.

Martin Smith

Further Reading

Pearn, Bertie Reginald. (1971) *History of Rangoon.* Farnborough, U.K.: Gregg.

Tin Nwe Maung, ed. (1990) *City of Yangon Modernization Record.* Yangon, Myanmar: Public Relations Information Division, Yangon City Development Committee.

Tinker, Hugh. (1967) *The Union of Burma: A Study of the First Years of Independence.* Oxford: Oxford University Press.

YANGTZE RIVER. See Chang River.

YAO The Yao are a minority people living in southern and southwestern China, mostly in the mountainous regions of Guangxi, Hunan, Yunnan, Guangdong, Guizhou, and Jiangxi Provinces. The Yao total 2.1 million people (1990 census) and rank as the thirteenth most populous of China's fifty-five minority nationalities. The majority of the Yao, more than 1.2 million, live in Guangxi; fewer than 1,000 live in Jiangxi. The Yao groups are scattered in many areas; their communities, usually small in size, consist exclusively of Yao. Before the founding of the People's Republic of China in 1949, the Yao groups identified themselves by over thirty names. But in the 1950s, the central government redefined all Yao groups and named them all "Yao."

History

The origin of the Yao is debated. Most Western, Chinese, and Yao scholars believe that the Yao became an ethnic group during the Tang dynasty (618–907 CE) when the term *mo yao* (not subject to corvée) was first used to refer to the upland people living in the mountains of Hunan and northern Guangdong and Guangxi. The central government allowed these people to search for arable land free from obligations—taxes and in particular corvée—to the imperial regime. After the identifier *mo* ("not") was dropped in later dynasties, the term *yao* gradually became associated more with the groups of upland people who traced their origins to an ancestral king, Pan Hu, than with a political category defining the people who were not subject to corvée.

It is conceivable that the Yao people did not become a distinct ethnic group until the Song dynasty (960–1279). During the Song and after, the central government ruled the Yao areas by *jimi* ("loose reins") policy and the *tusi* ("local chiefs") system, allowing the Yao chiefs to have autonomous power to govern their realms but requiring them to pledge loyalty to the imperial regime. By the early Ming dynasty (1368–1644), the central government replaced *jimi* and *tusi* with the policy of *gaitu guiliu* ("replacing locals with officials"), sending Han Chinese (the Chinese majority ethnicity) officials to rule the Yao areas; the Qing dynasty (1644–1912) continued the policy. The process of replacing locals, along with policies of ethnic discrimination during the Ming and Qing dynasties (for example, prohibiting the Yao from engaging in the salt trade) inspired tenacious resistance among the Yao.

During the Song dynasty and earlier, the Yao lived mainly in communes, in which families worked together and shared equally. Apart from a small portion who moved to valleys and plains and engaged in agriculture, most of the Yao lived in the mountains, basing their life on hunting, fishing, and slash-and-burn cultivation on hillsides. To flee the Mongol invasion and encroaching Chinese immigration from the north, in the early years of the Yuan dynasty (1279–1368), the Yao began to migrate southward. By the early Ming dynasty, the majority of the Yao had settled in Guangxi, and smaller portions had settled in other provinces. The migration changed the geographic distribution of the Yao population, a distribution that remains today. The migration also changed the economic life of many Yao. A large portion of them adopted agricultural production, although those who remained in the deep mountains preserved their traditional way of life.

Modern Era

In modern times, the Yao maintained their tradition of resistance against the penetration of the Chinese central authority. Uprisings continued; many Yao people joined the Taiping Rebellion (1850–1864) that originated in Guangxi. The Nationalists (Guomindang) adopted a policy of assimilation, attempting to promote Yao economy and culture. However, the Yao resisted and the assimilation attempts failed.

During the first two years after the founding of the People's Republic of China (1949), the government defined the Yao as a discrete nationality. Beginning with the establishment of the Longsheng Yao Autonomous County in Guangxi in 1951, the government in the next two decades established twelve Yao autonomous counties and over two thousand Yao autonomous towns or administrative villages. Under a policy of equality for all nationalities, the government trained many Yao cadres and extended its political administration to the Yao areas through these cadres. The Yao people in the deep mountains also began to give up slash-and-burn cultivation. During the Cultural Revolution (1966–1976), the government's minority work was halted when some Yao youths organized the Red Guards organizations to rebel against local authorities, who consisted of both Han and Yao officials; religious rituals and traditional festivals were prohibited.

In 1979, the government reassured the Yao of their rights and privileges as a minority nationality and promoted their equality more in the light of economic development. Since then Yao communities have experienced progress in agriculture, education, and health care. Reservoirs and hydroelectric power plants have been built; indigo, anise, and spices have been planted and are now important economic products; and the Yao mountainous regions have been developed for the timber industry and tourism. With more autonomous power under the government's reform policy, the Yao have also revived their traditions. But despite these developments, Yao communities are still poor in economic terms and far behind those of the Han Chinese.

Culture

Half the Yao speak the Yao language, a branch of the Sino-Tibetan language, but their dialects vary so significantly that Yao from different areas can hardly communicate with each other. The rest speak mainly Miao and Dong languages—the Sino-Tibetan languages of two other minority nationalities. Because of their long tradition of migration and association with the Han and Zhuang people in history, many Yao can also speak Han and Zhuang languages. The Yao write using Chinese characters. Although they have a long history of living with other nationalities, the Yao people usually marry only other Yao.

The Yao have a long tradition of oral literature, mostly legendary stories about their ancestors. Most of the Yao practice Taoism and ancestor worship, and the Taoist rituals and ancestor worship ceremonies, except during the Cultural Revolution, have always been practiced with great respect. The Yao also have many festivals, of which the most famous is the King Pan Festival to remember Pan Hu, celebrated by all Yao communities. The Yao are known for their unique ways of dressing, in particularly their men's turbans and women's clothes, which are very colorful. In the past, many of the Yao subgroups were actually named after their turbans and dresses, such as the "white-trouser Yao," "flowery Yao," "flat-turban Yao," and "red-turban Yao."

For most of their history, Yao economic and social development has been uneven, determined by their locations. Although the government defines them as one minority nationality, establishing a cohesive ethnic identity is still difficult, given the people's wide dispersion, the barrier of dialects, and the uneven socioeconomic development of their communities.

Yixin Chen

Further Reading

Litzinger, Ralph. (2000) *Other Chinas: The Yao and the Politics of National Belonging.* Durham, NC: Duke University Press.

Ma, Yin. (1989) *China's Minority Nationalities.* Beijing: Foreign Language Press.

YAP AH LOY (1837–1885), Chinese leader in Malaysia. Yap Ah Loy was born in Guangdong Province, China, on 14 March 1837, the son of a peasant. He arrived in Melaka, Malaysia, about 1854 and became Malaysia's most famous Kapitan Cina (a Malay word meaning "Chinese captain"). He also was head of the Hai San secret society in the state of Selangor and rose to fame by siding with Sultan Abdul Samad in the succession war in that state during the 1860s.

The title of Kapitan Cina acknowledged Yap Ah Loy and wealthy Chinese merchants like him as spokesmen or leaders of the Chinese immigrants then living in British Malaya. Through the appointment of the Kapitan Cina, the British recognized the separateness of the Chinese and their ability to govern themselves. In the first few decades of colonial rule, the British continued to rely on the Kapitan Cina–secret-society leadership system to administer revenue farms for opium, spirits, and gambling, develop the tin and plantation industries, and keep peace among the fractious Chinese dialect groups. Under Yap Ah Loy's stewardship, tin mining and other commercial activities in the Kuala Lumpur area developed rapidly. These activities transformed the previously backwater area into the nation's leading center of commerce and industry as well as the nation's capital city. He also contributed to the development of the city by supporting the building of schools, hospitals, churches, and facilities for the aged.

Kog Yue Choong

Further Reading

Middlebrook, S. M., and J. M. Gullick. (1983) *Yap Ah Loy: 1837–1885.* Kuala Lumpur, Malaysia: Malayan Branch of the Royal Asiatic Society.

Pann, Lynn, ed. (1998) *The Encyclopedia of the Chinese Overseas.* Singapore: Chinese Heritage Centre.

YASUKUNI SHRINE Yasukuni Shrine is a major Shinto shrine in Japan honoring the dead of the Imperial Japanese Army from the Sino-Japanese War (1899) to World War II. Established in 1869 in Kudanshita in Tokyo, the shrine encompasses gardens, a shrine, and a museum of the Imperial Army. It is marked by a giant torii (ceremonial gate), one of the largest in

Japan. The shrine's major festival, Mitama Matsuri, is celebrated around mid-July. The shrine was initially established to commemorate and venerate the dead of the Boshin Civil War, in which the new Imperial Army defeated rebellious feudal *han* (clans) during the Meiji Restoration (1868–1912). It is controversial largely because of its association with the militaristic period of the Japanese imperial past. The shrine is not supported by public funds because of constitutional prohibitions. Many conservative Japanese feel in consequence that their war dead are not properly honored. Moreover, the clause separating state from church in the constitution can be interpreted, and has been interpreted, to mean that national political figures, such as the prime minister, are forbidden from attending rituals at Yasukuni Shrine in their official capacity. As a result, ministers have attended Yasukuni memorial rituals only in their capacity as private citizens.

Michael Ashkenazi

Further Reading
Safier, Joshua. (1996) "Yasukuni Shrine and the Constraints on the Discourses of Nationalism in Twentieth-Century Japan." M.A. thesis. University of Kansas.

YASUKUNI SHRINE CONTROVERSY

The Yasukuni Shrine has been a source of antiwar sentiment in East Asia because of its association with the Shinto *bushido* warrior code. Yasukuni has been visited routinely by members of the royal family, but civil politicians have been criticized for visiting the shrine because the remains of Japanese soldiers convicted of war crimes are placed there. Controversy began in 1978 when the remains of General Tojo Hideki were brought to Yasukuni thirty years after he was executed. The placement of his remains there deified him. Prime Minister Fukuda Takeo was the first prime minister to visit Yasukuni since 1945. In 1985, Prime Minister Nakasone Yasuhiro made an official visit to the shrine.

Japan's Supreme Court ruled in 1997 that using public funds for ritual offerings violated the constitution. Nevertheless, annual visits by politicians on the anniversary of the end of the war (August 15) continue to be a point of contention with Japan's neighbors. In 1997, the Japanese prime minister chose not to attend Yasukuni prior to visiting China. Three years later, however, China cancelled a scheduled visit of Japan's Transportation Minister, who was to have presented his bid for Japanese construction of a high-speed rail line in China, two days after he had visited Yasukuni.

Thomas P. Dolan

YAYOI PERIOD The Yayoi period (c. 300 BCE to 300 CE) saw the introduction of a full-scale agricultural economy into the islands of Japan. This economy was initially associated with immigration from the Korean Peninsula. Population growth among early Yayoi farmers then led to the rapid expansion of Yayoi culture as far as northern Honshu. By the end of the Yayoi period, chiefdom-type societies had developed in Japan, laying the foundation for Japan's first early states.

The Jomon period (c. 14,500 BCE–300 BCE) that preceded the Yayoi had seen some small-scale plant cultivation but such practices seem to have had little influence on the organization of Jomon society. In contrast, the full-scale farming of the Yayoi period marked a very different intensive and expansionary economic system. A variety of studies within biological anthropology have shown that the people of the Yayoi period were physically quite different from the Jomon peoples but very similar to the inhabitants of mainland Japan in historical times. Currently the most widely accepted interpretation of this evidence is that continental rice farmers spread to Japan from the Korean Peninsula at the beginning of the Yayoi period. It has been argued that the Japanese language also spread to the archipelago at this time.

As well as rice farming, a variety of other items and technologies were introduced from Korea in the Yayoi.

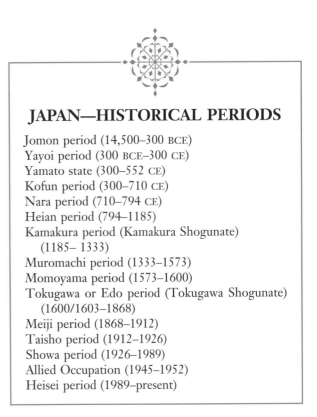

JAPAN—HISTORICAL PERIODS

Jomon period (14,500–300 BCE)
Yayoi period (300 BCE–300 CE)
Yamato state (300–552 CE)
Kofun period (300–710 CE)
Nara period (710–794 CE)
Heian period (794–1185)
Kamakura period (Kamakura Shogunate)
    (1185– 1333)
Muromachi period (1333–1573)
Momoyama period (1573–1600)
Tokugawa or Edo period (Tokugawa Shogunate)
    (1600/1603–1868)
Meiji period (1868–1912)
Taisho period (1912–1926)
Showa period (1926–1989)
Allied Occupation (1945–1952)
Heisei period (1989–present)

These include the use of bronze and iron, domesticated pigs, wooden and stone agricultural tools, megalithic burials, and certain types of pottery. The actual context of many of these finds, however, suggests close interaction between the native Jomon and immigrant Yayoi peoples, at least in the early stages of the Yayoi period.

Yayoi Cultural Expansion

During the Early Yayoi phase (c. 300–175 BCE), Yayoi culture spread rapidly through western Japan, with outlying sites in eastern Honshu as far north as Sunazawa in Aomori Prefecture. Some Yayoi pottery is known in Okinawa, but agriculture did not develop in the Ryukyu Islands until at least the eighth century CE. Hokkaido also lay outside the area of Yayoi culture, although the Epi-Jomon people of that island engaged in trade for iron and shell bracelets with their Yayoi neighbors.

The expansion of Yayoi culture is known from the excavation of over a hundred rice-paddy field sites dating to that period. Without doubt rice was an important crop during the Yayoi, but barley, millet, and other cultivated plants were also consumed in large quantities. Domesticated pigs and, more rarely, chickens are known from Yayoi contexts, but it is not clear how important these animals were as food sources. The hunting of deer and wild boar, practiced during the Jomon period, certainly continued through the Yayoi, as did river and marine fishing.

Bronze and iron appear to have been introduced simultaneously into Yayoi Japan. Iron was mainly used for agricultural and other tools, whereas ritual and ceremonial artifacts were mainly made of bronze. Some casting of bronze and iron began in Japan by about 100 BCE, but the raw materials for both metals were introduced from Korea and China. Han-dynasty (206 BCE–220 CE) bronze mirrors were the most important prestige items imported from China. Bronze mirrors were also cast in Japan, as were a variety of other ritual objects unknown on the continent. Bronze weapons and bells both evolved from practical tools to ornate, ceremonial artifacts. In northern Kyushu, bronze weapons are found as grave goods in elite burials at sites such as Yoshinogari, but elsewhere weapons and bells are usually discovered as isolated hoards buried away from settlements. At Kojindani in Shimane Prefecture, 6 bells, 16 spearheads and 358 swords were found on an isolated hillside. Such hoards are often interpreted as resulting from community-based agricultural rituals.

Although written records are unknown in Japan itself until the seventh century CE, Chinese dynastic histories make some mention of the Wa people, who are thought to be the Yayoi Japanese. The Chinese *History of the Wei Dynasty* (*Wei shu* or *Wei zhi*) was compiled in 280 CE and contains a short description of the economy and society of the Wa people and of the diplomatic relations between the Wei dynasty and the Wa polity of Yamatai and its queen, Pimiko. This text has long been a subject of great controversy. The location of Yamatai is unclear from the text itself; northern Kyushu and the Kinai region have been suggested as the two main possible locations but the *Wei shu* suggests Yamatai controlled most of western Japan in the third century CE. The archaeological record does not support such a degree of political unification until the late Kofun period (c. 300–710 CE).

Yayoi Polities

Archaeologists have proposed the existence of several chiefdom-type polities in western Japan in the Yayoi period. These were regional polities based on a large, central settlement with populations of perhaps several thousand people. Such polities may correspond to the "countries" (Chinese *guo*) described in the *Wei shu* but their political control did not extend beyond their particular basin or river valley. The site of Yoshinogari in Saga Prefecture was probably the center of one of these chiefdoms. Defensive ditches with watchtowers enclose an area of 25 hectares. The rulers of this settlement appear to have lived in a central residential precinct and to have been buried in a 40-by-26-meter burial mound.

Many of the Yayoi chiefdoms of western Japan were engaged in conflicts with neighboring groups to gain access to water and other resources and to extend their power. Such conflicts are mentioned in the *Wei shu* and are evidenced archaeologically by defended settlements, the widespread presence of weapons, and discoveries of human skeletons with war-related injuries. Over 150 Yayoi-period skeletons have been found with embedded arrowheads, cut marks, or decapitated skulls. Through warfare, trade, and alliance building, the chiefdoms of the Kinai region had considerably extended their power by the end of the Yayoi period. By the second half of the third century CE, the mound burials of the Yayoi period had developed into the huge, standardized, keyhole-shaped tombs of the Kofun period. Yoshiro Kondo has argued that the standardization of these tombs signifies not political unification but rather the creation of ties of fictitious kinship among powerful Yayoi chiefs. The Yayoi period is distinguished from the Kofun on the basis of these standardized tombs, but the underlying political processes straddle both periods.

Mark Hudson

Further Reading

Farris, William Wayne. (1998) *Sacred Texts and Buried Treasures: Issues in the Historical Archaeology of Ancient Japan.* Honolulu: University of Hawaii Press.

Hudson, Mark J. (1990) "From Toro to Yoshinogari: Changing Perspectives on Yayoi Period Archeology." In *Hoabinhian, Jomon, Yayoi, Early Korean States: Bibliographic Reviews of Far Eastern Archaeology 1990*, edited by Gina Barnes. Oxford: Oxbow, 63–111.

———. (1999) *Ruins of Identity: Ethnogenesis in the Japanese Islands.* Honolulu: University of Hawaii Press.

Imamura, Keiji. (1996) *Prehistoric Japan: New Perspectives on Insular East Asia.* Honolulu: University of Hawaii Press.

YELLOW SEA The Yellow Sea (Huang Hai), the shallow gulf between China and Korea, is 870 kilometers long from the south to the north and 556 kilometers wide from the east to the west and covers an area of 378,600 square kilometers. The northern part comprises the inlet of Bohai Bay in the northwest, which is almost enclosed by the Liaodong Peninsula in the northeast, the Shandong Peninsula in the south, and the Korea Bay in the northeast. The southern part of the Yellow Sea borders on the Shandong Peninsula in the north and the Chinese mainland in the west and meets the East China Sea where the Chang (Yangtze) River flows into the sea. In the east, it borders on Korea and the Korea Strait. The Yellow Sea, which has received its name from the yellowish silt deposited mainly by the Huang (Yellow) River, has a warm temperate climate. With an average depth of about forty meters, it is one of China's best fishing grounds.

The entire Yellow Sea, and especially its coastal regions, is presently being overexploited by Chinese, Vietnamese, Korean, and Japanese fishing vessels, and the environmental problems are critical. Important ports and fishing bases on the Chinese coast are Qingdao and Yantai in Shandong Province and Dalian on the Liaodong Peninsula in Liaoning Province. Bohai Bay in the northwest has been the traditional location for salt-works. Large offshore petroleum deposits have been discovered there, and a number of oil refineries have been set up.

Bent Nielsen

Further Reading

Choi, B. H. (1980) *A Tidal Model of the Yellow Sea and the Eastern China Sea.* Seoul: KORDI Report.

Chough, Sung Kwun, Homa J. Lee, and S. H. Yoon. (2000) *Marine Geology of Korean Seas.* Amsterdam: Elsevier.

Ichiye, Takashi, ed. (1986) *Japan, East China, and Yellow Sea Studies.* Oxford: Pergamon.

Jin, Xianshi. (1996) *Variations in Fish Community Structure and Ecology of Major Species in the Yellow/Bohai Sea.* Bergen, Norway: Universitetet i Bergen.

Morgan, Joseph, and Mark J. Valencia, eds. (1992) *Atlas for Marine Policy in East Asian Seas.* Berkeley and Los Angeles: University of California Press.

YEN, Y. C. JAMES (1890–1990) Chinese reformer. Born in the mountains of China's Sichuan Province in 1890, the young Y. C. James Yen (Yan Yangchu) was sent to mission schools, where he became, in his later words, not a "Christian" (implying membership in a foreign institution) but "a follower of Christ." After studying at Hong Kong University, Yen graduated in 1918 from Yale University and worked under the International Young Men's Christian Association (YMCA) with the Chinese Labor Corps in France. While there, he wrote a widely copied literacy primer that used one thousand basic Chinese characters.

Yen returned to China in 1921 to head a national mass literacy campaign under the Chinese National YMCA and to marry Alice Huie, an American-born Chinese with whom he had three sons and two daughters. He adapted the publicity and organization techniques of the YMCA's science education campaigns and combined them with the traditional village-school concepts of nonprofessionalized teachers, neighborhood classes, and flexible schedules to produce a campaign (*yundong*) model used in hundreds of localities that attracted more than five million students. In 1923, Yen and other leading intellectuals formed the National Association of Mass Education Movements (MEM).

Still, most illiterates lived in villages; nor was literacy their fundamental problem. In 1926, the MEM set up a village campaign in Ding Xian, a county some two hundred miles south of Beijing. Rejecting the radical approach, Yen saw "farmers," not "peasants," in need of education and support, not class war. In 1928, Yen received an honorary graduate degree from Yale, raised a substantial endowment in the United States, and then enlisted socially conscious specialists to develop a fourfold program in rural reconstruction. The Ting Hsien (Ding Xian) Experiment used people's schools to coordinate innovations ranging from hybrid pigs and economic cooperatives to village drama and village health workers. By 1931, these successes excited nationwide public and government interest. Yen joined Liang Shuming and other independent reformers to form a National Rural Reconstruction Movement comprising hundreds of organizations. The 1937 Japanese invasion drove MEM operations first to Hunan, then to Sichuan, but Yen spent much of the war in Washington, D.C. After 1945, Yen found himself increasingly at odds with the Nationalist government's military preoccupation; in 1948 he persuaded the U.S. Congress to fund an independent Joint Commission on Rural Reconstruction, of which he became one of the commissioners. After 1949, Yen led the Philippines Rural Reconstruction Movement and founded the International Rural Reconstruction Movement, which he headed until his death in New York City in the fall of 1990.

Charles W. Hayford

Further Reading
Hayford, Charles W. (1990) *To the People: James Yen and Village China.* New York: Columbia University Press.
Sun Enrong, ed. (1980) *Yan Yangchu Quanji* (Works of Yan Yangchu). 4 vols. Changsha, China: Hunan jiaoyu.
Wu Hsiang-hsiang. (1981) *Yan Yangchu Zhuan* (Biography of Yan Yangchu). Taipei, Taiwan: Shibao wenhua.

YEREVAN (2002 pop. 1.3 million). Yerevan is the capital and the largest city of Armenia, as well as its largest cultural, scientific, and industrial center (producing electronics, chemicals, textiles, and food products). The site was fortified as early as the eighth century BCE, when a ruler of the ancient kingdom of Urartu (thirteenth–seventh centuries BCE) established a fortress there in 782 BCE. In the sixth century BCE, Yerevan was the capital of Armenia when the region was under Achaemenid Persian rule.

Because of its strategic location on the trade route through the Caucasus, Armenia was overrun through the centuries by various powers, including the Romans, Parthians, Arabs, and Mongols. Between 1513 and 1735, it was repeatedly devastated by Persian and Turkish forces. The Russians conquered Yerevan in 1827; under the Treaty of Turkmanchai (1828), the city, together with east Armenia, became part of the Russian empire.

After a short-lived period of independence between 1918 and 1920, Yerevan became the capital of the Armenian Socialist Soviet Republic within the Soviet Union. Since 1991, it has been the capital of the independent Republic of Armenia.

Architectural monuments include the Katoghike Church (thirteenth century), the Church of Zoravar (1691–1705), and a sixteenth-century Ottoman fortress. In the 1930s–1950s, the city was completely redesigned in accordance with plans developed by A. I. Tamanian. Yerevan boasts a state university founded in 1919, several other institutions of higher education,

research institutions, and the Academy of Sciences. Cultural institutions include the opera house, several theaters, museums such as the National Museum of Armenia, art galleries, and the Matenadaran, a library with a large collection of Armenian manuscripts.

Pavel Dolukhanov

YESILIRMAK RIVER The Yesilirmak (from Turkish *Yesil*—green; known in antiquity as the Iris), a river in Turkey, has a course of approximately 418 kilometers. The area of its basin is around 20,000 square kilometers. The river rises in the mountains of northeast Turkey, flows northwest through narrow fertile valleys, and ends in the Black Sea, near the city of Samsun. The river's highest flow is from March to July, as snow melts in the mountains of Turkey, and its lowest flow is in November and December.

The Yesilirmak River is an important source of drinking and irrigation water for northern Turkey, and since ancient times it cities flourished along its course. The area along the river basin is known for its historical treasures and numerous architectural monuments from pre-Hellenic, ancient Greek, and Roman eras, as well as from the early Ottoman empire. This region has been inhabited since prehistoric times by various civilizations, including the Hittites (second millennium BCE) and Phrygians (early first millennium BCE), and was once part of Pontus, a kingdom bordering the Black Sea, which flourished from the fourth century BCE until it became part of the Roman empire in 63 BCE.

Several ancient cities in Asia Minor lie on the Yesilirmak River, including Amasia, the capital of Pontus, and Samsun, ancient Amisus, at the mouth of the river. Amasia was the birthplace of Strabo (64 or 63 BCE–after 23 CE), a Greek geographer who traveled over the known world and described it in his *Geographical Sketches.* Samsun, located on the Silk Road, flourished as a commercial center in medieval times.

In the modern era, the area along the Yesilirmak River has become an important agricultural and tourist region of Turkey. In 1980 Turkey built the Hasan Ugurlu dam on the river, which at the height of 175 meters was then one of the world's highest dams. The dam holds an estimated 1 billion cubic meters of water. In the 1990s, the government of Turkey became concerned about pollution, due to the overapplication of fertilizers and pesticides and the disposal of animal manure and wastes along the river's basin.

Rafis Abazov

YI The Yi people live in southwest China, in the mountainous regions of Yunnan, Sichuan, Guizhou, and Guangxi provinces. With 6.6 million people (1990 census), the Yi are the fourth largest minority nationality in China in terms of population. Yi groups in various areas described themselves with a variety of names until the 1950s, when the Chinese government redefined all Yi groups and named all of them Yi.

History

Scholars have different views about the origins of the Yi. Some believe that the Yi originated from the ancient nomadic Qiang peoples who had lived in northwestern China; others argue that the Yi people developed from the original inhabitants in Yunnan, as early as ten thousand years ago. In either case, scholars agree that starting from the early second millennium BCE, the people in central Yunnan, whether they were the original inhabitants or Qiang immigrants, migrated out of their homeland and mixed with the Han Chinese (the ethnic Chinese majority) and other minority groups. As a result, the Yi are a mixed group with diverse origins.

Their migration extended along the watersheds of the six rivers in the Sichuan-Yunnan region and the Yunnan-Guizhou plateau and divided the Yi into six branches. These six branches are the origins of the six branches of the modern Yi nationality: Southern Nisu Yi, Southeastern Sani Yi, Eastern Nasu Yi, Northern Nuosu Yi, Central Yi, and Western Yi. According to a Yi legend, the Yi people originated from an ancient ceremony of tribal division, the division of six ancestors (*liu zu*).

During the Han dynasty (206 BCE–220 CE), the ethnic minority peoples inhabiting the mountainous border region of Yunnan, Sichuan, and Guizhou were first referred to as *yi* (barbarians) in Chinese records; the Yi people were part of this group. The Han government established an administrative prefecture in the region and appointed a Yi chief to rule the region with the title King of Dian. During and after this time, large clans emerged in the Yi tribes; a caste system, which not only established various social statuses in the Yi communities but also defined a large number of common people as slaves, started to dominate the Yi societies.

From the Sui (581–618) to the Song dynasty (960–1279), the Yi people were generally referred to in the Chinese records as *wuman* (black barbarians) and *baiman* (white barbarians). While the former exclusively designated the Yi groups in central Yunnan, the latter referred to the minority groups inhabiting the border region of Yunnan, Sichuan, and Guizhou, including some of the Yi tribes. During these centuries, two independent kingdoms, Nanzhao (739–902) and Dali (902–1253), ruled Yunnan, organized by the Yi and other minority peoples. Under the reign of these authorities, a distinct Yi culture, including music, dance, ancestral worship, and architectural, culinary, and sartorial practices, began to develop from Yi tribal traditions and from contact with the cultures of neighboring minority groups.

In 1253, the Mongols invaded southern China and destroyed the Dali kingdom. After conquering the region, the Mongol Yuan dynasty (1279–1368) extended its administration to the Yi areas through a system of *tusi* (local chiefs). By pledging loyalty to the central government, the Yi local chiefs gained autonomy to govern their realms. During the Mongol period, the Yi people were referred to as *luoluo* (barbarians). Malaria and other epidemic diseases spread to the Yi areas and led to a loss of population and a setback to Yi socioeconomic development.

To consolidate its political control of Yunnan, the Ming dynasty (1368–1644) in the late fifteenth century decided to substitute for the *tusi* system a new policy whereby locals were replaced by Han Chinese officials. The process of replacing locals was not completed until the 1730s during the reign of the emperor Yongzheng of the Qing dynasty (1644–1912), and in most areas the Yi chiefs were powerful enough to maintain their rule and defy the penetration of the Chinese central government at least until the end of Republican China (1927).

The Modern Era

During the early period of the People's Republic of China (1949–), the government made efforts to redefine Yi nationality. After bringing the six branches of the Yi peoples together, the government changed their name from the barbarian term *yi* to "Yi," a different Chinese word, with connotations of respect. Beginning with the founding of the Liangshan Yi Autonomous Prefecture in 1952, the government established a total of fifteen Yi autonomous prefectures and counties. Viewing the Yi as the only existing slave society in the world, the government conducted a democratic reform of the Yi areas between 1956 and 1958 and abolished slavery. Under the policy of the equality of all nationalities, the government trained many Yi cadres and extended its political administration into the Yi areas through these cadres. However, the Cultural Revolution (1966–1976) brought chaos to all the Yi communities; the traditional Yi customs and religion became the targets of political campaigns, and former local chiefs and priests were scorned or even prosecuted.

With the beginning of reform in 1979, the government reassured the Yi of their rights and privileges as a minority nationality and promoted their equality more in terms of economic development. Since then, the Yi communities have made progress in agricultural economy, education, and health care, and many of the Yi people have become modern workers employed in the tin and coal mines in Yunnan and Guizhou. Yi trade with the outside world has developed, and modern railroads, highways, and communications have been extended through the Yi areas. Despite these developments, the Yi societies, disadvantaged by their geographic locations in remote mountains, are still poor in economic terms and are far behind the Han Chinese areas.

Culture

The Yi have a long and rich cultural history. Much traditional literature is written in the distinctive script used for the Old Yi language. Folk tales, epics, and songs have also been passed down orally. Yi traditional medicine has a rich variety of resources; *baiyao*, a white medical powder with a special efficacy for treating hemorrhage, wounds, bruises, and the like, is widely used by all Chinese. Yi religion, based on ancestor worship and a belief in many gods, has been revived in recent years after its practices were prohibited in the 1960s and 1970s.

Yi people speak the Yi language, a linguistic branch of the Chinese-Tibetan language family, which has six sets of major dialects and many more local dialects which are not always mutually intelligible. One million members of the Yi nationality do not speak the Yi language at all. In 1975, the Chinese government attempted to formalize a unified Yi language by defining 819 standard Yi words, but the effort has not been as successful as hoped, as isolation and language barriers have prevented the Yi from establishing a commonly shared ethnic identity. The development of their autonomous power and the modernization of their economy and society have yet to occur.

Yixin Chen

Further Reading

Harrell, Stevan, ed. (2001) *Perspectives on the Yi of Southwest China*. Berkeley and Los Angeles: University of California Press.

Ma, Yin. (1989) *China's Minority Nationalities*. Beijing: Foreign Language Press.

YI HA-UNG

YI HA-UNG (1821–1898), Korean statesman. Yi Ha-ung, also known as the Taewon'gun, served as the de facto regent of the Yi (Choson) dynasty (1392–1910) from the time his twelve-year-old son, Kojong, assumed the throne in 1864 until 1873 when he relinquished power to his son. During his tenure as regent, the Taewon'gun set about restoring the power and prestige of the Yi dynasty by inaugurating far-reaching reforms. He appointed officials to the bureaucracy on the basis of merit, regardless of clan or regional affiliation. In order to restore the financial stability of the monarchy, he closed the large, tax-exempt Confucian academies known as *sowon* and imposed taxes on *Yangban* (hereditary aristocracy) and commoners alike. The Taewon'gun succeeded in restoring financial stability, even though he undertook the rebuilding of Kyongbok Palace, destroyed two centuries earlier in the Hideyoshi Invasion.

Diplomatically, the Taewon'gun pursued a policy of isolation with regard to Japan as well as the West. He modernized the army and upgraded defensive installations along the Korean coastline, thus repelling military incursions by the French, Russians, Americans, and Chinese. Domestically, the Taewon'gun suppressed Catholicism, which he perceived as a threat. Eventually, Yi was forced to relinquish power to his son by Confucian officials and the family of Queen Min.

Keith Leitich

Further Reading

Eckert, Carter J., Ki-baik Lee, Young Ick Lew, Michael Robinson, and Edward W. Wagner. (1990) *Korea Old and New: A History*. Seoul: Ilchokak.

Lone, Stewart, and Gavan McCormack. (1993) *Korea since 1850*. New York: St. Martin's.

YI I (1536–1584), Korean philosopher and statesman. Yi I, whose honorific is Yulgok, forms with Yi Hwang (1501–1570) the most famous pair in the intellectual history of the Choson dynasty (1392–1910). Yi I was educated in his youth by his mother, Shin Saimdang, who is as famous as her son in Korea and is regarded as the paragon of Korean motherhood. Yi became famous by placing first in the civil service examination nine times. After entering officialdom, he was engaged in a wide scope of activities, from historian to diplomat.

However, Yi is mainly remembered for his contributions to Neo-Confucian thought. He participated in what was known as "Four-Seven Debate," arguing for the position that *li* and *ki*, ("principle" and "material force"—a pair of key terms in Neo-Confucian metaphysics) were ultimately inseparable. His position has often been interpreted as reflecting the practical character of his thinking, for Yi was also actively engaged in the effort to reform governmental institutions and strengthen the military system.

Youngmin Kim

Further Reading

Chung, Edward Y. J. (1995) *The Korean Neo-Confucianism of Yi T'oegye and Yi Yulgok: A Reappraisal of the "Four-Seven Thesis" and Its Practical Implications for Self-Cultivation.* Albany: State University of New York Press.

Kalton, Michael C., et al. (1994) *The Four-Seven Debate: An Annotated Translation of the Most Famous Controversy in Korean Neo-Confucian Thought.* Albany: State University of New York Press.

Ro, Young-Chan. (1989) *The Korean Neo-Confucianism of Yi Yulgok.* Albany: State University of New York Press.

YI KYU-BO

YI KYU-BO (1168–1241), Korean poet. Yi Kyu-bo, pen name Paegunkosa (White Cloud Hermit), lived during a very turbulent period of Korean history: Koryo was threatened to the north by barbarian tribes and from within by the struggle for power between the civil and the military factions in the bureaucracy. A child prodigy, Yi Kyu-bo had a penchant for wine, which accounts for his repeated failures in the civil service examination before finally passing in 1189. A chance meeting with General Choe Chung-hon, the most powerful figure in Koryo at the time, led to the recognition of his ability. Thereafter he had a long and distinguished public career, which culminated in his appointment as head of the Chancellery of State Affairs.

A Korean poet writing Chinese poetry attempts the equivalent of a Chinese poet writing classical Latin verse. Small wonder that many of the Korean *hanshi* poets (Korean poets writing in Chinese) did not meet a high standard; the wonder of Yi Kyu-bo is that he did. A prolific writer, he has more than two thousand poems to his credit, including the celebrated epic *The Lay of King Tongmyong.* His collected poems are in *Tongguk isangguk chonjip* (Collected works of Minister Yi of Korea). He was the greatest poet of the age and arguably the greatest poet in Korean history. His poems are vibrantly alive, rooted in the concerns of everyday life, redolent of the spirit of China's Tang (618–907 CE) and Song (960–1279) dynasties. They focus on an emotion, offering brief but brilliant illuminations of the heart. Yi Kyu-bo also left substantial prose writings.

Kevin O'Rourke

Further Reading

O'Rourke, Kevin, trans. (1995) *Singing Like a Cricket, Hooting Like an Owl: Selected Poems of Yi Kyu-bo.* Ithaca, NY: Cornell University Press, East Asia Series.

YI MUN-YOL

YI MUN-YOL (b. 1948), Korean novelist. Since he made his debut in 1977 with a short story in a Daegu newspaper, Yi Mun-yol (Lee Mun-yol) has published prolifically, producing novels dealing with a wide range of subjects, from experience of military service to serious religious and philosophical questions to traditional Korean cultural heroes. In his novels—most particularly in his two masterpieces, *Yongung shidae* (1984, An Age of Heroes) and *Pyongyong* (1989, The Outskirts/Borderlands)—he reveals himself to be a sensitive witness to the twists and turns of modern Korean history. He has received numerous Korean literary prizes: his *Hwangje rul wihayo* (1985; trans. 1986, Hail to the Emperor!) was awarded the Republic of Korea Literary Prize, and *Saram ui adul* (1979, Son of Man) received the Today's Writer Prize.

Yi is one of the most controversial literary figures in the contemporary Korean cultural arena. His conservative stance on political and gender issues (the latter motivated by his reappraisal of traditional Confucian values) has been severely criticized by many left-leaning intellectuals and feminists. His conservative stance toward Korean politics has sometimes been interpreted as reflecting his plight as the son of a communist who defected to North Korea during the Korean War.

Youngmin Kim

Further Reading

Lee, Mun-yol. (1986) *Hail to the Emperor!* Seoul: Si-sa-yong-o-sa.

Yi, Mun-yol. (1995) *The Poet.* London: Harvill.

———. (2001) *Our Twisted Hero.* New York: Hyperion.

YI SONG-GYE

YI SONG-GYE (1335–1408), Koryo general; founder of Choson dynasty. A prominent general serving the Koryo kingdom (918–1392), Yi Song-gye (later King T'aejo) eventually founded the Choson dynasty (sometimes referred to as the Yi dynasty), which would rule Korea from 1392 to 1910. He rose to prominence as a general defending the later Koryo dynasty from increasingly potent attacks by Japanese marauders and China-based brigands.

In 1388, the king of Koryo opted to oppose Ming China's incursions in the north by launching a counterattack. Despite Yi Song-gye's strong opposition to an anti-Ming policy, he joined in the military campaign, ostensibly as a deputy commander. Not long after setting out, however, Yi marched his army back toward the Koryo court and bloodlessly drove his rivals, including the Koryo king, from power. Yi and his supporters then set about an ambitious land reform program, and it soon became apparent that de facto power rested with Yi Song-gye rather than with the Koryo king. In 1392 he took the formal step of forcing the abdication of Koryo's last king, Kong'yang (1345–1394) and establishing himself as the first ruler of the Choson kingdom (whose name hearkens back to an ancient kingdom of the peninsula), moving the capital from Kaesong to Seoul.

Daniel C. Kane

Further Reading

Duncan, John B. (2000) *The Origins of the Choson Dynasty.* Seattle: University of Washington Press.

Henthorn, William E. (1963) *Korea: The Mongol Invasions.* Leiden, Netherlands: E. J. Brill.

Lee, Ki-baek. (1984) *A New History of Korea.* Cambridge, MA: Harvard University Press.

Lee, Peter H. (1975) *Songs of Flying Dragons: A Critical Reading.* Cambridge, MA: Harvard University Press.

YI T'AE-YONG

(1914–1998), Korean women's rights activist. Yi T'ae-yong (Tai-Young Lee) was born in North P'yongan Province in what is the present-day Democratic People's Republic of Korea (North Korea). Although her father died when she was only a year old, Yi grew up in a loving family with strong Christian values.

After graduating from Ewha Woman's College in 1936, Yi married Dr. Chong Il-hyong (Chyung Yil-Hyung), a Methodist pastor and Korean nationalist. After the end of World War II, Chong encouraged his wife to pursue her childhood dream of becoming a lawyer. At the age of thirty-two, she became the first female student at Seoul National University (SNU) College of Law. She graduated in 1949 and passed the National Judicial Examination in 1952.

In 1956 Yi founded the Women's Legal Counseling Center, which in 1966 became the Korea Legal Aid Center for Family Relations. Yi was also dean of Ewha's College of Law and Political Science from 1963 to 1971. While dean, she earned a doctorate in law from SNU in 1969.

Yi was a famous champion of women's legal rights in Korea. For her work, she earned the Ramon Magsaysay Award for Community Leadership, as well as numerous other international accolades. Lee and her legal aid centers in twenty-nine Korean and twelve U.S. cities assisted countless women. Her advocacy helped effect revisions of the Korean family law in the areas of divorce, custody, and inheritance.

Jennifer Jung-Kim

Further Reading

Strawn, Sonia Reid. (1988) *Where There Is No Path: Lee Tai-Young, Her Story.* Seoul: Legal Aid Center for Family Relations.

YOGA

Yoga, or Western-style painting, emerged in Japan in 1855 as a result of efforts by the Japanese government to establish a bureau (Bansho Shirabesho) for the study of Western documents. The Western paintings that formed one part of this bureau were studied not for their aesthetic value, but rather for the insights they might yield in understanding Western technology through the study of styles and materials.

Takahashi Yuichi (1828–1894) was a central figure at this time. He entered the Bansho Shirabesho and became the first artist to consider the Western concept of objective and subjective interpretations. He later studied Western painting techniques under Charles Wirgman, of the *Illustrated London News,* and was important in founding *Kokka,* Japan's first scholarly art journal, in 1889.

The establishment of the Technical Fine Arts School (Kobu Bijutsu Gakko) in 1877 enabled the Japanese to study under Italian artists. The school was interested in providing training in drafting and cartography; however, the Westerners who taught at Kobu Bijutsu Gakko had a strong impact on the development of *yoga.* One such painter was Antonio Fontanesi (1818–1881). A follower of the Barbizon school, for whom the dominant colors were browns and golds, Fontanesi was teacher to the artists Yamamoto Hosui (1850–1906) and Asai Chu (1856–1907).

The popularity of Western-style painting declined in the 1880s in favor of Japanese-style work. As a result, the Meiji Art Society was established in 1889 to promote Western-style art through its annual exhibitions, which led, in the 1890s, to a revival of popular interest in *yoga.* However, in the first half of the 1890s, a rivalry developed between the artists trained by masters of the Barbizon school and those who had been strongly influenced by the light colors of the French Impressionists. Kuroda Seiki (1866–1924), who spent ten years in France, influenced other Japanese artists who painted in the Western style. By 1896 the strained relationship between the two approaches led Kuroda and others to separate from the Meiji Art Society and form the White Horse Society. It was through the exhibitions of these societies that Western-style painting was promoted, creating an appreciation and interest in *yoga* that would influence later generations of artists in Japan.

Catherine Pagani

Further Reading
Harada Minoru. (1974) *Meiji Western Painting*. Trans. by Murakata Akiko. New York: Weatherhill.
Rosenfeld, John M. (1971) "Western-Style Painting in the Early Meiji Period and Its Critics." In *Tradition and Modernization in Japanese Culture*, edited by Donald H. Shively. Princeton, NJ: Princeton University Press.
Takashima Shuji and J. Thomas Rimer, with Gerald D. Bolas. (1987). *Paris in Japan: The Japanese Encounter with European Painting*. Tokyo: Japan Foundation.

YOGYAKARTA (2002 est. pop. 418,000). The city of Yogyakarta (pronounced "Jogjakarta")—known as the Javanese cultural heartland—is located in the Yogyakarta Special Territory (2002 est. pop. 3 million), surrounded on three sides by the province of Central Java. The city lies 27 kilometers north of the Indian Ocean and the sacred beach of Parangtritis, and a similar distance south of the active volcano Mount Merapi (2,900 meters). It is near such important ancient religious sites as Borobudur (constructed by the Sailendra kingdom between 778 and 842 CE) and Prambanan (constructed by the Mataram kingdom c. 900 CE).

The current Hamengkubuwono sultanate of Yogyakarta is descended from the Mataram kingdom of the sixteenth century. In 1755 Yogyakarta was founded when Mataram was divided into two, a related sultanate being established in nearby Surakarta (or Solo). Yogyakarta was invaded briefly by British forces in 1812 and was the center of an anti-Dutch rebellion (1825–1830) led by Prince Diponegoro. In recognition of the city's, and the royal family's, role in the Indonesian struggle for independence, Yogyakarta and its territory were granted special status as a province to allow its sultan to occupy the position of governor, a position currently held by Sultan Hamengkubuwono X. The principality of Pakualaman (founded 1812) is also situated in the city. Yogyakarta is also home to one of Indonesia's premier tertiary educational institutions, Gadjah Mada University.

Anthony L Smith

YOSHIDA SHIGERU (1878–1967), prime minister of Japan. Yoshida Shugeru served as Japan's prime minister from May 1946 to May 1947, and again from October 1948 until December 1954. After that, he continued to exercise influence as an elder statesman through his many disciples, including prime ministers Ikeda Hayato and Sato Eisaku. As prime minister, Yoshida guided Japan through the turbulent early postwar years, sometimes working with—and sometimes against—Occupation authorities to preserve Japan's *amour-propre*. His biggest accomplishments were the peace settlement signed in San Francisco in September 1951, which restored Japan's sovereignty, and the U.S.-Japan security treaty, which formed the basis of Japan's postwar foreign policy. At the same time, Yoshida resisted strong calls by the United States to rearm, forming one of the three tenets of what has been called the "Yoshida Doctrine": focus on the economy, light rearmament, and alignment with the United States and the West.

Shigeru was born in Yokosuka near Tokyo and adopted by a wealthy friend of his father, taking the family name Yoshida. In 1906, at the age of thirty-four, he entered the Foreign Ministry, and in 1909, he married Yukiko, the daughter of a prominent diplomat, Makino Nobuaki, and granddaughter of the Meiji statesman Okubo Toshimichi. Yoshida served as ambassador to Italy and England in the 1930s and foreign minister in the Shidehara Kijuro cabinet (October 1945–May 1946) before becoming premier.

Robert D. Eldridge

Further Reading
Dower, John W. (1988) *Empire and Aftermath: Yoshida Shigeru and the Japan Experience, 1878–1954*. Cambridge, MA: Council on East Asia Studies, Harvard University.
Kosaka Masataka. (1968) *Saisho Yoshida Shigeru* (Prime Minister Yoshida Shigeru). Tokyo: Chuko Sosho.
Yoshida, Shigeru. (1961) *The Yoshida Memoirs: The Story of Japan in Crisis*. Westport, CT: Greenwood.

YOSHIDA SHOIN (1830–1859), Japanese nationalist. Yoshida Shoin was born Yoshida Norikaka in the castle town of Hagi in Choshu. He was adopted by his uncle. At the age of eighteen he began a series of long journeys for the purpose of learning about the country and studying coastal defenses, traveling as far as Kyushu, Edo, and Mito, often without the travel documents then required by the shogunal government. Through his travels and readings of *kokugaku* (national learning), he developed strongly pro-emperor beliefs, as expressed by the slogan *sonno joi* ("revere the emperor; expel the barbarians").

Convinced that Japan's defenses needed to be strengthened immediately to protect it from incursions by the West, and believing that to accomplish this he had to see how such defenses were built in the West, he attempted to stow away on board the U.S.S. Powhatan, flagship of Commodore Matthew Perry, in 1854. Unsuccessful, he found himself in prison for a short time before his punishment was reduced to house detention in Choshu. He eventually received special permission to accept students at his private school, the Shoka Sonjuku, where his dedication and passion greatly influenced his students, among whom were some who would become cabinet ministers of the Meiji government.

Constantly inciting his students to take direct action, he himself became involved in a plot to assassinate a high shogunal official, Manabe Akikatsu. The plot was uncovered and Shoin was executed, but his ideals lived on in his students, who helped to bring about the Meiji Restoration in 1868.

James M. Vardaman, Jr.

Further Reading
Earl, David Magarey. (1964) *Emperor and Nation in Japan: Political Thinkers of the Tokugawa Period.* Seattle: University of Washington Press.

Rubinger, Richard. (1982) *Private Academies of Tokugawa Japan.* Princeton, NJ: Princeton University Press.

YU KWAN SUN (1904–1920), Korean independence fighter. Born 29 March 1904 in Pyongch'on, a small farming village outside the city of Ch'onan, South Ch'ungch'ong Province, Yu was sent to study at Ewha Girls' School in Seoul at the age of twelve. At this time nationalist resentment against the Japanese occupation of Korea was rising, and in 1919 this would lead to widespread resistance. Yu took part in the most memorable uprising, the Samil-undong uprising, which occurred in Seoul on 1 March of that year.

With her school closed by the Japanese, Yu continued to rally Koreans in outlying areas to continue the resistance; because of her young age and fervor, she is called by many the Korean Joan of Arc. With fellow students, Yu organized a mass demonstration in her province for 1 April. The signal to begin the uprising was to be a bonfire lit on a mountain near Ch'onan. Yu lit the fire herself, but the subsequent demonstrations resulted in the death of her parents and her own imprisonment. She died in prison more than a year later, on 12 October 1920. She is among the few women who were independence leaders in Korea.

Thomas P. Dolan

Further Reading
Saccone, Richard. (1993) *Koreans to Remember.* Seoul: Hollym.

YUAN DYNASTY The Yuan dynasty (1272–1368; as rulers of all China 1279–1368) marked the first instance in which Central Asian invaders succeeded in conquering all of China. Mongolian tribes, reorganized into military units by the famed conqueror Genghis Khan (whose name is more accurately transliterated from the Mongolian as Chinggis Khan, 1162–1227), descended upon China in repeated campaigns from the early years of the thirteenth century until the conquest process ended with the collapse of the Southern Song dynasty (1127–1279) under Genghis Khan's grandson, Khubilai Khan (1215–1294). North China had been ruled by other invaders from the north (first Kitans, then Jurchens) from 916 to 1234, but the Mongols were the first outsiders to conquer and reunify all of China.

After Genghis Khan's death, his heirs carved out separate imperial domains (khanates) that, while connected by trade and diplomacy, evolved into independent geopolitical units. In addition to the Yuan dynasty in China, these units consisted of the Il-Khan dynasty in Persia, the Golden Horde in Russia, and the Chagatai khanate in Central Asia. The Yuan dynasty in China was directly ruled by a branch of Genghis Khan's descendants who were based in the Yuan capital city of Daidu (modern Beijing). As such, the Yuan dynasty was an independent polity that was governed quite differently from the other Mongolian-ruled polities in Eurasia.

The Mongols as Rulers of China

Rulers of China after the fall of the Yuan dynasty castigated the Mongols for their inattention to the welfare of the people and for their abuses of privilege. The Mongols in fact did rule China in a manner different from that of previous dynasties. As a pastoral nomadic people, they relied on their traditional emphasis on military values and hereditary transmission of office. Yet, the Mongols also adapted many preexisting Chinese institutions to facilitate their rule. The structure of the Yuan civilian bureaucracy was very much in the traditional Chinese mold, but the fact that Mongols and Western and Central Asians (Turks, Uighurs, Persians, and others) held the higher-level positions meant that many Chinese scholars, accustomed to government service as a mark of status, felt disenfranchised.

The Yuan rulers did not allow the traditional Chinese examination system, which had determined entry into the civilian bureaucracy in previous centuries, to function until 1315; even then it was a minor source of recruitment. The Mongolian emphasis on heredity and the primacy given to the military sphere over the civilian sphere made government service less accessible and even unpalatable for many Chinese.

Yet, the Chinese viewed the Yuan dynasty as a legitimate dynasty that had won the Mandate of Heaven and reunified the empire. Khubilai Khan was largely responsible for winning Chinese acceptance of Mongolian rule. In 1272, Khubilai gave the dynasty its Chinese name, Yuan, and employed several prominent Chinese scholars as advisers at his court in Daidu. It was Khubilai also who selected the site of modern-day Beijing in 1260 as the dynasty's capital, thereby moving the symbolic center of Mongolian rule from Mongolia into China proper.

Khubilai also employed Tibetan Buddhist monks and Central Asian Muslim financiers as his court advisers. A multiethnic, multilingual entourage gave the Yuan court a cosmopolitan aura. Yet, from the point of view of contemporary Chinese observers, the Tibetans at the Yuan court were seen as arrogantly interfering with the administration of justice and claiming privileged status for themselves; Muslim financial advisers were criticized for imposing too severe a tax burden on the Chinese people and were accused of usury and embezzlement. While such criticisms may have been exacerbated by the factions at the Yuan court, it is true that the Tibetans and Central Asians rarely displayed any philosophical interest in Confucianism and its values of frugality and loyal, selfless service to one's ruler. Tensions ran high among the different ethnic groups that served the Yuan court during Khubilai's reign and in later Yuan times.

Culture and Society in the Yuan

Blocked from government service and alienated from their Mongolian rulers, some Chinese literati turned to the arts as an outlet for their untapped energies and talents. Popular drama, a genre that had existed in China for at least two centuries prior to the Mongolian invasion, benefited from elite participation in the writing of new plays. At least 160 Yuan plays are extant. The Yuan era also produced many great Chinese painters, some of whom, like Zhao Mengfu (1254–1322), served the Yuan court in official capacities.

CHINA—HISTORICAL PERIODS

Xia dynasty (2100–1766 BCE)
Shang dynasty (1766–1045 BCE)
Zhou dynasty (1045–256 BCE)
    Western Zhou (1045–771 BCE)
    Eastern Zhou (770–221 BCE)
Spring and Autumn period (770–476 BCE)
Warring States period (475–221 BCE)
Qin dynasty (221–206 BCE)
Han dynasty (206 BCE–220 CE)
Three Kingdoms period (220–265 CE)
North and South dynasties (220–589 CE)
Sui dyansty (581–618 CE)
Tang dynasty (618–907 CE)
Five Dynasties period (907–960 CE)
Song dynasty (960–1279)
    Northern Song (960–1126)
    Southern Song (1127–1279)
Jurchen Jin dynasty (1125–1234)
Yuan dynasty (1279–1368)
Ming dynasty (1368–1644)
Qing dynasty (1644–1912)
Republican China (1912–1927)
People's Republic of China (1949–present)
Republic of China (1949–present)
Cultural Revolution (1966–1976)

While Confucianism as a philosophy and as a way of life was never directly threatened with suppression by the Mongolian rulers of China, competing ways of thought were encouraged in the Yuan period. Uighurs reintroduced Islam, Tibetans promoted Buddhism, and Central Asian monks revived Nestorian Christianity. The Mongol rulers practiced religious toleration in China as elsewhere throughout Eurasia; they exempted the clergy of all religions from taxation and from military conscription. As long as clerics did not foment or support anti-Mongolian sentiments, their churches, temples, and mosques were left untouched. In spite of the coexistence of a variety of religions in China in the thirteenth and fourteenth centuries, however, the Chinese elite remained bonded to their own Confucian tradition. The Chinese lack of interest in foreign cultures was testimony to the strength of Confucianism.

Trade, Transport, and the Economy

The Mongols, like other pastoral nomadic peoples of Eurasia, saw trade with neighboring sedentary peoples as an acceptable method to obtain needed goods to supplement the products of their own economy.

MONEY OF THE YUAN DYNASTY

Marco Polo, the Venetian merchant who spent twenty years in China at the court of Khubilai Khan, described in great detail the manufacture and distribution of paper money, which in the thirteenth century was unknown in Europe.

> It is in this city of Khan-balik [Daidu] that the Great Khan has his mint; and it is so organized that you might well say that he has mastered the art of alchemy. I will demonstrate this to you here and now. You must know that he has money made for him by the following process, out of the bark of trees—to be precise, from mulberry trees (the same whose leaves furnish food for silkworms). The fine bast between the bark and the wood of the tree is stripped off. Then it is crumbled and pounded and flattened out with the aid of glue into sheets like sheets of cotton paper, which are all black. When made, they are cut up into rectangles of various sizes, longer than they are broad. . . . And all these papers are sealed with the seal of the Great Khan. The procedure of issue is as formal and as authoritative as if they were made of pure gold or silver.

> *Source:* Ronald Latham, trans. (1980) *The Travels of Marco Polo.*
> New York: Penguin, 147.

Trade and raids coexisted in the frontier history of China and Central Asia. Genghis Khan had employed Muslim merchants in long-distance trading ventures as early as 1218 in western Central Asia. By the generation of his grandson, Khubilai, the Yuan imperial family was experienced in world trade. Investing silver in Central Asian Muslim merchant companies that financed trade caravans to distant lands and loaned funds within China at usurious rates, Khubilai and his successors reaped enormous profits. Maritime trade also flourished in Yuan times, and the government treasury was enriched by trade taxes.

Within China itself, trade and communications were facilitated by the more than 1,400 government postal stations that allowed authorized officials and merchants to cover great distances in a short span of time with fresh mounts supplied at each station. With the use of some 3 million conscripted laborers and an enormous expenditure of government funds, Khubilai Khan extended the Grand Canal so that grain from the Chang (Yangtze) River region could be shipped north to the Yuan capital at Daidu. Both land and inland waterway transport routes were improved in Yuan times.

Paper currency had been in circulation to varying degrees in China before the Yuan dynasty, but during Khubilai Khan's reign it was used more widely than ever before. Taxes were paid in paper money, and merchants saw the advantages of the new currency. The Yuan court, however, never completely resisted the temptation to print more money when revenue demands generated by military campaigns of expansion and by fiscal mismanagement arose. Inflation was ultimately one of the economic factors contributing to the collapse of the dynasty in 1368.

Decline of the Yuan

During Khubilai's reign, the Mongols continued their campaigns outward from China, successfully subjugating Korea. They met defeat, however, in their naval attacks upon Japan in 1274 and 1281. Mongolian military expeditions into Southeast Asia in the 1270s and 1280s also met stiff resistance. After Khubilai's reign, the Yuan rulers abandoned further expansionist campaigns. The dynasty fell into decline during the course of the thirteenth century, as the once powerful military could not suppress widespread popular revolts in the 1350s–1360s. The last decades of the Yuan dynasty were marred by major floods, droughts, and epidemics, creating a confluence of natural disasters that would have undermined any dynasty, whether of foreign or Chinese origins. The Mongols fled their capital city of Daidu and returned to Mongolia in 1368, escaping before the arrival of the armies of Zhu Yuanzhang, a rebel leader who founded the Ming Dynasty (1368–1644).

Elizabeth Endicott

Further Reading
Franke, Herbert, and Denis Twitchett, eds. (1994) *The Cambridge History of China.* Vol 6: *Alien Regimes and Border States.* Cambridge, U.K.: Cambridge University Press.
Langlois, John D., Jr., ed. (1981) *China under Mongol Rule.* Princeton, NJ: Princeton University Press.
Latham, Ronald, trans. (1980) *The Travels of Marco Polo.* New York: Penguin.
Rossabi, Morris. (1988) *Khubilai Khan: His Life and Times.* Berkeley and Los Angeles, CA: University of California Press.

YUAN SHIKAI (1859–1916), first president of the Chinese Republic. Yuan Shikai was born in Xiangcheng, Henan Province, in 1859 and became an adopted son. In 1880 he joined the Qing army and was Chinese commissioner of commerce in Korea from 1885 to 1894. In 1899 he was appointed governor of Shandong Province, where he suppressed the rising tide of Boxers. He was made governor-general of Zhili Province and the high commissioner for the Northern Ocean (Beiyang Dachen) in 1901, in which position he was in charge of foreign and military affairs in North China. From 1901 to 1908 he directed various reform programs, including the establishment of a modern army, the creation of military schools, the organization of the police system, and the inauguration of modern industry.

With the outbreak of the revolution in 1911, Yuan was placed in charge of the imperial troops and negotiations with the revolutionaries. He used his immense military power to promote his own interests by clever manipulation of the negotiations. As a result, he was designated as the president of the first Chinese Republic by both the Qing court and the provisional government of the Chinese Republic in February 1912. He assumed the formal presidency in 1913, and in the next two years he outlawed the Nationalist Party, dissolved parliament, and assumed dictatorial control. Finally, in late 1915, he began preparations to assume the title of emperor. He announced that his imperial title, Hong Xian, would be used beginning 1 January 1916. Rebellion in the southern provinces against this monarchic scheme, however, forced him to revoke plans for his enthronement. He died on 6 June 1916.

Chen Shiwei

Further Reading
Mackinnon, Stephen. (1980) *Power and Politics in Late Imperial China: Yuan Shi-kai in Beijing and Tianjin, 1901–1908.* Berkeley and Los Angeles: University of California Press.
Young, Ernest. (1977) *The Presidency of Yuan Shih-k'ai: Liberalism and Dictatorship in Early Republican China.* Ann Arbor: University of Michigan Press.

YUE Speakers of Yue, or Cantonese, include Chinese speakers in Guangdong and Guangxi provinces and in many overseas Chinese communities. Cantonese is the most common form of the Chinese language or dialect heard in Chinatowns around the world. Hong Kong continued to use the dialect as a medium of instruction during British colonial rule. Yue is very different from Mandarin (*putonghua*; "standard" Chinese). Yuehua, or "Yue speech," is a more formal name given by linguists to the Cantonese language, particularly when they are referring to all of the many related subdialects and not just to the standard Cantonese that is centered on the cities of Guangzhou and Hong Kong. The speakers of Yuehua are among the most populous of Chinese people.

Guangdong and Guangxi are often referred to as the *liang guang*, or the "two Guangs"; as *liang yue*, the "two yue"; or as *Lingnan*, which means "south of the mountain range." Strictly speaking, the term Cantonese refers only to one subdialect of Yuehua, the vernacular spoken in the city of Guangzhou (Canton). The forms of Yuehua are actually diverse. Even in Guangzhou and the surrounding area, there are sharp subdialectical differences. Seven dialect areas have been identified in Guangdong, most of them in the Zhu (Pearl) River Delta and western Guangdong—Guangfu (the speech of Canton), Yongxun, Gaoyang, Siyi (four districts), Goulou, Wuhua, and Qinlan. These are spoken around specific geographical areas.

Origins of Yue

Sinitic people moved across the Nan Ling mountains, which run east to west, and into the Lingnan, or what subsequently became the provinces of Guangdong and Guangxi. A variety of indigenous people who were already living in the Lingnan were incorporated into new Sinicized cultural groups. The various Yue-speaking people originated in this way. The basic ideograph *yue* means "to exceed, go beyond." It has been extended to mean "frontier," or "beyond the borderland."

Being separated from the rest of China by the high Nan Ling range, the people in Guangdong and Guangxi have usually considered themselves different from other Sinitic peoples. The Yue speakers are more likely to identify themselves as *Tong yen* (Yue) or *Tang ren* (Mandarin), that is, "Tang persons," rather than as *Han ren*, or "Han persons," which is how most Chinese identify themselves. This is mainly because it was during the Tang period (618–907 CE) that the homeland of the Yue people became part of the Chinese cultural realm. In addition, the Cantonese have traditionally spoken of classical written Chinese as *Tong man* or *Tang wen*, that is, the Tang language. Yue is closer to ancient Chinese than Mandarin is.

Characteristics of Yue

The standard Cantonese that is spoken in Guangzhou and Hong Kong demonstrates the phonetic features that set Yuehua apart from other Sinitic sublanguages. Among these phonetic features are the following: First, Yuehua retains the ancient final consonants that have been lost in the north. These include -*m*, -*p*, -*t* and -*k*. Second, the retroflex consonants that characterize Northern Mandarin are absent. Third, Yuehua has syllables that begin in *ng*-. Fourth, there are nine tones, five more than the four of standard Chinese. Fifth, Yuehua lacks any phonetic distinction between *s*- and *sh*-, *ts*- and *ch*-, and *ts'*- and *ch'*-. Finally, there is a separate series of long and short vowels.

Yue and Mandarin also differ in terms of written Chinese characters. This is in part because new characters have been added to stand for the words that are apparently exclusive to Yuehua. In some instances, characters that are no longer in use among Mandarin speakers have been used to transcribe words in Yue. This means that there can be written texts that are uniquely Cantonese, and that would be difficult for someone from northern China to read without special study of Cantonese.

Yue also differs from standard Chinese in grammar. One such difference is the ordering of the indirect and direct object in a sentence. In Mandarin the ordering is similar to that in English: the sentence "give me something" would have the same sequencing in both Mandarin and English. For standard Cantonese, the ordering is more like "give something me."

It is generally assumed that the region in which Yue is spoken has been heavily influenced by the phonetic principles of the Tai peoples who lived there before the coming of Sinitic peoples. This influence is apparent in Yue's word order and grammar. In Tai-related languages, as in Yue, the adjective follows the noun. In English and standard Chinese, by contrast, the adjective precedes the noun. This is why many two-character terms in Yuehua appear to readers of standard Chinese to have been put together in backward sequence. The pattern is evident in subdialects of Yuehua, particularly in the southwest of Guangzhou.

Additional vowel sounds and the final consonants in standard Cantonese mean that Yuehua has practically twice the number of syllables that standard Chinese has. Because the language is so flexible, Yue has been able to absorb many foreign words, including English ones. Examples include "salad" (*sah-lud*), "bus" (*baa-see*), and "taxi" (*dik-see*).

The Yue sublanguage, unlike many of the other southern sublanguages, has little tone sandhi (modification due to context). It has none of the unaccented, toneless "neutral" syllables that form parts of compounds and other connected utterances in standard Mandarin. There is a pattern in Yue, however, in which a change in a word's tone can be used to modify it to mean a related term. One example is the word for tobacco, which is a tonal variant of the word for "smoke."

The number of tones in Yue varies from form to form. In Zhongshan County, which is located between Guangzhou and Sze-yap, there are only six tones, whereas in other counties, there are ten or even more tones. The Yue vernacular has also not borrowed as much from northern Chinese as, for instance, the Wu or Min dialects.

Yue Speakers

The best-known and most populous of the speakers of Yuehua are the Cantonese of Guangzhou and Hong Kong. The language form that these people speak is composed of many subdialects, known to linguists as the Yuehai dialect of Yuehua. The most influential subdialect is standard Cantonese. Linguistically, the Yuehai subregion is rather fragmented, but the core is the so-called Three Districts (Sam-yap in the vernacular). This would include the area around the city of Guangzhou. The districts are Namhoi, Punyu, and Shuntak.

Other well-known speakers of Yuehua are people of the Four Districts, or Sze-yap (Siyi in Mandarin). The Sze-yap dialect has many features that mark it from standard Cantonese so that speakers of the two would find it difficult to understand each other. Both the tonal pattern and vowels are different.

Guinan is the name usually given to the Yue subdialects of the interior of Guangxi. Among the Guinan subdialects are Wuzhou, Guixian, Cangwu, Guiping, and Tengxian. Many of these Guinan vernaculars include a sound shift that leads to pronunciations that are not at all characteristic of other Yuehua subdialects. There are initial consonants like *b*- and *d*- that might not be found in Yuehua.

The general impression among the Chinese is that, with the exception of speakers of standard Cantonese, Yue speakers haven't played much of a role in the cultural development of China. Consequently, the Guangxi part of the Yue region has been treated more as a cultural backwater even by other Yue speakers, especially Cantonese speakers or those living around Guangzhou.

Ooi Giok Ling

See also: **Guangdong; Guangxi; Hong Kong; Mandarin; Tang Dynasty**

Further Reading
Moser, Leo J. (1985) *The Chinese Mosaic: The People and Provinces of China.* Boulder, CO: Westview.
Pan, Lynn. ed. (1998) *The Encyclopaedia of the Chinese Overseas.* Singapore: Chinese Heritage Centre.
Whitaker, Donald P., Rinn-Suip Shinn, Helen A. Barth, Judith M. Heimann, John E. MacDonald, Kenneth W. Martindale, and John O. Weaver. (1972) *Area Handbook for the People's Republic of China.* Washington, DC: U.S. Government Printing Office.

YULGOK. See **Yi I.**

YUN SUN-DO (1587–1671), Korean poet.

Yun Sun-do, another in the long list of Korean poet-ministers who had turbulent political careers, passed the civil-service examination at the age of twenty-six, but did not serve under the tyrant Kwanghaegun (1556–1622). In 1616 he presented a memorial to the king remonstrating against corruption in the court, for which he was exiled to Kyonwon, where he is said to have written his earliest poems. He was recalled in 1623 when Injo (1595–1649) succeeded to the throne. In 1628, he was appointed personal tutor to the two young princes, Pongnim and Inp'yong. In trouble again during the Manchu invasion of 1636 for failing to attend on the king, he was sent into exile to Yongdok but soon released. Over the next number of years his memorials to the king kept him at the center of controversy. The final embroilment occurred over the length of the mourning period that was judged appropriate for the mother of King Hyojong (1619–1659). Again Yun Sun-do's opponents carried the day, and the poet was banished to Samsu, where he remained until his release in 1668.

Yun Sun-do is regarded by most Korean commentators as the master of the *shijo*, Korea's traditional short lyric poetry genre. His most celebrated work, *The Fisherman's Calendar*, is a cycle of forty poems describing the four seasons in one of the poet's favorite retreats. The fisherman is a time-honored symbol of the wise man who lives simply in nature. Yun Sun-do was inspired to write his poem when reworking the earlier "Fisherman's Song" by Yi Hyon-bo, which in turn was a reworking into nine verses of an anonymous poem from Koryo. Yun Sun-do was also a considerable poet in Chinese. He died in 1671.

Kevin O'Rourke

Further Reading
Lee, Peter, trans. and ed. (1991) *Pine River and Lone Peak.* Honolulu: University of Hawaii Press.
O'Rourke, Kevin. (2001) *The Fisherman's Calendar.* Seoul: Eastward.
O'Rourke, Kevin, trans. and ed. (1993) *Tilting the Jar, Spilling the Moon.* Dublin, Ireland: Daedalus.

YUNNAN

(2002 est. pop. 43.2 million). The southeastern China province of Yunnan (Yün-nan, "the cloudy south") borders in the west on Burma and Tibet, in the north on Sichuan, in the east on Guizhou and Guangxi, and in the south on Vietnam and Laos. The province covers an area of 394,000 square kilometers of mountains and plateaus. The northwestern part features the Hengduan mountain range, traversed by several big rivers and with peaks reaching over 4,000 meters. The eastern and southeastern part forms a lower plateau. The diversity of Yunnan's topography means there are three climate zones: temperate in the mountains and subtropic and tropic to the south. The rainy season between May and October accounts for about 80 percent of the annual precipitation, which averages over 1,000 millimeters.

Yunnan has a population of 43.2 million, of which about a third belong to twenty-two officially recognized minority peoples, the Yi being the largest. The Han Chinese, who constitute about 70 percent of the population, are mainly concentrated on the eastern plateau, which is also where the capital, Kunming (2002 est. pop. 871,000 million), is situated.

Yunnan was loosely incorporated into the Chinese empire during the Han dynasty (206 BCE–220 CE). It was the center of the independent Nanzhao and Dali kingdoms from the eighth to the thirteenth centuries and was reincorporated as a Chinese frontier area under the Yuan dynasty (1279–1368). During the Ming dynasty (1368–1644), the Chinese government encouraged Chinese immigration into Yunnan, and during the Qing dynasty (1644–1912), the province was repeatedly the seat of rebellion against the Manchu government. In the nineteenth century, the British and French colonial powers in Southeast Asia extended their activities into Yunnan, and the French built a railway connecting Kunming with Vietnam. During the Japanese occupation of eastern China, the Chinese Nationalist party (Guomindang) moved the government and various industries to the western provinces of Sichuan and Yunnan, and Yunnan became a stronghold against further Japanese advance.

Kunming developed into an important industrial center in the southwest, a position it still retains. Yunnan has one of the largest reserves of tin in the world, and the principal industries are tin and copper mining. Heavy industry such as iron and steel works are concentrated in the area around Kunming. The province is an important manufacturer of textiles, chemicals, processed foods, and light-industry products, and a major producer of tea, cigarettes, and sugar.

Bent Nielsen

Further Reading

Arvidsson, Sara-Stina. (2001) *Ethnicity and Economic Development in Yunnan.* Uppsala, Sweden: Uppsala University Department of Economic History.

Hall, J. C. S. (1976) *The Yunnan Provincial Faction, 1927–1937.* Canberra: Australian National University Department of Far Eastern History.

Hansen, Mette Halskov. (1999) *Lessons in Being Chinese: Minority Education and Ethnic Identity in Southwest China.* Seattle: University of Washington Press.

Sutton, Donald S. (1980) *Provincial Militarism and the Chinese Republic: The Yunnan Army, 1905–25.* Ann Arbor: University of Michigan Press.

Wang, Jianping. (1996) *Concord and Conflict: The Hui Communities of Yunnan Society in a Historical Perspective.* Lund, Sweden: Lund Studies in African and Asian Religions.

YURT The yurt is the traditional dwelling of nomadic Mongols and Turkic peoples in Siberia, Mongolia, China, and Central Asia. Although the yurt is no longer as common as in the past, there are still regions in Kazakhstan, western China, and Mongolia where the yurt is the primary form of dwelling, especially in summer months. In Buryiat Mongolian the word for yurt is *ger* (also *gher*), meaning "home" or "dwelling." Yurt, the more common term, is from the Russian *yurta*.

Like dwellings used by nomadic peoples around the world, the yurt is circular in shape and easy to assemble and transport. The major components are a collapsible, wooden latticework framework for the walls, wooden roof poles, a wooden tension smoke ring, large

pieces of felt (usually from sheep fleece) for the siding, tension ropes, a wooden door, and a white cloth covering. A more permanent wooden *ger* is used by more sedentary peoples in Mongolia and Siberia. These are eight-sided rather than circular. The entire yurt can be carried on one or two pack animals, a cart, or a truck.

In accord with Mongol and Turkic conceptions of the universe, the yurt is always set up with the opening facing south. The interior is divided into men's and women's areas, with a fire pit in the center over which a three-legged cooking frame is set. The north or northwest side is reserved for the family shrine, and all sacred objects are placed there. The floor is covered with felt carpets and bedding. The space opposite the door is reserved for important visitors or the male head of the household.

Yurts have become very popular in the West, and numerous companies provide modified yurt kits for home or vacation use. Why they are popular is not clear, although their association with a nomadic lifestyle and shamanism and the association of the circular shape with "symbolic circles" may be factors.

David Levinson

Further Reading

Vostrov, Veniamin V., and I. V. Zakharova. (1989) *Kazakhskoe Narodnoe Zhilishche* (Dwelling of the Kazakh People). Alma-Alta: Nauka Kazakhskoi SSR.

YUSHIN South Korean President Park Chung Hee (1917–1979) set forth the idea of *yushin* ("revitalization" or "reform") in October 1972 when he suspended the national constitution and dissolved the national assembly. *Yushin*, as an idea, policy, and set of actions, included the inculcation of values supporting the new authoritarian regime as well as institutions designed to repress political opposition and the labor movement.

Promulgation of the *Yushin* Constitution

Park, who came to power through a military coup in 1961, enjoyed relatively high popular approval as a result of his active role in driving South Korea's rapid economic development during the 1960s. This popularity, however, made him more politically ambitious, and he attempted to revise the constitution in 1969 to extend his presidency from two to three four-year terms. After having faced a strong challenge from the prominent opposition candidate Kim Dae Jung (b. 1925) in the 1971 election, Park drafted the Yushin Constitution of the Fourth Republic in 1972, explaining his actions as a national effort to achieve peaceful unification of the divided Korea. The Yushin Constitution was promulgated in December 1972, whereupon the Fourth Republic was inaugurated.

Through economic development, Park attempted to rationalize his past performance and his plans for the future. When he introduced *yushin*, Park restructured the industrial sectors to promote heavy and chemical industry. In this respect, the importance placed on economic development was a reflection of Park's strong commitment to strengthening industrialization and expanding national prosperity.

Consolidation of Power

To realize the values of *yushin*, Park designed formal and informal authority structures that guaranteed enormous power for the officeholders of his administration.

First, the authority structure provided Park with unprecedented power. The president as the top leader of the executive dominated not only the administration but also the legislature and the courts. According to the Yushin Constitution, the president had the right to dissolve the legislature, that is, the National Assembly, and to declare a presidential emergency measure (PEM) on internal and foreign affairs and national defense, economy, finance, and judicial affairs. Moreover, the president was not elected by the National Assembly nor the constituency but rather by a nonpartisan rubber-stamp organization, the National Conference for Unification (NCU), without any limitation in the number of terms.

Second, the role of political parties was severely undermined, and even the ruling party was not an exception. Neither the ruling party nor the opposition party had any chance of obtaining a majority in the National Assembly. This was so because the Yujonghoe political group, one-third of the National Assembly members, was elected by the NCU based on the recommendation of the president. Furthermore, the political parties lost one of their major functions, that is, nomination of presidential candidates, after the NCU was established. However, it is noteworthy that the authority structure ensured that the ruling camp, composed of the Democratic Republican Party and Yujonghoe, was always able to form an absolute majority in the legislature.

Third, civil rights were extremely vulnerable to infringement under the *yushin* regime. The PEM suspended the freedoms of speech, press, assembly, and association, and the labor law substantially restricted labor rights. These legal arrangements were effectively used to repress the opposition and labor forces. The notorious PEM No. 9, promulgated in May 1975, forbade civil activities such as denial of the Yushin Constitution or petition for its repeal; criticism of the PEM itself; and broadcasting of news about instances of violation of the PEM. The labor law, revised in 1973 and 1974, decentralized the union structure, weakening the role of seventeen overarching industrial sector unions. The law also provided for a cushion organization, the Labor-Management Council, to minimize the impact of erupting demands for better working conditions and human rights, protecting enterprises that pursued a goal corresponding to one of the *yushin* regime's values—economic development.

Opposition to *Yushin*

Opposition by students and churches undermined the legitimacy of the *yushin* regime. From the beginning, they conducted a campaign for revision of the Yushin Constitution and denounced the values of national security and economic development. In particular, they argued that restoration of civil rights and democracy were a precondition for national security on the ground that only democratic citizens voluntarily fight for their nation. Furthermore, they encouraged and supported labor's politicization, which meant not only the expansion of the magnitude of the opposition but also a serious threat to economic development. Eventually, the alliance among student, church, and labor groups and opposition parties to confront the harsh repression under the *yushin* regime resulted in violent clashes, such as the Y. H. Incident and the Pusan-Masan Uprising in 1979, which were followed by an internal conflict in the ruling bloc and the assassination of Park on 26 October 1979.

Sung Chull Kim

Further Reading

Oberdofer, Don. (1997) *The Two Koreas: A Contemporary History*. Indianapolis, IN: Basic Books.

Sohn, Hak-Kyu. (1989) *Authoritarianism and Opposition in South Korea*. New York: Routledge.

ZAGROS MOUNTAINS The Zagros Mountains, in western Iran, lie along and across the border between Iraq and Iran. Consisting of a series of ridges running parallel to the Persian Gulf and northward along portions of Iran's borders with Turkey and Iraq, the range is characterized by sheer, high cliffs and steep-walled canyons. Several of the highest peaks rise over 4,000 meters, with the highest, Zardeh Kuh, reaching 4,548 meters.

The range's rugged topography and high altitudes have made it virtually impassable, especially during winter months when heavy snows fall across the region. Throughout history, the Zagros have thus buffered the neighboring Iranian Plateau from invasions from the west. Iran's ethnic minority group, the Kurds, also found refuge in the Zagros, which form an important part of the larger but politically unrecognized Kurdistan region that occupies part of northern Iran, Iraq, and Turkey.

Archeologists estimate that the Zagros Mountains also served as one of the world's earliest cultural hearths for both plant and livestock domestication some 10,000 years ago. Today, sheep, goat, and cattle herding remain important industries, with herders seasonally moving their animals between high-altitude summer and lower-altitude winter pastures. Millennia of intensive human use, however, have led to the destruction of many of the region's native oak and juniper forests.

Ann DeVoll Brucklacher

Further Reading
Fisher, W. B., ed. (1968) *The Cambridge History of Iran.* Vol 1. Cambridge, U.K.: Cambridge University Press.

ZAHIR SHAH (b. 1914), king of Afghanistan. Zahir Shah was the king of Afghanistan from 1933 to 1973. Born in Kabul, he received his initial schooling at the Habibia and Istiqlal schools. Later, Zahir studied in France when his father, Mohammad Nadir Khan, moved there as a result of political pressure following a falling-out with King Amanullah. Zahir's father returned to Afghanistan soon after Amanullah was deposed and took the throne on 15 October 1929, establishing the Musahiban dynasty. One year later, Zahir returned to Kabul and enrolled in the Infantry Officers School. At a young age, Zahir held several government positions, such as assistant minister of war and minister of education, before assuming the throne on 8 November 1933 following his father's assassination. Although Zahir was king, two uncles and a cousin actually wielded power as prime ministers during much of his reign. When his cousin resigned after a disagreement, Zahir in 1963 appointed, for the first time, a non–family member as prime minister. For the next ten years, Zahir instituted an experimental program called *Demokrasy-I Now* (New Democracy), which allowed free elections and promoted democratic ideals such as a free press and freedom of association in addition to a constitution. Zahir was overthrown in 1973 by his cousin, Daud Khan, and witnessed Afghanistan's shift to communism, a Soviet invasion, and the Afghan civil war. He is currently in exile in Italy. Although some support his return to power, Zahir Shah has made no major overtures in that direction.

Houman A. Sadri

Further Reading
Adamec, Ludwig W. (1997) *Historical Dictionary of Afghanistan.* 2d ed. Lanham, MD: Scarecrow.

Edwards, David B. (1996) *Heroes of the Age: Moral Fault Lines on the Afghan Frontier.* Berkeley and Los Angeles: University of California Press.

ZAMBALES MOUNTAINS

The Zambales Mountains in the Philippines stretch from the northern part of Zambales Province to the northern edge of Bataan Province. This range comprises nearly the whole province of Zambales. There are eight named mountains in the range. Its highest peak is High Peak (2,037 meters). It also includes Mount Pinatubo, which erupted in 1991.

The mountains are sparsely populated, given their rugged topography, but are home to the Negritos or Aetas, an indigenous people known for their Negroid features. They live primarily by hunting and foraging. It is rich in natural and mineral resources, particularly bauxite deposits. The Zambales Mountains were formed by the shift of tectonic plates, which pushed the land upward during prehistoric times.

Aaron Ronquillo

Further Reading
Action Asia. (1999) *Adventure and Travel Guide to the Philippines.* Hong Kong: Action Asia.

Department of Tourism. (1994) *The Philippines: Spirit of Place.* Manila, Philippines: Department of Tourism.

Lancion, Conrado, Jr. (1995) *Fast Facts about Philippine Provinces.* Manila, Philippines: Tahanan.

Parkes, Carl. (1999) *Philippines Handbook.* Emeryville, CA: Moon Travel.

ZAMBOANGA

(2000 pop. 603,000). Located at the tip of the Zamboanga Peninsula in the Mindanao Island group in the Philippines, the City of Zamboanga is a chartered city independent of the province of Zamboanga del Sur in terms of funding, administration, and so on. The early Malay settlers known as Subanons ("people of the river") named the place Jambangan or Tambangan ("land of flowers"), and the city is still known for its many species of flowers, especially orchids. The Samal and Badjao ethnic groups who came to the city in their *vinta*s or native boats called it Samboangan, referring to the wood poles they used to dock their boats.

The Spanish established a small garrison on the site in 1596, but they failed to hold it in the face of repeated attacks by the Moros, various Muslim ethnic groups of Malay descent who had dominated the area from the 1400s. In 1636, the Spanish reestablished themselves in what is now known as Fort Pilar, which remained the center of Spanish rule in the southern Philippines for three hundred years. A testimony to this long Spanish presence is the use of Chavacano, the chief local dialect, which is based on Spanish.

When the Americans came in 1898, the city became the capital of Moro province, which encompassed all of Mindanao and Sulu Islands. Zamboanga City attained its cityhood status on 12 October 1936 under Commonwealth Act 9 and was formally inaugurated as the City of Zamboanga on 26 February 1937. The city became a headquarters for the Japanese during World War II but was retaken by U.S. troops in March 1945.

Today the city is a trade center and port for the southern Philippine products of copra, hemp, timber, and fish. It is also a center for Moro brass and bronze ware and a collection point for the many varieties of shells found locally. In terms of religious background, the population of Zamboanga City is 75 percent Christian and 25 percent Muslim. It is considered a Christian enclave in the heart of the Muslim region of the Philippines.

Aaron Ronquillo

Further Reading
Action Asia. (1999) *Adventure and Travel Guide to the Philippines.* Hong Kong: Action Asia.

Curaming, Lilian M., and Leonardo N. Mercado, eds. (1999) *100 Years of Filipino Muslim-Christian Relations.* Zamboanga City, Philippines: Silsilah.

Department of Tourism, the Philippines. (1994) *Spirit of Place.* Manila, Philippines: Department of Tourism.

Höbel, Robert. (1981) *The Philippines.* Hong Kong: Robert Rovena.

Lancion, Conrado, Jr. (1995) *Fast Facts about Philippine Provinces.* Manila, Philippines: Tahanan.

Mayuga, Sylvia, et. al. (1988) *Philippines.* Hong Kong: APA Publication.

ZEBU

Zebu, or brahminy cattle (*Bos indicus*; sometimes called humped oxen or Brahman), are a species of domesticated livestock native to India. According to some, they are the same species as common cattle (*Bos taurus*), but others think that the two are separate species. Zebu are usually white or gray, with a large hump over the shoulders, a deep undulating dewlap, and hanging ears. They do not bellow but give a short grunt.

Zebu are thought to have evolved from the wild ox of Java and Borneo and to have been domesticated in South Asia as early as the ninth millennium BCE. They were depicted on seals of the Indus Valley civilization (2700–1500 BCE). Today, zebu are the preeminent draft animals in Indian farming (though camels are used in some areas), and along with water buffalo they are used as beasts of burden in Africa as well. Some breeds of *Bos indicus* were selected for their milk-producing ability and serve as dairy animals in India. Their cooked flesh is abhorred by Hindus and Buddhists alike, but their leather forms the basis of a major industry in South Asia.

In some Hindu sects, white zebu are "sacred cows," the most sacred of all animals, because they are associated iconographically with the god Siva. Since the Kushan era (78–200 CE), they have been known as Nandi, the sacred mount or vehicle of Siva, and Siva temples have a figure of a white zebu facing the entrance to the shrine. In sacred cities like Varanasi (Benares), some zebu bulls are branded with Siva's insignia as a sign that they belong to the god, and are permitted to roam the streets. For this reason, the species has come to be known as "Brahman" outside India.

Zebu are resistant to extreme heat and to many of the insects that attack other cattle species, and thus are suited for the hot climates of their ancestral home areas. For this reason, cattle breeders in the southern United States and Latin America have imported them since the mid-nineteenth century to breed with native beef cattle and have produced hardy crosses such as the Santa Gertrudis (Brahman and Shorthorn), Charbray (Brahman and Charolais), and Brangus (Brahman and Angus).

Paul Hockings

Further Reading
Prater, Stanley H. (1971) "Origin of Domestic Breeds." In *The Book of Indian Animals.* 3d ed. Bombay (Mumbai), India: Bombay Natural History Society, 240–241.

ZENG GUOFAN

ZENG GUOFAN (1811–1872), Confucian scholar and official. A leading Confucian scholar and high official in the late Qing dynasty (1644–1912), Zeng Guofan was born into a peasant family in Hunan Province. Zeng received his degree and served in various positions in the central government. Typical of the scholar-official ideal, he preferred to support a foreign dynasty—the Qing—who respected Chinese norms than support an indigenous rebellion that threatened the social and political order in which he believed. When the Taiping Rebellion (1851–1864) threatened the Qing dynasty, he accepted an appointment to raise an army first to regain control over Hunan and later to suppress the rebellion. He sponsored various projects of China's Self-Strengthening Movement (an effort by the Qing dynasty to restore power to resist Western encroachments, especially after the Second Opium War) and tried to increase China's military and economic power by learning from Western nations.

Zeng was very successful. He demanded that his troops conduct themselves according to proper Confucian principles. Zeng recruited members of the local scholar-gentry class as officers who were loyal to him and then recruited troops from Hunan. They embodied such Confucian ideals as respect for superiors, concern for their fellow Chinese, and moral behavior. Zeng's very success helped pave the way for a devolution of power from the Qing government in Beijing and began the rise of regional authorities, leading, ultimately, to the period of warlordism in the 1920s and 1930s. He died in 1872.

Charles Dobbs

Further Reading
Chen, Gideon. (1968) *The Pioneer Promoters of Modern Industrial Technique in China: Three Studies.* New York: Paragon.
Hail, William J. (1964) *Tseng Kuo-fan and the Taiping Rebellion.* New York: Paragon.

ZERAFSHAN RIVER

ZERAFSHAN RIVER With a length of 877 kilometers and a drainage basin of 17,100 square kilometers, the Zerafshan, or "Golden," River is one of the most important of Central Asia, providing water for irrigation to some of the region's most famous cities, among them Bukhara and Samarqand. Known as the Matcha in its upper reaches, the Zerafshan has its source in the Zerafshan Glacier at an altitude of 2,800 meters in Tajikistan's Koksu range of mountains. For its first 300 kilometers, the river flows through a narrow valley that opens out near the city of Penjikent. Below this point the river has no tributaries. Near Samarqand the river divides into two main branches known as the Akdarya (White River) to the north and the Karadarya (Black River) to the south. As it approaches the Bukhara oasis the river becomes known as the Karakul Dar'ya.

The river's flow is entirely used for irrigation, particularly of cotton, which has been grown in the region since ancient times. As a result, it dries before reaching the Amu Dar'ya, which in recent times it has attained only in 1874 and 1921. Its lower reaches are, however, fed by the Amu-Bukhara Canal, one of several major irrigation works that also include the Kattakurgan Canal. More than three-quarters of the river's flow occurs between May and September, peaking in July with a rate of 250–690 cubic meters per second. Average flow is 162 cubic meters per second, and the lowest rate is 28–60 cubic meters per second, occurring in March.

Will Myer

ZHANG YIMOU

ZHANG YIMOU (b. 1951), Chinese film director. Zhang Yimou is currently China's best-known film director. Born in Xi'an, Sichuan Province, he began his film career in the early 1980s as a cinematographer. A leader among China's "Fifth-Generation" of film directors, he is credited with giving modern Chinese cinema an international profile. Since winning the Golden Bear Award (Best Picture) at the 1988 Berlin Film Festival for his debut film, *Red Sorghum* (1987), Zhang has garnered many awards at prominent international film festivals, including those at Venice and Cannes, while also achieving commercial success across the globe.

His film career can be divided thematically into two periods. In such early films as *Red Sorghum*, *Ju Dou* (1990), and *Raise the Red Lantern* (1991), his work takes on the quality of the historical epic. In *The Story of Qiu Ju* (1992), *To Live* (1994), *Keep Cool* (1997), *Not One Less* (1998), and *The Road Home* (1999), he shifts his cinematic focus to the realistic depiction of modern Chinese life. Throughout his career, Zhang has been troubled by censorship in China. Outside China, his films, ironically, have often been criticized as contributing to the Chinese government's overseas public relations activities.

Doobo Shim

Further Reading

Chow, Rey. (1995) *Primitive Passions: Visuality, Sexuality, Ethnography, and Contemporary Chinese Cinema.* New York: Columbia University Press.

Tam Kwok-kan and Wimal Dissanayake. (1998) *New Chinese Cinema.* New York: Oxford University Press.

ZHANG ZHIDONG (1837–1909), Chinese Confucian scholar-official. Zhang Zhidong (Chang Chih-tung), born in Nanpi, Zhili Province, was prominently associated with the "self-strengthening movement" in China. His distinguished career as an official in the Qing dynasty (1644–1912) (Manchu) imperial administration began in 1863 when he passed the highest-level civil service examination and was awarded the prestigious *jinshi*, or "presented scholar," degree. From 1867 to 1877 he held a variety of supervisory posts related to education and the Confucian examination system in Zhejiang, Hubei, and Sichuan provinces. During this time, he achieved renown for his energetic promotion of scholarship and exemplary rectitude in administrative affairs. In 1879 Zhang was inducted into the Imperial Academy, where he earned a reputation as an astute commentator on Chinese foreign relations and political reform.

In 1882 Zhang was promoted to the governorship of Shanxi Province, the first in a long series of administrative posts that would eventually include an eighteen-year tenure as governor-general of Hunan and Hubei Provinces. During this period, he gained the reputation as a modernizer and political reformer even while retaining a conservative devotion to Confucianism and the Qing dynastic order. The abbreviated formula as-

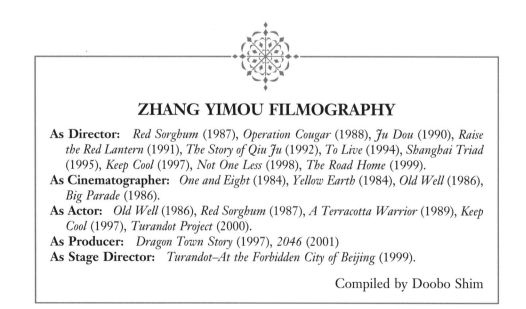

ZHANG YIMOU FILMOGRAPHY

As Director: *Red Sorghum* (1987), *Operation Cougar* (1988), *Ju Dou* (1990), *Raise the Red Lantern* (1991), *The Story of Qiu Ju* (1992), *To Live* (1994), *Shanghai Triad* (1995), *Keep Cool* (1997), *Not One Less* (1998), *The Road Home* (1999).

As Cinematographer: *One and Eight* (1984), *Yellow Earth* (1984), *Old Well* (1986), *Big Parade* (1986).

As Actor: *Old Well* (1986), *Red Sorghum* (1987), *A Terracotta Warrior* (1989), *Keep Cool* (1997), *Turandot Project* (2000).

As Producer: *Dragon Town Story* (1997), *2046* (2001)

As Stage Director: *Turandot–At the Forbidden City of Beijing* (1999).

Compiled by Doobo Shim

sociated with Zhang's philosophy of reform is *ti/yong*, or "Chinese learning as the essence, Western learning for practical development." His active promotion of railway development and his enthusiastic sponsorship of the Han-Ye-Ping iron and steel works are among the many projects that characterized his efforts to strengthen the Chinese state and economy.

Michael C. Lazich

Further Reading
Ayers, William. (1971) *Chang Chih-tung and Educational Reform in China*. Cambridge, MA: Harvard University Press.

Bays, Daniel H. (1978) *China Enters the Twentieth Century: Chang Chih-tung and the Issues of a New Age, 1895–1909*. Ann Arbor: The University of Michigan Press.

ZHAO ZIYANG (b. 1919), Chinese Communist Party leader and economic reformer. Zhao Ziyang was born as Zhao Xiusheng in Huaxian County, Henan Province, in 1919. He joined the Chinese Communist Party (CCP) in 1938. After the establishment of the People's Republic of China (PRC), Zhao served in numerous positions in Guangdong Province, where he played an instrumental role in consolidating CCP control and implementing land reform policies.

After being denounced and exiled during the Cultural Revolution, Zhao was rehabilitated by Zhou En-lai (1899–1976) and assigned as provincial first party secretary in Guangdong in 1971 and then in Sichuan in 1976. His market-oriented reforms there brought substantial progress to the economy and became a showpiece of the reforms of paramount leader Deng Xiaoping (1904–1997).

A strong supporter of Deng's economic reforms, Zhao became a member of the CCP Politburo in 1979, premier in 1980, and party secretary-general in 1987. He continued to advocate market-style reforms as well as ambitious plans to streamline the bloated PRC bureaucracy. While many of his reforms were praised, his economic liberalization program was blamed for the rising inflation of the late 1980s.

Zhao's most important moment and his political downfall came with the student protests in Tiananmen Square in May and June of 1989. Zhao openly sided with the student demonstrators and was ousted in the aftermath of the bloody crackdown on protests in Beijing. He remains a member of the CCP but has become almost completely absent from public life.

Kirk W. Larsen

Further Reading
Cheng, Chu-yuan. (1990) *Behind the Tiananmen Massacre*. Boulder, CO: Westview.

Liang, Zhang, Andrew Nathan, and Perry Link, eds. (2001) *The Tiananmen Papers*. New York: Public Affairs.

Shambaugh, David. (1984) *The Making of Premier Zhao Ziyang's Provincial Career*. Boulder, CO: Westview.

Vogel, Ezra. (1969) *Canton under Communism*. Cambridge, MA: Harvard University Press.

ZHEJIANG (2001 pop. 47 million). One of the most fertile and wealthiest provinces in China, Zhejiang lies on China's southeastern coast just south of the Chang (Yangtze) river delta and China's largest city, Shanghai. It is bordered on the north by Jiangsu province, on the west by Anhui and Jiangxi, and on the south by Fujian. It covers 101,800 square kilometers, including 3,061 offshore islands. About one-third of the province consists of plains, rivers, and lakes, while the other two-thirds is mountainous.

The province's capital is Hangzhou, China's capital during the Southern Song dynasty (1127–1279 CE) and a city described by Marco Polo in his travels as "beyond dispute the finest and noblest city" in the world. The province has 41 counties, 23 cities, and 23 county-level towns. The total population in 2001 was about 47 million, of which 300,000 are categorized as ethnic minorities. The largest of these minorities are the She and Hui nationalities.

Historically, Zhejiang has been in the forefront of China's economic and cultural development since the early Han dynasty (206 BCE–220 CE). Its emergence as a major producer of grain resulted in the extension of the Grand Canal to Hangzhou in the seventh century. Since the tenth century, the province has been a leading producer of grain, silk, tea, porcelain, and paper, and a center of trade and commerce. When the Southern Song dynasty established its capital in Hangzhou in 1127, Zhejiang also became China's political and cultural center. The province continues to be home to many of China's intellectual and political elite. Two of China's greatest modern writers, Lu Xun and Mao Dun, were from Zhejiang, as are nearly a fifth of the current members of the Chinese Academy of Sciences. The province also produced two of China's best-known contemporary leaders: Zhou En-lai, the premier of the People's Republic of China from 1949 to 1976, and Chiang Kai-shek, president of the Republic of China on Taiwan from 1949 to 1975.

Zhejiang has been a prime beneficiary of China's present economic reforms. Since 1978 the province's economy has grown faster than the national average, thanks in part to the rapid growth of collective and private firms. Currently the province is the fourth wealthiest in China behind such economic powerhouses as Guangdong and Shanghai. In addition to its traditional industries, the province has concentrated on the development of its machinery, electronics, chemicals, and pharmaceutical industries. Foreign trade, investment, and tourism have also flourished, especially in the coastal cities of Hangzhou, Ningbo, and Wenzhou.

Shawn Shieh

Further Reading
Rankin, Mary Backus. (1986) *Elite Activism and Political Transformation in China: Zhejiang Province, 1865–1911.* Stanford, CA: Stanford University Press.

Schoppa, Keith R. (1982) *Chinese Elites and Political Change: Zhejiang Province in the Early Twentieth Century.* Cambridge, MA: Harvard University Press.

ZHOU DYNASTY The era popularly known as the Zhou dynasty covers two time periods: the Western Zhou period (1045–771 BCE) and the Eastern Zhou period (770–221 BCE). During the Western Zhou period, the Zhou lineage ruled from the capital, Zongzhou, located near their ancestral burial grounds (near modern-day Xi'an in Shaanxi Province). In 771 BCE the Zhou elite fled east to the city of Chengzhou (located near modern-day Luoyang in Henan Province). During the Eastern Zhou period, former Zhou tribute states vied for power under the guise of upholding traditional Zhou moral authority. The Zhou royal descendants were themselves puppets of neighboring states.

Origins of Zhou
The original Zhou nation rose up in the Wei River valley in Shaanxi. Shang-dynasty (1766–1045 BCE) oracle-bone records dating from 1200 to 1000 BCE suggest that the Shang considered the Zhou group alternately as an enemy and as a tribute-paying subject. By the middle of the eleventh century BCE, the Zhou had built a coalition of partners, including former Shang subjects in northern Henan, and destroyed Shang hegemony. In texts compiled centuries later, this shift in power was attributed to the will of Heaven and called the Mandate of Heaven (*tianming*). In contemporary Zhou bronze texts, the term refers to the will of ancestral spirits, perhaps manifested as astral phenomena. By the Eastern Zhou period, however, the event was mythologized as a heroic military conquest commanded by Heaven and carried out by King Wu (who represented "martial" reckoning against immoral leaders), the son of the founder of the Zhou nation, King Wen (who represented "humane" treatment of inferiors and a system of utopian agrarian government). By the Han period (206 BCE–220 CE), the Mandate of Heaven clearly represented shifts in a system of natural forces, much closer to the five phases system (*wuxing*) popular by the third century BCE. The Mandate of Heaven theory became a permanent part of Chinese political thought, used by later Chinese reformers to frighten recalcitrant rulers as well as by those who took up arms against the government to justify their rebellion.

After the shift of hegemony from the Shang in the east to the Zhou in the west, the Zhou rulers spent the next two centuries consolidating their power through military coercion and trade. They focused on control over resources essential to their economic system of gift giving and award, a system inherited from the Shang and intimately tied to the spread of the worship of Zhou ancestral spirits. Cowries, bronze, and jade—all valuables in Shang religion and all requiring trade links with distant regions—continued to be important to the Zhou. Although the Zhou initially worshiped the Shang spirits, by the mid-tenth century BCE, their own ancestors had clearly become national icons. Nation building became a form of ancestor worship. The Zhou rewarded subjects with sacrificial vessels, ritual clothing, wines, and agricultural lands (for food production) to further the Zhou ritual system. Gift recipients used these items to present mortuary feasts to the ancestral spirits, often including the names of their Zhou benefactors and their ancestors in the inscribed prayers. The sophistication of Zhou bronze vessels, carved jades, and musical instruments attests to control over resources and production in regions outside the Zhou homeland. At the peak of Zhou hegemony, during the late tenth to the late ninth centuries BCE, they controlled a network that reached west into Gansu Province, southwest into Sichuan Province, northeast to Beijing, east into Shandong Province, and south into Hubei Province and beyond the Chang (Yangtze) River.

Eastern Zhou Period
The Eastern Zhou period is subdivided into the Spring and Autumn period (770–476 BCE) and the Warring States period (475–221 BCE). The names for both periods derive from chronicles of tales collected about each period that detail conflicts and alliances between former subject states of the Zhou. The entire Eastern Zhou era is characterized by larger states annexing smaller states, so that by the third century BCE,

only a few large states remained. During the Spring and Autumn period, the Zhou ruler was alternately a puppet of the states Jin, to the north; Zheng, to the south; and Qi, to the east—each of which took turns as "hegemon protectors" *(ba)*. States that were on the fringes of the Zhou world earlier rose to power and challenged the exclusionary protector system.

By the time of the Warring States period, powerful new players included the states of Qin, located to the west in the old Zhou homeland; Chu, spreading south and east out of the Han River valley in modern Hubei Province; Yue, spreading north into the lower Huai River valley from the southeastern coastal region; and Yan, in the northeast near modern-day Beijing. Jin (a powerful state that rose up in southern Shanxi not far from the Zhou administrative city of Chengzhou) in the meantime divided into territories run by the large lineage groups Wei, Zhao, and Han. Zheng was taken over by Han, but other states survived simply by allying themselves strategically with different, larger groups. Examples include Lu, the birthplace of Confucius (551–479 BCE), and nearby Song, birthplace of the anti-Confucian thinker Mozi (470?–391? BCE).

The art of strategic alliances, known as the Theory of Horizontal or Vertical Alliances, was promulgated by peripatetic "guests" *(ke)*, members of disenfranchised elite and artisan families who had studied under masters of military, ritual, and technical arts. By the Warring States period, literacy and text production, as well as technical or occult expertise, spread with the guest masters and their disciples from one site of patronage to another. The myriad new text types and ritual items discovered in Warring States tombs, particularly those associated with the southern state of Chu, attest to a cross-fertilization of ideas and practices over vast geographical distances. This was no doubt perpetuated not only by the roving guests, but also by the migrations of peoples, states, and armies. These guests took the cultural fabric, once identified as Zhou and rewove it, introducing new ideologies that better fit the cultural and economic realities of their far-flung patron rulers. During this time, they used tales about former Zhou-period rulers to warn and cajole regional leaders. Founder kings Wen and Wu were cast as paragons of honest humility and—most important to enhancing the precarious position of these guest advisers—the wise minister Zhou Gong (regent for Wu's son and cult founder of the state of Lu) was cast as essential to the foundation of a strong Zhou state. He took the helm while the king was weak, gave speeches about morality, quelled remnant Shang rebels, set up an administration, and politely retired when the king came of age.

CHINA—HISTORICAL PERIODS

Xia dynasty (2100–1766 BCE)
Shang dynasty (1766–1045 BCE)
Zhou dynasty (1045–256 BCE)
    Western Zhou (1045–771 BCE)
    Eastern Zhou (770–221 BCE)
Spring and Autumn period (770–476 BCE)
Warring States period (475–221 BCE)
Qin dynasty (221–206 BCE)
Han dynasty (206 BCE–220 CE)
Three Kingdoms period (220–265 CE)
North and South dynasties (220–589 CE)
Sui dyansty (581–618 CE)
Tang dynasty (618–907 CE)
Five Dynasties period (907–960 CE)
Song dynasty (960–1279)
    Northern Song (960–1126)
    Southern Song (1127–1279)
Jurchen Jin dynasty (1125–1234)
Yuan dynasty (1279–1368)
Ming dynasty (1368–1644)
Qing dynasty (1644–1912)
Republican China (1912–1927)
People's Republic of China (1949–present)
Republic of China (1949–present)
Cultural Revolution (1966–1976)

Social and Economic Changes

Comparison of the Warring States and early Western Zhou economies reveals drastic social changes. The economic network expanded by the Zhou from the eleventh through the ninth centuries BCE collapsed under its own ideological weight (a collapse that continued through the Spring and Autumn period). The rigid link to Zhou kinship through mortuary ritual and a gift-giving system was unsustainable. By contrast, the major states during the Warring States period developed their own monetary systems as well as individualized religious systems that incorporated both local practices and elements of the archaic but prestigious Zhou rhetoric. Smaller states participated in the expanded networks of larger states. Markets were commonplace in every city. The export of mass-produced trade goods and the import of exotic goods flourished. The network of interstate relationships was often multilateral, involving trade, marriage, warfare, and political covenants. Until the Qin dynasty (221–206 BCE) conquered the entire region and attempted unification, early China was a complex social web of competing philosophies, mingled social classes, and peoples from different cultural backgrounds. In the face of this cultural fluidity, individual states promoted their own calendar systems, script styles, musical styles, artistic styles, and occult practices. The Warring States period represented the end of Bronze Age Zhou culture. Writers and philosophers of this and later periods would commonly use an increasingly idealized vision of Zhou ritual and government as a rhetorical foil against which to criticize the political chaos of their own times.

Constance A. Cook

Further Reading

Cook, Constance. (1997) "Wealth and the Western Zhou." *Bulletin of the School of Oriental and African Studies* 60, 2: 253–294.

Hsu Cho-yun, and Katheryn M. Linduff. (1988) *Western Chou Civilization.* New Haven, CT: Yale University Press.

Li Xueqin. (1985) *Eastern Zhou and Qin Civilizations.* Trans. by K. C. Chang. New Haven, CT: Yale University Press.

Loewe, Michael, and Edward L. Shaughnessy. (1999) *The Cambridge History of Ancient China: From the Origins of Civilization to 221 B.C.* Cambridge, U.K.: Cambridge University Press.

ZHOU ENLAI (1898–1976), Chinese revolutionary. Zhou Enlai was one of the most important leaders of the Chinese Communist Party (CCP) and the government of the People's Republic of China (PRC, 1949–). He was born in 1898 in Jiangsu Province in a family native to Shaoxing in Zhejiang Province, with a family history typical of that locality, long noted for producing the educated aides who provided indispensable services to appointed officials in imperial times. Zhou's radical political career began with his participation in the May Fourth Movement in the city of Tianjin in 1919. This led to his arrest and imprisonment for several months, after which he traveled to Europe as a student and clandestine radical activist. Active mainly in France from 1920 to 1924, Zhou lived for shorter periods in Germany and Britain as well. He joined the Chinese Communist Party in 1921 and was the leading founder of the Paris-based Chinese Communist Youth Group. Returning to China in 1924, Zhou married Deng Yingchao, another former student activist with whom he had corresponded regularly for four years, and joined the work of the CCP in its new alliance with the Guomindang (Nationalist Party) of Sun Yat-sen (1866–1925), then based in Guangzhou (Canton). In preparation for the "Nationalist Revolution" to reunite China, Zhou served as deputy director of the Whampoa Military Academy, where Chiang Kai-shek (1887–1975) was commandant. During the Northern Expedition (1926–1927),

which was undertaken to combat warlords in the north, Zhou organized labor and directed a general strike in Shanghai, facilitating the Nationalist takeover of China's most important city. Chiang's subsequent crackdown on Communism drove Zhou and his comrades into hiding. After that, Zhou organized the Nanchang uprising and became one of the founders and leaders of the Red Army. Zhou began to work closely with Mao Zedong (1893–1976) after the Communist regime in Jiangxi was destroyed by the Nationalist government. During the Long March (the Communists' flight from Jiangxi to Shaanxi), Zhou's support of Mao decisively helped Mao in his rise to dominance in the CCP. From that time on, Zhou served as Mao's right-hand man until his death. While Mao formulated doctrine, Zhou translated doctrine into practical policies. His organizational talents featured a notable ability to maintain discipline and cohesion within the CCP. During the Xian Incident of 1936, when Chiang Kai-shek's generals held Chiang captive until he would agree to postpone fighting the Communists until after the Japanese were defeated, Zhou helped to negotiate a partial rapprochement between the Communists and Nationalists and as chief liaison officer maintained relations between the two until the end of the war against Japan. During the decisive struggle against the Nationalists during the civil war of 1946–1949, Zhou directed political indoctrination programs that induced captured Nationalist soldiers to fight on the Communist side. From the inauguration of the People's Republic of China until his death, Zhou was head of state (premier of the State Council) and was a popular paternal figure among the Chinese people. Zhou also served as foreign minister from 1949 to 1958 and was respected abroad as a skilful, urbane, and dignified diplomat. One of Zhou's leadership techniques was to acknowledge personal responsibility for problems faced by the CCP. For example, following the tragic failure of the Great Leap Forward (1958–1960), Mao's attempt to industrialize at the village level, Zhou was able to diffuse responsibility for the disaster and deflect blame from Mao. During the Cultural Revolution (1966–1976), Zhou used his political influence and skills to limit the chaotic effects of the campaign and protect some of the victims of leftist excesses. Before becoming ill during the 1970s, he played an important role in the emergence of the PRC from isolation and the adoption of a program of economic reform. Chinese leader Deng Xiaoping (1904–1997) was a protégé and close associate whose Four Modernizations program announced in 1978 was a continuation of Zhou's earlier work.

Following Zhou Enlai's death on 9 January 1976, preceding Mao's by precisely nine months, the Chinese people responded with an outpouring of grief. In April 1976, on the occasion of an annual festival honoring the dead, they gathered to mourn their loss in public. In Beijing, as crowds of citizens paying their respects to Zhou swelled tremendously in size, authorities became alarmed about their oblique expression of antigovernment sentiment and forcibly dispersed the crowds in an event known as the Tiananmen Incident of 1976.

Emily M. Hill

Further Reading
CCP Central Committee Editorial Committee on Party Literature. (1981) *Selected Works of Zhou Enlai*. Beijing: Foreign Languages Press.
Wilson, Dick. (1984) *Zhou Enlai: A Biography*. New York: Viking.

ZHOU SHUREN.   See **Lu Xun.**

ZHU DE   (1886–1976), founder of the Chinese Communist army.

Zhu De (Chu Teh), founder of the Chinese Communist army, was born on 30 November 1886, the son of a poor tenant farmer. After graduating from the Yunnan Military Academy in 1911, Zhu became active in anti-Manchu activities in Yunnan and Sichuan Provinces between 1912 and 1916. In 1922, on a work-study program, he left for Europe, where he participated in Communist Party activities. In 1926, Zhu returned to China and became involved in the Nationalist Guomindang army. After the failed Nanchang Uprising (1927), Zhu led his troops to Hunan Province, where he joined up with Communist Party leader Mao Zedong (1893–1976). In Hunan they formed an effective military force that would later become the Red Army. Under Zhu's command, the Red Army defended the Jiangxi Soviet and undertook the 6,000-mile Long March to Shaanxi Province.

During the war with Japan, Zhu commanded the Red Army's northern forces. Following Japan's surrender, Zhu served as the commander of the People's Liberation Army until 1955, when he became a marshal of the People's Liberation Army. He would later become the chairman of the National People's Congress Standing Committee and continually was listed in many high official positions, although he was not actively involved in Chinese politics after 1954.

Keith A. Leitich

Further Reading
Gelder, G. Stuart, ed. (1946) *The Chinese Communists*. London: Gollancz.

Smedley, Agnes. (1992) *The Great Road: The Life and Times of Chu Teh*. New York: Monthly Review Press.

ZHU RONGJI   (b. 1928), Chinese premier.

Following the end of Li Peng's term as premier of the Chinese Communist Party in 1998, Zhu Rongji was named premier. Zhu was born on 20 October 1928 in Changsha, Hunan Province. While an electrical engineering student at Qinghua University, Zhu joined the Chinese Communist Party and, following graduation in 1951, held a variety of posts within the State Planning Commission (SPC). While working at the SPC, Zhu was labeled as a rightist during the Hundred Flowers Movement of 1957.

Following the Cultural Revolution, Zhu became the director of the Industrial Economics Institute of the Chinese Academy of Science. He would later move to the State Economic Commission (SEC), where he was associated with the formation of economic reform policies. From there, Zhu's star began to rise. He was named a vice minister of the SEC and later a director at the China International Trust and Investment Corporation.

Zhu then became mayor of Shanghai following the elevation of Jiang Zemin to the Politburo following the June 4 Incident (when army tanks rolled into Tiananmen Square in 1989 killing civilians in their path). While the mayor of Shanghai, Zhu gained a reputation as a no-nonsense reformer who got things done. Zhu was then appointed to the post of vice premier where he worked to limit money supply while implementing fiscal and financial reforms.

Keith A. Leitich

Further Reading
Bartle, Wolfgang. (1991) *Who's Who in the People's Republic of China*. 3d ed. New York: K. G. Saur.

ZHU XI   (1130–1200), Chinese synthesizer of neo-Confucianism.

Zhu Xi (Chu Hsi) was born in Youzi in Fukien province; he is perhaps the greatest neo-Confucian philosopher. He developed and clarified the metaphysics of two earlier philosophers, Cheng Yi (1033–1107) and his brother Cheng Hao (1032–1085). According to their view, everything in the universe has two aspects, *li* (principle) and *qi*. *Li* is a structuring principle that accounts for both the way a thing is and the way it ought to be. Although the *li* is present in each and every thing, things are distinguished by having different endowments of *qi*. *Qi* is a

ZHU XI ON THE HEART

"The intelligence of the human heart never fails to have some knowledge, and the things of the world never fail to have principle (*li*). It is only due to the fact that principle is not exhausted that knowledge is not completed. Consequently, when the school of Greater Learning begins its teaching, it must direct students, in regard to all the things of the world that they encounter, to never fail to follow the principle that they already know and exhaust it, seeking to arrive at the limit. One day, after they have exerted effort for a long time, they will suddenly penetrate it, and then there will be nothing in the multitude of things—external or within, fine or coarse—that they do not reach. Then there will be nothing in the complete substance and great functioning of our heart that is not illuminated!"

Source: Zhu Xi. Collected Commentaries on the Greater Learning. Translated by Bryan Van Norden.

---

sort of self-moving ethereal substance, which has varying degrees of turbidity or clarity. Inanimate objects have the most turbid *qi*, with plants, animals, and humans having increasingly clearer *qi*.

Since the *li* is one, everything is part of a potentially harmonious whole. Consequently, a good person has concern for everything that exists. Because the *qi* differentiates things, people have greater obligations to those tied to them by particular bonds such as the five relations. The clearer one's endowment of *qi*, the easier it is to appreciate one's obligations.

Relying on one's own moral sense without education is dangerous, because selfish desires obscure the *li* within people. Instead, people should study the classic texts under a wise teacher, because the texts provide partial abstractions of the *li* from its particular embodiments in *qi*.

Prior to Zhu Xi, Confucian education emphasized the Five Classics: the Odes, the Documents, the Spring and Autumn Annals, the Record of Rites, and the Yi Jing. These works had been central to Confucian education since the Han dynasty (206 BCE–220 CE). Zhu Xi proposed a new curriculum, based on what came to be known as the Four Books. His *Collected Commentaries on the Four Books*, which gives a synthetic interpretation of these texts in the light of neo-Confucian metaphysics, became the basis of the Chinese civil service examinations in 1315 and was committed to memory by generations of scholars until the examinations were abolished in 1905. In the early twenty-first century, the views of the majority of Confucians in East Asian communities, including the "New Confucian" philosophers, are deeply influenced by Zhu Xi's interpretations.

Bryan W. Van Norden

Further Reading

Chan, Wing-tsit, ed. (1986) *Chu Hsi and Neo-Confucianism.* Honolulu: University of Hawaii Press.

Gardner, Daniel K. (1990) *Chu Hsi: Learning to Be a Sage.* Berkeley and Los Angeles: University of California Press.

Graham, Angus C. (1992) *Two Chinese Philosophers.* 2d ed. Chicago: Open Court.

ZHUANG The Zhuang are a minority people living in south and southwest China, mostly in the mountainous areas of the Guangxi Zhuang Autonomous Region and the Wenshan Zhuang-Miao Autonomous Prefecture of Yunan province. A number of Zhuang communities are also scattered in Guangdong, Hunan, Guizhou, and Sichuan provinces. With 15.5 million people (1990 census), the Zhunag are the largest of all Chinese minority nationalities in terms of population.

Before 1949, Zhuang groups described themselves with more than twenty different names. In the 1950s the government redefined all Zhuang groups and in 1965 it renamed all of them Zhuang.

History

The origin of the Zhuang is debated even by the Zhuang people themselves. Scholars generally believe that the Zhuang either migrated from outside the Guangxi area, developed from the original inhabitants of the area, or evolved from intermarriage between local and outside people.

It is conceivable that the Zhuang originated partially from the ancient peoples known as Baiyue ("Hundred Yues"), who were indigenous to Lingnan, a geographic region encompassing modern Guangxi and Guangdong. With the warm weather and rich water resources of Lingnan, the Baiyue had long engaged in rice agriculture.

In 214 BCE, the Qin dynasty (221–206 BCE) conquered Lingnan, moved people from the central plains to the Lingnan region, and built the Lingqu Canal to connect the Chang (Yangtze) and Zhu (Pearl) Rivers. These policies brought together the Baiyue and immigrant populations and established political, economic, and cultural ties between Lingnan and central China. On the collapse of the Qin dynasty, a general named Zhao Tuo founded Nanyue as an independent kingdom in Lingnan. In 111 CE, the emperor Wudi of the Han dynasty (206 BCE–220 CE) destroyed Nanyue and organized an administration in Lingnan that included the eastern portion of Guangxi. It was during the Han that some native groups in Lingnan were first referred to as Zhuang.

Rulers of the Tang (618–907) and Song (960–1279) dynasties administered the Lingnan region loosely. The central government appointed Zhuang local chiefs as magistrates and allowed them to hold their positions hereditarily, but the chiefs were required to renounce independent statehood. This indirect rule permitted the Zhuang local chiefs to become autocratic on the local level, and their autonomy grew to the point that they resisted the central state. Starting in the early Ming dynasty (1368–1644), the central government decided to rule the Zhuang areas directly, but the Zhuang strongly resisted. Between 1492 and 1571, Zhuang uprisings forced the Ming government to mobilize over 140,000 troops. The Qing dynasty (1644–1912) and the Republic of China (1912–1949) maintained a policy of replacing local leaders until 1929, when the central state held overall authority.

Concurrent with increasing Chinese control was a migration of Han Chinese (the ethnic group of the majority of the Chinese population) to the Zhuang areas. During the Ming and Qing dynasties, large numbers of Han people immigrated into Guangxi and other Zhuang regions to escape the warfare and famine in northern and central China and to look for agricultural land. By the end of the nineteenth century, Han Chinese represented 50 percent of the total population of Guangxi, whereas they had represented less than 20 percent of the population in the mid-sixteenth century. The continuing arrival of Han people brought advanced agricultural technology to the Zhuang communities and formed a social base for the central government to extend its authority, but it also sometimes led to ethnic conflicts between the Han and Zhuang.

The Modern Era

In modern times, the Zhuang people increased their resistance to the central government. In 1952, the government of Communist China founded the Western Guangxi Zhuang Autonomous Prefecture, the first step toward redefining all Zhuang groups and creating the Guangxi Zhuang Autonomous Regions in

1958. Though many Zhuang were trained and promoted to official positions, Zhuang communities suffered severely from the government's forced assimilation policy.

After China's reform in 1979, the government guaranteed the Zhuang people their rights and privileges as a minority nationality and began promoting their equality more in terms of economic development. Since then, various modern industries have begun to grow in the Zhuang areas, and the Zhuang economy has shifted from a self-sufficient agricultural base toward a more interdependent one through developments in trade, roads, and modern communication technology. Although the Zhuang economy still lags far behind that of the Han Chinese areas, it is the most advanced among the economies of China's minority nationalities.

Culture

The Zhuang have a rich cultural heritage; their traditional mountain songs and Zhuang brocade are famous. The third day of the third month of each lunar year is the most important Zhuang festival, when in each area people dance and sing before large audiences. Liu Sanjie, a Zhuang woman singer of the Tang dynasty, is considered Zhuang's music goddess (*ge xian*), known to all Chinese because of her beautiful voice and the lyrics of her songs. Zhuang brocade, originating in Tang times and woven in beautiful designs with cotton warp and dyed velour weft in five colors, is popular in China and is exported to foreign countries.

Zhuang people speak the Zhuang language, a linguistic branch of the Sino-Tibetan language family, although various distinct dialects remain in Zhuang communities. Zhuang culture has also been influenced by the Han culture because of the long interaction between the two peoples. Zhuang's old written language, the square Zhuang characters, developed from Chinese characters during the Tang dynasty, and throughout history a few Zhuang scholars passed imperial China's state examination and earned scholarly degrees.

To promote education among all the Zhuang people, the Chinese government in 1955 reformed the Zhuang language based on the Latin alphabet and then revised the alphabet system in 1982. The promotion of the Zhuang ethnic language has helped to elevate education among the Zhuang people; it has also helped to create a common Zhuang ethnic identity that was nearly nonexistent before the People's Republic.

Chen Yixin

Further Reading

Kaup, Katherine. (2000) *Creating the Zhuang: Ethnic Politics in China*. Boulder, CO: Lynne Rienner.

Ma, Yin. (1989) *China's Minority Nationalities*. Beijing: Foreign Language Press.

ZIA, KHALEDA (b. 1945), prime minister of Bangladesh. Khaleda Zia, the widow of former Bangladesh president Ziaur Rahman Zia (1936–1981), was born in Jalpaiguri (now in West Bengal, India), although her family was from the Feni district in Bangladesh. After her husband Zia's assassination in 1981, his party, the Bangladesh Nationalist Party (BNP), was without a leader and selected Khaleda as chairperson on 10 March 1984. As such, she was a leader of the opposition to the military regime of Hussain Muhammad Ershad along with Sheikh Hasina Wajid of the Awami League. The two frequently clashed with each other as well as with Ershad, but in late 1990 they united and brought about Ershad's fall. Following the election in February 1991, Khaleda became prime minister on 20 March 1991, an office she

Khaleda Zia appears before the media in Dhaka on 2 October 2001 when it became clear that the election would make her the next prime minister of Bangladesh. (REUTERS NEWMEDIA/CORBIS)

held until March 1996. In the June 1996 election, the BNP finished behind the Awami League and Khaleda became leader of the opposition. The enmity since 1991 between the BNP and Awami League has impeded the governance of Bangladesh. In 1999 the BNP formed an alliance with the Jatiya Party faction headed by Ershad and the Jama'at-e-Islami, an Islamic fundamentalist party, to attempt to destroy the Awami League government and prepare for the October 2001 parliamentary election. The alliance subsequently won by a substantial majority in the election.

Craig Baxter

Further Reading

Baxter, Craig. (1997) *Bangladesh from Nation to a State*. Boulder, CO: Westview.

Hakim, S. Abdul. (1992) *Begum Khaleda Zia of Bangladesh: A Political Biography*. New Delhi: Vikase.

ZIA-UL-HAQ, MOHAMMAD (1924–1988), president of Pakistan. Zia was born on 12 August 1924 in Jalandhar in Punjab. He graduated from the Indian Military Academy, Dehra Dun, in 1945, and served with the British army in Southeast Asia. Upon India's independence from Britain and the partition of the Indian subcontinent, Zia chose to live in Pakistan. He became a major general in 1972 and four years afterwards was made army chief of staff by Zulfikar Ali Bhutto (1928–1979), who was at that time prime minister. Next year Zia deposed Bhutto and became Pakistan's chief martial-law administrator.

Zia became president in 1978 and had Bhutto executed the following year, despite international appeals. Zia banned all political parties and imposed censorship of the press. Norms of *shari'a* (Islamic law) were strictly adhered to; the Islamic Ahmadiya sect, regarded as heterodox by the Islamic mainstream, was suppressed. The Soviet invasion of Afghanistan strengthened his position, and he collaborated with the United States administration fully in its opposition to the Soviets. In return, he received generous financial and military assistance from the United States. Under Zia there was no sign of substantial improvement of ties with India, and Zia launched Operation Topac in Kashmir. The operation was an attempt to stir up anti-Indian sentiment with a view to ultimately wresting Kashmir from Indian control. Ghulam Ishaq Khan (b. 1915) succeeded Zia after the latter died in a plane crash near Bahawalpur on 17 August 1988.

Patit Paban Mishra

Further Reading

Baxter, Craig, and Shahid Javed Burki, with contributions by Robert LaPorte, Jr., and Kamal Azfar. (1991) *Pakistan under the Military: Eleven Years of Zia ul-Haq.* Boulder, CO: Westview.

Burki, Shahid Javed. (1991) *Historical Dictionary of Pakistan.* Metuchen, NJ: Scarecrow.

ZIKIR   A *zikir* is a litany formula that usually follows an Islamic prayer, but which can also be practiced at other times. The Arabic word *dhikr*, which literally means "mention," "remembrance," "evocation," or "recollection," is part of the Malay-Indonesian vocabulary, sometimes written as *dzikir.* This concept and meditation tool is commonly linked with Sufi practices. Certain words or names of God are repeated as litanies after prayer, in accordance with the Prophet Muhammad's tradition, or the teachings of Sufi orders. The most common *zikir* formulas are "God is holy" (*Subhanallah*), "All praise to God" (*Alhamdulillah*), "God is most great" (*Allahuakbar*), and "There is no god but God" (*Lailaha-illallah*), repeated in either a low or a high voice.

The purpose of this practice is to increase piety. Since in Islam God is considered unimaginable and unthinkable, the *zikir* plays an important role in bringing one closer to or into union with God. Some *zikir* formulas also involve body movement and special breathing patterns, performed while counting beads. Correct practice is achieved when the practitioner consciously feels comfortable and at peace, which is sometimes inaccurately analogized with a state of trance. To be performed effectively, the *zikir* must be learned under the guidance of a teacher who can explain, among other things, the doctrines behind the words and the difference between the nature and essence of God.

Andi Faisal Bakti

Further Reading

Federspiel, Howard M. (1995) *A Dictionary of Indonesian Islam.* Athens: Ohio University, Center for International Studies.

Mittwoch, Eugen. (1971) "Dhikr." In *The Encyclopaedia of Islam.* Vol 1, edited by B. Lewis, V. Ménage, Ch. Pellat, and J. Schacht. New ed. Leiden, Netherlands: E. J. Brill, 223–227.

Sells, Michael A. (1995) "Dhikr." In *The Oxford Encyclopedia of the Modern Islamic World.* Vol 1, edited by John Esposito. New York: Oxford University Press, 372–374.

ZODIAC SYSTEM—EAST ASIA   The zodiac

system popular in China, Vietnam, Korea, and Japan has its origins in ancient East Asian cosmology, which developed during the centuries before the present era. It posits two basic complementary principles or primordial forces: yin and yang. They produce what are commonly known as the five elements: wood, earth, fire, metal, and water.

In its simplest and most familiar form, this zodiac consists of twelve signs, each represented by a different animal. The elements for which the animals serve as symbols are understood to be the twelve "earth branches." Thus, the first earth branch is symbolized by the rat (or mouse). The second is symbolized variously by the ox, the cow, or (in Vietnam) the water buffalo. The third is symbolized by the tiger. The fourth earth branch is symbolized by the rabbit in most places, but by the cat in Vietnam. The fifth earth branch is usually symbolized by the dragon, but as the system exists in Thailand the symbol is often a *naga*, a mythical aquatic beast with a more Southeast Asian ancestry. The sixth earth branch is symbolized by the snake; the seventh, by the horse; the eighth, by the goat or sheep; the ninth, by the monkey; the tenth, by the rooster; the eleventh, by the dog; and the twelfth by the pig.

A System of Symbols

But this twelve-part cycle is just one part of a larger system. These twelve earth branches operate in conjunction with ten heavenly stems. The full total cycle of twelve earth branches and ten heavenly stems provides a total of sixty units: six cycles of heavenly stems and five cycles of earth branches. (If each of the two cycles, one of ten and the other of twelve, lasts one year, the same combination [one earth branch, one heavenly stem] occurs every sixty years.)

Most people in the West think of the animals that symbolize the twelve earth branches as a means of designating years: the year of the dragon, the year of the pig, and so on. People in East Asia do this too; but they also can and do apply the entire system of categories to months, days, and even minutes for astrological and other purposes. These units are at the same time often categorized in terms of yin and yang and the five elements.

For example, all earth branches with odd numbers (represented by the rat, tiger, dragon, horse, monkey, and dog) are yang. Those with even numbers are yin. Also, the first and twelfth earth branches are associated with water; the third and fourth with wood, and so on. The five elements create and destroy each other in an eternal process. Wood produces fire, which produces earth, and so on; wood also destroys earth, which destroys water, which destroys fire, which destroys metal. Words like "create" and "destroy" are in some sense metaphors for a wide range of relationships between "elements" that are compatible or incompatible, mutually supporting or in opposition. The five elements, like yin and yang and the signs of the zodiac themselves, are primarily systems of symbols. "Water," for example, is not necessarily and not only water. It represents a category (of actions, things, segments of time and space) that is in a predictable relationship with other similar categories that are represented by other elements or signs.

Influence in Daily Life

The earth branches and heavenly stems, coded in terms of yin and yang and the five elements, can be related to (or used to represent) stars, directions, seasons of the year, landscape features, foods, flavors, parts of the body, and many other things. The zodiac is thus linked to astrology, geomancy, health, diet, selection of a marriage partner, and the best or worst time to travel, begin building a house, or perform certain religious rituals. Thus amid all the economic growth and development of modern science and technology in East Asia, the zodiac and the ancient concepts of yin and yang are still a vital part of many people's ways of life and thought.

Neil L. Jamieson

Further Reading:
Hickey, Gerald C. (1964) *Village in Vietnam*. New Haven, CT: Yale University Press.
Van Huyen, Nguyen. (1995) *The Ancient Civilization of Vietnam*. Hanoi, Vietnam: Gioi.

ZONGULDAK (2002 est. city pop 119,000). The city of Zonguldak is the capital of the province (estimated population in 2002 of 684,000) of the same name. It is located on the Black Sea coast of northwestern Turkey in the country's main coal district. The city has been inhabited since 1200 BCE. The Lydians came into power in 6 BCE, followed by the Persians around 546 BCE. Alexander of Macedon defeated the Persians in 334 BCE. Zipoetes ruled the kingdom of Bitinia around Zonguldak from 326 BCE until the Roman conquest in 74 BCE. When the Roman empire was divided into two in 395 CE, Zonguldak fell into the eastern half. Following their victory at Manzikert, the Seljuks temporarily occupied the area, but it reverted to Byzantine rule in 1086. When the fourth Crusaders conquered Constantinople in 1204, Zonguldak became part of the Nicaean kingdom until the

Byzantines reconquered it and gave it to the Genoese. Ottoman Sultan Mehmed II (1432–1481) conquered the whole area in 1461, and Zonguldak has been under Turkish rule ever since.

The city lost its economic importance during Ottoman rule and remained a small village until the discovery of coal in the second half of the nineteenth century. In 1939 after the official openings of the steel and iron plant in Karabük and the electricity-generating plant in Çatalağzı, the province of Zonguldak regained its importance. The city of Zonguldak has one of the largest ports in Turkey and houses the Technical School of Mining.

T. Isikozlu-E. F. Isikozlu

ZOPFAN ZOPFAN, the Zone of Peace, Freedom, and Neutrality, originated in a 1970 proposal by Malaysia for neutralizing Southeast Asia. The idea for such a zone has been attributed to Tunku Abdul Rahman Putra al-Haj (1903–1990), who was then a parliamentary backbencher (rank-and-file member of parliament) but later became the deputy prime minister of Malaysia. Calling for a neutrality system, the proposal had two levels of implementation. The first level specified that Southeast Asian nation-states adopt and practice nonaggression principles based on mutual respect for sovereignty and territorial integrity, as well as finding different ways and means to ensure peace and security among themselves. For the second level of implementation, the major superpowers at the time, the United States, China, and the Soviet Union, were singled out as prospective guarantors for ensuring that the Southeast Asian region would not become an arena for conflict among these major countries. Furthermore, the superpowers were also called on to implement supervisory means to ensure the neutrality of Southeast Asia. The declaration emphasized regional cooperation in economic, social, and cultural matters, as well as support for strengthening the economic and social stability of the region to ensure peaceful and progressive national development.

The Malaysian government drove the process of gaining support for ZOPFAN by first broaching the proposal at the Non-Aligned Summit in Lusaka in September 1970. In 1971, the proposal was again raised at the Commonwealth Conference held in Singapore. The Zone of Peace, Freedom, and Neutrality Declaration, Malaysia, was signed by the foreign ministers of Indonesia, Malaysia, the Philippines, and Singapore, and by the special envoy of the National Executive Council of Thailand on 27 November 1971.

The proposal and subsequent declaration by the foreign ministers, however, received only limited support from the superpowers as well as from Malaysia's fellow member states of the Association of Southeast Asian Nations (ASEAN, which in 1976 included Singapore, the Philippines, Indonesia, and Thailand, in addition to Malaysia; Brunei became part of ASEAN in 1984). Nevertheless, Malaysian officials pushed for two accords when the ASEAN member states met in Bali in 1976. These were the Declaration of ASEAN Concord and the Treaty of Amity and Cooperation signed at Bali. The two documents fell short of neutralizing the ASEAN states and the region as a whole.

Yet the second document, the Treaty of Amity and Cooperation, which is open to accession by other Southeast Asian states, was couched along lines that had been the basis of the proposal or plan for peace first mooted by Tunku Abdul Rahman Putra al-Haj. In the Treaty of Amity and Cooperation, the signatory countries agreed to be guided by the following principles in Article 2 of the treaty: mutual respect for the independence, sovereignty, equality, territorial integrity, and national identity of all nations; the right of every state to exist free of external interference, subversion, or coercion; noninterference in one another's internal affairs; settlement of differences or disputes by peaceful means; renunciation of the threat or use of force; effective cooperation among themselves.

In Chapter 4 of the Treaty of Amity and Concord, there is provision for peaceful settlement of conflict through a high council of ministerial-level representatives, which would include the parties to a dispute. The treaty has been considered a significant intergovernmental effort at initiating and achieving a Southeast Asian pact on security cooperation.

ZOPFAN has not progressed very much beyond the conceptual beginnings and terms set down during the Bali meeting in 1976. ZOPFAN remains an intra-ASEAN policy, but over the years, the principles of the proposal and the subsequent Treaty of Amity and Concord have been contravened by non-ASEAN states.

In the 1990s, there has been a call for the revival and review of ZOPFAN. Such a review, according to some analysts, should recognize that while regional cooperation on security must be promoted, the emphasis on national sovereignty severely limits the realization of ZOPFAN, which needs states to submit to a supranational authority. Furthermore, the concept of ZOPFAN seems increasingly irrelevant in the post–Cold War era. ZOPFAN is extremely limited in the contribution it can make toward the shaping or formulation of security arrangements and other such forms of regional cooperation among the member states of ASEAN.

Ooi Giok Ling

Further Reading
Alagappa, Muthiah. (1991) "Regional Arrangement and International Security in Southeast Asia: Going beyond ZOPFAN." *Contemporary Southeast Asia* 12, 4: 269–305.
Hamzah, B. A., ed. (1992) *Southeast Asia and Regional Peace.* Kuala Lumpur, Malaysia: Institute of Strategic and International Studies, Malaysia.
Saravanamuttu, Johan. (1984) "ASEAN Security for the 1980s: The Case for a Revitalised ZOPFAN." *Contemporary Southeast Asia* 6, 2: 186–196.

ZOROASTRIANISM Zoroastrianism (or Mazdaism) was born of a set of reforms attributed to the prophet Zarathushtra (in Greek, Zoroaster; traditional dates 628–551 BCE). A new ritual system gradually developed, revolving around a sacred fire, with a theology that envisions the world as an ongoing contest between good and evil. The religion originated around 1000 BCE in a pastoral society inhabiting what is now eastern Iran and Afghanistan, growing from archaic Indo-Iranian priestly ritual tradition, in which offerings of food and an invigorating plant juice (called soma in Old Indo-Iranian and Sanskrit; *haoma* in Avestan), directed to celestial divinities, were made in a ritual fire accompanied by poetic recitations. The religion survives in Iran and South Asia, with the total number of Zoroastrians worldwide at about 150,000. It is passed on mainly through family tradition; conversions are uncommon and are not sought.

Sources
Extant sources include the Avesta, compiled between the fourth and sixth centuries CE by priests, and recorded in the Avestan language by using a specially devised script based on the Aramaic script. The Old Avesta principally encompasses the *Gathas*, hymns traditionally ascribed to Zarathushtra himself and praising a supreme god, Ahura Mazda (Wise Lord; in Pahlavi, Hormazd). In language and meter they closely resemble the hymns of the Rig Veda of India, and many ideals of the Vedic religion appear in them. However in the Avesta the old Indo-Iranian gods (*daevas*) are relegated to the status of demons and are supplanted by a new class of divine entities who personify key Zoroastrian virtues. The Younger Avesta

Iranian Zoroastrian religious leader Jahangir Osheidari with Iranian president Mohammad Khatami in Tehran in October 2000. (AFP/CORBIS)

includes the *Yasht*s (hymns praising the divine entities), the *Vendidad* (a purity code), and several liturgical compilations of prayers. Only a small fraction of the original Avesta is thought to have survived.

Later but equally important are the Pahlavi texts written around the ninth and tenth centuries in the province of Fars in Persia. Notable among these are the *Zand*, a compendium of exegesis of the Avesta; the *Bundahishn*, presenting Zoroastrian cosmology and eschatology; the *Denkard* (Acts of Religion); and examples of didactic and catechistic teachings by eminent priests of the period, including the *Shkand-gumanig Vizar* (Teaching That Destroys Doubt), which demonstrates Zoroastrianism's superiority to Islam, Judaism, Christianity, and Manichaeism. In more recent centuries, collections of *Rivayat* (scholarly opinions on doctrinal, liturgical, and legal questions) have played an important role in adapting the tradition to changing times and in linking disparate communities of Zoroastrians.

The Old Persian inscriptions of the Achaemenid (sixth to fourth centuries BCE) and Sasanid (third to seventh centuries CE) dynasties provide invaluable information on the history of the tradition. Particularly important are the inscriptions of Kartir, high priest under the Sasanids, who helped establish Zoroastrianism as the state religion in the third century, and urged the vigorous suppression of other religions, such as Judaism, Nestorian Christianity, Buddhism, Manichaeism, and the Mandaean movement.

Theology and Cosmology

In the Zoroastrian religion the world is the scene of a continual struggle between truth (*asha*) and deceit (*druj*), forces personified in Spenta Mainyu (Benefi-

cent Spirit) and Angra Mainyu (Hostile Spirit; in Pahlavi, Ahriman), the children of Ahura Mazda. Alongside Spenta Mainyu are the six other Amesha Spentas (Beneficent Immortals), distinct entities embodying virtues: Vohu Manah (Good Thought), Asha Vahishta (Best Truth), Khshathra Vairya (Desirable Dominion), Spenta Armaiti (Beneficent Devotion), Haurvatat (Wholeness), and Ameretat (Immortality). Besides these, other "venerable beings" (*yazatas*) to whom *yasht*s are dedicated include Anahita, Mithra, Sraosha, and Rashnu, who sit in judgment over the soul after death; Verethraghna, who represents victory; and personifications of the sun, the moon, the star Sirius (called Tishtrya and associated with rain), and the wind.

After the soul is judged at death, it may tumble into hell, be relegated to "the region of the mixed" (limbo), or ascend via the stars, the moon, and the sun to heaven. Three days after death, the virtuous encounter their *daena*, a spiritual alter ego in the form of a girl. A final judgment is also envisioned in which a river of fire separates the good from the wicked, the world is transfigured, and the dead are revived and endowed with incorruptible bodies by means of a special offering to be performed by Saoshyant (the future savior).

Observances

Humanity, constantly faced with the choice between good and bad, true and untrue, can follow the *asha*, or truth, by adhering to the Zoroastrian purity code (canonized in the *Vendidad*) and by sponsoring performances of the fire-service (*yasna*), the central liturgy performed in the fire-temples (*atesh-gah*). The *haoma* drink, the offering itself, is prepared in the *paragra* rite. Then it is offered up while the *zot* priest recites the *yasna* chapters of the Avesta and the *raspi* priest fuels the fire.

Other important rites include the *naojot* (or *nozud*, "new birth"), the initiation of the seven- or ten-year-old child into religious responsibilities, symbolized by the putting on of a shirt (*sadre*) and waist-cord (*kusti*); *patet*, a penitential confession of sins; marriage; various purifications; and *zohr-i atash*, a funeral ceremony performed in the *dakhma* ("tower of silence"), where corpses are exposed to the elements. This latter rite involves pouring a libation of animal fat into the fire and is believed to release the soul of the deceased from the power of *druj* (implicit in bodily decay) and to send him or her along the path to heaven. The modern priestly hierarchy comprises the *mobed*, assisted by the *herbad*; major fire-temples are presided over by a *dastur*.

History

The tradition in the Younger Avesta developed under the Achaemenid empire's patronage of the priestly clan of the Magi, recorded in inscriptions of the Persian kings. In this cosmopolitan imperial setting Zoroastrianism was established more widely in Persia, in the regions of Fars and Media, and became the basis for a royal ideology, including the adoption in 441 BCE of the Zoroastrian calendar.

This period ended with Alexander of Macedon's conquest of Iran (323 BCE). In the following Seleucid period (312–246 BCE), when Alexander's generals ruled over large areas of his former empire, Hellenistic culture was an important influence in Zoroastrian circles, and Zoroastrian ideas were carried westward. They took the form of the mystery religion of Mithras in Greece and played a role in the development of dualistic Jewish and Christian doctrines. In the east Zoroastrianism interacted with Buddhism.

In the early third century CE Zoroastrianism was reestablished as the state religion of the Sasanid dynasty in Iran. After the Arab conquest of the seventh century, this period was remembered as a golden age, before Islam became the dominant religion. Despite the loss of many faithful to Islam, Zoroastrian culture remained vibrant, yielding a prolific literature in Pahlavi.

Attempts at revolt against Arab hegemony, however, led to repression, and from the tenth century, many Zoroastrians began an exodus to India, settling mainly along the western coast. These Parsis ("Persians"), as they are known in India, prospered and became the primary caretakers of the tradition. Toward the end of the fifteenth century formal contacts (in the form of *rivayat*) were forged between the Parsis and the remaining Zoroastrian communities in the regions of Yazd and Kerman in Iran.

Under British colonial rule in India the Parsis had a privileged position, and many became prosperous merchants and financiers. At the same time, the tradition was confronted with a welter of religious practices and theologies, leading to disputes between reformists and conservatives. The study of the Avesta by Western philologists beginning in the eighteenth century also gave rise to doctrinal disputes.

In 1947 with the partition of British India, the Parsis found themselves further separated into a small Pakistani community in Karachi and Lahore and the more numerous groups in India, with the largest concentration in Mumbai (Bombay). International conferences of Zoroastrians began to be held in 1960, as the Zoroastrian community found itself becoming further dispersed internationally. Today the tradition continues its efforts to sustain the priesthood and adapt its traditions to new circumstances.

Timothy Lubin

Further Reading

Boyce, Mary. (1992) *Zoroastrianism*. Costa Mesa, CA: Mazda Publishers.

———, ed. (1984) *Textual Sources for the Study of Zoroastrianism*. Chicago: University of Chicago Press.

Kellens, Jean. (2000) *Essays on Zarathustra and Zoroastrianism*. Trans. by Prods Oktor Skjærvø. Costa Mesa, CA: Mazda Publishers.

Malandra, William W., trans. and ed. (1983) *An Introduction to Ancient Iranian Religion: Readings from the Avesta and the Achaemenid Inscriptions*. Minneapolis: University of Minnesota Press.

The Zend-Avesta: Part I: The Vendidad. (1887) Trans. by James Darmesteter. Sacred Books of the East, no. 4. Oxford: Oxford University Press.

The Zend-Avesta: Part II: The Sirozahs, Yasts, and Nyayis. (1882) Trans. by James Darmesteter. Sacred Books of the East, no. 23. Oxford: Oxford University Press.

The Zend-Avesta: Part III: The Yasna, Visparad, Afrinagan, Gahs, and Miscellaneous Fragments. (1887) Trans. by L. H. Mills. Sacred Books of the East, no. 31. Oxford: Oxford University Press.

ZUO ZONGTANG

ZUO ZONGTANG (1812–1885), Chinese military leader and statesman. Born into a scholarly family in Hunan Province in 1812, Zuo Zongtang studied works in the fields of history, classics, geography, and agriculture in his early years. He participated in military affairs in 1852 in the campaign against the Taiping Rebellion and soon displayed his military ability and sagacity. In 1863 he was promoted to governor-general of Fujian and Zhejiang Provinces and remained in this position until 1866. During this period, Zuo founded China's first modern dockyard and naval school in Fuzhou. In 1866 Zuo was appointed governor-general of Shaanxi and Gansu Provinces to suppress the Muslim rebels there. Between 1868 and 1880, Zuo suppressed Nian rebels in Shandong Province and Muslim rebels in northwestern China and consolidated China's northwestern frontier. He militarily sustained China's negotiation with Russia in recovering Yili, a Chinese territory occupied by Russia during the Muslim rebellion. He also carried out several important economic reforms, including the encouragement of the cotton industry in Xinjiang and mobilizing soldiers to farm unused land. In 1881 Zuo was appointed to serve in the Grand Council of the central government. Later, in 1884, he was once again put in charge of all military affairs of China during the Sino-French War (1884–1885). After a settlement between China and France was reached, Zuo Zongtang died on 5 September 1885.

Chen Shiwei

Further Reading

Chu, Wen-chang. (1966) *The Moslem Rebellion in Northwest China, 1862–1878: A Study of Government Minority Policy.* The Hague, Netherlands: Mouton de Gruyter.

Wright, Mary C. (1957) *The Last Stand of Chinese Conservatism: The T'ung-chih Restoration, 1862–1874.* Stanford, CA: Stanford University Press.

Directory of Contributors

Abazov, Rafis
Columbia University
 Astana
 Bactria
 Baguio
 Caraballo Mountains
 Cebu
 Celebes Sea
 Davao
 Gafurov, Bobojan Gafurovich
 Great Game
 Herat
 Istanbul
 Japan-Philippines Relations
 Johor
 Karakalpaks
 Karakalpakstan
 Kazakhstan—Education System
 Kota Kinabalu
 Murgab River
 Myanmar—Profile
 Nabiev, Rakhmon
 Philippine Sea
 Philippines—Education System
 Rashidov, Sharof Rashidovich
 Sabah
 Shanghai Cooperation Organization
 Singapore—Education System
 Solo
 Suleimenov, Olzhas
 Tajikistan—Education System
 Usubaliev, Turdakun Usubalievich
 Visayan Islands
 Yesilirmak River

Abdullaev, Kamol
Tajik University
 Kalym
 Tajikistan—History
 Tajikistan—Political System
 Tajikistan—Profile
 Tajiks

Abdullah, Thabit
York University
 Abadan
 Al-Najaf
 Bandar Abbas
 Basra
 Gulf of Oman
 Iraq—History
 Karbala
 Persian Gulf

Abel, J.
Princeton University
 Eto Jun
 Oe Kenzaburo

Abuza, Zachary
Simmons College
 Anh Dao Duy
 Anwar, Ibrahim
 Badawi, Abdullah Ahmed
 Bumiputra
 Chart Thai
 Chavalit, Yongchaiyudh
 Chulalongkorn University
 Chulalongkorn, King
 Estrada, Joseph

Abuza, Zachary (*continued*)
  Federal Territories—Malaysia
  Federation of Malaysia
  Goh Chok Tong
  Hoa Hao
  Hoat, Doan Viet
  Khmer Rouge
  Linh Nhat
  Macapagal, Diosdado
  Malaysia—Political System
  Malaysian Chinese Association
  Manhattan Incident
  Marcos, Ferdinand
  Megawati Sukarnoputri
  National Peacekeeping Council—Thailand
  New Economic Zones
  Nguyen Thi Minh Khai
  Nguyen Van Thieu
  Onn Bin Jaafar
  Phieu Le Kha
  Priyayi
  Ramos, Fidel
  Sabah Dispute
  Tempo
  Tran Do
  Vietnam—Economic System
  Vietnam Communist Party

Achdian, Andi
University of Nottingham
  Cukong
  Flores Sea
  Irian Jaya
  Wayang Beber

Afsaruddin, Asma
University of Notre Dame
  Ibn al-Qasim, Muhammad
  Naqshbandiya
  Qadiriya

Akcali, Pinar
Middle East Technical University
  Kyrgyzstan—Profile

Akiba, Motoko
Mills College
  Gakureki Shakai
  Ijime

Allison, Anne
Duke University
  Settai

al-Musawi, Mushin Jassim
American University of Sharjah
  Arabic
  Poetry—Iraq

Al-Shawi, Manat H
University of Toronto
  Euphrates River
  Tigris River

Altany, Alan
Western Carolina University
  Asian-Christian Religious Dialogue

Ambikaibaker, Mohan
Austin, Tex.
  Jit, Krishen
  Lim, Shirley
  Maniam, K.S.

Amer, Ramses
Uppsala University
  Association of South-East Asian Nations
  Cambodia-Vietnam Relations
  China-Vietnam Relations
  Chinese in Vietnam

Amratisha, Klairung
Chulalongkorn University
  Literature, Khmer

Anderson, Eugene
University of Californi, Riverside
  Cuisine—China

Andressen, Curtis A.
Flinders University
  Aging Population—Japan
  Australia-Asia Relations
  Japan—Profile
  Malaysia—Education System

Andreyev, Sergei
United Nations Special Mission to Afghanistan (UNSMA)
  Ismaili Sects—Central Asia

Angles, Jeffrey
International Research Center for Japanese Studies
  Shakuhachi
  Shimazaki Toson
  Suzuki Daisetsu Teitaro

226

Arase, David
Pomona College
  Overseas Economic Cooperation Fund
  Recruit Scandal
  Shipbuilding Scandal
  Showa Denko Scandal

Arifkhanov, Sharaf
Hitotsubashi University
  Kafirnigan River
  Kariz Irrigation System
  Taimanov, Isatai

Arthur, Linda B
University of Hawaii, Manoa
  Clothing, Traditional—Indonesia
  Clothing, Traditional—Kyrgyzstan

Asaduddin, M.
Jamia Millia University
  Chughtai, Ismat
  Faiz Ahmed Faiz
  Ghalib, Mirza Asadullah Khan

Ashkenazi, Michael
Leamington Spa, Warwickshire, United Kingdom
  Anime
  Chugen
  Iwashimizu Hachiman Shrine
  Manga
  Shinto
  Yamato Damashii
  Yasukuni Shrine

Aspinall, Robert
Nagoya University
  Nikkyoso

Atabaki, Touraj
University of Utrecht
  Russification and Sovietization—Central Asia

Aydin, Mustafa
Ankara University
  European Union and Turkey
  North Atlantic Treaty Organization and Turkey
  Tanzimat

Ayres, David M
University of Sydney
  Cambodia—Civil War of 1970–1975
  Cambodia—Economic System
  Cambodia—Education System
  Cambodia—Political System

  Cambodia—Profile
  Cambodian People's Party
  FUNCINPEC
  Hun Sen
  Jayavarman II
  Jayavarman VII
  Khieu Samphan
  Lon Nol
  Phnom Penh Evacuation
  Sihanouk, Norodom
  United Nations Transitional Authority in
    Cambodia

Babicz, Lionel
Hebrew University of Jerusalem
  Japan-Korea Relations

Bahcheli, Tozun
King's College; University of Western Ontario
  Aegean Sea
  Bosporus
  Marmara, Sea of

Bai, Di
Drew University
  Heilongjiang
  Liaoning
  Nei Monggol

Baker, Don
University of British Columbia
  Buddhism—Korea
  Ch'ondogyo
  Confucianism—Korea
  Religions, New—Korea
  Taejonggyo
  Tan'gun Myth
  Taoism—Korea
  Tonghak
  Unification Church

Bakti, Andi Faisal
University of Victoria
  Angkatan Belia Islam Malaysia
  Bandung Institute of Technology
  Gadjah Mada University
  Hari Raya Puasa
  Indonesia—Education System
  Islam—Indonesia
  Islam—Malaysia
  Muhammadiyah
  Nahdlatul Ulama
  University of Indonesia
  Zikir

Balaeva, Jeren M.
Laramie, Wyo.
   Turkmenistan—Education System

Balim-Harding, Cigdem
University of Manchester
   Central Asian Languages

Banerji, Debashish
University of California, Los Angeles
   Chitra-Ardhachitra-Chitrabhasha
   Painting—South Asia
   Sculpture—South Asia

Banister, Judith
Hong Kong University of Science and Technology
   China—Profile
   Marriage and Family—China

Bardsley, Jan
University of North Carolina, Chapel Hill
   Hiratsuka Raicho
   Ito Noe

Bargen, Doris G
University of Massachusetts, Amherst
   Murasaki Shikibu

Barker, David
United Nations
   Textiles—Bhutan

Barker, Nick
East-West Center; University of Hawaii
   Religious Self-Mortification

Barkin, Gareth
Washington University
   Media—Insular Southeast Asia

Barrios, Maria Josephine
Osaka University of Foreign Studies
   Literature—Philippines

Bashir, Elena
University of Chicago
   Hindi-Urdu
   Panjabi

Bashir, Shahzad
Carleton College
   Anarkali
   Bakhsh, Data Ganj
   Multan
   Muslim Saints
   Nurbakhshiya

Basri, Muhammad Chatib
University of Indonesia
   Manufacturing Industry—Indonesia

Basu, Raj Sekhar
Rabindra Bharati University
   Lingayat
   Mauritius—Profile
   Nagarjuna

Bauer, Wolfgang
Berlin, Germany
   Hokkaido

Baumgartner, Jody
St. Petersburg College
   Kong Xiangxi
   Li Shizhen
   Song Ziwen

Baumler, Alan
Indiana University of Pennsylvania
   Christianity—China
   Opium
   Opium War

Baxter, Craig
Juniata College
   Awami League
   Bangladesh—Political System
   Bangladesh—Profile
   Bangladesh Nationalist Party
   Ershad, H.M.
   Hasina Wajid, Sheikh
   Jatiya Party
   Rahman, Ziaur
   Zia, Khaleda

Beer, Bettina
Universitat Hamburg
   Suki

Bennett, Gordon
University of Texas
   China—Political System

Betz, Joachim
German Overseas Institute
   Sri Lanka—Economic System
   Tea—South Asia

Bhandari, Vivek
Hampshire College
  Devi, Phoolan
  Laxmibai
  Raziya

Bichel, Anthony R.
Central Michigan University
  Central Asian Regionalism
  Mahalla
  Turkmenistan—Profile

Bichel, Rebecca M.
Pennsylvania State University
  Samarqand
  Termez
  Urgench

Bikkinin, Irek
Tatar Gazette
  Tatars

Biliouri, Daphne
Aberystwth, Wales, United Kingdom
  Balkhash, Lake
  Irtysh River

Bishop, Elizabeth
American University, Cairo
  Soil Loss
  Water Issues

Blaylock, David W.
Eastern Kentucky University
  Shibusawa Eiichi

Blom, Amélie
Centre D'Études et de Recherches Internationales
  Jama'at-e-Islami
  Mawdudi, Abu'l-A'la

Boulton, William
Auburn University
  High-Technology Industry

Braester, Yomi
University of Washington
  Lu Xun

Brandon, James R
University of Hawaii
  Bunraku
  Drama—Japan
  Kabuki

Breu, Marlene
Western Michigan University
  Clothing, Traditional—Turkey

Brook, Kevin
Khazaria Information Center
  Iznik
  Kyrgyz

Brown, Bess
OSCE Ashgabat
  Central Asia—Human Rights
  Westernization—Central Asia

Brown, Peter
Armidale, Australia
  Paleoanthropology—East Asia
  Paleoanthropology—Southeast Asia

Brown, Rebecca M.
St. Mary's College of Maryland
  Dhaka

Brown, Roger H.
University of Southern California
  Japanese Expansion

Brown, Sid
University of the South
  Dhammayut Sect

Brucklacher, Ann
DeLand, Fla.
  Cuisine—Iraq
  Heisei Period
  Pachinko
  Zagros Mountains

Buck, David D.
University of Wisconsin, Milwaukee
  Chinese Civil War of 1945–1949
  Guomindang
  Lee Teng-hui
  Shandong
  Sino-French War
  Sino-Japanese Conflict, Second

Buell, Paul D.
Seattle, Wash.
  Asian Economic Crisis of 1997
  Camel, Bactrian
  Chinese Communist Party
  Cuisine—Mongolia
  Damdinsuren, Tsendiyn

Buell, Paul D. *(continued)*
Ginseng
Islam—Southwest Asia
Jurchen Jin Dynasty
Khalkha
Khararkhi
Khubilai Khan
Mongolia—Economic System
Mongolia—History
Mongols
Muslim Peoples in China
Polo, Marco
Russians in Mongolia
Sukhbaatar, Damdiny
Tea—China
Tofu

Bunnell, Timothy G.
National University of Singapore
Petronas Towers

Buntrock, Dana
University of California, Berkeley
Arata Isozaki
Architecture—Modern Japan
Kurokawa Kisho
Tange Kenzo

Burkman, Thomas
State University of New York, Buffalo
Konoe Fumimaro

Butler-Diaz, Jacqueline
Mesa, Ariz.
Clothing, Traditional—Laos

Byard-Jones, Tim
Reading, Berkshire, United Kingdom
Arja
Bali Barong-Rangda
Balinese Sanghyang
Dance—Bali
Masks, Javanese
Mendu
Noer, Arifin C.
Pramoedya Ananta Toer
Puisi
Rendra, W.S.
Riantiarno, Nano
Wijaya, Putu

Caldwell, John C.
Australian National University
Fertility

Campbell, Joel
Kansai Gaidai University
Chen Yun
Kim Il Sung
Kim Jong Il
Korea Institute of Science and Technology
Li Peng
Science Towns—Korea

Campi, Alicia J.
US-Mongolia Advisory Group, Inc.
Bogdo Khan
Cashmere Industry
Forest Industry—Mongolia
Mongolian Social Democratic Party
Narantsatsralt, Janlavyn
United Party of Mongolia

Caprio, Mark E.
Rikkyo University
Communism—North Korea
Korea-Japan Treaty of 1965
North Korea—Profile
North Korea-South Korea Relations
Three Revolutions Movement
United Front Strategy

Carbo, Nick
Hollywood, Fla.
Poetry—Philippines

Cardona, George
University of Pennsylvania
Indo-Aryan Languages

Carlile, Lonny
University of Hawaii, Manoa
Denki Roren
Quality Circles
Shunto

Carr, Kevin G.
Kishihama
Judo
Jujutsu

Case, William
Griffith University
Malaysia—History

Cassidy, Carol
Lao Textiles Company
Textiles—Laos

Cavasin, Nathalie
Keio University
  Ando Tadao
  Araki Sadao
  Chubu
  Chugoku
  Citizen's Movement
  Ebina Danjo
  Etorofu Island
  Fuji, Mount
  Fujita Tsuguhara
  Fukuchi Gen'ichiro
  Fukumoto Kazuo
  Furukawa Ichibei
  Honshu
  Iriomotejima Island
  Ishihara Shintaro
  Japanese Firms Abroad
  Kansai Region
  Kanto Region
  Kawasaki
  Kinki Region
  Kodama Yoshio
  Kunashiro Island
  Kyushu
  Lockheed Scandal
  Maruyama Masao
  Matsumoto Shigeharu
  Minobe Tatsukichi
  Ringi System
  Sado Island
  Sasagawa Ryoichi
  Setouchi Region
  Shikoku
  Tatsuno Kingo
  Tokaimura Nuclear Disaster
  Whaling—Japan
  Yakushima Island

Chai, Winberg
University of Wyoming
  China-Taiwan Relations

Chakravorty, Ranes C.
University of Virginia; Virginia Polytechnic Institute
  Chatterjee, Bankim Chandra
  Gupta Empire
  Medicine, Ayurvedic
  Vivekananda, Swami

Chan, Timothy
University of Sydney
  Chuci
  Du Fu

  Li Bai
  Quan Tangshi
  Shijing

Chance, Linda H.
University of Pennsylvania
  Biwa

Chang, Jui-te
Academia Sinica
  Academia Sinica
  National Taiwan University

Chang, Teh-Kuang
Ball State University
  Mongolia—Profile
  Nepal—Education System
  Peking University

Charney, Michael W.
University of London, School of Oriental and African Studies
  Anawratha
  Andaman Sea
  Arakan Yoma Mountains
  Chinese in Myanmar
  Islam—Myanmar
  Moulmein
  Myanmar—Economic System
  Myanmar—Foreign Relations
  Myanmar—History
  Rakhine State
  Rohingya
  Tenasserim Division

Chen Chiu, Lee-in
Chung-hua Institute for Economic Research
  Taiwan Investment in Asia

Chen, Bao-xing
China Academy of Traditional Chinese Medicine
  Acupuncture
  Massage—China
  Medicine, Traditional—China
  Moxibustion

Chen, Shiwei
Lake Forest College
  Ci Xi, Empress Dowager
  Yuan Shikai
  Zuo Zongtang

Chen, Yixin
University of North Carolina, Wilmington
  Sui Dynasty

Chen, Yixin *(continued)*
Yao
Yi
Zhuang

Chhoki, Sonam
University of London, School of Oriental and African Studies
Bhutan—History
Bhutan—Profile
Bhutan—Religion
Bhutanese
Lhasa
Potala Palace
Tibetans

Chin, James
University of Papua New Guinea
Southeast Asia Treaty Organization

Cho, Hong Sik
Catholic University of Korea
South Korea-European Union Relations

Choe, Minja Kim
University of Hawaii
Marriage and Family—East Asia

Choi, Yearn Hong
University of Seoul
Han River
Naktong River and Delta
Pak Kyung-ri

Chouvy, Pierre-Arnaud
Courbevoie, France
Drug Trade
Golden Crescent
Golden Triangle

Chowdhury, Sima Roy
Lincoln Park, N.J.
Taxila

Chua, Beng Huat
National University of Singapore
New Rich

Chua, Ying
Ohio State University
Fu Baoshi

Chukhovich, Boris
Montreal, Québec, Canada
Fine Arts—Central Asia

Chung, Hyunsook
Seoul, South Korea
Clothing, Traditional—Korea

Chung, Stephanie
Hong Kong Baptist University
Hundred Flowers Campaign
Long March
Three and Five Antis Campaigns

Church, Gary
Huntsville, Tex.
Nukus
Osh
Petropavlovsk

Clark, Donald N.
Trinity University
Christianity—Korea

Clark, Ross
University of Auckland
Austronesian Languages

Clement, Victoria
Ohio State University
Turkmenistan—History

Clow, Kate
Antalya, Turkey
Anti-Taurus
Ararat, Mount
Archaeology—Turkey
Byzantines
Cilician Gates
Eastern Orthodox Church
Hittites
Miletus
Ottoman Empire
Pergamon
Saint Paul
Sardis
Tarsus
Taurus Mountains
Turkey, Republic of

Colak, Yilmaz
Eastern Mediterranean University
Menderes, Adnan
Turks—West Asia

Cole, Juan
University of Michigan
Babism
Baha'i

Collins, Diana
Textile Society of Hong Kong
    Kain Batik

Cook, Constance A.
Lehigh University
    Zhou Dynasty

Cook, Geoffrey
International Institute of India Studies
    British East India Company
    Mutiny, Indian

Cordonnier, Isabelle
French Institute for Political Studies
    Japan-Pacific Islands Relations

Cox, Sean
Dogus Universitesi
    Iraq-Turkey Relations

Coxhead, Ian
Australian National University
    Agriculture—Southeast Asia

Creighton, Millie
University of British Columbia
    Chrysanthemum
    Department Stores—East Asia

Cribb, Robert
University of Queensland
    Abangan
    Amboina Massacre
    Babirusa
    Bahasa Indonesia
    Batavia
    Bosch, Johannes van den
    Coen, Jan Pieterszoon
    Daendels, Herman
    Darul Islam
    Ethnic Colonial Policy—Indonesia
    Gerindo
    Gestapu Affair
    Hatta, Mohammad
    Hizbullah
    Indonesia—Economic System
    Mongol Empire
    Netherlands East Indies
    Repelita
    Santri
    Speelman, Cornelius
    Sukarno
    Treaty of Giyanti
    Umar, Teuku

Cumings, Bruce
University of Chicago
    Korean War

Cunha, Stephen F.
Humboldt State University
    Altay Mountains
    Badakhshan
    Dushanbe
    Karakoram Mountains
    Khorog
    Khunjerab Pass
    Leopard, Snow
    Pamir Peoples
    Pamir Range
    Sarez Lake
    Sheep, Marco Polo
    Tarim Basin
    Tian Shan
    Trans Alai

Cwiertka, Katarzyna J.
Leiden University
    Cuisine—Korea

Daftary, Farhad
Institute of Ismaili Studies
    Ismaili Sects—South Asia

Dai, Yingcong
William Paterson University
    Boxer Rebellion
    Taiping Rebellion

Dallapiccola, Anna L.
Edinburgh, U.K.
    Vijayanagara Empire

Dalloz, Jacques
l'Institut d'Etudes Politiques de Paris
    Indochina War of 1940–1941

Daly, M. Catherine
St. Paul, Minn.
    Clothing, Traditional—Afghanistan
    Omar, Mullah Muhammad

D'Amicantonio, John
California State University, Long Beach
    Royal University of Phnom Penh

Darian, Steven
Rutgers University
    Ganges River
    Silk Road

Das Gupta, Sanjukta
Rabindra Bharati University
Aurangabad
Awadh
Bhubaneshwar
Bihar
Chittagong
Dadra and Nagar Haveli Union Territory
Gujarat
Hyderabad
Indigo
Indore
Khasi
Munda Languages
Nagas
Pondicherry
Pune
Puri
Rubab
Sikhism
Srinagar

Dass, Nirmal
Toronto, Canada
Afghanistan—Human Rights
Azad Kashmir
Baltistan
Bamian
Baraka
Bitab, Sufi
Calendars—East Asia
Calendars—West Asia
Dawai, Abdul Hadi
Din Mohammad, Mushk-e Alam
Durrani
Greeks in Turkey
Mamadali Mahmudov
Marriage and Family—West Asia
Muhajir
Pakistan—Human Rights
Shah, Lalon
Shah, Mihr Ali
Shahbaz Qalandar Lal
Wakhan

Davis, C. Roger
Northampton, Mass.
Agartala
Ahmadabad
Ajodhya
Amritsar
Arunachal Pradesh
Assam
Bodh Gaya

Calcutta
Chandigarh
Darjeeling
Dehra Dun
Delhi Union Territory
Gangtok
Guwahati
Haryana
Himachal Pradesh
Imphal
Jaipur
Jodhpur
Kanpur
Kohima
Leh
Lucknow
Manipur
Mathura
Meghalaya
Mizoram
Nagaland
Patna
Rajasthan
Shillong
Simla

Davis-Kimball, Jeannine
Center for the Study of Eurasian Nomads
Nomadic Pastoralism—Central Asia

D'Costa, Anthony P.
University of Washington, Tacoma
Steel Industry—Korea

De Bary, Wm. Theodore
Columbia University
Neo-Confucianism

de Silva, K.M.
Sri Lanka International Centre for Ethnic Studies
Ethnic Conflict—South Asia
Jammu and Kashmir

Degtiar, Mikhail
Jewish Cultural Center of Uzbekistan
Bukharian Jews

DeMarco, Michael A.
Journal of the Asian Martial Arts
Wushu

Derris, Karen
Harvard University
Buddhism, Theravada—Southeast Asia

Desser, David
University of Illinois
  Cinema, Contemporary—Japan

Dewan, Deepali
University of Minnesota
  Anand, Mulk Raj

Dickinson, Frederick R.
University of Pennsylvania
  Goto Shinpei
  Ikeda Hayato
  Kato Takaaki
  Saionji Kinmochi

Diller, Anthony
Australian National University
  Tai-Kadai Languages

Dimitrov, Dimitar L.
Sofia University
  Agriculture—West Asia
  Fishing Industry—Korea
  Industry—West Asia
  Jakarta
  Java
  Kalimantan
  Malaysia-Europe Relations
  Manufacturing Industry—Philippines
  Organization of Petroleum Exporting Countries
  Woodworking—Central Asia

Do, Thuy
Australian National University
  Refugees—Southeast Asia

Dobbs, Charles M.
Iowa State University
  Hart, Robert
  Hundred Days Reform
  Kang Youwei
  Li Hongzhang
  Lin Biao
  Manchurian Incident
  Northern Expedition
  Self-Strengthening Movement
  Sino-Japanese War
  Xi'an Incident
  Zeng Guofan

Dolan, Thomas P.
Columbus State University
  Comfort Women
  Democratization—South Korea
  Haeju

Han Yong-un
Japan-Taiwan Relations
Keumkang, Mount
Namp'o
Northern Territories
Status of Forces Agreement
T'aebaek Mountains
World War II
Yasukuni Shrine Controversy
Yu Kwan Sun

Dolukhanov, Pavel
University of Newcastle upon Tyne
  Architecture—Central Asia
  Black Sea
  Yerevan

Dombrowsky, Patrick
*Center for Studies and Research on Middle Asia
(CERAM)*
  Garabil Plateau
  Ishim River

Domroes, Manfred
Mainz University
  Andaman and Nicobar Islands
  Bay of Bengal
  Climatology—South Asia
  Colombo
  Indian Ocean
  Lakshadweep
  Maldives—History
  Maldives—Profile
  Sri Lanka—Profile

Donnelly, Peter
University of Toronto
  Mountaineering

Donovan, Deanna G.
University of Hawaii
  Forest Industry—Southeast Asia

Dorian, James P.
State of Hawaii
  Energy—Central Asia

Dorji, Karma
Ministry of Health and Education, Bhutan
  Clothing, Traditional—Bhutan

Duke, Benjamin C.
International Christian University
  Imperial Rescript on Education

Dunham, Mary Frances
Columbia University
  Music—Bangladesh

Duschinski, Anna Haley
Harvard University
  Sabri Brothers

Dutton, George E.
University of California, Los Angeles
  Nguyen Du
  Truong Vinh Ky

Dwyer, Arienne
University of Kansas
  Turkic Languages

Eade, Chris
Australian National University
  Calendars—Southeast Asia

Earns, Lane R.
University of Wisconsin, Oshkosh
  Nagasaki
  Tokugawa Period
  Tsushima Island
  Twenty-Six Martyrs

Eberstadt, Nicholas
American Enterprise Institute for Public Policy
  North and South Korean Economic Ventures

Edgington, David W.
University of British Columbia
  Japanese Firms Abroad

Efegil, Ertan
Eastern Mediterrannan University
  Central Asia-Russia Relations

Eissenstat, Howard
University of California, Los Angeles
  Adana
  Ankara
  Circassians
  Izmir

Eldridge, Philip
University of Tasmania
  Southeast Asia—Human Rights

Eldridge, Robert D.
Research Institute for Peace and Security
  Amami Islands
  Hatoyama Ichiro

  Higashikuni Naruhiko
  Kishi Nobusuke
  Nakasone Yasuhiro
  Okinawa
  San Francisco Peace Treaty
  Sato Eisaku
  United States Military Bases—Japan
  United States-Japan Security Treaty
  Yoshida Shigeru

Elias, Jamal
Amherst College
  Shari'a

Elsie, Robert
Olzheim, Germany
  Albanians

Emch, Michael
Portland State University
  Disease, Tropical
  Jute

Endicott, Elizabeth
Middlebury College
  Yuan Dynasty

Eng, Robert Y.
University of Redlands
  Agriculture—China
  Chen Kaige
  Courtyards
  Fishing Industry—China
  Foot Binding
  Machinery and Equipment Industry—China
  Textile and Clothing Industry—East Asia
  Toy Industry—China

Entessar, Nader
Spring Hill College
  Iran-United States Relations

Erdemir, Aykan
Dorchester, Mass.
  Guney, Yilmaz

Erhan, Cagri
Ankara University
  European Union and Turkey
  North Atlantic Treaty Organization and Turkey
  Tanzimat

Ettner, Charles
California State University, Fresno
  Tai Chi

Evered, Emine O.
University of Arizona
Children's Day—Turkey
Music—Turkey

Evered, Kyle T.
Illinois State University
Abkhazia
Amu Dar'ya
Ardabil
Dagestan
Kandahar
Mashhad
Qom
Shiraz
Syr Dar'ya
Tabriz

Fan, C. Cindy
University of California, Los Angeles
China—Population Resettlement
Jiangsu
Rural Workers, Surplus—China

Fanany, Rebecca
Deakin University
Randai

Fattah, Hala
Amman, Jordan
Iraq—Education System

Faustino, Marie-Hélène F.
École Nationale des Ponts et Chaussées
Architecture—Korea

Felix, Mark S.
Sunway College
Cuisine—Malaysia

Fet, Victor
Marshall University
Camel, Arvana Dromedary
Horse, Akhal-teke
Horse, Karabair
Horse, Lokai
Sheep, Karakul

Feulner, Frank
University of London, School of Oriental and African Studies
Belo, Bishop Carlos
Dili
Fretilin

Gusmao, Xanana
Mohamad, Goenawan
Ramos-Horta, Jose

Fiacconi, Giorgio
Central Asia Times
Christianity—Central Asia

Field, Stephen
Trinity University
Feng Shui

Forage, Paul
Florida Atlantic University
Grand Canal
Great Wall
Junk
Magnetism
Needham, Joseph
Printing and Papermaking
Science, Traditional—China
Sericulture—China

Forêt, Philippe
Zurich, Switzerland
Chengde
Summer Palace

Foroughi, Payam
University of Utah
Bakhtaran
Elburz
Karun River and Shatt al Arab River
Kerman
Khurasan

Forrest, Francesca M.
Berkshire Publishing Group LLC
Kamakura Period
Shi

Fortna, Benjamin C.
University of London, School of Oriental and African Studies
Turkey—Education System

Fox, Stacey
Saratoga Springs, N.Y.
Ci
Dance—Korea
Kathmandu
Komodo Dragon
Music—West Asia
Naguata

Fox, Stacey (*continued*)
Sarod
Shamisen
Sun Bear

Frank, Adam D.
University of Texas, Austin
Birds and Bird Cages

Freedman, Robert O.
Baltimore Hebrew University
Iran-Russia Relations

Frerichs, Warren
Greenhill School
Qigong

Frost, Peter
Williams College
Japan—Political System

Fry, Gerald W.
University of Minnesota, Twin Cities
Bhumipol Adulyadej
Buddhadasa, Bhikku
Chintanakan mai
Chuan Leekpai
Ekaphap
Laos—Education System
Laos—Political System
Laos-Thailand Relations
Lee Kuan Yew
Longboat Racing
Mechai Viravaidya
Mittaphap Bridge
October 6 Crisis—Thailand
Pathet Lao
Phalang Dharma Party
Pridi Banomyong
Student Uprising of 1973—Thailand
Sulak Sivaraksa
Thailand—Education System
Thaksin Shinawatra
Thompson, Jim
Westernization—Southeast Asia

Fulton, Bruce
University of British Columbia
Hwang Sun-won
Literature—Korea

Gale, Robert
Royal Roads University
Energy Industry—China
Shanghai Pudong New Area

Gatzen, Barbara
Australian National University
Media—Japan

Gavin, Masako
Bond University
Shiga Shigetaka

Georg, Stefan
University of Leiden
Altaic Languages
Hmong-Mien Languages
Indo-European Languages
Mongolian Languages
Sino-Tibetan Languages
Tibeto-Burman Languages
Tungus Languages
Uralic Languages

Ghanoonparvar, M. R.
University of Texas, Austin
Cuisine—Iran

Gleason, Greg
University of New Mexico
Kazakhstan—Political System
Turkmenistan—Economic System
Turkmenistan—Political System
Uzbekistan—Economic System
Uzbekistan—Political System

Goldin, Paul R.
University of Pennsylvania
Warring States Period—China

Goldman, Robert P.
University of California, Berkeley
Literature, Sanskrit
Mahabharata
Ramayana
Upanishads

Goldstein, Darra
Williams College
Cuisine—Central Asia

Golkin-Kadonaga, Arline
Los Angeles Pierce College
Famine—China

Gombosurengiin, Ganzorig
Supreme Court of Mongolia
Mongolia—Political System

Goodwin, Mike
College Station
    April 19 Revolution—Korea

Gopinath, R.
Jamia Millia University
    Calicut
    Kerala
    Mangalore
    Trivandrum

Gorjão, Paulo
Lusiada University
    Dili Massacre
    United Nations in East Timor

Gottesman, Brian
Cambridge, Mass.
    Bakhtiari
    Karabag
    Sind

Govindasamy, Geetha
University of Malaya
    Anglo-Dutch Treaty
    Bangkok Declaration
    Dutch East India Company
    Koreans in Japan
    Malayan Emergency
    Malayan People's Anti-Japanese Army
    North Korea-United States Relations
    South Korea-United States Relations
    Treaty of Amity and Co-operation of 1976

Graburn, Nelson
University of California, Berkeley
    Tourism

Gray, Laurel Victoria
Alexandria, Va.
    Dance—Central Asia

Greene, Megan
University of London, School of Oriental and African Studies
    Beijing
    Calligraphy—China
    Hong Kong

Grimes, William W.
Boston University
    Economic Planning Agency
    Japanese International Cooperation Agency

Grimes-MacLellan, Dawn
University of Illinois, Urbana Champaign
    Kyoiku Mama

Grodzins Gold, Ann
Syracuse Univeristy
    Pilgrimage—South Asia

Groot, Gerry
University of Adelaide
    Communism—China

Gülalp, Haldun
Bosphorus University
    Refah and Fazilet Parties

Gullett, Warwick
Australian Maritime College
    Transportation System—China
    Ustyurt Plateau

Gunn, Geoffrey C.
Nagasaki University
    Brunei—Political System
    Brunei—Profile
    East Timor—Profile
    Islam—Brunei

Gupt, Bharat
University of Delhi
    Dance—Bangladesh
    Hindu Philosophy
    Jatra
    Music—India
    Music, Devotional—India
    Nataka
    Possession
    Prakarana
    Rasa

Guttmann, Allen
Amherst College
    Olympics
    Sports—China
    Sports—India
    Sports—Islamic Asia
    Sports—Japan
    Sports—Korea

Haas, Michael
California State University, Fullerton
    Acehnese
    Buddhist Liberal Democratic Party—Cambodia
    Goh Keng Swee

Haas, Michael (*continued*)
Marcos, Imelda
Pibul Songgram
Thai Revolution of 1932
United Nations

Hafner, James Allen
University of Massachusetts, Amherst
Boat People
Earthquakes
Endangered Species
Typhoons
Volcanoes

Haghayeghi, Mehrdad
Southwest Missouri State University
Kyrgyzstan—Economic System
Kyrgyzstan—Political System
Madrasahs
Minaret
Muslim Religious Board of Central Asia

Halabi, Awad Eddie
University of Toronto
Arabs
Muslims, Sunni

Handrahan, L. M.
Finvola Group
Akaev, Askar
Aksakal
Mongolia—Human Rights

Hara, Abubakar Eby
Jember University
Hamengku Buwono IX, Sri Sultan
Madurese
Malik, Adam
Moerdani, Leonardus Benjamin
Rais, Muhammad Amien

Hardy, Andrew
National University of Singapore
Vietnam—Internal Migration
Vietnamese, Overseas

Harper, Katherine Anne
Loyola Marymount University
Jade
Jainism
Women in South Asia

Harpviken, Kristian Berg
International Peace Research Institute, Oslo (PRIO)
Afghanistan—Political System

Ethnic Conflict—Afghanistan
Land Mines

Harris, Rachel
University of London, School of Oriental and African Studies
Beijing Opera
Dombra
Music—Central Asia
Music—China
Twelve Muqam

Hashmi, Taj I.
Independent University
Bangladesh—History
Islam—South Asia

Hassanpour, Amir
University of Toronto
Language Purification
Media
Media—West Asia
Self-Censorship

Hayase, Shinzo
Osaka City University
Philippines—History

Haydari, Nazan
Ohio University
Pamuk, Orhan

Hayes, Louis D.
University of Montana
Democratic Socialist Party—Japan
Japan Communist Party
Japan Socialist Party
Komeito
Liberal Democratic Party—Japan

Hayford, Charles
Evanston, Ill.
Yen, Y.C. James

Heberer, Thomas
Gerhard-Mercator University, Duisburg
Cadre System—China
Corruption—China
Guanxi
National Minorities—China
Political Participation, Unofficial—China
Social Associations—China

Hegel, Robert E.
Washington University, St Louis, Mo.
Literature—China
Poetry—China

Heim, Maria
California State University, Long Beach
Buddhism—South Asia
Buddhism—Vietnam

Henderson, Mark
University of California, Berkeley
Air Pollution

Herbert, Patricia M.
British Library
Bassein
Burmese Arts
Magwe Division
Mandalay
Myanmar—Education System
Pegu
Yangon

Hernandez de Leon, Josie
Laurentian University
People Power Movement
Philippines—Political System

Hill, Emily M.
Queen's University
Chang Fee Ming
Chinese in Southeast Asia
Chuah Thean Teng
Siemens Incident
Tay Hooi Keat
Zhou Enlai

Hill, Ronald D.
University of Hong Kong
Guizhou

Hillman, John
Trent University
Tin Industry

Hirai, Hajime
Shiga University
Baseball—Japan

Ho, Khai Leong
National University of Singapore
Chinese-Language Newspapers—Singapore

Federated Malay States
Malay States, Unfederated
Malaysia—Profile
Nanyang Technological University
Singapore Democratic Party
Straits Settlements
Straits Times, The
Workers' Party—Singapore

Hockings, Paul
University of Illinois
Abdullah, Muhammad
Abu, Mount
Afghan Hound
Africa-Asia Relations
Afzal Khan
Ali Janhar, Mohamed
Anglo-Indians
Anglo-Mysore Wars
Aryan
Asoka
Assamese
Banteng
Bengal, West
Bhil
Bhopal
Birla Family
Blavatsky, Helena Petrovna
Bolan Pass
Bose, Subhas Chandra
Brahman
Bustard, Hubara
Calendars—South Asia
Chagos Archipelago
Chaudhuri, Nirad Chandra
Chenab River
Chera
Chhattisgarh
Chicken
Chola
Coimbatore
Coomaraswamy, Ananda Kentish
Cormorant
Cranganur
Curzon, George Nathaniel
Dance, Kandyan
Dekkan
Dogra Dynasty
Duck and Goose, Domesticated
Eastern Ghats
Everest, Mount
Fazl, Abu'l
Garo
Goat

Hockings, Paul *(continued)*
Godavari River
Godse, Nathuram Vinayak
Gond
Gujarati
Haidar, Ali Khan
Harsa
Hill Tribes of India
Himalaya Range
Hindu Kush
Hindu Values
Hinduism—India
Holkars
Indian Subcontinent
Indo-Gangetic Plain
Indus River
Islamic Banking
Jharkhand
Jhelum River
Jones, William
Jumna River
K2, Mount
Kalidasa
Kandy
Kangchenjunga, Mount
Kautilya
Kaveri River
Kistna River
Ladakh
Lion, Asiatic
Literature—India
Madhya Pradesh
Madras
Madurai
Mahanadi River
Medicine, Unani
Mohenjo Daro
Narayan, R.K.
Narmada River
Nilgiri District
Ootacamund
Pandit
Pandya
Peripatetics
Pig
Poros
Raipur
Rajkot
Rajput
Ramachandran, Marudur Gopalamenon
Ramakrishna
Rann of Kachchh
Rao, Raja
Ravi River

Refugees—South Asia
Reunion Island
Rhinocerous, Asiatic
Sankara
Sarnath
Satpura Range
Satyagraha
Siddhartha Gautama
Sikkim
Sindhia Family
Singh, Jai
Sundarbhans
Sutlej River
Tata Family
Teresa, Mother
Thanjavur
Thimphu
Tripura
Tungabhadra River
Uttar Pradesh
Uttaranchal
Varanasi
Vindhya Mountains
Vishakapatnam
Western Ghats
Yak
Zebu

Hossain, Akhtar
University of Newcastle
Bangladesh—Economic System

Houtman, Gustaaf
Royal Anthropological Institute, London
Anti-Fascist People's Freedom League—
    Myanmar
Aung San
Aung San Suu Kyi
Burmans
Mandalay Palace
National League for Democracy—Myanmar
Ne Win, U
Nu, U
Pagodas, Burmese
Pali Canon
Spirit Cults
State Law and Order Restoration Council—
    Myanmar
Thakins
Than Shwe
Thant, U
Union Solidarity and Development Association—
    Mya

Hruschka, Daniel
Emory University
 Aimag
 Darhan
 Erdenet
 Gandan Lamasery
 Gobi Desert
 Hangai Mountains
 Hentii Mountains
 Horse, Przewalski's
 Karakorum
 Mongolia—Education System
 Trans-Mongolian Railway
 Ulaanbaatar

Hsieh, Ding-hwa Evelyn
Truman State University
 Buddhism—China
 Buddhism, Chan
 Buddhism, Pure Land

Hsu, Madeline Y.
San Francisco State University
 Chinese, Overseas

Hu, Xiaobo
Clemson University
 China—Economic System
 China—Internal Migration
 Special Economic Zones—China

Huang, Shu-Min
Iowa State University
 Dragon Boat Festival
 Mid-Autumn Festival
 Qingming
 Spring Festival—China

Hudson, Mark
University of Tsukuba
 Jomon Period
 Yayoi Period

Huffman, James L.
Wittenberg University
 Abe Iso
 Nitobe Inazo

Huong, Ha
Technology Management Centre, Singapore
 Ho Chi Minh
 Vietnam—Political System

Hwang, Eui-Gak
Korea University
 North Korea—Economic System
 South Korea—Economic System

Hyer, Eric
Brigham Young University
 Central Asia-China Relations
 China-Russia Relations
 Mongolia-China-Russia Relations
 Spratly Islands Dispute

Idris, Hazinah
University of Malaya
 Batik

Iezzi, Julie A.
University of Hawaii, Manoa
 Music—Japan
 Noh-Kyogen

Irem, Nazim
Dokuz Eylul Universitesi
 Etatism—Turkey
 Turkey—Economic System

Isikozlu, E.F.
Whitby, Canada
 Anatolia
 Antakya
 Antalya
 Bursa
 Diyarbakir
 Edirne
 Erzurum
 Gaziantep
 Halide Edib Adivar
 Kars
 Kemal, Yasar
 Kutahya
 Samsun
 Sivas
 Trabzon
 Urfa
 Van
 Zonguldak

Isikozlu, T.
Whitby, Canada
 Amasya
 Anatolia
 Antakya
 Antalya
 Bursa

Isikozlu, T. *(continued)*
  Diyarbakir
  Edirne
  Erzurum
  Gaziantep
  Halide Edib Adivar
  Kars
  Kemal, Yasar
  Konya
  Kutahya
  Samsun
  Sivas
  Trabzon
  Urfa
  Van
  Zonguldak

Islamov, Bakhitor
Tashkent University
  Kafirnigan River
  Kariz Irrigation System
  Taimanov, Isatai

Jacq, Pascale
Autralian National University
  Austroasiatic Languages
  Mon-Khmer Languages

Jain, B. M.
University of Rajasthan
  Bangalore
  Bangladesh-India Relations
  Bangladesh-Pakistan Relations
  India—Human Rights
  India—Political System
  India-Myanmar Relations
  India-Pakistan Relations
  Kama Sutra
  Sinhalese
  Sri Lanka—Human Rights
  Westernization—West Asia

Jamieson, Neil L.
Callao, Va.
  Cuisine—Vietnam
  Plowing Ritual—Vietnam
  Vietnamese
  Vietnamese Language
  Wandering Souls
  Zodiac System—East Asia

Jay, Jennifer
University of Alberta
  Wu Zetian

Jenkins, Martha C.
Western Kentucky University
  Clothing, Traditional—Iraq

Jennings, John M.
United States Air Force Academy
  Tojo Hideki
  Wang Jingwei
  Yamamoto Isoroku

Jha, Ganganath
Jawaharlal Nehru University
  Malay-Indonesian Languages

Jia, Wenshan
State University of New York, New Paltz
  Cinema—China
  Hu Jintao

Jian, Ming
William Paterson University
  Social Realism—China

Jiang, Yonglin
Grand Valley State University
  Han Dynasty
  Ming Dynasty
  Qing Dynasty
  Song Dynasty
  Tang Dynasty

Johnson, Carter
Open Society Institute (OSI), Uzbekistan
  Semipalatinsk Movement

Jung-Kim, Jennifer
University of California, Los Angeles
  Chagang Province
  Ch'ongjin
  Kim Myong-sun
  Korean Language
  Koreans
  Kwangju
  Kyonggi Province
  North Cholla Province
  North Ch'ungch'ong Province
  North Hamgyong Province
  North Hwanghae Province
  North P'yongan Province
  Paper Crafts and Arts—Korea
  Park Chung Hee
  Pojagi
  Sejong, King
  Seoul

Shin Saimdang
South Cholla Province
South Ch'ungch'ong Province
South Hamgyong Province
South Hwanghae Province
South P'yongan Province
Taedong River
Taegu
Taejon
Tanch'ong
Women in Korea
Yanggang Province
Yi T'ae-yong

Jurgenmeyer, Clemens
Arnold-Bergstraesser-Institut
Hindu Nationalism

Jussawalla, Meheroo
University of Hawaii
Information Technology Industry

Kagan, Richard C.
Hamline University
Chen Duxiu
Chen Shui-bian
China—Human Rights
Nanjing Massacre
South Korea—Human Rights
South Korea—Profile
Taiwan—Education System
Taiwan—Human Rights
Taiwan, Modern
Taiwan-United States Relations
Vietnam War

Kaldis, Nicholas A.
Binghamton University
Ba Jin

Kalyuzhnova, Yelena
University of Reading
Kazakhstan—Economic System
Kazakhstan—Profile

Kane, Daniel C.
University of Hawaii, Manoa
Kim Pu-shik
Kim Yu-sin
Korea—History
March First Independence Movement
Sadaejuui
Yi Song-gye

Kang, Chul-Kyu
University of Seoul
Chaebol

Kangas, Roger D.
George C. Marshall European Center for Security Studies
Basmachi Movement
Communism—Central Asia
Karimov, Islam
Kunaev, Dinmukhamed
Nazarbaev, Nursultan
Oil and Mineral Industries—Central Asia
Rakhmonov, Imomali
Uzbekistan—Profile

Karan, Pradyumna P.
University of Kentucky
Japanese Foreign Investments

Karasik, Theodore
RAND
Medicine, Traditional—Central Asia

Karlsson, Anders
University of London, School of Oriental and African Studies
Ch'oe Nam-son
Nobi
Yangban

Karpova, Elena
University of Missouri
Clothing, Traditional—Tajikistan
Clothing, Traditional—Turkmenistan
Clothing, Traditional—Uzbekistan

Kartomi, Margaret
Monash University
Music—Indonesia

Katahira, Miyuki
International Research Center for Japanese Studies
Bonsai

Kaul, Chandrika
University of St. Andrews
Akbar
Aurangzeb
Babur
Canning, Charles John
Humayun
Jahangir
Khilafat Movement

Kaul, Chandrika *(continued)*
Macaulay, Thomas B.
Montagu-Chelmsford Reforms
Morley-Minto Reforms
Muslim League
Nehru, Motilal
Quit India Movement
Sai Baba, Satya
Shah Jahan
Tagore, Rabindranath

Kawakami, Akihiro
Chiba, Japan
Taisho Period

Kazi, Aftab
Washington, D.C.
Pakistan—History
Pakistan People's Party
Siraiki

Keller, Shoshana
Hamilton College
Russians in Central Asia

Kendall, Harry
University of California, Berkeley
Mongolia-Soviet Union Relations

Kenley, David L.
Marshall University
May Fourth Movement
Republican China
Republican Revolution of 1911

Kennedy, Kenneth
Cornell University
Paleoanthropology—South Asia

Kerlogue, Fiona
The Horniman Museum
Marriage and Family—Insular Southeast Asia
Marriage and Family—Mainland Southeast Asia
Women in Southeast Asia

Ketels, Christian
Harvard University
Export-Led Development

Khabibullaev, Akram
Al-Beruni Institute for Oriental Studies
Uzbekistan—History

Khalid, Adeeb
Carleton College
Alisher Navoiy Samarkand State University
Bukhara
Central Asia—Modern
Jadidism
Tashkent
Uzbekistan—Education System

Khan, Abdul Karim
University of Hawaii, Leeward
Constitution—India
French East India Company
Hadood
Khushal Khan Khatak
Kipling, Joseph Rudyard
Muhajir Qawmi Movement
Pashtunwali
Rahmat Ali, Chauduri
Taliban

Khan, Natalya Yu.
Tashkent State Institute of Oriental Studies
Almaty
Ashgabat
Central Asia—Late Medieval and Early Modern
Fergana Valley
Guliston
Karshi
Khujand
Kulob
Mary
Paleoanthropology—Central Asia
Qurghonteppa
Turkmenabat

Kidd, Laura Klosterma
Southern Illinois University at Carbondale
Clothing, Traditional—China
Clothing, Traditional—Mongolia
Clothing, Traditional—Tibet

Kilic, Ayla H.
University of Winnipeg
Adalet Partisi
Constitution—Turkey
Demirel, Suleyman
Hikmet, Nazim
Nesin, Aziz
Ozal, Turgut
Turkey—Political System
Turkey—Profile

Kim, Byounglo Philo
Korea Institute for National Unification
Food Crisis—North Korea

Kim, Jun-hee
Berkshire Publishing Group LLC
Cappadocia

Kim, Robert H.
Western Washington University
North Korea—Education System

Kim, Shin-il
Seoul National University
Seoul National University
South Korea—Education System

Kim, Sung Chull
Korea Institute for National Unification
North Korea—Political System
South Korea—Political System
Yushin

Kim, Youngmin
Harvard University
Yi I
Yi Mun-yol

Kirkpatrick, Joanna
Boise, Idaho
Conveyance Arts

Kislenko, Arne
Ryerson University
Anand Panyarachun
Chiang Mai
Louangnamtha
Luang Prabang
Peninsular Thailand
Sukhothai
Thailand—History
Thailand—Profile

Klein, Thoralf
University of Erfurt
Atheism, Official—China

Knapp, Ronald
State University of New York, New Paltz
Architecture, Vernacular—China

Knight, Nick
Griffith University
Cultural Revolution—China

Kobayashi, Tetsuya
Poole Gakuin University
Cram Schools
Japan—Education System

Kobayashi, Victor
University of Hawaii, Manoa
Ceramics—Japan

Koenberg, Cyrus
Salt Lake City, Utah
Twelver Shi'ism

Kog, Yue Choong
National University of Singapore
Bali
Barisan Sosialis
Cagayan River
Coastal Malays
Green Revolution—Southeast Asia
Jeyaretnam, Joshua Benjamin
Lim Chin Siong
Maguey
Majapahit
Marshall, David
Melaka Sultanate
Orang Asli
Singapore—Political System
Tan Siew Sin
Terrace Irrigation
Westernization—East Asia
Yap Ah Loy

Kohl, Stephen W.
University of Oregon
Basho
Haiku
Literature—Japan

Kolb, Charles C.
Washington, D.C.
Afghanistan—History
Afghanistan—Profile

Kolenda, Pauline
University of California, Berkeley
Marriage and Family—South Asia

Komelski, Matthew F.
University of Hawaii, Manoa
Funakoshi Gichin

Kowalewski, Michael
The Old School, Dorchester, U.K.
Bhutan—History

Kowalewski, Michael *(continued)*
    Bhutan—Profile
    Bhutan—Religion
    Bhutanese
    Lhasa
    Potala Palace
    Tibetans
    Wangchuck, King Jigme Singye

Krotov, Pavel
University of Wisconsin, Madison
    Kyrgyzstan—Education System

Kuehnast, Kathleen
Alexandria, Va.
    Marriage and Family—Central Asia
    Women in Central Asia

Kuru, Selim S.
University of Washington, Seattle
    Literature—Turkey

Kwak, Ki-Sung
University of Sydney
    Media—South Korea

Laird, Peter Frederick
Massey University
    Shamanism

Lam, Truong Buu
University of Hawaii, Manoa
    An Duong Vuong
    Ba Trieu
    Bac Son Uprising
    Dai Viet Su Ky
    Doan Thi Diem
    Ho Xuan Huong
    Hoang Ngoc Phach
    Huynh Tan Phat
    Khai Hung
    Lac Long Quan
    Ngo Dinh Diem
    Revolt of the Short Hair
    Sino-Vietnamese Culture
    Tu Luc Van Doan
    Vietnam—History
    Vietnam—Profile

Lam, Y. L. Jack
Chinese University of Hong Kong
    Single-Child Phenomenon—China

Lanti, Irman G.
Center for Information and Development Studies, Jakarta
    Candi of Java
    Mataram
    Nusa Tenggara
    Pribumi
    Sailendra
    Sundanese

LaPorte, Jr., Robert
Pennsylvania State University
    Pakistan—Economic System
    Pakistan—Political System

Larsen, Kirk W.
George Washington University
    Zhao Ziyang

Lazich, Michael C.
Buffalo State University
    Liang Qichao
    Zhang Zhidong

Leaf, Murray J.
University of Texas, Dallas
    Agriculture—South Asia
    Green Revolution—South Asia
    Rice and Rice Agriculture

LeCompte, Garé
Hollins Communications Research Institute
    Acupuncture
    Massage—China
    Medicine, Traditional—China
    Moxibustion

Lee, Byongwon
University of Hawaii
    Music—Korea

Lee, Hyo Sang
Indiana University
    Hangul Script
    Romanization Systems, Korean

Lee, Sing Kong
National Institute of Education
    Mangroves

Lee, Wei-chin
Wake Forest University
    Defense Industry—China

Lefferts, Leedom
Drew University
Clothing, Traditional—Laos

Leitich, Keith A.
Seattle, Wash.
Chang River
Chun Doo Hwan
Corruption—Korea
Deng Xiaoping
Fujian
Guangzhou
Henan
Huang River
Hunan
Inchon
Kim Dae Jung
Kim Young-sam
Koreans in Central Asia
Kwangju Uprising
Pusan
Rhee, Syngman
Roh Tae Woo
South China Sea
Taiwan Strait
Yi Ha-ung
Zhu De
Zhu Rongji

Lessard, Micheline R.
University of Ottawa
Catholicism, Roman—Vietnam
Co Loa Thanh
Con Dao Islands
Doumer, Paul
Duong Van Minh
Franco-Viet Minh War
Hanoi
Ho Dynasty Citadel
Ho Tung Mau
Iron Triangle
Le Duan
Le Duc Anh
Nguyen Cao Ky
Nguyen Thieu Gia
People's Army of Vietnam
Tran Van Giau
Vo Van Kiet

LeTendre, Gerald K.
Pennsylvania State University
Ijime

Levinson, David
Berkshire Publishing Group LLC
Afghanistan—Economic System
Arnis
Asian Games
Bedaya
Bengalis
Buh
Buzkashi
Cockfighting
Fish fighting
Hakka
Ibn Battutah
Iglesia ni Christo
Kendo
Kizel Irmak River
Manila
Mindanao
Muay Thai
Musharraf, Pervez
Nu Shooting
Philippine Independent Church
Philippines—History
Preface
Raffles, Thomas Stamford
Sati
Sepak Takraw
Siberia
Tae Kwon Do
Yurt

Lewis, Elaine T.
International Ministries, American Baptist Churches
Clothing, Traditional—Tribal Southeast Asia

Lewis, Glen
University of Canberra
Media—Insular Southeast Asia
Media—Mainland Southeast Asia

Li, Chris Wen-Chao
National Taiwan Normal University
Chinese, Classical
Mandarin

Li, Dian
University of Arizona
Falun Gong

Li, Narangoa
Australian National University; University of Queensland
Mongol Empire

Liechty, Mark
University of Illinois, Chicago
Kathmandu Valley

Lim, Paulino
California State University
Philippines—Profile

Limaye, Satu
Asia-Pacific Center for Security Studies
India-United States Relations

Lin, Jian-Zhong
Eastern Connecticut State University
Guo Moruo
Hu Shi
Mogao Caves
Qin Tomb
Temple of Heaven
Thirteen Ming Tombs
Wuyi, Mount

Lincicome, Mark E.
College of the Holy Cross
Meiji Period
Mori Arinori
Textbook Scandal

Littell-Lamb, Elizabeth A.
Carnegie Mellon University
Women in China

Littleton, C. Scott
Occidental College, Los Angeles
Confucianism—Japan
Religion, Folk—Japan

Lodrick, Deryck O.
University of California, Berkeley
Cricket
Hawkins, William
Nomadic Pastoralism—South Asia

Loh, Anthony A.
Harvard University
China-Korea Relations
Tiananmen Square

Lone, Stewart
University of New South Wales
Russo-Japanese War

Long, Daniel
Tokyo Metropolitan University
Ogasawara

Loomis, Craig
Sacramento City College
Bulosan, Carlos
Constitutional Crisis of 1881
Magsaysay, Ramon
Rizal, José
Romulo, Carlos Peña

Lubin, Timothy
Washington and Lee University
Orientalism
Tamils
Zoroastrianism

Lunsing, Wim
University of Tokyo
Homosexuality
Kanno Suga

Lutz, Hazel
University of Minnesota
Clothing, Traditional—India

Lynch, Daniel C.
University of Southern California
Media—China
Socialist Spiritual Civilization—China
Thought Work—China

Lynn, Leonard
Case Western Reserve University
Electronics Industry—Japan

Mackerras, Colin
Griffith University
Cultural Revolution—China
Gang of Four
Han
Hui
Jiang Zemin

Mackie, Vera
University of Melbourne
Women in Japan

Maeda, Hitomi
University of Minnesota, Twin Cities
Hirohito

Magat, Margaret C.
University of Pennsylvania
Cuisine—Philippines

Magnarella, Paul J.
University of Florida
Iran—Human Rights

250

Kazakhs
Turkey—Human Rights
Turkmen
Uzbeks

Maharjan, Keshav L.
Hiroshima University
Nepal—Economic System
Nepal—Profile

Malik, Hafeez
Villanova University
Iqbal, Muhammad

Malik, J. Mohan
Asia-Pacific Center for Security Studies
China-India Relations
Nuclear Arms

Malkeyeva, Aygul
New York, N.Y.
Dauylpaz
Sarangi

Manaf, Nor Faridah A.
International Islamic University
Bangsawan
Mak Yong
Manora
Tarian Asyik

Mansurnoor, Iik A.
University of Brunei Darussalam
Bedil
Borneo Peoples
Hosen, Ibrahim

Marashi, Ibrahim
Oxford University
Iraq—Economic System
Iraq—Human Rights
Iraq—Political System
Iraq—Profile
Persian Miniature Painting

Masud-Elias, Mehrin
Montague, Mass.
Islam, Kazi Nazrul
Rahman, A.R.

Mathieson, Daniel
Australian National University
Pagan

Matthews, Rebecca
University of Iowa
Social Stratification—China

May, Ronald J.
Australian National University
Autonomous Region of Muslim Mindanao
Islam—Philippines
Moro Islamic Liberation Front
Moro National Liberation Front
Nur Misuari

May, Timothy
University of Wisconsin, Madison
Batmonkh, Jambyn
Buddhism—Mongolia
Central Asia—Early Medieval Period
Chormaqan, Noyan
Choybalsan, Horloogiyn
Genghis Khan
Geser Khan
Golden Horde
Gurragchaa, Jugderdemidiyn
Natsagdori, Dashdorjiyn
Ochirbat, Punsalmaagiyn
Shamanism—Mongolia
Timur
Tsedenbel, Yumjaagiyn

McBride, II, Richard D.
University of California, Los Angeles
Cheju Province
Cult of Maitreya
Kaema Plateau
Korea Bay
Nangnim Range
North Kyongsang Province
South Kyongsang Province
Ulchi Mundok

McCann, David
Harvard University
Kim Sowol

McCargo, Duncan
University of Leeds
Thailand—Political Parties
Thailand—Political System

McCarthy, Joseph
Suffolk University of Boston
Iran—Education System

McCurley, Dallas L.
Queens College; City University of New York
Drama—China
Drama—Korea
Drama—South Asia
Drama—Southeast Asia
Qin Dynasty
Shadow Plays and Puppetry
Shang Dynasty
Xiqu

McDaniel, June
College of Charleston
Bhakti

McGirk, James B.
Berkshire Publishing Group LLC
Federally Administered Tribal Areas—Pakistan
Mazar-e Sharif
Toxic-Waste Disposal

McIntosh, Linda S.
Seattle, Wash.
Ayutthaya, Kingdom of
Basi
Bun Bang Fai
Chao Anou
Civil War of 1956–1975—Laos
Clothing, Traditional—Cambodia
Clothing, Traditional—Thailand
Cuisine—Thailand
Fa Ngoum
Ho Chi Minh Trail
Ikat Dyeing
Kaysone Phomvihan
Khmer
Lao People's Revolutionary Party
Lao-Tai Languages
Literature—Laos
Music, Folk—Laos
Palm-Leaf Manuscripts
Prabang
Setthathirat
Sisavangvong University
Souphanuvong, Prince
Souvanna Phouma, Prince
That Luang
That Luang Festival
Wat Xieng Khouan

McKay, Alex
International Institute for Asian Studies, Leiden
Dalai Lama
Tibet

Tibet—Image in the Modern West
Tibetan Uprising

Mehta, Monika
University of Minnesota
Ray, Satyajit

Mellen, Joan
Temple University
Cinema—Japan

Merchant, W. D.
Chimayo, N.M.
Parsi

Michael, Bernardo A.
Messiah College
Rana

Micklin, Philip P.
Western Michigan University
Aral Sea

Millay, Lea
Lake Oswego, Oreg.
Poetry—Japan

Milner, Jr., Murray
University of Virginia
Caste

Mir, Farina
Cornell University
Hir Ranjha Story
Shah, Waris

Mir, Shabana
Indiana University
Farid, Khwaja Ghulam

Mishra, Patit Paban
Sambalpur University
Bandaranaike, Sirimavo Ratwatte Dias
Bentinck, William Cavendish
Bhosle, Shivaji
Borobudur
Budi Utomo
Cambodia-Laos Relations
Chishtiya
Dev, Nanak Guru
Drama—India
Forster, E.M.
Hinduism—Thailand
India—Medieval Period
India—Profile

India-Southeast Asia Relations
Indonesia—Political Parties
Indonesia—Profile
Indonesian Revolution
Indonesia-United States Relations
Jakarta Riots of May 1998
Khusrau, Amir
Kumar, Dilip
Laos—Profile
Mangeshkar, Lata
Mauryan Empire
Mongkut
Nur Jehan
Orissa
Oriyas
Panini
Phya Taksin
Poetry—India
Premchand
Rama Khamheng
Rama Tibodi I
Ramanuja
Sarit Thanarat
Singapore—Profile
Soviet-Vietnamese TFOC
Sufism—South Asia
Thanom Kittikachorn
Tipu Sultan
Trailok
Vietnam-United States Relations
World War I
Xayabury
Zia-ul-Haq, Mohammad

Mitter, Rana
University of Oxford
Taipei

Miyake, Marc Hideo
Aiea, Hawaii
Chu Nom
Sinitic Languages

Mizenko, Matthew
Ursinus College
Uchimura Kanzo

Moghadam, Valentine M.
Illinois State University
Women in West Asia

Mohamad, Zulkifli
Association of South East Asian Nations (ASEAN)
Dance—Malaysia

Moller, Catherine
International Rescue Committee (IRC)
North Korea—Human Rights

Moore, Ray A.
Amherst College
Constitution, Postwar—Japan

Morel, Jeanne
Antioch University Seattle
Cambodia—History
Heng Samrin
Ranariddh, Norodom
Sam Rainsy

Moss, Lucy D.
London, United Kingdom
Aoi Matsuri
Bon Matsuri
Children's Day—Japan
Elephant, Asian
Geisha
Gion Matsuri
Hakata Matsuri
Harappa
Hina Matsuri
Leopard, Clouded
Mongoose
Three Imperial Regalia—Japan
Tiger

Moxham, Roy
Covet Garden, London, United Kingdom
Salt Tax

Muhutdinova-Foroughi, Raissa
Salt Lake City, Utah
Bakhtaran
Elburz
Karun River and Shatt al Arab River
Khurasan

Munshi, Shoma
University of Pennsylvania
Media—South Asia

Munson, Todd S.
Indiana University, Bloomington
Choshu Expeditions
Oh Sadaharu

Murakami, Kyoko
University of Kansas
Fukuda Hideko

Murakami, Kyoko (*continued*)
Ichikawa Fusae
Ienaga Saburo

Musselwhite, Diane
Poole Gakuin University, Osaka
Cram Schools
Japan—Education System

Myer, Will
London, United Kingdom
Ariq Water System
Ataturk
Islam—Mongolia
Islam—West Asia
Kara-Kum Canal
Oriental Orthodox Church
Surkhob River
Tedzhen River
Turgay Plateau
Zerafshan River

Na, Young-il
Seoul National University
Ssirum

Nagano, Yoshiko
Kanagawa University
Philippines—Economic System

Nakano, Koichi
Sophia University, Tokyo
Japan-France Relations

Nalle, David
Central Asian Monitor
Caravans

Nanda, Ram Shankar
Sambalpur University
Andhra Pradesh
Kabaddi
Karnataka
Khan, Vilayat
Literature—Vietnam
Maharashtra
Mysore
Tamil Nadu

Nanji, Azim
Institute of Ismaili Studies, London
Ismaili Sects—South Asia

Neary, Ian
University of Essex
Burakumin
Japan—Human Rights

Neff, Andrew
Dulles, Va.
Caspian Sea

Neuman, Dard
Columbia University
Ali Khan, Bade Ghulam

Ngooi, Chiu-Ai
National University of Singapore
National University of Singapore

Nguyen, Ursula
Humboldt University, Berlin
Doi Moi
Vietnam—Education System

Nichol, Jim
Library of Congress
Kyrgyzstan—History

Nichols, Jennifer L.
Ohio State University
Dasht-e Margo
Hazara
Hunza
Kabul
Waziri

Nielsen, Bent
University of Copenhagen
Ang Lee
Anhui
Bamboo
Bramaputra River
Cao Xueqin
Cathaya Tree
Chengdu
Chilung
Chongqing
East China Sea
Gansu
Greater Xing'an Range
Guangxi
Hainan
Hebei
Hengduan Ranges
Hubei
Jiangxi
Kao-hsiung

Kunlun Mountains
Lao She
Ningxia
Qinling Range
Qiu Jin
Quemoy and Matsu
Shaanxi
Shanxi
Taklimakan Desert
White Terror
Xi'an
Yellow Sea
Yunnan

Nuridinova, Munavvara
Tajik Academy of Sciences
Tajikistan—Economic System

Oakman, Daniel
Australian National University
Alghoza
Ban Chiang
Burma-Thailand Railway
Dazu Rock Carvings
Emerald Buddha
Mei Lanfang
Pan-Philippine Highway
Ustyurt Plateau
Xu Guangqi

Ochner, Nobuko Miyama
University of Hawaii, Manoa
Enchi Fumiko

Ochs, Michael
Helsinki Commission
Niyazov, Saparmurat

O'Connell, Jr., J. Barry
U.S. Department of State
Carpets—Central Asia

O'Connor, Noelle
Pace University
Dance Drama, Mask—Korea
Gardening—China
Longmen Grottoes
Lu, Mount
Masks—East Asia
Puppetry, Water
Qinghai

Oda, Juten
Toyohashi Sozo College
Uighurs

Oddie, Geoffrey
University of Sydney
Christianity—South Asia

Ohnishi, Hiroshi
Kyoto University
Pacific Rim

Olafsson, Kevin
University of Hawaii, Honolulu
Koto

Olesen, Alexa
Brooklyn, NY
Cui Jian
Dai Qing
Gong Li
Xu Beihong

Olson, Robert
University of Kentucky
Kirkuk
Kurds
Sulaymaniya

Onder, Sylvia Wing
Georgetown University
Rize
Sinop

Ooi, Giok-Ling
University of Singapore
Bangkok
Buffalo, Water
Ethnic Relations—Southeast Asia
Fishing Industry—Southeast Asia
Habibie, B.J.
Hakka
Kinabalu, Mount
Lacquerware
Lim Chong Eu
May 13 Ethnic Riots— Malaysia
Medan
Porcelain—East Asia
Sustainability
Wu
Xiang
Yue
ZOPFAN

Ooi Keat Gin
Universiti Sains Malaysia
Abdul Razak
Abu Bakar

Ooi Keat Gin *(continued)*
Albuquerque, Afonso de
Azahari, A.M.
Bandar Seri Begawan
Birch, James W. W.
British Military Administration
Brooke, James
Clifford, Hugh
Haji, Raja
Hassanal Bolkaih
Hussein Onn
Iskandar Muda
Mahmud Shah
Malaysia—Economic System
Mansur Shah
Manufacturing Industry—Malaysia
Mat Salleh Rebellion
Mineral Industry—Malaysia
Pangkor Treaty
Parti Rakyat Brunei
Rubber Industry—Malaysia
Swettenham, Frank
Timber Industry—Malaysia
Universiti Brunei Darussalam
Universiti Sains Malaysia
Wan Ahmad
White Rajas

O'Rourke, Kevin
Kyunghee University
So Chongju
Yi Kyu-bo
Yun Sun-do

Pagani, Catherine
University of Alabama
Architecture—Japan
Bunjinga
Cloisonne
Emakimono
Nihonga
Origami
Painting—China
Painting—Japan
Teahouses
Yoga

Paget, Roger
Lewis and Clark College
Wahid, Abdurrahman

Pakkan, Mujdat
Mountain View, Calif.
Pamuk, Orhan

Paksoy, H. B.
Franklin University
Dastan, Turkic
Literature—Central Asia

Palmer, Brandon
University of Hawaii, Honolulu
Amnok River
Kangwon Province
Korea Strait
Kum River
Tumen River

Panda, Hrushikesh
Delhi University Enclave
Diwali
Holi

Panini, M. N.
Jawaharlal Nehru University
Sanskritization
Westernization—South Asia

Park, Chan E.
Ohio State University
P'ansori

Pauka, Kirstin
University of Hawaii, Manao
Opera—Vietnam

Paulson, Linda Dailey
Ventura, CA
Agra
Ajanta
Allahabad
Bokeo
Bolovens Plateau
Chao Phraya River and Delta
Cordillera Central
Dangrek Range
Doi Inthanon
Gulf of Thailand
Khon Kaen
Nakhon Ratchasima
Phuket
Three Pagodas Pass
Vientiane

Peebles, Patrick
University of Missouri, Kansas City
India-Sri Lanka Relations
Jaffna
Literature, Sinhalese
Polonnaruva

Sinhala
Sri Lanka—History

Peimani, Hooman
Commugny, Switzerland
Alevi Muslims
Armenians
Kazakhstan—History
Pakistan—Education System

Peiser, Benny
Liverpool John Moores University
Karate

Perlin, John
Santa Barbara, Calif.
Deforestation

Perrin, Ariane
University of London, School of Oriental and African Studies
Hamhung
Kaesong
Pyongyang
Sinuiju

Perrin, Serge
University of Paris I-Sorbonne
South Korea-European Union Relations

Perrins, Robert
Acadia University
Guangdong
Harbin
Kyoto
Macao
Manchu
Manchuria
Nanjing
Shanghai
South Manchuria Railway
Tianjin
Xinjiang

Phillips, Steven
Towson University
China-United States Relations

Pollard, Vincent Kelly K.
University of Hawaii, Manoa
Philippines-United States Relations

Powers, John
Australian National University
Buddhism—Tibet

Prendergast, David K.
Cambridge University
Kye

Pretes, Michael
Australian National University
Balinese
Bin Laden, Osama
Dardanelles
Dujiangyan
Emerald Buddha
Huang Shan
Maluku
Pacific Ocean
Pagan
Panda
Sulawesi
Tai Shan
Thar Desert
Wudang Shan
Wulingyuan

Priddy, Greg
Z, Inc.
Oil Industry—West Asia

Prior, D.
Indiana University
Bishkek
Chagatay
Folklore—Central Asia
Kurmanjan Datka
Nava'i, Mir' Ali Shir

Privratsky, Bruce G.
Turkistan Academic Research Associates
Islam—Central Asia

Pryde, Philip R.
San Diego State University
Radioactive Waste and Contamination—Central Asia

Puntasen, Apichai
Thammasat University
Ungphakorn Puey

Puri, Rajika
New York University
Dance—India

Quah, Jon S.T.
National University of Singapore
Corruption

Quddus, Munir
Prairie View A&M University
    Bangladesh—Education System

Raben, Remco
Netherlands Institute for War Documentation
    Romusha

Raendchen, Jana
Southeast Asia Communication Center (SEACOM)
    Damkoeng, Akat
    Nation-Religion-Monarch
    Phumisak, Chit
    Plain of Jars

Raendchen, Oliver
Southeast Asia Communication Centre (SEACOM)
    Muang
    Nation-Religion-Monarch
    Phra Pathom Chedi
    Shan

Raghibdoust, Shahla
Tehran University of Medical Sciences
    Persian

Rahman, Syedur
Pennsylvania State University
    Grameen Bank

Raju, Shanti
Urbana, Ill.
    Telugu

Ramos, Teresita V.
University of Hawaii, Manoa
    Philippine Languages

Ramsing, Kenneth D.
University of Oregon
    Thailand—Economic System

Ramstedt, Martin
International Institute for Asian Studies, Leiden
    Airlangga
    Gajah Mada
    Gambuh
    Gamelan
    Golkar
    Indonesian Democratic Party
    Kain Songket
    Ludruk
    New Order
    Old Order
    Pancasila
    Partai Kebangkitan Bangsa
    Partai Persatuan Pembangunan
    Prambanan Hindu
    Sarekat Islam
    South Asians in Southeast Asia
    Spice Trade
    Srivijaya
    Suharto
    Taman Siswa
    Wayang Kulit
    Wayang Topeng
    Wayang Wong

Rangaswamy, Padma
University of Illinois, Chicago
    Remittances
    South Asians, Overseas

Rapp, Jr., Steve H.
Georgia State University
    Caucasia

Rashid, Salim
University of Illinois, Urbana-Champaign
    Bangladesh—Economic System
    Bangladesh—Education System

Ravi, Kokila
Atlanta Metropolitan College
    Mumbai

Reader, Ian
Lancaster University
    Aum Shinrikyo Scandal

Redaelli, Riccardo
Catholic University of the Sacred Heart
    Azad, Abu'l-Kalam
    Bagram
    Bahadur Shah
    Bhitai, Shah Abdul Latif
    Daud, Muhammad
    Dost Muhammad
    Ghazna
    Khan, Abdul Ghaffar
    Nizam ad-din Awliya
    North-West Frontier Province Sarhad
    Pashtun
    Punjab
    Sayyid, Ahmad Khan
    Wali Allah, Shah

Refsing, Kirsten
University of Hong Kong
    Ainu

Reichert, Allen
Otterbein College
Mahathir Mohamad
Nara Period

Reichl, Karl
University of Bonn
Alpamish
Edige
Gorkut Ata
Kalmakanov, Bukharzhrau
Koroghli
Kuli, Maktum
Makhambet Utemisov
Manas Epic
Shahnameh Epic

Reynolds, Douglas
Georgia State University
China-Japan Relations

Reynolds, Katsue Akiba
University of Hawaii, Manoa
Feminine Language

Rhodes, James
National Graduate Institute for Policy Studies
Japan—Economic System
Japan—Money

Richey, Jeffery L.
University of Findlay
Bureau of Religious Affairs

Ridgeway, William Nelson
University of Hawaii, Manoa
Baba Tatsui
Eda Saburo
Enomoto Takeaki
Fujieda Shizuo
Fujisawa Takeo
Fukuda Takeo
Futabatei, Shimei
Mori Ogai
Natsume Soseki
Tanizaki Jun'ichiro

Ringer, Greg
University of Oregon
Angkor Wat
Cardamon Mountains
Elephant Range
Khmer Empire
Killing Fields
Kompong Som Bay

Mekong River and Delta
Pol Pot
Tonle Sap

Rixon, Diane
Yale University
Sufism—Southwest Asia

Rizvi, Kishwar
Yale University
Bhit Shah
David, Collin
Gulgee
Makli Hill
Naqsh, Jamil
Rohtas Fort
Sadequain
Sehwan

Rocheleau, Danielle
University of Colorado, Boulder
Japanese Language

Roden, Donald
Rutgers University
Fukuzawa Yukichi

Röesel, Jakob
Rostock University
Bandaranaike, Solomon West Ridgeway Diaz
Sri Lanka—Education System
Sri Lanka—Political System
Trincomalee

Ronquillo, Aaron
De la Salle University
Agno River
Baltazar, Francisco
Guerrero, Fernando M.
Luna Y Novicio, Juan
Luzon Group
Ruiz, Saint Lorenzo
Sierra Madre
Urdaneta, Andres de
Zambales Mountains
Zamboanga

Rood, Judith
Biola University
Architecture, Islamic—West Asia

Rose, Leo
University of California, Berkeley
Nepal—History
Nepal—Political System

Rosen, George
University of Illinois
India—Economic System

Ross, Heidi
Colgate University
China—Education System

Ross, Marcy
Berkshire Publishing Group LLC
Cuisine—Afghanistan

Rothermund, Dietmar
Heidelberg University
Bhutto, Zulfiqar Ali
Gandhi, Indira
Gandhi, Mohandas K.
Hindu Law
India—Education System
Nehru, Jawaharlal
Rajagopalachari, Chakravarti

Roy, Olivier
Centre National de la Recherche Scientifique (CNRS)
Tajikistan Civil War

Roy, Ranjit
Rabindra Bharati University
Colombo Plan

Roy, Tirthankar
Indira Gandhi Institute of Development Research (IGIDR)
British Indian Empire
Hastings, Warren
India-United Kingdom Relations
Marxism—South Asia
Raga
Roy, Rammohan
Shehnai
Veena

Rozman, Gilbert
Princeton University
Japan-Russia Relations

Rudolph, Jennifer
State University of New York, Albany
Pingyao, Ancient City of

Ruohomaki, Olli
Ministry of Foreign Affairs, Finland
Khmu

Russell, Terence C.
University of Manitoba
Religion, Folk—China
Ricci, Matteo

Saaler, Sven
German Institute for Japanese Studies (DIJ), Tokyo
Hara Takashi
Japan-Germany Relations
Tanaka Giichi
Yamagata Aritomo

Sabol, Steven
University of North Carolina, Charlotte
Abdalrauf Fitrat
Ai Qap
Altynsarin, Ibrahim
Auezov, Mukhtar
Baitursynov, Akhmet
Bokeikhanov, Alikhan
Dulatov, Mirzhaqyp
Kazak
Kobyz
Kunanbaev, Abai
Leninshil Zhas
Mailin, Beiimbet
Seifullin, Saduakas
Seralin, Mukhammedzhan
Valikhanov, Chokan

Sadri, Houman A.
University of Central Florida
Afghani, Jamal ad-din
Afridi
Amanollah
Ayub Khan
Baluchi
Bazargan, Mehdi
Bhutto, Benazir
Brahui
Constitution, Islamic—Iran
Dari
Esfahan
Fars
Hamadan
Iran—Economic System
Iran—History
Iran—Political System
Iran—Profile
Iran-United States Hostage Crisis
Islamabad
Islamic Revolution—Iran
Jinnah, Mohammed Ali
Karachi

Karakoram Highway
Khomeini, Ayatollah
Lahore
Mahmud of Ghazna
Mujahideen
Muslims, Shi'ite
No-ruz
Pahlavi Dynasty
Pashto
Persians
Peshawar
Qajar Dynasty
Rahman, Mujibur
Shariati, Ali
Sindhi
Tehran
Treaty of Gandomak
Veleyet-e Faqih
Zahir Shah

Safi, Omid
Colgate University
Khwaja Mu'in al-Din Chishti
Literature, Persian
Rudaki
Sana'I

Sanada, Hisashi
University of Tsukuba
Balisong
Board Games
Chajon Nori
Kites and Kite Flying

Sankey, Margaret
Auburn University
Abacus
Red Guard Organizations

Sarkissian, Margaret
Smith College
Dikir Barat
Jikey
Tarian Portugis

Sato, Yoichiro
University of Auckland
Farmer's Movement
Fishing Industry—Japan

Schaberg, David
University of California, Los Angeles
Five Classics

Schafer, Elizabeth
Loachapoka, Ala.
Agricultural Collectivization—China
Hongcun and Xidi
Measurement Systems

Schatz, Edward
Southern Illinois University, Carbondale
Tribes and Tribal Federations—Central Asia

Schneider, Axel
Leiden University
Taiwan—Political System

Schneider, Michael A.
Knox College
Showa Period

Scholberg, Henry
University of Minnesota
Daman and Diu Union Territory
Gama, Vasco da
Goa
Jesuits— India

Schroeder, Carole
Boise State University
Hangzhou
Suzhou

Schuepp, Chris
Internews Network
Media—Central Asia

Schwartzberg, Joseph
University of Minnesota
South Asia—History

Scupin, Raymond
Lindenwood University
Islam—Mainland Southeast Asia

Secter, Mondo
Simon Fraser University
Calligraphy—Japan

Seliger, Bernhard J.
Hankuk University of Foreign Studies
Juche
Shenzhen Special Economic Zone

Sellmann, James D.
University of Guam
Analects

Sellmann, James D. *(continued)*
Confucian Ethics
Confucianism—China
Confucius
Five Phases
Four Books
Laozi
Mencius
Mozi
Taoism
Xunzi

Selsor, Marcia L.
Montana State University
Architectural Decoration—Central Asia
Tile Work—Central Asia

Selvaraju, Mala
University of Malaya
Light, Francis
Malayan Union
Resident System
Rukunegara
Templer, Gerald

Serra, Régine
Institut Français des Relations Internationales
Europe-Asia Relations

Sethi, K. N.
Sambalpur University
India—Profile
Iran-Iraq Relations
Khusrau, Amir

Shaffer, Brenda
Harvard University
Azerbaijanis

Shaffer, David E.
Chosun University
Calligraphy—Korea
Ceramics—Korea
Choson Kingdom
Ch'usok
Hanshik
Koryo Kingdom
Parhae Kingdom
Poetry—Korea
Seshi Customs
Sol
Sottal
Tano
Three Kingdoms Period
Unified Shilla Kingdom

Shah, Ami P.
University of California, Santa Barbara
Bachchan, Amitabh
Manto, Sadaat Hasan

Sharma, Shalendra
University of San Francisco
International Monetary Fund

Sharp, Andrew
State College, Pa.
Aitmatov, Chingis
Dungans
Germans in Central Asia
Ibn Sina
Islamic Renaissance Party—Tajikistan
Khiva, Khanate of
Kishlak
Oral
Quqon, Khanate of
Saryshaghan

She, Xiaojie
Jinan University
Ding Ling
Hong Shen
Tian Han
Xu Zhimo

Shefer, Miri
Tel Aviv University
Medicine, Traditional—West Asia

Shen, Kuiyi
Ohio University
Wang Yiting
Wu Changshi

Shepherd, Eric Todd
US/China Links
Qingke

Shieh, Shawn
Marist College
People's Liberation Army
Zhejiang

Shih, Chuan-kang
University of Illinois, Urbana-Champaign
Miao—China
Moso
Tujia

Shim, Doobo
National University of Singapore
Zhang Yimou

Shishida, Fumiaki
University of Warwick
Aikido

Shultz, Edward
University of Hawaii
Wang Kon

Sidwell, Paul
Australian National University
Austroasiatic Languages
Mon-Khmer Languages

Sieber, Patricia
Ohio State University
Hong lou meng
Jin ping mei

Simidchieva, Marta
York University
Ansari, Abdullah
Azerbaijan
Baluchistan
Bulgarians
Jami, 'Abdurrahman
Khuzestan
Khwarizm
Sistan

Simon, Scott
University of Ottowa
Tainan
Taiwan—Profile
Taiwan Economic Miracle

Singh, Udai Bhanu
Institute for Defence Studies and Analyses (IDSA)
Thich Nhat Hanh

Sioris, George A.
Asiatic Society of Japan
Asiatic Society of Japan
Buddhism—Japan

Sluglett, Peter
University of Utah
Aleppo
Baghdad
Hussein, Saddam
Judaism—West Asia

Marsh Arabs
Mosul
Persian Gulf War

Smith, Anthony L.
Institute of Southeast Asian Studies
Aceh Rebellion
Bali Summit
Bandung Conference
British in Southeast Asia
British-Dutch Wars
Dutch in Southeast Asia
Five Power Defence Arrangements
Indonesia—Political System
Indonesia-Malaysia Relations
Irian Jaya Conquest
Java War
Konfrontasi
Padri War
Pakualaman
Peranakan
Piracy—Southeast Asia
Portuguese in Southeast Asia
Timor Sea
Volksraad
Yogyakarta

Smith, David R.
Ohio Northen University
Kara-Kum Desert
Kazakh Uplands
Mangyshlak Peninsula
Tura Lowland
Turugart Pass

Smith, Larry E.
International Association of World Englishes
English in Asia

Smith, Martin
Buckhurst Hill, United Kingdom
Akha
All Burma Students Democratic Front
Burma Independence Army
Burma Road
Chin
Chin State
Christianity—Myanmar
Communist Party of Burma
Ethnic Conflict—Myanmar
Inle Lake Region
Irrawaddy Division
Irrawaddy River and Delta
Kachin

Smith, Martin (*continued*)
Kachin Independence Organization
Kachin State
Karen
Karen National Union
Karen State
Kayah State
Mandalay Division
Mon
Mon State
Mong Tai Army
Myanmar—Human Rights
Myanmar—Political System
National Unity Party—Myanmar
Palaung State Liberation Party
Pao National Organization
Sagaing Division
Salween River
Shan State
Shan State Army
Sittang River
United Wa State Party
Yangon Division

Smitka, Michael J.
Washington and Lee University
Automobile Industry

Smyth, David
University of London
Bidyalankarana
Dokmai Sot
Drama—Thailand
Khun Chang, Khun Phaen
Literature—Thailand
Nirat
Ramakien
Saek
Siburapha
Sot Kuramarohit

Sobti, Manu
Georgia Institute of Technology
Architecture—India
Bukhara, Khanate of
Mughal Empire
Persepolis
Taj Mahal

Soni, Varun
University of California, Santa Barbara
Nusrat Fateh Ali Khan

Spagnoli, Cathy
Vashon, Wash.
Storytelling

Spark, Patricia H.
North American Felters' Association Network
Felting—Central Asia

Sperling, Gerald
University of Regina
Jilin

Srinivas, Tulasi
Boston University
Cuisine—South Asia

Stainton, Michael
York University
Aboriginal Peoples—Taiwan

Stapleton, Kristin
University of Kentucky
Humor in Chinese History
Sichuan

Steinhardt, Nancy
University of Pennsylvania
Architecture—China

Stimpfl, Joseph
Webster University
Clothing, Traditional—Malaysia

Stone, Jacqueline
Princeton University
Nichiren

Stone, Leonard A.
Jadaupur University
Abdullah Quaisi

Strahorn, Eric A.
Florida Gulf Coast University
Indus River Dolphin
Narmada Dam Controversy
Tarai

Strand, Jonathan R.
University of Nevada, Las Vegas
Nixon Shock
Nuclear Allergy
Plaza Accord

Stuart-Fox, Martin
University of Queensland
   Laos—History
   Laos-Vietnam Relations

Suganuma, Unryu
Hokuriku University
   Asia-Pacific Economic Cooperation Forum
   China-Japan Peace and Friendship Treaty
   Civil-Service Examination System—China
   Hayashi Razan
   Household Responsibility System—China
   Japan-Africa Relations
   Jiuzhaigou
   Liu Shaoqi
   Sixteen Kingdoms

Sugita, Yone
Osaka University of Foreign Studies
   Japan-United States Relations
   Open Door Policy

Swan, Suzanne
Kas, Antalya, Turkey
   Afyon
   Amasya
   Bodrum
   Kas
   Konya
   Mersin

Tachau, Frank
University of Illinois, Chicago
   Turkey-Russia Relations
   Turkey-United States Relations

Takasaki, Izumi
University of Wisconsin, Madison
   Clothing, Traditional—Japan

Tan, Eugene K. B.
Singapore Management University
   Military, Indonesia
   Ningkan, Stephen Kalong

Tan, Leo
National Institute of Education
   Mangroves

Tapp, Nicholas
National University of Australia
   Hmong
   Thai

Taylor, Kim
University of Guelph
   Iaido

Teele, Rebecca
International Noh Institute
   Utai

Teh, Yik Koon
Universiti Utara Malaysia
   Kelantan
   Negeri Sembilan
   Pahang
   Penang
   Perak

Terauchi, Naoko
Kobe University
   Kouta
   Music, Ryukyuan

Terwiel, Barend Jan
Hamburg University
   Sanskrit

Thadathil, George
Paul Quinn College
   Indonesia—History
   Singapore—History

Thambiah, Shanthi
University of Malaya
   Batik
   Gawai Dayak
   Kuching
   Labu Sayong
   Pesta Menuai
   Sarawak
   Songket

Thiesenhusen, William C.
University of Wisconsin, Madison
   Agriculture—Central Asia

Thorsten, Marie
Macalester College
   Economic Stabilization Program

Timmermann, Martina H.
Institute of Asian Affairs (IFA)
   Buraku Liberation League
   Philippines—Human Rights

Tiourine, Alexandre
Netanya, Israel
Marxism-Leninism-Mao Zedong Thought

Tohme, Lara G.
Masschusetts Institute of Technology
Architecture—West Asia

Tokuda, Noriyuki
Heisei International University
Mao Zedong

Traphagan, John W.
University of Texas, Austin
Social Relations—Japan

Tseo, George
Pennsylvania State University, Hazelton
Privatization—China

Tun, Saw
Northern Illinois University
Literature—Myanmar

Tuttle, Gray
Harvard University
Emei, Mount
Huanglongsi

Tyabji, Amina
National University of Singapore
Banking and Finance Industry—Singapore

Upshur, Jiu-hwa Lo
Eastern Michigan University
Chiang Kai-shek
Sun Yat-sen

van den Berg, Gabrielle
Cambridge University
Farsi-Tajiki

Van Norden, Bryan W.
Vassar College
Zhu Xi

van Olphen, Herman H.
University of Texas, Austin
Cinema—India

Van Wie Davis, Elizabeth
Asia-Pacific Center for Security Studies
Hu Yaobang

Vander Lippe, John M.
State University of New York, New Paltz
Bayar, Mahmut Celal
Democrat Party—Turkey
Inonu, Mustafa Ismet
Republican People's Party—Turkey

Vander Ven, Elizabeth
University of California, Los Angeles
Lijiang, Old Town of
Shen Congwen

Vardaman, Jr., James M.
Waseda University
Ancestor Worship—East Asia
Atsuta Shrine
Christianity—Japan
Daigaku
Dazai Osamu
Edogawa Rampo
Endo Shusaku
Hayashi
Honen
Ikkyu
Ise Shrine
Izumo Shrine
Kawabata Yasunari
Kukai
Motoori Norinaga
Nishida Kitaro
Religions, New—Japan
Saicho
Sendai
Shinran
Tohoku Region
Yoshida Shoin

Varley, Paul
University of Hawaii, Honolulu
Muromachi Period
Tea Ceremony

Vasavakul, Thaveeporn
Council on International Educational Exchange
Communism—Vietnam

Verrone, Richard Burks
Texas Tech University
Ao Dai
Army of the Republic of Vietnam
August Revolution
Bao Dai
Cam Ranh Bay
Cao Dai

Da Nang
Dalat
Ha Long Bay
Haiphong
Ho Chi Minh City
Hoan Kiem Lake
Hoi An
Hue
Le Duc Tho
National Front for the Liberation of South
  Vietnam
Ngo Dinh Nhu
Nhu, Madame Ngo Dinh
Paracel Islands
Phan Boi Chau
Red River and Delta
Revolutionary Youth League of Vietnam
Tay Son Rebellion
Tet
Tonkin Gulf
Trung Sisters
Vo Nguyen Giap

Wachs, Iris
Ben Guron University of the Negev
  Qi Baishi

Walsh, John
Zayed University
  Laos—Economic System
  Mekong Project
  New Economic Policy—Malaysia

Walter, Michael
Indiana University
  Buddhism—Central Asia

Wang, Ju
L'École des Hautes Études en Sciences Sociales (EHESS)
  Agricultural Collectivization—China

Ward, Julian
University of Edinburgh
  Imperial Palace
  International Labor Day—China
  National Day—China

Ware, Stephanie L.
Chicago, Ill.
  Pahari
  Santal
  Vedda

Warren, Carol
Murdoch University
  Adat

Watkins, Justin
University of London
  Burmese

Weber, Eva
Northampton, Mass.
  Aichi
  Akita
  Aomori
  Chiba
  Ehime
  Fukui
  Fukuoka
  Fukushima
  Gifu
  Gumma
  Hiroshima
  Hyogo
  Ibaraki
  Ishikawa
  Iwate
  Kagawa
  Kagoshima
  Kanagawa
  Kochi
  Kumamoto
  Mie
  Miyagi
  Miyazaki
  Nagano
  Nara
  Niigata
  Oita
  Okayama
  Osaka
  Saga
  Saitama
  Sapporo
  Shiga
  Shimane
  Shizuoka
  Tochigi
  Tokushima
  Tokyo
  Tottori
  Toyama
  Wakayama
  Yamagata
  Yamaguchi
  Yamanashi

Weil, Shalva
Hebrew University
  Judaism—South Asia

Weinstein, Brian
Howard University
  Judaism—China

Weintraub, Andrew
University of Pittsburgh
  Gambang Kromong
  Sandiwara
  Wayang Golek

Weiss, Anita M.
University of Oregon
  Pakistan—Profile
  Women in Pakistan

Whalen, Robert K.
Madison, N.J.
  Asian Development Bank
  Bogor Declaration
  Intellectual Property
  Manila Action Plan
  Osaka Action Plan
  Rubber Industry
  World Bank in Asia

Whitby, Adrienne
Australian National University
  Cinema—West Asia

White, Merry
Boston University
  Bento
  Cuisine—Japan
  Danchi
  Fugu

Widodo, Johannes
National University of Singapore
  Architecture—Southeast Asia

Wieringa, Edwin
University of Leiden
  Amangkurat
  Bandung
  Bendahara
  Hikayat Amir Hamza
  Javanese
  Laksamana
  Sumatra
  Surabaya

  Temenggong
  Weld, Frederick

Wilce, Jim M.
Northern Arizona University
  Bengali Language

Williams, Catharina
Australian National University
  Cuisine—Indonesia

Wilson Trower, Valerie
Hong Kong Polytechnic University; London Institute
  Clothing, Traditional—Hong Kong
  Clothing, Traditional—Taiwan
  Clothing, Traditional—Vietnam
  Kain Batik

Wilson, Peter
National University of Singapore
  Singapore—Economic System

Winter, Frank H.
National Air and Space Museum
  Gunpowder and Rocketry

Wolz, Carl
Hong Kong Academy for Performing Arts
  Dance, Modern— East Asia

Wong, Poh Poh
National University of Singapore
  Banda Sea
  Borneo
  Cameron Highlands
  Java Sea
  Monsoons
  Strait of Malacca

Wong, Valerie C.
East-West Center
  Chinese in Japan

Woods, Damon L.
University of California, Irvine
  Aquino, Benigno
  Aquino, Corazon
  Bagonbanta, Fernando
  Catholicism, Roman—Philippines
  Garcia, Carlos P.
  Godparenthood—Philippines

Woods, L. Shelton
Boise State University
  Chinese Influence in East Asia

Chinese Influence in Southeast Asia
Protestant Fundamentalism—Southeast Asia

Wray, William D.
University of British Columbia
Financial Crisis of 1927

Wright, Carolyne
University of Central Oklahoma
Literature, Bengali

Xenos, Peter
East-West Center
AIDS

Xu, Jian
University of Wisconsin, Milwaukee
Gao Xingjian

Yagasaki, Noritaka
Tokyo Gakugei University
Japan-Latin America Relations

Yamada, Teri Shaffer
California State University
Poetry—Vietnam

Yamazaki, Hirohisa
Hokuriku University
Heian Period
Japan-United Kingdom Relations

Yan, Margaret Mian
Indiana University, Bloomington
Hakka Languages
Min

Yang, Dali L.
University of Chicago
Great Leap Forward

Yano, Christine R.
University of Hawaii, Manoa
Karaoke

Yaseer, Rahmeen
University of Omaha
Afghanistan—Economic System

Yeoh, Seng-Guan
Sunway College
Chinese New Year
Christianity—Southeast Asia
Hungry Ghost Festival

Kapitan Cina
Kedah
Kuala Lumpur
Melaka
Perlis
Thaipusam
Trengganu
University of Malaya

Yilmaz, Emel
Rome, Italy
Cuisine—Turkey

Yim, Seong-Sook
University of Montreal
Ch'onmin
Paik, Nam June
Painting—Korea

Yoon, Hong-key
University of Auckland
Koreans, Overseas
New Zealand-Asia Relations

Young, John
South Orange, NJ
Romanization Systems, Chinese

Youngblood, Robert L.
Arizona State University
Huk Rebellion
MacArthur, Douglas
Sin, Jaime
Sulu Archipelago

Zamar, Maria Sheila
University of Hawaii, Manoa
Philippine Languages

Zeldovich, Mikhail S.
Harvard University; Dewey Ballantine, LLP
Kabul River
Khyber Pass
North Cyprus, Turkish Republic of

Zeller, Anne
University of Waterloo
Orangutan

Zelliot, Eleanor
Randolph, Minn.
Ambedkar, B.R.
Untouchability

Zhang, Xing Quan
University of Hong Kong
    Development Zones—China
    Three Gorges Dam Project

Zimmermann, Gerd
Technical University of Braunschweig
    Central Highlands of Vietnam
    Phnom Penh

Zvelebil, K. V.
Cabrespine, France
    Dravidian Languages
    Literature, Tamil
    Tamil Language

Index

Boldface page numbers refer to the main entry on the subject.
Italic page numbers refer to illustrations, tables, and maps.

Communist regime in, **1**:29a

constitutions and govern-
ment reforms, **1**:28,
28a–29a, **2**:343b

interim government of, **1**:30a

loya jirga (council of local
leaders) in, **1**:28b, 29b,
30a, 30b

monarchic and local institutions and, **1**:27b–28a

in Taliban era, **1**:30a–30b,
2:*495b*, 495b–496a

profile of, **1:19b–24b**

refugees and, **2**:502a, **4**:81b

Silk Road and, **2**:504b

sociopolitical characteristics of,
1:21b–23b

Tajikistan and, **1**:457b

Tajiks in, **5**:406a

Turkic empire and, **1**:451b

women in, **4**:244a

See also Durrani; Kabul; Kandahar; Sufism: in Southwest
Asia; Taliban; *uzkashi*

Afghanistan Is Everywhere movement, **1**:26a

Afghanistan-Russia/Soviet relations, **1**:19b, 27b, 89b, 216b,
296b, 462a, **2**:3007b, **3**:296a,
6:218b

mujahideen and, **4:208b–209a**

Soviet invasion, **1**:23b, 25a, 29b,
296b, **2**:254a, 343b, 369b,
505a, **4**:92b, 384b,
429a–429b, **5**:439b, **6**:207b

Afghanistan-United States relations

mujahideen and, **4**:209a

U.S. military campaign (2001)
in, **1**:23b, **2**:517a, **3**:172b,
5:407b, **6**:47b

protests against, **4**:*18a*

AFO. *See* Anti-Fascist Organization.

AFPFL. *See* Anti-Fascist People's
Freedom League.

Afrasiab (Uzbekistan), **2**:379a

Africa

AIDS in, **1**:67a

East, **1**:33b, **3**:186b

bombing of embassies in,
1:297a

media in, **4**:97b

mining industry in, **4**:149b

North

Arabic-speaking peoples of,
1:118a

architecture in, **1**:138b

Sevener Muslims in, **4**:242b

South, **1**:31a, 32

cricket in, **2**:184a

Gandhi in, **1**:32,
2:420b–421a, **5**:136a

Indian immigrants in,
2:420b–421a

Japanese relations with,
3:230a–231a

Natal Indian Congress,
2:421b

Natal Indian Congress in,
2:421a, 421b

telephone services in, **3**:88a

Africa-Asia relations, **1:31a–35a**

ancient voyagers and, **1**:33a–33b

Chinese voyages to, **2**:41b, 47a,
4:151b

colonial phase of, **1**:34a–35a

early civilization and, **1**:31a–31b

India and, **1**:33b, **4**:209b

Iron Age, **1**:31b

Japan and, **3**:229b–231b

prehistoric, **1**:31a–31b

religions and, **1**:31b–33a

Afridi people, **1:35b**

Afrika no zento (The Future of
Africa; Tomizu Hirondo),
3:230a

AFTA. *See* ASEAN Free Trade
Area.

Afyon (Turkey), **1:35b–36a**

Afzal Khan, **1:36a–36b**, 284a,
3:365a

Aga Khan, **3**:184a, 184b, 185a,
186b, 187a, **4**:236b, 239b

Agalega Islands (Mauritius), **4**:86a

Agamas (Hindu texts), **2**:526b

Agaoglu, Adalet, **3**:517a

Agartala (India), **1**:*36*, **36b–37a**,
248a, 248b, **5**:532b

Agence Lao Presse, **3**:502a

aging population (Japan),
1:37a–39a, **3**:210a

alternative sources of labor and,
1:38a–38b

costs of, **1**:37b

Golden Plans, **1**:37b

labor shortages and, **1**:38a

trade and, **1**:38a, 39b8a

Agir Roman (Heavy Novel; Kacan),
3:517b

Aglipay y Labayan, Gregorio,
4:488a, 488b

Agno River (Philippines),
1:39a–39b

Agon-shu (Buddhist sect),
5:72b, 73a

Agra Fort, **1**:39b, 135a, **3**:170a

Agra (India), **1:39a–40b**, *40a*, 76a,

84b, 135b, **2**:494a–494b,
5:392b, 393b

Agrava Commission (Philippines),
1:115b

agricultural collectivization

in Cambodia, **1**:412b, **4**:543a

Khmer Rouge and,
1:420b–421a, **3**:358b

in Central Asia, **1**:467a

marriage and family and,
4:49b

in China, **1:40a–41b**,
505b–506a, 523b, 525a,
4:545a–545b, **5**:9b, 105b

agricultural producers' cooperatives (APC) and, **1**:40b,
41a, 46a

command economy and,
1:510a

decollectivization and,
2:448a–448b

Great Leap Forward and,
2:447a–449a

land reform and, **1**:40b, 45b

mutual aid teams (MATs)
and, **1**:40b, 46a

people's communes and,
1:41a, 46b

political system and, **1**:523b,
525a

results of, **1**:41b

third stage of, **1**:40b, 46a

See also household responsibility system

in Kazakhstan, **1**:467a

Khmer Rouge and, **3**:358b

in Laos, **3**:447b, 455a

marriage and family and, **4**:53a

in Mongolia, **4**:174a,
183a–183b, 189b

in North Korea, **3**:372b

in Vietnam, **2**:154a, 154b, **6**:64a

Agricultural Cooperative of Cotia
(Brazil), **3**:238b

agriculture

in Bangladesh, **1**:241b, *242*,
3:51a

jute cultivation, **3**:292a–292b

calendars and, **1**:396b

in Cambodia, **1**:409a, 412b,
413, 420b–421a, **3**:358b

in Central Asia, **1:41b–45a**,
453a–453b, **3**:425a, 426a,
5:363a–363b, **6**:107b

cuisine and, **2**:186a

economic problems of,
1:42a–43a

future implications of,
1:44b–45a

agriculture *(continued)*
  in Central Asia *(continued)*
    Gobi Desert and, **2**:438b
    group farming and,
      1:44a–44b
    irrigation and, **1**:157a–157b,
      2:186a, **4**:36a, 215a,
      5:513a, **6**:*107b*, 109a
    land reform and, **1**:44a, 44b
    monoculture farming and,
      1:42a, 462a, 463a, 467a,
      470b
    restructuring of, **1**:43a–44a
    Russian conquest and,
      1:462a, 462b, 463a–463b
  in China, **1**:45a–51a,
    505b–506a, **2**:455b, 456b,
    459b–460a, 475a, 496b,
    499a, 559b–560a, 566a,
    3:471b, **5**:155a, 166b, 361b
    command economy and,
      1:509a
    Confucianism and, **2**:158a,
      158b
    constitution and, **1**:524b
    cuisine and, **2**:188a, 188b
    in Cultural Revolution, **1**:47a
    dissolution of communes
      and, **1**:47b
    in early twentieth century,
      1:45b
    feminization of, **1**:529a
    Four Modernizations and,
      1:47a
    future prospects for,
      1:50a–50b
    Great Leap Forward and,
      1:46b, 47a, **2**:150b, 260b,
      364a, 447a–449a
    Han dynasty, **2**:481b
    incentives for, **1**:495a, 506a
    internal migration and,
      1:521a
    irrigation and, **1**:496a
    Jiangxi, **3**:274b
    kariz irrigation system, **3**:325a
    labor surplus and, **1**:522a,
      528b, **5**:105b
    land ownership and, **1**:49b,
      2:555b–556b
    land reform and, **1**:45b
    local governments and,
      1:49b–50a
    from mid-1980s to the pre-
      sent, **1**:47b–50a, **2**:475a,
      499a
    Ming dynasty, **4**:152b, 153a
    ninth Five-Year Plan and,
      1:50b

northern, **2**:425a
policies between 1950 and
  1958, **1**:45b–46b
policies of Deng Xiaoping,
  1:47a–47b
population resettlement and,
  1:527b
Qing dynasty, **5**:30a
reform of, **1**:511a, **2**:151a
self-sufficiency in food and,
  1:49b
sericulture and, **5**:150b
Shang dynasty, **5**:167b
Shanxi, **5**:172a
southwestern, **2**:459b–460a
Sui dynasty, **5**:348a
trade and, **1**:49a, 49b
TVEs and, **1**:47b, 506a,
  511a, 522a, **2**:151a,
  5:106a
World Trade Organization
  (WTO) and, **1**:50b
See also agricultural collectivization: in China
Gond women and, **2**:444a
of Hittites, **2**:532b
in India, **2**:227b, 423b, 460b,
  461a, **3**:11b, 13a, 380b,
  383b, 536a, 543b–544a,
  4:38b, 129a, 396b, 548a,
  5:181a, 207a, 410a, **6**:209a
  cotton and, **2**:114b
  Ganges River and, **2**:423a
  Goa, **2**:436b
  irrigation and, **2**:142b, 225b,
    423b, **5**:17b
  in Karnataka state, **3**:325b
in Indo-Gangetic Plain, **3**:51a
in Indonesia, **3**:53b, *55*, 55a,
  55b, 56a, 58a–58b, 61b, 66a,
  5:78a, 131a
  GDP and, **4**:40a
information economy and,
  4:98b
intensive, **2**:454a–454b
in Iran, **3**:99a, 99b, 101a, 349b,
  364b
in Iraq, **4**:76b
  earliest, **2**:196a
in Japan, **2**:81b, 83a, 463a,
  502a–502b, 531a, **3**:1b, 150b,
  190b, 206b, 214a–214b,
  378a, 382b, 434a–434b,
  4:143a, 143b, 155b, 156a,
  381b, **5**:117a, 179a, 180b,
  181a, 504a–504b, **6**:189b
  cuisine and, **2**:200a
  early, **5**:120a
  irrigation and, **2**:197a

  of Kagawa prefecture, **3**:300a
  of Kagoshima prefecture,
    3:300b
  truck farms, **2**:463a
  Yayoi period, **6**:189b
in Karakalpakstan, **3**:315b,
  316a–316b
in Kazakhstan, **3**:149a,
  338a–338b, 346a, **6**:107b
in Korea, **5**:144b, 273a–273b
  Chinese influence and, **2**:14a
  failure of, **2**:61b
  land reform and, **2**:60b
in Laos, **3**:445a, 447b, 455a
  swidden, **3**:446b, 448a
in Malaysia, **1**:58a, 58b,
  429a–429b, **4**:1b, 9b, 42a,
  137b, 477b
  British colonialism and,
    4:7b–8b
  Sabah, **5**:113a
in Maldives, **4**:23a
in Mesopotamia, **3**:131b
in Mongolia
  subsistence, **4**:168b
monsoons and, **4**:194a
in Myanmar, **3**:89a, 146b, 147a,
  149a, 541a, **4**:248b,
  249a–249b, 250a–250b,
  251b, *252*, 252b, 258b–259a,
  260b, 262b, 264b, 268b,
  5:117b, **6**:186b
  irrigation and, **4**:31a
  in Kachin state of, **3**:298b
  in Kayah state of, **3**:332a
  Shan, **5**:164a, 165a
  swidden, **1**:502a, 502b, **4**:268b
New World
  China and, **4**:153b
  Chinese cuisine and, **2**:188b
  South Asian cuisine and,
    2:210b
in North Korea, **1**:485a
  farm system, **2**:396a
in Pakistan
  irrigation and, **1**:495b,
    5:210a, 211a
  labor force and, **5**:211b
in Philippines, **1**:394a, 451a,
  3:540b–541a, **4**:44a, 148b
  irrigation and, **1**:433a, **5**:441
rituals and, **2**:429a–429b
settled, **2**:443b, **3**:380a
shifting, **2**:428b, 429a, 443b
  of Garo, **2**:428b, 429a
shifting *vs.* settled, **1**:51a
in Siberia, **5**:195b, 196a, 196b
in Singapore
  forest fire haze and, **1**:61a, 74a

in South Asia, **1:51a–57b**, *51b*, 2:227b
　agrarian reform and, 1:54–55
　animals and, 1:53a–53b
　climate and, 2:101a, 101b
　cropping and, 1:51b–53a
　Green Revolution and, 2:451b–453b
　irrigation and, 1:56a–56b, 2:101a
　modern and traditional methods in, 1:52
　organization of, 1:53b–57a
　Persian wheels and, 1:53a
　physiography of, 1:51a
　prospects of, 1:57a
　shifting *vs.* settled, 1:51a
in South Korea, 1:493a, 5:269a, 270b
　irrigation and, 5:273a
in Southeast Asia, **1:57b–62a**, 2:534a, 6:129a
　coastal Malays and, 2:141a
　commercialization of, 1:15a
　globalization and, 1:61b
　Green Revolution and, 2:453b–455a
　history of, 1:58a–59a
　Integrated Pest Management (IPM) and, 1:61a
　population growth and, 1:59a–59b
　technology and, 1:59b–61a
in Sri Lanka, 5:315b, 317b, 319a, 325b, 326b
　irrigation and, 5:317a, 319a, 319b, 324a
subsistence
　in Indonesia, 4:26a
　in Malaysia, 4:4b
sustainability and, 5:359a
swidden (slash and burn), 1:78b, 429a, 478a, 502a, 502b, 2:399a, 4:192b, 6:88b, 187b
　in Laos, 3:446b, 448a
　in Myanmar, 1:502a, 502b, 4:268b
of Tai people
　irrigation and, 4:203b, 204a
in Thailand
　irrigation and, 1:490b
in Turkey, 1:432b, 3:382a, 386b–387a, 5:543b, 6:126a
　irrigation and, 6:*107b*
in Turkmenistan, 6:6b, 7b, 8a, 9a
in Uzbekistan, 6:45a, 107b
　irrigation and, 6:209b

in Vietnam, 2:281b, 282a, 4:527b, 5:61a, 6:63a, 63b, *64a*, 65a, 88b–89a
　reforms in, 2:154b, 281a–283a
in West Asia, **1:62a–65a**, 3:78b, 79a
　contemporary status of, 1:63b–64b
　livestock and, 1:65a
　natural conditions and, 1:62b–63a
　structure of, 1:64b–65a
See also farmer's movements; Green Revolution; water issues
Aguda (ruler; Jurchen), 3:290b, 291a
Aguilar, Faustino, 3:506a
Aguinaldo, Emilio, 3:529b, 4:494b, 507a, 512b, 515
Agung, Mount (Bali; Indonesia), 1:*60*
Agung (sultan; Java), 1:89b, 3:63a, 4:84b
Ahaseuerus (biblical king), 3:284b
ahimsa (nonviolence), 3:197b–198b, 5:127a
Ahmad, Aijaz, 4:395b
Ahmad, Imtiaz, 4:71b
Ahmad, Qazi Husain, 3:201a
Ahmad, Sultan Mahmud Perdasa, 4:96a
Ahmad al-Ahsa'i, 6:18b
Ahmad al-Asaʿi, Shaikh, 1:18b
Ahmad b. Hanbal, 5:21a
Ahmad Khan, Sayyid, 1:202b, **5:136b–137a**
Ahmad Shah Abdali (Durrani dynasty), 2:307a, 434a, 446b, 4:468a, 5:17b
Ahmad Shah (Melaka), 3:545b
Ahmad Shah (Qajar dynasty), 1:222b, 4:408a, 5:21b, *22b*, 23a, 23b
Ahmad Shah (sultan; Mughal empire), 1:65b
Ahmadabad (India), **1:65a–66a**, *65b*, 135a, 2:460a
Ahmed al-Safi al-Najafi, 4:532b
Ahn Ae-soon, 2:242a
Ahn Chung-gun, 2:473b
Ahn Jung-hyo, 5:281a
Ahom people (India), 2:469b
　language of, 3:460b
Ahura Mazda, 1:335a, 4:465a, 6:221b, 222b
Ai (emperor; China), 2:544a
Ai Khanum (Central Asia), 1:128b

Ai Qap (journal; Kazakhstan), **1:66a**, 5:149b
Aichi prefecture (Japan), **1:66a–66b**
AIDS (Acquired Immune Deficiency Syndrome), **1:66b–69a**
　among Akha people, 1:78b
　behavior and, 1:68b
　demographic and social impacts, 1:67a–67b
　HIV and, 1:66b–67a, *67b*, 67b–68a
　in India, 5:77a
　intravenous drug users (IDU) and, 1:67a, 67b, 68a
　men having sex with men (MSM) and, 1:67a
　in Mongolia, 4:175b
　in Myanmar
　　Shan State, 5:165a
　prospects for behavior change and control, 1:67b–68b
　spread of, 1:67a, 67b
　in Thailand, 4:95b
Aigun, Treaty of, 2:15b
Aik Mone, 4:441b
aikido (Japanese martial art), **1:69a**
Aiko, princess (Japan), 2:502b
aimag (Mongolian provinces), **1:69a–70b**
Ain-i-Akbari (Institutes of Akbar), 2:368a
Aini, Sadriddin, 2:367a–367b
Ainu language, 1:70b, 71a, 71b, 3:264b
Ainu people, **1:70b–73a**, 3:280b, 412a, 5:129b
　customs of, 1:71b–72a
　early description of, 1:71, 72
　Japanese and, 1:72a–73a, 3:223b
　origins of, 1:71a–71b
　rebellions of, 2:542a
air pollution, **1:73a–74b**
　acid rain and, 1:73b, 2:335b
　from biomass fuels and forest fires, 1:73b–74a
　in China, 2:335b
　　Shanghai, 5:171b
　combating, 1:74a–74b
　future of, 1:74b
　Indonesia and, 3:73a–73b
　industrial, 1:73a–73b
　　greenhouse gases and, 1:73b
　sustainable growth and, 5:359b, 360a
See also environmental issues
Airlangga (king; Java), **1:74b–75a**, 3:62a
Aitmatov, Chingis, **1:75a**, 2:147a

elephant, **2:326b–327a,**
361a, **5:**164a, *327a*
in Mongolia, **4:**168a–168b
water buffalo, **1:**_370_,
370a–371b, 4:76b
yak, **5:**31b, 32a, **6:**100b,
181a–181b
zebu (brahminy cattle),
6:208b–209a
in mangroves, **4:**35a
wild
in Afghanistan, **6:**100
babirusa (pig deer),
1:210a–210b
banteng, **1:261b–262a,** _262_
of Garabil Plateau, **2:**426a
of Gobi Desert, **2:**438b
Hubara bustard, **1:389a–389b**
in India, **1:**161b
of Iriomotejima Island,
3:145b
lion, **3:476a–476b**
in Malaysia, **3:**376a
mongoose, **4:190b–191a**
orangutan, **4:**390b
in Sundarbans National
Park, **2:**424a
in zodiac, **6:**219b
See also camels; chickens; endangered species; goats;
horses; pigs
anime (Japanese animation),
1:108a–108b, 2:95b, 96b
manga and, **4:**34a
See also cinema: Japanese
animism, **5:**300a
Christianity and, **2:**77b
in India, **1:**100b, **4:**156b
Indonesian music and, **4:**227a
Miao, **4:**142b
nomadic pastoralism and,
4:340a
rites of, **1:**265b
Thai people and, **5:**448b
Tujia people and, **5:**536b
Anitta (king; Hittites), **2:**531b
Ankara Agreement (1963),
2:356a–356b
Ankara (Turkey), **1:108b–110a,**
176a, **2:**86b, **3:**82a, 188b, **5:**61a,
562b
architecture in, **1:**_109_, 155b
Haci Bayram Mosque in,
1:109b
history of, **1:**108b
museum at, **1:**125b
in twentieth century,
1:108b–109b
universities in, **1:**109b

Ann Chae-hong, **5:**281b
Annadurai, C. N., **5:**49b
Annam, **1:**402a, **2:**402b, 403a
Sino-French War and, **2:**8b
See also Vietnam
Annan, Kofi, **6:**31a
Annapurna, Mount, **2:**513a, **4:**200b
Anp'yong (prince; Korea), **4:**418a
Anquetil-Duperron, A. H., **4:**393b
Ansar-e-Hezbollah (Helpers of the
Party of God; Iran), **3:**108a, 109a
Ansari, Abdullah, **1:110a–110b**
quatrain by, **1:**110a
Ansari, Abu Ayyub, **4:**241a
Ansari, Bayazid, **4:**467b
Ansari, M. A., **1:**82b
Ansei earthquake (Japan), **5:**509b
Antaki, Dawud, al-, **1:**117b
Antakya (Antioch; Turkey),
1:110b–111a, 2:86b
Christianity in, **1:**111a, **5:**119b
Antalya (Turkey), **1:111a–111b**
Antara News Agency (Indonesia),
4:25b
Antep. *See* Gaziantep.
anti-Americanism, **3:**361a
Anti-Comintern Pact (1936), **3:**233a
anti-Communism, **1:**375b,
6:81b, 93a
of Chiang Kai-shek, **2:**466a,
466b, **5:**391b
Anti-Fascist Organization (AFO;
Myanmar), **1:**111b
Anti-Fascist People's Freedom
League (AFPFL; Myanmar),
1:111b–112a, 181a, 325a,
2:155a, **4:**248a, 257b,
264a–264b, 269a, **5:**471a
Anti-Japanese Malay Resistance
Movement (Wataniah), **1:**3b
Anti-Rightist Campaign (China;
1957), **2:**150a, 447a
Anti-Taurus (Guney Dogu Toros)
Mountains, **1:112a–112b**
Antioch. *See* Antakya.
Antiochus III (emperor; Seleucid
empire), **4:**476a
Antiquities of Dacca (paintings;
D'Oyly), **2:**272b
Antrasen, Ja-eam, **2:**234a
Anuradhapura kingdom (Sri
Lanka), **5:**317a, 323b–324b
Anuvong (king; Laos), **3:**452b,
5:474a
Anvari (Persian poet), **3:**520b
Anwar, Chairil, **5:**15b
Anwar, Ibrahim, **1:**103a, 112b,
112b–113a, 214a, **3:**163a, 164a,
4:16a, 18b

Anwar-ud-Din, **2:**404b
Anyang (China), **2:**503b,
5:167a–167b
ANZUK. *See* Australia, New
Zealand, and the United King-
dom.
ANZUS Treaty (Australia, New
Zealand, U.S.; 1952), **3:**240a
ao dai (traditional Vietnamese
dress), **1:113a–113b, 2:**138a,
_139_, 139b
Aoi Matsuri (festival; Japan),
1:113b–114a
Aomori prefecture (Japan),
1:114a–114b
Aoyoma Shinji, **2:**96b
Ap Bac, battle of (1963; Vietnam),
6:78b, 81b
Aparajito (film; The Unvanguished;
Ray), **2:**88b
Aparri (Philippines), **1:**394a
APEC forum. *See* Asia-Pacific
Economic Cooperation forum.
APFNHRI. *See* Asia-Pacific Forum
of National Human Rights In-
stitutions.
Aphaiwong, Kowit, **4:**521b
Apita (The One Who Cannot Be
Touched; Ramamirtham),
3:492b
Appar (Tamili poet), **3:**492a
April 19 Revolution (1960; Korea),
1:114b–115a
corruption and, **2:**182a
See also Rhee, Syngman
Apte, Narayan, **2:**440a
Apu Trilogy, The (Bandyopadhyay),
3:509b
Apu trilogy (films; Ray), **2:**88b,
89a, **3:**509b
Apur sansar (film; The World of
Apu; Ray), **2:**88b, 89a
aquaculture
in China, **2:**383a–383b
Japanese fishing industry and,
2:384a–384b, 385a
in Korea, **2:**386b–387a
mangroves and, **4:**35a–35b
in southeast Asia, **2:**_388_, 388a
Aquino, Benigno, **1:115a–116a,**
115b, 446a, **4:**48a, 104b, 472b,
508b, **5:**53a
assassination of, **1:**115b–116a,
4:538b
Aquino, Corazon Cojuangco,
1:115a, 116a, **116a–116b,** 446a,
2:340a, **4:**48a, 197a, 472b, 508b,
510b, **5:**209b, **6:**124b
agrarian reform law of, **4:**499a

Avar people, **2**:229a
    invasions of Central Asia by,
        1:477a
Avarodbhasini (Secluded Women;
    Hossain), **3**:509b
Aves y Flores (Guerrero), **2**:459b
Avesta, **4**:393b, 465a, **5**:399b,
    6:221b–222a, 223a
    See also Zoroastrianism
Avicenna. *See* Ibn Sina.
Aw Boon Haw, **2**:49b
Aw Boon Par, **2**:49b
Awadh (India), **1**:198b
Awami League (AL; Bangladesh),
    1:198b–199b, 240b, 247b,
        249a, 251b, 252b, 253a, 253b,
        254a, 256b, 258a, **2**:172a, 492a,
        3:266a–266b, **4**:434a, **6**:218a,
        218b
    founder of, **1**:251a, **5**:43b
    supporters of, **1**:199a, 248a,
        249b
Ayhan, Ece, **3**:516b
Aylak Adam (Free Man; Atilgan),
    3:517b
Aynanm Icindekiler (Inside the Mir-
    ror; Ilhan), **3**:517a
Ayodhya (India)
    destruction of mosque in,
        5:128a
Ayub Khan, Muhammad,
    1:199b–200a, 200, 200a, 247b,
        248a, 248b, 251b, 252a, 295a,
        4:426a, 428b–429a, 433b–434b,
        437a–437b, 440a
Ayusawagawa River (Japan), **2**:407a
Ayutthaya, kingdom of (Thailand),
    1:200a–202b, 387b, **2**:297b,
        3:513a–513b, 525b, **4**:199b,
        203b, 204b, 257a, 550a, **5**:154b,
        218b, 460a–460b, 480a
    Burmese sack of, **1**:202a, 383a,
        4:520a, 521a
    founding of, **5**:49a, 49b
    poetry of, **1**:201b
    See also Trailok
Azad, Abu'l-Kalam, **1**:202b–203a
Azad Hind Fauj (AHF; Indian Na-
    tional Army), **1**:312a
Azad Kashmir (Free Kashmir),
    1:4b, 203a–203b, **4**:424a
Azahari, A. M., **1**:203b–204a,
    330a, 332a, **4**:466b–467a
Azato Yasutsune, **2**:412a
Azerbaijan, **1**:43a, 156b,
    204a–205a
    Armenia and, **1**:204b, **3**:311b
    Armenians in, **1**:158b
    boundaries of, **1**:204b

camels in, **1**:428a
Caspian Sea and, **1**:437a, 437b
Caucasia and, **1**:448a
Central Asian music and,
    4:219a
CIS and, **1**:472b
Democratic Republic of, **1**:206b
fertility rates in, **2**:376b
independence of, **1**:204b, 450a,
    5:562b
Iran and, **1**:206b, **4**:409a
Iran-Russia relations and,
    3:117a–117b, 118a
map of, **1**:*205*
Mongols in, **4**:188b
oil exports from, **4**:379b
Russia and, **1**:450a
Shi'ite Muslims in, **4**:241b
Soviet Union and, **1**:159b, 204b
Sunni Muslims in, **4**:243b
Tabriz and, **5**:366a
war with Armenia of, **3**:311b
See also Karabag
Azerbaijani people, **1**:205a–207b
    culture of, **1**:206b–207b
    in Iran, **1**:206b
    language and culture of,
        1:206b–207b
    religions of, **1**:205b–206a
    Shirvanshah dynasty and,
        1:205b
    territory of, **1**:204b, 206a
    in Transcaucasus, **1**:206a
Azim Shah (prince; Mughal em-
    pire), **2**:272b
Aztech Technology (Singapore),
    2:509b
Azucena (De Gracia Conception),
    4:538b

B
Ba, state of (China), **2**:58b, **5**:535b
Ba Cut, **2**:306b
Ba Jin, **1**:209a–209b, **5**:244a–244b
Ba Maw, **1**:181a, **4**:264a
Ba Thoung, **5**:471a
Ba Trieu, **1**:209b–210a
Ba'ath Party (Iraq), **2**:569a–569b,
    3:124b, 125a, 127a, 130a, 130b,
        135b, 138b, **4**:115a
    control of political system by,
        3:138b, 140a, 141a
    human rights and, **3**:136b, 137a
Baba Shah Muzzafar, **1**:183a
Baba Tatsui, **1**:210a
Babakhanov, Zia al-din, **4**:238b
Babil Corporation (Iraq), **2**:93a
babirusa (pig deer), **1**:210a–210b

Babism, **1**:210b–211a, 217b–218a
    baha'i and, **1**:218a
Bab,the (Sayyid 'Ali Muhammad
    Shirazi; Mirza 'Ali Muham-
    mad), **1**:210b, **6**:18b
Babur (Zahir ud-Din Muhammad;
    founder; Mughal empire),
    1:76a, 135a, 198b, **211a–211b**,
        485b, 486a–486b, **2**:210b, 519b,
        562b, **3**:174a, 536a, **4**:206a,
        5:17b, 58a, **6**:148a
    as author, **3**:480b
    conquest of South Asia, **4**:485a
    grave of, **1**:*211b*
    Mosque of, **1**:76a
Baburnama , *The* (Babur), **1**:211a,
    486b
Babylon, **2**:117a, **5**:497a
    calendar of, **1**:396b, 399b, 400b
    Hittite capture of, **2**:531b
    See also Euphrates River
Bac Son Uprising (Vietnam),
    1:211b–212a
Bach Long Vi (Vietnam), **2**:471b
Bacha-e-Saqao (king; Afghanistan),
    2:343a
Bachchan, Amitabh, **1**:212a–212b,
    2:89b, **4**:111
Bactria (Central Asia), **1**:128b,
    212b–213a
    art in, **2**:379a
Badakhshan (Central Asia), **1**:23a,
    213a–213b, **6**:100a
Badakshani language, **4**:456a,
    5:395a
Badarayana (Hindu teacher),
    2:523a
Badawi, Abdullah Ahmed,
    1:213b–214a, *214a*
badminton, **5**:308a
Badr Ahaki al-Sayyab, **4**:533a
Badshahi Mosque (Pakistan), **3**:439a
Baelz, Erwin von, **3**:232b
Bagabandi, Natsagiin, **4**:167a, 375a
Bagan. *See* Pagan kingdom; Pagan
    kingdom (Myanmar).
Baghdad (Iraq), **1**:117a, 118b,
    156a, **214a–216a**, **3**:82a
    architecture in, **1**:137b, 215a
    Britain and, **1**:215b
    decline of, **1**:215a–215b
    fall of (1258), **1**:117b, **4**:532a
    formation of OPEC in, **4**:391a,
        391b
    founding of Baha'i in,
        1:218a–218b
    housing in, **1**:*215*
    Nestorian (Assyrian) Church in,
        4:393a

Bandaranaike, Solomon West
Ridgeway Diaz, **1**:232a, **5**:322b,
325b, 326a
assassination of, **5**:326b
Bandit Queen (film), **2**:271b
Bandung Conference (1955), **1**:34,
233a, **233b**, 234, **3**:34b, 539,
4:383a
Bandung Institute of Technology,
1:**233b**, 235a, **2**:472a
Bandung (West Java, Indonesia),
1:**233a–233b**, 268a, **3**:51b,
268a, **6**:110b
Bandyopadhyay, Bibhutibhushan,
3:509b
Banerji, R. D., **4**:158b
Bangadarshan (Review of Bengal;
journal), **1**:491b
Bangalore (India), **1**:106b,
235a–235b, **3**:325b
Bangkok Conference, **4**:516a
Bangkok Declaration,
1:**236b–237a**, **5**:292b
Bangkok (Thailand), **1**:202a,
235b–236b, *236a*, 312a, 359a,
381a, **4**:471b, 472a, **5**:451a,
6:151b
Asian Games in, **1**:166a
automobiles in, **6**:124a
Buddhist monks in, **1**:*361b*
demonstrations in, **1**:96a,
4:487a, **5**:464b
in eighteenth century, **5**:460b
Emerald Buddha in,
2:**329a–329b**, **4**:521b
population of, **5**:452a
Thai kickboxing in, **4**:205b
Vietnam War and, **5**:463b,
464b
Wat Sutat in, **1**:360b
Bangla language, **1**:278b
Bangladesh, **1**:36b, 51a, 53a, 269b,
278a, **2**:348a, **3**:43b, 172b, 507b
agriculture in, **1**:241b, *242*,
3:51a, 292a–292b
ascetics in, **5**:156b
Christianity in, **2**:74b
climate of
cyclones in, **2**:101a
typhoons in, **6**:19b, 20a
Communism and, **4**:78b
Constitution of, **5**:44a
conveyance arts in,
2:171b–172b, *172a*
creation of, **1**:203b, 249b,
3:203b, **4**:433b, 434a, 438a,
5:43b, 44a
cricket in, **2**:184a
cuisine of, **2**:209b, 210a, 210b

dance in, **2**:**235b–237a**
economic system of,
1:240b–241a, **241a–243a**
agriculture, **1**:241b, *242*
finance, **1**:242b–243a
future prospects, **1**:243a
industry, **1**:242a–242b
education system of,
1:**243b–245b**, *244a*
primary and secondary
schooling, **1**:244a–244b
Private University Act of
1992, **1**:244b–245a
public and private tertiary,
1:244b–245a
recent trends and statistics,
1:243b–244a
structure of, **1**:244a
English language in, **2**:336a
ethnic groups in, **5**:128a, 128b
fertility rates in, **2**:377a
folk opera in. *See* Jatra.
Grameen Bank in, **2**:445a–445b
Green Revolution in, **2**:451b,
452b, 453a
history, timeline of, **1**:246
history of, **1**:239a–240a,
245b–250b, **2**:273a
beginning of separatist
movement, **1**:247a–249a
East Bengal at partition,
1:247a
General Rahman's assuption
of power, **1**:249a–250b
premodern, **1**:245b, 247a
immigrants from, **1**:172b
independence of, **5**:44a, 44b
Internet in, **4**:111a
Islamization of, **3**:169a, 169b,
170a
Jama'at in, **3**:201a
jute cultivation in, **3**:292a–292b
languages in, **1**:239a, **2**:349b
leaders of, **6**:218a–218b
literacy in, **4**:97b
in literature, **3**:509b
mangroves in, **4**:35a
map of, **1**:*237b*
marriage and family in, **4**:69a,
70a, 71a
media in, **4**:97b, 110a–112a
mosques in, **2**:56b
Mukti Bahini (Freedom Force)
of, **1**:253a
music of, **4**:**216b–218b**
people of, **1**:238a–239a
phone services in, **3**:88a
poetry of, **3**:509b
political parties of, **2**:492a

political system of,
1:240a–240b, **250b–253b**,
6:218a
colonial heritage,
1:250b–251a
constitution and, **1**:252
after independence,
1:253a–253b
independence and, **1**:249a,
250b, 252, 253a, 255a
Pakistan period, **1**:251a–253a
women in, **6**:148b
See also Awami League;
Bangladesh Nationalist
Party; British Indian em-
pire; Jatiya Party; Mughal
empire
presidents of, **5**:342b
profile of, **1**:**237a–241a**
rivers of, **1**:316b, 317a
Rohingyas and, **5**:94b
statistics on, **1**:238
Sunni Muslims in, **4**:243b
tea production in, **5**:432a
toxic-waste disposal and, **5**:523a
United Front in, **1**:251a–251b
universities in, **1**:56b
See also ethnic conflict: in South
Asia
Bangladesh-India relations,
1:**254b–256b**
in 1980s, **1**:255a–256a
ancient, **1**:255a
Bangladesh secession and,
2:420a, **3**:32b
current, **1**:256a
Bangladesh Institute of Development Studies (BIDS), **2**:445b
Bangladesh Nationalist Party
(BNP), **1**:199a–199b, 240a,
240b, 249b, 253a, 253b, *254*,
254a, **254a–254b**, **2**:492a,
3:266a–267b, **5**:44b
See also Awami League
Bangladesh-Pakistan relations,
1:**256b–258a**, *257b*, **4**:424a,
432a
Bangladesh secession and,
1:295b
era of friendship, **1**:257a–257b
Harare Commonwealth sum-
mit, **1**:257a
Organization of Islamic Conference summit (Dakar; 1991),
1:257a
See also Awami League; India-
Pakistan relations
Bangsa Moro (Moro Nation;
Philippines), **3**:168b, 169a

BBCAU. *See* British Borneo Civil
Affairs Unit.
Beaufort, Leicester P., **4**:84a
Beck, Brenda E.F., **3**:491a
Becrooni, al-, **4**:24b
bedaya (Javanese dancers), **1**:271a
Bedi, Rajinder Singh, **2**:82b
bedil (cannon), **1**:271b–272a
Beihai Park (China), **2**:428a
Beijing (China), **1**:272, **272a–275a**
air pollution in, **1**:73b
Boxer Rebellion and, **3**:469b,
5:28b
as capital city, **2**:496b, **6**:199a
cuisine of, **2**:191b
in Cultural Revolution, **2**:222b,
223b
demographics of, **1**:274b
economy of, **1**:274b
education in, **1**:514b, 515b
examination system in, **1**:273a
gardens in, **2**:427a, 428a
geography of, **1**:274a–274b
Grand Canal and, **2**:446a
history of, **1**:272b–274a, 273
Imperial Palace in, **3**:6b–7a
internal migration and, **1**:521a
Japanese attack on, **6**:162a
Mandarin and, **4**:31b, 32a
in Ming dynasty, **4**:151b
Mongols and, **4**:162b, 164b
Taiping Rebellion and, **5**:374b
vending machines for, **1**:274a
See also Tiananmen Square
Beijing Foreign Language Insti-
tute, **2**:425b
Beijing Opera (China), **1**:*275a*,
275a–275b, **2**:561b, **4**:129b,
221a, **6**:178a
masks in, **4**:82a
Beijing University (China), **2**:507a
Beijing Zhongguancun Science and
Technology Park (China),
2:507a
Beiyang Fleet (China), **3**:469b
Bek, Ibrahim, **1**:266a
Bektashiyya (Sufi order), **4**:240a
Belarus
Central Asia and, **1**:472a, 472b
CIS and, **1**:472b
Belgium
in Africa, **1**:34a
Bell, Alexander Graham, **2**:323b
Bell, Gertrude, **4**:532b
Bell, Johann Adam Schall von,
1:396a
Bell Trade Act (1947; Philippines),
4:514b
Belli, Oktay, **1**:126a

Belo, Bishop Carlos, **1**:275b–276a,
2:315a, **5**:54a
Beloe Dvizhenie (White Move-
ment; Kazakhstan), **1**:85a
Benares. *See* Varanasi.
Bencao gangmu (Compendium of
Materia Medica; Li Shizhen),
3:470b, **4**:123b, 154a
bendahara (Malay state official),
1:276a–276b, **3**:439b–440b
See also Laksamana
Bene Israel, **3**:285a–285b
Benedict, Ruth, **2**:80a
Benedict XIV (pope), **3**:271b
Benegal, Shyam, **2**:89b
Bengal, East (India), **2**:273a,
4:427b–428a, 432b–433a, 436b
Bengal, West (India),
1:276b–277a, 278a, 394a,
2:252a
Bangladesh and, **4**:216b
borders of, **1**:285b
colonial life in, **1**:277a
Communism in, **4**:78b
ethnic groups in, **5**:128a
Garo in, **2**:428b
government of, **2**:493a
Bengal Atlas (Rennell), **2**:272b
Bengal (India), **1**:77a, 238a, **5**:502b
anti-British revolutionaries in,
1:202b
architecture in, **1**:135a
ascetics in, **5**:156b
Bangladesh and, **1**:245b, **4**:216b
British India and, **1**:247a, 250b,
251a, 317b
capital of, **1**:394a–394b
cuisine of, **2**:209b, 210b, 212b
earliest references to, **1**:239a
famine in, **5**:38a
folk opera in, **3**:266b
Ganges River and, **2**:424a–424b
influence of, **4**:38b
jute cultivation in, **3**:292b
literature of, **3**:507a–510a
Munda languages in, **4**:213a
Pakistan and, **1**:276b
partition of, **1**:394b, **4**:432b
salt tax and, **5**:121a
split of, **2**:225b
spread of Islam in, **1**:238b
treaty with British East India
Company, **1**:318–319
See also Laksamana
Bengal Liberation Front, **1**:248a
Bengal Renaissance, **1**:277b, 394b
Bengali language, **1**:37a, 172b,
251a, 277a, **277a–278a**, **3**:44a,
44b, 50b, **5**:48a, 100a, 532b

in Bangladesh, **2**:349b
in Calcutta, **1**:277a–277b, 394b
in cinema, **2**:88a
dialects of, **1**:277a
films in, **2**:89a
literature in, **1**:491a, **3**:179b,
490a–491a, **507a–510a**
mass media and, **4**:98a
Munda languages and, **4**:211b
Oriya and, **4**:397a
in Pakistan, **1**:247a–247b
poetry in, **4**:530b, 531a
terms from, **5**:134a
Bengali people, **1**:238a, 247a,
247b, 248a, 248b, 249a, 250a,
256b, **278a–279a**, *278b*
Benten kozo (Benten the Thief;
Kawatake Mokuami), **3**:294a
Bentham, Jeremy, **1**:279a
Bentinck, William Cavendish,
1:279a–279b, 317b
bento (lunchbox meal),
1:279b–280a, **2**:197b
Benyamin S., **2**:418a
Berjaya (United People's Party of
Sabah; Malaysia), **2**:569a
Berke (Mongol empire), **2**:442a,
3:165a
Berlin Film Festival, **2**:444a, 463a
Berlin Wall, **1**:269a
Berreman, Gerald, **1**:440b
Besant, Annie, **6**:161b
Beschi, C.G.E., **3**:490b
Bessus (ruler; Bactria), **1**:212b
Bey, Selim Sirry, **5**:307b
Beyaz Kale (The White Castle; Pa-
muk), **3**:517a
Beyond Life Sentences (Tabios),
4:538b–539a
Bhaduri, Jaya, **1**:212b
Bhagavad Gita, **1**:280b, **2**:491b,
3:13a, 488b, 510a, 541b, 542b,
5:124b, **6**:38a
Bhagavata Purana, **3**:489a
Bhagirathi River (India), **2**:424a
Bhai Gurdas Bhalla, **2**:528b
bhakti (devotional practice; India),
1:280a–282a**, 357a, 440a,
2:523b, *526a*, 526b, **3**:23a, 25a,
4:530b, **5**:125b, 127a, 202b,
204a, 204b
early developments,
1:280b–281a
groups, **1**:281a
Indian music and, **4**:226b–227a
practices, **1**:281a–282a
See also caste; Hindu philosophy; Hindu values; Hin-
duism; Sanskritization

Bismillah Khan, **5**:175b

Bitab, Sufi, **1:299a**

Biwa, Lake (Japan), **2**:552a–552b, **5**:178b, 179a

biwa (Japanese lute), **1:299a–299b**, **4**:230a

Bizen ware (Japan), **1**:*479b*, 480, 481a

Bizim Koy (Our Village; Makal), **3**:517a

Black, Davidson, **4**:446b

Black Flags (Vietnam), **5**:230b–231b

"Black Hole of Calcutta," **1**:394b

Black Satsuma ceramics (Japan), **3**:301a

Black Sea, **1**:64b, 96b, 98a, **299b–300a**, 312a, **2**:250b
  pollution in, **4**:49a

Blackburn, Anne, **1**:361a

Blake, William, **4**:376b

Blancas de San Jose, Francisco, **3**:505b

Blavatsky, Helena Petrovna, **1**:167b, **300a–301a**, *300b*, **5**:487a–487b

blowfish (fugu), **2**:405b–406a

Blue Shirts (GMD; China), **2**:466a–466b

BNP. *See* Bangladesh Nationalist Party.

Bo Hai Gulf (China), **2**:558a
  oil fields in, **5**:484a

Bo Mya, **3**:323a

board games, **1:301a–301b**

boat people (Vietnamese), **1:301b–302a**, **6**:92b
  See also refugees

Boaventura rebellion (1911–1912; East Timor), **2**:314b

Bodawpaya (king; Myanmar), **4**:262a

Bodh Gaya (India), **1:302a–302b**, 354a, 357b, **5**:200a

Bodhidharma, **1**:335b, 336a, 344a, 367b

bodhisattvas, **5**:141b–142a

Bodic languages (Tibet), **5**:234a–236a

Bodoo, Dogsomyn, **4**:182a, 182b

Bodrum (Turkey), **1:302b–303a**

Boer War (South Africa)
  Gandhi and, **2**:421a

Bogazkoy (Turkey), **1**:124b, 126a, **2**:*531b*, 532a, 533a

Bogdo Khan (Jebtsundamba Khutukhtu), **1:303a–303b**, 349b, 350a–350b, 351a, **4**:173b, 174a, 180a, 180b
  USSR and, **4**:182a, 182b, 183a

Bogor Declaration, **1:303b–304a**, **4**:397b

Bogor (Indonesia), **1**:268a
  APEC meeting in, **1**:170a, **4**:397b

Bohol (Philippines), **2**:426a, 426b

Bohras (Shi'a sect), **3**:171b, **4**:210b

Bokeikhanov, Alikhan, **1**:66a, **304a–304b**, **3**:333a

Bokeo (Laos), **1:304b**

Bokor, Mount (Elephant Range), **2**:327a

Bolan Pass (Baluchistan), **1:304b–305a**

Bolivia, **4**:149b

Bollywood (India), **2**:89b, **4**:211a
  See also cinema: in India

Bolor Erike (The Crystal Rosary; Mongolia), **1**:349a

Bolovens Plateau (Laos), **1:305a–305b**

Bolshevik Revolution, **2**:489b, **5**:561b
  Central Asia and, **1**:464a, **2**:145a–145b
  Jadidism and, **1**:465a
  Karakalpakstan and, **3**:315a
  literature and, **3**:481a–482a
  Sun Yat-sen and, **6**:130a
  See also Russian Revolution (1917)

Bolsheviks, **1**:3a, 5a, 85a, 221b, 266a, 304a, 350b, **2**:284b, 306a, 446b
  in Armenia, **1**:159b
  in Central Asia, **1**:470b–471a, 471b, **3**:313a
  education and, **1**:465a, **6**:48a–48b
  in Kazakhstan, **1**:179a, **5**:144a
  Leninism and, **4**:79b
  in Mongolia, **2**:62b, **4**:180b
  in Siberia, **5**:196a

Bom Waktu (Time Bomb; Nano Riantiarno), **5**:85a

Bombay. *See* Mumbai.

Bon Matsuri (Bon Festival; Obon), **1:306a–306b**
  "Dance of the Ginger" at, **1**:306
  See also ancestor worship; Buddhism: in Japan

Bonaparte, Napoleon, **4**:394b

Bondo people (India), **2**:114a

Bonifacio, Andres, **3**:505b–506a
  "A Primer for Philippine Independence," **4**:506–507, 507a

Bonjol, Tuanku Imam, **4**:405a

bonsai (miniature tree cultivation), **1:306b–307b**, *307*
  Japanese ceramics and, **1**:479a

Book of Agriculture (Xu Guangqi), **6**:179a

Book of Changes. *See* Yijing.

Boris I (ruler; Bulgarian kingdom), **1**:374b

Borlaug, Norman, **2**:451b, 452b

Borneo, **1**:105b, **307b–308b**, **3**:385b, **4**:4b
  British in, **1**:319b–320a, **4**:13b
  Chinese in, **2**:47a
  Dayak in, **1**:308b, 309a, 309b, 310a
  Federation of Malaysia and, **2**:370a
  forest fires in, **1**:74a, 331b
  language groupings of, **1**:308b
  logging contractors in, **2**:398b
  Malaysia and, **4**:1a
  map of, **1**:*308a*
  North, **1**:204a, 325b
    See also Sabah
  orangutan in, **4**:390b
  Penan in, **1**:309b–310a
  piracy and, **4**:525a
  religion in, **1**:310a
  ritual festivals in, **2**:429a–429b
  See also Brunei; Kalimantan; Sabah; Sarawak

Borneo Company Limited (BCL), **4**:7a, 150b

Borneo peoples, **1:308b–310b**, **5**:5b

Borobudur (Java), **1:310b–311b**, *311*, 429b, 430a, **3**:54b, 61b, **4**:227b, **5**:332b, 515a, 520a, **6**:197a

Borodin, Michael, **6**:130a

Boromaraja II (king; Ayutthaya), **5**:525b

Borommatrailokanat (king; Ayutthaya), **1**:201a

Bosch, Johannes van den, **1:310b–311b**, **3**:64b

Bose, Buddhadeva, **4**:531a

Bose, Khudiram, **2**:172a

Bose, Subhas Chandra, **1:311b–312a**, *312a*, **3**:11b

Boshin War (Japan), **4**:130b

Bosporus, **1**:96b, **312a–313a**, **2**:250b, **3**:187a

Bouchier, Guillaume, **3**:319a

Boulle, Pierre, **1**:382b

Boun Oum, Prince, **2**:99b

Bouphanovong, Sonvanthone, **3**:502b

Bourbon Island (Indian Ocean), **2**:404b

Bovaradej (prince; Thailand),
5:451b
Boven Digul (Dutch New Guinea),
2:493b
Boworadet (prince; Thailand),
4:521b
Bowrey, Thomas, 2:272b
Boxer, C. R., 2:68b
Boxer Rebellion (1900; China),
1:313a–314b, *313b*, 2:24a–24b,
566b, 3:469b, 4:386b, 5:28b,
31a, 166a, 6:201a
Christianity and, 2:65b
Empress Dowager and, 2:86a
Hongdengzhao (Red Lanterns;
women's martial arts organization) in, 1:314a
international army and, 5:484a
Protocol of, 1:314a
U.S. - Philippines relations and,
4:515a
See also Qing dynasty
Bradley, Dan Beach, 5:457b,
6:122b, 123b
Brahma (Hindu concept),
2:521a–521b, 523a, 524a, 526a,
5:51a
Brahma Sutra, 5:124b
Brahman (Hindu concept), 5:124b
Brahmanas (Hindu texts), 2:521b,
526b, 3:488b
Brahmanism, 1:77b, 169a, 239b
Brahmans, 1:201a, **314b–316a,**
315, 323a, 3:488b, 4:395a–395b,
5:410b
caste and, 1:440a, 440b, 2:517b,
520a, 522a, 524b,
3:475a–475b, 4:407a
four Hindu castes of, 1:225a
literature and, 3:491a
marriage and, 4:69a
ritual purity of, 1:316a, 6:145a
Sanskritization and, 5:126a,
126b
in Thailand, 2:527a, 527b
women and, 6:145a
See also caste; pandit
Brahmaputra River, 1:161a, 172a,
172b, 237a, 254b, 269a, 276b,
316b–317a, 2:272a, 469b,
3:10a, 51a
flooding and, 2:101a, 5:87b
map of, 1:*317a*
Brahmasutra Bhasya (Sankara),
5:124b
Brahmi script, 1:172a, 3:281b,
5:323b
Asokan, 5:409a
Brahmo Samaj movement, 5:135a

Brahui people, **1:316a–316b**
Brang Seng, 3:297b
Brazil, 3:91a, 4:149b
Japanese economic development
and, 3:239a–239b
Japanese migration to,
3:238a–239a
Breaking Away (Linh Nhat), 3:476a
Brecht, Bertolt, 5:85a
Breda, Peace of, 1:326a
Bretton Woods Conference
(1944), 6:157a
Bretton Woods system, 3:212a
Brezhnev, Leonid, 1:467a, 3:337b,
411a, 5:534a, 6:114a
Central Asia and, 2:147a
bride stealing, 3:422b
Bridge over the River Kwai (film),
1:186a, 382b
Briggs, Sir Harold, 3:548b
Briggs Plan (Malaya), 3:548b
Brihadaranyaka Upanishad, 6:144b
Brihadratha (Mauryan empire),
4:89a
Brihaspati Sutra, 2:523a
British Borneo Civil Affairs Unit
(BBCAU), 1:325b
British colonial rule, 3:201a,
6:115a
in Afghanistan, 4:92b
in Africa, 1:34a–34b
in China, 5:168b
Opium Wars and, 4:28a
in Hong Kong, 1:503b,
2:547b–549b, 550b
independence and, 1:320a–320b
in Iraq, 4:76b
Karen people and, 3:322a
in Korea, 5:312b
in literature, 2:401a
in Malaya, 1:325a, 2:100a–100b,
391a, 3:548a, 4:6b–9a,
6:113a
agriculture and, 4:7b–8b
coastal Malays and, 2:141a
education system and, 4:10b,
12a
Islam and, 3:161a, 162a,
162b
in Malaysia, 1:429b, 4:6a–8b,
13a–14a, 20b–21a, 90a
cuisine and, 2:204b
influence of, 4:4a, 19a
Kapitan Cina and, 3:310b
mineral industry and, 4:149a,
150a–150b
Sabah, 5:113b–114a
in Maldives, 4:22b, 25a
in Mauritius, 4:87b–88a

in Middle East, 4:243a
Mon and, 4:159b
in Myanmar, 1:111b, 501b,
502a, 2:344b, 534a, 4:30a,
31b, 160a, 199b, 246a–246b,
248a, 249a–249b, 257a–257b,
258, 262a–264a, 268b–269a,
5:164a
Christianity and, 2:72a,
4:254a
Islam and, 3:166b
in Pakistan, 2:368b–369a
in Singapore, 2:179a
in South Asia, 4:110b
cuisine and, 2:210a, 210b,
211a–212a
in Southeast Asia, 1:9b, 151a,
319a–320b, 4:244a, 6:123b
in Sri Lanka, 3:307a, 5:316b,
317b, 322a–322b,
325a–325b, 327b, 328b
Thailand and, 4:161b, 162a,
5:461a, 461b, 462a
See also British Indian empire
British Commonwealth, 3:37b,
38a, 38b–39a
Colombo Plan and, 2:143a
members of, 4:87a, 88b
Sri Lanka in, 5:328b
British-Dutch Wars, **1:326a–326b**
British East India Company (EIC),
1:25a, 76a, 106b, 198b, 279a,
317a–319a, 2:272b–273a, 404b,
476a, 491b, 493a, 494a–494b,
571a, 3:11b, 462b, 472b,
508a–508b, 536a–536b, 4:459b,
470a, 471a, 497a, 5:100a, 409b
Bengal and, 1:318a–319, 320b,
321a
Calcutta and, 1:394a
cricket players and, 5:305a
Dutch East India Company
and, 1:91a–91b
employees of, 5:136b
founding of, 1:317a
Governor-Generals of, 1:430a
India-Sri Lanka relations and,
3:35b
Indian Mutiny and, 4:244b
Jahangir contact with, 3:196b
Mumbai and, 4:210a–210b
Orientalism and, 4:394b
Second Anglo-Maratha War
and, 2:543a
South Asian cuisine and,
2:210b
in Sri Lanka, 5:325a
Straits Settlements and,
5:219a–219b, 339b

Brunei *(continued)*
  sultans of, **1:**320a, 325b, 330a,
    6:128a
    net worth of, **1:**330b
  See also Borneo; Islam: in
    Brunei; Universiti Brunei
    Darussalam
Brunei-Malaysia Commission,
  1:204a
BSPP. *See* Burma Socialist Pro-
  gramme Party.
bubble economy (Japan), **3:**209b,
  212b–213a
  emigration and, **3:**238b
  foreign investment and, **3:**263a
  Japanese firms abroad and,
    3:261a
Buch, Harry Crowe, **5:**305b
Buck, Pearl, **2:**24b
Buddha. *See* Amitabha (Amida)
  Buddha; Maitreya; Siddhartha
  Gautama.
Buddha era, **1:**398a
Buddha Vairocana, **3:**526a
Buddhacarita, **3:**510b
Buddhadasa, Bhikku,
  1:333b–334a
Buddhism, **1:**2a, 10a, 19b, *293,*
  2:495a
  in Afghanistan, **2:**495b, **3:**173a
  ancestor worship and, **1:**100a
  Ari sect of, **1:**97b
  art and architecture of, **1:**133b,
    2:174b, 512a, **3:**526a–526b
    Ghandaran style in, **5:**428b
  Asoka and, **4:**89a
  atheism and, **1:**176b
  Ayurvedic medicine and,
    4:119a
  in Bactria, **1:**213a
  in Bangladesh, **1:**239a
    music and, **4:**217a
  in Bengal, **1:**239b
  in Bhutan, **1:**285b, 353a
  in Brazil, **3:**238b
  British description of, **1:**354
  in Cambodia, **3:**449b
  Cao Dai and, **1:**430b, 431a
  celibacy in, **5:**182b
  centers of, **1:**216b, 227a, 230a,
    4:485a, **5:**428b
  in Central Asia, **1:**128b,
    334a–335b, 453a, 454b
    historical record of, **1:**334b
    importance for China,
      1:334b–335a
    interaction with other reli-
      gions, **1:**335a
  Central Asian art and, **2:**381b

  in China, **1:**131b, 334b,
    337a–341b, *340,* **2:**481b,
    484b–485a, 564a, 564b,
    5:64b, 68b, **6:**199b
    arrival of, **1:**337a–337b
    Buddhist schools and,
      1:337a, 339b–340a
    Chinese culture and, **1:**337a,
      340b
    in contemporary China,
      1:340b–341a
    cuisine and, **2:**188b
    cult of Maitreya and,
      2:220b–221b
    growth and expansion,
      1:337b–339a
    music and, **4:**220b
    period of maturity, **1:**339a
    poetry of, **4:**529a
    statues in, **5:**172a
    suppression of, **1:**339a,
      5:415a–415b
    syncretism, **1:**339a–339b
    timeline, **1:**338
    See also Buddhism, Chan
  China-India relations and, **2:**1b
  China-Japan relations and, **2:**6a,
    6b–7a, 7b, 13b
  China-Korea relations and,
    2:14a, 14b
  Chinese influence in East Asia
    and, **2:**37a–38b
  Christianity and, **1:**100a, 169a,
    2:76–77, **5:**14b
  clothing and, **2:**108a
  Confucianism and, **2:**159a, 160b
  conversion literature and,
    3:480a
  conversion to, **1:**91a, **2:**272a
  Diamond Sutra of, **5:**8a
  Drukpa sect of, **1:**289a, 289b,
    290a, 292a–292b, 294b
  at Dunhuang, **4:**157b, 158a
  Esoteric, **1:**346a
  Falun Gong and, **2:**362b
  feminine power in, **5:**142b
  Festival of the Dead, **1:**100a,
    306a–306b
  Fifth Buddhist Council and,
    4:30a
  Gesar Kahn in, **2:**432a–432b
  Hinayana, **1:**302b, 334b, 335a,
    354b, 355b, 367a, **6:**88a
    in Srivijaya, **5:**332b
  Hinduism and, **1:**169a, 357a,
    357b, 360
  Hokke (Lotus) sect,
    4:330a–330b
  homosexuality and, **2:**544b, 545a

  Huayan school of, **1:**339a, 339b,
    340a, 346a
  Hungry Ghost Festival and,
    2:567b
  icons of, **1:**201b
  in India, **1:**161b, 173a, **2:**490b,
    512a–512b, **3:**13a, 438b,
    4:85a, 85b, **5:**143b, 410b
    Gupta era, **2:**468a
    Islam and, **3:**173b
    music and, **4:**226b
    sculpture and, **5:**139b
    tribal peoples, **4:**156b
  in Indonesia, **3:**51b, 61b
    music and, **4:**227b
  in Inner Mongolia, **1:**381a
  in Japan, **1:**336a, 336b,
    341b–345a, **2:**498a–498b,
    3:206b, **4:**276a–276b, 414b,
    5:71a
    basic characteristics,
      1:342a–342b
    Buddhist-Shinto synthesis,
      1:342a, **5:**69a, 71b
    calligraphy and, **1:**404b
    ceramics and, **1:**479a, 481a
    Christianity and, **2:**67b
    Confucianism and, **2:**8a,
      161a
    cuisine and, **2:**197b, 198b
    government and, **4:**284b
    historical development,
      1:342b–344b
    kokugaku and, **4:**199a
    literature of, **3:**494a
    Madhyamika (The Middle
      Way), **4:**276b
    monuments, **4:**284a
    Mount Emei, **2:**328a–329a
    music and, **4:**229a, 230a
    Nara period, **4:**284b–285a
    Obaku school, **1:**344a
    poetry of, **4:**534a–534b
    Pure Land, **3:**304b–305a
    Rinzai school, **1:**344a
    Ryobu Shinto, **1:**343a–343b
    Shingon school,
      1:342b–343a, **4:**414b
    Shinto and, **5:**183a–183b
    Six Nara schools, **1:**342b
    Soto school, **1:**344a
    Tendai school, **3:**409a
    Tokugawa and later times,
      1:344b
  in Java
    candi and, **1:**429b, 430a
    Islam and, **5:**129a
  Kargyu sect of, **1:**289b, 292a,
    292b

in Khmer empire, **3**:357a
in Korea, **1**:336b, 342a,
    345a–351a, **2**:15a, 61a,
    3:400b, 405a, **6**:26b, 103a
    Chinese influence and, **2**:38
    Chogye order in, **1**:346b
    Christianity and, **2**:70b
    Confucianism and, **2**:163a,
        163b, **4**:535b, 536a, **5**:479b
    cuisine and, **2**:201b–202a
    eclectic nonsectarianism,
        1:346a–346b
    hangul and, **5**:144b
    history, **1**:345a–346a
    literature and, **2**:15a,
        3:497a–497b, 500a–500b
    sports and, **5**:312b
    twenty-first century,
        1:346b–347a
in Lao People's Democratic Re-
    public, **3**:455a, 457a, 457b
in Laos, **1**:490a, **2**:50b, **3**:444a,
    445b, 447b, 449b, 452b,
    501b–502b, **5**:14b
Lay, **1**:339b
literature of, **3**:488b
Madhyamika school of, **1**:355b
Mahanikaya, **2**:273a, 273b
in Malaysia, **4**:1b
masks and, **4**:82a
in Mauritius, **4**:87a
meditative, **1**:346a, 346b, 361b
Mon people and, **4**:159b
monasteries of, **1**:75b, 366a,
    2:424b, 484b, 485b, 512a,
    544b, **3**:438b, 466a, 527a,
    4:261a
in Mongolia, **1**:347a–351a,
    349a–350a, *350a*, **2**:419b,
    3:165a, 165b, 166a, 363a,
    4:173a, 189b, **5**:161b, 163b,
    6:23b
    monasteries of, **1**:70a
    Mongol empire,
        1:347b–348a
    post-Mongol empire,
        1:348a–349a
    pre-Mongol empire, **1**:347a
    Red Hat sect, **1**:348b
    timeline, **1**:348
    in twentieth century,
        1:350a–351a
    Yellow sect, **1**:348b, 349a
    See also Buddhism, Tibetan
in Myanmar, **1**:78b, *383b*, 386b,
    502a, **3**:503a–503b, **4**:*30*,
    30a, 30b, 253b, 257a,
    260b–261a, 262b–263a, 266a,
    268b, 269b, **5**:48a

Christianity and, **2**:72b,
    5:14b
    Islam and, **3**:166b, 167a
    pilgrimage sites of, **5**:117b
Neo-Confucianism and, **4**:302b,
    303a, 303b
in Nepal, **1**:353a
Nichiren sect of, **1**:344a,
    3:305a, 383b, **4**:330a–330b**,
    5:72a, 72b, **6**:184b
nirvana and, **2**:523b
official recognition of, **1**:177b
in Pakistan, **3**:173a
peace movement and, **2**:541b
poetry and, **3**:477a–477b, 484b
rebellion and, **2**:221a
Ritsu sect of, **2**:6b
sacred sites of, **2**:514a
Sarnath and, **5**:133b
sculpture and, **5**:140a, 140b,
    141b–142a, 142b, 143a, 143b
sects of, **2**:485b, 498a, 523a,
    540a–540b, 544b, 547b
shamanism and, **5**:158b
Shingon, **2**:498a
Shingon esoteric, **3**:408b, **409a**
Shingon (Zhenyan), **2**:7a
shrines of, **3**:189b–190a
in Singapore, **5**:214a
South Africa and, **1**:31b
in South Asia, **1**:353a–358a,
    3:51a, **4**:419b
    Mahayana, **1**:354b–357a
    origins, **1**:353a–354b
    recent developments,
        1:357b–358a
    Tantric, **1**:357a
in South Korea
    canons of, **5**:288b
in Southeast Asia, **2**:41a, **3**:449b
    marriage and family and,
        4:65b
spirit cults and, **5**:300b
sports and, **5**:304b
spread of, **1**:128b, 148b, 150a,
    353b, 357b
in Sri Lanka, **1**:353a, 354a, *355*,
    357b, 358a, 359b, 362a,
    2:142b, **3**:35a, **4**:454b, 523b,
    5:316b, 323b, 326b
    civil war and, **5**:327a, 329a
    education and, **5**:322a, 322b,
        323a
    introduction of, **1**:172a
in Srivijaya, **5**:332a–332b
storytelling and, **5**:337a, 337b
stupas (reliquary mounds) of,
    1:172a, *355*
T'aego order of, **1**:346b

of Tai people, **4**:203b, 204b
in Taiwan, **1**:341a
Tantric, **1**:289b, 303a, 339a,
    339b, 343a, 357a, **3**:409a,
    507b, **5**:143b, 486b, 487b
    Black Sect, **2**:374a–374b
temples and
    libraries of, **3**:501b–502b,
        511b, 512a–512b
    Mount Emei, **2**:328a–329a
    Todaiji, **4**:284b
in Thailand, **1**:499a, **2**:526b,
    527a, **3**:*449b*, **4**:161b, 162a,
    487a, 521b, **5**:14b, 133a,
    449, 460a
    clothing and, **2**:132a
    Islam and, **3**:159a–159b
    Lankavamsa, **5**:454a
    literature and, **3**:513a–513b
Theosophy and, **1**:167b
in Tibet. *See* Buddhism, Ti-
    betan.
tolerance of, **1**:167a
transcendentalism and, **1**:167b
transmigration of souls and,
    1:97b
Turkic empire and, **1**:452a
Uighur people and, **6**:21b
Vajrayana, **1**:357a, 357b
vegetarianism and,
    2:201b–202a, 212a, **3**:198b
in Vietnam, **1**:160a, **367a–369a**,
    5:14b, **6**:62b, 65a, 65b, 89b
    beliefs and practices, **1**:368b
    Catholicism and, **1**:446a,
        448a
    history, **1**:367a–368b
    Hoa Hao sect, **1**:368a
    Ngo Dinh Diem and, **4**:326a
    poetry of, **4**:540a
    Thao Duong school, **1**:367b
    Thien (Chan; Zen), **1**:367b,
        368b
    Truc Lam school, **1**:367b
the West and, **1**:169b
Western scholarship and,
    6:179b
Won, **1**:346b
Yogacara school of, **1**:355b,
    5:332b
Zen. *See* Buddhism, Chan.
See also Amitabha (Amida) Bud-
    dha; Maitreya; Siddhartha
    Gautama
Buddhism, Chan (Zen), **1**:168b,
    264b, 307a, 333b, **335b–337a**,
    339a, 339b, **3**:389a, 518b,
    5:415a, 419a
    archery and, **5**:310a

People's Republic of, **1**:471a, **6**:51a

Seljuk Turks and, **1**:454a

Bukharan People's Soviet Republic (BNSR), **1**:465a

Bukharian Jews, **1**:373b–374a

Bulbul Lachman Raina, **4**:531a

Bulgarian Orthodox Church. *See* Eastern Orthodox Church.

Bulgarians, **1**:374a–375a
    ancient history, **1**:374a–374b, 390b
    Ottoman rule, **1**:374b–375a, **4**:400a
    World War II and after, **1**:375a

Bulleh Shah, **4**:461b

bullet train (*shinkansen*; Japan), **2**:98a, **5**:147a, 520a

Bulletin of Concerned Asian Scholars, **6**:82a

bullfights
    in Korea, **2**:85b

bullying (*ijime*)
    in Japan, **3**:5a

Bulosan, Carlos, **1**:375a–375b, **3**:506a, **4**:538b

Bulwer-Lytton, Victor, **4**:29b

Bumiputra (indigenous Malays), **1**:375b–376a, **4**:11b

Bun Bang Fai, **1**:376b

Bun Rany, **2**:565b

Bunga Semerah Darah (A Blood-Red Flower; W. S. Rendra), **5**:77a

Bungakuza Theater (Japan), **3**:496b

bunjinga (literati painting; Japan), **1**:376b–377b
    See also calligraphy: in Japan; painting: in Japan; poetry: in Japan

Bunker, Ellsworth, **6**:79a, 80a

Bunraku (Japanese puppet theater), **1**:377b–378b, *378a,* **2**:288a, 572b, **3**:495a, 496b, **4**:230a
    characteristics, **1**:378a–378b
    history, **1**:377b–378b
    kabuki troupes and, **1**:378a
    music of, **5**:163b
    Three Great Masterpieces of, **1**:377b
    See also drama: in Japan

Buon Pimai (festival; Laos), **3**:445b

Buongnang Vorachit, **3**:445a

Buqar-zhyrau (Kazakh singer), **2**:393a

Buraku Liberation League (BLL; Buraku Kaiho Domei), **1**:378b–379b, 380a, **3**:223b

burakumin (outcastes; Japan), **1**:378b–379a, **379b–380b**, **3**:223b, 227b
    background of, **1**:379b–380a
    improvements for, **1**:380a–380b
    novel about, **5**:181b

Burdick, Eugene, **6**:122b

Bure, Lev, **2**:380a

Bureau of Religious Affairs (People's Republic of China), **1**:380b–381a

Burges, William, **5**:427b

Burgess, Anthony, **6**:122b

Burgos, José, **1**:445b, **4**:505b

Burinsk, Treaty of (1727), **2**:15b

Burlingame Treaty (1868), **2**:24a

Burma. *See* Myanmar.

Burma, Communist Party of (BCP), **1**:111b, 382a, **2**:155a–155b, 345a, **3**:297b, **4**:252b, 269a, 269b, 463a, **5**:165b, **6**:33b
    Shan and, **5**:165a

Burma Independence Army (BIA), **1**:381a–381b, **2**:344b, **4**:257b, 264a

Burma Road, **1**:*381b,* 382a, **6**:162b

Burma Socialist Programme Party (BSPP), **2**:72b, 345b, **3**:504b, **4**:31b, 160a, 248a, 264b, 266a–266b, 269a–269b, 271a–272a, **5**:117b
    SLORC and, **5**:333b

Burma-Thailand Railway, **1**:382b–383a, **5**:99b

Burma Workers and Peasants Party, **1**:111b, **4**:269a

Burmah Oil Company, **3**:541a

Burman people, **1**:121a, **383a–384b**, 501b, 502a, 502b, **3**:89a, **4**:31a, 160a, 247, 260b, 262a, **5**:117b, 164a
    colonial history of, **1**:383b–384a, 386b, **4**:268b
    CPB and, **2**:155a
    marriage and family of, **4**:65a, 65b–66b
    Mon and, **4**:159a, 159b
    Montagu-Chelmsford Reforms and, **1**:384a
    royal dynasties of, **1**:383a

Burmese arts, **1**:386a–389a**
    arts and crafts, **1**:386b–387a, *387*
    performing arts, **1**:387a–388a
        classical drama, **1**:387a–387b
        music and song, **1**:387b–388a
        preservation and sponsorship, **1**:388b
        puppet theater, **1**:387a

See also literature: of Myanmar; Mon; Pagan; pagodas: Burmese

Burmese language, **1**:383a, **384b–386a**, **4**:246b, 247, **5**:48a
    grammar, **1**:385b–386a
    nationalism and, **4**:247, 254b
    origins of, **2**:46b
    script, **1**:385a–385b

"Burmese Way to Socialism," **4**:248a, 249b, 264b, 266a, 269b

Burmic languages, **5**:234b

Burnouf, Eugène, **4**:393b

Burns, Peter, **1**:16a

burqa (Muslim women's covering), **2**:114a, **4**:71b, 385a, **5**:408a

Bursa (Turkey), **1**:79b, 138b, 139a, **389a**, **2**:321a

Burton, Sir Richard, **4**:394a

Buryat people
    shamanism and, **5**:158b

Buryatia, **4**:182b, 187b
    Mongolia and, **4**:181b
    Republic of, **4**:190a
    Soviet Autonomous Republic of, **4**:183b

See also Mongols: Buryat

Burzuya, **4**:127a

Bus Stop (Gao Xinjiang), **2**:425b

Bush, George H. W.
    China-U.S. relations and, **2**:27a–27b
    Iraq and, **4**:482a–482b
    Pakistan and, **4**:429b
    Turkey and, **5**:559a

Bush, George W., **1**:170a, 170b, **3**:257b–258a, **6**:86a
    China-U.S. relations and, **2**:27b
    Iran and, **3**:98b, 121b
    Philippines and, **4**:517b
    war on terrorism and, **5**:407b

Bushru'i, Mulla Husayn, **1**:210b

Bustan (Orchard; Sa'di), **3**:520b

Bustani, al-, **1**:117b

bustard, Hubara, **1**:389a–389b

Butoh (dance), **2**:241a–241b, 289a

Buxar, battle of, **1**:198b

Buyid dynasty (Iraq), **1**:214b, 454a, **3**:133a–133b, **4**:242b

buzkashi (Afghan game), **1**:*389,* **389b–390a**, **5**:306b

Byzantines, **1**:36a, 90a, 97a, 137a, 139a, 374b, 390a, **390a–392b**, **2**:250b, 280a, **4**:476b, 547a, **5**:556a, **6**:57b, 220b
    army of, **1**:391a
    Asia Minor and, **5**:123a, 131b, 424a
    Caucasia and, **1**:449a, 449b, 450a

Candragupta II (king; Gupta empire), **1**:296a, **5**:142b

Candragupta Vikramaditya, **1**:296a

Canglang shihua (Canglang Remarks on Poetry; Yan Yu), **5**:37a

Cannes Film Festival, **2**:463a

Canning, Charles John, **1**:430a–430b

Cansever, Edip, **3**:516b

Canton system (China), **2**:65b, **4**:153a

Cantonese. *See* Yue language; Yue people.

Cao Cao, **2**:483a

Cao Dai (Vietnamese religion), **1**:430b–432a, *431b*, **6**:90a

Cao Pi (Wendi; Wei state), **2**:483a

Cao Xueqin, **1**:432a, **2**:551a, **3**:486b

Cao Yin, **5**:36b–37a

Cao Yu, **2**:287a, **6**:178b

Cape of Good Hope, **1**:31a, 81a, **3**:42b

Capitulations (extraterritoriality regulations; West Asia), **3**:287b

Cappadocia (Turkey), **1**:432a–432b

Caraballo Mountains (Philippines), **1**:394a, **432b–433a**, **2**:175a

Carajoas Shoals (Mauritius), **4**:86a

caravans, **1**:433a–434a

in Central Asia, **1**:460a, **3**:466a

caravansaries, **1**:433b

Cilician Gates and, **2**:86b

in Turkey, **4**:144b

Carchemish (Kargamis; Turkey), **2**:532a

Cardamon Mountains (Cambodia), **1**:407a, 408, **434a–434b**, **5**:512b

See also Elephant Range

Cardus, Neville, **5**:305b

Carian kingdom, **1**:126a

Carmine, Giovanni da Pian del, **2**:63b

Carnatic, kingdom of (India), **2**:404b

Carpenter Agreement (1915), **4**:507a

carpets

in Central Asia, **1**:434a–436a

Kerman, **3**:349b

Nepali, **3**:329b

Persian, **2**:479a, **3**:349b, **5**:365b

Turkmen, **1**:435a

Uzbek, **1**:434b, 435a–435b, **3**:326b

felt and, **2**:371a–372b

in Iran, **3**:98b, 100b

Karakul sheep yarn and, **5**:174b

in Mongolia, **4**:168a

Carter, Jimmy

China-U.S. relations and, **2**:27a, **5**:391b–392a

hostage crisis and, **3**:119a–119b

Casabar, Constante, **3**:507a

cashmere industry, **1**:436a–437a, **3**:88a

in China, **1**:436a–436b, 437a

in Mongolia, **4**:168a

Caspian Sea, **1**:20b, 204a, 227b, 312b, **437a–437b**, **2**:228b, **4**:35b, **6**:5a, 40b

climate change and, **4**:36a

Iran-Russia relations and, **3**:116a, 118a

tourism and, **3**:101a–101b

caste, **1**:353a, 358a, **438a–443a**, **2**:443b, **6**:35b

in ancient China, **6**:193a

Ayurvedic medicine and, **4**:117a

in British India, **6**:118b, 119b

Christianity and, **2**:73b

clothing and, **2**:114a, 114b, 115a

cuisine and, **2**:210a

Dalit, **1**:239a, **5**:127a, **6**:36b, 37b

in India

constitution and, **2**:165b, 166a

contemporary, **1**:441b–443a, **3**:11a, **6**:120a, 121b

medieval, **3**:23a, 23b

traditional, **1**:438a–440a, **2**:517b, 520a, 522a, 524b, **6**:145b

Julaha, **6**:119a

Kshatriya (ruler-warrior), **2**:522a, 524b, **4**:407a, **5**:47a–47b

Sanskritization and, **5**:126b–127a

marriage and family and, **4**:69a, 74a

Nadar, **6**:36

in Nepal, **5**:54b

opposition to, **1**:440a, **5**:156b, 157a, **6**:118a

Pahari and, **4**:407a

Sanskritization and, **5**:125b–128a

scheduled, **6**:36a–36b, 37a, 94b, 118a

Sikhism and, **5**:203a, 203b

in South Asia

marriage and family and, **4**:74b

in Sri Lanka, **3**:35b, **5**:322a, 322b, 325a

Sudra (server), **2**:522a, 525a

theories of, **1**:440a–441a

Vaisya (merchant and farmer), **2**:522a, 525a

varnas and, **3**:489a

vegetarianism and, **2**:212a, **5**:126b, 127a

violence and, **1**:441b, 442

See also untouchability

Castes and Tribes of Southern India (Thurston), **1**:439

Castiglione, Giuseppe, **4**:413b

CAT. *See* torture: Convention against.

Cat Tuong, **1**:113b

Catalhuyuk (Turkey), **1**:124b, **5**:556a

cathaya tree, **1**:443a–443b

Catherine II (empress; Russia), **2**:432a, **4**:389a

Catherine of Braganza, **4**:210a

Catholicism, Roman, **1**:168a, **2**:436a–436b

in Albania, **1**:80b

in Central Asia, **2**:64a, 64b

in China, **2**:65a, 65b, **5**:85b–86a

Ming dynasty, **4**:154a

in East Timor, **2**:315b

Eastern Orthodox Church and, **2**:316b, 318a

in India, **2**:73b, *74a*, **3**:536b

in Japan, **2**:67a–68a, 68b

in Korea, **2**:61b, 70a, 71a–71b, **5**:510b, 511a, **6**:194b

in Macao, **3**:531a

in Mauritius, **4**:87a

in Melaka, **4**:5a

mendicant orders of, **1**:443b–444a

in Myanmar, **2**:72a, 72b, 77b

official recognition of, **1**:177b

in Philippines, **1**:443b–446a, *445*, **2**:49a, 77a, **3**:505a–505b, 530b, **4**:148b, 488a, 488b, 493a, 538a, **5**:209b

introduction of, **1**:443b–444b

nature of, **1**:444b–445b

recent, **1**:445b–446a

See also *Iglesia ni Christo*: Philippine Independent Church

ritual kinship and, **2**:439a

in South Asia, **2**:74b

in Southeast Asia, **2**:75a, 75b,
78a, 78b
spread of, **4**:550a
in Sri Lanka, **5**:322a
Vatican II and, **1**:168b, 445b,
2:78a, 318a
in Vietnam, **1**:160a, **446a–448a**,
4:540b, **6**:89b
colonial government and,
1:446b–447b
persecution and, **1**:446b
Vietnamese government and,
1:447b–448a
writing system and, **2**:80b
cattle
brahminy (zebu), **6**:208b–209a
in Mongolia, **4**:168a, 168b
sacred, **5**:127a, **6**:209a
Cau Moi Hamlet (Linh Nhat),
3:476a
Caucasia, **1:448a–450b**
Bagratids in, **1**:449a–449b
Christianity in, **1**:449a
German settlers in, **2**:432a
languages in, **1**:448a–448b, 450a
map of, **1**:*449b*
mountains in, **4**:199b, 200b
Persia and, **1**:448b, 449a, 449b
Russia and, **1**:449b–450a
Russians in, **1**:460a, 461b
Sunni Muslims in, **4**:243a,
243b–244a
Caucasian languages, **2**:97a
Caucasus Mountains, **1**:448a
Cauvery River. *See* Kaveri River.
Cave of 10,0000 Buddhas (Long-
men Grottoes; China), **3**:526b
Cave of the Immortals (Mount Lu;
China), **3**:527a
caviar, **1**:437b, **3**:100b, 101a
Cavite Mutiny (Philippines; 1872),
1:445b
Cayetano, Benjamin J., **4**:517a
Cbap (Code of Conduct; didactic
Khmer poetry), **3**:477a
CCP. *See* Chinese Communist
Party.
Cebu (Philippines), **1:450b–451a**,
6:95a
Cebuano language, **1**:192a
media and, **4**:104b
CEDAW. *See* Convention on the
Elimination of All Forms of
Discrimination against Women.
Cefu yuangui (Outstanding Models
from the Storehouse of Litera-
ture), **5**:255b
Celebes Sea (Sulawesi Sea),
1:451a–451b

Cemal, Ahmed, **5**:557b
Cennai. *See* Madras.
censorship, **4**:98b
in Central Asia, **4**:100a
in China, **2**:87a–87b,
4:100b–101b, **5**:175b
in India, **2**:88b
in Indonesia, **4**:158a, **5**:145a
in Iran, **4**:115b
in Iraq, **4**:115a–115b
in Japan, **2**:95a, 95b,
4:106a–106b
Meiji period, **4**:132b
in Malaysia, **4**:18b
in Singapore, **5**:340b
in South Korea, **4**:114a, **5**:282b
in Southeast Asia, **4**:101b–105a
in Sri Lanka, **5**:328a
in Turkey, **4**:115b
in West Asia, **2**:93a, 94b
See also self-censorship
Central Asia, **1:451b–468a**
agriculture in, **1**:41b–45a,
157a–157b, 453a–453b,
3:380a, **5**:363a–363b, **6**:107b
irrigation and, **1**:157a–157b,
2:186a, **4**:36a, 215a,
5:513a, **6**:*107b*, 109a
Anglo-Russian rivalry in,
2:446a–446b, **5**:395b–396a
architectural decoration in,
1:127a–127b
architecture in, **1:128a–130a**
arts in, **1**:465b, **2**:378b–382b
Buddhism in, **1:334a–335b**, 354a
caravans in, **1**:433a–433b, 460a,
3:466a
China-India relations and, **2**:1b
China-Russia/Soviet Union relations and, **2**:19b
Chinese music and, **4**:220b
Chinese settlers in, **2**:20b
Christianity in, **2:63a–65a**
Communism in, **1**:179a, 467a,
2:145a–148b
cuisine of, **2**:184b, **186a–187b**
dance in, **2:237a–240b**
declining health in, **6**:108a–108b
early medieval, **2**:504b
Ghaznavids and Karakhanids
in, **1**:453b–454a
Kara Kitai in, **1**:454b–455b
Muslim conquest of,
1:452b–453b
Seljuks in, **1**:454a–454b
Turkic empire in,
1:451b–452b
economy of
marriage and, **4**:49b

Muslim saints and, **4**:240b
relations with China and,
1:469b
Russian conquest and,
1:462a, 462b, 463a–463b
Soviet control of,
1:462a–462b, 463a–463b,
467a, 467b, 470b, 472a,
472b–473a, **2**:148a
trade and, **1**:469b, 477a
UN and, **1**:466
educational system in
Communism and, **2**:146a
Jadids and, **1**:470b, **3**:154b
leaders of, **5**:149b
Muslim, **1**:465b, 469a,
3:152b, 154b, 155b
Russia and, **1**:462b, 463b,
465a, 474a
in Soviet period, **1**:465b,
2:148a, **3**:154b, 155b
energy in, **1**:469b, 473a,
2:331b–334a
ethnic groups in, **2**:145b, 146a,
147a
ethnic unrest in, **1**:468b,
469a–469b
famine in, **1**:463b–464b, 470b
festivals in
music and, **4**:219a
folklore in, **2:392a–395b**, 444b
foreign influence in, **4**:26b
gas industry in
Karshi (Uzbekistan) and,
3:326b
Genghis Khan and, **2**:431a
Germans in, **2:432a**
Great Game in, **1**:19b, 25a,
2:446a–447a, **4**:456a, 458a
horses of, **2:552b–554a**
human rights in, **1:455b–459a**,
472b
Indian music and, **4**:226a
Islam in, **3:152a–156b**
shrines of, **3**:152b, 154b,
155a–155b, 156a
kalym (bride-price) custom in,
3:303a–303b, 333a
languages of, **1**:465b,
473b–476b, 477b, **3**:152b,
154a, 154b, 156a
Communism and, **2**:147a,
147b
Indo-Iranian, **1**:476a–476b
Turkic, **1**:474b–476a
late medieval and early modern,
1:459a–463a
in Kazakh steppe,
1:459b–460a

Central Asia (continued)
late medieval and early modern
(continued)
Russian conquest and,
1:461b–462b
in Transoxiana, 1:460a–461b
legends of, 4:547a
literature of, 3:478b–482b
conversion literature,
3:480a–480b
dastans and, 3:479a–480a
"Mirrors for Princes" and,
3:479a
under Russian authority,
3:480b–482a
media in, 4:99a–100b
modern, 1:463a–468a
colonial, 1:463a–464b
cooperative agreements in,
1:472b–473a
post-Soviet, 1:466,
467b–468a, 3:482a
Russian dominance in,
1:473a–473b,
3:480b–481a
Soviet, 1:465a–465b,
467a–467b, 3:481a–482a
timeline, 1:464
Mongols in, 4:163a, 163b
moutains of, 2:511b–514a,
516b–517a
music of, 2:392a–393b, 394b,
3:382a, 4:218b–220a
Twelve Muqam, 6:17a–18a
Muslim Religious Board of,
4:238b–239a
national identity in,
1:465a–465b, 467b, 472a
natural resources of, 1:467b,
468b, 469b, 470a, 473a, 474a
non-Russians in, 1:265b
oil and mineral industries in,
4:49a, 377b–379b
obstacles facing,
4:378b–379b
paleoanthropology in,
4:441b–445b
postmodernism in, 2:381b
puppetry in, 5:155b
radioactive waste and contamination in, 5:41a
railroads in, 1:470b
refugees in, 1:463b
regionalism in, 1:476b–478a
ethnicity and, 1:477a–477b
geography and history and,
1:476a–477a
language and, 1:477b
religion and, 1:477b

rivers in, 5:362b–363a, 6:209b
Russian settlers in, 1:20b, 463a,
463b–464a, 470b, 471a,
473a, 2:17a, 63b, 380a
Sunni Muslims in, 4:243a,
243b–244a
trade routes of, 1:230a
traditional medicine in,
4:119b–120b
tribes and tribal federations in,
5:530b–532a
westernization in, 6:113b–115b
women in, 6:131b–132b
Communism and,
2:146a–146b
USSR and, 2:148a
woodworking in, 6:156a–156b
See also particular countries
Central Asia-China relations,
1:93a, 452b–453a, 468a–470a
boundaries and, 1:468a–468b
Central Asian refugees in,
1:463b
Chinese cuisine and, 2:188b
Dunhuang and, 4:157b
economic interests and, 1:469b
ethnic unrest and, 1:469a–469b
Genghis Khan and, 2:431a
Kara Kitai and, 1:454b
Muslims and, 4:243b
Russia and, 1:468a–468b, 469a,
469b, 473b
Samarqand and, 5:122b
SCO and, 5:169b–170a
strategic concerns and,
1:468b–469a
trade and, 2:425a
traditional medicine and, 4:120a
Central Asia-India relations
traditional medicine and, 4:120a
Central Asia-Russia/Soviet relations, 1:85a, 159b, 373a, 373b,
374a, 459b–460a, 463a–467b,
470a–473b, 2:380a,
3:480b–482a, 5:39a
Afghanistan and, 1:473b
architecture and, 1:129b
Bolshevik Revolution and,
1:470b–471a, 3:481a
Britain and, 2:446a–446b,
5:395b–396a
China and, 1:468a–468b, 469a,
469b, 473b
China-Russia/Soviet Union relations and, 2:17a
Christianity and, 2:63b–64a,
64b
clothing and, 2:130b, 136b,
137b

in Cold War, 1:471b–472a
collapse of Soviet Union and,
1:472a–472b
Communism and, 2:145a–148b
cuisine and, 2:186a, 187b
dissidents and, 4:26b
early modern, 1:459b–461b
economic development and,
1:462a–462b, 463a–463b,
467a, 467b, 470b, 472a,
472b–473a
economy and, 1:462a–462b,
462b, 463a–463b, 467a,
467b, 470b, 472a,
472b–473a, 2:148a
educational system and
Russia and, 1:462b, 463b,
465a, 474a
in Soviet period, 1:465b,
2:148a, 3:154b, 155b
energy and, 2:333a
ethnic unrest and, 1:469a
Great Game and, 1:19b, 25a,
2:225b, 446a–447a
Iran and, 1:473b
Khiva khanate and, 1:461b,
6:51a
literature and, 3:480b–482a
media and, 4:99a, 99b
modern, 1:465a–465b,
467a–467b, 473a–473b,
3:480b–481a, 481a–482a
music and, 4:219a
Muslims and, 4:243b
nineteenth-century,
1:461b–462b, 470a–470b
post-Cold War, 1:472b–473b
Russian conquest and,
1:461b–462b
under Soviet regime, 1:266a,
471a–472a, 5:531b
trade and, 1:460b–461a, 470a
Central Asian Union, 3:433a
Central Asiatic Expedition (1922;
Andrews), 2:438b
Central Bank of China, 3:386a
Central Highlands of Vietnam,
1:478a–478b
peoples of, 2:139a–139b
Central Intelligence Agency (CIA;
U.S.), 1:305a, 2:304a, 3:454b
Iran and, 4:409a, 409b
Phoenix program of, 6:77a, 80a
in South Korea, 1:115a
Tibet and, 5:490a
Central Office for South Vietnam
(COSVN), 3:463a
Central Provident Fund (Singa-
pore), 5:214a, 215b

Central Treaty Organization, 3:32a

Centrality and Commonality. See *Zhong yong*.

ceramics
  in Central Asia, 2:381b
  in China
    Ming dynasty, 4:152b–153a
  in Iran, 5:188a
  in Japan, **1:478b–482a**,
    3:279b–280a, 4:143b, 5:117a
    Black Satsuma, 3:301
    mass production of, 1:480a, 480b, 481a
    modern, 1:481a–482a
    origins of, 1:479a
    porcelains, 1:479a–480a
    variety of, 1:481a–481b
    Western influence on, 1:480a–481a
  Japanese
    Black Satsuma and, 3:301
  in Korea, **1:482a–483a**, 5:273a
    Chinese influence and, 2:14b
  in Thailand, 5:49a
  in Turkey, 3:191b–192a
CERD. *See* Convention on the Elimination of All Forms of Racial Discrimination.
Cerularious, Michael, 2:317b
Ceyhan River (Turkey), 1:112a
Ceyhan (Turkey), 1:312b, 4:381a, 5:565a
Ceylon. *See* Sri Lanka (Ceylon).
Ceylon Indian Congress (CIC), 5:328b
Ceylon National Congress (CNC), 1:232b, 5:325b, 328b
chaadaree (chador; Afghanistan), 2:103b
Chaderji, Rifat, 1:156a
chaebol (Korean conglomerates), **1:483a–485a**, 2:509a–509b, 5:271b, 272b
  development of, 1:483b–484a
  IT sector and, 3:82b
  negative impact of, 1:484a, 5:336b
  reforms and, 1:484a–485a
  reorganization of, 5:272a, 272b
Chagang province (North Korea), **1:485a–485b**
Chagatai (khan; Mongol empire), **1:**485b, 4:163a, 163b, 6:22b, 50b, 198b
  descendants of, 4:206a, 546b
Chagatay language, 1:476a, **485b–487a**, 3:174a, 480b, 6:54a
  literature in, 1:486a–486b

Chagilli Tepe (Turkmenistan), 1:128a
Chagos Archipelago, **1:487a–487b**, 3:42a, 4:86a
Chaguan (Teahouse; Lao She), 3:443a
Ch'ah'ae Man-shik, 3:500a
Chaim See Tong, 5:223a
Chaitanya (Bengali poet and revivalist), 3:266b, 508a, 4:218a
Chaitanya Chandrodaya Kaumudi (performance text), 3:266b
Chaitanyamagal (narrative poems), 3:508a
Chajon Nori (battle game; Korea), **1:487b**
chajusong (self-determination), 3:281a
Chakama refugees, 1:255b
Chakri dynasty (Thailand), 1:284b, 285a, 2:83b, 329b, 5:460b
Chalcedon, Council of (451), 2:317a, 4:392b
  Caucasia and, 1:449a
Chalcolithic Age, 1:128a, 4:449b
Chalukyas kingdom (India), 2:460b, 5:143a
Cham people, 1:105a, 2:560b, 3:160a–160b, 6:88b
  in Cambodia, 1:409b, 3:160a–160b
  in Cardamon Mountains, 1:434b
  Khmer empire and, 1:419a, 2:537b
  textiles of, 2:106a, 106b
  in Thailand, 3:160a
Chamberlain, Basil Hall, 1:171a, 2:474b
Chamlong Srimuang, 4:486b, 487a, 5:466a
Champa, kingdom of, 3:356b, 357a
Champa, kingdom of (Vietnam), 1:148b, 367b, 409b, 426b, 2:41a, 537b, 541b, 560b, 3:*34a*, 160a, 356b, 357a, 4:387a, 6:71b
  calendar in, 1:397b
  Mongols and, 4:163b
Champasak, kingdom of, 1:490a
Chamundi Hill (India), 4:273b
Chan Lien, 2:467a
Chanakya (Mauryan empire), 4:88b
Chandana, 6:146b
Chandarnagar (India), 2:404b
Chandella dynasty (India), 5:143b
Chander, Krishan, 2:82b
Chandidas (Bengali poet), 3:490a, 508a

Chandigarh (India), 1:136a, **487b–488a**
Chandra River. *See* Chenab River.
Chandragupta (ruler; Mauryan empire), 1:171b, 4:88b, 549b
  salt tax and, 5:121a
Chandralekha (film; India), 2:88b
Chanel, Coco, 1:436a
Chang, John Myon (Chang Myon), 2:264b, 5:282a, 284a
Chang, P. C. (Zhang Pengqun), 1:519a
Chang Fee Ming, **1:488a–488b**
Chang Kil-san (Hwang Sog-yong), 3:500b
Chang River (Yangtze River; China), 1:107b, **488b–490a**, 2:313b, 334b, 446a, 496b, 559b, 5:31b, 198b, 374a, 528a, 6:168b, 191a, 211b, 217a
  cuisine and, 2:188a
  electricity production and, 5:199a
  fish culture and, 2:383b
  high-technology industry and, 2:507a
  map of, 1:*488a*
  Opium Wars and, 4:389a
  population resettlement and, 1:528a
  Taiping Rebellion and, 5:374a, 374b
  trade and, 6:200a
  See also Three Gorges Dam Project
Chang Shi Ji (The Trials; Hu Shi), 2:557a
Chang Sung-op, 4:418b
Chang'an (China), 1:131a, 131b, 2:38b, 482a, 5:207b, 412b, 414a, 414b, 415a, 6:174a
Changhon, Crown Prince (Sado; Korea), 3:391
Changsheng dian (Palace of Long Life; Hong Sheng), 3:487a
Changsu (king; Koguryo), 5:479b
Chantarat (king; Laos), 5:2b
Chao Anou (ruler; Laos), **1:490a–490b**
Chao Fa Ngiew, 2:361a
Chao Lam (people of the sea; Thailand), 4:520a
Chao Nor Far, 4:441b
Chao Phraya River and Delta (Thailand), 1:235b, **490b**, 5:450a, 452a
  timber industry and, 2:399b
Chao Shwe Thaike, 5:164a
Chao Tzang Yawnghwe, 5:165b

Chikugogawa River (Japan), **2**:410a
child labor
  in India, **3**:21b
children
  abuse of, **4**:177a
  with AIDS, **1**:*67b*
  Confucianism and, **2**:156b
  homeless
    in Mongolia, **4**:175b
  Indonesian music and, **4**:228a
  in Iranian cinema, **2**:94b
  in Japanese theater, **3**:294a
    banning boys from stage in
      and, **3**:294a
  in Korea
    music and, **5**:*277b*
  labor of
    in China, **1**:515b
  malnutrition and, **2**:396
  marriage and family and
    in Southeast Asia,
      4:64a–64b
  marriages of, **4**:69b, 70b–71a
  in South Korea
    rights of, **5**:281a
  in Southeast Asia
    health of, **4**:66a
    marriage and family and,
      4:66b, 68a
  UN Convention on the Rights
    of the Child and,
    3:223a–223b, **5**:291b
Children of Heaven (Bachchah 'ha-
  yi Aseman; film), **2**:94a
Children's Day
  in Japan, **1**:**500a–500b**, **5**:69b
  in Turkey, **1**:**500b–501a**
Chile
  wood exports from, **2**:400a
Ch'ilsok (festival; Korea),
  5:153a–153b
Chilung (Taiwan), **1**:**501a–501b**
Ch'in dynasty. *See* Qin dynasty.
Chin National Front movement,
  1:502a, 502b
Chin Peng, **3**:548a–548b
Chin people, **1**:120b, **501b–502a**,
  2:72a, 344b, **4**:268b, 269a, 464a,
  5:117b
Chin state (Myanmar),
  1:**502a–503a**
China
  abacus in, **1**:1a
  agriculture in, **1**:**45a–51a**,
    505b–506a, **2**:455b, 456b,
    459b–460a, 475a, 496b,
    499a, 559b–560a, 566a,
    3:471b, **5**:155a, 166b, 361b
    advances in, **5**:254a–254b

Great Leap Forward and,
    1:46b, 47a, **2**:150b, 260b,
    364a, 447a–449a
  kariz irrigation system,
    3:325a
  reforms of, **5**:247a–248b
  TVEs and, **1**:47b, 506a,
    511a, 522a, **2**:151a,
    5:106a
AIDS in, **1**:67b, 68a
anarchism in, **2**:149a, **4**:92a
ancestor worship in, **1**:98
archeology in, **2**:503b, 558b,
  5:424a
architectural decoration in,
  1:127b
architecture in, **1**:**130a–133a**,
  3:473a, **5**:361a
  courtyards, **2**:**182a–182b**
  vernacular, **1**:**152b–154b**
  Western-style, **5**:168b, 170b
authoritarian corporatism and,
  5:243a–243b
automobiles in, **1**:192b, 193b,
  195b–196a, **5**:527a–527b
autonomous regions of,
  4:293b–294a
  See also particular regions
Autonomy Law of, **4**:293b
bamboo in, **1**:228b–229a
banking in, **5**:254b
boundaries of, **1**:19b
Buddhism in, **1**:**337a–341b**
  Chinese Buddhist Associa-
    tion and, **1**:341a
  cult of Maitreya,
    2:220b–221b
Bureau of Religious Affairs in,
  1:177b, **380b–381a**
bureaucracy of, **1**:510b
  Chinese economic system
    and, **1**:509a
  Cultural Revolution and,
    2:221b
  influence of, **2**:38b–39a
  Ming, **4**:151b
cadre system in, **1**:**393a–393b**
calendar in, **1**:**395a–395b**,
  396b, 398a
camels in, **1**:428b
caravan routes from, **1**:434a
cashmere industry in,
  1:436a–436b, 437a
cathaya tree in, **1**:443a
Chinese in Japan and, **2**:34a
Christianity in, **2**:63a, 70a
cinema in
  social realism and,
    5:243b–244b

cloisonné in, **2**:102a–102b
clothing in, **2**:**107b–111a**, 133a
coastal open cities in, **5**:298a
comfort women from, **2**:143b
Communism in, **1**:365a,
  2:**148b–152a**
  CCP and, **2**:32a
  literature and, **3**:527b
compass and, **3**:538b–539a
cooperatives in, **1**:48
cormorant fishing in, **2**:175b
corruption in, **2**:176a, 177b,
  178a, 180a
cuisine of, **1**:507a, **2**:184b,
  187b–192a, **4**:142b–143a
culture of, **1**:507a
dance in, **4**:154a, **5**:536b, **6**:178b
  modern, **2**:242a–242b
  in opera, **6**:178a
defense industry in,
  2:**257a–259b**
  achievements of,
    2:258a–259a
  challenges of, **2**:259a–259b
  nuclear industry in, **2**:257b
department stores in,
  2:269a–269b
"Developing the West" program, **6**:177a
drama in, **2**:**285a–287b**,
  551a–551b
  Ming, **2**:286b
  in PRC, **2**:287a
  Qin-Han, **2**:286a–286b
  Qing, **2**:286b–287a
  Song, **2**:286a
  Tang, **2**:285b–286a
  Yuan, **2**:286a–286b
earthquakes in, **2**:312a, 313a
economic indicators for, **1**:511b
economic system of,
  1:505b–506a, **508b–513a**
  agricultural reforms and,
    1:511a, 511b
  agriculture and, **1**:509a
  banking and, **1**:509a, 512a,
    515a
  bureaucracy and, **1**:510b,
    512a
  CCP and, **2**:32a, 32b
  centralization of,
    1:509b–510a
  China-Russia/Soviet Union
    relations and, **2**:17a,
    20a–20b
  China-Taiwan relations and,
    2:23a
  China-U.S. relations and,
    2:27b

Chinese Youth Society, **1**:493a

Ch'ing dynasty. *See* Qing dynasty.

Chinggis Khan. *See* Genghis Khan.

Chinmoku (Silence; Endo Shusaku), **2**:331b

chintanakan mai (New Economic Mechanism; Laos), **2**:50a–51a, **3**:442b–443a

Chinul, **1**:346a–346b

Chirac, Jacques, **3**:232a

Chirippu-date (Etorofu Island; volcano), **2**:352a

Chishtiya (Sufi order), **2**:51a–51b, **4**:240a, 524a
Khwaja Mu'in al-Din Chishti, **3:366a–366b**

Chitra-Ardhachitra-Chitrabhasha (sculpture, relief, painting; South Asia), **2:51b–56b**
distinctions among, **2**:51b–52b
in painting, **2**:54b–56a
in sculpture, **2**:*52a*, 52b–54b, *53b*

Chittagong (Bangladesh), **1**:238a, 238b, 248b, 277a, **2**:56b

Chittagong Hill Tracts (CHT; Bangladesh), **2**:349b

Cho Chong-nae, **3**:500b

Cho Se-hui, **3**:500b

Cho Suk Jin, **4**:*418a*

Choda Ganga Deva (king; Ganga dynasty), **5**:19a

Ch'oe Che-u, **2**:58a, **5**:74a, 510a, 510b, 511a, 511b

Ch'oe Chong-hui, **3**:501a

Ch'oe Chung-hon, **6**:195a

Ch'oe family (Korea), **3**:389b, 390a

Ch'oe In-ho, **3**:500a

Ch'oe In-hun, **3**:500a

Ch'oe Kyu-ha, **2**:85a, 265a

Ch'oe Myong-hui, **3**:500b

Ch'oe Namson, **2**:57a, **5**:115a

Ch'oe Shi-hyong, **2**:58a, **5**:510b–511a, 511b

Ch'oe Yun, **3**:501a

Choi Chung-ja, **2**:242a

Choi Seung-hee, **2**:241b

Chola kingdom (India), **1**:497a, 497b, **2:57a–57b**, **3**:22b, 61b–62a, **4**:460a, **5**:143a, 218a–218b, 332b, 409b, 410b, 472a, 532a, 532b, **6**:146a
Sri Lanka and, **4**:547b, **5**:324b
temples, **3**:23a

Cholla province (South Korea), **3**:417b

Chomolungma ("mother goddess of the land"). *See* Everest, Mount.

Chon Pong-jun, **5**:511a, 511b

Ch'ondogyo kyongjon (Sacred Writings of Ch'ondogyo), **2**:58a

Ch'ondogyo (Religion of the Heavenly Way; Korea), **2**:15a, **57b–58a**, **5**:74b, 510a, 511b, 512a
See also Tonghak

Chong Chi-yong, **3**:499b, **4**:537a

Chong Ch'ol, **3**:498a, **4**:536b

Chong Il-hyong (Chyung Yil-Hyung), **6**:196a

Chong Son, **4**:418a

Chong Yag-yong, **3**:390b

Chong yong (Doctrine of the Mean)
Zhu Xi on, **4**:303b–304a

Ch'ongch'un (Youth; Korean literary journal), **3**:374a

Ch'ongjin (North Korea), **2:58a–58b**

Chongjo (king; Korea), **3**:391

Chongqing (China), **2:58b–59a**, **5**:80a

Chongzhen (emperor; China), **4**:152b

ch'onmin (lowest social class; Korea), **2:59a**

Chora Batir, **3**:479b, 481a

Chormaqan, Noyan, **2:59a–59b**

Choshu Civil War (1865; Japan), **2**:60a

Choshu clan (Japan), **2**:488b

Choshu domain (Japan), **4**:130b, 131a, 132b, **5**:411b

Choshu Expeditions (Japan), **2:59b–60a**

Choson kingdom, **3**:233b, 236b

Choson kingdom (Yi dynasty; Korea), **1**:144a, 144b, 345b, **2:60a–62b**, 182a, 480a, **3**:299b, 390a–392a, 395b, 400b, 401a, 405b, 497b–499a, **5**:144b, 412a, 417b, 510a, **6**:196a
calligraphy in, **1**:406a, **2**:486a–486b, **3**:497a
ceramics of, **1**:482b
China-Korea relations and, **2**:14a, 14b
Chinese influence in, **2**:39b, **5**:115a
clothing in, **2**:121a
Confucianism in, **2**:162b, 163a–164a
drama in, **2**:289b, 290a
early, **2**:60b–61a
education in, **5**:277a
elite in, **6**:185a
emancipation movements in, **2**:59a

fishing industry in, **2**:386a
founding of, **5**:416b, **6**:195b
human rights in, **5**:278b
laquerware in, **3**:437b–438a
later, **2**:61a–62a
Neo-Confucianism in, **4**:305a
painting in, **4**:417b–418b
paper crafts in, **4**:463a
poetry of, **4**:536b–537a
private schools in, **5**:20b
relics from, **5**:269b
rulers of, **5**:537a, **6**:194a–194b
Seoul during, **5**:147a
sports in, **5**:312b
Taoism in, **5**:422a–422b
women in, **6**:140a
wrestling in, **5**:333a

Chosuk festival (Korea), **4**:82a

Chota Nagpur, **3**:272b

Chotmai Changwang Ram (Letters of Deputy Ram; Bidyalankarana), **1**:296a

Chotongpyung Liaison Committee (North Korea), **3**:283a

Chou dynasty. *See* Zhou dynasty.

Chou En-lai. *See* Zhou Enlai.

Choybalsan, Horloogiyn, **1**:350b, **2**:62b, **4**:174a, 182a, 183a, 183b–184a, **5**:534a

"Ch'oyong ka" (Song of Ch'oyong; Korea), **3**:497a

Christian Conference of Asia (CCA), **2**:78a–78b

Christianity, **1**:6a, 7a, 77b, 82a, **2:62b–79a**, **6**:196a
Anglo-Indians and, **1**:106a
in Antioch, **1**:110b, 111a
Armenians and, **1**:158b
in Asia Minor, **4**:144a, **5**:119a, 119b, 556a
Asian religions and, **1:167a–169b**
Buddhism and, **1**:335a, **2**:76–77
Cao Dai and, **1**:430b
in Bangladesh, **1**:239a, **2**:73b, 74b
Byzantines and, **1**:391a
calendar of, **1:397a–397b**
in Calicut, **1**:401a
in Cambodia, **2**:77*b*
in Caucasia, **1**:448b, 450a
in Central Asia, **2:63a–65a**, **3**:153a, 154a, **6**:5b
contemporary, **2**:64b
early, **2**:63a–63b
Eastern Orthodox, **2**:63b–64b
Islam and, **2**:63b

in Sri Lanka, **5**:317b, 322a,
325a
in Taiwan, **1**:501a, **2**:21b
See also Dutch East India
Company
European
in China, **2**:148a, **4**:90b, 91b
China-India relations and,
2:1b
Chinese influence in Southeast Asia and, **2**:41b–42a
in India, **2**:114b
Indonesia and, **3**:56a, 56b
Maldives and, **4**:24b–25a
Meiji Restoration and,
4:130a
overseas Chinese and,
2:47b–48a, 48a–48b
Thailand and, **2**:84a
in Vietnam, **6**:69b–70b
French, **4**:487b, **6**:92a, 116b
in Africa, **1**:34a
in Cambodia, **1**:416b, 419a,
419b–420a, 424a, **2**:106a,
3:522b
in China, **5**:145b
Christianity and, **2**:75b, 77a
in India, **2**:473b
in Laos, **3**:332a–332b, 442b,
444b–445a, 447b, 449b,
456a–456b, 502a, 528a
in Maldives, **4**:25a
in Mauritius, **4**:87b
Mekong River and, **4**:136a
in Middle East, **4**:243a
in Myanmar, **2**:72a
Opium Wars and, **4**:28a
Thailand and, **4**:161b, 162a
in Vietnam, **1**:446a,
446b–447a, 478a, **2**:28a,
152b, 153a, 155b, 402a,
488a, 537a, 537b, 542a,
560b, 570a, **3**:476a,
518a–519a, **4**:109b, 540b,
6:68, 71a, 93a
See also Franco-Viet Minh
War; French East India
Company; Indochina:
French colonialism in
German
in Africa, **1**:34a
in China, **1**:151a, **2**:149a,
4:91b, **6**:116a
Italian
in Africa, **1**:34a
Japanese, **3**:208a–208b, **6**:141a
expansion of, **3**:208a–208b,
6:162a–162b
in Indonesia, **5**:124a

in Korea, **3**:*235*, **4**:46b–47ab,
5:115a, 115b
in Malaya, **6**:163b–164a
in Manchuria, **4**:28b,
29a–29b
Meiji Restoration and,
4:134b
in Myanmar, **2**:155a
in Philippines, **4**:514a
mass media and, **4**:97b–98a
mountaineering and, **4**:200a
Orientalism and, **4**:395a
Portuguese
in Africa, **1**:34a
in East Timor, **2**:314a–315b
in India, **2**:113b, **4**:34b, 210a
in Indonesia, **4**:26a
in Malaysia, **4**:4b–5b, 13a,
139a
in Maldives, **4**:24b–25a
in Mauritius, **4**:87a
in Southeast Asia, **1**:151a
in Sri Lanka, **3**:512a–512b,
5:316b, 317b, 322a, 323b,
325a
Thailand and, **4**:161b
Prussian
Thailand and, **4**:161b
Russian
in Central Asia,
1:462a–462b, 463a–465b,
467a–467b, **4**:81a
in Manchuria, **4**:28a–28b
Spanish
in Africa, **1**:34a
corruption and, **2**:176b
in Philippines, **2**:208a, **4**:6a,
37b, 44a, 148b
Sunni Muslims and, **4**:243a
in Thailand, **2**:77a
U.S.
in Philippines, **2**:208a,
4:148b, 512b–514b
Thailand and, **4**:161b
See also *individual countries*
Columbus, Christopher, **4**:546b
comfort women, **2**:**143b–145a**,
144a, **5**:193a, **6**:141a
Comintern (Communist International), **3**:233a, 523b, 524b,
4:78b, **6**:130a
CCP and, **2**:31b, 149a
Mongolia and, **4**:174a, 182b,
183a
Vietnam and, **2**:153b
Commission of Science, Technology, and Industry for National
Defense (COSTIND; China),
2:257b, 259b

Commonwealth of Independent
States (CIS), **1**:6b, 19b, **3**:343b
Central Asia and, **1**:472b–473a,
5:396a, **6**:49b
China and, **5**:170a
Kyrgyzstan and, **3**:427a–427b,
431a
shamanism and, **5**:161a
See also Russia
Commonwealth of Nations. *See*
British Commonwealth.
Communism
in Afghanistan, **1**:25a, **6**:207b
mujahideen and, **4**:209a
Asian Development Bank and,
1:163a
in Australia, **1**:185a
in Bulgaria, **1**:375a
in Cambodia, **2**:503b–504a,
565a–565b, **3**:523a,
4:542b–543b
See also Khieu, Samphan
in Central Asia, **1**:179a, 467a,
2:**145a–148b**, **6**:55a
collapse of, **2**:148a–148b
Gorbachev and, **2**:147b–148a
introduction of, **2**:145a–145b
postwar, **2**:146b–147a
Stalin and, **2**:146a–146b
in China, **1**:176b, 365a,
2:**148b–152a**, **3**:6a,
249a–250a, 443a, **6**:28b, 81b
early period, **2**:149a–149b
human rights and, **1**:517a,
517b
literature of, **3**:527b
Maoism and, **2**:150a–151a
May Fourth Movement and,
4:92a
music and, **4**:221b
Nationalists and, **6**:130a,
164b, 214b
post-Mao, **2**:151a–152a
in PRC, **2**:149b–150a
Shanghai, **5**:168b
Soviet Union control and,
3:524a–524b
China-U.S. relations and, **2**:25b
Christianity and, **2**:67a, 77a
domino theory and, **6**:77b, 83b
fall of (1989–1990), **1**:350b,
2:148a–148b, 154b, **6**:93a
in Indochina, **2**:534a, **4**:376a
in Indonesia, **2**:493b, **5**:4b, 129b
Suharto and, **3**:72b, 158a
international, **1**:173b
CCP and, **2**:31b, 149a
See also Comintern
in Iraq, **4**:77a

festival, **4**:142b–143a
history of, **2**:188a–189a
influence of, **2**:197b, 198b,
201a, 201b, 202a,
204b–205a, 206b–207a,
208a, 208b, 209a, 213a
regional, **2**:191b–192a
of India, **2**:209b–212b, *210*
influence of, **2**:204b,
205a–205b, 213a, 213b
of Indonesia, **2:192a–194b**,
4:475a
international, **2**:214a
in Japan, **2**:200b
of Iran, **2:194b–196a**
of Iraq, **2:196a–197a**
of Japan, **2:197a–201a**
bento (lunchbox meal),
1:279b–280a, **2**:203a
ceramics and, **1**:478b–479a
chrysanthemum and, **2**:79b
history of, **2**:197a–199b
influence of, **2**:202b
sashimi, **2**:406a
of Kashmir, **2**:*210*
of Korea, **2:201a–204b**,
5:269b–270a
festivals and, **2**:85a–85b
kimchi, **2**:*202*, 202a–202b,
203
of Malaysia, **2**:*204b*, **204b–206b**
influence of, **2**:208a, 209a,
213a, 213b
of Mongolia, **2**:*206a*,
206b–208a
Muslim influence on, **4**:237b
of Pakistan, **2**:209b, 210a, 210b,
212b
of Philippines, **2:208a–209a**,
208b
regional, **2**:208b
of Russia, **2**:207a
of South Asia, **2**:184b,
209b–212b, *210*
curries in, **2**:211a–212a
regional, **2**:209b
of Southeast Asia
influence of, **2**:213a
of Spain
influence of, **2**:208a, 209a
of Thailand, **2**:*212b*,
212b–214a
regional, **2**:213b
of Turkey, **2:214b–217a**
pilaf in, **2**:215b–216a
vegetarian, **2**:201b–202a, 205a,
209b–210a, 212a
of Vietnam, **2:217a–220a**, *217b*
regional, **2**:219b–220a

cuju (ballgame; China), **5**:301b
cukong (Chinese businessman in
Southeast Asia), **2:220a–220b**
Culavamsa (Pali chronicle), **3**:511b
cult of Maitreya. *See* Maitreya:
cult of.
Cultural Agreement (1953), **3**:232a
Cultural Revolution (1966–1976;
China), **1**:176b, 177b, 275b,
341a, 365b, 381a, 495a, 505a,
2:151b, **221b–225a**, *222a*,
266b, 276a, 287a, 422a–422b,
557b, 561b, 564b, **3**:443a, 468b,
474b, 483, 521a, 534b, **4**:293b,
542b, **5**:303a, **6**:187b, 188a
art and, **4**:413b–414a
assessment of, **2**:224b–225a
barefoot doctors in, **4**:124a
causes of, **2**:221b–222b, 225a
CCP and, **2**:32a, 221b, 222b,
223a, 223b, 224b
change and, **5**:11b
China-Japan relations and, **2**:11b
China-Russia/Soviet Union relations and, **2**:17b
China-U.S. relations and, **2**:26a,
224b
Christianity and, **2**:67a
courtyards and, **2**:182b
Cultural Revolution Group in,
2:222b, 422b
destruction in, **1**:496a, 507a,
6:22a
early stages of, **2**:222b–223a
ethnic groups and, **4**:293b
film and, **2**:87a
"Four Olds" in, **1**:177b, **2**:222b
Gao Xinjiang in, **2**:425b
Great Leap Forward and,
2:221b, 222a, 448a,
4:293a–293b, **5**:176a
in Guangzhou, **2**:456b
human rights and, **4**:177a
influence on Pol Pot of, **4**:542b
Japan Communist Party and,
3:229a
Japan Socialist Party and,
3:229b
later stages of, **2**:224a–224b
Mao and, **1**:526a, **2**:150b–151a,
221b–224b, **4**:46b, **5**:9b,
483b, 516b, 517b
Marxism-Leninism-Mao Ze-
dong Thought and, **4**:80b
media and, **5**:477a
model operas in, **1**:275b, **4**:221b
music and, **4**:221b
Ninth CCP Congress and,
2:223a–224a

Peking University and, **4**:470b
political exile in, **1**:521b, **2**:224a
population resettlement and,
1:528a
religion and, **1**:178a
traditional clothing and, **2**:111b
traditional medicine and, **4**:124a
writings on, **3**:483
Yi people and, **6**:193b
Zhao Ziyang and, **6**:211a
Zhou Enlai and, **2**:32a, 224b,
6:211a, 214b
See also Red Guard organizations
Cuman people, **3**:480a
Cumings, Bruce, **2**:152b
cuneiform script, **2**:532a, 532b,
533a, **4**:393b, 479b
discoveries of, **1**:126a
Cunningham, Merce, **2**:241a
Cuong De, **4**:487b
Curzon, George Nathaniel,
2:225b, **4**:31b, 194b, 394b,
478a
Cushing, Caleb, **5**:29
customary law. *See* adat.
Cyprus
disputes over, **5**:559a, 560a,
564b, 565a
missiles in, **5**:562b–563a
Cyrillic script, **1**:206a–207b
in Central Asia, **1**:465b,
474a–476b
in Mongolia, **4**:183a
Mongolian languages and,
4:185a, 185b, 190a
Cyrus the Great, **1**:212b, **4**:477b,
484a, **5**:131b, 399b, 428b, **6**:49b
Czechoslovakia
San Francisco Peace Treaty
and, **5**:123b
Soviet invasion of, **2**:26b

D

Da Costa, Rafael Zulueta, **4**:538b
da Cruz, Father, **6**:122b
Da Nang (Vietnam), **2:227a–227b**,
542a, **4**:526a, **6**:62b
da wah (religious awakening;
Southeast Asia), **3**:160b, 161a
Da Xue (Great Learning), **4**:303b,
304a, **6**:65a
Dada Qorqut (Azerbaijani epic),
1:207b
See also *Gorkut Ata*
Dadra and Nagar Haveli Union
Territory (India), **2:227b–228a**
Dae-Sook Suh, **5**:481a

Dandin, **3**:489b, 511a

Dang Tran Con, **2**:280b

dangdut (Indonesian popular music), **4**:228b

Dangrek Range, **1**:407a, **2:249b–250a, 5**:512b

Danjuro II (Japanese actor), **3**:294a

Danshoku okagami (Great Mirror of Male Love; Ihara Saikaku), **2**:544b

Dante Alighieri, **2**:423a, **4**:376b, 394b

Danzan, Soliyn, **4**:182a, 182b, 183a

Daoan (monk), **2**:221a

Daochuo, **1**:351b

Daodejing (The Way and Its Power; Laozi), **2**:158a, 563b, **3**:461b–462b, 485a
See also Laozi; Taoism

Daoism. *See* Taoism.

Daoud, Muhammad, **1**:25a

Daqing oil field (China), **2**:499a

Daqiqi (poet), **5**:158a

Dara Shikoh, **1**:183b

D'Arcy, William Knox, **4**:379b

Dardanelles, **1**:96b, 139b, 176a, 312b, 313a, **2**:*250*, **250a–251a**, **5**:558b
Gallipoli campaign and, **2**:250b, **5**:558a

D'Argenlieu, Georges Thierry, **2**:402b

Darhan (Mongolia), **1**:69a, **2:251a**, **4**:190a

Dari language, **2:251a–251b**, 366b, **4**:467a, 479a, **5**:395a
poetry in, **2**:251b, 256a

Darius I (the Great; ruler; Achaemenid empire), **2**:366a, **4**:393b, 477b, 479b, 485a, **5**:17a

Darius III (ruler; Achaemenid empire), **1**:212b, **2**:479a, **5**:139b

Darjeeling Himalayan Railway, **2**:252a

Darjeeling (India), **2:251b–252a**, **3**:308a, **5**:514b

Darul Arqam (House of Arqam), **3**:163a

Darul Islam movement (Indonesia), **2:252a–252b**, 533b, **3**:158a, **4**:459a

Darwin, Charles, **4**:452b

Darwinism, **5**:13b

Das, Jibanananda, **3**:509b, **4**:531a

Das, Kamala, **4**:531b

Das Baul, Purna Chandra, **3**:507b

Dasakumaracharita (Story of Ten Princes; Dandin), **3**:489b

Dasas tribe (India), **2**:512a

Dasehra Festival (India), **4**:273b

Dashakumaracarita (Adventures of the Ten Princes; Dandin), **3**:511a

Dasht-e Margo desert (Afghanistan), **1**:20b, **2:252b**

Dasranya, **3**:272b

Dast-i Saba (Fingers of the Morning Breeze; Faiz), **2**:362a

dastan (Central Asian epics), **2:252b–253b**, **3**:479a–480a, 481a, 481b, **4**:26b
cultural values in, **2**:253a–253b, **6**:13a
hero of, **2**:253a
occasions for, **2**:253a
performers of, **2**:253a

Dastan Dede Korkut, **3**:482a

Dastan Koroglu, **3**:481a

Dastanbu (Pellet of Perfume, Ghalib), **2**:433b

Date Masamune, **5**:146b, 504a

Dato Onn bin Jaafar, **4**:14a

Datta, Narendranath. *See* Vivekananda, Swami.

Daud, Muhammad, **2:253b–254a**

Daud Beureueh, **2**:252a

Daud Khan, **1**:29a, **2**:343b, **6**:207b

dauylpaz (kettledrum), **2:254a–254b**

Davao (Philippines), **2:254b–255b**, *255*

David, Collin, **2:255b–256a**

David-Neel, Alexandra, **5**:487b

Daw Khin Kyi, **1**:182a

Daw San San Nweh, **4**:267a, 268a

Dawai, Abdul Hadi, **2:256a–256b**

Dawna Range (Myanmar), **3**:323b

Daxinganling Forest (Inner Mongolia, China), **4**:302b

Day, Francis, **3**:536a

Day Lasts Longer than 100 Years, The (Chingis Aitmatov), **1**:75a

Dayabhaga (Jimutavahana), **2**:517b

Dayak people (Borneo), **2**:429a–429b, **3**:73a, 538a, **5**:131a, **6**:128a

Dayananda Saraswati, **2**:523b

Dazai Osamu, **2:256b–257a**, **3**:495b

Dazu rock carvings, **2:257a**
See also Sichuan; Song dynasty; Tang dynasty

De Gracia Conception, Marcelo, **4**:538b

De Jesus, José Corazon, **4**:538b

De Los Reyes, Isabelo, **4**:538a

de Melo, Sergio Vieira, **2**:315b

de Paul, Saint Vincent, **5**:439a

de Rhodes, Alexandre, **1**:446a–446b

de Silva, John, **3**:512b

Death Kye Document (1651; Korea), **3**:*418*

Deccan plateau. *See* Dekkan plateau.

Deewar (film; India), **1**:212b

defense industry (China), **2:257a–259b**
See also military

deforestation, **2:259b–261b**, *260*, **3**:89a, **6**:95a, 156b
in China, **2**:192a
mangroves and, **4**:35a
See also forest industry; Mangroves; Mongolia: forest industry in; Southeast Asia: forest industry in

Dehra Dun (India), **2:261b**, **6**:42b

Dekkan plateau (India), **2**:101a, **261b–262a**, 316a, **3**:325a, 380b

del Pilar, Marcelo H., **3**:505b, **4**:505b, 538a

Delhi (India), **1**:134a, 183b, 198b, 217b, 239b
Punjab and, **5**:17b

Delhi sultanate, **1**:39b, 76a, 134a, 211a, 239b, 247a, 296a, 498a, **2**:56b, 491b, **3**:536a, **4**:96a, **5**:58b
Islam in, **3**:169b
in Pakistan, **4**:209a

Delhi Union Territory (India), **2:262a–263a**

Delphi, oracle of, **5**:131b

Demetillo, Ricaredo, **4**:538b

Deming, W. Edwards, **5**:36a

Demirel, Suleyman, **1**:12a, **2:263a–263b**, **5**:555b, 559a–559b, 560b, *564*

democracy
Asian, **5**:292b
in Cambodia, **1**:410a, 422b, 424a, 424b, **5**:122a
in Central Asia, **1**:472b
in China, **1**:508a, 508b, 517b, 519a, 519b, 522a, 522b, 526b, 527b, **2**:151b, 152a
May Fourth Movement and, **4**:91b, 92a
media and, **4**:101b
Tiananmen Incident and, **5**:483a
Christianity and
in Southeast Asia, **2**:78b
global human rights and, **1**:258a
in India
British rule and, **4**:196a

Indonesian Revolution and,
3:76a–76b
in Japan, 2:68a, 197b
in Muromachi period,
4:216a
trade and, 2:8b
Java War and, 3:269a–269b
Kapitan Cina and, 3:310
legal studies and, 1:13b
Malaysian cuisine and, 2:204b
Padri War and, 4:405a
seige of Melaka and, 2:476a,
4:550b
in Southeast Asia, 1:6b, 9b,
151a, 225a, 233a, 267b,
319b, 320a, 326a–326b,
2:228a, *309*, **309a–310b**,
479b, 5:252a, 408a–408b,
6:98a–98b, 122b, 164a
spice trade and, 1:58b, 326a,
2:142a, 4:550b
in Sri Lanka, 3:307a
in Taiwan, 1:501a, 2:21b,
3:310a, 5:379a
See also colonialism: Dutch
Dutch East India Company
(Verenigde Oostindische Com-
pagnie; VOC), 1:267b, 2:228a,
308a–309a, 404b, 3:531b,
4:470a, 497a, 5:252a, 358a
British East India Company
and, 1:91a–91b
ethnic colonial policy and,
2:342a–342b
formation of, 2:309a
governors-general of,
2:141b–142a, 5:298b–299a
in Indonesia, 3:55b–56b,
63b–64a, 5:252a
insignia of, 2:*308*
Japanese ceramics and, 1:479b
in Java, 1:89b
Java and, 1:89b
Malay language and, 1:220a
in Malaysia, 4:6a
Mataram and, 4:84b, 5:252a,
529b
opium trade and, 4:388a
porcelain trade and, 4:549a
Sri Lanka and, 5:322a, 532b
Dutch language, 1:220b, 4:208a
Dutch New Guinea, 2:493b
Dutta, Michael Madhusudhan,
3:508b, 4:530b
Duval Rani-Khizr Khan (Romance
of Duval Rani and Khizr
Khan;Khusrau), 3:365b
Dzongkha language, 1:294b
Dzunghar people, 4:173b

E

E-commerce, 3:82b, 83a
Earhart, H. Byron, 5:71a, 71b
Early Events in Akita (Fujitu; painting), 2:408a
earthquakes, **2:311a–313b**, 338b
in Andaman Islands, 2:312a
in Bhuj, 2:461a, 5:56a
in China, 2:496b
in Constantinople, 3:188a
disaster preparedness for,
2:313a
in Greece, 5:560a
in India, 5:180b
in Indonesia, 3:51b
in Iran, 5:365a, 365b
in Iraq, 3:364b
in Japan, 2:499b, 502b, 572a,
3:189b, 305a, 378a, 5:378a,
509b, 514a
bills for and, 2:378a
Tokyo (1923), 2:378a,
5:417a
in Korea, 5:367a
in Tashkent (1966), 5:425a
tsunamis caused by, 2:312b
in Turkey, 4:49a, 5:132a, 559b,
560a
East Africa. *See* Africa: East.
East Asia
calendars in, **1:395a–396a**
Communism in, 1:162b
department stores in,
2:267b–270a, *268*
intellectual property rights and,
3:90a
Japanese expansion in, 3:258b,
259b, 260a
kites in, 3:380b
marriage and family in,
4:57a–62b, 60a
missionaries in, 3:531a
New Zealand and, 4:323b–325a
textile and clothing industry in,
5:443a–445b
tourism in, 5:522a
westernization in, **6:115b–117a**
See also particular countries
East China Sea (Dong Hai),
2:313b
East India Company. *See* British
East India Company; Dutch
East India Company; French
East India Company.
East Indies, 1:105b
East Timor, 1:224b, 275b, 276a,
2:274a
Australia and, 1:187, 187b,
5:499b

Catholicism in, 2:315b
independence of, 2:468b–469b,
3:65b, 5:53b, 293b
Indonesia and, 1:224b, 2:314a,
315a–315b, 405a, 468b–469a,
3:53a, 65b, 74b, 4:321b,
5:499b, 6:30b–31b, 123b
languages of, 2:315b
map of, 2:*314a*
media in, 4:105a
Nobel Prize for freedom fighters in, 2:315b
peacekeeping in, 2:502a
political movement in, 2:405a
politics of
Boaventura rebellion of
1911–1912, 2:314b
Fretilin party in,
2:315a–315b
Indonesian colonialism in,
2:314a, 315a–315b,
4:157a
Portuguese colonialism in,
2:314b–315a
traditional political system
of, 2:314b
Portuguese colonialism in,
4:550b
profile of, **2:314a–316a**
topography of, 2:314a–314b
UN and, 2:274b, 314a,
315b–316a, 4:105a, 5:53b,
6:28a, 30b–32a
U.S. and, 3:74b
See also Dili Massacre; Fretilin;
United Nations
Eastern Ghats (India), **2:316a**,
3:10b
See also Western Ghats
Eastern Jin dynasty (China),
2:477b
Eastern Learning. *See* Tonghak.
Eastern Orthodox Church, 1:168a,
2:316b–318a, 3:187b
beginnings of, 2:316b
in Central Asia, 2:63b–64b
ecumenical councils and, 2:317b
Greek
Albanians and, 1:80b
Greco-Turkish attrocities
and, 2:317a–318b
Islam and, 2:317a–317b
patriarchates of, 2:317a–317b
priest of, 2:*317a*
Roman Catholicism and, 2:318a
Russian, 2:63b–64a, 64b
Central Asia and, 3:154a
in Japan, 2:68b
in Siberia, 5:194b

endangered species, **1**:437b, 443b,
2:**330a–331b**, **3**:467b, **5**:116a
birds, **2**:330b
in China, **2**:330b, 331a, **3**:277b,
6:171a
CITES treaty on, **2**:330b,
3:466b
elephant, **2**:327a, 331a
in Japan, **5**:116a
in Java, **3**:267b
Komodo dragon, **3**:384a–384b
sun bear, **5**:160b, **355b–356a**
Enderuni, Fazil-i, **3**:515b
Endo Shusaku, **2**:**331a–331b**
energy
in Central Asia, **1**:469b,
2:**331b–334a**
coal, **2**:332b–333a
major trends in, **2**:333b–334a
natural gas, **2**:332a–332b,
335a
nontraditional resources,
2:333a–333b
oil, **2**:332a
China-Russia/Soviet Union relations and, **2**:20b
electricity, **3**:332a
in Central Asia, **2**:333a,
5:358a
Chang River and, **5**:199a
Ganges River and, **2**:423b
Mekong River and, **4**:135b,
137a
Surkhob River and, **5**:358a
Sutlej River and, **5**:361a
in West Asia, **3**:80, 80a, 80b
Japanese crisis in (1970s),
2:378a
in Myanmar, **5**:165a
in South Korea, **5**:286a
sustainability and, **5**:358b, 359a,
359b
energy industry
in China, **2**:**334a–336a**
Central Asia and, **1**:469b
coal in, **2**:334a–334b
environmental issues and,
2:335b
restructuring of,
2:334b–335b
in Malaysia, **4**:9a, 9b, 17a
Mekong River and, **4**:137a
in Myanmar, **5**:121b
in North Korea, **5**:273a–273b
See also natural gas industry; oil
industry
Engbekshi Kazak (*Kazak Worker*;
Soviet-Kazakh newspaper),
2:306a

English language, **1**:106a
in Asia, **2**:**336a–337a**, **4**:432b
in Central Asia, **1**:474a
education system and,
4:10b–12a
in India, **3**:11a, 533b, **4**:129a,
5:411a
Calcutta, **1**:394b
education and, **3**:*18a*, 18b,
19, **5**:136a
as official language, **1**:279a
in Indonesia, **4**:208a
in Japan
Meiji period, **4**:195a
Muromachi period, **4**:216a
in Malaysia, **3**:550b, **4**:2a
Malaysian literature in, **4**:37a
media and, **4**:98a, 103a, 104a,
104b, 110a, 110b
in Pakistan, **4**:431a
in Philippines, **4**:490b, 491a,
492b, 494b, 500b, 502a,
513b
media and, **4**:104b
in Singapore
school system and, **2**:441a
in South Asia
ethnic conflict and, **2**:348a
media and, **4**:110a, 110b
in Southeast Asia, **4**:108a, 108b,
5:454b
media and, **4**:103a
in Sri Lanka, **2**:336a, **4**:*111b*,
5:317a, 323a
Sinhalization and, **5**:323a
in Vietnam, **6**:66b
Enhanced Structural Adjustment
Facility program (Kyrgyzstan),
3:427a
enlightenment (*kevalajnana*),
3:197a
Enlightenment,the, **1**:167b, **5**:75b,
6:118a, 141a
mass media and, **4**:97a
Enomoto Takeaki, **2**:**337a–337b**
Enrile, Juan Ponce, **5**:53a
Enryakuji temple (Japan), **2**:547b,
5:179a, 182a
Enver, Ismail, **5**:557b, 558a
environmental issues, **2**:**337b**
in Black Sea area, **1**:300a, 312b,
313a
in Cambodia, **1**:434b,
5:513a–513b
in Cardamon Mountains,
1:434a–434b
in Caspian Sea, **1**:437a–437b
in Central Asia, **1**:467a, **4**:215a,
5:363b

certified wood products, **2**:400a
in China, **1**:506a–506b, 508a,
520a, **2**:187b, 192a
air pollution, **1**:73b, 74a, 74b
of Greater Xing'an Range,
2:449b
greenhouse gases in, **5**:528a
Manchuria and, **4**:29a
Shanghai, **5**:171a, 171b
China-India relations and, **2**:4b
in forest areas, **2**:400b
global warming, **2**:261a
Maldives and, **4**:22a, 24a
of Gobi Desert, **2**:438b
Green Revolution and, **2**:454a,
454b, 455a
Gulf of Thailand and, **2**:462a
in Japan, **2**:98a, **5**:135b,
153b–154a
endangered species, **5**:116a
in Kathmandu Valley (Nepal),
3:329b
in Malaysia, **4**:20b
Sabah, **5**:113b
in Maldives, **4**:22a, 24a
mangroves and, **4**:35a–35b
measurement systems and,
4:93a
Mekong River and,
4:137a–137b
in Mongolia, **4**:168b, 177a
in Nepal
Kathmandu Valley, **3**:329b
nuclear testing and,
5:146a–146b
in Nukus (Uzbekistan),
4:371b–372a
in Philippines, **1**:433a, 450b
virgin forests, **5**:201b–202a
Philippines and, **4**:517a
pollution
in China, **2**:425a
in Japan, **1**:500a, **2**:83a
in Taiwan, **3**:310a
in Turkey, **6**:192b
salinization, **3**:313a, 315b, 319b,
320a
SCO and, **5**:170a
Sea of Marmara and, **4**:49a
in Siberia, **5**:196a, 196b, 197a
in Singapore, **5**:212b
in South Korea, **5**:269a
sustainable growth and,
5:359b–360a
in Turkmenistan, **1**:458a
in Uzbekistan, **4**:371b–372a
See also air pollution; Aral Sea;
Bhopal; deforestation; earthquakes; endangered species;

Funan, state of, **1**:418a, 425a, **2**:41a

FUNCINPEC (United Front for an Independent, Neutral, Peaceful and Cooperative Cambodia), **1**:408b, 421a, 421b, 422a, 422b, 423a, 428a, **2**:412b–413a, **3**:359a, **359a**, **5**:55a

Sam Rainsy and, **5**:121b, 122a

Furukawa Ichibei, **2**:413a–413b

Fushimi-Inari Shinto Shrine (Kyoto, Japan), **3**:*420*

Futabatei Shimei (Hasegawa Tatsunosuke), **2**:413b, **3**:495a

Futen rojin nikki (Diary of a Mad Old Man; Tanizaki Junichiro), **3**:495b

Fuzhou (China), **2**:407a
dialects of, **4**:145b–146a

G

G-8 (Group of Eight), **2**:3a

G-30-S. *See* Gestapu affair.

Gabbay family, **3**:287a

GABRIELA federation of women's organizations (Philippines), **4**:516b

Gadjah Mada University (Indonesia), **2**:415a–415b, **6**:197a

Gafurov, Bobojan Gafurovich, **2**:415b–416a

Gajah Mada, **2**:416a–416b, **3**:546b, **5**:218b

gakureki shakai (educational record society; Japan), **2**:416b–417a

Gakusei (First National Plan for Education; Japan), **3**:7a–7b

Galdan Khan, **6**:22b

Galen, **4**:125a, 476b
Greco-Islamic medicine and, **4**:126b–127b

Galland, Antoine, **4**:393b

Galle (Sri Lanka), **5**:299b

Gama, Vasco da, **1**:33a, 58b, 81a, 400b, **2**:417a–417b, **3**:42b, 62b, **4**:550a

gambang kromong (type of musical ensemble; Indonesia), **2**:417b–418a

gambuh (Balinese dance drama), **2**:*418a*, 418a–418b, *419a*, **6**:112b

gamelan (Indonesian music ensemble), **1**:157b, 225b, **2**:418b–419b, **3**:54a, 54b, **4**:227b, 228a, 228b, **5**:124a, **6**:111a, 112a, 112b

games
board, **1**:301a–301b
computer, **4**:34a
See also sports

Games of the New Emerging Forces (GANEFO), **4**:384a, **5**:307b

Gamperaliya (Wickramasinghe), **3**:512b

Gan language, **2**:477a, **5**:229a

Gandan lamasery (Mongolia), **2**:419b

Gandhara (India), **5**:428b–429a

Gandhara style, **5**:141b–142a

Gandhi, Feroze, **2**:419b

Gandhi, Indira, **1**:85a, 166b, 193b, 255a, **2**:166a, **419b–420a**, *420a*, **3**:25b, 26a, 28b, 204a, **4**:460a, **5**:50a, **6**:148b
assassination of, **1**:92b, **2**:420a, **3**:13b, **5**:206b
India-Pakistan relations and, **3**:32b

Gandhi, Mohandas K. (Mahatma), **1**:32, 34b, 65b, 83a, 95a, 298a, 300b, 311b, **2**:336b, **420a–422a**, 523b, **3**:11b, 14b–15a, 198b, 277a, 353b, 492b, **4**:523b, **6**:118a
assassin of, **2**:439a–439b
assassination of, **1**:85a, **2**:422a
caste and, **1**:438a, **2**:166a, **6**:36a
Christianity and, **1**:168b
clothing and, **2**:114b
education and, **3**:20a, 20b
education of, **5**:47a
imprisonment of, **2**:421b
Indian constitution and, **2**:165b
influence of, **5**:5a, 38a, 46a, 56a
on land ownership, **2**:420b
law practice of, **2**:420b, 421a
manifesto of, **2**:421a
in Mauritius, **4**:88a
nonviolent resistance of, **2**:420a, 421a, 421b, 439b, **5**:136a–136b
salt tax and, **5**:121a
Sanskritization and, **5**:127a
Southeast Asia and, **3**:34b
Tagore and, **5**:369a
vow of chastity of, **2**:421a
women's rights and, **6**:147, 148a
work with untouchables of, **2**:421b

Gandhi, Rajiv, **2**:419b, *420a*, **3**:15b, 16a, 25b, 26a, 204a, **5**:206b, 411a
Myanmar and, **3**:29b
Sri Lanka and, **3**:36a, 37a

Gandhi, Sanjay, **2**:419b, *420a*

Gandhi, Sonia, **3**:*27b*

Gandhi Hall declaration, **4**:291b

Gandhinagar (India), **2**:460a, 461a

GANEFO. *See* Games of the New Emerging Forces.

Gang of Four (China), **2**:32a, 151a, 267a, 287a, **422a–422b**
corruption and, **2**:181b
fall of, **2**:224b, **4**:376a, **5**:516b

Ganga dynasty (India), **4**:273b, **5**:19a, 143b

Ganges River (India), **1**:*84b*, 85a, 237a, 237b, 254b, 255a, 255b, 269a, 276b, 296a, 316b, **2**:422b–424b, **3**:10a, 51a, **4**:396b
in Indian history, **2**:423a–424b
irrigation and, **2**:423b, **5**:87b
map of, **2**:*423a*
in Medieval thought, **2**:423a
mystical pull of, **4**:524a
in religious ceremonies, **2**:423b, 424a, **6**:58a
sharing waters of, **1**:255a, 255b, 256a, **6**:*58a*

Gangotri glacier (Himalayas), **2**:424a

Gangtok (India), **2**:424b, **5**:207a

Gani, A.K., **2**:431b

Ganj Ali Khan, **3**:349a

Ganjin (Jianzhen), **2**:6b, 13b

Gansu corridor (China), **2**:425a

Gansu province (China), **2**:425a–425b, **5**:32a, **6**:223b

Gao E, **1**:432a

Gao Gang, **3**:524b

Gao Jianfu, **4**:413b

Gao Qifeng, **4**:413b

Gao Xingjian, **2**:287a, **425b–426a**, **3**:483

Gao Yihan, **1**:517b, 518a

Gaozong (emperor; China), **5**:253b–254a, 413a, **6**:170a

Gaozu (emperor; China), **5**:412b, 414b

GAP Project (*Guneydogu Anadolu Projesi*; Southeastern Anatolia Project), **2**:430a, **4**:141a

Garabil Plateau (Turkmenistan), **2**:426a
plants of, **2**:426a

Garcia, Carlos P., **2**:426a–426b, **3**:532b

Garcia Villa, Jose, **4**:538b

gardens
in China, **1**:130b, *427b*, **2**:426b–428b, **5**:355a, 361a
cosmology of, **2**:427a, *427b*

Ghats. *See* Eastern Ghats; Western Ghats.
ghazal (Persian lyric poetry), **3**:170b, **5**:188a
Ghazali, al- (Persian poet), **3**:364b, 520b
Ghazna, Mahmud of, **3**:520a, **4**:85a, 163b
Ghazna (Ghazni; Afghanistan), **1**:453b, **2**:434a–434b
Ghaznavid dynasty (Central Asia), **1**:453b–454a, **2**:434a, **3**:438b, 480a, 545a, **5**:17a, **6**:50b
  Islam and, **3**:173b
  Kara Kitai and, **1**:454b
Ghazni. *See* Ghazna.
Ghiyas-ud-din Tughluq, **1**:134b
Ghulab Singh, **1**:227a
Ghulam Ishaq Khan, **1**:295a, **4**:439b, **6**:218b
Ghulam Muhammad, **4**:433b
Ghulam Shah Kalhoro, **1**:282b–283a
ghulam (slave) system, **1**:453a–453b, 454a
Ghurids, **2**:434a, **3**:173b
Gia Long (emperor; Vietnam), **2**:227a, 488a, **4**:387a
Giap, Vo Nguyen. *See* Vo Nguyen Giap.
Gifu prefecture (Japan), **2**:434b
Gil, Fluvio, **2**:459a
Giles, H. A., **5**:95b
Gilgamesh, **2**:259a–259b
Gilgit (Pakistan), **4**:424a
Gillette, P. L., **5**:312b
ginseng, **2**:435a, **3**:299b
Ginzburg, Moisei, **2**:381a
Gion Matsuri (festival; Japan), **2**:435a–435b, 476a
Gir Forest National Park (India), **3**:476a–476b
Giscard d'Estaing, Valéry, **3**:232a
Gita Govinda (Sanskrit poems), **3**:23a
Gitanjali (Song Offerings; Tagore, R.), **3**:509a, **4**:531a
Giyanti, Treaty of (1755), **4**:84b
glaciers
  in Karadoram Mountains, **3**:b
  in Karakoram Mountains, **3**:318a, b
  See also Gangotri glacier (Himalayas); Zemu glacier (Himalayas)
glasnost (openness), **3**:344b, 432b
global economy
  Cambodia and, **1**:415b
  Central Asia and, **1**:467b

China and, **5**:171a
  cuisine of, **2**:188b–189a
  education system of, **1**:514b
clothing and, **2**:135b
Malaysia and, **4**:13a
  mineral industry, **4**:150a
overseas Chinese and, **2**:48b, 49a
South Korea and, **5**:285b
Southeast Asian agriculture and, **1**:61b
global warming, **2**:261a, **3**:43a, **5**:62b
  Maldives and, **4**:22a, 24a
Global Water Partnership (GWP), **6**:109b
globalization
  China and, **1**:507a
    education system of, **1**:516b
  of clothing, **2**:114a, 115a–115b
  in Japan
    cuisine and, **2**:200a
  Korean music and, **4**:231a
  languages and, **4**:192b
  Malaysia-EU relations and, **4**:19b
  mass media and, **4**:98a
  shamanism and, **5**:159a
  in Southeast Asia
    marriage and family and, **4**:65a, 68a
globefish (fugu), **2**:405b–406a
Gloria, Angela Manalang, **4**:538b
GMD. *See* Guomindang.
Gneist, Rudolf von, **3**:232b
Go-Komatsu (emperor; Japan), **3**:6a
Go-Sanjo (emperor; Japan), **2**:498a–498b
Goa (India), **1**:81a, **2**:435b–437b, **3**:531a
  churches in, **1**:436, **2**:436a, 436b
  Jesuits in, **3**:271a–271b
  printing in, **4**:530b
  trade in, **2**:210b
goats, **2**:437b–438a
  angora, **1**:65a, **2**:371a
  cashmere, **1**:436a–437a
  cheese from, **2**:437b
  felt from, **2**:370b, 371a
  in Filipino cuisine, **2**:208b
  as food, **1**:437a, **2**:185b, 186a
  in Iraq, **2**:196a
    cuisine and, **2**:196b
  milk from, **2**:186b
  in Mongolia, **4**:168a
Gobi Desert, **1**:69b, 70b, 88a, 428b, **2**:438a–438b, **4**:164b

cashmere industry and, **1**:436a, 436b
  in China, **2**:425a
  dinosaur fossils in, **2**:438b
  flora of, **2**:438b
  herding in, **4**:168a
  map of, *2:438a*
Gobind Singh, **4**:470a, **5**:205a–205b
God of Small Things, The (Roy), **3**:491a
Godaigo (emperor; Japan), **4**:215b, **5**:181a
Godan Khan, **1**:364b
Godavari River (India), **1**:102a, **2**:316a, **438b–439a**, **3**:10b, **4**:396b, 397a
Godber, P. F., **2**:179b
godparenthood (Philippines), **2**:439a–439b
Godse, Nathuram Vinayak, **2**:439b–440a
Godzilla (*Gojira*; film), **2**:95b
Goethe, **4**:480a
Goh Chok Tong, **1**:170a, **2**:353b, **440a–440b**
Goh Keng Swee, **2**:441a, **3**:473b
Goi Teru, **2**:241b
Gok (Tengri) belief system, **6**:11b
Gok-Tepe, battle of, **6**:12a
Gokalp, Ziya, **3**:516a
gold
  Lydia and, **5**:131b
  in Malaysia, **4**:150a–150b
Golden, Arthur, **2**:430b
Golden Crescent, **2**:441a–442a
Golden Horde, **2**:97a, **442a–442b**, **3**:342b, 367a, 480a, **4**:163b, 164b, 172b, 173a, 546b, **6**:54b, 198b
  Islam and, **3**:165a
  See also Edige
Golden Lotus. *See Jin ping mei.*
Golden Triangle, **1**:499b, **2**:441b, **442b–443a**, **4**:160b, 388b
Golkar (Joint Secretariat of Functional Groups; Indonesia), **3**:67b, 68a, 71a, 75b
Golkar Party (Golongan Karya; Indonesia), **2**:443a–443b, 472b
Golkonda, sultanate of (India), **5**:436a
Golodnaia Steppe Economic Region (Uzbekistan), **2**:462b
Golwalkar, M. S., **2**:518b
Gomes, Mariano, **1**:445b, **4**:505b
Gomes, Sebastiao, **2**:274b–275a
gompas (Sherpa dieties), *2:513b*
Gon Jerng (Mo Heing), **4**:161a

Hirohito (emperor; Japan), **2**:499b, 505a, 505b, **529a–530b**, *529b*, **5**:190a–190b, 191a, 193a, 193b, 377a, 378b
  Japanese constitution and, **2**:168a–168b
Hirosaki, **1**:114b
Hiroshi Kume, **4**:106b
Hiroshige, **5**:508a
Hiroshima (Japan), **2**:530b–531a, **3**:208b, **6**:167b
  U.S. bombing of, *2:530*, 530a, 531a, **3**:495b
Hiroshima Noto (Hiroshima Notes; Oe Kenzaburo), **3**:496a
Hiroshima Peace Memorial Park, **1**:147a, **4**:396a, **5**:416b
Hirsch, Emil, **1**:168a
Hisari, **5**:405b
Hisham Munir, **1**:156a
Hishida Shunso, **4**:331a
Hishikawa Moronobu, **5**:508a
Hisoris, **5**:401b
History. See *Shujing*.
History of England (Macaulay), **3**:533b
History of the Wei Dynasty (*Wei shu*; *Wei zhi*), **6**:190b
Hitachi (electronics firm), **2**:324a, 326a
Hitler, Adolph, **1**:312a, **2**:493b, **6**:164b
Hitome Kinue, **5**:311b
Hittite empire, **1**:126a
Hittite language
  written, **2**:532a–532b
Hittite people, **1**:31b, 35b, 90a, 96b, 124b, 1226a, **2**:429b, **531a–533a**, **3**:387a, **5**:556a, **6**:192b
  Cappadocia and, **1**:432b
Hizbul Muslimin party (Malaysia), **3**:162a
Hizbullah, **2**:533a–533b
Hkakabo Razi (mountain, Myanmar), **3**:298b
Hla Pe, Thaton, **4**:463a
Hmong (Meo) people, **2**:99b, 304a, **533b–535b**, **3**:443b, 446b, 526b
  clothing of, **2**:123a–123b, *123b*, 127a
  diaspora of, **2**:536a, **3**:447a, 455a
  in Laos, **4**:526a
  marriage and family of, **4**:67b–68a
  in Vietnam, **2**:138b, 139a
  in Vietnam War, **3**:454b
  See also Miao people

Hmong-Mien languages, **2**:535b–536a, **3**:452a
Hmoob Dawb (White Hmong), **2**:535b
Ho Bieu Chanh, **3**:519a
Ho Chi Minh, **1**:107b, 179b, 425b, **2**:488a, *536b*, **536b–537a**, 539b, **3**:34b, 48a, 463a–463b, *536b–537a*, **6**:74, 77b, 78a, 92b, 96a, 96b, 124b
  death of, **6**:76a, 97a
  Democratic Republic of Vietnam and, **2**:402b, **6**:69b
  end of World War II and, **1**:179b, **6**:77a
  on foreign dominance, **1**:179b
  in France, **6**:92a
  literacy campaigns of, **6**:65b
  mausoleum of, **6**:*73b*
  National Day speech of (1957), **6**:84
  North Vietnam and, **6**:73a
  Phan Boi Chau and, **4**:487b
  PRC and, **2**:42b
  Revolutionary Youth League and, **5**:83a–83b
  victory of, **4**:495a
  Viet Minh and, **2**:404a, **6**:77b, 83a
  Vietnamese Communism and, **2**:153a–154a
  Vietnamese Communist Party and, **2**:402a, **6**:73b, 75b
  World War I and, **6**:161a
Ho Chi Minh City (Saigon; Vietnam), **1**:179b, **2**:36a, *153*, 227a, **537a–538a**, **6**:62b, 66a, 72b, 86a, 86b, 88a, 97b
  cuisine of, **2**:*217b*, 220a
  fall of, **1**:426a, **6**:81a, 81b, 85a
  French capture of, **6**:69b, 77a
Ho Chi Minh Trail, **1**:305a, 425b, **2**:538a–539a, **3**:454b, **6**:*82a*, 83b
  map of, **2**:*538*
Ho dynasty Citadel (Vietnam), **2**:539a–539b
Ho dynasty (Vietnam), **2**:488a
Ho Guom (Sword Lake; Vietnam), **2**:487b
Ho Kyun, **3**:498b
Ho language, **4**:211a, 213b
Ho Nansorhon, **3**:498b
Ho Quy Ly, **2**:488a, 539a–539b
Ho Saeng chon (Tale of Ho Saeng; Pak Chi-won), **3**:499a
Ho Tay (West Lake; Vietnam), **2**:487b
Ho Tung Mau, **2**:539b

Ho Xuan Huong, **2**:540a, **3**:519a
Hoa Hao sect (Vietnam), **1**:431b, **2**:306b, **540a–540b**, **6**:90a
Hoan Kiem Lake, **2**:540b—541a, **5**:19a
Hoang Ngoc Phach, **2**:541a–541b, **3**:519a
Hoat, Doan Viet, **2**:541b
Hobhouse, L. T., **1**:517b
Hocart, A. M., **1**:440b
Hockings, Paul, **2**:524b
Hoei, Mount (Japan), **2**:406b
Hoi An (Vietnam), **2**:541b–542a
Hojo family (Japan), **3**:304b
Hojoki (An Account of My Hut; Kamo no Chomei), **3**:494a
Hokkaido Former Aborigines Protection Act (1899; Japan), **1**:72b–73a
Hokkaido (Japan), **1**:114a, **2**:352a, **542a–542b**, **3**:205a, 239b
  Ainu in, **1**:71a, 72a, 72b–73a, **5**:129b
  Japanese expansion and, **3**:259b
  Jomon period and, **3**:281a
Hokkien language, **1**:329b, **4**:475a, **5**:381b
Hokomat-e Eslami (Islamic Government;Khomeini), **3**:361a
Holi (festival; India), **2**:542b–543a
Holkar, Tukoji, **2**:543a
Holkar dynasty (India), **2**:543a–543b, **3**:76b
Homer, **2**:450a
homosexuality, **2**:543b–547b
  Ayurvedic medicine and, **4**:117b
  in China, **2**:545b–546a
  female, **2**:543b, 545b–546a, 546b
  in India, **2**:546a
  in Iran
    in film, **2**:94b
  in Japan, **2**:544b
  literature and, **2**:401a
Hon'ami Koetsu, **1**:405a
Honda Motor Company, **3**:261a
Honda Toshiaki, **5**:508a
Honen (founder of Pure Land Buddhism), **1**:344a, **2**:547b, **5**:182a–182b
Hong, Lady (Princess Hyegyong), **3**:391
Hong Bang dynasty (Vietnam), **6**:67a
Hong gaoliang jiazu (Red Sorghum; Mo Yan), **3**:487b
Hong Kil-dong chon (Tale of Hong Kil-dong; Ho Kyun), **3**:498b

Hugo, Victor, **4**:40a, **5**:533b
   Cao Dai and, **1**:431a
Hui (king; Chu kingdom), **4**:202b
Hui people, **2**:481b, 496b,
   560b–562a, *561*, **4**:244a,
   6:211b
Huichigadake, Mount (Japan),
   2:411a
Huie, Alice, **6**:191b
Huiguo, **2**:7a, 13b, **3**:409a
Huineng, **1**:336a
Huiyuan, **1**:351a
Huizong (emperor; China), **4**:412a
Huk Rebellion, **1**:115a,
   2:562a–562b, **4**:495a, 499a,
   508a–508b, 516a
Hukbalahap (People's Anti-Japan-
   ese Army; Philippines), **2**:562a
Hukbong Mapagpalaya ng Bayan
   (HMB; Philippines),
   2:562a–562b, **4**:516a
Hulegu (ruler; Mongol empire),
   1:215a, **4**:163b, 172b, 173a,
   532a
Hum aap ke hain kaun (film; Who
   Are We to You?), **2**:89b
human rights
   in Afghanistan, **1:25b–27b**
   Asia Pacific Region and, **5**:53b
   in Cambodia, **2**:565b
   in Central Asia, **1:455b–459a**,
      472b
   in China, **1:517a–520b**, 522b,
      2:27b
   China-U.S. relations and, **4**:38b
   devolution and, **5**:293a–293b
   EU and, **5**:559b–560a
   global, **1**:258a
   in India, **3**:20b–22a
   in Indonesia
      military and, **4**:145a
   in Iran, **1**:270b, **3**:98a,
      107b–110b, 182a, 182b,
      4:409b
   in Iraq, **3**:136b–138b, **4**:482a
   in Japan, **3**:222b–224a
   in Korea
      Christianity and, **2**:71a,
         71b–72a
      Malaysia-EU relations and,
         4:19b
   in Mongolia, **4**:167b, 179b
   in Myanmar, **4**:21a
   in Pakistan, **4:435a–436b**
   in Philippines, **4**:47b,
      509a–510b
   in Siberia, **5**:196a
   in Southeast Asia, **5**:290a–295b
   in Sri Lanka, **5**:326b, 331a

   in Taiwan, **5:384a–384b**
   in Tibet, **5**:492a
   in Turkish Republic, **4**:402b,
      5:543a, **549a–551b**, 565a
   UN Commissioner for (UN-
      HCHR)
      China and, **1**:520a
      comfort women issue and,
         2:145a
      Mongolia and, **4**:175a, 175b,
         176a–176b
      South Korea and, **5**:281a
   in USSR
      Semipalatinsk movement
         and, **5**:146b
   in Uzbekistan, **3**:324b, **4**:26b
   See also civil rights
Human Rights and Fundamental
   Freedoms, European Convention for the Protection of,
   5:549a, 550a, 551a
Human Rights (journal), **1**:517b
Human Rights Watch, **3**:482a,
   4:482a
   Iran and, **3**:108a, 110b
   Mongolia and, **4**:175a, 177a
   on refugees, **5**:64a
Humann, Carl, **4**:476b
Humay (queen; India), **5**:306b
Humayun-nameh (Gulbadan Begum), **6**:148a
Humayun (Nasin-ud-Din Muhammad; emperor; Mughal empire),
   1:77a, 135a, **2**:262b,
   562b–563a, **4**:206a–206b, 420b,
   6:148a
humor in Chinese history,
   2:563a–565a
Hun Sen, **1**:408b, 413a, 421a,
   421b, 422a, 422b, 428a, **2**:412b,
   503b–504a, **565a–565b**,
   3:565a–565b, **5**:55a
Hunan province (China), **2**:284b,
   566a, **6**:171a, 174b, 175a, 175b,
   176a, 209a, 209b, 215a
   cuisine of, **2**:191b
   governors of, **6**:210b
Hundred Days Reform (1898;
   China), **2**:86a, **566a–567a**,
   3:307b, 470b, **5**:28b
Hundred Flowers Campaign
   (China), **2**:150a, **567a–567b**,
   4:544a, **6**:215b
   human rights and, **4**:177a
Hung kings (Vietnam), **3**:436a
Hungary
   Mongol invasion of, **2**:442a
   Mongols and, **4**:163a
   Ottoman empire and, **4**:398b

Hungnam (North Korea), **2**:480a
Hungry Ghost Festival, **2**:*567b*,
   567b–568a
Huns
   invasions of Central Asia by,
      1:477a
   invasions of India by, **5**:429a
   See also Xiongnu
Hunza (Pakistan), **2:568a–568b**,
   4:*201*
Hurley, Patrick, **2**:29b
Hurri people (Anatolia), **2**:531b,
   532b
Husain ibn Ishaq, **4**:127a
Husain Muhammad Ershad,
   1:239a, 240b, 253a, 253b, 254a,
   257a
Husain Shahid Suhrawardy,
   1:198b, 251a, 251b, 253a
Husayn (third imam; son of 'Ali),
   3:312b, **4**:234b, 242a, 242b,
   5:75a
Huseyin Baykara, **3**:480b
Hushmand Fatheazam, **1**:219a
Hussain, Altaf, **4**:207b, 208a
Hussein, Saddam, **1**:156b, 216a,
   2:172a, **569a–570a**, **3**:361a,
   4:380b, 481a, 482a, 482b–483a,
   6:127a
Hussein, Shah (Sufi poet), **2**:528b,
   4:461b
Hussein, Sharif, **1**:215b
Hussein, Sultan (1438–1506),
   2:379b–380a
Hussein Onn (Tun Hussein bin
   Dato Onn), **2:568b–569a**,
   3:544b, **4**:385b
Huy-Can, **4**:541a
Huynh Phu So, **1**:368a, **2**:540a
Huynh Tan Phat, **2:570a–570b**
Hwang Chin-i, **3**:498b
Hwang Jang Yup, **2**:396b
Hwang Sog-yong, **3**:500b
Hwang Suk-young, **5**:281a
Hwang Sun-won, **2:570b–571a**,
   3:500a
Hwanung, **5**:367a
Hwaseong (Korea), **2**:61b
Hydaspes River, **3**:273a
Hyder Ali, **1**:106b, **4**:34b, **5**:502a,
   502b
Hyderabad (India), **1**:101b, 102a,
   106b, 235b, 283a, **2:571a–571b**,
   3:77b, 490a, **5**:436a
Hyegyong, Princess (Lady Hong;
   Korea), **3**:391, 499a
Hyogo (Japan), **2:571b–572b**
Hyojong (king; Korea), **6**:203a
Hyon Chin-gon, **3**:499b

"In the Beginning, Woman Was the Sun" (Hiratsuka Raicho), **2**:529a

In the Realm of the Senses (film; Oshima), **2**:92a–92b

Ince, Kamran, **4**:236a

Ince Memed (Memed, My Hawk; Kemal), **3**:347b, 517a

Ince Memed II (They Burn the Thistles;Kemal), **3**:347b

Inchon International Airport (South Korea), **3**:8b

Inchon (South Korea), **3:8b**, 419b, **5**:312b

   MacArthur at, **3**:533a

Indawgyi (lake, Myanmar), **3**:298b

La Independencia (Independence; newspaper), **2**:459a

India, **1**:18b, **3**:*9*, **9a–29a**, 43b

   agriculture in, **2**:227b, 424b, 460b, 461a, **3**:11b, 13a, 51a, 380b, 383b, 536a, 543b–544a, **4**:38b, 129a, 396b, 548a, **5**:181a, 207a, 410a, **6**:209a

      irrigation and, **2**:142b, 225b, 423b, **5**:17b

   AIDS in, **1**:67a, 67b, 68a, 68b

   air pollution in, **1**:74a, 74b

   airlines in, **5**:426a

   Anglo-French wars of, **2**:473b, **5**:261a–261b

   anti-Brahman movement in (1916–1940), **1**:440a

   architecture in, **1**:133a–136a, **133a–136a**

      See also Taj Mahal

   art of, **2**:51b–56b

      Gupta empire, **2**:51b, 53a, 53b

      Hinduism and, **2**:174b, 175a

      Mauryan, **2**:52a, 52b–53a, 54a

      medieval, **3**:24a, 24b

   ascetics in, **5**:156b

   Asian Games and, **1**:165b

   automobile industry in, **1**:193a, 195b–196a

   Ayurvedic medicine in, **4:116a–119b**

   baha'i in, **1**:218a

   Brahmanic period in, **1**:397a

   British East India Company and, **5**:261b

   Buddhism from, **2**:37a

   calendars in, **1:396b–397a**, 397b

   Cambodia and, **1**:418a

   caste in, **3**:11a, 508a

   Christianity in, **2:73a–75a**

   churches in, **2**:183b

      Cathedral of San Thome, **3**:536b

   cities in, **1**:65a–66a

   Civil Disobedience Movement in, **1**:83a, **5**:136a–136b

   climate of, **3**:10b, **4**:34a

   clothing in, **2:112b–115b**

   Colombo Plan and, **2**:143a

   constitution of, **2:165b–167a**, **3**:26a, 27a, 28a, **6**:118a

      on caste, **1**:441

      Christianity and, **2**:74b

      hill tribes and, **4**:129a

   conveyance arts in, **2**:172b–173b

   corruption in, **2**:176a, 177a, 177b, 178a–178b, 180a, **3**:20a

   cricket in, **2**:183b–184a

   culture of, **3**:13a–13b

   Dalai Lama in, **5**:489

   Dalits (downtrodden) in, **1**:239a, **5**:127a, **6**:36b, 37b

   dance drama in, **4**:39a

   dance in, **2:243b–245b**, **3**:383b, **5**:1a–1b

   diversity of, **3**:11a, 12a–12b

   dowries in, **6**:121a, 146a

   drama in, **2:287b—288a**

   earthquakes in, **2**:311b

   economic system of, **3**:11a, 13a, **14a–17b**, **6**:158b

      agriculture and, **3**:14b, 15a, 15b, 17a

      China-India relations and, **2**:4a, 4b

      companies in, **3**:14a

      Constitution and, **3**:15a

      corruption and, **3**:15b, 16a

      credit and, **3**:16a

      financial system and, **3**:15a, 16b

      foreign investment in, **2**:461a, **3**:16a–16b

      foreign trade and, **3**:15a, 16a, 16b

      gross domestic product and, **3**:14a

      gross national product and, **3**:14a

      health and, **3**:14b, 17a

      after independence, **3**:14b–15b

      under Indira Gandhi, **3**:15b

      industrial policy and, **3**:14b, 15a–17a

      industry and, **3**:14b, 15b

      infrastructure and, **3**:16b–17a

      literacy and, **3**:14b

      money lending in, **2**:461a

      Mumbai and, **4**:211a

      under Nehru, **3**:15a–15b

      poverty and, **3**:14b, 17a

      production and, **3**:14a–14b

      public-sector firms and, **3**:15a–15b, 16b

      under Rajiv Gandhi, **3**:15b, 16a

      reforms of, **3**:15a–17a

      rural sector and, **3**:14b, 15b, 17a

      under R.V.N. Rao, **3**:16a

      Soviet model and, **4**:79a

      technology sector and, **3**:16b

      urban sector and, **3**:14b, 15b

   education system of, **1**:514b, **3:17b–20b**, 28a

      agricultural universities in, **1**:56b

      Anglicists in, **3**:18b

      Brahmans and, **3**:17b

      before British colonization, **3**:17b–18a

      under British rule, **3**:17b, 18a–18b, 20a

      Christian missionaries and, **3**:18b

      gurukul (family of the teacher) and, **3**:17b

      Hindu tradtion in, **3**:17b, 18b

      after independence, **3**:20a–20b

      Indian culture and, **3**:17b–18a

      languages in, **3**:*18a*, 18b, 19, 28a

      leaders in, **5**:136b–137a

      literacy and, **3**:20b

      lower classes and, **3**:17b

      Muslim tradition in, **3**:17b–18b

      "national education" and, **3**:17b, 20a

      primary schooling in, **3**:20a–20b

      women and, **3**:17b

   emergency (1975) in, **2**:177a, 420a

   emigration of professionals from, **1**:441b–442a, **5**:267b–268a

   emigration of unskilled workers from, **5**:267a–267b

   endangered species in, **2**:330b

   English language in, **2**:336a, **3**:533b, **4**:110b, 531b

nonviolent resistance in, **1**:83a,
2:420a, 421a, 421b, 439b,
5:136a–136b
nuclear weapons and, **3**:13b,
4:368a–371b, 369
opium in, **4**:388a
overpopulation in, **3**:13b
painters in, **5**:115b
partition of, **1**:83a, 202b, 227a,
245b, 250b, **2**:2a, 422a,
491a–491b, **3**:11b, 94a, 94b,
351a, **4**:40a, 236b, 427b,
430a, **5**:16b, 18a, 262a–263b
people of, **3**:11a
pledge of national integration
in, **3**:12
poetry in, **4:530a–531b**
political system of, **3:25b–29a**,
4:300a–301a, 301b–302a
under A.B. Vajpayee, **3**:26b,
27b
caste and, **1**:442a–442b
Cold War and, **3**:28b
contemporary, **3**:13a–13b
decentralization of power
and, **3**:27a
degeneration of, **3**:27a
under Desai, **3**:25b–26a, 28b
evolution of, **3**:25b–27a
federalism in, **3**:27a–27b
foreign policy and,
3:28a–28b
Indian National Congress
party and, **3**:25a, 26a, 26b
under Indira Gandhi, **3**:25b,
26a, 28b
Israel and, **3**:28b
judiciary and, **3**:27b
law enforcement and,
3:26b–27a
literacy and, **3**:25b
media and, **3**:28a
National Democratic Al-
liance and, **3**:26b–27a
nonalignment policy and,
3:28a–28b, 41a
party system in, **3**:25b–27a
poverty and, **3**:27a
under P.V.N. Rao, **3**:26b
under Rajiv Gandhi, **3**:25b,
26a–26b
secularism and, **3**:28a
under Singh, V.P., **3**:26b
Soviet Union and, **3**:26b,
28b
trade and, **3**:28b
United States and, **3**:26b,
28b
women and, **3**:25b, 27a

population of, **3**:11a
ports in, **2**:469b
poverty in, **3**:11b, 27a
prime ministers of, **2**:419b–420a
profile of, **3:9a–13b**
Queen Victoria's Proclamation
of 1858 to, **1**:319a
railroads in, **3**:529a
religions in, **3**:11a
religious minorities in, **1**:440a,
3:198b
rivers in, **5**:361a
rocketry in, **2**:464b
Saka era in, **1**:397a
salt law in, **2**:421b
salt tax in, **5**:121a
sati/suttee in, **6**:145b–146a
sculpture in, **5**:*139b, 140a, 141,
142a*
separatist movements in, **2**:519b
sericulture in, **5**:150a
service sector in, **3**:11b, 13a
Sikkim and, **2**:424b
socialism and, **6**:120a
software industry in, **2**:506b,
4:111a
South Africa and, **5**:267a–267b
spice trade and, **5**:299b
sports in, **5**:304b–306a
Srivijaya and, **5**:332a
states of, **1**:498a
States Reorganization Act of
1956, **1**:101b, **2**:348b
storytelling in, **5**:337a, 337b,
338a
Tamil people from,
5:316a–316b
tea business in, **2**:469b, **5**:431b
television in, **4**:110b, 111
temples of, **4**:273b
textiles from, **2**:131b, 132b
tourism in, **2**:228a, 460b,
3:440b, 466a, 536a, **4**:548a
traditional medicine in, **4**:126a
tribes of, **2**:165b, **4**:38b, 87b
unifying, **3**:9a–9b, 12
universities in, **3**:18b, 20a,
6:58b
for women, **2**:571a
untouchables in, **3**:21a, 21b
Urdu speakers in, **2**:516b
Vasco da Gama and,
2:417a–417b, **5**:261a
Vedic Sanskrit in, **1**:162a,
2:491b
Vikrama era in, **1**:397a
women in, **1**:323a, **2**:518a,
6:*119b*, 120b–121a, 143a
in art, **2**:54b

clothing of, **2**:113b–114a
constitution and, **2**:166a
education of, **2**:166a
rights of, **2**:518a, **6**:147
as writers, **2**:82b–83a
See also Agartala; Agra; Ajanta;
Allahabad; Andhra Pradesh;
Bangladesh-India relations;
British Indian Empire;
British Indian empire;
China-India relations; cin-
ema: in India; Mughal em-
pire; Muslim League
India-Myanmar (Burma) relations,
3:29a–30b, **4**:256b
ASEAN and, **3**:30a–30b
China and, **3**:30a, 30b
common border and, **3**:29b, 30a
estrangement of, **3**:29b
Gandhi, R. and, **3**:29b
Great Britain and, **3**:29a
"Memorandum of Understand-
ing" and, **3**:29b
Pakistan and, **3**:30a
pro-democracy movement and,
3:29b
ties between, **3**:29a–29b
India-Myanmar relations
smuggling and, **3**:29b, 30b
India-Pakistan relations, **1**:1:203a,
4b–5a, 203a, 204a, 247a, 248a,
250a, 324a, **2**:420a, **3**:13b, 30a,
30b–33b, 318b, **4**:430a,
5:262a–263b
1965 war and, **1**:248a, **4**:434a
1970 war and, **4**:434a
China and, **3**:33b
Cold War and, **3**:32a
Indian cessions to, **1**:172b, 173b
Indian National Congress party
resolution on (1950), **3**:31
Japan and, **3**:33a
Kashmir and, **3**:30b, 32a, 32b
muhajir and, **4**:207a–208a
nuclear weapons and, **3**:30b,
33a–33b
partition of India and, **2**:422a
post-Shimla Accord, **3**:32b–33a
separation from India (1947),
1:227a
Shimla Accord and, **3**:32b
Soviet Union and, **3**:32a
terrorism and, **3**:*32b*, 33a, 33b
U.S. and, **3**:32a, 33a
war and, **3**:203a–203b
war with India (1965), **1**:199b,
200b
wars between, **3**:30b
See also India-Pakistan relations

Caspian Sea and, **1**:437a, 437b
censorship in, **4**:98b
Central Asia and, **1**:43a, 93a
Central Asian music and,
  4:219a, 219b
China-India relations and, **2**:3b
China-U.S. relations and, **2**:27b
Christianity in, **2**:63a
cinema in, **2**:*93*, 94a–94b
cities in, **3**:95b–96a
constitution of, **3**:96b, 97a, 97b,
  107a, 108b, 109b, 111a, 112,
  183a
Constitutional Revolution
  (1905–1911) in, **1**:218b,
  4:115a, **6**:126b
cuisine of, **2:194b–196a**
currency in, **3**:101b
drug trade and, **2**:304b
economic system of,
  3:98b–102a
    construction industry and,
      3:101a
    diversification in, **3**:98a, 99a,
      100a
    future of, **3**:101b–102a
    historical perspective on,
      3:99a–100a
    hostage crisis (1979–1981)
      and, **3**:99b–100a
    industry and, **3**:100a–100b
    internal debate about, **3**:99a
    Islamic Republic and,
      3:99a–100a
    manufacturing and, **3**:101a
    mining and, **3**:101a
    natural resources and, **3**:99a
    telecommunications and,
      3:101a
    transportation and, **3**:100b
    U.S. trade embargo and,
      3:99a, 100b
education system in, **3**:98a,
  102a–103b
    cycles of, **3**:102a
    higher, **3**:102a, 103a–103b
    after Islamic revolution,
      3:103a–103b
    before Islamic revolution,
      3:102b–103a
    secular, **3**:102b, 103a, 182a
    women and, **3**:102a, 103a,
      182a
ethnic groups in, **2**:194b, **3**:96a
exports of, **3**:100b
faqih (spritual leader of the nation) in, **3**:97a, 107a, 107b,
  111a
    See also *veleyet-e-faqih*

fishing industry in, **3**:101a
Genghis Khan and, **2**:431a
government of
    constitution and,
      2:167a–167b
    Islam and, **3**:97a, 97b
history, timeline of, **3**:**104**
history of, **3:103b–107b**, *106a*,
  545a, **5**:158a
    ancient, **3**:103b–105b
    Arab conquest and,
      3:104b–105a
    Constitutional Revolution
      and, **3**:106a–106b
    Islamic Republic and,
      3:96a–96b, 107a–107b,
      112
    modern, **3**:105b–107b
    Mongol conquest and,
      3:105a
    Pahlavi dynasty and,
      3:106b–107a
    Safavid dynasty and,
      3:105a–105b
    Seleucid and Sasanid dynas-
      ties in, **3**:104a–104b
    See also Qajar Dynasty
human rights in, **3**:98a,
  107b–110b
    court system and,
      3:108b–109a
    freedom of assembly and,
      3:109a–109b
    freedom of expression and,
      3:109a, 113a, 114a, 114b
    Human Rights Association,
      1:270b
    in Islamic Republic,
      3:108a–110b
    under Pahlavi monarchy,
      3:107b, 182a, 182b
    political dissidents and,
      3:108a–108b, *113a*
    political rights and, **3**:110a
    privacy rights and,
      3:109a–109b
    religious freedom and,
      3:109b–110a
    torture and, **3**:108a–108b
    of women, **3**:110a–110b
Il-Khanid period, **1**:138b
imports of, **3**:100b
Indian music and, **4**:222b, 225a,
  226a
intellectuals in, **5**:174a–174b
invasions of, **2**:478b–479a
Islam in
    government and, **3**:97a
    introduction of, **3**:176a

modern, **3**:178b–179a
    Muslim saints' shrines, **4**:239b
    society and, **3**:97b–98a
Islamic constitution of,
  2:167a–167b
Islamic Republic of, **3**:361a,
  5:35b, **6**:126b
    creation of, **3**:96a–96b
    opium production and,
      2:441b
Ismailis in, **3**:185b
Kurds in, **2**:94a, **3**:116a
languages of, **1**:222b, 366b,
  367a, 475b, 476a, **2**:366a,
  3:97a, **4**:479a
literacy in, **3**:*102b*, 103a
literature of, **3**:97a,
  5:157b–158a
map of, **3**:*96*
marriage and family in, **4**:75b
measurement systems in, **4**:93b,
  94a
media in, **3**:100b–101a, 109a,
  113a, 114b, **4**:98b,
  114b–115b
military in, **3**:114a, 119b
miniature painting in, **4**:483b,
  5:188a, 188b
Mongols and, **2**:59a–59b,
  4:172a, 172b, 173a, 188b
mountains in, **4**:199b, **6**:207a
Mughal empire and, **4**:206b
music in, **4**:234b
nationalism in, **3**:106b, 182a
nationalist movement
  (1951–1953), **6**:126b
nomads in, **1**:222b–223a,
  3:364b
nuclear weapons and, **4**:368a,
  369b, 370a, 371b
oil in, **3**:365b–366a
oil industry in, **3**:98a, 98b, 99b,
  100a, 101b, **4**:379b–380b
    Iraq and, **3**:115a–115b
    nationalization of, **3**:106b,
      182a
    before W.W.II, **3**:99a
opium production in,
  2:441a–441b, 443a
political system of,
  3:110b–114b
    civil service and, **3**:114a
    executive branch and, **3**:111b
    freedom of the press and,
      3:113a, 114a
    Islamic law and, **3**:110b–111a
    judiciary and, **3**:113a
    legislative branch and,
      3:111b–113a

in India, **1**:356b, **4**:34b, 85a,
85b, **5**:410b
sculpture and, **5**:139b
Indian music and, **4**:226b
literature of, **3**:490a
manuscripts of, **4**:419b
marriage and, **4**:68b
vegetarianism and, **3**:198b
Jains
marriage of, **4**:68b
Jaintia people (India), **4**:129a
Jaipal Singh, **3**:272b
Jaipur (India), **3**:**199a–199b**, **5**:46b
Jakarta (Batavia; Indonesia),
1:224b, 233a, **267b–268a**, 326a,
2:228b, 252b, 308a, **3**:63a, 71b,
199b–200a, 200a, 267b, 268a,
4:384a, **6**:34b, 35a
air pollution in, **1**:73b
Dutch East India Company
and, **2**:142a
music in, **2**:417b–418a
popular theater in, **2**:417b
spice trade and, **4**:5b
theater in, **5**:85a
Jakarta Riots (May 1998),
3:**b200a–200b**
See also New Order; Suharto
Jalal al-Din Khwarazmshah, **2**:59b
Jalalabad (Pakistan), **1**:22a
Jalandoni, Magdalena, **3**:506b
Jallianwala Bagh Massacre (1919;
Amritsar, India), **1**:92b
Jam Mizam al-Din, **3**:547b
Jama al-Din al Afghani, **5**:22b–23a
Jamaʿat-e-Islami (JI), **1**:253b, 254a,
469a, **2**:343b, 344a,
3:**200b–201b**, **4**:89b, *437b*
Jamal Effendi, **1**:218b
Jamal ul Kiram II, **4**:507a
James I (king; England), **2**:494a
Jami, ʿAbdurrahman, **1**:110b,
3:**201b–202a**
Jamiat-ul-Ulema, **3**:353b
Jamil Sidqi al-Zahawi, **4**:532b
Jammu and Kashmir, **1**:5a, **2**:280b,
3:26b, 27a–27b, 32a,
202a–204b, **4**:460a
map of, **3**:*203b*
Jammu and Kashmir Disturbed
Areas Act, **3**:21a
Jamnagar (India), **2**:460a
Jamtar Mantar observatory (Jaipur,
India), **3**:199b
Jan Beg Tarkhan, **3**:547b
Janakiraman, T., **3**:492b
janapadas (tribal republics; India),
2:*512a*
Janata Party (India), **3**:25b, 26b

Janata Vimukti Peramuna (JVP;
People's Liberation Front; Sri
Lanka), **5**:326b, 327a, 331a
Janes, Leroy Lansing (1838–1909),
2:318a
Janid dynasty (Central Asia),
1:460b
Janmashtami (festival; India),
2:460b
Japan, **1**:1a
1960s economic growth in, **3**:5b
academic competition in, **3**:5a
agriculture in, **2**:81b, 83a, 463a,
502a–502b, 531a, **3**:1b, 150b,
190b, 206b, 214a–214b,
378a, 382b, **4**:143a, 143b,
155b, 156a, 284b, 381b,
5:117a, 179a, 180b, 181a,
504a–504b, **6**:189b
air pollution in, **1**:74b
Allied Occupation of, **2**:11b,
34a, 69a, 493b, 505b,
530a–530b, **4**:95a
comfort women and, **2**:143b
constitution and,
2:167b–168b
democracy and, **5**:280b
end of, **5**:123b
Japanese cinema and, **2**:91a,
91b–92a
media and, **4**:106b
Shinto and, **5**:183b
Showa Denko scandal and,
5:189b–190a
ancestor worship in, **1**:97b, 98b,
99b
archeological remains in,
2:572b, **4**:284a–284b
architectural decoration in,
1:127b
architecture in, **1**:140b–143a,
140b–143a, 142a,
145a–148a, **145a–148a**,
2:434b
ancient period, **1**:140b–141b
architects in postwar,
1:147a–148b
Buddhist influence,
1:141b–142b
Bunri-ha (Secessionist
School) and, **1**:145b
castles in, **1**:142b–143a,
3:190a, **4**:276a
Imperial Roof Style in,
1:145b
Momoyama period,
1:142b–143a
Shinto, **1**:141b
sukiya style in, **1**:145b

taisha-zukuri (great-shrine
building) style in,
3:192a–192b
Tokugawa period, **1**:143a
traditional, **3**:150b
variety of, **1**:141
Western-style, **5**:428a
aristocracy of, **2**:497b–498a
Asian Games and, **1**:165b
Australia and, **1**:185a
automobile industry in, **1**:192b,
194b–195b
unveiling of Isuzu model
Z.E.N., **1**:197a
Axis Pact and, **3**:260a
banking industry in, **2**:319a,
500b, **3**:212b–213a, 213b,
214a, 215b–216b, 264a,
4:401a, 401b, **5**:178b
banking crisis (1990s), **3**:216a
financial crisis (1927) and,
2:378a
Meiji period, **4**:134a
baseball in, **1**:**263b–264b**
early years of, **1**:263b–264a
popularity in Japan,
1:264a–264b
U.S. and, **1**:264a
big bang reforms in, **3**:216a
bilateral diplomacy by, **3**:240b
bilateral friendship associations
in Africa of, **3**:*231a*
Boshin Civil War in, **6**:189a
British model and, **4**:132b
"Bubble Economy" in, **5**:193a
bullying (*ijime*) in, **3**:5a
business entertainment in,
5:154a
business in, **5**:154a
Confucianism and, **5**:178b
business philosophy of, **3**:249b
calendar in, **1**:395b
capitalism in, **3**:213a–214a
carpets in, **2**:372b
Central Asian music and,
4:219b
ceramics of, **1**:**478b–482a**
Children's Day in,
1:**500a–500b**, **5**:184b
Christianity in, **2**:67a–70a, *69b*,
3:309a, **6**:19a
chrysanthemum in, **2**:79a–80a
Chrysanthemum throne and,
2:529b
civil wars of 1867–1868, **6**:183a
climate of, **2**:552a–552b, **5**:116a,
153b
clothing in, **2**:108b, **118b–120a**,
4:*229*

Imperial Japanese Army (IJA) in, **1**:382b
Imperial Way faction (Kodoha) in, **1**:121a
imperialism of, **3**:223b
income distribution in, **3**:210b
in India, **4**:38b
India-Pakistan relations and, **3**:33a
Indo-U.K. relations and, **3**:37b
Indochina and, **1**:211b–212a, **6**:162b
in Indonesia, **2**:533a, 554b, **3**:56a, 302b, 550b–551a
military and, **4**:144b
Indonesia and, **2**:431b, **3**:157b
industry in, **1**:499b, 500a, **2**:434b, **3**:1b–2a, 378a, 382b, **4**:276a, 277b, 278, 284b, 331b, **5**:179a, 180b
industrial zones, **1**:66b, **2**:463a, **3**:378a
industrialization and, **5**:443b
silk production in, **2**:462b
influence on Korean sports of, **5**:312a, 312b
interior design in, **4**:61
invasion of China by, **1**:493b, **2**:530a, **4**:447a, 470b, **5**:9b, 191a, 484a
invasion of Myanmar and, **4**:264a
invasion of Southeast Asia, **1**:185a, **4**:248a, 249b
invasion of Thailand by, **5**:462a
IT and, **3**:82b, 85a–86a
jusen scandel in, **2**:500b
Kabo reforms and, **6**:141a
kites in, **3**:380b
in Korea, **3**:235, **4**:537a
Korea-Japan Treaty of 1965 and, **3:395a–395b**
Korea-U.S. relations and, **5**:286b
Koreans in, **5**:193a
labor unions in
wages and, **5**:193b–194b
land prices in, **3**:210b
in Laos, **3**:444b, 453a
laquerware in, **3**:436b, 438a
largest companies of, **3**:212
leaders of, **5**:119b–120a, 135a–136a
legal profession in, **3**:222a–223a
legal system of
SOFA and, **5**:335a
Liberal Democratic Party (LDP) and, **3**:471b–472a
literacy in, **3**:265a, **4**:98a

literature in, **3**:150a, **493a–497a**
See also Kawabata Yasunari
Manchuria and, **3**:245, 534a, **4**:106b, **6**:160a, 162a
Manchurian Incident (1931) and, **4**:29a–29b
map of, **3**:207
marriage and family in, **4**:57a–62a
martial arts in, **1**:69a, **3**:1a
masks in, **4**:81b, 82a
Matsumae clan in, **1**:72b
May Fourth Movement and, **2**:31a
measurement systems in, **4**:94b, 95a
media in, **4**:98a, **105a–107b**
China and, **4**:101a
Mencius in, **4**:140a
militarism in
China-Japan relations and, **2**:11a
education and, **3**:7b–8a
militarism of, **2**:490a, 497a, 498a–498b, 530a, **5**:183b
China-Japan relations and, **2**:11a
education and, **3**:7b–8a
military in, **3**:386b, **5**:190b, 191a, 191b, 192a, 193a
Ministry of International Trade and Industry (MITI), **2**:359b
minority groups in, **1**:70b–73a
Mitsubishi shipyards, **4**:277b
modern
economy of, **2**:499b–502b
invasion of Southeast Asia, **2**:475b
Liberal Democratic Party (LDP) and, **3**:471b–472a
money in, **3**:211
money system in, **3**:211, **224a–224b**
mountaineering and, **4**:201a
mountains in, **2**:552a, **3**:205b–206a, **4**:199b
music of, **2**:182b, 494b, **4**:228b–231a**, 229, **5**:158a–158b, **6**:41a–41b
instruments, **5**:163b
utai, **6**:41a–42a**
See also karaoke
in Myanmar, **4**:264a, **5**:164a
nationalism in, **3**:383a, **4**:195a
neoclassical economists in, **3**:215a–215b
New Zealand and, **4**:323b–325a
nihonga art in, **4**:330b–331a
Noh-Kyogen theatre in and, **4**:337a–338a, *337b*

nuclear weapons and, **4**:368a, 369b, 370a–371b
Obon Festival in, **5**:69b–70a
oil and gas reserves in, **4**:331b
Olympics and, **4**:384a–384b
opium trade in, **4**:388aa–b
painters in, **1**:376b–377a, **4**:330b–331a
painting in, **1**:376b–377a, **4**:330b–331a, **414a–417b**
See also emakimono
parks in, **2**:572b, **4**:143b, **5**:120b, 130a, 153b
people of, **3**:206a
pilgrimage sites in, **4**:276a
poetry in, **4**:533a–535b**
political reform in, **2**:501a–501b
political system of, **2**:444b–445a, 493b, **3**:224b–228b**, 383a
analyses of, **4**:78a
Chinese influence and, **2**:6a, 6b
Diet, **3**:226b, 227b, 228a, 257a, 257b
Jiyu-to (Liberal Party) in, **1**:210a
media and, **4**:106b–107a
Nihon Shakaito (Japan Communist Party), **5**:377a
Seiyukai (Friends of Government Party) in, **5**:377a
Shakaishugi Doumei (Japanese Socialisti League) in, **5**:377a
See also Japanese expansion; Meiji period; Showa period; Taisho period
pollution in, **1**:500a, **3**:210b, **5**:193a
population resettlement in, **5**:130a
porcelain of, **4**:549a–549b**
postwar recovery of, **2**:530a–530b
pottery in, **3**:279b–280a
prefectures of, **1**:499b–500a
pressure to achieve in, **3**:217
prime ministers of, **3**:5b–6a, 7b, 379b–380a, 383a, 386a–386b, **5**:189b, 192b
real estate in, **3**:209a
rearmament of, **3**:6a
recesssion in, **2**:500b–501a
rice production and, **2**:502a–502b
right-wing leaders in, **5**:134b
ringi system in, **5**:90b–91b**
rocketry in, **2**:464b

art and architecture of,
3:329a

religions of, 3:328b

the Shah kings and Rana era of,
3:329a–329b

trade routes through,
3:328a–328b

Katip Celebi, 5:123a

Katipunan (Philippine revolutionary organization), 3:505b

Kato Kiyomasa, 3:410a

Kato Takaaki, 3:329b–330a,
5:377b

Kato Tomosaburo, 5:377b

Katsuhika Hokusai, 5:508a

Katsumi Jiro, 2:407a

Katsura: Tradition and Creation in Japanese architecture (Gropius),
1:146

Katsura Taro, 3:227a, 6:183a

Katyayana, 4:460a

Kaufman, K. P. von, 1:470a

Kautilya (Indian author), 2:1a,
517a–517b, 3:330a, 489a

Kaveri River (Cauvery;India),
2:316a, 3:10b, 330a–330b,
5:409b

falls of the, 3:330b

islands of, 3:330b

Kavirajamarga, 3:490a

Kavsilumina, 3:512a

Kawabata Yasunari, 2:408a,
3:330b–331a, 495b, 5:378a

Kawagoe (Japan), 5:120b

Kawaguchi, Lake, 2:407a

Kawaguchi, M., 2:68

Kawai, Kanjiro, 1:481a

Kawakami Hajime, 2:365a, 410a

Kawakami Otojiro, 2:288a–288b

Kawasaki, 3:331a–b

Kawasaki Shozo, 3:331a

Kawase Naomi, 2:96b

Kawatake Mokuami, 3:294a

Kawi Kanmuang (Kawi Srisayam).
See Phumisak, Chit.

Kaya, Ahmet, 4:234a

Kayah (Karenni) state (Myanmar),
2:344b, 3:89a, 331b–332a

ethnic groups in, 3:331b

history of, 3:331b

natural resources of, 3:332a

political system of, 3:332a

population of, 3:331b

Kayin state. *See* Karen state.

Kaymakli (Cappadocia, Turkey),
1:432b

Kaysone Phomvihan, 2:50a,
3:332a–332b, 442b, 443a,
454b, 455b, 457a

Kazak (Kazakh newspaper), 1:221a,
304a, 3:332b–333a

Kazakh horde. *See* Kazakh people.

Kazakh language, 1:66a, 456b,
474a, 475b

poetry of, 3:546a, 547a

Kazakh people, 1:66a, 70b, 88a,
88b, 221a–221b, 2:306a,
3:333b–335b, 411a–411b,
4:371b

carpets of, 1:435b, 3:335a

in China, 4:244a

diaspora of, 3:333b, 334b–335a

discrimination against, 1:464a

epics of, 1:86a, 2:320b

folklore of, 1:393a

impact of Soviet culture on,
3:335a

Karakalpaks ("black hat people") and, 4:371b

Khiva khanate and, 1:461b

leaders of, 3:411a

literature of, 3:335a

in Mongolia, 4:164b

Islam and, 3:165b–166a

music of, 3:382a

nomadic, 4:340a–340b

nomadic pastoralism and,
3:333b, 335a

political confederations of,
1:459b–460a

Quqon khanate and, 1:461a,
5:39a

religion of, 3:333b, 335a

Russia and, 1:461b, 462b, 463a

the Russian/Soviet periods,
3:334a–334a

effect of colonization program and, 3:334a–334b

population decline and,
3:334b

Soviet Union and, 5:531b

tribal groups of, 3:334a, 335a,
342b

uprising of, 5:372a

Kazakh SSR Communist Youth
Group, 3:466a–466b

Kazakh Uplands (Kazakhstan),
3:333a–333b

natural resources of, 3:333a

rivers of, 3:333a

Kazakhstan, 1:41b, 42a, 44b, 85a,
93b, 174b–175a, 175a, 2:306b,
4:297b–298a, 5:0

agriculture in, 3:149a, 6:107b

Altay Mountains in, 1:88a, *88a*

Aral Sea and, 1:121b, 6:106b

camels in, 1:428a, 429a

Caspian Sea and, 1:437a, 437b

Central Asia-Russia relations
and, 1:470a

Central Asian separatist movements and, 1:469b

China and, 1:468b, 469a, 2:19b

Christianity in, 2:63b, *64a*

CIS and, 1:472b, 473a, 3:343b

clans in, 1:477a

See also Kazakh people: tribal
groups of

climate of, 3:335b

collectivization of agriculture
in, 3:337a

Communism in, 2:147a, 147b,
4:297b–298a

Communist Party of, 1:85a,
3:345b

cuisine of, 2:186a, 186b, 187a

disease in, 3:346a

economic system of, 1:456a,
3:338a–340a, 346a

agriculture and, 3:339b

banking and, 3:339b

early, 1:460a

post-Soviet financial crisis,
3:338b

privatization and, 3:339a, b

production of raw materials
and, 3:338a, 339a

security market and, 3:339b

education system of, 3:338b,
340a–341b

constitution and, 3:340b

post-Soviet, 3:341a

under Soviets, 3:340a

structure of, 3:340b

energy in, 2:331b–334a

ethnic groups in, 1:456b,
3:335b, 341b

Europe and, 6:114b

falconry in, 2:254a

geography of, 3:335b

German settlers in, 2:432a

history, timeline of, 3:342

history of, 3:336b–337b,
341b–344a

Kara Kitai in, 1:454b

Mongol era in and,
3:342b–343a

post-Soviet era in and,
3:343b–344a

Russian conquest of,
1:459b–460a, 3:343a

Soviet era in and,
3:343a–343b

tribal confederations in,
3:312b

Turkic era in and,
3:341b–342a

Kim Yu-jong, 3:500a
Kim Yu-sin, **3:376a–376b**, 6:24b
Kim Yuk, **1**:396a
Kimak Turks, 3:342a
kimchi (pickled cabbage; Korea), *2:202*, 202a–202b, 203
kimono (Japanese garment), 2:118b, 119b, 129b
Kimura Yuriko, 2:243a
Kinabalu, Mount (Malaysia), **1**:307b, **3:376b–377b**, *377*
Kinabalu National Park (Malaysia), 3:377a
Kinchenjunga, Mount. *See* Kangchenjunga, Mount.
King, Martin Luther, Jr., 5:136b, 475a, 6:80a
King and I, The (film), 2:83b, 4:162a
Kinh-Vietnamese people, 1:478a–478b, 6:86b
Kinki Region (Japan), **3:377b–378a**
Kinoshita Junji, 2:289a, 3:496b
Kinoshita Keisuke, 2:92a
kinship
  Central Asian regionalism and, 1:477a–477b
  joint families, 4:69a–70a
  in Korea
    chaebol and, 1:483a, 484b
  Miao, 4:142a–142b
  in Mongolia, 4:171b
  overseas Chinese and, 2:48b–49a
  in Philippines, **2:439a–439b**
  in Southeast Asia, 4:62b–63a, 66b
  of Tai people, 4:203b
  See also marriage and family; matrilineality
Kinugasa Teinosuke, 2:90a
KIO. *See* Kachin people: Kachin Independence Organization.
Kipchak language, 1:475a, 475b, 486a, 3:421a, 425a, 5:427a
Kipchak people, 1:455a, 3:342a, 4:163a, 5:39a
Kipling, Joseph Rudyard, 2:446b, 491b, 3:296b, **378a–378b**, *378b*, 491a, 4:190b
  on Calcutta, 1:394b
Kiranti languages (Nepal), 5:234b–236a
Kirghiz language, 2:367b
Kirghizia, 3:424a
"Kirgizy" (The Kazakhs; Bokeikhanov), 1:304a
Kirishima-Yaku National Park (Japan), 3:301a

Kiritamati Island
  nuclear monitoring on, 3:241a
Kiriyama Seiyu, 5:72b
Kirk Kiz, 3:479b
Kirkpinar Festival (Edirne, Turkey), 2:321b
Kirkuk (Iraq), 3:80a, 124b, **378b–379b**
Kisakurek, Necip Fazil, 3:516b
Kisegawa River (Japan), 2:407a
Kishi Nobusuke, **3:379b–380a**, 5:135b, 187b
Kishida Kunio, 3:496b
Kishida Toshiko, 2:409a, 5:192b
kishlak, **3:380a**
Kisogawa River (Japan), 2:434b
Kissinger, Henry, 2:11b, 3:250a, 464b, 6:80b, 81a, 85a
  China-U.S. relations and, 2:26b, 5:391b
Kistna River, 2:316a, **3:380b**, 5:537a
Kita-Kyushuy Industrial Area (Japan), 3:434b
Kitab-i Dede Qorqut (Book of Grandfather Qorqut), 2:392b
  See also *Gorkut Ata*
Kitabatake Chikafusa, 6:184b
Kitabi Aqdas (Most Holy Book; Bahaullah), 1:218a–218b
Kitagawa, Joseph, 1:342b
Kitagawa Utamaro, 5:508a
Kitan political group (China), 3:290b, 291a
Kitchener, Lord, 2:225b
kites and kite flying, **3:380b–381b**, *381b*
  in China, 5:302a
  in Korea, 3:381a, 5:312b
Kitingan, Joseph Pairin, 1:308b
Kittikhachorn, Thanom, 4:375b, 5:463a, 464a, 465b, 467b, 6:25a
Kiyayi Maja, 3:269b
Kiyoura Keigo, 5:377b
Kizel Irmak River, **3:381b–382a**
Kizudarake (Song of the Bruised and Battered; Fujisawa Takeo), 2:408a
Kkunley, Drukpa, 1:293b
Klaproth, Heinrich Julius, 4:393b
Klunggkung court (Bali), 6:112b
Knight in the Panther's Skin (Rustaveli), 1:449b
KNU. *See* Karen National Union.
Ko-Fuji, 2:406b
Ko Un, 3:500b, 4:537a
Kobayashi Hideo, 2:351b
Kobayashi Issa, 4:534b
Kobayashi Masaki, 2:90b, 92a

Kobe (Japan)
  earthquake in, *2:311*, 313a, 499b, 502b, 572a
Kobe University (Japan), 2:572b
kobyz, **3:382a–382b**
Koch, C. J., 6:122b
Kochi prefecture (Japan), **3:382b**
Kodai Andal, 6:146a
Kodama Gentaro, 5:411b
Kodama Yoshio, **3:382b–383b**
Koenigsberger, Otto, 1:284b
Koenigswald, Ralph von, 4:453a
Kofun period (Japan), 3:410a, 4:143a, 414a–414b, 6:190b
  artifacts from, 5:509a
  tomb mounds from, 5:514a
Koguryo kingdom (Korea), 1:345a, 2:60b, 289b, 3:376a–376b, 387b, 389a, 400b, 404b, 405a, 4:464a, 5:20a–20b, 479a, 479b, 6:24a, 24b, 26a
  architecture in, 1:144a
  ceramics of, 1:482b
  Chinese influence on, 2:37a, 37b, 4:535b–536a
  Confucianism in, 2:162b
  Later, 6:26b
  painting in, 4:417b
  relics from, 5:269b
  sports in, 5:312a
  Sui dynasty and, 5:348b–349a
  Tang China and, 5:480a
  Taoism in, 5:422a
  wrestling in, 5:332b, 333a
Kohima (India), **3:383b**
Koimala Kalo legend (Maldives), 4:24b
Koizumi, Junichiro, 2:501b–502a, 3:247b, 257b–258a, 4:107a
Kojiki (Record of Ancient Matters; Japan), 2:5b, 3:493a, 4:199a, 285a–285b, 533b, 5:183a, 183b, 184a, 6:127b
  Confucianism and, 2:161b
Kojinteki no kaiken (A Personal Matter; Oe Kenzaburo), 3:495b
Kojong (king; Korea), 4:47a, 6:194b
  education and, 5:277a
Kok-Gumbez Mosque, 3:326b
Kokand, 5:396a
  Fergana valley and, 2:375a
Kokbarak language, 1:37a
Kokinwakashu (Collection of Ancient and Modern Poems; Ki no Tsurayuki), 3:493b, 4:533b, 534a
Kokka (scholarly art journal), 6:196b

Kyrgyz Committee for Human
Rights, **1**:457a
Kyrgyz-Kazakh nomads,
4:340a–340b
Kyrgyz language, **1**:474a, 475b,
3:421a, 428b
Kyrgyz people, **3**:362a, 415a,
421a–423a, 423b, 425a–425b,
4:458a, **6**:17a, 22a, 100b
carpets of, **1**:435b
folklore of, **1**:393a
literature of, **3**:478b
Quqon khanate and, **1**:461a
Russia and, **1**:461a
Kyrgyz Turkish Manas University,
3:429a
Kyrgyzstan, **1**:41b, 42a, 44b, 75a,
76b, **2**:306b, **4**:398a, **6**:17a
Aksakal courts and, **1**:79a
Aral Sea and, **1**:121b
architecture in, **1**:128a
Central Asia-Russia relations
and, **1**:470a
Central Asian separtist movements and, **1**:469b
China and, **1**:468b, 469a, **2**:19b
Christianity in, **2**:63b, 64a, 64b
CIS and, **1**:472b, 473a
clans in, **1**:477a
clothing in, **2**:121b–122a
constitution of, **4**:99b
cuisine of, **2**:186a, 186b, 187a
dams in, **2**:375a
economic system of,
3:426a–428a, 430b–431a
education system of,
3:428a–429b
energy in, **2**:331b–334a
history of, **3**:429b–432a
human rights in, **1**:455b,
456b–457b
Koreans in, **3**:401a
languages of, **1**:474a
Manas epic of, **2**:395a, **3**:422a,
425b, **4**:26b–27a, **6**:57a
map of, **3**:424
marriage and family in, **4**:49b
media in, **4**:99b
mineral deposits in, **4**:378b
oblasts of, **3**:424a–424b
oil and gas industries in, **4**:378b
people of, **3**:421a–422b
political system of, **1**:457a,
3:424a–425a, 430a–430b,
432a–434a
politicians in, **6**:41a
profile of, **3**:423a–426a**
Quqon khanate and, **1**:461a
SCO and, **5**:169b

Soviet regime and, **1**:471b
Soviet Socialist Republic of,
1:465b
statistics for, **3**:*423*
Sunni Muslims in, **4**:243b
trade of, **1**:469b
tribal dominance in, **5**:531b
water resources in, **6**:109a
the West and, **6**:114b
kyudo (the way of the bow), **5**:310a
kyujutsu (techniques of the bow),
5:310a
Kyushu (Japan), **1**:89a, **3**:205a,
434a–434b
Kyushu-Yamaguchi Economic
Sphere, **3**:434b
Kyzyl Kum Desert, **1**:93a, **5**:538a

L

Laan Naa, kingdom of. *See* Lan
Na, kingdom of (Thailand).
Laan Saang, kingdom of, **4**:203b
Labarnas I (king; Hittites), **2**:531b
Labaw Donggon (Philippine epic),
3:505a
labor
costs of
in high-technology industry,
2:505b, 507
in South Korea, **5**:274a,
274b, 275b
forced
in Java, **5**:99b
in Siberia, **5**:196a
in Sui dynasty, **5**:346b, 347b,
348b, 349a
indentured, **4**:87b, 88a
in South Africa, **5**:136a
in India
child, **3**:21b
in Indonesia
in Dutch colonial period,
3:55b–56a
in Korea
reciprocal arrangements,
3:418a
overseas Chinese and, **2**:48a
in Philippines
surplus, **4**:44a
surplus
in China, **5**:105b–106a**
sustainability and, **5**:358b,
359a–359b, 360a
labor unions
in Cambodia, **1**:410a, 413a,
5:122a
chaebol and, **1**:483b
in China, **6**:130b, 131a
Shanghai, **5**:168b

in India
Communism and, **4**:79a
in Japan, **3**:213a–213b, 229b
in Kazakhstan, **1**:456b
in Korea, **5**:279a
in Myanmar, **2**:155a
in Poland, **2**:151b
in South Korea, **5**:272b, 275b
in Sri Lanka, **5**:328a
Labourdonnis, Mahe de, **4**:87b
Labu Sayong, **3**:435a, *435b*
Labuan (Malaysia), **1**:327a, 328a,
2:368b
Lac Long Quan, **3**:435a–436a**
Laccadive Islands, **3**:440b
lacquerware, **3**:150b, **436a–438a**
Edo period, **5**:189a
makie, **1**:405a
Ladakh Festival (India), **3**:466a
Ladakh (India), **1**:294b, **3**:77b,
438b
view of Karakorum Mountains
from, **3**:*318*
Laguna Lake (Philippines), **3**:530a
Lahawri, Abdul Hamid, **5**:156a
Lahore Fort, **3**:439a, 439b
Lahore (Pakistan), **1**:4b, 51b, 83a,
96a–96b, 221b, 487b,
3:438b–439b**, **4**:*206*, 427a,
5:17b, 18a, **6**:143a
architecture in, **1**:135b
Lahore Resolution (1940), **3**:277a,
439b
India-Pakistan relations and,
3:32b–33a
Lahu people, **1**:78a, **2**:123a,
3:526b, **5**:164a
clothing of, **2**:127b
Lai, Helen, **2**:242b
Lak witthaya (Stealing Knowledge;
journal; Thailand), **1**:295b,
3:514a
laksamana (Malay military com-
mander), **3**:439b–440b**
Lakshadweep (India), **3**:41b, **440b**
Lal, Madan, **2**:440a
Lalan Shah, **4**:218a
Lalla (poet), **3**:490a, **6**:146a
Lam-ang (Philippine epic), **3**:505a
Lam Duc Tho, **4**:487b
Lamaism. *See* Buddhism, Tibetan.
lamas
clothing of, **2**:126a, 133a
See also Buddhism, Tibetan
Lamma Mas-Oodhi, **4**:24b
Lamvong (dance; Laos), **3**:445b
Lan Na, kingdom of (Thailand),
1:499a, **4**:203b, **5**:154a, 525b
Lan Xang Hom Khao (kingdom;

Laos), **1**:425a, **2**:361a, **3**:444b, 449b, 451b–452b, 456a, 459a, 501b, **4**:526a, 526b, **5**:154a–154b, **6**:173a
  Myanmar and, **4**:256b
land mines, **3**:441a, **441a–442a**
  in Cambodia, **3**:370a
  in Kandahar (Afghanistan), **3**:305b, 306a
Land of the Rising Sun. *See* Japan.
land ownership
  in Cambodia, **1**:410a
  in China, **1**:49b
  in India, **2**:420b
  in Philippines
    Catholicism and, **1**:445a–445b
land reform
  in Central Asia, **1**:44a, 44b
  in China, **1**:40b, 45b, 46a
  in Japan
    Confucianism and, **2**:161a
  in Sri Lanka, **5**:319b, 328b
Lan ʿdan ʾsva" ne zin ʿ hmat ʿ tam" (Journal of a Trip to London; Kan ʿ" van ʿMan ʿ"kri" U" Kon ʿ"), **3**:503b
Lang Bac, battle of, **5**:533a
Lang Darma (king; Tibet), **1**:363b, **5**:485b
Langenois, Henri, **6**:122b
language purification, **3**:441a–442b**
Lanling Xiaoxiao Sheng (The Scoffing Gentleman of Lanling). See *Jin ping mei.*
Lansbury, George, **1**:*312a*
Lansing-Ishii Agreement (1917), **2**:24b, **5**:376a, 377b
Lanzhou (China), **2**:425a
Lanzin Party (Myanmar's Socialist Programme Party), **4**:248a
Lao Dong Party (LDP; Vietnam), **1**:107b, **3**:463b, **6**:63b, 76a
Lao Grammar (Phoumi Vongnichit), **3**:450, 460b
Lao Issara (Free Laos), **3**:453a, 456b, **5**:296a–296b
Lao Khamhom. *See* Srinawk, Khamsing.
Lao language, **2**:322a, **5**:116a, 370b
Lao Lum people (Lao Loum), **3**:443b–444a, 446b, 460a–460b
Lao Nhay (newspaper; Laos), **3**:502a
Lao Patriotic Front, **3**:453b, 502b
Lao people, **3**:*445b*
  in Cambodia, **1**:409b, 425a

Tai-speaking, **5**:450a
  Thai people and, **5**:454a
  in Vietnam, **2**:138b
Lao People's Democratic Republic, **1**:305b, **2**:100a, **3**:445a, 449b, 450a, 451b, 452a, 454b–455b, 458b–459a, **6**:60a
  Buddhism in, **3**:455a, 457a, 457b
  formation of, **3**:459b
  founding of, **3**:456a
  proclamation of, **5**:296b
  See also Kaysone Phomvihan; Laos
Lao People's Liberation Army, **3**:459b
Lao People's Party. *See* Lao People's Revolutionary Party.
Lao People's Revolutionary Party (LPRP), **3**:442b–443a, 449a, 454b–455a, 456b–457a, 459a, **4**:469b
  clothing and, **2**:123b
  economic reforms and, **2**:50a
Lao She (Shu Qingchun), **2**:223a, 287a, **3**:443a, **5**:244a–244b, **6**:178b
Lao Sung people (Lao Soung), **3**:443b, 446b, 461a
Lao-Tai languages, **1**:265b, **3**:446b, **460a–461a**
Lao Theung (Lao Thoeng), **3**:443b–444a, 446b, 461a
Lao-Tzu. *See* Laozi.
Laos, **5**:133a
  agriculture in, **3**:445a, 447b, 455a
  Akha people in, **1**:78b
  architecture of, **3**:528a
  as ASEAN member, **1**:174a, **3**:445a
  Buddhism in, **1**:358b
  calendar in, **1**:397b
  Chinese in, **1**:425b, **3**:459a
  Chinese influence in, **2**:42b
  Civil War (1956–1975) in, **2**:99, **99a–100a**, **5**:296a
  clothing in, **2**:122b–125a, **5**:447a
  Colombo Plan and, **2**:143a
  Communism in, **1**:173b, 224b, **3**:442b–443a, 444a, 502a–502b, **5**:62b
  communist victory in, **2**:100a, 534a
  cuisine of, **2**:213a
  culture of, **3**:445a–445b
  drug trade in, **1**:499b
  economic system of, **1**:58a,

3:445a, **446a–449a**, 448a–449a
  market economy and, **1**:426a, **2**:50a
  New Economic Mechanism for, **2**:50a–51a**, **3**:448a, 450a, 455a, 502b
  1997 economic crisis in, **2**:50b, **3**:445a, 447a, 449b, 452a, 455b, 457b, 459a, 460a
  reforms and, **4**:98b
education system of, **3**:449a–451b**, *451a*, 456b
ekaphap (unity), political slogan in, **2**:322b
ethnic groups in, **4**:65b
  clothing of, **2**:122b–124a, **5**:448a–448b
fertility rates in, **2**:376b
festivals in, **1**:376b, **3**:445b, 502b
folk music of, **4**:232b–233b**, *233a*
forest industry in, **2**:399a
Franco-Laotian Convention (1949) and, **3**:444b
Friendship Bridge and, **4**:155a
Green Revolution in, **2**:453b
history, timeline of, **3**:*452a*
history of, **3**:444a–445a, **451b–455b**, **5**:154a–154b
  French colonial rule, **1**:447a, **2**:402a, **3**:332a–332b, 442b, 444b–445a, 447b, 449b, 452a–453a, 456a–456b, 458b, 502a, 528a
Hmong in, **2**:99b, 534a, 535a, 535b–536a
human rights in, **3**:445a
ikat dyeing in, **3**:5a–5b
independence of, **3**:449b, 453a, 453b, 456b, 458b, **5**:296b
Khmer empire and, **1**:418a
Khmu people of, **3**:359b–360b**
kingdom of, **3**:452a, 453a–453b
land mines in, **3**:441a–441b
languages of, **5**:116a, 116b
literacy in, **3**:460b–461a
literature of, **3**:501b–503a**
longboat racing in, **3**:525b–526a**
map of, **3**:*443b*
measurement systems in, **4**:94b
media in, **4**:98b, 107b–110a
Mekong River and, **4**:135b–137b
Mon-Khmer languages in, **4**:191a

MacMichael, Sir Harold, **3**:549b

McNamara, Robert, **6**:79a, 79b, 82b

Madagascar, **1**:31a, 31b, 33b, 34a, 34b, 191a, 191b, **3**:42b
  language of, **1**:191a, 191b, 192a, **4**:488b

Madali Khan, **1**:461a, **5**:38b

Madame Butterfly (Puccini), **2**:80a, 430b

Madame Chrysanthemum (Loti), **2**:80a

Madan, J. F., **2**:88a

Madd-wa-Jazr-e-Islam (Ebb and Flow of Islam; Hali), **4**:530b

Madhavakar, **4**:118b

Madhavrai fair (India), **2**:460b

Madhi (twelfth imam of Twelvers), **4**:242a

Madhya Pradesh (India), **1**:51a, 51b, 282b, 283b, **3**:76b, **535b–536a**, **5**:45a

Madras (India), **1**:101b, 102b, 106b, 107b, 279a, 300b, **2**:473b, **3**:536a–536b**
  British in, **5**:409b–410a, 436a
  capture of, by France, **2**:404b
  film industry in, **2**:88b, *89*, 89b
  name change to Chennai, **5**:411a
  in World War I, **6**:161a

madrasahs (Muslim religious schools), **1**:119a, 129a, 136b, 138b, 140a, 372a, **2**:262b, **3**:102a–102b, 128b–129a, 129b, 152b, 172a, **536b–537a**, 546a, **4**:81b, **5**:21a, **6**:48a, 48b
  in Central Asia, **4**:385a, **5**:35b, 122a
    Communism and, **2**:146b
  in Malaysia, **3**:161b
  in Philippines, **3**:168b
  in Turkey, **4**:144b
    closing of, **5**:548b, **6**:126b
  ultraorthodox, **3**:172a

Madura, **3**:62b, 63a

Madura (Indonesia), **3**:52a, 62b, 63b

Madurai (India), **3**:537a–538a**, **4**:460a

Madurese language, **3**:268a

Madurese people, **3**:51b, 63b, **538a–538b**

Maebashi (Japan), **2**:462b

Maeda family, **5**:524b

Magadhan empire, **1**:296a, **4**:469b

Magahi language, **3**:44b

Magat River (Philippines), **1**:394a

Magellan, Ferdinand, **1**:58b, 59a, 443b, **2**:208b, **4**:538a, **6**:122b

in Philippines, **1**:450b, **4**:494a, 503b, 504–505, **6**:95a

magnetism, **3**:538b–539a**

Magsaysay, Ramon, **1**:115a, 116a, **2**:426b, 562a–562b, **3**:539a–540b**

Magtumguly (poet), **6**:13a

maguey, **3**:540b–541a**

Magwe Division (Myanmar), **3**:541a**

Maha Kumbh Mela (Grand Pitcher Festival), **1**:84b, 85a

Mahabalipuram (India), **2**:526a

Mahabharata, **1**:133b, 134a, 157b, 172b, 173a, 201b, 202b, 280b, **2**:262a, 290b, 293a, 469b, 491b, 514a, 520b, 526b, **3**:34a, 44b, 51a, 488b–489a, 508a, 510a, 511a, 537b, **541a–542b**, **4**:530a, **5**:49a
  Bangladeshi music and, **4**:217a
  dance drama and, **4**:39a, **6**:112a
  deforestation in, **2**:260b–261a
  in Indian drama, **5**:2b
  pilgrimage and, **4**:523a
  in puppet theater, **6**:110a, 110b, 111a
  Sanskrit and, **5**:125a, 126b
  sports and, **5**:304b
  See also *Ramayana*

Mahagiri (spirit; *nat*), **5**:300b

Mahajana Eksath Peramuna (MEP), **1**:232b

Mahakasyapa, **1**:335b

mahalla, **3**:542b–543a**

Mahanadi River (India), **3**:543a–543b**, **4**:396b
  flooding and, **2**:101a

Mahanatakam, **2**:524a

Mahaprajapati Gotami, **6**:146b

Maharashtra (India), **1**:02b, 68a, 68b, 75a, 76a, 183a, 184a, **2**:227b, **3**:543b–544a**, **5**:15b, 436a, **6**:37a

Maharshi Vatsyayana, **3**:303b

Mahathir Mohamad, **1**:103b, 104b, 113a, 114a, 170b, 171b, 193b, 194b, 196b, 197a, 213b, **3**:73b, **544a–545a**, *544b*, **4**:8, 15b, 16a, 17a, 18a, 19b, **5**:295a, **6**:158b
  Malaysia-Europe relations and, **4**:21a
  media and, **4**:103b

Mahavamsa (Sinhalese chronicle), **3**:511b, **5**:324b

Mahavira (Jain founder), **3**:*196b*, 196b–197b, **6**:146a–146b

Mahdi al-Hassani, **1**:156a

Mahdi (Rightly Guided One), **6**:18a, 18b

Mahendradatta (queen; Bali), **1**:74b, 75a

Maher, Ahmed, **4**:*432*

Mahikari, **5**:73a

Mahkota, Pangiran, **3**:408b

Mahmud II, **4**:399, 400a, **5**:418a, 548a

Mahmud of Ghazna, **1**:453b, 454a, **2**:434a, **3**:545a–545b**, **5**:158a, **6**:50b

Mahmud Shah (sultan; Malaka), **2**:283b, **3**:279a, **545b–546a**, **4**:139a, 474a

Mahmud Talequani, **1**:270b

Mahmud Tarabi, **6**:50b

Mahmudov, Mamadali, **3**:481b, 482a

Mahn Ba Zan, **3**:323a

Mailin, Beiimbet, **3**:333a, **546a**

Maithili language, **3**:44b

Maitland, Julia C., **2**:212a

Maitreya (Mile; Metteyya), **1**:340b, 346a, 355a, 359b, 361a
  cult of, **2**:220b–221b**
  images of, **5**:142a

Majalis an-Nafais (Assemblies of Refined Men; Nava%i), **1**:486a

Majapahit empire (Java), **1**:89b, 90a, 224b, **2**:41a, 41b, 293b, 416a, 418a, **3**:52a, 268a, 347a, **546a–546b**, **4**:84b, **5**:332b, **6**:112a, 112b
  Melaka and, **4**:39b, 138b
  music in, **4**:227b

Majapahit (Java), **1**:430a, **3**:62a, **4**:503a, 525a, **5**:436b

Majid Khan, Ishon Babakhan Ibn, al-, **4**:238b

Majidi, Majid, **2**:94a

majlis (parliament; Iran), **3**:97a, 99a, 106a, 106b, 107b, 108a, 110a, 181b

Majumdar, D. N., **4**:68b

Mak Yong (Malaysian dance drama), **3**:546b–547a**, **4**:39a

Makal, Mahmut, **3**:517a

Makar Sankranti (festival; India), **2**:460b

Makassar (Dutch East Indies), **5**:299a

Makhambet Utemisov, **3**:547a–547b**

Makhmudov, Mamadali, **2**:147a

Maki, Fumihiko, **1**:147a, 147b, 148b

Makiguchi Tsunesaburo, **5**:72b

Makino Masahiro, **2**:90a

Makino Nobuaki, **6**:197b

Makino Shozo, **2**:95a

Makiya, Mohamad, **1**:156a
Makli Hill (Pakistan), **3**:547b
Makmalbaf, Mohsen, **2**:94b
Makpon dynasty, **1**:227a
maktab (Islamic elementary
   school), **3**:102a, 536b
Malabar district (India), **1**:400b,
   5:82b
   Judaism in, **3**:285b
   spice trade and, **5**:299b
   See also Kerala
Malacanang palace, **2**:340a, **4**:472b
Malacca, kingdom of (Malaysia),
   5:332b
Malacca, Strait of, **1**:101b, 102a,
   105b, 106b, 149a, 149b, 269a,
   269b, 270a, 319a, **3**:42a, **4**:4b,
   257a, **5**:339a
   China-India relations and, **2**:3b,
      4a
   map of, **5**:*339a*
   piracy in, **4**:460b
   Portuguese control of, **4**:550a
   Srivijaya and, **5**:332a
   trade and, **4**:5a, **5**:339a
Malacca (Malaysia), **1**:276a, 276b,
   319a, 326b, 332b, **2**:368b
   cuisine of, **2**:204b
   Portuguese community in,
      5:423b
Malagasy language, **1**:33b, 34a,
   4:488b
Malat, **2**:418a
Malay, Islam, Beraja (Malay, Islam,
   Kingship; MIB), **1**:332a–332b
Malay Annals (*Sejarah Melayu*),
   1:276a, **2**:510b
Malay archipelago, **1**:105b, 106a,
   149a, 149b, 271b, 326b, 327a,
   2:308b, 429a, **3**:151a
   Dutch-Bugis war and, **2**:476a
   Dutch control of, **4**:6a
   Moluku and, **4**:26a
   Srivijaya and, **5**:332a
   See also Malaysia
Malay Dilemma, The (Mahathir
   Mohamad), **3**:544b
Malay-Indonesian archipelago,
   1:13a, 16b
Malay-Indonesian languages,
   1:13a, 220a–220b, 376a,
   3:550a–551b
Malay language (Bahasa Malaysia),
   1:189b, 190b, 191b, 192a, 192b,
   193a, **3**:72b, 157a, 270b, **4**:2a,
   11a, 11b, 12a, **6**:34a, 35b, 98b
   coastal Malays and, **2**:141a
   education system and,
      4:10b–12a

Indonesian music and, **4**:227a
   in Java, **4**:475a
   mass media and, **4**:98a
   media and, **4**:103a, 104a
   Vietnamese and, **4**:192a
Malay Peninsula, **1**:105b, 106a,
   150a, 151a, 276a, **3**:472b, **5**:212a
   British in, **1**:319a–319b, 320a,
      4:6a–6b, 460b–461a, **5**:82a,
      362a–362b
   history of, **4**:4a–4b
   indigenous population of,
      4:389b–390a
   Japanese occupation of, **3**:549a,
      549b
   Melaka and, **4**:39b
   monsoons in, **4**:194a
   mountains in, **4**:200a
   piracy in, **4**:525a
Malay people, **1**:329b, 330b, 332b,
   375b–376a, **2**:140a–141b,
   3:51b, 72a, **4**:1b, 11b
   Chinese and, **4**:12b, 13b, 14a,
      21b–22a, 89b–90b
   clothing of, **2**:131a, 131b
   coastal, **2**:140a–141b, 141a
   cuisine of, **2**:204b
   education system and, **4**:10b–12a
   in Indonesia, **4**:96b
   Malaysian political system and,
      4:17a, 18b, 19a, **5**:294b
   marriage and family of, **4**:63a,
      63b, 64a, 64b
   NEP and, **4**:16b
   in Philippines, **4**:37b
   in Sarawak, **5**:131a
   Skrang, **1**:327a
Malay States, Unfederated,
   3:547b–548a, 549b
   See also Federated Malay States
   (FMS)
Malay sultanate. *See* Melaka sultanate.
Malaya, Federation of, **2**:369b,
   370a, **3**:548a, 550a, **4**:21a, 471b,
   474b, 477b
Malaya, University of, **4**:2a,
   6:35a–35b
   Asia-Europe Institute at, **4**:20a
Malayalam language, **1**:497a, 497b,
   2:299a–299b, 301a, **3**:348b,
   490a0491a, 490a–491a
   conveyance arts and, **2**:173a
Malayan Chinese Association
   (MCA)
   ethnic conflict and, **4**:90a
Malayan Communist Party (MCP),
   3:473b, 548a–549a, **4**:14a, 21b,
   5:438a

Malayan Emergency,
   3:548a–549a, **4**:14a, 21b, 149b,
   5:438a
Malayan People's Anti-Japanese
   Army (MPAJA), **3**:549a–549b
Malayan Union, **1**:325a, **3**:548a,
   549b–550a, **4**:14a, 15, 21a
Malayo-Polynesian languages,
   3:265a, 550a
Malaysia, Federation of, **1**:320a,
   2:369b–370b, **3**:408a, 548a, **4**:9a
Malaysia-Europe relations,
   4:19b–21b
   Anglo-Malaysia relations and,
      4:20b–21a
   trade and, **4**:20a–20b
   See also colonialism
Malaysia-Japan relations
   Japanese firms and, **3**:261b
   Japanese occupation of, **1**:3b,
      3:161b–162a, 550b, **4**:9a,
      14a, 149b, 150b, 164a, 477b,
      6:162b
Malaysia (Malaya), **1**:319a, 325a,
   326b, **4**:149b, 319a–320a
   adat controversies in,
      1:13a–16b, **5**:436b–437a
   agriculture in, **1**:58a, 58b,
      429a–429b, **4**:1b, 9b, 42a,
      137b, 477b
   AIDS in, **1**:68a, 68b
   air pollution in, **1**:74a, 74b,
      3:72a–72b
   aquaculture in, **2**:*388*
   archeology in, **3**:346b
   art in, **2**:81a
   artists of, **1**:488a–488b
   automobile industry in, **1**:192b,
      193b, 194b
      National Champion policies
         in, **1**:196b, 197a–198a
   batik industry in, **1**:268a, *268a*,
      268b
   bumiputras, peoples of,
      4:319a–320a
   censorship in, **4**:18b
   Chinese in, **1**:429a, **2**:35a, 42a,
      46b, 48a, **3**:544b, 549a,
      549b, **4**:1b–2a, 6a, 6b, 7a, 9a,
      9b, 319a–319b
      expulsion of, **2**:49b
      mineral industry and, **4**:150a
   Chinese languages in, **4**:146a
   Christianity in, **2**:75b, 77b,
      5:14b
   clothing in, **2**:124a–125a, *124b*
   cockfighting in, **2**:141b
   colonialism in, **1**:297a,
      2:100a–100b, **6**:124b

maquiladoras (industrial zones; Mexico), **3**:261b
Maratha people (India), **1**:84b, 85a, 106b, 107b, 183b, 184a, 235b, 284a, **2**:227b, 473b, 543a, **3**:24b, 76b, 171b, 172a, 543b–544a, **4**:207a, **5**:15b, 17b, 211b
Jodhpur and, **3**:278b
Marathi language, **3**:44a, 47a, 50b, **4**:34b
literature of, **3**:490a–491a
March First Independence Movement (Korea), **4**:46b–47b
Marco Polo Bridge Incident (1937), **1**:498b, **2**:11b
Marcos, Ferdinand, **1**:115b, 116b, 198a, 446a, **2**:42b, 340a, **3**:532b–533a, **4**:38a, *47b*, **47b–48b**, 538b, **5**:53a, 99a
constitutions and, **4**:511a
corruption and, **2**:178b, **4**:47b, 48a–48b
declaration of martial law, **4**:508b
fall of, **2**:255b, **4**:48a, 472a, 472b, 510b, 512a, **5**:209b
human rights and, **4**:509b, **5**:292a, *293b*
media and, **4**:103b
New Society of, **4**:499a
Philippines - U.S. relations and, **4**:516b
Sabah Dispute and, **5**:114a
United States and, **4**:495a
U.S. - Philippines relations and, **4**:515a
Marcos, Imelda, **4**:38a, 48a, *48b*, **48b–49a**
Mardan, Hussein, **4**:533a
Mardhekar, B. S., **4**:531a
Margao (Goa), **2**:437a
Maritime Customs Service (China), **2**:491a, **5**:30b
Marjani, Shihabeddin, al-, **3**:194b
Mark Antony, **4**:476a, **5**:424a–424b
Markandaya, Kamala, **3**:491a
Marlowe, Christopher, **5**:500a
Marmara, Sea of (Turkey), **1**:96b, 97a, 97b, 98a, 312a, 312b, **2**:250a, **4**:49a
Maro Akaji, **2**:241b
Marpo-Ri (Red Hill; Tibet), **3**:468a
marriage and family
among Garo, **2**:428b–429a, **4**:68b
caste and, **1**:438b, 439b, 440a, 441a, 442b, **4**:69a, 74a

in Central Asia, **4**:49b–51a
bride stealing in, **4**:50a–50b
guardian parents and, **4**:50b
kalym (bride-price) custom and, **3**:303a–303b, 333a
kalym (bride-price) custom in, **3**:303a–303b, 333a
reforms of, **5**:149b
in China, **4**:51a–57a
adoptions and, **4**:55
economic reforms and, **4**:56a–56b
family planning and, **1**:513b, **4**:53b, *54*, 54a–56a
female infanticide and, **4**:53b–54a, 54b
male dominance and, **4**:53b
Ming, **4**:151b
New Year and, **5**:315a, 315b
traditional, **4**:51a–52
twentieth-century, **4**:53a–57a
community and, **4**:58
divorce and, **2**:444a, **3**:110b, **4**:53a, 56a, 59b, 60a, 60b, 64a–64b, 66a–66b, 67b, 68a, 74a, 76a
dowry and bride price and, **4**:50a, 65b–66a, 66b, 67b–68a, 72a–74a, 75b–76a, **5**:127a
in Central Asia, **3**:303a–303b, 333a
dowry-deaths and, **4**:72b–73a
reforms of, **5**:149b
in East Asia, **4**:57a–62b, *59b*
changes in, **4**:60a–62a
intergenerational relations and, **4**:57b, 59a, 60b–61a
traditional, **4**:57a–60a
education and, **4**:71a, 72a, 72b
geisha and, **2**:430b
in India, **4**:68b–75a, *71b*
Sanskritization and, **5**:127a
in Iran
divorce and, **3**:110b
in Japan, **4**:57a–62a, *59b*
joint families, **4**:74b, 75a
Khmer people and, **3**:355a
Miao, **4**:142a–142b
monogamy in, **2**:444a, **4**:63a, 67b, 68b
in Moso culture, **4**:197b
overseas Chinese and, **2**:48b–49a
in Philippines, **2**:439a–439b
polyandry in, **4**:68b
polygyny in, **2**:444a, **4**:49b, 53a, 63a, 65b, 67a, 67b, 68b, 76a
remarriage and, **2**:444a, **4**:49b,

59b, 60a, 60b, 66b, 68a, 74a–74b, 76a
in South Asia, **4**:68b–75a, *69b*, *71b*, **6**:145b–146a
matchmaking and, **4**:73
northern, **4**:70a–71b
southern, **4**:71b–72a
in Southeast Asia
Insular, **4**:62b–65a, *63b*, *64*
Mainland, **4**:65a–68b
in Taiwan, **4**:58, 60a, 60b, 61b–62a, **5**:381b–382a
in Vietnam, **4**:66b–67b, 68a
Communism and, **2**:153b–154a
in West Asia, **4**:75a–76b
pleasure marriages and, **4**:76a–76b
Marriott, McKim, **1**:440a, 440b
Marsden, George, **5**:14a
Marsden, William, **1**:13b
Marsh, Mabel, **5**:307b
Marsh Arabs, **4**:76a–77b, 77
Marshall, David, **3**:272a, **4**:77b–78a, **6**:156b
Marshall, George C., **2**:29b, 30b
Chinese Civil War and, **2**:30a
Marshall, Sir John, **4**:158b
Marthanda Varma, **5**:533a
martial arts
at Asian Games, **1**:165b, 166b
in China, **6**:171b
Chinese, **1**:313a, 313b, **5**:301b, 369b, **6**:171a, 171b
women's, **1**:313b–314a, **5**:35a
in film, **2**:87a
Indonesian, **5**:55b
in Japan, **1**:69a, **3**:1a, 321a
Japanese, **1**:69b, **2**:182b, **3**:1a, **5**:311b
in Korea, **5**:313a
Zen and, **2**:8a
judo, **3**:288b–289a
Jujutsu, **3**:289a–289b
in Korea, **5**:366b
Korean, **5**:312a, 313a, 366b
Okinawan, **2**:412a
in Philippines, **1**:160b, 226a
in Thailand, **4**:205a–206a
See also karate; kendo
Martin, François, **2**:404b
Martin, Graham, **6**:81b
Marubeni Corporation (Japan), **3**:521b
Marudevi, **6**:146b
Ma'ruf al-Rusafi, **4**:532b
Maruyama Masao, **4**:78a–78b
Marvandi, Sheikh Osman. *See* Shahbaz Qalandar Lal.

Minamata mercury poisoning
(Japan), **2**:98a
Minamoto family (Japan), **2**:498b,
572b, **3**:304a, 494a, **4**:415a
Minangkabau people, **1**:13a, 13b,
14a, 14b–15a, **2**:140b, **4**:404b,
5:55b, 437a, **6**:149b
in Indonesia, **4**:96b
marriage and family of, **4**:62b,
63a, 63b
music of, **4**:227b, 228a
Padri War and, **4**:404b, 405a
minarets, **4**:147b–148a, *206*, 206b
Mindanao (Philippines), **1**:451a,
4:148a–149a, 462a, 491b,
5:93a, **6**:208b
Autonomous Region of Muslim
(ARMM), **1**:198a–198b,
198b–199a, **4**:196a, 197a,
372b, 517b, **5**:354a
cuisine of, **2**:208b
Islam in, **4**:492b, 510b, **5**:354a
map of, **4**:*148a*
Muslims in, **3**:167b
piracy in, **4**:525a
Mindon (king; Myanmar), **3**:331,
4:30a, 31a
Mindon Min (king; Myanmar),
4:257b, 262a
mineral industry
in Kyrgyzstan, **3**:425a, 426b
in Malaysia, **4**:8a, 13b, 41b,
42b, **149a–151a**, *150a*
Chinese and, **2**:42a, **4**:149a,
149b, **5**:500b
in Mongolia, **2**:337b–338a,
4:189b
in Myanmar, **5**:117b
See also mining industry; oil and
mineral industries
Ming dynasty (China), **1**:1a, 133a,
133b, 150b, 272b, 336b, 339b,
2:477b, **3**:310a, **4**:151a–154b,
5:379b, **6**:170b, 171a, 187a,
187b, 195b, 196a, 203b
architecture of, **1**:132b, 153b,
4:524b
bans on emigration in, **2**:47b
Buddhism and, **1**:349b
China-Japan relations and, **2**:8a,
11b
Chinese influence and, **2**:39b
Christianity and, **2**:65a
cloisonné in, **2**:102b
clothing in, **2**:108b, 121a,
4:151b
commercialization in, **4**:153a
Confucianism in, **2**:159b
cuisine in, **2**:188b

cultural and intellectual changes
in, **4**:153b–154b
decline of, **2**:564b
drama in, **3**:487a
ethnic groups in, **5**:536a
eunuchs in, **4**:152a
folk religion in, **5**:67b, 68b
foot binding and, **2**:396b
founding of, **4**:151a, **6**:201a
Fujian and, **2**:407a
gardens in, **1**:132b, **2**:427a
Grand Canal in, **4**:152b
Great Wall in, **2**:449a, 449b,
4:152a
Han Chinese officials and,
6:193b
homosexuality in, **2**:544a–544b
Korea and, **1**:396a, **2**:61a,
3:390a, 390b, 405b
language in, **2**:45b
maritime expeditions in, **1**:150a,
150b, 151a, **2**:47a, **4**:151b
medicine in, **3**:470b
Mongols and, **4**:143a, 151b,
164a, 164b, 188b
Myanmar and, **4**:256a
national minorities in, **6**:217a
overthrow of, **4**:152b, **5**:27b
painters of, **1**:376b
painting in, **4**:412b–413a
Wu school of, **4**:412b, 413a
Zhe school of, **4**:412b, 413a
peasant rebellions in, **4**:152b
poetry in, **4**:529a
political changes in,
4:151a–152b
population resettlement and,
1:528a, **4**:152b
porcelain in, **4**:549a
puppetry in, **5**:155b
rent revolts in, **4**:153a
Shanghai in, **5**:168b
socioeconomic changes in,
4:152b–153b
Southeast Asia and, **2**:41b–42a,
4:151b
Taiwan and, **2**:21a, 21b, **5**:372b
Temple of Heaven in, **5**:437a
Tianjin in, **5**:484a
tombs of, **1**:132b, 133a, **5**:67b,
475b
trade in, **2**:410b, **4**:152a
trade with Macao and, **3**:531a
traditional medicine in, **4**:123b
Tumu incident in, **4**:152a
Vietnam and, **4**:151b, **6**:69a
Zeng Chenggong and, **2**:47a
Ming dynasty (Uzbek), **1**:461a,
5:38b

Mingdi (emperor; China), **2**:484b
mingei (people's crafts) movement
(Japan), **1**:481a, 481b
Minh Mang (emperor; Vietnam),
2:488a, **4**:387a
miniature painting
in Central Asia, **2**:379b–380a
Persian, **4**:483a–483b, **5**:188a,
188b
Minicoy Island, **3**:440b
mining industry
aluminum, **3**:336a
in China
Shang dynasty, **5**:167a
Shanxi, **5**:172a
copper, **3**:333b, 336a
in Dutch East Indies, **5**:501a
in Indonesia, **5**:131a, 500b
iron ore, **2**:436b, **3**:333b
in Japan, **2**:413a, **3**:190b,
5:116a, 117a, 130a, 181a
silver, **2**:413a
in Malaysia, **4**:6a, 6b–7a, 8a,
42a, 150a–150b
Sabah, **5**:113a
in Mongolia, **4**:168b
in Myanmar
Shan State, **5**:165a
in North Korea, **1**:485b
in Philippines, **1**:451a, **2**:175a
in Siberia, **5**:195b, 196b
in West Asia, **3**:78a, 78b, 79b
See also mineral industry
Ministry of Education (Japan),
3:218a
banning of sports by,
5:310b–311a
Ministry of Finance (Japan),
3:215b, 216a–216b, 264b
Ministry of Foreign Affairs
(Japan), **3**:264b
Japan-African relations and,
3:231a
Ministry of International Trade
and Industry (MITI; Japan),
3:215a, 250b–251b, 264b
Ministry of Justice (Japan), **3**:222b
Ministry of Military Affairs
(Japan), **3**:226b
Ministry of Posts and Telecommu-
nications (Japan), **3**:216a
Minobe Ryokichi, **4**:155a
Minobe Tatsukichi, **4**:154b–155a,
5:134b, 376b
Minseito party (Japan), **3**:330a
Minto, Lord (Gilbert John Elliot),
1:326a, **4**:194b, 236b
"Minute on Education"
(Macaulay), **3**:533b

min'yo (folk songs), **5**:163b
Mir, Samad, **4**:531a
Mir Ahmed Khan I, **1**:316b
Mir Ali Shir Nava%i, **3**:480b
Mir Jalal Khan, **1**:227b
Mir Sayyid Ali, **4**:420b
Mira Bai, **1**:280b, **6**:146a
Mirbaqeri, Davoud, **2**:94b
Mirsaidov, Shukhrulla, **6**:44a
Mirz Fath Ali Akhundzade,
    1:207b, 208b
Mirza, Iskander, **1**:199b, 200b,
    4:437a, 437b
Mirza, Shafqat Tanveer, **4**:461b
Mirza 'Ali Muhammad. *See* Bab,
    the.
Mirza Buzurg Nuri, **1**:218a
Mirza Hosayn Ali Nuri (Ba-
    haullah), **1**:218a
Mirza Muhammad 'Ali, **1**:218b
Mirza Taqi Khan Amir Kabir,
    5:22a
mishima technique (type of inlay),
    1:481b
Mishima Yukio, **2**:241a, 289a,
    3:495b, 496b
Misri Khan Jamali, **1**:82b, 83a
"Miss Sophie's Diary" (Ding
    Ling), **2**:276a
missionaries, **1**:168a, **6**:117a, 129a,
    141a, 183b
    Buddhist, **2**:160b
        in India, **2**:57a
    Catholic
        in China, **4**:154a–154b,
            5:85b, 95b, **6**:179a
        in Japan, **2**:67a–68a, 68b
        in Philippines, **1**:450b,
            4:505a
        in Vietnam, **1**:446a–446b,
            4:540b
    in China, **2**:65a–66b,
        4:154a–154b, **5**:31a, 166a,
        302a, **6**:135b
        Jesuit, **5**:85b, 95b, **6**:179a
    China-U.S. relations and, **2**:24a
    Christian, **5**:487b
        in Myanmar, **4**:253b–254a
    in India, **2**:74b, **4**:129a
    in Japan, **2**:67a–68a, 68b
        cuisine and, **2**:198b
        education and, **2**:69a
        Japanese music and, **4**:230b
        in Muromachi period, **4**:216a
    Jesuit, **1**:167a
    Jesuit, in Korea, **4**:418b
    in Korea, **2**:62a, **3**:391a
        education and, **2**:70a
        sports and, **5**:312b

Korean, **2**:71a, **5**:368a
    in Laos, **3**:452b
    in Macao, **3**:531a
    in Mongolia, **4**:164b
    in Philippines, **1**:450b
    Protestant
        in China, **5**:31a
        in Japan, **2**:68b
        in Korea, **2**:62a
    Protestant fundamentalist,
        5:14a–14b
    in South Asia
        Norwegian, **5**:128b
    in Southeast Asia, **2**:77a, 77*b*,
        6:122b, 123b
        education and, **2**:75b
    in Sri Lanka, **5**:322a, 322b
        education and, **5**:325a
    in Thailand, **2**:76–77, **3**:513b,
        4:162a, **5**:457b
        clothing and, **2**:132b
    in Vietnam, **1**:446a–446b
        writing system and, **2**:80b
    writing systems and, **5**:128b
Misuari, Nur, **4**:196a, 196b, 197a
Mitakshara (Vijnanesvara), **2**:517b
Mithridates II (king; Pontus),
    1:90a, 91a
MITI. *See* Ministry of Interna-
    tional Trade and Industry.
Mito (Japan), **3**:1b
Mito school, **3**:1b
Mitsubishi, **3**:260b
Mitsubishi Electric, **2**:324a, 326a
Mitsubishi Motors, **3**:261b
Mitsubishi shipyards, **4**:277b
Mitsui, **3**:260b
Mitsui Bank (Japan)
    financial crisis (1927) and,
        2:378a
Mittaphap Bridge (Friendship
    Bridge; Laos-Thailand), **4**:137a,
    155a–155b
Miyage Michio, **4**:230b
Miyagi prefecture (Japan), **4:155b**
Miyazaki Hayao, **1**:108a, 109a,
    2:95b, 96b
Miyazaki prefecture (Japan),
    4:156a
Miyazaki Yuzensai, **2**:119a
Miyazawa Kiichi, **5**:59a
Mizo (Lushai) people (India),
    1:501b, 502a, **4**:156a–156b
Mizo National Front (MNF; In-
    dia), **4**:156b
Mizoguchi Kenji, **2**:92a–92b, 95a
Mizoram (India), **1**:172b, 173b,
    4:156a–156b
Mizutani Yaeko, **2**:288b

MNLF. *See* Moro National Liber-
    ation Front.
Mo Yan, **3**:487b
Modern Critic (Chinese journal),
    5:175b
modernization
    caste and, **1**:441, 442b
    in Central Asia, **1**:465b
        Communism and, **2**:145b
    in China, **1**:527a
        calendar and, **5**:315a
        civil service examination sys-
            tem and, **2**:98b
        classical Chinese and, **2**:46a
        family and, **4**:51a
        music and, **4**:221b
    China-Japan relations and, **2**:13a
    in East Asia
        marriage and family and,
            4:60a
    fertility and, **2**:376a–376b
    in Indonesia
        Islam and, **4**:208a–208b
    in Japan
        media and, **4**:105b
        Meiji period, **4**:130a, 132b
    Japanese cinema and, **2**:90b, 91a
    Japanese music and, **4**:230b
    Khmer Rouge and, **1**:420b
    in Korea, **2**:62a
        education and, **5**:277a
    mass media and, **4**:97b–98a,
        98b, 114b–115a
    in Mongolia, **4**:170a
    in South Korea, **5**:282b
    Sunni Muslims and, **4**:243a
    in Thailand, **1**:499a, **2**:83b–84a,
        4:161a–161b
    traditional clothing and, **2**:104b,
        111b
Moe Thee Zun, **1**:84a, 84b
Moerdani, Leonardus Benjamin,
    4:156b–157a
Mogao Caves (Dunhuang, China),
    4:*157*, 157a–158a
Moggallana II (king; Sinhala),
    3:511b
Moghul empire. *See* Mughal em-
    pire.
mohajirs (immigrants from India
    to Pakistan), **2**:349a
Mohamad, Goenawan,
    4:158a–158b, **5**:438a
Mohamed, Prince (Brunei), **1**:330a,
    330b, 332a
Mohamed of Jais, **3**:490a
Mohammad. *See* Muhammad.
Mohammad Sadiq Al-Sadr, Ayatol-
    lah, **3**:137b

272b, 491b, 526b, 562b, 571a,
3:76b, 295b, 365a, 439a–439b,
528b, 4:206a, **206a–207a**, 470a,
5:156a, 223b, 261a–262a,
6:148a
Afghanistan and, 5:17b
clothing of, 2:103a
architecture of, 1:127b, 128a,
134a, 135a, 135b, 136a,
136b, 138b, 139b, 182, *183*,
2:262b, 3:529a, 4:*206*,
5:393a
Bangladeshi music and, 4:217a
Bengal and, 1:247a
Britain and, 2:494a–494b
British India and, 5:136b
Calcutta and, 1:394b
China and, 2:1b
creation of, 4:206a, 5:17a, 500a
cuisine of, 2:210a–210b
decline of, 1:135b, 136a,
4:206b–207a, 5:46b
emperors of, 3:195b–196a, 285a
establishment of, 3:480b
expansion of, 1:183b, 184a,
4:206b, 5:223b
founder of, 1:211a, 486a,
4:206a, 5:17b
gardens in, 5:332a
in India, 2:519b, 3:11b, 4:206a,
206b
Indian Mutiny and, 4:244b
Indo-Gangetic Plain and, 3:51a
invasions by, 1:172b, 173b,
3:364b
Islam and, 3:169b, 170b,
171a–171b, 172a, 174a–174b
Islam in, 1:184a, 184b, 4:206b
jade art and, 3:194a
Jodhpur and, 3:278b
language of, 2:514b
mosques of, 3:466a
Mumbai and, 4:210b
opium trade and, 2:302b
in Pakistan, 4:209a
pandits and, 4:460a
Persian miniatures in, 4:483b
salt tax and, 5:121a
state system of, 1:320b
statistical account of, 2:368a
Sunni Muslims and, 4:243b
Mughal-Gothic architecture,
3:439b
muhajir (migrants), **4:207a–207b**
Muhajir Qawmi Movement
(MQM; Pakistan), **4:207b–208a**
Muhajir Qawmi Movement
(MQM: Pakistan), 4:427a
Muhakamat al-lughateyn (Judgment

of Two Languages; Nava%i),
1:486a
Muhakemat al-lughateyn (Consider-
ation of Two Languages;
Huseyin Baykara), 3:480b
Muhammad, Caliph Hasan, 1:222a
Muhammad Akbar Khan, 2:256b
Muhammad Ali, 5:22a
Muhammad Amin Inaq, 3:354a
Muhammad 'Aufi, 3:520a
Muhammad b. Qasim, 5:17a
Muhammad Ghuri, 5:17a
Muhammad Hatta, 2:310a, 310b
Muhammad Ibn Abdallah (the
Prophet), 1:118b
Muhammad ibn Jarir at-Tabari,
3:480b
Muhammad II, 'Ala al-Din (Kara
Kitai leader), 1:455a
Muhammad Khatami, 6:126b
Muhammad Mahdi al-Jawahiri,
4:532b–533a
Muhammad Nadir Khan, 6:207b
Muhammad of Ghor (Pakistan),
3:438b
Muhammad (Prophet of Islam),
1:82a, 82b, 85b, 86b, 111a,
136b, 137a, 138a, 214b, 227a, b,
2:473a, 3:133a, 4:436a
calendar and, 1:400a
descendants of, 4:239a–239b,
5:157a, 6:4a
hadiths and, 4:243a, 5:173a
hegira (flight to Medina) of,
1:397a
Indian music and, 4:225a
pilgrimage sites and, 4:92b, 93
sacred sites of, 4:398a
shari'a and, 5:172b, 173a
shi'ism and, 4:241b
spice trade and, 5:300a
traditional medicine and,
4:125b
traditions of, 6:18a, 219a
women and, 6:147b
Muhammad (prophet of Islam),
4:436a
descendants of, 3:321a
Muhammad Sa'id al-Habubi,
4:532a–532b
Muhammad Shah, 1:210b, 3:105b,
4:138b, 421b
Muhammadiaya (Indonesia),
3:157a
Muhammadiyah (Islamic socioreli-
gious organization),
4:208a–208b, 5:45b, 129a
Muhammed Amin, khan (Kazan),
3:481a

Muhammed Quli Qutb Shah,
2:571a, 3:490a
Muhammed Qutb Shah, 2:571a
Muhbir (journal; Tashkent), 3:482a
Muhtadee Billah, al-, 1:333a
Mui Chek-yin, 2:242b
Mujahideen (Afghan freedom
fighters), 4:485b
mujahideen (Afghan freedom
fighters), 1:23b, 25a, 26a, 29b,
30a, 30b, 31a, 31b, 296b,
2:304a, 3:296a, 305b,
4:208b–209a, 385a, 485b,
5:408a
clothing of, 2:103b
*Mujh se pahli si muhabbat meri
mahboob na maang* (My Beloved,
Do Not Ask of Me My Former
Kind of Love; Faiz), 1:362a
Mujiz (historian), 4:219a
Mujong (Heartlessness; Yi Kwang-
su), 3:499b
Mukden Incident (1931)
media and, 4:106b
Mukherjee, Ashutosh, 4:196a
Muktibahini (Freedom Fighters;
East Pakistan), 1:256b
Mukundaraj (poet; India), 3:490a
mukyokai (no-church movement;
Japan), 2:69a, 5:71b
Mullens, Hannah Catherine,
3:509a
Müller, Friedrich Max, 4:394a
Muller, Max, 1:168b, 169a, 4:211a
Müller, Max, 1:167b, 168a
Mulsims
Thai
in Thailand, 3:160a
Multan (Pakistan), 3:2a,
4:209a–209b, 5:17a, 17b
multinational corporations, 2:326a
Mumbai (Bombay; India), 1:66a,
68a, 68b, 183a, 184a, 2:437a,
3:544a, **4:209b–211a**, 5:38a
cricket in, 2:183b, 184a
description of, 4:*210*
film industry in, 2:88a, 89b,
115a
Judaism in, 3:285b, 286a
Parsi in, **4:465a–465b**
Mumtaz Mahal, 1:40a, 40b, 5:156a
Munda languages, 1:189b, 190b,
4:192a, **211a–214b**, 452a,
5:128b
Ho, 4:211a, 213b
Mundari, 4:211a, 213a–213b
Santali, 4:211a, 211b–213
Mundari language, 4:211a,
213a–213b

Muslim saints, **4:239a–241b**, *240*, 243a
  roles of, **4:**240a–241a
  Shi'ite, **4:**239a–239b
  Sufi, **4:**239b–240a
  women and, **4:**244a
Muslims, **1:**5a, 10b, 18b, 28a, 29b, 30a, 32, 204a, **3:**11a
  in Afghanistan, **1:**27a
  in Albania, **1:**80b, 81a
  Alevi, **1:82a–82b, 82b–83a,** **5:**540a, 559a, 559b, **6:**16b, 126a, 166
  in Anatolia, **1:**97a, 98a
  Arab, **1:**23a, 25a, 25b, 33b, 34a, 117a, 117b, 118a, 119a
  architectural decoration and, **1:**127b, 128b
  in Asia, **1:**81a, 81b
  in Bengal, **3:**507b
  Bihari, **1:**256b, **5:**62b
  Bolshevik Revolution and, **1:**470b–471a
  Bolsheviks and, **1:**471b
  in British India, **4:**196a
  Buddhists and
    in Thailand, **3:**158b–159b
  in Cambodia, **1:**409b, **3:**160a–161a
  Caucasia and, **1:**448b, 449a, 449b
  in Central Asia, **1:**454b
  discrimination against, **1:**464a
  in China, **2:**560b–561b, **4:237a–238b**
    as national minority, **1:**506b
    rebellions of, **4:**238a
  Chishtiya Sufism and, **2:51a–51b,** **3:**366a–366b, **4:**240a, 524a
  Christians and
    in Indonesia, **2:**78a
  cleanliness of, **4:**238
  control of Guwahati by, **2:**469b
  cuisine of, **2:**205b, 208b, 210a, 213b, **4:**237b
  Greeks in Turkey and, **2:**450a–451a
  Hanafi school, **1:**21b, 23a, 214b, **5:**173a, 173b, 395a, 540a
  Hanbali school of, **1:**214b, **5:**173a, 173b
  Hindus and, **4:**243b, **5:**128a
    in India, **3:**28a, 440b
    Indian nationalism and, **3:**353b
  Hui, **2:**481b, 496b, **560b–562a**

  in India, **1:**173a, 174a, 239b, 240a, **2:**56b, 512a, 518a, 519a–520a, **6:**100b
  caste and, **1:**440a, 442a, 442b–443a
  clothing and, **2:**113b, 114b, 115a
    Hindus and, **1:**77b, 78a, 83b, 323b–324a, **2:**439b–440a, **4:**207b
    in Karnataka state (Mysore), **3:**325b
  Indian education and, **3:**17b–18a, 18a–18b, 20a
  Indian Mutiny and, **4:**244b
  in Indonesia, **1:**397b, **2:**554a–555a, **3:**61a, 62b, **4:**96b, 128a, 128b, **5:**5b, 132a
  influence in Indonesia of, **4:**458b
  in Iraq, **4:**198a
  in Java, **1:**2a, 2b
    heterodox, **1:2a–3a,** **5:**129a, 129b
    orthodox, **5:129a–129b**
  Javanese, **1:**2b
  in Karakalpakstan, **3:**314b
  in Kashmir, **1:**1:203a
  Kashmir and, **3:**32a
  in literature, **2:**83a
  mahalla and, **3:542b–543a**
  Malay
    in Thailand, **3:**159a–160a
  in Malaysia, **1:**103b, 104b, 113a, 114a, **2:**124a, 490a–490b
  Maliki school of, **5:**173a, 173b
  marriage and family of, **4:**68b, 69a, 70b, 71b–72a, 74a
  medicine of, **4:**237b
  in medieval India, **3:**22a, 23b, 24a, 25a
  in Melaka, **4:**550a
  national populations of, **3:**157b
  nationalism of, **3:**201a
  in Pakistan, **4:**209a, 435a, 437a, **6:**142b
  in Philippines, **1:**198a, 198b–199a, **4:**37a, 492b, 503b, 505a, 509b, 510b
    insurgencies of, **4:**196a–197b
  poetry of, **3:**490a
  prayer and, **1:**137a, 137b
  progress and, **3:**195a
  Ramadan and, **2:**490a–490b
  refugees
    from Myanmar, **3:***167*
  Shafi'i school of, **5:**173a, 173b
  Sind and, **5:**210a–210b

  in South Asia
    separatist movements of, **2:**351a
  in Sri Lanka, **5:**317a, 322b, 323b, 325a, 328b
  of Sulu archipelago, **5:**354a
  in Tajikistan, **5:**395a, 400a, 405a, 406a
    clothing of, **2:**130b
  Thai
    in Thailand, **3:**159a, 160a
  in Thailand, **5:**454a
  in Turkey, **1:**36a, 36b
  Turks and, **1:**80a, 80b, 245b, **6:**16b
  in Uzbekistan
    clothing of, **2:**136b, 137b
  women
    clothing of, **2:**114a, 135b
  Zikri sect of, **1:**227a
  See also Dungan people; Islam; Jadidism; khilafat movement; Sufism
Muslims, Shi'ite, **1:**18b, 21b, 23a, 23b, 26a, 85b, 86b, 205b, 206b, 214b, 215a, **4:**210b, **241b–243a**
  in Afghanistan, **2:**495b–496a
  in Azerbaijan, **1:**204a–204b, 205a–205b
  in Baghdad, **1:**216a, **4:**481a
  in Central Asia, **1:**454a, **4:**244a
  fasting and, **1:**119, 120
  in India, **3:**438b, 529a
  in Iran, **1:**217b, 218a, 222b, **3:**97b, 105a, 114b, 175b–176a, 178a, 178b, 179a, **4:**481a, **5:**35a, 35b, 75a, 400a
  in Iraq, **1:**266b, **3:**125a, 138b, 175b–176a, 178a, 178b, **4:**76b, 481a
    human rights and, **3:**137a, 137b, 138b
    political parties of, **3:**141a–141b
  Ismaili sects of, **3:**183a–184b
  Ismaili (Sevener), **1:**21b, 23a, 238b, **4:**242a, 242b, **5:**104b, 395a, 405a, 406a, **6:**18a
  Ja'fari school of, **5:**173b
  in Pakistan, **4:**426b, **5:**75a
  pilgrimage centers of, **3:**124b
  pilgrimage sites of, **4:**81b, 92b, *93*
  pleasure marriages and, **4:**76a
  saints in, **4:**239a–239b
  in South Asia, **3:**185a
  traditional medicine and, **4:**125b

Napoleon, **1**:326a, 326b, 436a
  India and, **2**:307a
  invasion of Egypt (1798) by,
    1:120a, 121a
Napoleon, Louis, **2**:228a
Naqsh, Jamil, **4:283a–283b**
Naqsh-i Faryaadi (Supplicant's
  Prayer; Faiz), **2**:361b
Naqshbandiya (Sufi order), **3**:201b,
  4:240a, **283b–284a**
Nara (Japan), **1**:141b, 142a, b,
  2:6b, 38b, **4:284a–284b**
  Buddhist monuments in, **4**:284a
  Todai-ji Temple in, **1**:*343*
  tourism in, **5**:515b
  See also Kyoto
Nara period (Japan), **1**:342b,
  2:497a, **4:284b–285b**
  centralized government and,
    4:284b
  clothing in, **2**:118b
  Confucianism in, **2**:161b
  cuisine of, **2**:197a–197b
  Dokyo Incident in, **4**:285a–285b
  laquerware of, **3**:436b
  literature in, **4**:285a–285b
  masks in, **4**:82a
  music in, **4**:229b
  painting in, **4**:414b
  poetry of, **4**:533b
  Sado Island in, **5**:116a
  temple building and, **4**:284b
Narai (Phra Narai; king; Ayutthaya), **1**:202a, 203a, **3**:513b
Narakasura (legendary king; Assam), **1**:172b, 173a
Narantsatsralt, Janlavyn,
  4:285b–286a
Narayan, R. K., **1**:95a, 96a, **3**:491a,
  4:286a
Narayana, Bhatta, **3**:511a
Narbuta Biy, **1**:461a
Naresuan (king; Siam), **4**:205a,
  5:460b
Narita Airport (Japan), **2**:98a
Narita (Japan), **1**:500a
Narmada Dam Controversy (In-
  dia), **4:286a–286b**
Narmada Man, **4**:450a, 450b
Narmada River, **4:286b–287a**,
  450a
narrow money (Japan), **3**:*211*, 224
Naruhito, prince (Japan), **2**:503a
Narukami (Narukami The Thun-
  der God; Ichikawa Danjuro I),
  3:294a
Naruse Mikio, **2**:92a, 92b
NASDA. *See* National Space De-
  velopment Agency.

Naser al-Din Shah, **1**:19a, 211a,
  5:22a, 22b, 23a, 435b
Nasir, Ibrahim, **4**:25a
Nasir al-Din Shah, **1**:211a
Nasr ibn Ahmad (ruler; Samanid
  Persia), **3**:520a, **5**:104b
Nasr Ilis, **1**:454a
Nasrallahi, 'Abdallah, **1**:486b
Nasser, Gamal Abdel, **3**:134b–135a
Nastaliq script, **2**:516a
Nastikas (Hindu sects), **2**:522a
Nasution, A.H., **2**:432b
Nataka (Indian drama genre),
  4:287a–288b
  dance and music of,
    4:288a–288b
  heroes and heroines of,
    4:287b–288a
Natakusuma. *See* Paku Alam.
Natal Indian Congress
  in South Africa, **2**:421a, 421b
Nation-Religion-Monarch,
  4:288b–290b
  national integration and destiny,
    metaphor of, **4**:288b–289a
National Assembly (*al-Majlis al
  Watani*; Iraq), **3**:140a, 140b
National Association of Mass Edu-
  cation Movements (MEM),
  6:191b
National Awakening Party (PKB:
  Indonesia), **3**:66b
National Awakening Party (PKB;
  Indonesia), **3**:67b–68a, 71a
National Coalition Government of
  the Union of Burma
  (NCGUB)292, **4**:292a
National Cultural Congress
  Malaysian theater and, **3**:277b
National Day (China), **4:290b**
National Democratic Alliance
  (NDA; India), **3**:26b–27a
National Democratic Front (NDF;
  Myanmar), **2**:345b, 346a,
  3:298a, 323a
National Front for the Liberation
  of South Vietnam, **3**:358b
National Front for the Liberation
  of South Vietnam (National
  Liberation Front; NLF; Viet
  Cong), **1**:411a, **4:290b–291b**,
  291a, 326a, **6**:63b, 70a, 77a,
  78a, 83a, 83b, 85a
  People's Liberation Armed
    Forces (PLAF) of, **4**:291a
National Front (Malaysia)
  human rights and, **5**:294a–294b
National Integration Conference
  (India; 1961), **3**:12

National League for Democracy -
  Myanmar, **2**:b
National League for Democracy
  (NLD; Myanmar), **2**:345b,
  346a, b, **4**:248a–248b, 251a,
  259a–259b, 261, 265a, 265b,
  266b, 267a, 268a, 270,
  291b–292a, **5**:334a, **6**:27a
National Levelers' Association
  (Suiheisha; Japan), **1**:379a, 380a
National Liberation Front (NLF;
  South Vietnam), **2**:154b,
  4:290b–291b, **5**:526a
  Cambodia and, **1**:426b–427a
  establishment of, **6**:83a
  Iron Triangle and, **3**:145b–146b
National Mandate Party (PAN; Indonesia), **3**:68a
national minorities (China),
  1:506b–507a, **2**:449a,
  476b–477a, 533b–534a,
  560b–561b, **4**:197b,
  292b–294b, 293a
  clothing of, **2**:108a, 112a–112b
  in constitution, **1**:525a
  cuisine of, **2**:192a
  education and, **1**:515a,
    515b–516a
  rights of, **1**:520a
  See also ethnic groups
National Order Party (Turkey),
  2:170b
National Peacekeeping Council
  (NPC;Thailand), **4:294b–295a**
National People's Congress
  (China), **1**:527a, **3**:521a
National Science and Technology
  Board (NSTB; Singapore),
  2:507b
National Socialist Council of Na-
  galand (NSCN), **1**:256a
National Space Development
  Agency (NASDA; Japan), **3**:241a
National Student Center of Thai-
  land (NSTC), **5**:340b, 341a
National Sugar Institute (India),
  3:309b
National Taiwan University,
  4:295a–295b
National Trade Union Congress
  (Singapore), **5**:221b
National United Front for an In-
  dependent, Neutral, Peaceful
  and Cooperative Cambodia. *See*
  FUNCINPEC.
National Unity Party (Myanmar),
  4:271b
National Unity Party (NUP;
  Myanmar), **4:295b–296a**

leadership of Kazakhstan and,
3:344b–345a, 411a
Nazarbaeva, Dariga, 4:99b
Nazik al-Mala'ikah, 4:533a
Nazir (Indian poet), 3:490b
NDF. *See* National Democratic
Front.
Ne Win, U, 1:111b, 112b, 182a,
183a, 381a, 382a, 2:72b, 345a,
477a, b, 3:29b, 298a, 322b,
4:160a, 249b, 250b, 252b, 254b,
259a, 261, 264b, 266a,
269a–269b, 271a, *298*,
298a–299a, 463a
Shan and, 5:164a, 165a
SLORC and, 5:333b
near money (Japan), 3:*211*, 224a
Nebuchadnezzar, 5:497a
Nebuta Festival, 1:114b,
115a–115b, 5:504b
NEC Corporation, 2:324a, 326a,
509a
Nedum-Cheliyan, 4:460a
Needham, Joseph, **4:299a**
Negara Brunei Darussalam. *See*
Brunei.
Negara Kesatuan Kalimantan
Utara (NKKU, the Unitary
State of North Borneo), 1:204a,
204b
Negeri Sembilan (Malaysia), 1:8b,
13b, 15a, 16b, 319b, 2:369b,
3:549b, **4:299a–300a**
Federated Malay States and,
4:474b
matrilineal inheritance in,
1:15a, 4:299a–300a
resident system in, 5:81b, 82a
Negoro ware (Japanese laquer-
ware), 3:436b–437a
Negritoes people
Orang Asli, in Malaysia, 4:389b
in Philippines, 3:530b,
4:502b–503a
Negritos, 4:502b–503a
Nehru, Jawaharlal, 1:5a, 85a, 161a,
233b, 234, 291a, 2:262a, 336b,
348a, 419b, 3:11b, 13b, 25b,
4:34b, **300a–301a**, *301*
Ceylon (Sri Lanka) and, 3:36b
Chandigarh and, 1:488a
China-India relations and, 2:2a
Five Year Plans of, 4:300b
"Independence Resolution" of,
4:301a–301b
Indian constitution and, 2:166b
Indian foreign policy and,
3:28a, 34b
as Kashmiri pandit, 4:460a

Myanmar and, 3:29b
Rajagopalachari and, 5:46a, 46b
reform of Hindu law and, 2:518a
on U.S.-Pakistan relations,
3:40b
Nehru, Motilal, **4:301b–302a**
Nei Monggol. *See* Inner Mongolia
Autonomous Region.
nembutsu, 2:547b
Nemichandra, 3:490a
Nena at Neneng (Pena), 3:506a
Neo-Confucianism, 1:336b, 340b,
345b, 2:157b, 158b, 160a,
495a–495b, **4:302b–307a**,
6:171b, 172a, 179a, 215b–216b
Cheng-Zhu school of, 2:159b
in China
Ming dynasty, 4:153b
China-Korea relations and,
2:14a
Chinese education and,
4:302a–305b
in Choson dynasty, 5:422a,
6:140a–140b, 194b–195a
Five Classics and, 1:389b
foot binding and, 2:397a
Four Books and, 2:401a–401b,
4:304a
human rights and, 1:519a
individual development and,
4:302a–307b
in Japan, 2:39b, 161b,
4:305b–307a, 5:508a
in Korea, 2:60b, 61a, 182a,
4:304a–306a, 462b
Choson period, 2:162b,
163a–164a, 3:390a,
5:422a, 422b
human rights and, 5:278b
Korea and, 5:115a
Mencius and, 4:140a
in Ming dynasty, 5:67a
in Qing dynasty, 5:30b
in Song dynasty, 4:411b, 5:67a,
415b
in Vietnam, 4:539b
See also Confucianism
Neohren, A. G., 5:306a
Neolithic era, 1:109b, 130b,
131a–131b, 144a, 4:443a–444b,
449a–449b, 451a, 5:535b, 556a
in China, 1:130a, 130b, 5:166a
in Japan
Forest, 3:279b
in Korea, 1:143a–143b
in Turkey, 1:108b
NEP. *See* New Economic Policy.
Nepal, 3:43b, **4:307a–317b**, *310,*
311, 313, 315

1990 constitution and
preamble of, 4:316a–316b
agriculture in, 4:309b–310a
AIDS in, 1:68a, 68b
Bhutan and, 1:287b–288a, 294b,
6:104a
Britain and, 5:54b
Buddhist shrines in, 4:523b
cashmere industry in, 1:436a
Christianity in, 2:74b
Colombo Plan and, 2:143a
constitutional monarchy in,
4:317a–317b
economic system of,
4:309b–311a
education system of, 4:*311,*
311a–313a
women's access to, 4:312a
endangered species in, 2:331a
ethnic groups in, 4:308b–309a,
313a–313b, 5:128a
Green Revolution in, 2:451b,
452b, 453a
Himalayas and, 2:*512*–514a
history, timeline of, **4:314a**
history of, 4:309a–309b, *313,*
313a–315a
industry in, 4:309b–310b
international trade of,
4:310b–311a
Internet in, 4:111a
Islam in, 3:169a
King Birendra and,
4:316b–317a
languages of, 5:234b–236a
map of, 4:*307*
marriage and family in, 4:71a
marriage in, 4:68b
media in, 4:110a–112a
mountaineering in, 5:519b
nature tourism in, 5:519b
political system of,
4:313a–315a, *315,*
315a–317b
profile of, 4:307a–309b
refugee camps in, 1:287b–288a
rulers of, 5:54a
sculpture in, 5:142a
Shah dynasty of, 4:313b–314b
See also Kathmandu; Kathmandu valley
Nepal Darbar Library, 3:507a–507b
Nepalese people
in Bhutan, 2:104b, 105b
Nepali, 3:47a, 50b
Nepali language, 1:293b, 3:44a,
47a, 50b, 4:308b–309a
Nerchinsk, Treaty of (1689),
2:15b, 16, 3:244a

economic stagnation of, **4**:352a
economic system of,
    4:348b–350a, **350b–353b**
    South Korea and,
      5:273a–273b
economic turnaround of,
    4:352a–352b
education system of,
    4:**354a–355a**, **5**:0
    kyoyuk and *kyoyang* and,
      4:354a
    role of class background and
      party loyalty in, **4**:354b
    school quality and, **4**:354a
energy shortages in,
    4:352a–352b, 353b
establishment of, **3**:392b, **6**:141b
farm improvement programs in,
    4:352a
food crisis in, **2**:**395b–396b**,
    4:351b–352a, 356a–356b
foreign relations and,
    4:350a–350b
human rights in, **4**:**355a–357a**
    censorship and, **4**:355b
    control of judiciary and,
      4:355b–356a
    International Covenant on
      Civil and Political Rights
      (ICCPR) and, **4**:355b,
      356b–357a
    labor camps and,
      4:355b–356a
    treatment of foreigners and,
      4:355b
incentive systems of, **4**:351b
industry in, **2**:58b, 473a, 480a,
    4:281a, 347b, 364a,
    5:336a–336b
Kangwon province and,
    3:308a–308b
Korean Communist Party in,
    6:141b, 195b
Korean Workers Party (KWP)
    of, **4**:357a–357b, 359a–359b,
    360b, **5**:510b, 511b
    Organization Department of
      the secretariat and,
      4:359a–359b
    Ten Principles for Establish-
      ment of the Monolithic
      Idea and, **4**:359b
literature in, **3**:501a
mining in, **1**:485b
missile threat from, **3**:248a
nuclear energy and, **5**:286a
nuclear weapons and, **4**:348b,
    350a–350b, 368a–368b,
    369b, 370a–371b

open door policy and,
    4:353a–353b
origins of, **3**:397b–398a
political system of, **4**:348a,
    350a, 351a, 353a, *357*,
    357a–361a
    Kim Il Sung and,
      4:357b–360b, 362b
    Kim Jong Il and, **4**:357b,
      359a–361a, 362b
    socialist constitution (pref-
      ace) for, **4**:358
    Supreme People's Assembly
      (SPA) and, **4**:360a
poverty in, **5**:313a
prison camps (9-27 camps) in,
    4:356b
Pyongyang in, **5**:**20a–20b**
socialist corporatism in, **2**:152b
South Korea and, **2**:85a
South P'yongan province of,
    5:289b–290a
special economic zones in,
    4:350a, 353a
sports in, **5**:303a, 313a
starvation in, **4**:356a–356b
statistics of, **4**:349
suppression of religion in, **2**:15a
Taedong River in, **5**:**367a**
tourism in, **2**:473a
trade in, **2**:58b, **4**:352a–353b
water pollution in, **4**:281a
See also China-Korea relations;
    Juche ideology; Kim Il Sung;
    Kim Jong Il; Korea; South
    Korea
North Korea-South Korea rela-
    tions, **2**:85a, **3**:376a,
    4:342b–343b, *361*, 361a–362b,
    5:283b
    calligraphy and, **1**:*406a*
    economic, **4**:342b–343b
    economic ventures and,
      4:342b–343b
    energy and, **5**:286a
    human rights and, **5**:280a
    Korean War and, **4**:362a,
      5:270a, 271a
    movement toward reunification
      and, **5**:336b
    negotiations in, **5**:272a–272b,
      286a
    reunification and, **4**:362a–362b,
      5:284b
    sadaejuui ("toadyism") and,
      5:**115a–115b**
    sports and, **5**:313a
    trade and, **4**:342b–343b
    U.S. and, **5**:286b–287b

North Korea-Soviet relations,
    2:40a
    North-South division and,
      4:361a–362a
North Korea-United States rela-
    tions, **2**:152b, **4**:**362a–362b**
    North-South division and,
      4:361a–362a
North Korean Central Bank, **3**:283a
North Korean Workers' Party
    (NKWP), **3**:281a–283a, 400b
North Kyongsang province (South
    Korea), **4**:**363b–364a**
    Buddhist sites in, **4**:364a
    industry in, **4**:364a
    mask dance in, **4**:364a
North P'yongan province (North
    Korea), **4**:**364a–364b**
    agriculture in, **4**:364a–364b
    industry in, **4**:364a–364b
North Sulawesi, **3**:52b
North Vietnam. *See* Vietnam, So-
    cialist Republic of.
North-West Frontier province
    (NWFP; Pakistan), **1**:19b,
    4:**365b–366a**, 424a, 427a, 427b,
    433a, 436b, **6**:142b
    Pashtun tribes of, **4**:365b–366a
Northern Alliance (Afghanistan),
    1:19a, 19b, 23b, 25b, 26a, 28b,
    30a, **4**:92b, **5**:407b
    opium and, **1**:24b, 25a
Northern and Southern dynasties
    (China)
    Buddhism in, **2**:221a, **4**:411a
    classical Chinese and, **2**:46a
    painting in, **4**:411a
Northern Expedition (China),
    2:31b, 455b, 465a, 466a,
    4:**364b–365a**, **5**:169a, **6**:102b,
    214a–214b
    Chiang Kai-shek and, **1**:498b,
      4:364b–365a, **5**:79a
    China-U.S. relations and, **2**:24b
    Chinese Communist movement
      and, **4**:365a
    Chinese warlords and,
      4:364b–365a
Northern Territories (Kurile is-
    lands;Japan), **3**:244a,
    4:**365a–365b**
    control of, **4**:365a–365b
    Russian-Japanese relations and,
      3:244a, **4**:365a–365b
    See also Southern Kuriles
Northern Wei dynasty (China),
    5:172a
Northwest Frontier, **4**:424a, 427a,
    427b, 433a, 436b

4:396a–396b, **5:**143b, 425b
jatra and, **3:**266b
Orita Katsuko, **2:**241a
Oriya language, **3:**44a, 44b, 50b, **4:**396b, 397a
Munda languages and, **4:**211b
Oriya (language), **3:**44b, 50b
Oriya (Sabat), **4:**531a
Oriyas people, **4:396b–397a**
Orogens people (China), **2:**449b
Orta Direk (The Wind from the Plain; Kemal), **3:**347b
Osaka Action Plan, **4:397b–398a**
Osaka Castle, **4:**397a, 397b
Osaka (Japan), **3:**206a, **4:397a–397b**, **5:**507b
tourism in, **5:**515b
World's Fair (1970) in, **5:**510a
Osaka Jijoden (Osaka Autobiography; Fujisawa Takeo), **2:**408a
Osanai Kaoru, **2:**90a, 288b, 289a, **3:**496b, **5:**378a
Osh Aymagi (Kyrgyzstan), **3:**432b
Osh (Central Asia), **4:398a–398b**
invasions of, **1:**477a
Osh (Kyrgyzstan), **3:**430a
Oshima Nagisa, **2:**92a, 96a
Osman I (founder of Ottoman empire), **1:**389a, **6:**16a
Osman tribe (Turkey), **4:**398b
Osmania University (India), **2:**571a
Osmeña, Sergio, **3:**243a
Ota Dokan, **5:**509a
Otgan Kunlar (Past Days; Abdullah Quaisi), **1:**5a
Otgon Tenger (mountain; Mongolia), **2:**486a
Otto, Rudolph, **1:**168b, 169b
Ottoman
literary traditions of, **3:**514b–517b
Ottoman empire, **1:**1b, 3a, 6a, 12b, 79b, 80b, 81b, 82a, 85b, 86b, 97a, 97b, 111a, 112a, 125a, 125b, 139b, **3:**187b–188a, 387a, **4:398b–401a, 398b–401b**, **6:**192b
administration of, **4:**141a
Afghani clothing and, **2:**103a
Albanians and, **1:**80, 80b–81a, 81a
Albanians in, **1:**80b–81a, 81a
ancient Iran and, **3:**105a
architecture in, **1:**138b–140a, 140a, 140b, 155b, 433b
architecture of, **1:**138b
Asia Minor and, **5:**123a, 424a, 556a
Baghdad and, **1:**215a, 215b

Bulgarians and, **1:**374b
Caucasia and, **1:**449b, 450a
character of, **4:**400a–400b
Circassians and, **2:**97a–97b
clothing of, **2:**134b, 135a
conversion of churches to mosques, **5:**525a
culture of, **4:**400b–401a
Dardanelles and, **2:**250b
demise of, **1:**35b, 36b, 215b, **3:**188b, **5:**543a, 556b, 557b, 563b, **6:**16a
khilafat movement and, **3:353a–353b**
Eastern Orthodox Church and, **2:**317b–318a
Edirna, second capital of, **2:**321b
education in, **5:**547b–548a
expansion of, **4:**398b–399b
impact of, **4:**401a
in Iraq, **4:**198a
Iraq and, **1:**267a, **3:**114b, 115a
Iraq-Turkey relations and, **3:**142a–142b
Islam in, **4:**400b
Janissaries in, **4:**400a, 400b, **5:**418a
Judaism and, **3:**286b, 287a–287b
Kirkuk and, **3:**379a
Kurds in, **3:**413b
later history of, **4:**399b–400a
literary traditions of, **3:**480a, 514b–517b
literature of, **4:**532a–532b
measurement systems in, **4:**95a
minarets in, **4:**148a
music in, **4:**233b
Muslim saints' shrines and, **4:**241a
in 1900, **5:**556b–557a
occupation of Kermanshah (Bakhtaran), **1:**222a
Persia and, **5:**365b
Persian miniatures in, **4:**483b
printing and, **4:**114b
reforms in, **5:**418a
spice trade and, **5:**300a
sultan of, **4:**399
Tanzimat in, **1:**215b, **5:**418a
traditional medicine and, **4:**125b
Tulip Era (1718–1730) of, **5:**418a
Turkey and, **1:**90a, 91a, 108b, 109a, 109b, 110a, 110b, 111b, 500b, **2:**280a, **3:**190b, 191a, **4:**476b, **5:**80b, 93b, 539a, 556b, **6:**16a

Turkish cuisine and, **2:**214b
Turkish Islam and, **3:**176a
Turkish Republic and, **1:**176a, 177a
in World War I, **4:**400a, **5:**561b
Ottoman Turkish language, **4:**401a, **5:**548b
Ou Mountains (Japan), **1:**114a, 115a, **2:**410b
Oudh (India), **1:**84b, 85a, **4:**244b
Oudh princes, **3:**528b
Ouichi Hiroyo, **6:**183a–183b
Oun Huenen (Sam Sene Thai), **2:**361a
Outline History of Vietnamese Culture, An (Anh Dao Duy), **1:**107a, 108a
Overbeck, Baron Von, **5:**113a
Overseas Economic Cooperation Fund (OECF), **4:401a–401b**
Ovid
Ganges River and, **2:**423a
Oz Beg (Uzbek) Khan, **2:**442a–442b, **6:**54b
Ozal, Turgut, **2:**263a, **4:401b–402b**, **5:**555b, 559a, 560a, 565a
Ozawa Seiji, **4:**230b
Ozu Yasujiro, **2:**90b, 91a, 92a, 95a

P
Pa-O-Rocket Festival (Shan states), **2:**464a
pachinko, **4:403a–403b**
Pacific Charter, **4:**516a
Pacific Islands-Japan relations, **3:**239b–241a
Pacific Ocean, **4:403b–404a**, 491b
migrations into, **1:**6b
war in, **3:**240a
Pacific Rim, **4:404a–404b**
Padas Raja, **3:**503b
Padmasambhava, Guru (Guru Rimpoche), **1:**285b, 287a, 292a, 292b, 293a, 294b
Padmavat (Mohamed of Jais), **3:**490a
Padmini (queen; India), **6:**146a
Padoh Ba Thin, **3:**323a
Padri War (Sumatra; 1821–1837), **3:**269a, **4:404b–405a**
Padshahnama (Lahawri), **5:**156a
P'aegwan chapki (Storyteller's Miscellany; O Suk-kwon), **3:**498b
Paekche kingdom (Korea), **2:**60b, 289b, 290a–290b, **3:**376a, 376b, 389a, 400b, 401a, 405a, 410a, 416b, **5:**479a, **6:**24b, 26a, 103a, 289b

Rupamati of Malwa, **6**:146a
rural areas
  in Central Asia
    media in, **4**:99a
  in China
    CCP and, **2**:31b
    family planning and, **4**:54b,
      56a–56b
    industrialization and, **2**:151a
    sericulture in, **5**:150a, 152b
    Shang dynasty, **5**:167b
  Cultural Revolution and, **2**:224a
  in India
    Communism and, **4**:79a
    government of, **2**:165b
  in Malaysia
    ethnic groups and, **4**:90a
  in South Asia
    marriage and family in, **4**:75a
    media in, **4**:112a
  in Southeast Asia
    marriage and family and,
      4:62b, 64a, 66b, 68a
    marriage and family in,
      4:63b
    traditional medicine in, **4**:125a
  in Vietnam
    clothing in, **2**:138b
    marriage and family and,
      4:67a
Rural Trilogy (Hong Shen), **2**:551b
rural workers, surplus
  in China, **5:105b–106a**
Rushdie, Salman, **3**:98a, *109b*,
  113a, 201a, 491a, **4**:115b, 436a
Rusk, Dean, **4**:515a, **6**:79b
Rusk-Thanarat Agreement (1962),
  5:133a
Ruskin, John, **2**:175a
Russell, Bertrand, **1**:517b
Russell, George William (AE),
  1:300b
Russia, **1**:1a, 5b, 6a, 6b, 19a, 66a,
  66b
  Altay Mountains in, **1**:88a, 88b,
    89a
  Bolshevik Revolution in, **1**:85a,
    86a, 159b, **2**:489b, 511a,
    3:546a
  Britain and, **5**:561a
    in Central Asia, **4**:81b,
      5:395b–396a
  Bukhara and, **5**:400b
  Caspian Sea and, **1**:437a, 437b
  Caucasia and, **1**:448b, 460a
  China-India relations and, **2**:2a,
    2b
  China-U.S. relations and, **2**:24a
  Chinese settlers in, **2**:20b

  Circassians and, **2**:97a–97b
  Circassians in, **2**:97b
  CIS and, **1**:472b, 473a
  economic system of
    China-Russia/Soviet Union
      relations and, **2**:20a–20b
  economy in, **1**:165b, 166b
  in Far East, **2**:446a, 542a–542b
  Fergana valley and, **2**:375a
  German settlers in, **2**:432a
  goat-meat market in, **1**:437a
  influence of
    on Central Asian carpets,
      1:435b
  Iran and, **1**:206a, 207a,
    3:105b–106b, 115a,
    116b–118b
    Islamic Revolution and,
      3:181b, 182a
  Ismaili sects and, **3**:184a
  Jadidism in, **3**:194a
  Japanese expansion and, **3**:259a
  Kyrgyz people and, **3**:421b,
    424a, 429b–430a
  modern pastoral nomads and,
    4:340a–340b
  Mongol empire and,
    4:339b–340a
  Mongolian languages in,
    4:185a, 185b
  Mongols in, **4**:189a, 190a
  Muslim Turks and, **5**:561a
  Napoleonic invasion of, **2**:228b
  nuclear weapons and,
    4:368a–371b, 369b,
    370a–371a
  pre-Revolution parties in,
    5:149b
  in Samarqand, **5**:122b
  SCO and, **5**:169b
  trade with Japan and,
    3:247a–247b
  Zakaspiiskaia oblast (Tran-
    scaspian province) of, **1**:162a
  See also Siberia; Soviet Union
Russia-Great Britain relations,
  1:23a
  Central Asia and, **2**:446a–446b,
    5:400b
Russia-United States relations,
  3:117a–118a
Russian Civil War (1918–1922),
  1:3a, 179a, 180a, **2**:306a
  Central Asia and, **1**:471a, **2**:145b
  Siberia and, **5**:196a
  U.S -Philippines relations and,
    4:515a
Russian language
  in Central Asia, **1**:462b, 470b,

    472a, 474a–474b, 477b,
    5:395a, 399a, **6**:8a, 10a, 10b,
    11a, 48b, 49a, 55b, 114a
  influence of
    on Farsi-Tajiki language,
      2:367a
  in Mongolia, **4**:170b
  Mongolian and, **4**:190b
  in Vietnam, **6**:66a
Russian Orthodox Church. *See*
  Eastern Orthodox Church.
Russian people
  in Central Asia, **1**:19b, 20a,
    463a, 463b–464a, 470b,
    471a, 473a, **4**:340a–340b,
    5:106a–107a
  cuisine of, **2**:207a
  invasions of Central Asia by,
    1:477a
  in Mongolia, **4**:164b,
    5:107a–107b
  White, **2**:446b
Russian Revolution (1905)
  Central Asia and, **1**:470b
Russian Revolution (1917)
  Central Asia and, **1**:463b, 465a,
    470b–471a, **2**:130b, 380b,
    4:389b, 486b, **5**:366a, 401a,
    424b, **6**:55a
  Japan and, **5**:377a
  Japanese cinema and, **2**:90b
  Kazakhstan and, **5**:149b
  Mongolia and, **4**:180b
Russian-Turkish wars, **2**:321b
Russians
  in Central Asia, **1**:20a
Russification and Sovietization
  in Central Asia, **1**:471b–472a,
    5:108a–111a, 405b
Russo-Japanese War (1904–1905),
  1:121a, 122a, **2**:11a, 489b,
  3:208a, 236a–236b, 244b, 252b,
  259a, 309a, 395a, **4**:134b,
  5:111b–112b, 376b, 377b,
  411b, **6**:183b
  Chinese in Japan and, **2**:33b
  decisive naval battle in,
    5:534b–535a
  Japanese cinema and, **2**:95a
  Korea and, **2**:62a, **3**:392a
  Manchuria and, **2**:11a, **4**:28b
  See also Sino-Japanese War
Russo-Turkish War, **1**:374b, 375a
Rustaveli, Shota, **1**:449b
Ryohaku mountain range (Japan),
  2:434b
Ryskulov, Turar, **3**:466b
Ryukyu Islands (Japan), **2**:313b,
  3:249a, 438a, **6**:190a

Sankhyapravachana Sutra (Kapila),
2:522b
Sannai Maruyama, 3:280b
Sansho Daiyu (*Sansho the Bailiff;
Mori Ogai*), 3:495a
Sanskrit language, 1:172a, 173a,
192a, 192b, 277b, 278a, 280a,
335a, 353b, 358b, 2:514b–515b,
517b, 3:34a, 47a, 491a, 4:276b,
461a, **5:**125a–125b, 6:119a
Arthasastra (Kautilya) and, 3:330a
Ayurvedic medicine and, 4:116a
borrowings from, 5:409b
Brahmans and, 1:314b
in Cambodia, 1:418a
Central Asian literature and,
3:480a
drama in, 2:291a–291b, 490b,
5:3b
epic poetry and, 3:541a–542b
in Gupta dynasty, 2:468a
Hindi and, 1:219b
Indian Buddhism and, 4:276b
Indian literature and,
3:488a–490a, 507a–508b,
510a–511b, 512a,
541a–542b
during Indian medieval period,
3:23a
Indian music and, 4:224a, 226b
inscriptions in, 1:367a, 3:302b,
328b
at Dunhuang, 4:158a
Japanese writing system and,
2:7a
languages of Europe and, 3:49,
50b
in Laos, 3:445a
literature in, 3:44b–45a, 4:530a
mass media and, 4:98a
medical texts in, 4:127b
Mongolian literature and,
4:189a
Munda languages and, 4:213a,
214a
music and, 4:222b
in poetry, 3:477a
in Southeast Asian calendars,
1:397b, 399a
speakers of, 3:44a
in Srivijaya, 5:332a
study of, 4:393b
terms from, 5:134a
texts in, 4:523a
Vedic, 1:162a, 167b, 168b,
2:491b, 5:56b
Vedic, in India, 4:452a
Sanskrit Siksastaka (Lesson in Eight
Verses; Chaitanya), 3:508a

Sanskritization, 2:514b,
5:125b–128a
changing forms of, 5:127b–128a
criticisms of, 5:127a–127b
cultural, 5:127a
Dalit movement and, 5:127a
models of, 5:126b–127a
as structural process,
5:125b–126b
vegetarianism and, 2:212a,
5:126b, 127a
women and, 5:126b–127a, 127a,
127b
Sansom, George B., 1:171a, 172a
Santal people (South Asia),
5:128a–129a
Santali language, 4:211a,
211b–213a, 5:128b
Santo Tomas, University of
(Philippines), 1:445a, 2:459a
Santos, Al, 1:446a
Santos, Bienvenido N., 4:538b
Santos, Lope, 3:506a, 4:538b
santri (putihan; orthodox Javanese
Muslims), **5:129a–129b**
Sao Shwe Thaike, 2:345a
Sapalli Tepe, 1:128a, 129a
Sapporo (Japan), 2:542a,
5:129b–130a
high-technology industry and,
2:542b
Sarachchandra, Ediriweera,
3:512b, 513a
Sarada Kinenbi (Salad Anniversary;
Tawara Machi), 4:535a
Sarangadeva, 4:217a
sarangi (stringed instrument),
5:130a–130b
Sarasvati River, 2:424a, 3:76b
Saraswati, Dayanand, 2:518b
Saraswati (Hindu goddess), 4:460a
Sarawak (Borneo, Malaysia),
1:105b, 106b, 204a, 204b, 307b,
308b, 309a, 325b, 326b, 2:429a,
4:1a, 4b, **5:130b–131a**
British in, 4:13b, 21a, 6:128a,
129b
Brooke in, 4:6b, 5:131a, 498a
Brunei and, 1:327a, 328a, 332b,
4:466b
Chinese in, 5:131a, 6:129a,
129b
colonial control of, 2:370a,
6:128b–129a
ethnic groups in, 5:130b–131a
Federation of Malaysia and,
2:370a, 4:332a–332b, 406b,
471b, 5:114a, 498b
foreign investment in, 4:20b

independence of, 4:9a
Japanese occupation of, 6:129b
languages in, 4:488b
Malaysia and, 4:14b, 19a, 474b,
5:131a
map of, 5:*130b*
media in, 4:104a
mineral industry and, 4:150b
mining industry in, 4:7a, 149b,
150a, 5:131a
Ningkan, Stephen Kalong and,
4:332a–332b
oil industry in, 4:41b–42a, 42b
paleoanthropology in, 4:454a
parks in, 5:131a
political system and, 4:17a, 19a
religion in, 4:2a
timber industry in, 5:498a
conservation issues in,
5:499a
in World War II, 4:9a
See also Brooke, James; Kuching; White Rajas
Sarawak (Malaysia)
rubber industry in, 5:104a
Saray Mulk Khanum, 5:122a
Sardar Sarovar dam project (Gujarat), 4:286a–286b
Sardis (Turkey), **5:131a–132a**
Sarekat Islam (Islamic Association;
Indonesia), 1:369b, 3:52b, 64b,
5:129a, **132a–132b**
Sarez Lake (Tajikistan), **5:132b**
Sargon II, 3:324b
Saribas, 1:327a
Sarit Thanarat, 4:36b, 522a,
5:132b–133b, *133a,* 458a, 463a,
472b
Sarkhej, 1:135a, 135b
Sarmad, Hazrat Saeed, 3:285a
Sarmatians, 1:448b
Sarnath (India), 4:523b, **5:133b,**
6:58b
sculpture and, 5:142b
sarod (stringed instrument), **5:134a**
Saroya (queen; Iran), 4:*408*
Sary arka (newspaper), 3:466a
Saryshaghan (Kazakhstan), **5:134a**
Sasagawa Ryoichi, **5:134b**
Sasame yuki (The Makioka Sisters;
Tanizaki Junichiro), 3:495b
Sasanid dynasty (Iran),
3:104a–104b, 122a, 133a,
5:158a, 365a, 395b
Sasanid empire (Iran), 1:23a, 25a,
25b, 110b, 111b, 128b, 129b,
137a, 138a, 214b, 222a, 390b,
2:339a, 3:122a, 133a, 4:198a,
484a, 5:35a, 429a, 6:222a, 223a

Index

Sikhism *(continued)*
  fundamentalist, **5**:206b
  Guru Nanak and, **5**:202b–204a
  independence and,
    2:491a–491b, **5**:206b
  in Kashmir, **1**:1:203a
  Khalsa (Order of the Pure) in,
    5:205a–205b
  separatist movement in, **5**:204,
    206a
  Sikh Panth (brotherhood) and,
    5:204a–205a
Sikhs, **2**:270a, **4**:245a, **5**:202b, *203b*
  clothing of, **2**:113a, 114b
  gurus and, **4**:461b
  in India, **2**:261b, 512a, 519b,
    520b, **3**:13b, **5**:17b, 18a
    caste and, **1**:440a
  in Indonesia, **4**:96b
  marriage and family and, **4**:69a
  marriage of, **4**:68b
  Mughal empire and, **4**:207a,
    5:204b, 205a, 205b
  in Pakistan, **3**:439a, **4**:209a
  texts of, **3**:490b
Sikkim, **2**:251b
Sikkim state (India), **1**:285b, 294b,
  2:424b, **5**:207a–207b
Silappadigaram (Stolen Anklet;
  Ilango Adigal), **3**:489b, 492a,
  537b
Silhara dynasty (India), **4**:210a
silk
  in Bhutan, **5**:445b
  Cambodian
    ikat, **2**:106a, 106b
  in carpets, **1**:434b
  in China, **1**:496b, **2**:483b, 487a
    clothing and, **2**:107b
  Gansu corridor and, **2**:425a
  in India, **2**:115a, **4**:273b
  in Iraq, **2**:117a
  in Japan, **2**:462b, **5**:506b
    exports and, **2**:413a
  in Karakalpakstan, **3**:315b
  in Korea, **2**:120b
  in Laos, **2**:122b, **5**:448b
  in Mongolia, **2**:125a
  production in Japan, **3**:150b
  in Tajikistan, **3**:363b
  in Thailand, **2**:131a, 131b,
    5:476a
  in Tibet, **2**:133a
  in Turkey, **2**:135a
  in Turkmenistan
    clothing and, **2**:136a
  in Vietnam, **2**:138b
  See also kain songket
silk industry, **5**:150a–152b

in China, **2**:107b, 483b, 487a,
  3:471b, **5**:150a–152b, *152a*,
  198b, 361b
  Ming dynasty, **4**:153a
in India, **3**:537b, **5**:181a
in Japan
  Meiji period, **4**:134a
See also sericulture
Silk Road, **1**:81b, 82a, 92a, 93a,
  94a, 150a, 150b, 212b, **2**:441b,
  482b, **3**:431a, **5**:207b–209b,
  363a, **6**:17a, 100a, 176b
  Afghani cuisine and, **2**:185a
  Buddhism and, **1**:337b, **5**:208a
  camels and, **1**:428b, **5**:208a
  caravans on, **1**:433b, **3**:466a,
    5:208a
  Caucasia and, **1**:448b
  Central Asia-Russia relations
    and, **1**:470a
  Central Asian regionalism and,
    1:476b
  Chinese cuisine and, **2**:188b
  cities on, **1**:216b, 371b, 373a,
    5:207b, 208a, **6**:174a, 192b
  demise of, **5**:209a
  Dunhuang and, **4**:157a–157b
  in Fergana valley, **2**:374b,
    4:398a
  goods on, **5**:207b
  Iraqi cuisine and, **2**:196a
  Japan and, **2**:118b
  Japanese music and, **4**:229a
  Karakalpakstan and, **3**:316b
  the Karakoram Highway and,
    3:317b, 318b
  Khujand, Tajikistan and, **3**:363b
  map of, **5**:*208*
  music and, **4**:221a
  Muslims and, **4**:237a
  opium trade and, **2**:302a
  in Pakistan, **4**:425b
  route of, **5**:207b–208b
  sericulture and, **5**:150a
  significance of, **5**:209a
  textiles and, **2**:121b
  Tian Shan and, **5**:481b
  in Turkey, **2**:86b
  Turkic empire and, **1**:452a,
    6:21b
  Turkic nomads and, **4**:339b
  World Heritage sites on, **4**:81a
Silva, W.A., **3**:512b
Sima Qian, **2**:5b, 230a, 485a,
  3:485a
Sima Xiangru, **4**:528b
SIMEX. *See* Singapore Interna-
  tional Monetary Exchange.
Simla Accord (1972), **1**:1:203b,

204a, 295b, **3**:203b–204a,
  5:209b
  Muslim League and, **4**:236b
Simla (India), **1**:182a, 182b,
  2:512a–512b, **5**:209b, 514b
Sin, Jaime, **1**:116b, 117b,
  5:209b–210a
Sin Ch'ae-ho, **5**:115a, 368b
Sin Chew Jit Poh (newspaper; Sin-
  gapore), **2**:49a
Sin Yoon-bok, **4**:418a–418b
Sinan, Mimar (Ottoman architect),
  2:321b, **4**:148a, 401a
Sinan Pasha, **1**:139b, 140b
Sinasi, **3**:515b
*Sind, and the Races That Inhabit the
  Valley of the Indus* (Burton),
  4:394a
Sindh (Pakistan), **1**:53b, 55a, 82b,
  83a, 247b, 282b–283a, **3**:2a,
  277a, 311b, 547b, **4**:424a, 425b,
  427a, 432b, 433a, 436b, **5**:17a,
  210a, 210a–210b, **6**:143a
  Arab invasion of, **4**:432a
  Islam in, **3**:169b
  Ismaili sects in, **3**:185a,
    185b–186a
  patron saint of, **5**:157b
  See also Karachi (Pakistan)
Sindhi language, **1**:283a, **3**:44a,
  47a, **4**:426b, **5**:210a,
  210a–211b, 211a, 211b
  British standardization of, **5**:238b
Sindhi people, **5**:210b–211b
Sindhia family, **2**:543a,
  5:211b–212a
Sinekli Bakkal (Grocery with Flies;
  Halide), **2**:478b
Sinekli Bakkal (The Clown and His
  Daughter; Adivar), **3**:516a–516b
Singan Kilich (Broken Sword;
  Kasimbekov), **3**:481b
Singapore, **1**:270a, **4**:471b, **5**:*214b*
  agriculture in, **5**:212b
    forest fire haze and, **1**:61a,
      61b, 74a, 74b
  APEC secretariat in, **1**:170b,
    171a
  aquaculture in, **2**:*388*
  Australian POWs and, **1**:186a,
    186b–187a
  Bank of Hong Kong in, **1**:*259*
  banking and finance industry in,
    1:259a–261b, **5**:104a, 213b,
    215a, 215b, 216b
    Asian Currency Units (ACU)
      in, **1**:260a
    banking services,
      1:259b–260b

capital markets, **1**:260b–261a

contractual saving institutions, **1**:260b

financial reforms, **1**:261a–261b

financial structure, **1**:259b, 260a

merchant banks, **1**:260b

British in, **4**:13a, 21a, **5**:213a, 438b

British occupation of, **1**:105b, 106b, 319a, 319b, 325a, 327a, **2**:179a, **3**:64a, **5**:218b–219b

CCP and, **2**:32b

censorship in, **4**:98b, **5**:340b

Chinese from, **2**:34b

Chinese in, **2**:35a, *35b*, 42a, **5**:212b, 220a, 222b

Chinese-language newspapers in, **2**:49b–50a

Chinese languages in, **4**:146a

Christianity in, **2**:77b, 78a

civil service of, **2**:440a, **5**:221a, 221b, 222a

colonial buildings of, **6**:124b

Communism in, **5**:220b–221a, 221b

companies in, **5**:216

corruption in, **2**:175b, 176a, 176b, 179a–179b, 180a

currency in, **5**:216a

Democratic Party of, **5**:223a

drama in, **2**:296b

Dutch and, **5**:218b, 219a

Dutch-British agreement on, **5**:219a

Dutch-British dispute over, **1**:326b

economic system of, **5:215a–217a**

challenges to, **5**:216a–217a

characteristics of, **5**:215a–215b

economic growth of, **1**:259a, 261b, **5**:215a, 218a

economic policy and, **5**:215b–216a

1997 economic crisis and, **1**:164a, 165a, 166a, 259a

education system of, **2**:441a, **5:217a–218a**

engineering and technology in, **4**:282b–283a

English acquisition of, **3**:64a

English language in, **2**:336a, **5**:217a, 217b

ethnic relations in, **2**:350a, b

Europeans in, **5**:213a

export-led development in, **2**:358b

Federation of Malaya and, **5**:114a

Federation of Malaysia and, **2**:370a–370b, **3**:549b

fertility rates in, **2**:376b

fesitivals in, **5**:214b

financial services in, **5**:215a

Five Power Defence Arrangements and, **2**:391a–391b

foreign investment in, **5**:221b

founding legend of, **2**:140b

GDP in, **2**:506, **5**:213b, 215a, 217a, 220a

geography of, **5**:212a–212b

Han population and, **2**:480b

high-technology industry in, **2**:505b–510a, **5**:216a

history, timeline of, **5:219**

history of, **5:218a–220a**

ancient, **5**:218a–218b

colonial period (1819–1959), **1**:259a, **5**:217a, 218b–219b

World War II to present, **5**:219b–220a

housing in, **5**:213b, 220b, 222b

human rights and, **5**:294a

human rights in, **5**:218a

immigrants in, **5**:212b–213a, 213b, 215a–215b, 216a

Independence Bill (1965), **1**:263b

independence of, **3**:464b–465a, 473a–473b, **4**:9a, **5**:220b

as independent nation-state, **1**:320a

Indian immigrants in, **3**:34a

industrial development of, **2**:441a

infrastructure of, **5**:215b, 220b

Internet in, **4**:111a, **5**:216b

IT industry and, **3**:82b, 83b, 84b

Japanese firms in, **3**:262a

Japanese foreign investment and, **3**:263a

Japanese occupation of, **5**:219b

labor unions in, **5**:221b

languages in, **5**:214a, 217a, 217b

languages of, **3**:550a

leaders in, **4**:77b–78a

literacy in, **5**:214a, 217a, 322b

Malaysia and, **4**:14b, 19a, 21b, **5**:221b

trade with, **4**:20b

map of, **5**:*212b*

measurement systems in, **4**:93b, 94b

media in, **4**:98b, 102a, 102b, 103a–103b, 104a, 104b, 109b, **5**:340a–340b

Melaka and, **4**:138b

National University of, **4**:296a

New Year in, **5**:315b

New Zealand and, **4**:324b–325a

people of, **5**:212b–214a, 220b

People's Party of, **5**:223a

Philippines and, **4**:517a

political system of, **2**:440a–440b, 441a, **5:220a–223a**

administrative state in, **5**:221b–222a

parties in, **4**:77b, **5**:221a, *221b*, 222a–222b, 223a

People's Action Party and, **5**:220a, 220b–**221**a–**222b**

prime ministers of, **2**:440a–440b, **5**:218a, 220a, 221b

shaping of, **5**:221a–221b

since 1984, **5**:222a–222b

pollution in, **5**:212b

Portuguese in, **5**:213a

prime ministers of, **5**:220a

profile of, **5:212a–215a**

puppetry in, **5**:155b

Raffles College in, **1**:3b, **2**:440a

recession (1985) and, **5**:222a

religions in, **5**:214a–214b

Republic of

founding of, **2**:370b

service sector in, **5**:215a

smelting in, **5**:501a

socialism in, **3**:464b, **5**:220b–221a

society and culture in, **5**:214a–214b

South Korea and, **5**:275a

sports in, **5**:148b

statistics on, **5**:213

storytelling in, **5**:338a

Straits of, **1**:105b, 106b

temples in, **5**:214a–214b

trade and, **5**:215a, 216a–216b, 218b–219a, 219b

unemployment in, **5**:216a

Workers' Party in, **6:156b–157a**

workforce in, **5**:213b, 214b, 215b, 216a, 217a, 221b

See also Raffles, Thomas Stamford

Singapore, University of, **2**:440a

Singapore-Cambridge General Certificate of Education (GCE), **5**:217b

Spanish-American War (1898)
  Philippines and, **4**:512b
  See also Philippine-American
    War
SPDC. *See* State Peace and Devel-
  opment Council.
SPECA (UN Special Programme
  for the Economies of Central
  Asia), **1**:466
Special Armed Forces (Korea),
  3:417a–417b
special economic zones (SEZs;
  China), **2**:151a, 270b,
    506b–507a, **5**:176a–177b,
    297a–298b, **297a–298b**, 484a
  Hainan, **2**:506b
  Shantou, **2**:455b, 506b
  Shenzhen, **2**:455b, 506b,
    5:176a–177b, *176b*
  Xiamen, **2**:506b
  Zhuhai, **2**:455b, 506b, **3**:532b
  See also development zones
Speelman, Cornelis, **5**:298b–299a
SPF. *See* South Pacific Forum.
Spice Islands, **1**:326a, **4**:26b,
  550a–550b
spice trade, **1**:58b, 59a, 81a, 81b,
  82a, 326a, **2**:308a, 308b, 309a,
  3:55a, 62b–63a, 63b,
  5:299a–300a
  Dutch East India Company
    and, **2**:142a
  Malaysia and, **4**:5a
  Malaysian cuisine and, **2**:204b
  Maluku and, **4**:26a
  Melaka and, **4**:4b
  monsoons and, **4**:194a
  South Asian cuisine and,
    2:210a, 210b
  Sri Lanka and, **5**:325a
  Srivijaya and, **5**:332a
  Venice and, **5**:300a
  Vereenigde Oostindische Com-
    pagnie and, **5**:300a
spices
  in Afghani cuisine, **2**:185b
  in Central Asian cuisine, **2**:187a
  in Chinese cuisine, **2**:191a
  in Indonesian cuisine, **2**:194a,
    194b
  in Iranian cuisine, **2**:194b
  in South Asian cuisine, **2**:209b
  in Sri Lanka, **5**:315b, 317b
  in Thai cuisine, **2**:*212b*, 213b
  in Turkish cuisine, **2**:216b
  in Vietnamese cuisine,
    2:218a–218b
spirit cults (Myanmar),
  5:300a–301a

Spivack, Gayatri Chakravorty,
  3:509b
sports
  in Central Asia
    buzkashi, **1**:*389b*, **389b–390a**
  in China, **5**:301a–304b
    ball games, **5**:301a–301b
    basketball, **5**:302a
    Nu archery, **4**:366b
  in India, **3**:8b, 293a,
    5:304b–306a
    wrestling, **5**:304b–305a
  in Islamic Asia, **5**:306a–308a,
    306a–312a
  in Japan, **3**:293a
    baseball, **1**:263b–264b, **2**:80a
    business entertainment and,
      5:154a
    fencing, **5**:310a–311a
    golf, **5**:311b
    gymnastics, **5**:311a
    television and, **4**:107
  kendo, **3**:348a
  in Korea, **5**:312a–313b
    baseball, **5**:*312*, 312b, 313a
    bullfights, **2**:85b
    Chajon Nori, **1**:487b
    Western, **5**:312b–313a
    wrestling, **4**:82a, **5**:312a,
      332b–333a
  in Mongolia
    Buh wrestling, **1**:371b, **2**:126a
  polo
    in China, **5**:302b
    in India, **3**:8b
    in Islamic Asia, **5**:306b
  in South Asia
    cricket, **2**:183b–184a
  in Southeast Asia
    longboat racing,
      3:525b–526a
    sepak takraw, **5**:148b–149a
    Thai kickboxing,
      4:205a–206a
  wrestling
    in India, **5**:304b–305a
    in Islamic Asia, **5**:306b
    in Turkey, **2**:321b
Spratly Islands
  dispute over, **1**:333a, **2**:29a,
    5:313b–315a
  map of, **5**:*314a*
  Philippines and, **4**:516a
Spring and Autumn Annals (Confucius). See *Chunqiu.*
Spring and Autumn period
  (China), **6**:212b, 213a, 213b
Spring Festival (New Year; China),
  5:315a–315b

Sri Aurobindo, **2**:523b
Sri Aurobindo Ashram (India),
  4:548a
Sri Jayawardenapura Kotte (Sri
  Lanka), **2**:142b–143a
Sri Lanka (Ceylon), **1**:269a, 302a,
  3:42a, 43b
  agriculture in, **5**:315b, 317a,
    317b, 319a, 319b, 324a,
    325b, 326b
  Buddhism in, **5**:226b–227b
  capital of, **2**:142b–143a
  cave sites of, **4**:450b
  censorship in, **5**:328a
  civil war in, **3**:513a, **5**:317a,
    318b, 319a, 321b, 323b,
    326a, 326b, 327a–327b
    human rights and, **5**:328a
    political system and,
      5:331a–331b
    refugees and, **5**:327b, 328a
  climate of, **2**:101b,
    5:315b–316a, 323b
  Colombo Plan and, **2**:143a
  colonial rule and, **3**:195b
  colonialism in, **5**:316b, 329a
    British, **5**:316b, 317b,
      322a–322b, 325a–325b,
      327b, 328b
    Dutch, **5**:317b, 322a, 325a
    education and, **5**:322a–322b
    Portuguese, **3**:512a–512b,
      5:316b, 317b, 322a, 323b,
      325a
  constitutions of, **5**:325b,
    326b–327a, 327b–328a,
    328b–331a
  corruption in, **2**:179b
  cricket in, **2**:184a
  cuisine of, **2**:209b
  currency of, **5**:318b
  dance in
    Kandyan, **2**:*247*, 247b–248a
  economic system of,
    5:317b–318a, **318a–321b**
    banking and finance sector,
      5:320a–320b
    civil war and, **5**:323a, 326b,
      329a
    colonialism and, **5**:325a, 325b
    export-processing zones
      (EPZs) in, **5**:321a–321b
    external sector, **5**:321a–321b
    free-trade zones in, **2**:142b,
      5:318b
    GNP and, **5**:318a
    government policy on,
      5:318a–318b, 319a,
      319b–320a, 321b

Tagore, Rabindranath *(continued)*
film on, **2:**88b–89a
Indian education and, **3:**20a
influence of, **5:**408a–408b
Southeast Asia and, **3:**34b
Tagore, Sharmila, **2:**89a
Tahdhib al-Akhlaq (Social Reform;
journal), **5:**137a
Tahir, Kemal, **3:**516b
Tahtali Mountains, **1:**112a, 113a
Tai Chi (martial art),
5:369b–370a, 483b, **6:**171a
in PRC, **5:**369a
Tai-Kadai languages, **1:**385a,
5:163b, **370b–372a**
Lao language and, **5:**370b
relation to Chinese, **5:**371b
sound and writing systems of,
5:371a–371b
subfamilies of, **5:**370b–371a
syntax and semantics in, **5:**371b
Thai language and, **5:**370b
tonal contrasts in, **5:**371b
Tai-Kadai people
clothing of, **2:**122b–123a
Tai kingdom, **4:**256a
Tai languages, **5:**116a–116b, 450a,
460a
Tai people, **3:**443b, 446b,
447a–447b, 452a–452b, 460b,
5:460a
marriage and family of, **4:**65a,
65b–66b
Mong Tai Army and,
4:160b–161a
muang and, **4:203b–205a**
in Vietnam, **2:**138b
See also Shan people
Tai Shan (Mount Tai; China),
5:166a, **370a–370b**
Taibei. *See* Taipei.
Taihang Mountains, **2:**496a
Taiho Code (702; Japan), **2:**6a
Confucianism and, **2:**161a
Taijiquan. *See* Tai Chi.
Taika Reforms (Japan), **2:**5b, 6a
Confucianism and, **2:**161a
Taima no Keyaha, **5:**308b
Taimanov, Isatai, **5:372a**
Taimaz (Mongol ruler), **2:**59b
Tainan (Taiwan), **5:372a–372b**
Taipei Economic and Cultural
Representative Office, **3:**251b
Taipei (Taiwan), **1:**501a, **3:**251b,
5:372b–373b, 378b, 389b
architecture in, **5:**373a
Chiang Memorial in, **5:***373*, 373a
February 28th Incident of 1947
in, **5:**373a, 380a, 384a, 389b

pollution in, **5:**373b
Taiping Rebellion (China), **2:**99a,
181a, 456a, 559b, 566a, **3:**274b,
469b, **4:**389a, **5:**28a,
373b–375b, **6:**187b, 209a, 223b
Chinese in Southeast Asia and,
2:42a
Christianity and, **2:**65b, **5:**373b,
374a, 374b, 375a
Ever-Victorious Army in,
5:375a
Xiang (Hunan) Army in,
5:374b, 375a
See also Zeng Guofan
Taiping yulan (Imperially Reviewed
Encyclopedia of the Taiping
Era), **5:**255b
Taipingjing (Classic of Great
Peace), **5:**420a
Taira family (Japan), **2:**531a, 572b,
3:304a, 305a, 494a, **4:**415a
Taira no Kiyomori, **1:**404b, **2:**498b
Taisho Democracy, **3:**227a,
5:375b, 377a
Taisho (emperor; Japan), **2:**529b
Taisho period (1912–1926; Japan),
2:529b–530a, **5:375b–378b**,
6:182b
cuisine in, **2:**199a–199b
Free Educational Movement in,
5:378a
impact of World War I in,
5:376a–376b
intellectuals in, **5:**376b–377a,
378a–378b
Kanto earthquake in, **5:**378a
literary schools in
Shin-Shichou (New Trend
of Thoughts), **5:**377a
Shirakaba ha (White Birch),
5:377a
Tanbi-Ha (Aestheticism
school), **5:**377a
New Theater (Western-style
theater) in, **5:**377a, 378a
postwar depression in,
5:377b–378a
postwar politics in, **5:**377a–377b
from Taisho to Showa, **5:**378b
See also Meiji period; Russo-
Japanese War; Showa period;
Sino-Japanese War
Taisho Political Crisis (1913;
Japan), **3:**227a
Taiwan economic miracle, **2:**25b,
5:386b–387b
Taiwan (Formosa; Republic of
China; ROC), **1:**7a–8a, 9a,
2:465b, **5:78b–80b**, **6:**201a

aboriginal peoples of, **1:6b–8a**,
191b, 192a, **2:**21a,
128b–129a
architecture on, **5:**382a
Austronesian language groups in,
1:192a, 193a, **5:**379a, 381a
Bank of
financial crisis (1927) and,
2:378a
Buddhism in, **1:**341a
Ciji Foundation and, **1:**341a
CCP and, **2:**32b
censorship in, **2:**87b
Chiang Kai-shek and, **1:**498b,
6:211b
China-Japan relations and,
2:11b, 12a
China-U.S. relations and, **2:**25a,
25b, **5:**37b
Chinese from Myanmar in,
2:34b
Chinese languages in, **4:**32a,
146a
Chinese migration to, **1:**6b
Chinese settlements on, **5:**372b
cinema and, **1:**102b, *103b*,
103b–104a, **3:**103a
cities in, **1:**501a–501b
clothing in, **2:128b–130a**
comfort women from, **2:**143b,
144b
Confucianism in, **2:**160a
contemporary issues of, **5:**382a
corruption in, **2:**176
Council of Aboriginal Affairs in,
1:8a
culture of, **5:**381b–382a
democratization in, **5:**272a
destruction in, **1:**496a
early, and warlordism,
5:78b–79a
earthquakes in, **2:**311b, 313a
economic crisis in, **1:**164a
economic system of
China-Taiwan relations and,
2:23a
China-U.S. relations and,
2:27a
success of, **1:**499a
economy of, **5:**380b–381a
education system of,
5:382b–384a
cram schools and, **2:**183a
expenditures and enroll-
ments, **5:**382b–383a
policies before 1990s,
5:383a–383b
reforms in 1990s,
5:383b–384a

Tamil language, **1**:497a, 497b, **2**:299a, 300a, 301a, **3**:489b–492b, **4**:460a, **5**:323b, **408b–409b**, 410a–410b
  in cinema, **2**:88a, 88b
  in Malaysia, **4**:2a
  media and, **4**:104a
  poetry in, **2**:183b
  in Southeast Asia, **5**:410a
    media and, **4**:103a
  in Sri Lanka, **3**:195b, 512a
    civil war and, **5**:329a
    Sinhalization and, **5**:323a
  in Sri Lankan ethnic conflict, **2**:348b
Tamil Nadu, **1**:53b, 101b
Tamil Nadu (India), **1**:*51b*, 53b, 55a, 101b, 102b, **4**:385b, **5**:49b, 50a, **409b–410a**, 411a, 436a, **6**:37a, 37b
  agriculture in, **5**:410a
  AIDS in, **1**:68a, 68b
  Brahmans in, **1**:316a
  Carnatic music in, **5**:410a
  cities in, **5**:472a
  civil war in, **5**:62a
  dance style (Bharatanatyam) in, **5**:410a
  Kongu kingdom in, **1**:314b
  Sri Lankan civil war and, **3**:36b
Tamil people, **1**:232a, **5**:49b, **410a–411a**, 532a
  civil war and, **5**:326a
  cuisine of, **2**:209b
  education and, **5**:322a, 323a
  Hindu festival of, **5**:76a
  human rights and, **5**:328a
  Indian, **3**:36a, 36b–37a
  literature of, **5**:410b
  in Mauritius, **4**:87b
  separatism of, **5**:327a, 327b
  separatist movement in Sri Lanka, **2**:349a–349b
  in Sri Lanka, **5**:316a–317a, 317a, 324b
    civil war and, **5**:327a
    political system and, **5**:328b–331b
    rights of, **5**:325b
  Sri Lankan, **3**:36a, *36a*, 36b–37a, 38b
Tamil Sangam, **3**:489b
Tamil Tigers, **5**:228a–228b
Tamil Tigers (Liberation Tigers of Tamil Eelam; LTTE; Sri Lanka), **5**:327a–327b, 328a, 329b, 331a
Tamil United Liberation Front (Sri Lanka), **5**:329b

Tamil Youth League (Sri Lanka), **5**:323a
T'amna, kingdom of, **1**:492b
Tan Cheng Lock, **3**:474a, **4**:14a, 21b
Tan Kah Kee, **2**:49b
Tan Siew Sin, **5**:411a–411b
Tan Sitong, **2**:159b
Tan Zhenlin, **2**:447b
Tanabata Festival (Japan), **5**:147a
Tanaka Chikao, **2**:289a
Tanaka Giichi, **5**:411b–412a, **6**:183a
Tanaka Hiroyuki, **2**:96b
Tanaka Min, **2**:241b
Tanaks Kakuei, **3**:250b
tanch'ong (decorative technique; Korea), **5**:412a
Tang dynasty (China), **1**:128b, 131a, 131b, 132a, 142a, 336a, 352b, b, **2**:289b, 306b, 487a, **3**:376a–376b, **5**:155a, **412b–416a**, **6**:170a, 170b, 174a, 176b, 177b, 187a, 195a, 202a
  agriculture in, **5**:415a
  An Lushan rebellion and, **2**:305a, **5**:413b, 414a, 414b, **6**:22a
  architecture in, **1**:127b, 130a
  Buddhism in, **1**:339a, 347b, **2**:221a, **5**:415a–415b
  Central Asia and, **1**:452b–453a
  China-Japan relations and, **2**:6a, 6b
  China-Korea relations and, **2**:14a
  Chinese influence and, **2**:37a, 37b, 38b, 39a
  Christianity and, **2**:65a
  civil service examination system in, **2**:98b, 163a
  classical Chinese and, **2**:46a
  clothing in, **2**:108a–108b, 120b
  commerce in, **5**:415a
  Confucianism in, **2**:159a, **5**:415b
  cultural and intellectual changes, **5**:415a–415b
  cultural relics of, **4**:524b
  drama in, **3**:487a
  economic system of, **2**:497a
  equal field system in, **5**:414b
  fishing industry in, **2**:383a
  folk religion in, **5**:66b
  Fujian and, **2**:407a
  gardens in, **2**:427a, 428a
  Grand Canal and, **2**:446a
  influence of eunuchs in, **5**:414a
  Japan and, **1**:307a, 342a, 404b

  Korea and, **3**:389a, **4**:464a, **6**:24b, 26a, 26b
  Korean literature and, **2**:15a
  language in, **2**:45b
  legacy of, **5**:415b–416a
  literature of, **3**:486a
  Middle Chinese of, **6**:175a
  Ming dynasty and, **4**:151b
  Mongols and, **4**:187a
  opium in, **4**:387b
  painting in, **4**:411b, 414b
  poetry and, **3**:483b–485a
  poetry in, **2**:85b, **4**:528b–530a, 540a, **5**:36b, 178a, 430b
  poetry of, **3**:469a
  political changes in, **5**:412b–414a
  population resettlement and, **1**:528a
  porcelain of, **4**:548a
  puppetry in, **5**:155b
  rock carvings in, **2**:257a
  rulers of, **6**:217a
  Shanxi and, **5**:172a
  socioeconomic changes iin, **5**:414b–415a
  Taoism in, **5**:415a, 421b
  taxation in, **2**:365a, **5**:414b
  tea in, **5**:430b–431a
  Tibet and, **2**:133a
  traditional medicine in, **4**:123a
  Turkic empire and, **1**:452a
Tang-wai (Opposition) Party (Taiwan), **1**:494b
Tang Xianzu, **3**:487a
Tang Yin, **4**:413a
Tange Kenzo, **5**:416a–416b
Tangshan (China), **2**:496b
  earthquake in
    courtyards and, **2**:182b
Tangshi ji (Records of Tang Poetry; Wu Guan), **5**:37a
Tangshi jishi (Events of Tang Poetry; Ji Yougong), **5**:37a
Tangun, **3**:400a, **5**:367a, 368a, 368b
Tan'gun Myth (Korea), **5**:74b, **416b–417a**
Tangut language, **5**:234b–236a
Tangut Xi Xia, **5**:253b
Tangyin tongqian (Comprehensive Booktags of Tang Sounds; Hu Zhenheng), **5**:37a
"Tanhaai" (Solitude; Faiz), **2**:362a
Tanhuan, **1**:351b
Tani, Jinzan, **1**:395b
Tani Buncho, **4**:417a
Taniguchi, Yoshio, **1**:148a, 148b
Tanikalang Guinto (Golden Chains; Abad), **3**:506a

Yue Fei, **5**:254a
Yue kingdom, **2**:407a
Yue people, **6**:168a, 168b, 171b,
 201b–203a
 cuisine of, **2**:204b, 205a
Yue Zhi (Tokharians), **5**:485b
Yueh-chih confederation, **1**:216b
Yugoslavia, **1**:80b
 bombing of Chinese embassy
 in, **2**:27b
Yuk Wan-sun, **2**:241b
Yukiguni (Snow Country; Kawa-
 bata Yasunari), **3**:330b, 495b
Yulgok. *See* Yi I.
Yun Hung-gil, **3**:500b
Yun Po-son, **5**:279b
Yun Sun-do, **3**:498a, 499a,
 6:203a–203b
Yun Tong-ju, **4**:537a
Yungang grottoes (China), **5**:172a
Yunnan province (China), **1**:78a,
 78b, 383a, **2**:284a, 302b, **6**:193a,
 193b, **203b–204a**, 215a
 as center of tin production,
 5:500b, 501b
 languages in, **5**:235a–236a, 370b
 minorities in, **5**:517a
 Muslim rebellion in, **5**:28a
 in nineteenth century, **6**:204a
 terrace irrigation in, **5**:442a
 Yi tribe in, **5**:535b
Yunus, Muhammad, **2**:445a
Yurdakul, Mehmet Emin, **3**:516a
Yuri (king; Korea), **4**:535b
Yuri Ng, **2**:242b
Yuriko Kimura, **2**:243a
yurts (*ger*), **2**:371, **4**:168a, 171a,
 187b–188a, **6**:204a–204b**
 Kazakh people and, **3**:333b
 Kyrgyz people and,
 3:421b–422a
yushin (revitalization, reform),
 6:204b–205b**
 consolidation of power and,
 6:205a–205b
 opposition to, **6**:205b
 South Korean constitution and,
 2:85a, **5**:279b, 282b,
 6:204b–205a
Yuson, Alfred A., **4**:538b
Yusuf of Balasagun, **3**:479a
Yuzuru (Twilight Crane; Kinoshita
 Junji), **3**:496b

Z

Zabaan-e-Urdu-e-Mu'alla (language
 of the royal; India), **2**:514b
Zabulistan, **2**:434a

Zagros Mountains (Iran), **1**:63a,
 63b, 112a, 113a, **3**:95b, 326b,
 5:35a, **6**:207a
Zahir Shah (king; Afghanistan),
 1:25a, 29a, **2**:253b, 256b, 307a,
 343a, **6**:207b–208a**
Zahir ud-Din Muhammad. *See*
 Babur.
zaibatsu (Japanese conglomerates),
 1:484a, **3**:211b, 213b, 227b
Zainal Arifin, **2**:533b
Zakariyya, Baha' al-Din (Sufi
 leader), **4**:209b
Zambales Mountains (Philippines),
 6:208a**
Zamboanga (Philippines),
 6:208a–208b**
Zamora, Jacinto, **1**:445b, **4**:505b
Zamorins (Calicut; India), **1**:400b,
 2:417a
Zanjeer (Indian film), **1**:212b
Zanskar Range (India), **3**:438b
Zaoshen (God of the Stove;
 China), **5**:67b
Zarathushtra, **6**:221b
Zargana, **4**:267a
Zau Mai, **3**:298a
Zau Seng, **3**:297b
Zayid ibn Salih, **1**:452b
Zayn al 'Abidin (fourth imam),
 4:242a
Zdansky, Otto, **4**:445b, 446a
Zeami, **3**:494b, **4**:82a
zebu (brahminy cattle), **6**:208b–209a**
Zeliangrong Movement (India),
 4:38b
Zemu glacier (Himalayas), **3**:308a
Zen Buddhism. *See* Buddhism,
 Chan.
Zen-Nippon Aikokusha Dantai
 Kaigi (National Council of Pa-
 triotic Societies; Japan), **5**:134b
Zen no kenkyu (A Study of Good;
 Nishida), **4**:334a
Zenan-name (Enderuni), **3**:515a
Zeng Fengrong, **5**:302b
Zeng Guofan, **2**:566a, **3**:469b,
 5:28a, 374b–375a, **6**:209a–209b**
Zenkoku Rono Taishuto Move-
 ment (Japan), **2**:365a
Zenkyo teachers' union (Japan),
 4:332a
Zerafshan River (Golden River;
 Central Asia), **1**:128b, 129b,
 6:209b–210a**
Zhang Chunqiao
 Gang of Four (China) and,
 2:422a–422b

Zhang Congzheng, **4**:123b
Zhang Daoling, **2**:484b
Zhang Guodao, **3**:524b
Zhang Jue, **2**:484b
Zhang Junmai, **1**:519a, **6**:179b
Zhang Juzheng, **4**:152a–152b
Zhang Pengqun (P. C. Chang),
 1:519a
Zhang Sanfeng, **5**:369b, **6**:171a
Zhang Shiyi, **4**:32a
Zhang Xueliang, **6**:174a–174b
Zhang Yan, **2**:86a
Zhang Yimou, **2**:87a, 444a,
 6:210a–210b**
 filmography of, **6**:210
Zhang Zai, **2**:157a, **4**:303b
Zhang Zhidong, **6**:210b–211a**
Zhang Zhongjing, **4**:122b–123a
Zhang Zuolin, **2**:11a, **4**:28b
Zhangjiang High-Tech Park
 (Shanghai, China), **2**:509a
Zhangzong, **3**:291a
Zhao Kuangyin (Taizu)
 the Song dynasty and, **5**:252b
Zhao Mengfu, **4**:412b, **6**:199a
Zhao Tuo, **1**:94a, 95, **6**:217a
Zhao Ziyang, **2**:151a, 151b, 555b,
 3:470a, **5**:10b, 483a,
 6:211a–211b**
Zhejiang province (China), **2**:313b,
 487a, **6**:211b–212a**
 internal migration and, **1**:521a,
 5:415a
 music of, **6**:177b
 Wu speakers in, **6**:168a–168b,
 169b
Zhen yuan miao Dao yao lue (Classi-
 fied Essentials of the Mysteri-
 ous Tao), **2**:463b
Zhenbao Island (Damansky Island;
 Ussuri River), **2**:17b
Zheng Chenggong (Koxinga),
 2:21b, 47a, **5**:372b, 379b
Zheng He, **1**:150a, 150b, 151a,
 2:47a, **4**:151b, 238a
Zhengtong (emperor; China),
 4:152a
Zhengyan (Buddhist leader),
 1:341a
Zhengzhou (China), **2**:503a, 503b,
 5:167b
Zhiyi (Zhikai; founder of Tiantai
 Buddhism), **1**:339b, 340a
Zhong yong (Doctrine of the Mean;
 Centrality and Commonality),
 2:158a, 401b, **6**:65a
 vs. Golden Mean, **2**:156a, 401b
Zhongguo Nübao (Chinese
 Women's Journal), **5**:35a

Index